AROUND THE SHORES OF LAKE MICHIGAN

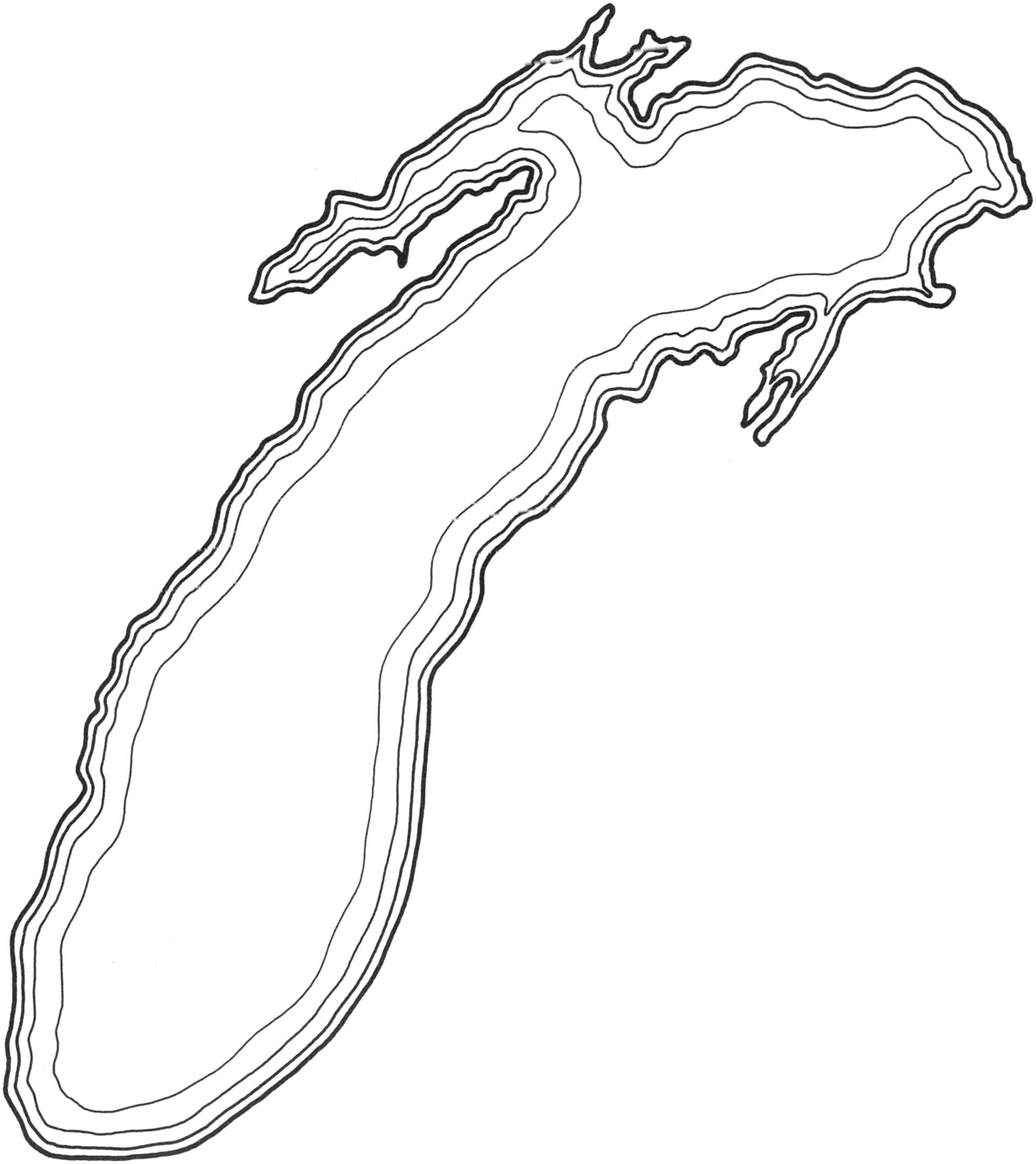

Around the Shores of

Lake Michigan

A Guide to Historic Sites

Margaret Beattie Bogue

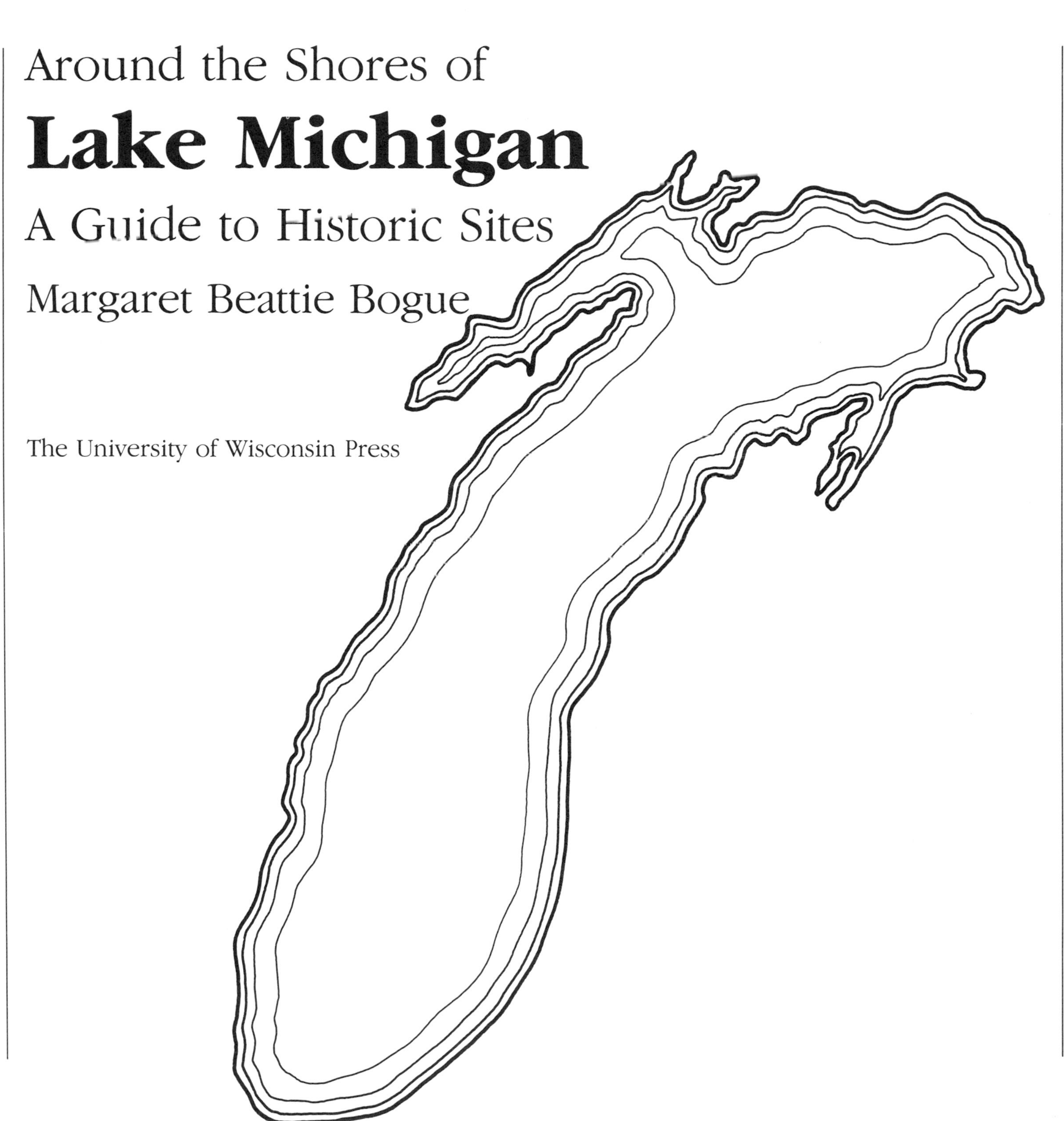

The University of Wisconsin Press

Published 1985

The University of Wisconsin Press
114 North Murray Street
Madison, Wisconsin 53715

The University of Wisconsin Press, Ltd.
1 Gower Street
London WC1E 6HA, England

First Printing

Printed in the United States of America

For LC CIP information see the colophon

ISBN 0-299-10000-6 cloth; 0-299-10004-9 paper

This work was funded in part by the University of Wisconsin Sea Grant College Program under grants from the National Sea Grant College Program, National Oceanic Atmospheric Administration, U.S. Department of Commerce, and from the State of Wisconsin (Federal grant #NA80AA–D–00086, Project #SGA–1). The U.S. government is authorized to produce and distribute reprints for government purposes notwithstanding any copyright notation that may appear hereon.

Cover photograph by Jean Lang
Courtesy of the University of Wisconsin Sea Grant Institute

To Allan

Contents

Maps

Key to Symbols in Part 2

B boating

C camping

F fishing

H hiking

P picnicking

S swimming

$ admission charged

* included in the National Register of Historic Places

Highways are designated as follows:

US U.S. Highway

I Interstate Highway

IL Illinois State Highway

IN Indiana State Highway

M Michigan State Highway

W Wisconsin State Highway

Preface

From the quiet, sandy, wave-washed beaches of the northern shore to the bustling urban-industrial communities at the southern rim, Lake Michigan's beautiful blue waters on a sunny summer day invite swimming, fishing, boating, and a long appreciative look. Today's admirers of Lake Michigan stand in a long line of people who have enjoyed its natural beauty. At the head of the line stand Lake Michigan's Indian peoples, who fished and canoed its waters and whose legends and tales are filled with the natural world around them. The lake's name comes from the Algonkian "Michigami" or "Misschiganin," meaning "large body of water."

When the Stephen H. Long expedition to the source of the St. Peter's River reached the shores of southern Lake Michigan on its way west from Philadelphia in April, 1823, William H. Keating, geologist and expedition journal keeper, noted, "We found ourselves transported, as it were, to the shores of an ocean . . . the view, towards the north, was boundless; the eye meeting nothing but the vast expanse of water, which spread like a sea. . . . The beach . . . reminded us of that of the Atlantic on the coast of New Jersey." E. P. Hendricks, surveyor of Indiana's northern boundary in 1827, admired the hills of "beautiful white sand," the dunes lying along the shore. Juliette Kinzie, who went by steamboat from Detroit to Green Bay in the fall of 1830, was captivated by the Michilimackinac area. Of the island she rhapsodized, "Michilimackinac! that gem of the Lakes! How bright and beautiful it looked. . . . A finer sight can scarcely be imagined. . . . Then those pure, living waters, in whose depths the fish might be seen gliding and darting to and fro; whose clearness is such that an object dropped to the bottom may be discerned at the depth of fifty or sixty feet. . . ." She was also impressed with the northern shore of the lower Michigan peninsula with its "gigantic forest-trees, and here and there the little glades of prairie opening to the water."

Harriet Martineau, during her western travels in 1836, came to the Michigan City area eagerly anticipating a look at "the mighty fresh water sea." From atop a dune she saw it. "There it was, deep, green, and swelling on the horizon, and whitening into a broad and heavy surf as it rolled in towards the shore." The impression was unforgettable.

Margaret Fuller in 1843 traveled from north to south and back again on "this majestic sea." The Manitou Island beach, a "most beautiful beach of smooth white pebbles, interspersed with agates and cornelians," the sunsets, the moonlight and starlight on the water, the colors of the lake changing hourly in the late afternoon, and the golden and flamelike prairie flowers set against blue waters near the Chicago shore affected her deeply.

Early in the twentieth century, after development had seriously eroded much of the original beauty of the lake, the Prairie Club of Chicago launched a campaign to save the Indiana dunes from further industrialization. The sculptor Lorado Taft, one of the club's many eminent members, said of the Chicago area: "Now, there are two great beauties of this region, two things which are distinctive. One is the lake and the other is its product, the Dunes."

A drive around Lake Michigan or along part of its shoreline still provides an impression of great natural beauty. In addition it can give the traveler insights into the political, economic, and cultural history of the area, from the time of the prehistoric Indians to the present. How better to get a feeling for the French explorers and missionaries and the era of the fur trade than to visit the Father Marquette Memorial at St. Ignace and Forts Mackinac and Michilimackinac at the Straits? How better to sense the heterogeneous character of Chicago and Milwaukee's people than to visit those cities and the many places of interest that reflect their ethnic diversity?

This book is designed to provide such experiences to those who travel Lake Michigan's shores. Given the diversity of the area's population and the wide variety in economic and cultural development from north to south, Lake Michigan's history is representative of many themes in regional and national history, comprising as it does the histories of the Indians, the first to live there, the French explorers and missionaries, the fur trade, the American Revolution, and the War of 1812. In the nineteenth and twentieth centuries, developmental themes have dominated: the westward movement of the American people, immigration, canal building, lumbering, mining, agriculture, fishing, commercial shipping, industrialization, recreation, and conservation and environmental protection efforts.

Lying in a richly endowed part of the mid-continent, with soils and climate suitable for intensive agriculture, with iron ore deposits lying to the north and coal to the east and south, with magnificent original stands of timber and abundant fish and furbearing animals, the Lake Michigan area has made a major contribution to national wealth. The geographic location of the lake, its long north-south thrust deflecting the lines of land communication east and west to its southern shore, gave Chicago prominence as a national commercial, transportation, and industrial center.

The first part of this guide explains the main themes in the lake's history, tying together the bits and pieces of it found scattered all around the lakeshore. Most of it, however, focuses on locations around the lakeshore to help people traveling the shoreline understand the historical relation of the lake to the great open spaces of natural beauty and to the development of lakeside cities, towns, and villages. Brief histories of these communities emphasize their origins and evolution to the present. The locational materials are arranged in a numbered sequence of 182 places, beginning at Chicago and running north through Illinois, Wisconsin, and Michigan to the Straits of Mackinac, and from there south through the Michigan lower peninsula and Indiana and back to Chicago. The numbered locations are keyed to the large map that accompanies the book.

The treatment is selective in many ways. The Indian reservations, communities, historic places, museums, parks, national lakeshores, forests, natural sanctuaries, and fish hatcheries described are found, with few exceptions, close to the Lake Michigan shore. Other locations, not in the immediate vicinity of the shore, but with a direct bearing on lake history, are also included. For example, a side trip to Iron Mountain is suggested at Escanaba, the great ore-shipping port of the northern shore, to give the traveler some idea of the Menominee Iron Range mines, whence came much of the ore shipped at Escanaba.

The guide is also selective rather than exhaustive in noting locations of historical importance within communities. Representative examples are identified, and the history and importance of each selected location noted. Because most businesses and industries discourage public tours, opportunities for such visits are not included unless they are part of a well-established, long-term "open" policy. Such visits materially add to one's understanding of a community, however, and persons especially interested should check with the local chamber of commerce to find out what firms may welcome visitors.

Selectivity has also been practiced in the case of Milwaukee, whose ethnic neighborhoods are described in some detail: its diversity is an example of a theme treated more generally in the materials on other communities. Moreover, Milwaukee locations representative of a number of diverse groups can be visited without major logistical problems. The section entitled "A Heterogeneous People" gives an area overview that puts differing treatments from community to community into balance.

Curiosity will, no doubt, lead many to explore beyond the locations described here. Publications that will help them do so are mentioned in the materials for a number of communities. To help travelers enjoy the lake's natural environment, opportunities for picnicking, camping, hiking, fishing, swimming, and boating are noted for parks, forests, and national lakeshores, all of which reflect the efforts of many people to conserve Lake Michigan's shoreline beauty. Open hours for all museums and sites noted herein are for the 1984 season.

Acknowledgments

Many scholars whose research touches on parts of Lake Michigan's history have provided valuable insights and information for this study. High on that roster stand Bessie Louise Pierce, Bayrd Still, Jack L. Hough, George I. Quimby, John B. Brebner, Alice E. Smith, Powell A. Moore, Milo Quaife, Louise P. Kellogg, Willis F. Dunbar, and Harlan Hatcher. To them, I am much indebted. To the dozens of people in Lake Michigan communities—librarians, historic site and museum directors, chamber of commerce staffs, local historians, and personnel of the U.S. Coast Guard, state departments of natural resources, national forests, and national lakeshores—who took time to discuss the project and offer helpful leads during the many weeks of field work around the lakeshore, I owe a special thank you.

To Virginia A. Palmer of the Division of Urban Outreach, University of Wisconsin–Milwaukee, I am especially indebted for valuable research assistance in identifying and describing historic buildings, parks, and natural sites along the lakeshore in Illinois and Wisconsin, and for writing some of the materials about them included herein. I am responsible for the broad conceptual plan for the book, final selection of materials, emphasis, interpretation, and all field work, as well as 95 percent of the research and writing. The reverse side of the coin is that I am also responsible for errors.

To Mark Marlaire and Rebecca Williams, project assistants, who spent days digging out census data and government documents, telephoning, and writing letters to improve the quality of the study, I am very grateful. Myrna Williamson and Christine Schelshorn gave perceptive guidance in locating and selecting illustrations in the photo archives of the State Historical Society of Wisconsin. James A. Hilliard and Onno Brouwer of the University of Wisconsin Cartographic Laboratory are responsible for the excellence of the map work.

To the five principal readers of the manuscript, who carefully reviewed various portions, offered suggestions for changes and additions, and pointed the way to additional resources for research, I am most grateful. They are: George May, professor of history, Eastern Michigan University, Ypsilanti, Michigan; Lance Trusty, professor of history, Purdue Univeristy–Calumet campus, Hammond, Indiana; Frederick I. Olson, professor of history, University of Wisconsin–Milwaukee; Gail Farr Casterline, associate editor, Chicago Historical Society; and John Holzhueter, associate editor, State Historical Society of Wisconsin, Madison.

To Allan, Susan, Margaret, and Elinor Bogue, my family, who heartily supported the project during the days I was buried in my study and the weeks I was absent on the road, I owe heartfelt thanks for their encouragement, patience, and willingness to pinch hit at home.

I am especially indebted to the University of Wisconsin Sea Grant College Program, which funded part of the research for this study, to University of Wisconsin–Extension for project assistance and funds for cartographic work, and to the staff of the University of Wisconsin Press, who worked on this book.

THE NATURAL AND HISTORICAL SETTING

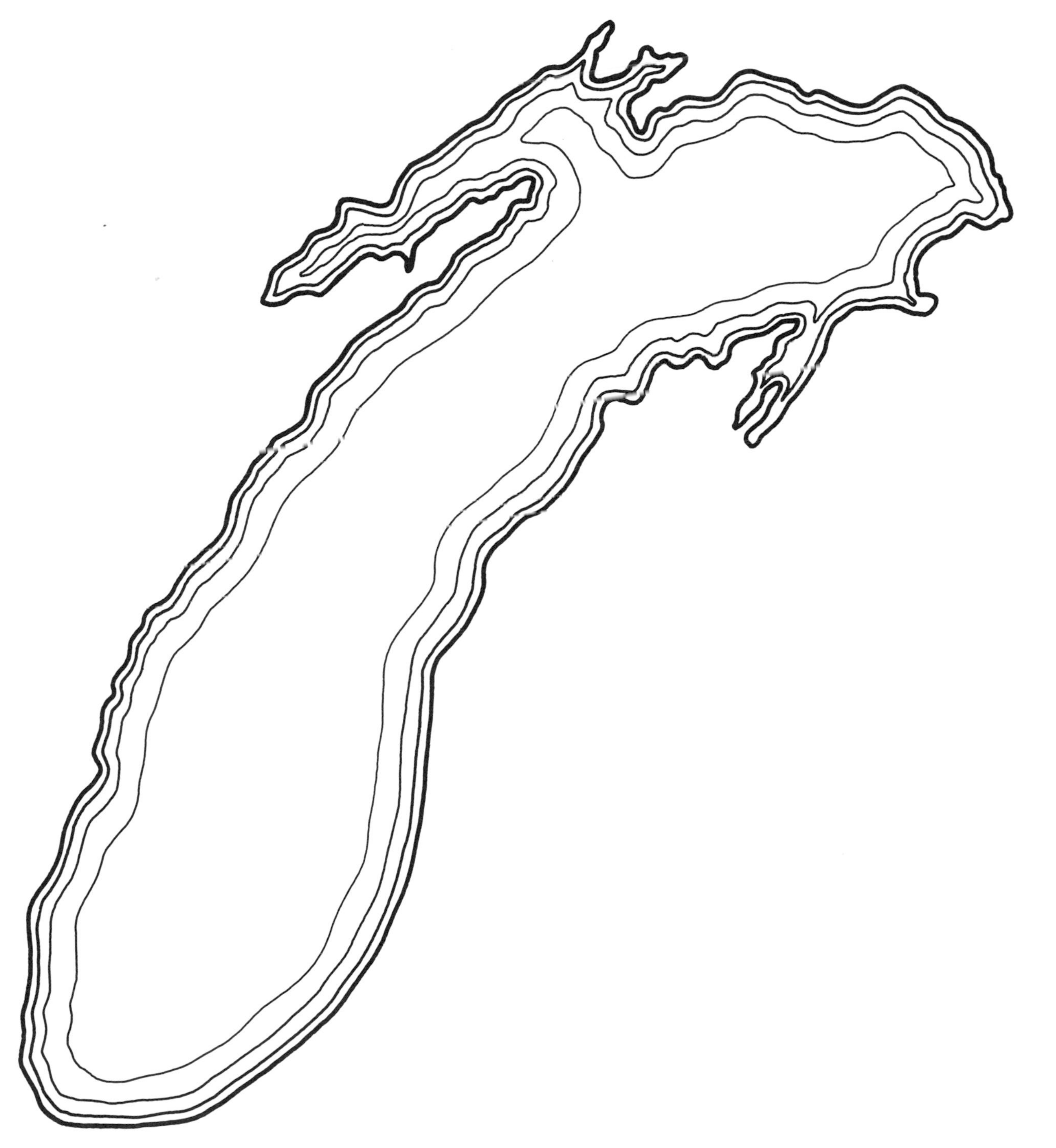

The lake between Manitowoc and Two Rivers, Wisconsin, on a sunny September day. Photo by Margaret Bogue.

The Lake

One of the five Great Lakes that form the largest group of freshwater lakes in the world, Lake Michigan extends 307 miles from north to south and 118 miles from east to west, with a surface area of 22,300 square miles in a beautiful expanse of blue water. Its shoreline, relatively regular in the south and broken by Green Bay and Grand and Little Traverse bays in the north, extends for 1,660 miles. Standing 531 feet above sea level, Lake Michigan's waters cover a geologically varied lake floor, descending to a depth of 923 feet at their deepest point in the northern basin. Of the Great Lakes, only Superior plunges to a greater depth. Largely sand and pebble beaches lie around its shores, and the prominent rock cliffs that characterize portions of Lake Superior's western and northern shores are absent. Lower cliffs lie on the Garden Peninsula, on the islands strewn across the mouth of Green Bay, and on the Door Peninsula, where the gray dolomite of the Niagara Escarpment protrudes above the water.

Along the eastern and southern shores (see p. 305), majestic sand dunes lend striking beauty to the lake's natural environment. Once extensive but now endangered by industrial development in the south (see sites 174 and 177) and recreational development in the east, dune formations are preserved for public enjoyment in the Sleeping Bear Dunes National Lakeshore (site 140), Warren Dunes State Park (site 172), and the Indiana Dunes National Lakeshore and Indiana Dunes State Park (site 175). Glacial deposits and wind and wave action produced these sand formations over a period of thousands of years. Ever changing, they nurture trees, grasses, wildflowers, and wildlife. At many locations along Lake Michigan's eastern shore, dunes have dammed up river waters flowing into the lake and created small inland lakes close to the shoreline.

Lake Michigan discharges into Lake Huron at the Straits of Mackinac at a rate that allows for a complete change of water about every hundred years. While tides are negligible in Lake Michigan, surface currents produced by wind action, especially the prevailing westerly winds, and changes in barometric pressure, follow a varied and complex pattern. Generally they move from north to south along the western shore and in a northerly direction along the eastern one. The U.S. Bureau of Fisheries has identified swirling current patterns in the southern end of the lake. Another counterclockwise swirl circles the Beaver Island group in the northern end. Lake Michigan's waters move vertically as well as horizontally when temperatures of surface and deep waters equalize at about 39°F, each spring and fall. Then, with the help of the wind, the waters at top and bottom mix thoroughly.

The lake's moderating influence on air temperatures is noticeable immediately adjacent to the shore. The water is cooler than air temperatures in spring and summer and warmer in fall and winter. This moderating influence has made the lake an attractive place for people to escape the summer heat and, for 25 to 30 miles inland on the eastern shore and on the Door Peninsula, a good place to grow fruit susceptible to early spring frosts.

Lake Michigan is rain fed at an average rate of 31 inches per year and river fed from a drainage basin of 45,460 square miles, most of which lies north of Kenosha, Wisconsin, and Michigan City, Indiana, at no point extending more than 100 miles inland from the shoreline. The Chicago and the Grand Calumet rivers, which once emptied into the lake, now discharge into the Illinois River, a rearrangement of nature designed to solve the Chicago metropolitan area's water supply and sewage disposal problems.

How did Lake Michigan, an important water resource and national avenue of transportation for more than 150 years, come into being? The question intrigued nineteenth-century geologists, who offered a number of explanations, including the action of earthquakes. The glacial theory suggested by Louis Agassiz continues to be the most widely supported. Jack L. Hough has explained it in his *Geology of the Great Lakes*, from which the materials below have in large part been drawn.

Between 500 and 185 million years ago, the Paleozoic sedimentary rocks that form the bedrock of the Lake Michigan basin developed slowly as seas flooded the continent and marine life deposited shell and skeletal remains, layer after countless layer. A sinking of the land, very marked in the Lake Michigan basin, led ultimately to the formation of Paleozoic rock, thousands of feet thick—limestones, dolomites, sandstones, and shales. The depth and extent of the seas varied over time. Apparently the Lake Michigan basin area was isolated at some point from the main sea, leading to extensive deposits of salt and gypsum. At the end of the Paleozoic era, with the building of the Appalachian Mountains, the seas retreated from the continent and, so far as is known, did not return to the Lake Michigan area.

Streams developed, sculpturing the land into drainage systems. The Mississippi, Missouri, Wabash, and Ohio rivers took on their preglacial contours, and others flowed in areas now occupied by the Great Lakes, forming portions of present lake floors. The glacial ages, or Pleistocene epoch, followed, lasting probably from one to two million years. Great ice sheets alternately advanced and retreated, carving out the Great Lakes basins by their sheer weight, scraping and grinding and recasting the landscape. Their great loads of glacial till, left behind as the climate alternated between warm and cold, covered most of the bedrock of the Lake Michigan area.

Geologists believe, on the basis of the evidence offered by shore terraces, beaches, erosion, and deposits (see sites 24, Schlitz Audubon Center, and 50, no. [7]), that a number of lakes occupied parts of the Lake Michigan basin in the intervals between glacial advance and retreat. These were lakes of various sizes, small compared to present-day Lake Michigan and bordered by ice, all falling under the rubric of glacial Lake Chicago because

Niagara limestone formations along the west shore of Washington Island. Photo by Paul Vanderbilt (August 1964). Courtesy State Historical Society of Wisconsin. WHi(X2)15942

they drained southward into the Des Plaines River. They dated from roughly 16,000 to 7,000 B.C. By the latter date, glacial ice was gone from the Lake Michigan region; prehistoric Indian peoples lived there. The earlier spruce and fir forests were declining, and pine forests were increasing. Mastadons slowly retreated northward. Deer, elk, and caribou remained. Some whales still swam in the lake waters.

From about 7,000 to 500 B.C., postglacial lakes occupied either portions or all of the present Lake Michigan basin (see Ridges Sanctuary, site 50, no [7]). The last of these, Lake Algoma, filled an area slightly larger than that of all of the present Great Lakes combined. In this postglacial lake phase, Lake Michigan's waters stood at a higher level than at present and drained southward. A gradual tilting of the land southward over a period of thousands of years helped alter the level and discharge pattern into the present one. Particularly significant in creating the present drainage system through the Straits of Mackinac into Lake Huron was a deepening of the St. Clair River, where rock formations were not strong enough to resist erosion by the outpouring waters of the combined Huron and Michigan basins. The Chicago outlet, on the other hand, is partly Niagaran bedrock, which the outlet stream could not cut through. By about 500 B.C. Lake Michigan had taken on its modern appearance. The flora and fauna were closely akin to those found by the seventeenth-century explorers.

Paleozoic bedrock, preglacial rivers, and the grinding pressure of the great, thick ice sheets left Lake Michigan with certain notable geological characteristics. Above water level, three escarpments alter the generally gentle, sloping shoreline: the Niagara (see above); the Bois Blanc along the south shore of the Straits of Mackinac (site 110) through Waugoshance Point (Wilderness State Park, site 117), and traceable on Beaver, Garden, and their adjacent islands; and the Traverse Group escarpment, which forms the shoreline from Bay View, Michigan, west and southwest to Petoskey, Charlevoix, and the headlands of Grand Traverse Bay.

Underwater the lakebed varies from a relatively gently sloping southern section, underlain by shale covered by several hundred feet of glacial drift, to the more rugged contours of the northern basin. In the latter, drowned riverbeds form a ridge and valley province running roughly twenty miles into the lake from the shoreline east of Grand Traverse Bay and including the bay itself. By contrast, the lakebed off the northern shore is a plane with water only about 75 feet deep, cut through by a 150-to 250-foot-deep river valley that extends through the Straits of Mackinac and into Lake Huron. The lake's northern deep basin area, lying about mid-lake northwest of Manistee, is very irregular, plunging as deep as 923 feet. Geologists believe that this basin, the ridge and valley province, and the Straits of Mackinac resulted in part from the dissolving of salt and gypsum deposits lying between relatively thin layers of limestone and a subsequent collapse.

On land, Pre-Cambrian and Paleozoic bedrock and the deposits of the glaciers left the upper Great Lakes with a storehouse of natural resources destined to have great impact on Lake Michigan's subsequent history. Iron ores in the Upper Peninsula of Michigan, in Northern Wisconsin, and in Minnesota; copper in the Keweenaw Peninsula; abundant limestones; salts and gypsum in Michigan; and glacial deposits that left soils suitable for forest growth and agriculture—to these natural riches, nineteenth- and twentieth-century developers fell heir.

Lake Michigan's Indian Peoples

For thousands of years before the coming of the Europeans, prehistoric Indians lived around the shores of Lake Michigan. By systematically analyzing the evidence of these early people found at hundreds of grave and village sites, archaeologists have pieced together the broad outlines of early human life in the Lake Michigan region, deducing from artifacts general ways of life and cultural changes over many centuries. Given the ravages of time and the nature of the physical evidence, many questions about why and how change took place will never be answered. Yet, however limited the knowledge of their ways of life, the ancient Indians, the real pioneers in Lake Michigan's natural environment, will always form a significant part of the region's human heritage.

Archaeologists have identified a series of broad epochs in the development of prehistoric Indian life, all of them greatly influenced by the physical environment. About 9500 B.C., in the presence of retreating glaciers, the earliest people roamed the area, hunting the mastadon, giant beaver, deer, elk, and caribou. For thousands of years these nomadic hunters were apparently few in number.

By 3500 B.C. a real transformation in human life had occurred. Responding to climatic changes and the evolution of plant and animal associations similar to those of today, the Indian population grew, using a wider variety of animals and plants for food and a wider variety of stones to fashion weapons and tools. Whereas in the earliest period the diet was primarily red meat from large animals, around 3500 B.C. foods included fish, small and large game, nuts, seeds, and fruits.

Notable among the cultures associated with the transformation were the Old Copper Culture Indians (5000–1500 B.C.), a group that appears to have been most heavily concentrated in the Lake Winnebago area, Fox River Valley, and western Green Bay shoreline of Wisconsin, where a large number of artifacts have been found, but whose geographic distribution included the Great Lakes region and the lands lying west to the headwaters of the Mississippi and Red rivers. The cold-hammered and annealed copper tools, weapons, and ornaments they crafted distinguished them from other contemporary cultures, which worked in stone, bone, and wood. They were probably the first metal fabricators in America (see Copper Culture State Park, site 73, no. [3]).

During the first millennium B.C., further changes in the ways of human life marked the beginning of the Woodland Indian culture, materially different from past cultures because of the increasing importance of agriculture—chiefly the cultivation of corn, beans, and squash—the use of earthenware pottery, mound burials, and new styles of craftsmanship, and the introduction of new tools, weapons, utensils, and ornaments.

Many archaeologists regard the Hopewell culture of the Middle Woodland period as the climax of prehistoric Indian life in the Lake Michigan region because of its comparatively more complex social structure, elaborate burial mounds, and the fine artistry and craftsmanship of the remaining artifacts. How and why the culture evolved in its major centers in the Mississippi, Ohio, and Illinois river valleys we do not know, nor are the reasons for its spread into the Lake Michigan area understood. Was the success of the Hopewells based on trade, political organization, religious ideas, military might, or an adaptation to agriculture that made the food supply so secure that time and energy could be devoted to mound building and crafts? While archaeology does not reveal the answers, it does reveal a society with class distinctions, a people who built very sizable mounds for their leaders whom they buried with fine examples of Hopewell art and wealth and probably with considerable ceremony.

The archaeological record shows that during the period from 100 B.C. to 700 A.D., the Hopewell Indians flourished in the St. Joseph, Kalamazoo, Grand, and Muskegon river valleys of lower Michigan and as far north as the coastal area between Traverse City and Mackinaw City. They also lived in northern Indiana and in Wisconsin. The largest Hopewell ceremonial center in the Lake Michigan region was the present site of Grand Rapids. On the west side of the Grand River in the center of the present city once stood a group of 30 to 40 mounds, the largest of which was 200 feet in circumference and 30 feet high. Two miles south of the city there re-

This display of Old Copper Culture Indians mining copper portrays their labor as accurately as knowledge of the ancient past permits. It is no longer on display at the Milwaukee Public Museum. Courtesy Milwaukee Public Museum.

mains a group of 17 Hopewell mounds, the Norton group.* (See Key to Symbols.) Originally they were probably enclosed within low earth walls.

Travelers and traders, the Hopewell Indians gathered raw materials for tools, weapons, ornaments, and ceremonial objects from many places: obsidian from the Rocky Mountains, shells from the Atlantic Ocean and the Gulf of Mexico, copper and silver from the Lake Superior region, mica from the Middle Atlantic coast, and lead from northwestern Illinois. Among their artifacts are musical instruments, tobacco pipes, fine pottery and utensils, and finger-woven cloth. George I. Quimby characterized the Hopewell Indians as "the outstanding artists of the Upper Great Lakes region." The reasons for the decline of the Hopewell culture after 800 are as elusive as its origins.

The Late Woodland Indians (800–1600 A.D.) developed a number of distinctive cultures in the Lake Michigan region, all dependent upon farming, agricultural goods secured by trade, hunting, fishing, and gathering. They differed mainly in pottery styles, housing, tools, weapons, ornaments, burial customs, and language. The Indian population continued to grow; Hopewell cultural traits disappeared; warfare and walled villages increased.

Notable among the many cultures of the Late Woodland period were the Effigy Mound builders, who lived mainly in Wisconsin from Green Bay to just south of the Wisconsin-Illinois border. In contrast to other cultures, they built mounds for burial and ceremonial purposes in circular and oval shapes and in the forms of buffalo, deer, bears, dogs, cranes, eagles, hawks, lizards, and the long-tailed panther. Their grave goods, compared with those of the Hopewells, were quite spartan. Of obscure origins, the Effigy Mound culture lasted from about 700 to 1300 A.D. Probably simple farming along with hunting, fishing, and gathering supplied their food. Many thousands of effigy mounds have been destroyed, but others remain, now protected from destruction. One excellent example is found at Lizard Mound State Park, northwest of Port Washington near West Bend, where 31 of these low earthworks remain. A beautiful 15-acre wooded park south of Sheboygan preserves 18 of the orig-

Each tribe was politically autonomous, but neither authority nor power was centralized. Members of a tribe shared a common culture and language and collectively utilized a loosely defined area of land. Although each tribe spoke a different language, the Indians of Lake Michigan belonged to two main lingual stocks: Algonkian (Chippewa, Menominee, Sauk, Fox, Miami, Potawatomi) and Siouan (Winnebago). Sources of food differed. The Chippewa were mainly hunters and fishers; the Menominee depended on farming, hunting, fishing, and wild-rice gathering; the balance combined farming and hunting. All but the Chippewa lived in permanent villages to which they returned after the hunt. The Chippewa congregated in villages along the lake to fish during the summer. The Indians organized their lives around a seasonal routine designed to ensure an adequate food supply.

Lake Michigan Indians lived in oval or elongated dome-shaped wigwams built with a sapling framework covered with bark or mats of woven rushes. They traveled on foot, by dugout and birchbark canoe, snowshoe, and toboggan. They made utensils, implements, tools, domestic wares, and ornaments from stone, bone, antlers, wood, bark, hide, plant fibers, sinews, clay, and, to a very minor extent, copper. The women fashioned clothing from animal skins. By trade they secured the items they could not themselves supply. The excellent birchbark canoes of the Chippewa, capable of long journeys on streams, rivers, and open lakes, the beautiful dyed porcupine quill and moose hair enbroidery work of the Ottawa and Potawatomi, and the fine woven mats and bags that the Menominee made from vegetal fiber and spun buffalo hair are prime examples of Lake Michigan Woodland Indian craftsmanship and artistry.

Religion—beliefs based on the unity of the physical and the spiritual, whether in inanimate or in plant, animal, or human form—played an important part in their lives. The souls or spirits of all animate things lived after the physical being had perished. They embraced the idea of a Great Spirit and deities such as the sun. Religious practices were traditional and varied from tribe to tribe. Although ceremonies were directed by religious leaders and organizations, religion, nevertheless, stressed the individual experience. Religious leaders and healers of the sick were one and the same.

Social structure was based on families organized into bands and clans. Sex roles were clearly defined. To the men went the tasks of hunting, fishing, and fighting, and heavy work like clearing land for cultivation and building fortifications. Men were healers of the sick and leaders in band, clan, village, and tribal affairs and in religious ones. The women attended to a wide variety of domestic duties that included planting and harvesting crops, building wigwams, and gathering fruits, nuts, berries, wild rice, and maple sap. They tanned hides and made pottery, clothing, and many household necessities. They were wives and mothers.

As in European cultures, indigenous war brought out the worst in upper Great Lakes Indian culture. These people fought to avenge the death of a tribesman, or to achieve individual glory, or to secure hunting territory from rivals. Generally small-scale and involving relatively few combatants, wars were nonetheless lethal and fierce, and the victims of bows, arrows, spears, and clubs could include women, children, infants, and the very old.

Such was the way of life of Lake Michigan's Indians when missionaries, explorers, and fur traders ventured into the area to make Christian converts, to claim territory for European monarchs, and to pursue the trade in beaver pelts. Within two hundred years that way of life would change under the impact of European political and economic competition and technology.

Locations that reflect prehistoric Indian life include a number of museums and natural sites. Excellent museum displays are found at the Field Museum of Natural History in Chicago (site 1, no. [10]), the Neville Public Museum of Brown County at Green Bay, Wisconsin (site 67, no. [3]), the Beyer Home Museum Annex at Oconto, Wisconsin (site 73, no. [8]), and the Grand Rapids Public Museum at Grand Rapids, Michigan. Natural sites specifically designed for public viewing are the Sheboygan Indian Mound Park at Sheboygan, Wisconsin (site 31, no. [15]), Copper Culture State Park at Oconto, Wisconsin (site 73, no. [3]), and the Norton Mound Group at Grand Rapids, Michigan.

The French Explorers

"It would be useless for me, my lord, to give you a description of Lake Michigan. . . . This route is fairly well known," wrote the missionary priest Jean St. Cosmé to his Quebec superior in 1699 after a canoe journey from Michilimackinac to the lower Mississippi. The Canadian-born priest was quite right. The French knew Lake Michigan well by the end of the seventeenth century, and they used it as a vital link in the complex system of waterways that bound together New France, from its vast claims on the lower Mississippi to the settlements on the St. Lawrence.

The discovery and exploration of Lake Michigan grew from the rival efforts of France and England to lay claim to North America, to reap the rewards of the fur trade with the Indians, and to find that elusive northwest passage to the Orient. Involving a wide range of people—Indians, governors of New France, the king of France and his ministers, fur traders, missionaries, and pathfinders—Lake Michigan's initial exploration by the French took place gradually between 1634 and 1679.

The names of many involved are lost. The countless Indians who told the French what they knew about the lake and helped paddle the canoes and guide the way left no written record of their friendliness and cooperation, without which the French would have been stymied. Nor do we know the names of the many *voyageurs* and *coureurs de bois*, the "trailmakers," as John B. Brebner has called them. The major pathfinders of the Lake Michigan region are well-known figures in American history: Jean Nicollet, Médard Chouart Des Groseilliers, Jacques Marquette, Louis Jolliet, and René-Robert Cavelier de La Salle. They were inspired by various motives: the quest for wealth or fame, loyalty to France, or the desire to make Christian converts. Hardy, adventuresome, inquisitive, ambitious, daring, and willing to make the great physical sacrifices essential to life in an unknown wilderness, all contributed to the growth of New France.

When Samuel de Champlain established Quebec in 1608 as a base for exploration and the profitable conduct of the fur trade, the French had long since tapped the wealth of fish and furs in the Newfoundland–Gulf of St. Lawrence region. The fur trade was at first a side business for European fishermen, who found the Indians eager to trade beaver, marten, elk, deer, and bear skins for iron kettles, axes, and hatchets. At the end of the sixteenth century, it became an end in itself. Fashionable Europeans prized felted beaver hats, and manufactures needed great quantities of pelts to supply the demand. Scandinavian and Russian fur-bearing animals that had supplied the market were in a decline.

The combined pressures of French entrepreneurs' eagerness for a monopoly of the North American fur trade, King Henry IV's desire to expand French territory, and Champlain's personal ambitions as the royal geographer led to his exploration of the St. Lawrence in 1603 and to the founding of Quebec in 1608. The French discovery of the upper Great Lakes in the seventeenth century was a logical outgrowth of the quest for beaver skins.

Champlain recognized that success in exploration and in serving his fur merchant employers depended upon the Indians. During the 1603 exploration they furnished him with abundant information on the lake and river routes connected to the St. Lawrence system. As founder of Quebec, he hastened to develop a system of cooperation with the Indians, geared to the realities of the struggle between rival native groups—on the one hand the Hurons, who lived around Georgian bay and on the eastern side of Lake Huron, and their allies, and on the other the League of the Iroquois, whose territory, lying to the south, stretched from Lake Champlain to Lake Erie. Champlain chose the Hurons as suppliers of furs, a choice that made the French and the Iroquois adversaries and shaped the direction of French exploration and fur trade thereafter. He adopted a policy of choosing energetic young Frenchmen to go into the wilderness, establish friendships with Indian tribes, live among them, learn their languages, and find out what they knew about the waterways of the continent. One of Champlain's young men, Jean Nicollet, is credited with the French discovery of Lake Michigan in 1634.

Nicollet came to Canada in 1618 in the employ of French fur-trading mer-

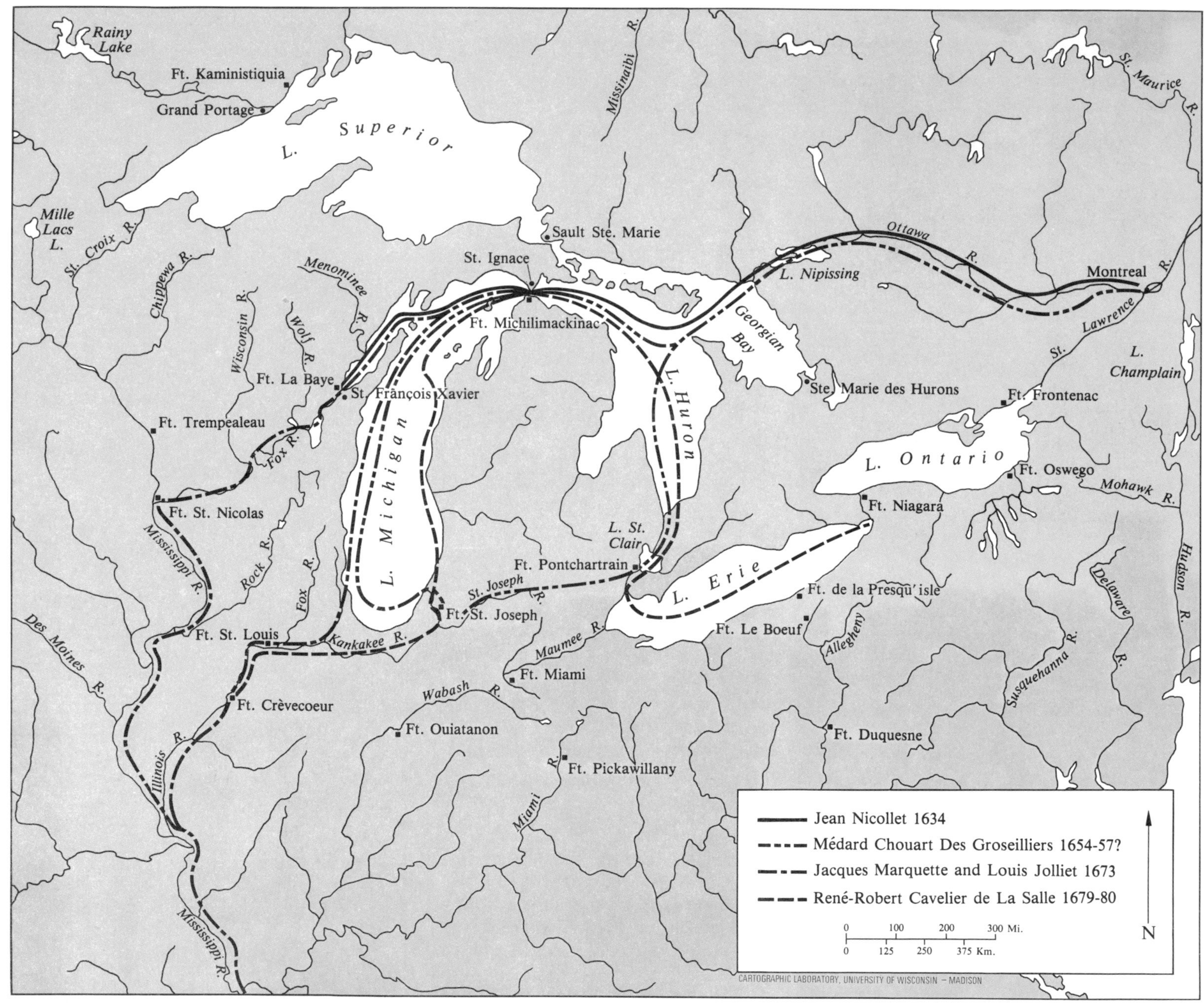

French Explorations of Lake Michigan. Adapted from Alice E. Smith, The History of Wisconsin. Volume I: From Exploration to Statehood *(Madison, Wis., 1973), map by Barbara Anne Wick. Adapted by permission of the State Historical Society of Wisconsin.*

Landfall of Nicollet, E. W. Deming, artist. Courtesy State Historical Society of Wisconsin. WHi(X3)30553

chants and went almost immediately to live among the Algonkian allies of the French on the upper Ottawa River. Two years later he was sent to the Nipissings. He had proven himself compatible, tactful, and diplomatic in Indian relations before being requested in 1633 to undertake a mission to facilitate the fur trade by smoothing out frictions between Algonkian tribes and the Winnebagos of the Green Bay area, "the people of the sea." His instructions included investigating information gleaned from the Indians about the "China Sea" near Green Bay.

In company with seven Hurons, in the summer of 1634 he followed the well-established route up the Ottawa River, Lake Nipissing, and the French River to Lake Huron. From there the party proceeded south through the Straits of Mackinac into Lake Michigan, and into Green Bay. Unfortunately Nicollet's memoirs of the journey were lost, and what is known about the discovery of Lake Michigan comes mainly from the account of Father Vimont, written just after Nicollet's death in 1642 as a memorial to his 25 years of service in the French cause. Vimont's often-quoted description of the Green Bay landing records the Indian's reactions:

They meet him; they escort him, and carry all his baggage. He wore a grand robe of China damask, all strewn with flowers and birds of many colors. No sooner did they perceive him than the women and children fled, at the sight of a man who carried thunder in both hands—for thus they called the two pistols that he held. The news of his coming quickly spread round about, and there assembled four or five thousand men. Each of the chief men made a feast for him, and at one of these banquets they served at least sixscore beavers. The peace was concluded.

Because the evidence is scanty, much controversy has arisen among historians about Nicollet's discovery of Lake Michigan. Some contend that the date was 1638, not 1634; others that he did not enter Lake Michigan at all, but rather landed somewhere on Lake Superior. To be sure, no one knows exactly where Nicollet landed, but an official marker of the State Historical Society of Wisconsin and an imposing bronze statue of Nicollet, traditional discoverer of Lake Michigan, stand near Red Banks (see site 65). As for Nicollet, he met an untimely death in 1642 in a canoe accident at Quebec while en route to Three Rivers to save an Iroquois prisoner from Huron torture. A strong wind overturned his canoe, and he drowned because he could not swim.

By the time of Nicollet's death, New France faced very serious challenges. Initially the French had no European rivals for the fur trade, but the hostility of the Iroquois forced them to pursue trade and exploration through the difficult and tortuous Ottawa River route west to Lakes Huron and Superior. As early as 1609, however, the Dutch made commercial contact with the Iroquois on the Hudson River, and by 1615 the Iroquois were acting as their middlemen, acquiring beaver pelts from various tribes in exchange for Dutch trade goods. Moreover, the longstanding interest of the English in the Gulf of St. Lawrence turned into a threat to New France's very existence when in 1628 and 1629 London merchants sent out an expedition to capture Quebec and the St. Lawrence trade. Lacking aid from France, New France fell into British hands, only to be returned to the French a few years later by Charles I of England. The English colonies along the Atlantic coast to the south spawned fur traders eager to make their fortunes. The presence of the Dutch and English sharpened the Iroquois-Huron conflict as these two groups of middlemen competed for the beaver pelts of the interior.

Nearly two decades of Iroquois wars against the French and their allies, beginning in 1643, disrupted the fur trade, brought a halt to western exploration, and all but extinguished New France. The Iroquois swept across the St. Lawrence north of Lake Ontario and Lake Erie, systematically destroying their Huron competitors and their allies. By the mid-century they were triumphant from the eastern shores of Lake Michigan to Tadoussac, northeast of Quebec on the St. Lawrence. The French fur-trading system lay in ruins. With the Hurons and their allies badly beaten and dispersed, no canoes laden with furs came down the St. Lawrence, and commerce with France languished. A truce in hostilities from 1653–1658 permitted the resumption of trade, missionary, and exploration activity.

During the lull one of New France's more daring, shrewd, and resourceful explorer-traders, Médart Chouart Des Groseilliers, probably learned much about the Michigan lower peninsula. "Probably" is the most that can be said because the written record is vague, a poor English translation of Pierre Radisson's original account. Apparently Des Groseilliers crossed the lower Michigan peninsula from present-day Detroit to Lake Michigan, virtually emptied of people by the Iroquois hostilities, and then passed up the western shore of the lake to the Straits of Michilimackinac. A desire to locate New France's terrified Indian allies, to find new sources of furs, and to investigate reports of a great river emptying into a great sea, brought by western Indians who came to the French settlement at Three Rivers on the St. Lawrence in the late summer of 1654, apparently prompted Des Groseilliers to explore.

Jean Nicollet may have been very close to the discovery of the Mississippi two decades earlier if, as the *Jesuit Relation* reports, he discovered the Fox River and ascended it in an effort to find the "China Sea." Exact knowledge of the Mississippi route to the Gulf of Mexico came only after New France had passed through the critical period of the mid-seventeenth century. In 1661 Louis XIV assumed personal control of the monarchy and turned his attention to establishing French hegemony in Europe and enhancing its colonial prestige. As money, equipment, military force, and men and women poured overseas, New France received a new lease on life. Marquis de Tracy curbed the Iroquois with an expedition into the Mohawk Valley in 1666, and a rush of *coureurs de bois* and missionaries into the western Lake Michigan and Upper Peninsula areas ensued.

Information flowed back to Quebec about the Great River and the sea to the south. New France's intendant, Jean Talon, zealous to advance the cause of territorial expansion as a check on the British and the Spanish, chose Louis Jolliet to find the passage to the south sea. The Jesuits persuaded Talon, despite his desire to curb their power, to permit Father Jacques Marquette, a man with important map-making and language skills, to go along. Marquette and Jolliet set out from St. Ignace in mid-May 1673 to solve the mysteries of the Mississippi: to determine whether it flowed north or south and whether it emptied into the Gulf of Mexico or the Pacific Ocean.

The Canadian-born Louis Jolliet, once a candidate for the priesthood, a talented organist, a highly educated man already experienced as an explorer and fur trader, stood at the beginning of a distinguished career as a hydrographer that gained him international distinction before his death in 1700. Jacques Marquette, scion of a family of warriors and officials who chose the priesthood in 1654, had arrived in New France seven years be-

Here Frederic Remington depicts the Marquette and Jolliet voyage of 1673, picturing a birchbark canoe unusual in design for the region and time. Generally, the French explorers of Lake Michigan used canoes with a more rounded profile at both ends. Engraved after a painting and published in Harper's Monthly, *April 1892, p. 131. Courtesy State Historical Society of Wisconsin. WHi(X3)14540*

fore the eventful voyage down the Mississippi. Only two years of life remained for him to fulfill his desire to undertake a mission to the Illinois Indians.

The Menominee Indians did their best to discourage the pair from their venture, warning of ferocious and warlike peoples along the way, the great river, treacherous and "full of horrible monsters, which devoured men and canoes together," and a demon as well. If all this were not discouragement enough, they were also warned of the intense summer heat, which would inevitably cause death.

Undaunted, they proceeded on the famous voyage that revealed the Fox-Wisconsin route to the Mississippi and the Chicago–Des Plaines–Illinois portage as well. Probably they were not in fact the first white men to use these portages, but it was they who made them well known. Lake Michigan became a vital link in the chain of waterways that led from the St. Lawrence to the Gulf of Mexico and to the entire watershed of the Mississippi River.

On the return journey in September 1673, Jolliet explored the shores of southern Lake Michigan. The ailing Marquette again passed along Lake Michigan's shores a year later—the western shore in the fall of 1674, on his way to establish a mission among the Kaskaskia Indians, and the southern and eastern shores in the spring of 1675. Now in failing health, he traveled as far north as present-day Ludington, Michigan, where he died. No other explorer of Lake Michigan has received as much recognition in commemorative plaque and statue as Marquette (see, for example, site 23, no. [9]). None has so stirred local historians to claim his presence, however fleeting in their communities. A beautiful marble figure of Father Marquette, executed in 1895 by Gaetano Trentanove, a prominent Florentine sculptor, stands in the nation's capitol, one of Wisconsin's quota of two for Statuary Hall. The Marquette memorial at St. Ignace, a site funded by the state and federal governments, depicts the Jesuit priest's missionary labors and the lives of the Indian peoples among whom he worked (see site 111).

The perimeters of Lake Michigan were reasonably clear to the French by the 1670s, but among the surviving early maps of the Great Lakes, those of the 1680s are the first that show the lake in a shape approximating its actual contours.

The last of the famous French explorers of the seventeenth century to make his mark around the shores of

Lake Michigan was René-Robert Cavelier de La Salle, a man of grand ambition and bold plans, whose life of service to New France remains controversial. Although he is chiefly remembered for his voyage to the mouth of the Mississippi in 1682 and his later efforts to explore and perhaps colonize the Gulf of Mexico as a deterrent to Spanish influence, La Salle occupies a very special place in Lake Michigan's seventeenth-century history as an explorer and fur trader. Original explorations were not his forte, and a massive fur trade, rather than fame or service to New France, may have been his goal. He envisioned escalating territorial conflicts between France and both England and Spain and developed imaginative schemes to stymie these powers.

Although officials in New France were keenly aware of the threat of English encroachment into the French fur trade in North America, they were hamstrung in their efforts to counteract it, for in 1672 Louis XIV plunged into a long series of costly European wars that diverted support from New France. In 1670 the British were trading on Hudson's Bay under the leadership of the intrepid Radisson and Des Groseilliers, to whom the French had turned a deaf ear when they urged the Hudson Bay route to European fur markets. They had gotten a better hearing in London and helped to organize the Hudson's Bay Company, to which the English crown granted a royal monopoly of the fur trade within the bay's watershed.

From the early 1670s until the French lost the Hudson Bay area to the British in 1713, French Canada's leaders struggled with mixed results to retain a foothold there. Governor Frontenac took measures in the 1670s both to protect New France's interests in the area and to follow up the Marquette-Jolliet voyage with an expedition to the mouth of the Mississippi. La Salle, who may have discovered the Ohio and Mississippi Rivers before 1673, received royal permission in 1678 to explore the western portions of New France and build forts, along with a five-year trade monopoly in the Mississippi Valley, provided that he did not pursue the fur trade in conflict with the Montreal traders. With Frontenac's support La Salle set about fulfilling his dream of establishing on the lakes and on the Mississippi a fur trade serviced by cargo sailing ships. On the Lake Erie side of Niagara Falls, he had *Le Griffon* (named in honor of Frontenac's coat of arms) built in 1678–1679. The 45-ton vessel, equipped with seven cannons, slipped into Lake Erie waters in August 1679, and La Salle set off on a 20-day journey into Lake Michigan.

Despite his promise not to trade furs in the Montreal traders' territory, La Salle assembled a cargo of furs in the Green Bay–Washington Island–Rock Island area. Recent digs on Rock Island confirm the presence of a seventeenth-century French trading post, probably that of La Salle's party (see site 56). Sending the *Griffon* back to Niagara, La Salle went south along Lake Michigan to the St. Joseph River and there built Fort Miami, a 40-by-30-foot structure (see site 168). He hoped to have the *Griffon* rendezvous at that point, but Lake Michigan's first sailing ship disappeared without a trace. Did it sink in a storm? Was it destroyed by hostile Indians? The mystery has never been solved.

La Salle meanwhile, in December 1679, pushed up the St. Joseph River, portaged to the Kankakee, and thence canoed into the Illinois River, using yet another Lake Michigan linkage with the Mississippi, one that other Frenchmen must have used before him. On the Illinois he established Fort Crèvecoeur and built a second sailing vessel for the Mississippi River fur trade. Over the next year he traveled Lake Michigan's waters repeatedly in connection with planning the voyage to the mouth of the Mississippi. The balance of his extraordinary life as an explorer does not relate closely to Lake Michigan, whose waters he had come to know so well. His controversial career ended in 1687 when one of his men murdered him on the Texas coast, where he was presumably attempting to plant a French colony to thwart the Spanish.

Most of the seventeenth-century French explorers of Lake Michigan do not cut such a swath in history as do Nicollet, Marquette, Jolliet, and La Salle. Of the many *coureurs de bois* who pressed into the area south of Lake Superior, west of Lake Michigan, and east of the Mississippi after 1666 and who used the lake, learning the peculiarities of its shoreline and its rivers, no record remains. Of the Jesuit missionaries who struck out into the wilderness we know more because of their reports to superiors, which were recorded in the *Jesuit Relation*. Although exploration was a secondary goal for them, these men made significant contributions to the power of New France in the upper Great Lakes and the Mississippi Valley, supplying vital information about the area's Indian peoples, waterways, and natural resources. The experiences of two of them are representative.

Artist George Catlin portrays the landing of Le Griffon *at Mackinac Island in the summer of 1679. Courtesy Department of Library Services, American Museum of Natural History. 15128*

Nicolas Perrot, explorer, interpreter, fur trader, and briefly French commandant at Green Bay, came to New France in 1660 as a lay assistant to the Jesuits. In 1667, utilizing the knowledge of Indians gained through his work with the missionaries, he formed a trading company and came to Green Bay, where he visited many of the Indian tribes and established friendly relations with them. French authorities quickly recognized his skill as an interpreter and diplomat. He was repeatedly sent by intendant and governor to assist in strengthening French alliances and friendships with western Great Lakes Indians, and in the all-important task of securing their help against the Iroquois.

Perrot traveled widely in the Great Lakes region and spent much time in Green Bay. He built three trading posts on the east bank of the Mississippi River between 1685 and 1687, one at Prairie du Chien, another, Fort St. Antoine, on Lake Pepin, and a wintering post at Trempealeau. Although he was often unappreciated during his lifetime and was repeatedly denied any relief from his debts by the authorities of New France, he has been described by modern historians as "France's best representative among the Indians of the west."

Claude Allouez, Jesuit missionary/explorer of Lake Michigan, a contemporary and acquaintance of Perrot, was among the many Frenchmen who filtered into the Green Bay area in the

many different tribes, forming pan-Indian rather than tribal villages. Thanks to its location, Mackinac remained the largest and most important of the garrisoned rendezvous points for Indians and traders well into the nineteenth century.

The late seventeenth-century reorganization of the French fur trade posed severe problems for Indians, traders, French colonial authorities, and the French crown. Undeniably the fur trade surged ahead and produced an abundance, even a glut of furs in the French market after the traders took to the woods, and their activities created crises in French-Indian diplomacy, for they stimulated among the Indians a competitive spirit as the hunt for fur-bearing animals accelerated. Intertribal competition led to friction and warfare among tribes and to the disruption of traditional tribal life.

Moreover, soon after the British captured New York in 1664, they and their Iroquois allies began to threaten the French fur trade. After 1670 the Hudson's Bay Company gained a foothold in the Hudson Bay fur trade and funneled away to the north some furs formerly traded with the French. The threat presented by the New York colony's aggressive traders grew in the eighteenth century. Indians perceived British trade goods as better in quality than the French, and they were cheaper. The British and Iroquois engaged in intrigues with Indian tribes nominally the allies of the French, and French traders smuggled their pelts to Albany for sale—consorting with the British came easily to traders critical of French official policies that, they felt, cut into their profits. All the while the sources of beaver retreated farther to the west, north, and south, and the expenses of the traders grew as distances increased. So effective was the hunt that beaver prices fell in European markets at the end of the seventeenth century. To make matters worse, the French-British competition led to a renewal of the Iroquois wars between 1682 and 1701.

"Beavers and Their Dams," from George Catlin, Letters and Notes on the . . . North American Indians. *Courtesy State Historical Society of Wisconsin. WHi(X3)27627*

The French were operating within the framework of mercantilism, which endorsed colonial controls for the benefit of the mother country. From the 1660s to 1700, policies intended to control the fur trade were a hodgepodge including the licensing of traders, ceilings on the number of trade licenses granted, price fixing, and prohibition of smuggling, with exceptional privileges granted to explorers like La Salle (see p. 16) and persons sent on special diplomatic missions to the Indians. These measures failed to control the supply of furs sent to market. They were an attempt to control the virtually uncontrollable—a few hundred free and independent spirits trading in a vast wilderness without official supervision. The French were the first of the western nations which tried to administer the fur trade. Neither the British nor the Americans who followed them did any better.

At the royal court in Paris, advisors differed on how New France should be developed. One school advocated French expansion over North America; the other urged concentration of settlements along the St. Lawrence and the fostering of agriculture. The debacle in fur prices in the 1690s, plus Jesuit warnings that the fur traders were debauching the Indians, led to official retrenchment in the trade. Governor Frontenac was ordered to restrict settlement to the St. Lawrence, to issue no more fur-trading licenses, to recall traders, soldiers, and settlers from the West, to abandon and destroy all western forts, and to make peace with the Iroquois. Had all these things been done, all of New France probably would have been lost to the British long before 1763. As it was, the French and British fought three international wars involving the fur trade in the North American theater in the eighteenth century before the French bowed out.

The French remained as long as they did first because the fur traders did not leave the wilderness, and second because officials of New France modified the orders to pull out of the West. They substituted a plan to hold the West by establishing three well-fortified locations to keep open the line of communications from Quebec to the mouth of the Mississippi. The plan involved garrisons at New Orleans to control the mouth of the Mississippi; a strengthening of Fort Crèvecoeur, on the northern Illinois River, established by La Salle in 1680 to guard the Lake Michigan–Illinois River connection to the Mississippi; and a third garrison at the straits between Lakes Huron and Erie, the site of present-day Detroit, strategic to the defense of the upper lakes and important in guarding the Maumee-Wabash-Ohio route to the Mississippi. Construction of French fortifications at Detroit and at the mouth of the Mississippi forestalled British plans to occupy those strategic locations by a matter of months. At these three points the French concentrated groups of Indians to assist in the conduct of the fur trade and in defense, arguing that they would in exchange teach them French ways of life and convert them to Christianity.

Despite these efforts, New France quickly lost ground to the English in the struggle to control the fur trade of North America. Even as the French were implementing their new plan, war broke out between England and the French and their Spanish allies. Queen Anne's War (1702–1713) was fought in Europe and in North America; in America, the competition for territory and the fur trade was the issue. Peace terms in 1713 placed the British in a stronger position than ever before, for they acquired from the French all the territory draining into Hudson Bay, Newfoundland, and Acadia (Nova Scotia and part of New Brunswick). The French recognized the Iroquois as British subjects, and another treaty provision gave British and French subjects equal trade rights with the North American Indians.

Meanwhile, the French had become embroiled in a major war with the Fox Indians, in part an outgrowth of the Indian concentration at Detroit (then Pontchartrain). This war kept Indian affairs and the fur trade along the western side of Lake Michigan in a state of turmoil from 1701 until 1737. The Fox held a very strategic position in the French line of communication, for they occupied territory astride the Fox-Wisconsin route to the Mississippi. Disappointed because the French had established direct trade in furs with the Sioux, their enemies, the Fox began intercepting French traders as a protest. Fuel was added to the flames by French treatment of their tribesmen at Detroit. Antoine de la Mothe Cadillac, the founder of the Detroit post, invited the Fox to settle just outside the fort: about a thousand accepted. After Cadillac was reassigned to Louisiana, the Fox at Detroit became embroiled in an intertribal conflict. To settle it, the new commandant virtually annihilated them. The massacre at Detroit heightened the conflict along the Fox-Wisconsin route.

Thus, the French, having finally put the conflict with the Iroquois to rest in 1701, were locked into another Indian war at the very time that the British challenge to the fur trade was mounting. They adjusted their tactics in 1714 to meet both threats. The western posts received commandants and garrisons. At the Straits of Michilimackinac, the French built a new fortification, not at the St. Ignace site of old Fort de Buade, evacuated in 1698 (site 111), but on the lower peninsula at present-day Mackinaw City (site 115). In 1716 they sent soldiers, militiamen, and Indian warriors, 800 in all, equipped with mortars and ammunition, to Green Bay to subdue the Fox. The Fox surrendered but then proceeded to organize a confederacy of tribes to combat the French. A year later the Fox attacked the Illinois country and seized the Chicago–Des Plaines portage, cutting another main line of communication between the St. Lawrence and the lower Mississippi. A general peace concluded in 1726 failed to end the struggle. In 1728 and again in 1733, the French sent new expeditions against the Fox. Finally peace came in 1737 after almost 40 years of bloody, brutal turmoil.

During the Fox wars French prestige fell among the Indians, and the popularity of British trade goods grew. In an effort to hold on, the French repeatedly reorganized the supply system of the fur trade after 1700, making garrisons in the West key centers of trade and utilizing a mixture of licensed traders, leased posts, and crown-administered posts as controls. The post leasing system, initiated in 1742, worked particularly to the disadvantage of the Indians because the lessees, who were assigned monopoly rights to the fur trade in competitive bidding, tried to maximize profits and displayed little concern for the well-being of their Indian suppliers of furs.

The short-lived experiment lasted only seven years on Lake Michigan. On the advice of Paul Marin, French subduer of the Fox, the licensing system came back into use. Marin believed that it offered greater opportunities for profit for himself and a ring of associates, including the governor of New France, who proposed to monopolize the fur trade at Green Bay and at La Pointe on Lake Superior. From that time until the collapse of the French regime in 1763, licensing continued, and so did the system of favoritism, corruption, and excessive profits to high colonial officials and their favorites. In the twilight of New France, fur trading on Lake Michigan at Mackinac, Green Bay, and St. Joseph became part of the general pattern of official dishonesty, bribery, and corruption that contributed to the collapse of the French regime in North America.

The French-British rivalry for the fur trade of the mid-continent entered its final phase with the outbreak of open warfare between the British and French in the upper Ohio country in 1754. British American colonists from the east coast had made steady inroads there since the beginning of the century, establishing friendships and trade with tribes whom the French considered their allies. The French system of defense, based on control of the St. Lawrence, the Mississippi, and the Great Lakes through strategically located garrisons, was weak in the Ohio Valley. Perceiving the danger, the French began in 1749 to construct garrisoned trading posts to counteract the British Americans. This precipitated the French and Indian War, which began with the rout of George Washington's forces at the forks of the Ohio in 1754. The slaughter of General Braddock and his soldiers followed on July 9, 1755. Nearly two years of bloody frontier warfare passed before France and England formally declared war.

The French, largely because of a show of military prowess early in the struggle, had massive Indian support for a time. Ultimately, however, British and colonial regulars overwhelmed New France. The climax of the struggle in North America came at the battle for Quebec in 1759, when General James Wolfe surprised and overwhelmed the forces of the Marquis de Montcalm on the Plains of Abraham. The British emerged triumphant in the contest for the fur trade, and France in 1763 relinquished all its North American continental possessions.

Politically the era of the French fur trade had passed, but the legacy of the French lingered on. Around the shores of Lake Michigan it continued in the small communities of active or retired French fur traders and their descendants who remained at Mackinac, Green Bay, and Fort St. Joseph during the British and American periods. It lingered in the minor Lake Michigan posts on the rivers tributary to the lake—the Muskegon, Kalamazoo, Grand, Calumet, Chicago, Waukegan, Milwaukee, Sheboygan, Manitowoc, Kewaunee, Oconto, and Menominee. And it lingered in the organization, techniques, and personnel of the fur trade itself. The French, allied with the Indians, pioneered in the fur trade, exploring the water routes, adapting the birchbark canoe to the needs of the trade, introducing the Indians to European trade goods, and practicing skills of Indian-white diplomacy. They developed a trading structure that included the large merchant suppliers of trade goods in Montreal and Quebec, traders operating in the remote western country, and inland depots for rendezvous points. The system of business partnership between merchant and fur trader used credit and settlement of accounts after a one-two year voyage of trade. The French colonial government developed the system of licensing traders and using post commandants as supervisors of the trade, in part to maintain standards of fairness in Indian-trader relationships, although intent and practice were often far apart. The nuts and bolts of the trade were a French legacy as well—the methods of bundling trade goods and furs in packs, stowing canoes, portaging, and camping. The widespread use of Indians as guides and of young Frenchmen from the farms of the lower St. Lawrence as canoemen was an important part of that legacy.

So, unfortunately, was the whetting of Indian appetites for European-made trade goods, which led them to cast off the skills that had made them self-sufficient in the natural environment. The trade occasioned loss of human life, the disruption of tribal life, and the alcoholic debauchery of the Indians. Indians died from European diseases and from an increase in inter-

The taking of Quebec, September 13, 1759. General Wolfe's forces land to join British forces already engaged in battle with troops of the Marquis de Montcalm on the Plains of Abraham. Public Archives Canada. C1078

Frederic Remington's "Voyageurs in Camp for the Night" captures the romantic vision of the voyageurs. From Harper's New Monthly Magazine, *March 1892. Courtesy State Historical Society of Wisconsin. WHi(X3)15472*

tribal warfare brought on by competition for hunting grounds. Equipped with guns and ammunition, they became the allies of the French, the Dutch, and the British, helping them to fight their battles and dying by the thousands.

The romantic image of the French fur traders, the *voyageurs*, and their Indian companions—traveling thousands of miles through the wilderness in canoes, navigating rapids, carrying heavy packs over long portages, and camping at night in beautiful wilderness settings survives. The marvelous achievement of the Frenchmen who penetrated thousands of miles inland to the foothills of the Rockies, the incredible physical exertion required by the 36 portages of the Ottawa–Lake Nipissing route to Georgian Bay, the great 36 foot birchbark canoes capable of carrying a crew and 6,000 pounds of cargo used on the Great Lakes, all capture the imagination. Yet these romantic impressions need to be tempered with the sobering realities of the business. The price in human life and misery was high, but not too high for the British and American inheritors of the fur trade to pursue it vigorously for profit using the techniques developed by the pioneering French.

Indians at Fort Michilimackinac by Bert Thom portrays the game of lacrosse before the open gates with British soldiers relaxed and watching. Such must have been the scene in June 1763 just prior to the Indian attack and capture of the garrison. From the Collections of the Michigan State Archives, Department of State. 05356

Furs and Lands: British-American Rivalries

With the conclusion of peace between France and Great Britain in 1763, the British acquired France's continental North American possessions and the responsibility for governing them. Indian affairs and the fur trade demanded immediate attention, for already the Great Lakes region seethed with discontent. Even before British troops occupied western posts, fur traders from Pennsylvania, Maryland, and New York, as well as Montreal entrepreneurs who had come to Canada with the British armies, had pushed into the upper Great Lakes area to pursue trade. There they found experienced French traders still engaged in the business.

The fur trade had already taken on a fiercely competitive character when Indian discontent erupted into Pontiac's Rebellion in the spring and summer of 1763. A combination of grievances led to hostilities: unauthorized British settlements on Indian lands, the tactless and unscrupulous behavior of some British fur traders and military personnel, lingering preferences for the French, and perhaps some encouragement from French and Spanish partisans in the West. The Ottawa chief Pontiac moved against the British at Detroit, arousing other Indian groups from Mackinac to Niagara. In quick succession they too struck at British outposts. On Lake Michigan, the British garrison at Green Bay escaped trouble largely because of the tact and diplomacy of its commandant. Fort St. Joseph, on the eastern side of the lake, fell, and at Fort Michilimackinac a Chippewa uprising, inspired by the activities of Pontiac, ended with the killing of a trader, several officers, and two-thirds of the British soldiers stationed there (see site 115).

British authorities were well aware that the fur trade could not flourish unless the Indians supported it and that unauthorized settlements on Indian lands kept Indian affairs in turmoil. After wrestling with the issue, the British home government adopted in October 1763 a plan to confine settlement to the territory east of the Alleghenies. For the next 11 years, the great challenge was to find a way to organize the fur trade that would stabilize Indian relations, harmonize the conflicting interests of traders from Montreal and those from the Atlantic coastal colonies, meet the needs of the French fur-trading population in the wilderness, and protect Britain's newly acquired western territories.

Britain faced exactly the same problem that the French had struggled with for well over a century: how to bring peace and order to a remote, sparsely populated area where it was virtually impossible to enforce any law or regulation. But the British problem was even more complex, because the Atlantic coastal colonies laid claim to the western country on the basis of their original charters, insisted that a large degree of home rule belonged to their legislatures, and grew increasingly resentful of parliamentary taxes levied to pay for the costs of crown government and defenses in the colonies.

Sir William Johnson was placed in charge of Indian affairs north of the Ohio River in 1756. An astute man who had the confidence of the Iroquois and fully understood the complexities of Indian-trader-settler relationships, he wanted a comprehensive, centrally administered plan for the West. He argued for restraining agricultural settlement, maintaining well-garrisoned western posts, restricting the fur trade to the posts under the supervision of superintendents, licensing traders, prohibiting the use of liquor in the trade, and fixing prices. Parliament did not adopt his plan because of the high cost entailed in administering it. Instead, in 1768, the Lords of Trade turned the regulation of the fur trade over to the individual colonies, as had been customary before the French and Indian War, and urged the colonies to cooperate and develop a uniform set of rules. Attempts at cooperation foundered, and competitive chaos and Indian dissatisfaction continued. Disreputable traders dealt heavily in rum. Crime and disorder grew.

In 1774 the British Parliament acted to establish a fur-trading policy for the West. In the restive coastal colonies, the Quebec Act, which embodied the new policy, became known as one of the Intolerable Acts and added fuel to the flames of controversy with Britain. The act extended the boundaries of Quebec to include the area bounded by the Appalachians, the Ohio River and the Mississippi, provided civil government for its French inhabitants, granted religious toleration to French Catholics, and ordered courts in the region to administer French civil law. The fur trade of the Great Lakes came under the authority of British officials in Quebec.

The act in effect made the area bounded by the Great Lakes, the Ohio, the Mississippi, and the Allegheny Mountains into a great Indian preserve where the rules for the fur trade would be made by Quebec, not the various coastal colonies. Fur traders in the 13 colonies were outraged because they perceived an advantage for the Quebec traders who already dominated the trans-Allegheny trade; British Canadians were outraged because the act gave French residents religious toleration and a form of civil government to their liking. The Quebec Act, many of whose provisions were, incidentally, never put into practice, helped the cause of those American colonists advocating independence from Britain. The Montreal traders, enterprising Scots and English, who dominated the fur trade in the Ohio country and the upper Great Lakes region, rapidly learned the techniques of the French and opened new fields in the interior, going beyond the areas previously exploited by the French particularly in the northwest. The outbreak of the American Revolution gave the Montreal group a further trade advantage on the upper Great Lakes where the British succeeded in maintaining territorial control.

Lake Michigan felt the impact of the Revolution. Partisans of the revolting colonies and of the British mingled among its Indian peoples seeking their allegiance and support in the conflict. As early as 1775, the British solicitated the help of Charles de Langlade of Green Bay, a French officer during the French and Indian War, in gathering Indian volunteers at Green Bay to help raise the American siege of Quebec. The British repeatedly used Indian recruits from the northern Lake Michigan region in eastern warfare and encouraged Indian raiding parties on outlying American settlements on the Pennsylvania and Kentucky frontiers.

"George Rogers Clark Raids Fort Sackville," February 1779. From a painting by George I. Parrish, Jr., in a series commissioned by Illinois Bell Telephone Co. to commemorate Illinois' Sesquicentennial year. Courtesy Illinois Bell Telephone Co.

After the George Rogers Clark expedition into the Northwest in 1778, which led to the American occupation of Kaskaskia, Cahokia, and Vincennes, the Americans began to erode the British loyalties of the Lake Michigan Indians. Clark assembled 4,000 representatives from Wisconsin and upper Mississippi tribes at Cahokia in August 1778 and so successfully presented the cause of the American revolutionaries that for a time the Lake Michigan tribes were split in their nominal allegiance, the northern Indians loyal to the British, and the Indians of Milwaukee and the Potowatomi, Sauk, Fox, and Winnebago in the Wisconsin, Rock, and Mississippi river areas sympathetic to the Americans. Probably the French alliance with the revolutionary colonies in 1778 and seeming Spanish sympathy for the Revolution bolstered the American position with the Indians of lower Lake Michigan, for the old French loyalities still lingered and many Indians traded directly with the Spanish at St. Louis.

Fear of American influence and a possible attack on Detroit and Mackinac led the British to send the sloop

Land gate entrance to replication of North West Company trading fort at Grand Portage. Photo by Allan Bogue.

Felicity on a diplomatic cruise around Lake Michigan in October 1779. Braving high winds, rain, and sleet, it landed near Muskegon and at Milwaukee. British officers learned little about potential American military moves and little to encourage them about Indian loyalities. During the next year the British moved Fort Michilimackinac from the southern peninsula to Mackinac Island, a more defensible location. In 1780 and 1781 the Illinois country, St. Louis, Chicago, the Rock River, Prairie du Chien, St. Joseph, and the Michigan City area all figured in raiding and counterraiding expeditions of the British and Americans. British sloops sailed Lake Michigan in support of British efforts. Notable among the 1781 raids was the Spanish overland thrust that seized Fort St. Joseph, unoccupied by British troops since 1763, in February. The Spanish left after 24 hours, but their action gives the present city of Niles its claim to being a city of four flags (see site 170). American influence on Lake Michigan was never strong but the British while in control had the uncomfortable feeling that their Indian allies would desert them and open the way for American military moves.

Ironically, when peace was finally made between Great Britain and the 13 former colonies in 1783, the raiding and counterraiding in the western theater had little to do with Britain's decision to let the young United States have the territory between the Appalachians and the Mississippi River. The United States fell heir to the Great Lakes country because Britain hoped that this would thwart the designs of its two European enemies, France and Spain.

With peace concluded, the fur trade of Lake Michigan and the region south of the lakes revived and entered a new era that the British dominated from 1783 to 1815. Why were they there? Had not the territory been ceded to the United States? The British traders remained because the Treaty of Paris left two loopholes that enabled them to do so. One was a provision calling for the British-held forts in American territory, including Michilimackinac, to be turned over to the Americans "with all convenient speed." "Convenient speed" was not defined. Second, the British and the Americans both had free navigation of the Mississippi, an important trade artery. The young United States was a relatively weak nation saddled with debts incurred in fighting the Revolution. It did not have the military strength to oust the British.

Most telling of all, the British had a competitive advantage over the Americans in the Great Lakes fur trade. During the years of the American Revolution, the Montreal traders came to the conclusion that excessive competition hurt everyone involved, and that combination and cooperation held greater possibilities for profit. During the 1770s combinations of merchants and traders formed to pursue the trade. Paramount among them was the North West Company, a loose association of merchant-trader partnerships that began cooperating informally in 1778 and organized formally during the winter of 1783–84. The company played a major role in the fur trade of North America until 1821, when the British government forced it to consolidate with the Hudson's Bay Company to stop open warfare between the two. The North West Company's spectacular success came largely from an expansion into the areas north and west of Lake Superior. Far-flung trade routes brought the wintering partners of the wilderness together with the Montreal merchant partners at an annual rendezvous held first at Grand Portage and later, after 1803, at Fort William.

This spectacular business, involving several thousand traders, *voyageurs*, and others engaged in bartering trade goods for furs with the Indians, also had a southwestern component involving the Great Lakes, the Illinois country, and the Mississippi Valley both east and west of the great river. The Revolutionary War did not seriously interfere with the company trade of the Lake Superior region. After peace was restored in 1783, the North West

Company and other, smaller Canadian trading combinations were ready once again to pursue vigorously the trade of the entire upper Great Lakes region. The North West Company's Mackinac Island depot soon bustled with activity. The trading partners established minor posts on Lake Michigan at Kewaunee, Manitowoc, Sheboygan, and Milwaukee, on the American shore of Lake Superior, and south into the interior. They had the capital, the organization, and the knowledge and personnel of the French, and they knew the techniques of the trade. In 1791 they got the Canadian government to drop all regulations covering the fur trade.

British domination of the fur trade in American territory irked the young United States. The new nation was convinced that the British were not only harvesting its furs and occupying its forts, but also stirring up the Indians against its authority. During the 1790s the U.S. government took a number of steps to counteract the British, including military expeditions against the Indians in the Ohio country. To avert the threat of open hostilities in the lower Great Lakes and on the high seas, it sent John Jay to England in 1794 to negotiate a settlement. The British agreed to evacuate their military posts in U.S. territory, seven in all, stretching from Lake Champlain to Fort Michilimackinac. But the fur trade was still accessible to the Canadians, for Jay's Treaty freely opened the Great Lakes and the rivers of the two countries to Canada and the United States alike and sanctioned trade and commerce between them.

In an effort partly designed to counteract the British, Congress initiated a fur-trading policy in 1796 with legislation calling for the establishment of government-operated factories where U.S. factors supplied with modestly priced goods, would trade at fair prices with the Indians. Liquor would be prohibited. Private trade was not banned, but traders had to be licensed, and they would have to trade in competition with government factories. First introduced among tribes south of the Ohio River, government factories were established at Chicago in 1805, two years after the establishment of Fort Dearborn, and at Mackinac in 1809.

In 1799 the U.S. government established a revenue district for the Northwest, making Michilimackinac a port of entry. British traders would now have to pay duties on trade goods brought into American territory. A few years later, it insisted that the vast region west of the Mississippi acquired in the Louisiana Purchase of 1803 was out of bounds to British traders: Jay's Treaty of 1794 did not apply there. In 1805 President Jefferson sent Zebulon Pike on an expedition to the headwaters of the Mississippi, at least in part to oust foreign traders. The Lewis and Clark expedition of 1804–1806 and the Pike expedition into the lower Louisiana Purchase of 1806–1807 had a similar purpose. Well before the War of 1812, the British traders could foresee the day when trade south of the border would be out of the question.

American commercial interests played a key role in wresting the fur trade away from the British. John Jacob Astor, the leading figure in the struggle, made real inroads into the British dominance in the U.S. Great Lakes region before the outbreak of the War of 1812. Astor, born and raised in the Duchy of Baden in southwestern Germany, came to New York in 1783 and established a mercantile business in furs and musical instruments, which grew, diversified broadly, and prospered. In 1800 he had well-established trading connections in Montreal, London, and China. By 1807 Astor's agents were purchasing furs from the British at Mackinac, and three years later he sent his own outfits from Mackinac into Indian country for direct trade.

In 1808 Astor founded the American Fur Company with the objective of building a vast organization that would monopolize the fur trade in all parts of the United States. He tried to buy the Michilimackinac Company, a Canadian fur-trading group organized in 1806 and containing many partners of the North West Company, whose sphere of trade was defined as the Great Lakes region. He failed and stepped up his competition at Michilimackinac. Convinced that they had to come to terms with Astor, a group of prominent Montreal merchants and traders journeyed in 1811 to New York, where they and Astor agreed to establish the South West Fur Company as successor to the Michilimackinac Company. The Montreal group and Astor would each contribute one-half the costs and share profits or losses equally. Each would send an agent to Michilimackinac. The North West Company assigned its U.S. posts to the South West Company, and the latter agreed not to trade in Canada save in specified exceptional circumstances. This division of territory applied to the region east of the Rocky Mountains only. The Canadians believed that by cutting Astor into the business of the South West Company, they could lessen U.S. custom payments and enlist

Astor's aid in eliminating the U.S. government's factory system. Astor thought that at least he would reap significant benefits from the Great Lakes fur trade. He followed up this coup with an ambitious leap to the west coast where he established Astoria near the mouth of the Columbia in 1811. Astor's well-laid plans ran awry because of strained relations between the U.S. and Britain: the long-simmering disputes over the rights of neutral ships on the high seas, which boiled over repeatedly after the onset of the Wars of the French Revolution, and frictions in the Great Lakes country engendered by the British presence in the fur trade and in Indian affairs. These strains finally culminated in the War of 1812, which disrupted the Great Lakes fur trade for three years.

Those pioneer settlers who lived south of the Great Lakes and in the West generally wanted war with Britain in 1812. They were convinced that the British presence was causing violent Indian unrest and failed to recognize that their own presence and the policies of the U.S. government so irritated the Indians that they were open to friendly overtures from the British or any other group that sought to help them.

Responding to the pressures of land hungry frontiersmen, the U.S. government used the army to quell Indian resistance to settlement and pressured Indian tribes into making treaties that ceded their tribal lands to the United States. Open warfare and treaty making characterized the two decades before 1812 in Ohio and Indiana country.

Tecumseh and the Prophet, Shawnee tribesmen, saw the handwriting on the wall and led the opposition to land cessions, gaining a widespread following that included the tribes of the upper Great Lakes and areas south of the Ohio River. Tecumseh regarded the British as his friends, for they gave him both presents and firearms. William Henry Harrison, territorial governor of Indiana and tough negotiator of land cession treaties, tried to crush Tecumseh's threatened rebellion at the so-called Battle of Tippecanoe in November 1811. This battle may in a sense be regarded as the beginning of the War of 1812. Settlers living in the interior surely thought so because of the widespread Indian attacks that followed it. The conflict in the West merged with the general war between the United States and Britain on June 18, 1812.

The second and last contest between Britain and the United States deeply affected the Lake Michigan region. On July 17, 1812, Fort Mackinac fell to combined British and Indian forces (Sioux, Winnebago, Menominee, Ottawa, and Chippewa) without a shot: the U.S. commander did not even know that war had been declared. The British arrived in a trading schooner furnished by the South West Company, the *Caledonia*, which landed on the western side of the island. At night the forces came ashore, climbed a hill overlooking the fort, and trained their cannon it. The next morning the U.S. commander had little choice but to surrender. The Americans never succeeded in retaking Mackinac during the war (see site 113).

Under orders from General Hull at Detroit to evacuate Fort Dearborn, Captain Heald, the commandant, led fort personnel outside the stockade on August 15 and south along the lakeshore. They had gone only a short distance when they were ambushed and captured by Indians (see site 1). On August 16 Detroit fell before British regulars and Tecumseh's Indian army. The British were in undisputed control on Lakes Michigan and Superior and had the confidence of the Indians, who willingly fought for them because they believed that the British planned to retake and keep the western posts and to establish a neutral Indian state west of the Great Lakes. Surely those measures would relieve U.S. pressures on tribal lands. The Indians paid a high price for their hopes. Uncounted hundreds died in battle, and Tecumseh, commissioned as a British general, died in 1813 fighting the forces led by William H. Harrison at the Battle of the Thames in southwestern Ontario. When the peace treaty was written in 1815, all the Indians had fought for was lost. U.S. territory was returned to the United States, boundaries remained unchanged, and the neutral state never materialized.

At last the fur trade in U.S. territory belonged to U.S. citizens, and John Jacob Astor soon emerged with the lion's share. Astor moved quickly to pick up the Great Lakes trade where he had been forced virtually to drop it in 1812. Congress helped him in 1816 by restricting licenses for the trade to U.S. citizens, "unless by the express direction of the President of the United States." Perhaps Astor, a very powerful and influential man, was responsible for the law, but that cannot be documented. In 1816 Astor needed to use British traders to wind down the business of the South West Company. He appealed to the president for help, and shortly thereafter the gov-

A Heterogeneous People

Few places in the United States can claim a richer and more varied ethnic history than the area lying around the shores of Lake Michigan. Here people from dozens of nations and from varying religious and racial backgrounds have mingled for three centuries as they sought a livelihood in a changing physical and economic environment. Conscious of their group identities and their differences from others, they nevertheless devised ways to coexist, and despite economic, social, and cultural frictions, all contributed to the area's development. Some came and stayed. Others came and went, giving the area an ever-changing population profile. Here the major sources of in-migration are discussed in a historical framework to provide a context for the material on ethnic groups included in the descriptions of specific lakeside cities, towns, and villages.

The Indians were the Lake Michigan area's first inhabitants. In the seventeenth and eighteenth centuries the French fur traders came establishing a few small communities, some of which have endured. The British came and went with the fur trade, leaving no lasting centers of settlement. In the vanguard of American settlers came U.S. Army personnel to garrison Mackinac, Chicago, and Green Bay and federal representatives to negotiate treaties of land cession with the Indians.

The westward tide of American settlers did not reach the Lake Michigan region until after 1830. Earlier, the fertile lands of the Ohio River Valley satiated the hundreds of thousands of easterners bent on starting life anew in the West. A less well known and more remote frontier, the Lake Michigan area suffered from adverse publicity. Michigan, popularly regarded as a pesthole of malaria and typhoid fever in the 1820s, became the subject of an eastern rhymester's warning:

Don't go to Michigan, that land of ills;
That word means ague, fever, and chills.

During the 1820s a developing transportation system opened the area to settlers. The Erie Canal, completed in 1825, linked New York City via the Hudson River to Buffalo on Lake Erie. Montreal merchants fearful of competition from New York's rising port, an ice-free entree all year round, pressed for development of a St. Lawrence–Great Lakes linkage by further waterway improvements. The Welland Canal bypassing Great Falls, completed in 1829, overcame the 326-foot difference between Lakes Ontario and Erie. Thus, by 1830 two major water routes connecting the Great Lakes with the Atlantic Ocean had improved access to the Lake Michigan region. Steamboat transportation on the lakes was then in its infancy, but sailing vessels aplenty served the flow of traffic westward from Buffalo.

Meanwhile, the U.S. government had begun building roads through the lower Michigan peninsula. Construction of a military road to connect Fort Dearborn and Detroit, known as the Chicago Military Road, began in the late 1820s and was completed in 1835. A branch of this road connecting Detroit and St. Joseph, Michigan, on the eastern lakeshore opened to stagecoach traffic in 1834. In 1828 the Indiana legislature planned a road to run from the Ohio River to Lake Michigan's southern shoreline, a project completed in 1833. In 1830 Chicago was surveyed as the potential terminus for the Illinois-Michigan Canal, which was to connect the lake with the Mississippi River via the Illinois River.

With the lines of water communication open, roads in the process of construction, and plans for future transportation linkages on the drawing board, southern Lake Michigan appealed to some of the thousands of Americans moving westward in the prosperous years from 1834 to 1837. The lower one-third of present-day Michigan, Chicago, northern Illinois, and, to a lesser extent, Lake Michigan's western shore attracted settlers. As the national speculation in western lands rose to a fever pitch, town site promoters infested the southern and western shores of Lake Michigan, platting towns at locations with a potential for port development.

This first wave of settlement around the lake came primarily from New England and upper New York State, where economic forces propelled the population westward. The declining fertility of hill farms and a shift to wool production led many New England farmers to seek more fertile lands in the West, and in upper New

The Detroit harbor by the mid-1830s was a very busy place filled with sailing vessels and steamboats carrying passengers westward. William James Bennett's painting, "View of Detroit in 1836," captures this port activity. Gift of the Fred Sanders Company in memory of its founder, Fred Sanders. Courtesy Detroit Institute of Arts.

York State many descendants of an earlier generation of New Englanders who had settled there felt the impact of "crowding," rising land values, and the uncertainties of the wheat harvest. With them came aspiring merchants, businessmen, and professionals who perceived better opportunities in an urban frontier than in older, established communities. This New England–New York stream of settlers, who arrived in the 1830s and continued to come in succeeding decades, exerted a significant influence upon the area in the formative years, laying the foundations of government, agriculture, business, and the professions and shaping the area's educational, religious, and cultural life.

If they expected to turn Lake Michigan into a replica of New England, their aspirations were short-lived, for beginning in the late 1840s and continuing for the next seven decades, Lake Michigan's cities, forests, and farmlands attracted a veritable flood of emigrants from Europe. Hundreds of thousands, representing every northern, western, central, and eastern European country, established themselves around the shores of the lake in search of a livelihood.

A complex of economic, social, and political forces induced them to leave their homes and start anew in America. While the specific reasons varied from country to country and from one period to another, there were common causes behind this exodus of millions. Living standards were threatened by a sharp increase in population, notable in Britain and the Scandinavian countries early in the nineteenth century and in eastern and southern Europe by the end of it. Should one stay and struggle against heavy odds or relocate overseas? Land tenure problems vitally affected the livelihood of many—the subdivision of arable land into very small holdings that could scarcely support a family; the consolidation of small holdings in response to a rising commercial agriculture, increasingly mechanized and responsive to a world market; and unsatisfactory leaseholds that left many in despair of ever becoming landowners.

Changes in the European economy presented problems for artisans too. The spread of the industrial revolution and the growth of factory production threatened the time-honored ways of the small, individual producer. While industrial jobs might ultimately absorb many, the years of transition were fraught with despair, discouragement, and, in extreme cases, worker riots and the smashing of industrial machinery.

Other considerations induced many to leave their homelands. Sometimes religious dissatisfaction weighed heavily in the decision. Religious motives played an important part in bringing the Norwegian Moravian settlers to Ephraim (site 59), the Dutch to the Holland area (site 160), and the German Catholics to St. Nazianz (site 35). Others smarted under a restricted franchise, compulsory military service, heavy taxes, or—as in the case of Jews from Rumania and Russia—discrimination that restricted their access to work and education and made them victims of organized massacres. Individual motives for migrating to America varied widely. While most Europeans stayed at home, millions left.

A revolution in transportation, a major component of nineteenth-century economic change, opened land and sea routes of departure. Roads, canals, railroads, and improved ocean passenger service facilitated the exodus. Transatlantic vessels made the transition from sail to steam and greatly reduced the length and discomfort of the ocean passage. The five- to six-week passage in a sailing ship under the best of circumstances in the 1840s shrank to 12 days or less on small steamships bound from northwestern European ports to New York in 1914.

Moreover, America received widespread publicity as a land of promise. Travelers' accounts, immigrant guide books, "America letters" (letters written home by established immigrants), the advertising and recruiting of steamship companies, land grant railroads, immigration societies, and American businessmen seeking cheap labor spelled out in glowing terms the economic opportunities in America and lauded its natural resources, its healthy, attractive climate, its cheap federal lands, its low consumer prices, its religious freedom, and its democratic political system. Catholic and Protestant churches actively sought immigrants to enlarge their membership.

Midwestern state governments joined the siren song of opportunity. Around Lake Michigan, the state legislatures of Michigan, Indiana, and Wisconsin, but not Illinois, appropriated public money to attract European settlers. Both Michigan and Wisconsin established New York offices for their agents. Wisconsin hired a traveling agent to distribute publicity to the eastern and Canadian press and in 1854 opened a branch office in Quebec, an important port of entry. Meanwhile the states published attractive pamphlets extolling their virtues in English, German, and other languages for distribution at ports of entry and in Europe. Not to be outdone by its neighbors, Wisconsin had Chancellor John Lathrop of the State University write some of its propaganda, a rhapsodic piece claiming that Wisconsin had the most healthy climate, the greatest beauty, and the greatest farming potential. Wisconsin's literature also emphasized its political advantages. Male aliens 21 or over could vote after one year of residence by simply declaring their intention of becoming citizens, and they were eligible to hold many public offices.

These glowing promises fell on receptive ears. Before the outbreak of the Civil War, thousands of people from the Germanies, the British Isles, Norway, Holland, and Belgium experienced the trauma of leaving their homelands, families, and friends and making a long, tedious passage across the Atlantic in crowded immigrant ships, where facilities for eating and sleeping were minimal, sanitation poor, and sickness and death common.

Most of those bound for Lake Michigan ports came via New York and Quebec. From the depot at Castle Gar-

The Erie Railroad transfer barge carried newly arrived immigrants from Castle Garden in the New York harbor shown on the right to the railroad's short line to Buffalo. Collection of Business Americana, Archives Center, National Museum of American History, Smithsonian Institution.

den in New York, they made their way west by Hudson River steamboat, Erie Canal boat, and Great Lakes sailing vessels or steamboats. After the Erie Railroad opened a short line from New York to Buffalo, some used the train instead of the Erie Canal. At Buffalo they joined the immigrants who had come via the St. Lawrence to Quebec and then made their way through the canals of the upper river, Lake Ontario, and the Welland Canal. From there in good weather it was about four days' travel by steamboat to Lake Michigan.

The immigrant's travel alternatives increased as the northern United States experienced a railroad-building boom in the 1840s and 1850s. In those decades tracks were laid parallel to the southern Lake Erie shore from Buffalo to Detroit and thence across the southern Michigan peninsula. By 1853 one could go by train from New York to Chicago. In the 1850s the railroads began siphoning off westbound passenger traffic from lake carriers. After the Civil War the railroads emerged as the major passenger carriers.

In the heyday of immigrant travel by ship on Lake Michigan, passengers could use comfortable cabin accommodations if they could afford them. Most elected the more economical steerage, with curtained berths two and three tiers high and corridors heaped with baggage. As on their ocean voyages, immigrants on lake steamers often suffered from cramped quarters, for agents arranged passage with profit margins, not passenger comfort, in mind. Passage in good weather could be quite inspiring, and travelers standing on deck absorbed the beauty of Mackinac Island, "that gem of the Lakes," and the passing panorama of forests, sand dunes, beaches, and the beautiful deep blue lake waters. In stormy weather the passage was uncomfortable and even frightening. Johan Gasmann, a Norwegian immigrant bound for Milwaukee in 1844 aboard the *Illinois*, noted: "I do not regard these long, three-storied steamships as seaworthy vessels."

Fire and storm produced perhaps the most noted immigrant tragedy on Lake Michigan. The 302-ton steam-propelled *Phoenix*, a passenger and freight vessel en route from Buffalo to Chicago, heavily laden with freight and carrying a maximum passenger load, mostly emigrants from Holland, left Manitowoc in stormy weather at midnight on 21 November 1847. About four in the morning the ship caught fire. Forty-three of the passengers and crew took to lifeboats and made shore safely. For all but three of the 200 left behind, assistance arrived too late. They perished either by fire or in icy lake waters. At least 127 of them were Dutch immigrants.

Milwaukee and Chicago were the

major ports of debarkation. For many, they were the destination, but for hundreds of thousands they were merely a stop, a place to change ships or begin the overland leg of their journey. Both also served as outfitting points for new Americans. The two towns flourished on the commerce generated by westbound passenger traffic. Margaret Fuller, a traveler on the Great Lakes in 1843, left a memorable picture of the new arrivals at Milwaukee: "The torrent of emigration swells very strongly toward this place. During the fine weather, the poor refugees arrive daily in their national dresses all travel-soiled and worn. . . . Here on the pier, I see disembarking the Germans, the Norwegians, the Swedes, the Swiss. . ."

The foreign component in the Lake Michigan area's population grew during the nineteenth century to very substantial proportions, reaching its height in the counties ringing the lake during the decade from 1890 to 1900. At that point people of foreign birth and those born in the United States with one or two foreign-born parents were the predominant element in the population. The heaviest concentration lay from Chicago northward on the western and northern shores to Mackinac. There the percentage of persons of foreign birth and parentage ranged as high as 90 percent in Manitowoc County, Wisconsin, and from a low of 68 percent upward in the other counties. In Cook and Milwaukee counties, whose port cities for years had served as principal immigrant arrival points, the percentage of persons of foreign origins stood at 80 and 86 percent respectively in 1890. On the eastern shore, county percentages were generally lower, but very few fell below the 50 percent level, and in counties were lumbering still flourished, such as Manistee and Muskegon, people of foreign birth or of American birth with foreign parentage constituted 70–80 percent of the population.

Although this concentration of persons of foreign birth or parentage was not unique in the United States at the time, the variety of national and racial groups, and the variety of rural and urban environments in which these people worked, made the area exceptional. Chicago, because of its opportunities for employment and its role as rail hub of the nation, was an extreme case. There in 1900 lived small minorities form Asia, Africa, Australia, South America, and the islands of the Atlantic and Pacific, in addition to the great mass of people from Europe. The majority of Europeans were from Germany, the British Isles, and the Scandinavian countries, but southern and eastern European countries were well represented. Immigrants from Central America, Cuba, Mexico, and the West Indies constituted a small Spanish-speaking group, and nearly 35,000 Canadians of English and French background lived in Chicago. More than 30,000 Blacks and 1,300 Mongolians levened the predominantly Caucasian racial character of the city.

The sources of immigration to the United States as a whole and to the Lake Michigan region in particular changed between the 1840s and 1920. While the majority of immigrants came from northern and western European countries between 1840 and 1900, during the 1880s substantial numbers arrived from eastern and southern Europe—the so-called new immigration—harbingers of many more to come. In 1910 Chicago's Poles numbered more than 125,000, the largest group among the "new immigrants," and its Italian-, Bohemian-, and Lithuanian-born residents numbered in the tens of thousands. Similar shifts occurred in "German" Milwaukee's population profile, and most smaller Lake Michigan cities with an industrial component also reflected this trend.

The Lake Michigan region attracted such large numbers of new Americans because it afforded a wide variety of ways of making a living. The rich natural-resource base of farmlands, forests, mines, quarries, and fisheries provided a livelihood for many. Commerce, construction, transportation, and industry required hundreds of thousands of workers. The jobs were there. Furthermore, Lake Michigan began attracting immigrants early in its developmental history. Foreign-born people, once established in Lake Michigan communities, fostered further foreign in-migration by ties of kinship and friendship and by their formal organizations. While group migration was the exception rather than the rule, networks of communication within national groups produced communities in the countryside and the cities where people of like nationality grouped together, speaking their native languages, establishing common cultural institutions, and, when their group was large enough, as in the case of Milwaukee's Germans, creating a largely self-sufficient economic life.

Lake Michigan's geographic setting was also a factor in the high concentration of immigrants—a direct one during the 1840s and 1850s, when it was a carrier of the main stream of immigrant arrivals at Quebec and New York. In the long run the lake's 307-mile north-south thrust, which so in-

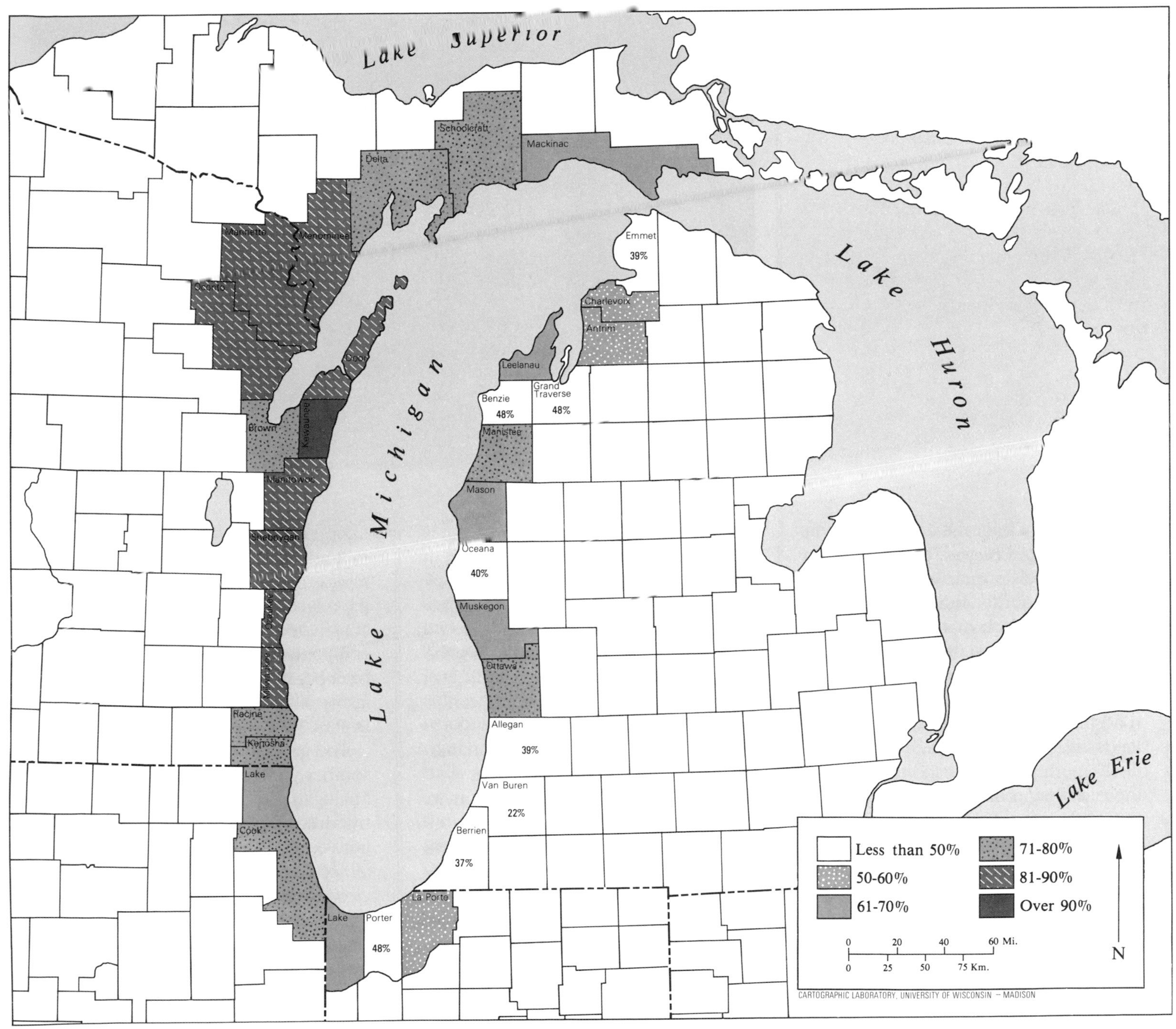

Percentage of Foreign-Born People and Persons with One or Both Foreign-Born Parents in Lake Michigan County Populations, 1890.

bers remained. By 1873 a "Canadian colony," made up of workers in machine shops, in trades, and in commercial establishments, included 15,000 persons. A Canadian newspaper reported in 1884 that the young men of Ontario "look upon Chicago as the Mecca of their ambition."

Within the United States American-born people by the hundreds of thousands, from the 1830s to the present, moved into the Lake Michigan area, attracted by its rich resources and job opportunities. From 1870 on, although the overwhelming majority of the American-born people in the counties surrounding the lake were born in the states in which they lived, the census-takers found a continuing sizable population born out of state, largely in New York or New England. In the late nineteenth century, Lake Michigan's cities attracted rural people from surrounding states who became an important source of labor in the developing industrial area stretching from Chicago to Milwaukee.

When World War I and immigration restriction in the 1920s disrupted the flow of cheap immigrant labor from overseas, domestic labor sources became critically important. Industry attracted people from many parts of the United States. Two groups among them—southern Blacks and Mexicans or Mexican Americans—added new dimensions to the population profile of Lake Michigan's industrial cities. Like so many other people, they believed that they could improve their economic status by making the move.

Wages offered for unskilled labor in Lake Michigan's industrial communities were attractive compared with those in Mexico and the American Southwest. While the vast majority leaving Mexico between 1900 and 1930, "pushed" by poverty and political disruption, settled in the borderlands of the Southwest, a small minority, hired by railroad companies as track maintenance workers, formed the nucleus of Mexican and Mexican American communities in Chicago and Gary beginning about 1916. Mexicans had long worked for the western railroads as section hands. Their appearance in the nation's rail hub was a logical outgrowth of several decades of railroad company recruitment of low-cost Mexican labor. They moved from these occupations into industrial jobs, working primarily in steel mills, packing plants, and tanneries. Milwaukee's Mexican and Mexican American people arrived to take tannery jobs in the city's expansive economy in the 1920s. Chicago, with its more plentiful jobs, remained the focus of Mexican migration. There the Mexican population grew from 3,854 in 1920 to 19,632 in 1930.

American industrial, railroad, and agricultural employers used their influence to keep the Mexican labor pool available. They lobbied to prevent the restriction of immigration from Mexico in the 1920s and 1930s. They pressured the federal government during both world wars to permit contract Mexican labor to enter the country, and they got their wishes.

Movement from Mexico and the Southwest into Lake Michigan's industrial communities, as elsewhere in the United States, has ebbed and flowed with the economy. The most notable disruption came in the 1930s. During the Great Depression, with masses of unemployed and critical public relief problems, many unnaturalized Mexicans were forcibly repatriated, and others went back to Mexico of their own volition. The depression experience disrupted and destroyed the developing social and economic life of the barrios. Rebuilding began when Mexican laborers were needed to fill critical shortages during World War II and succeeding conflicts. Prosperous times in the United States in the 1950's and 1960's lured still more people of Mexican origins into the industrial Midwest.

Along with them, beginning especially after World War II, came Puerto Rico's U.S. citizens. Leaving their island home, where overpopulation, low wages, and job shortages, bred discontent, most settled in New York City, but a substantial group came to Chicago, and smaller numbers to Milwaukee, in search of jobs. Chicago also acquired a much smaller Cuban community in the 1960s.

Of these Spanish-speaking groups (classified in the 1980 census as persons of "Spanish origins"), the people of Mexican origin were far the largest category in the Lake Michigan area. The 1980 census showed Chicago with the largest number—422,000. In the industrial cities ringing the lake, from Muskegon on the east around the south shore and north through Milwaukee, lived another 100,000. Milwaukee, with 26,100, had the second-largest group. Communities with 5,000 to 17,000 persons of Spanish-speaking origin are East Chicago, Gary, Waukegan, Hammond, and Racine.

Present in relatively small numbers in the populations of Chicago and Milwaukee during the formative years, Blacks assumed a new and very important place in Lake Michigan's industrial cities in the twentieth century. The great migration to Chicago during

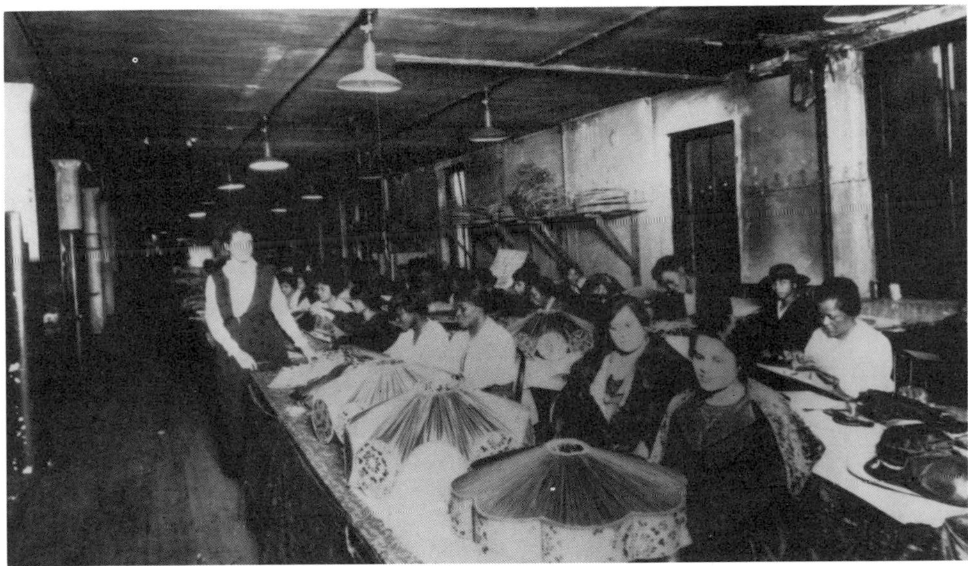

Black women and girls working in a Chicago lampshade factory in the World War I period. From The Chicago Commission on Race Relations, The Negro in Chicago. *Courtesy University of Chicago Press.*

World War I was the first movement of massive proportions. Blacks chose to leave the rural South in part because of serious, long-standing agricultural problems, compounded by the ravages of the boll weevil, floods, or low cotton prices—and at times all combined—from 1913 to 1916. An intensification of racism, Jim Crow legislation, violence, and disfranchisement, beginning in the 1890s, further eroded the quality of life for southern Blacks.

Labor shortages created by World War I forced northern employers to suppress their racial prejudices and welcome all workers. Agents sent by railroad and steel companies actively recruited southern workers, and a kind of northern fever infected the southern states. Letters home from those who had made the move to Chicago helped bring others. The *Chicago Defender*, an enthusiastically edited Black paper widely read in the South, championed migration. It soon emerged as the nation's leading Black newspaper. Blacks left Mississippi, Georgia, Alabama, and Louisiana by the thousands for the northern industrial cities. In Chicago's packing houses, steel mills, and foundries, they found jobs. The city, easily accessible by two major southern railroads and long well known to southern Blacks, attracted probably 50,000 between 1916 and 1920. While northward migration slackened in the 1920s and especially during the depression years of the 1930s, the availability of industrial jobs in the North renewed the movement during World War II and the two decades thereafter. Blacks in Lake Michigan industrial communities became the area's largest and most influential racial minority group. The 1980 census showed the Black population in the city of Chicago as 1,197,000—40 percent of the total. An additional 420,000 lived in the industrial towns east of Chicago as far north as Muskegon and north of Chicago through Milwaukee.

What impact did this heterogeneous gathering of people have upon the Lake Michigan area? The American-born and the foreign-born alike provided the leadership and the workforce that made intensive development possible. They produced cultural variety by founding ethnically oriented churches and educational facilities and by contributing to the area's literature, architecture, music, and visual and performing arts. While heterogeneity did not basically change the social institutions, political system, and economic organization common to the nation, it did modify them and influence the way they functioned.

The two social institutions most obviously affected were the churches and the schools. The foreign-born, Blacks, and people of Spanish origin challenged the Catholic and Protestant churches to meet their needs. The

St. Joseph's Catholic Church, Oconto, Wisconsin, resolved ethnic problems by offering sermons in English, Dutch, German, and Bohemian on an established schedule (see site 73). Photo by Margaret Bogue.

Catholic hierarchy responded by sanctioning parishes based on language and nationality, staffed with priests of the appropriate ethnic background. The Protestants followed similar policies. Moreover, ethnic differences within the American Catholic hierarchy led to a major policy struggle, primarily between Irish and German clergy, over the "Americanization" of the Catholic church in the United States. At the local level, priests and ministers working with relatively low-income ethnic groups found it essential to broaden traditional spiritual fare to include programs meeting economic and social needs. Ethnic congregations supported a profusion of parochial schools and raised the political issues of state assistance to parochial schools and relief from taxes for the support of public schools. Ethnic groups forced public educational facilities from the elementary level on up to include foreign language and ethnic studies in their curriculums.

The political system has also felt the ethnic impact at the local, state, and national levels. In the nineteenth century, midwestern state legislatures often encouraged immigrants to come by giving them the franchise whether naturalized or not. Established in their New World homes, they entered the political mainstream. Their presence in sizable groups with specific needs and ideas forced political parties to take heed and make concessions. Party bosses learned to manipulate the votes of newly arrived Americans in large urban centers like Chicago and Milwaukee. Progressive reformers in the early twentieth century attacked corruption and boss rule and demanded a restructuring of city government along city manager lines. Many, but not all, Progressives also called for restrictive national immigration policies. Many advocated prohibition as a way of purifying election day procedures and curbing the drinking habits of new Americans. Others worked for the repeal of state laws permitting aliens to vote.

Some Progressives responded with more positive programs, including settlement houses and pressures for increased social services, housing and tenement codes, laws regulating working hours and conditions, better law enforcement, higher health and sanitation standards, expanded educational programs, and a reorganization of charity. The Jane Addams Hull House experiment is an outstanding example of positive Progressive thinking (see site 1, no. [31]).

The foreign-born, Blacks, and people of Spanish-speaking origin have also had a major impact on the region's economy. A developing nation needed people to help it grow: hence an open national immigration policy with little restrictive legislation until the 1920s. Employers seeking low-cost labor emphatically supported the open policy. The American labor movement, on the other hand, resented employer tactics of hiring the newest comers at the lowest wages and found the newcomers, from many nations and speaking many languages, hard to unionize. Immigrant workers hampered the efforts of struggling unions in their pitched battles with management. Employers used new Americans and southern Blacks as strikebreakers and scabs. These tensions were never resolved, and the unions made real organizational progress only after New Deal legislation sanctioned their existence and the rights to bargain collectively and to strike.

Although most foreign-born immigrants were wage earners, a very small elite emerged as managers and entrepreneurs in the brewing, lumbering, meat-packing, tanning, steel, transportation, and plumbing-fixture industries, as well as in banking, insurance, industrial engineering, and trade. Relatively few among the foreign-born, Black, and Spanish-speaking minority groups in Lake Michigan communities have advocated a complete change of the U.S. economic system; most have sought to make a place for themselves within it. Unquestionably socialism made a substantial appeal to some, particularly in the early twentieth century. In industrial Milwaukee in the Progressive period, a socialist movement that had many foreign born followers veered away from doctrinaire rigidity and achieved success at the polls through gradualism and political coalition tactics. Despite widespread fears during the Red Summer of 1919 and again after World War II, Communism never appealed to more than a minority.

The presence of minority ethnic groups created social tensions. Sometimes they took the form of frictions between new arrivals and older, established groups of American-born residents or between new arrivals and more established members of the same ethnic group. Sometimes they were between ethnic groups—for example, Irish versus Germans. Sometimes race or religion was the divisive issue. Often the frictions had strong economic overtones or cultural dimensions. Five times over the last 130 years, such social tensions reached pronounced climaxes. The first was in the 1850s, when strong anti-foreign feelings accompanied a peak period of immigration, giving birth to the Know Nothing party, with its anti-foreign and anti-Catholic agenda. Early in the twentieth century, when European immigration reached an all-time high, anti-foreign sentiments again became widespread, taking the form of a conviction that immigrants were spoiling the democratic system, impeding reform, and changing the very character of society. During World War I anti-German feeling led on the one hand to suppression of German culture and harassment of German Americans suspected of disloyalty to the war effort, and on the other to a feverish attempt to "Americanize" the nation's foreign-born. In the excessive and misdirected nationalism of the 1920s, antiforeign sentiments led to immigration restriction and to the revival of the anti-foreign, anti-Catholic, anti-Jewish, and anti-Black Ku Klux Klan. The Klan gained a substantial following in Lake Michigan's urban centers. More recently the Civil Rights movement of the 1960s, spearheaded by an aggrieved Black minority, forced the majority to make concessions. Milwaukee and Chicago played major roles in the national Black protest against longstanding racial discrimination in housing, education, the job market, and law enforcement.

Today the Lake Michigan area's nationality neighborhoods, rural and urban, are less distinctive than they were in the late nineteenth and early twentieth centuries, but Black, Mexican American, and Puerto Rican neighborhoods are very evident in industrial centers. Although they are superficially like the old immigrant neighborhoods that they often now occupy, the experience of their residents is very different. These people are not, in a generation or two, fusing with the economic and social mainstream of American society. They look different from the majority population, and they have not been readily accepted. Their average incomes are lower, and their battles to pass out of the ranks of the unskilled and semiskilled into the ranks of skilled, managerial, and professional workers have been longer and harder than those of foreign-born whites. Meeting their needs remains possibly the biggest challenge of a democratic society in Lake Michigan's cities and towns.

The region's ethnic history is well illustrated in Chicago's ethnic museums (see site 1, no. [32]); the reminders of Milwaukee's nineteenth-century immigrant neighborhoods (see site 23, no. [2]); the churches of ethnic origin cited and described throughout this book; businesses founded by first-generation Americans, like Svaboda Industries in Kewaunee (see site 42); the Black and Spanish-speaking neighborhoods in Michigan City, Gary, Chicago, Kenosha, Racine, and Milwaukee; and Old World Wisconsin, the outdoor ethnic museum of the State Historical Society of Wisconsin (site 17).

Lake Michigan: Artery of Transportation

All manner of craft have plied Lake Michigan's waters over the centuries, from canoes to luxury cruise boats and thousand-foot freighters, using the lake's 307 mile north-south thrust for access to adjacent shorelands and as an entree into vast segments of the mid-continent. A procession of people have navigated its waters—prehistoric Indians, French explorers and missionaries, fur traders, soldiers and government officials, pioneering American and immigrant settlers, fishermen, travelers, vacationers, and captains and crews of ships serving the needs of commerce and industry. In every era of national development, the lake has played an important and ever-changing role as an artery of transportation.

The Indian peoples who prized the lake for its wealth of fish also used it for travel and learned the rivers, lakes, and streams of its drainage system as well as portage routes that carried them into the Mississippi River basin. The Chippewa became masters at building and paddling the birchbark canoe, the first of the eminently practical and beautifully designed light craft used on the lake. They often used Jack pine or spruce roots for sewing and binding, spruce and pine gum for waterproofing, hardwood for ribbing, and split cedar for flooring, and they always used white birch bark for covering. Family canoes were usually less than 18 feet long. Light, sturdy, and easy to portage, they worked well in very shallow water, on streams, on lakes, and in whitewater, yet skill and good judgment were essential, for the birchbark canoe was unstable, especially in turbulent Lake Michigan waters, and easily damaged by rocks and logs.

Chippeway Canoe by Peter Rindisbacher. Courtesy West Point Museum Collections, United States Military Academy.

When European explorers, fur traders, and missionaries entered the St. Lawrence–Great Lakes region, they quickly recognized the worth of the birchbark canoe, and they adopted and modified it. On large lakes and rivers, fur traders used the largest of these adaptations, the *canot du maître* or Montreal canoe, 35 to 40 feet long and capable of carrying 6 to 12 crewmen and 6,000 pounds of freight. They used the *canot du nord* ("north canoe"), about 25 feet long and capable of carrying a crew of 4 to 8 and a 3,000-pound load, on smaller rivers and lakes. Generally paddled, but sometimes poled or on the lake, fitted with a sail, these birchbark canoes served French, British, and American fur traders well in the seventeenth and eighteenth centuries.

When the British took control of France's continental North American possessions in 1763, they introduced a new era in the navigational history of Lake Michigan, characterized by the use of sailing vessels. British fur-trading and naval vessels came and went at Michilimackinac, but not until the American Revolution was well in progress is there a definite record of a British sailing ship entering Lake Michigan. In 1778 John Askin, a prominent British fur trader, sent the schooner *Archange* to Green Bay and Milwaukee to buy corn. Perhaps it was not the first sailing vessel since La Salle's *Griffon* (see "The French Ex-

The Detroit Harbor in 1820 showing the Walk-in-the-Water. *Courtesy The Mariners Museum of Newport News, Va. LP-57*

plorers") on Lake Michigan, but its voyage marked the beginning of a period when the British and American struggle to dominate the upper Great Lakes frontier brought many more. Prominent among the sloops that helped the British retain control of Lake Michigan during the Revolution were the *Felicity* and the *Welcome*, which sailed from Michilimackinac to the southern shores in 1779 on missions to forestall George Rogers Clark from a northward thrust toward Detroit and Fort Michilimackinac. A reproduction of the *Welcome* lies at anchor at Mackinaw City (see site 115).

During the years of the British-American contest for control of the fur trade of the upper Great Lakes, sloops, brigs, bateaux, and freight canoes of both nations sailed the lake. The United States had no Great Lakes naval fleet until the late 1790s. It established a shipyard at River Rouge in 1797 and here launched the brig *Adams* and the sloop *Tracy*, both of which assisted in establishing Fort Dearborn in 1803. Driven from the lake during the War of 1812, U.S. naval vessels returned in the summer of 1816, bearing troops and materials to rebuild Fort Dearborn and to construct Fort Howard at Green Bay.

Determined to exert their influence over the Indians and to extinguish their British loyalties, the United States embarked on a program of forcing Indian land cessions, surveying the public domain for sale, beefing up its military presence, and regulating the fur trade. The same program brought the first steam-powered vessel to Lake Michigan's waters. The United States hired the *Walk-in-the-Water*, the first successful Great Lakes steamboat, launched in 1818, to bring 200 troops from Detroit to Green Bay in 1821. When, in 1832, the army wished to dispatch troops speedily to Chicago to defeat Black Hawk, the owners of four Lake Erie passenger steamboats—the *Henry Clay*, *Sheldon Thompson*, *Superior*, and *William Penn*—agreed to transport them. Cholera struck the expedition, creating a panic among soldiers and crew alike. Even the surgeon aboard the *Sheldon Thompson* panicked, got drunk, and took to his bed, leaving a thoroughly disgusted General Winfield Scott to deal with the sick. Only two of the vessels got to Chicago, the first steamboats to navigate the entire length of the lake. Prophetic of a new era in Lake Michigan's navigational history, their coming also symbolized the fading of the frontier era. A lightly traveled wilderness area for hundreds of years, Lake Michigan's southern and western shores stood on the eve of settlement and development, and the lake would quickly become a natural avenue for ships and people by the thousands.

The intensive use of Lake Michigan as a major transportation artery from 1835 to the present falls into well-defined periods of growth and change closely tied to the exploitation of the region's natural resources, the expansion of agriculture in the mid-continent, the rise of industry, business cylces, and changing national and international transportation systems. The first of these, the canal era, began as the westward tide of settlement touched the lake's shores in the 1830s and grew to major proportions by the outbreak of the Civil War. These be-

Chicago's busy harbor in the 1850s at the Rush Street Bridge. Courtesy The Mariners Museum of Newport News, Va. LP-1908

ginnings owed much to the canal-building boom that extended roughly from 1817 to the early 1850s, a period when enthusiasm for improving natural waterways with canals captured the public imagination. New York's success in building the Erie Canal (1817–1825) sparked the enthusiasm and deeply influenced the development of the wilderness areas around Lake Michigan, for it opened an avenue of water transportation between New York City (and the Northeast generally) and the Great Lakes, diverting population into that region.

The Great Lakes shipping industry blossomed as companies built and launched sailing ships and steamboats which by 1850 served hundreds of thousands of people and a vast freight tonnage moving west and east. Eleven steamboats and far more numerous sailing ships served the traffic westward from Buffalo in 1833. At the close of the decade, the fleet included 61 steamboats and 225 sailing vessels on Lakes Erie, Michigan, and Superior. Steamboat arrivals at Chicago grew from 3 in 1833 to 70 in 1841. Twenty steamboats and an uncounted but seemingly endless number of sailing craft carried the trade between Chicago and Buffalo in 1846. At Milwaukee passenger and freight traffic mushroomed in the 1840s. The growing Wisconsin port claimed 1,376 ship arrivals in 1848 and 30,000 passenger arrivals in 1850. Both port cities at the mid-century served as emigrant entrepôts, and both exported sizable tonnages of agricultural produce from the developing farms of their hinterlands. Regular stops on the steamboat routes, they fostered a thriving coastal trade, for at both points homeseekers changed ships for other destinations on the lake. Lake Michigan's growing coastal communities depended on boats outbound from Chicago and Milwaukee to bring goods and supplies. The beginnings of commercial lumbering in response to rural and urban development added lumber schooners to the lake in the prosperous 1850s.

The shipping companies, eager to capture the east-west passenger and freight traffic in the canal age, engaged in a competitive scramble. They built new and larger vessels as they vied with one another to increase passenger and freight capacity, speed, and quality of service and at the same time to cut costs. Innovation was the order of the day. They tried the screw propeller invented by the Swedish engineer John Ericsson and brought to America in 1839. Its advantages compared with paddle wheelers—of compact engine and low fuel consumption—led to quick acceptance. In 1844, three years after its introduction, 10 propellers served Chicago; 50 operated on the Great Lakes at mid-century. A climax in steam passenger ship construction came in the 1850s when the impact of the railroads made itself felt on boat passenger service. The Michigan Central, in an effort to overcome the advantage of its rival, the Michigan Southern, built a series of huge, impressive steam-powered passenger ships to run from Buffalo to Detroit, whence its line would transport passengers westward. In 1849 it built the *Atlantic* and the *Mayflower*, considered marvels of lake transportation at the time. The *Mayflower*, weighing 1,354 tons, had 85 staterooms, cabin space for 300 passengers, and steerage capacity for 300 to 500 more. The Central added the *Plymouth Rock* and the *Western World* (2,000 tons each) five years later. Their launchings marked the beginning of a rapid decline in east-west lake passenger traffic. The railroads had gained the edge.

Canal-building projects aimed at enhancing Lake Michigan's usefulness characterized the years before the Civil War. The example of the Erie Canal inspired the lake's coastal town promoters to champion canals as a way to extend their commercial domain: what the Erie did for New York might be duplicated if Lake Michigan and the Mississippi River could be linked. Three Lake Michigan ports—Chicago, Milwaukee, and Green Bay—pushed the idea. Chicago's route would follow the Marquette-Jolliet return route (see p. 97), and Green Bay's the route the two used on the way to the Mississippi (see p. 12); Milwaukee's would follow the Milwaukee and Rock rivers to the Mississippi. All three projects received generous land grants from the federal government.

The Illinois-Michigan Canal, begun in 1836 and opened to traffic in 1848, proved to be a boon to Chicago and Lake Michigan commerce, initially because of the large quantities of northern Illinois agricultural produce it funneled into Chicago. The two Wisconsin projects turned out to be flops. Yet the idea of improving the lake's potential as an artery of commerce by building canals lingered on. It eventually bore fruit in the construction of the Sturgeon Bay Ship Canal (see site 46) and achieved its most elaborate expression in Great Lakes history in the St. Lawrence Seaway, opened to traffic in 1959 (see below).

During the canal era, Lake Michigan communities set the precedent for federal assistance for river, harbor, and navigational improvements. Coastal town promoters of the 1830s all envisioned their infant villages as potentially great commercial ports, if only harbors could be freed from sand bars and dredged. They pressed their representatives and senators for river and harbor improvements and for lighthouse construction. Considering the navigational hazards presented by shoals, islands, currents, and peninsulas and the well-known violence of storms on the lake, lighthouses were badly needed. In the 1830s the flow of federal funds for such improvements began, modestly at first, but destined over a century and a half to grow into multimillion dollar expenditures. Between 1829 and 1839, Racine, St. Joseph, Chicago, Michigan City, Sheboygan, Manitowoc, and South Manitou acquired lighthouses. Sixteen were operating at critical locations on Lake Michigan by 1848. By 1866 10 more had been added. In locations where lighthouse construction presented great difficulties, the government authorized the use of lightships. The first of these on the Great Lakes was stationed at the junction of Lakes Huron and Michigan at the Straits of Mackinac. Poorly designed for the task, the lightship repeatedly ran aground in high winds. Again and again the Lighthouse Service recommended that the lightship be replaced with a lighthouse on Waugoshance shoal, but Congress took its time. Finally, in 1851, the lighthouse went into operation, and the lightship was decommissioned.

The coming of the railroads to lower Lake Michigan in the 1850s marked the beginning of a new era in the lake's use as a major waterway. A close relationship grew up between the lake and the railroads, each at times obstructing and at times complementing the other. Railroad competition began to affect lake carriers in 1852–1853, when the rails linked New York and Chicago. In 1854 rail lines surrounded Lake Erie, and Lake Erie and Lake Michigan passenger vessels began to lose the east-west passenger traffic. In the long run, however, Lake Michigan fairly blossomed as an avenue of transportation in the railroad era. Rail lines promoted lake traffic by stimulating both agricultural and industrial development of the mid-continent, by serving as carriers of bulk cargoes and finished products to lakeports for transfer to ships, and by serving as aids in coal- and iron-mining operations and lumbering.

As early as the canal age, promoters of Lake Michigan's ports envisioned a close relationship between lake and rail. As they dreamed of developing the largest possible marketing areas

This engraving, which depicts the opening of the Illinois-Michigan Canal, appeared in Frank Leslie's Weekly, *August 26, 1871. Courtesy Chicago Historical Society.*

for their growing towns, they supported all manner of transportation capable of bringing commodities to port for shipment. To them railroads had great potential because they promised year-round service and could reach areas where natural water transportation did not exist.

Because of its location at the southern end of Lake Michigan's long north-south thrust, Chicago gained the greatest advantage from the railroads, emerging as the lake's principal port and as the rail hub of the nation with lines extending north, south, east, and west. The hub effect had taken shape by 1860, and it grew in intricacy over the next 60 years.

Extending roughly from the Civil War to 1940, the age of railroad influence might be dubbed the era of diversity—diversity in boats and ships, in passengers and cargo, and in services rendered. Then Lake Michigan's many faceted commerce took on a different character than ever before or since. Passenger ships of many sizes and purposes, package freighters, bulk cargo carriers large and small, a sizable fishing fleet (see "The Lake and the Fish"), railroad car ferries—literally hundreds of vessels carrying millions of tons of cargo and millions of people made Lake Michigan over that 80-year period a very busy waterway, one where the nature of its traffic changed from decade to decade.

The lake held the competitive edge in carrying bulk cargoes. By far the greatest tonnage passing over Lake Michigan included iron ore, lumber, coal, grain, stone, and petroleum products. From the forests of northern Lake Michigan, billions of board feet of lumber moved southward, principally to Chicago, but in sizable quantities to Milwaukee as well. The opening of the Illinois-Michigan Canal in 1848 sparked the traffic. By 1857 a large fleet of lumber schooners valued at $1.5 million moved 444.0 million board feet to Chicago, a small amount compared to the 30.3 billion feet delivered there between 1871 and 1893.

At first the beautiful white-masted lumber schooners dominated the trade. In 1867, just one year before the number of sailing vessels on the Great Lakes reached its height, William B. Ogden, a wealthy Chicago entrepreneur, introduced wooden steam barges as lumber carriers from his Peshtigo sawmills. Many schooners stripped of their sails were converted into barges towed by steam barges or tugs, sometimes six in a row, during the last quarter of the century. Although Lake Michigan lumber production declined after the 1890s, the lake continued as a lumber carrier until the 1920s as part of the harvest of Lakes Superior and Huron made its way to Chicago for distribution to the western market.

As the volume of lumber declined, the tonnage of iron ore and limestone needed for the expanding steel industry of the south shore grew. Almost unbelievable innovations in ore carrier design proliferated during the age of diversity (see p. 73). Coal made a convenient return cargo for home and industrial use and, increasingly in the twentieth century, for power generation in the communities lying north of Chicago. Pipelines would ultimately cut into the tonnage of petroleum products passing north from the refineries in the Chicago area, but during the age of diversity they were carried in tank freighters. Although Lake Michigan once carried more grain to market than any of the other lakes, it declined in importance as the center of wheat production moved westward and Lake Superior, water highway for east-bound grain from the wheat fields of the U.S. and Canadian plains country, rose to prominence.

A major innovation in the age of diversity, the car ferries most obviously illustrate the interdependence of rail and lake. In the 1890s the lake-locked railroads of Michigan's lower peninsula, suffering from a decline in lumber traffic, adopted the strategy of stimulating freight traffic by making direct connections with rail lines running west from the lake's western shore. For decades some of the lower peninsula roads had used break bulk freighters that carried freight and passengers across the lake to Milwaukee from Ludington and Grand Haven, but this involved an extra loading and unloading. The use of car ferries over shorter expanses of water was well established by 1890. The first Great Lakes car ferries spanned rivers: the Niagara, the Detroit, and the St. Clair. A more daring project to span the Straits of Mackinac went into successful operation in 1888.

The Toledo, Ann Arbor, and Northern Michigan Railroad took the plunge in 1892 by building a car ferry capable of operation over large areas of open lake to link Frankfort-Elberta, Michigan (see sites 142, 143), and Kewaunee, Wisconsin. The *Ann Arbor No. 1*, the pioneer of the Lake Michigan car ferries, went into service on September 29, 1892—1,128 gross tons, oak-hulled and covered with steel to four feet above the water line, with a capacity of 24 railroad cars.

That was the beginning of a significant feature of Lake Michigan transportation for decades to come. The car ferries carried hundreds of millions of tons of freight, hundreds of thousands of passengers, and, by the mid-twentieth century, tens of thousands of automobiles across the lake. The Ann Arbor line extended its services, and other lines followed its example. The Pere Marquette plunged into the business in 1897, destined to become the largest car ferry service on Lake Michigan. The Grand Trunk initiated car ferry service in 1903, and two smaller, short-lived companies entered the business early in the century. By 1910 a fleet of 16 car ferries bridged the lake, most of them with 1,300- to 1,700-ton capacities. Even after railroad passenger service had declined severely and trucks had challenged railroad freight traffic, in 1961 the Chesapeake and Ohio ferries (successor to the Pere Marquette) carried 132,000 freight cars, 153,000 passengers, and 54,000 automobiles over the lake.

The Lucia B. Simpson, *the last of the lake lumber schooners on her final voyage in 1929. Photo by J. Robert Taylor. Courtesy State Historical Society of Wisconsin. WHi(T35)32*

Package freighters also plied Lake Michigan's waters in the age of diversity, carrying a wide variety of manufactured products to and from port cities, principally Chicago and Milwaukee. Their entree in the lake's commerce dated from the 1850s. The railroads came to dominate the package freight business, but independents operated as well. Through much of the late nineteenth century, package freight moved on vessels that included passenger accommodations and even space for bulk cargoes. The Anchor Line's four iron propellers, a real innovation when they were built in 1871—The *Alaska, China, Japan,* and *India*—sailed between Lake Erie and Chicago, combining freight and rather

The Grand Rapids of Milwaukee *ferry entering the Milwaukee harbor.* Milwaukee Journal *photo. Courtesy State Historical Society of Wisconsin. WHi(X3)40551*

elegant passenger services as an adjunct to the railroads. As traffic grew after 1890, the carriers introduced newer steel vessels designed specifically for package freight and others designed specifically for passengers. In 1907 large, fast freighters carried 6,650,000 tons of package freight on the Great Lakes for the railroads. Buffalo, Chicago, Milwaukee, and Duluth-Superior were the major shipping and receiving points.

At the end of the nineteenth century, passenger traffic on the Great Lakes underwent a spectacular revival involving millions of people. A byproduct of rapid industrialization and urbanization, the efforts of the railroads to promote lake travel, and the search for new business alternatives in Lake Michigan's lumbering towns (see p. 93), lake travel boomed through the 1920s. While relatively small proprietors developed the resort business in Lake Michigan's lumbering towns, the railroads made huge investments. In 1901 the Ann Arbor Road built the Royal Frontenac on the Frankfort waterfront specifically for vacationers (see site 142). At Mackinac Island, long regarded as a vacation paradise, three major carriers in 1887 built the Grand Hotel, a wonderful white-pillared structure overlooking the straits, reputedly the largest summer hotel in the world (see site 113). Moreover, James J. Hill's Great Northern Railroad launched a promotional campaign to popularize transcontinental travel via the Great Lakes. Hill's two luxury Great Lakes passenger liners, the *North West* and the *North Land*, traveling between Buffalo and Duluth and Buffalo and Chicago respectively, went into service in 1894–1895. These 5,000 ton steel-hulled luxury liners, much like transatlantic vessels, were soon known as "the wonder of the tourists."

Less luxurious Lake Michigan carriers offered day, night, and excursion service between Lake Michigan ports. Resort locations like Washington Island, Mackinac Island, Ottawa Beach near Holland, Michigan City, and Benton Harbor, where the House of David's amusement park attracted thousands of Chicagoans (see site 168), were well served during the summer months. Outstanding among the excursion steamers, the *Christopher Columbus*, pride of the Goodrich Transportation Company, oldest and largest of the transportation companies on Lake Michigan in 1910, was the largest on the lake. It was Captain McDougall's only whaleback passenger ship. Between Chicago and Michigan City the Indiana Transportation Company ran two excursion steamers with 3,500 and 2,500 passenger capacity—the *Theodore Roosevelt* and the *United States*—twice daily. The latter was indeed a boatload of patriotism, featuring the American flag in "suspended electrical effects" that flashed on and

The Christopher Columbus *passing through the Broadway Street drawbridge in Milwaukee. Photo by Joseph Brown. Courtesy State Historical Society of Wisconsin. WHi(W6)6347*

off. The decor included pictures and tablets depicting the nation's history and a map of the United States made from wood furnished by the governors of the various states. Pearl stars designated the state capitals. In an age when patriotism ran high, the company fully understood how to make its vessels attractive to Chicagoans headed for the cool and beautiful beach at Michigan City.

In the early twentieth century, 2 million lake-borne passengers passed through the port of Chicago annually, many of them tourists and excursionists. No aesthetic prize, Chicago's harbor was nevertheless very busy. As James Cooke Mills noted in *Our Inland Seas*, published in 1910, vessel entrances and departures exceeded those of any port on the continent, and the volume of Chicago's commerce stood second only to the port of New York. There in 1910 the thoughtful observer could see a passing parade of vessels old and new that profiled the revolution in ship technology since 1850—the occasional schooner; steam barges with demasted schooners loaded with lumber in tow; wooden and iron steamers; steel freighters; the new 600-foot ore carriers; the steel-hulled *North Land* cruise ship; the whaleback *Christopher Columbus*, queen of the day and excursion boats; a wealth of smaller steel passenger and package freighters; tug boats. By the early twentieth century only a few hundred sailing ships remained. Steam triumphed, and iron (and later steel) replaced wood.

Gone is the age of great diversity that gradually grew and then flowered in the first two decades of the twentieth century. Even then a wave of change in transportation technology—first the automobile, then trucks, and finally the beginnings of aviation—laid the groundwork for the undoing of diversity. With mass production of automobiles and their widespread popularity in the 1920s, public pressure for better roads mounted. Massive road construction culminated in the interstate systems of the 1950s and 1960s. Automobile travel hurt the Great Lakes passenger business. Cruise ships gradually lost their popularity as people elected to travel by car or by air. Fortunately the *S.S. Keewatin*, cruise ship of the Canadian Pacific Railroad, lies at anchor at Saugatuck-Douglas, where visitors can go aboard and capture the flavor of the Great Lakes luxury cruise (see site 162). Truck transportation eroded the lake package freight service, and the railroads curtailed passenger service to the point that railroad-owned vessels that had served both types of traffic disappeared from the lake. American-operated package freighters disappeared from Lake Michigan just before World War II. Railroad car ferries continued to operate, but in the 1960s and 1970s they

The Prins Johan Willem Friso*, a Dutch freighter, the first to arrive at Chicago through the St. Lawrence Seaway, participating in the Seaway opening ceremony at Chicago, April 30, 1959. Photo by F. Dober. Courtesy Chicago Historical Society.*

reported declining traffic and sought operating subsidies from Wisconsin and Michigan. One by one their services ceased, until in the summer of 1984 only two remained in service.

During World War II Lake Michigan's use as a major waterway entered a new era in which bulk cargo tonnage grew to unprecedented heights and international trade assumed a greater importance than ever before. Carriers loaded with iron ore and limestone dominated the tonnage figures. In 1945 wartime demands for steel sent tonnage figures to a record high of 80 million, surpassing the earlier record of 67 million set in 1929. From 1945 to 1979 tonnage edged upward. In every year except 1977, Lake Michigan carried more than 100 million tons of cargo annually, the largest component by far being the materials of steel production. The recession of the 1980s has substantially lowered those figures.

The opening of the St. Lawrence Seaway in 1959 was the culmination of years of support for the project by business interests in Great Lakes port cities. The dream of linking the Atlantic Ocean, the St. Lawrence River, and the lakes was clearly expressed by Toronto merchants early in the nineteenth century, and ways of increasing foreign commerce had been on the agenda of Chicago and Milwaukee promoters from the 1850s on. World War I sparked the growth of direct trade. Small tramp vessels made their way into the lakes in the 1920s, but not until 1931 did the first regularly scheduled cargo vessel from overseas make its way to Chicago—the *Anna*, outbound from Antwerp with a load of chicken wire and barbed wire for Montgomery Ward. World War II focused attention as never before on the limitations of the mid-continent's linkage to the Atlantic. For example, submarines built in Manitowoc had to be transported in sections down Lake Michigan, the Calumet Sag Channel, the Illinois River, and the Mississippi, and then reassembled before going into service.

The number of vessels engaged in service between Europe and Chicago grew steadily, from a few dozen in 1945 to 120 a decade later, when Lake Michigan ports received two-thirds of all the U.S. traffic between Great Lakes ports and foreign markets. Small wonder that Lake Michigan port cities wanted the seaway. To Grand Haven, South Haven, and Green Bay came wood pulp in small liners and tramps from the Scandinavian countries, and to Sheboygan came clay from England for use in Kohler plumbing fixtures. To the port of Chicago came cement, sugar from the Caribbean, glass from Italy and Scandinavia, raw materials for iron and steel production, whiskey, beer, wine, Italian marble, Spanish olives, and German and English cars—products either unavailable in the domestic market or available more economically overseas. Out from Lake Michigan's ports went agricultural products, machinery, automobiles, trucks, and buses.

The possibilities for foreign trade were well established when Congress in May 1954, after 52 years of procrastination and Canada's announcement that it would go it alone if neccessary, approved construction of the seaway as a joint Canadian-American effort. In addition to the foreign trade and national defense arguments, the hydroelectric generating potential of the seaway appealed to northeastern interests.

After the opening of the seaway in 1959, overseas commerce grew. Lake Michigan's totaled 470,300 tons in 1958. It jumped to 1.5 million in 1959 and in most years from 1968 to 1979 topped 5 million. Moreover, commerce with Canada, quite significant for a century, reached new heights. During the 1950s, 4 million tons was a common annual figure; in the 1960s and 1970s, 8–10 million was.

Iron and steel shapes and coke and petroleum products made up the greatest tonnage of foreign imports into Chicago and Milwaukee in 1979. The heaviest outbound cargoes for overseas delivery included corn, soybeans, grain products, and iron and scrap steel. To Canada went corn, soybeans, and coke. Canada supplied nonmetallic minerals and over 2 million tons of iron ore and concentrates from its Lake Superior mines, which were very competitive with Minnesota's Mesabi.

Two decades after its opening, the seaway was beset with problems: the ever-increasing size of ocean-going vessels, many of which cannot come through its locks and canals; heavy competition from trucks and railroads; rising tolls for the use of the waterway, averaging $30,000 per ship in 1983; the need for a system for handling containerized general cargo; the failure of the ports to cooperate in pressing their needs; and an economic recession that by 1983 had sharply diminished iron ore shipments. Grain continued to be a bright spot in the gloomy picture. Creative thought in both the government and private sectors can turn around the seaway's future as economic conditions improve.

Lake Michigan's second major waterway connection with the ocean is the Calumet Sag Channel, originally built in 1922 to provide through barge traffic to the Mississippi. In 1955 improvements began that widened it from its original 60 feet to 225 feet. The Sag Channel has both supplied Lake Michigan with additional tonnage and competed with it as a carrier of foreign-bound cargoes.

Through the history of Lake Michigan as a major avenue for water-borne commerce run the themes of adapting to changes in transportation technology, to the ups and downs of the national and international economies, and to political realities. These themes became part of the complexities of lake use during the era of the fur trade and they continue in modern times.

Lake Michigan's transportation history is illustrated at a number of places. The following sites are especially noteworthy.

1. At both Milwaukee and Green Bay, visitors can get close enough to get a good view of harbor activity.
2. At Port Washington pleasure craft, commercial fishing boats, and a coal carrier are often found in harbor in the vicinity of Smith Brothers Restaurant. See site 26.
3. The Manitowoc Maritime Museum and World War II submarine *U.S.S. Cobia* are both excellent places to visit. See site 36.
4. The Kewaunee railroad car and auto ferry pier is still operational. See site 42.
5. Visitors can get a good look at shipbuilding operations at Sturgeon Bay, see its small Marine Museum, and at specified times visit the U.S. Coast Guard cutter *Mobile Bay*. See site 46.
6. At Gills Rock, where the ferry leaves for Washington Island, the Door County Maritime Museum has a number of displays on aspects of Great Lakes maritime history. See site 53.
7. The *Alvin Clark* "Mystery Ship" Marine Museum at Menominee features a Great Lakes cargo schooner raised from the lake bottom in 1969 and now rapidly deteriorating. See site 75.
8. The iron ore docks at Escanaba can be visited. See site 81.
9. On Mackinac Island the Grand Hotel stands, a fine example of the summer resort hotels built by the

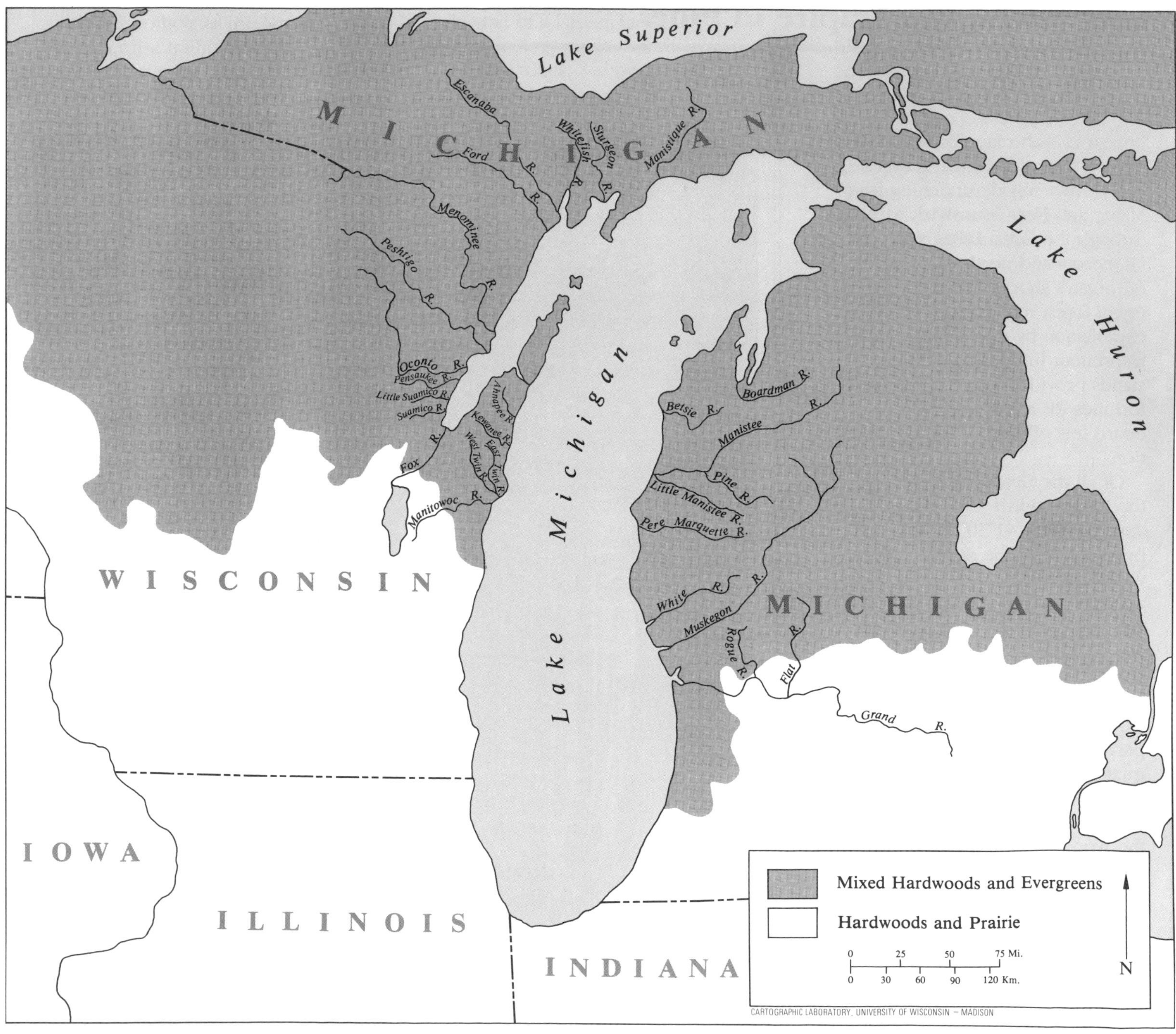

Lake Michigan's Logging Rivers and its Forests.

Nevertheless, in popular parlance the hardwood forests interspersed with white and red or Norway pines were called the pineries. They began on the western lakeshore near Sheboygan, Wisconsin, and extended northward around the head of the lake and south as far as South Haven, Michigan.

On most nineteenth-century Lake Michigan residents, the aesthetics of the fine timber stands made little impression. For farmer-settlers, trees were a source of wood for homes, fences, farm buildings, and fuel. If they chose timbered land, as many German immigrants did along Lake Michigan's western shore, the trees presented a challenge, an impediment to cultivation that had to be cleared away with backbreaking labor. Lumbermen eyed the trees with board footage in mind, and to their logging crews and sawmill workers, trees meant a living. Few reflected on the beauty of the great black walnut stands of southern Michigan, the magnificent old maples, or the majestic black-barked climax white pines, some as much as 20 feet in circumference and 100 feet tall, or the equally impressive giant yellow birch. Even in the wake of the devastating forest fire at Peshtigo in 1871, a local observer describing the horror paused to pay tribute to the lumbering industry because it utilized the woods, "making them, instead of a curse, the source of our wealth."

Americans of the 1980s can get some sense of the magnificence of these woodlands at places like the Ridges Sanctuary–Tofts Point–Mud Lake Area Natural Landmark site near Baileys Harbor, Wisconsin (site 50), and at Interlochen State Park, Interlochen, Michigan (site 134). Lake Michigan's present forests represent subsequent growth on cutover lands.

Nature's bounty provided the lumbermen with a delivery system as well as fine timber stands. Lake Michigan and the rivers flowing through the forests into the lake made the harvest easy. Pine floated readily, and logs could be driven downstream from the inland pineries to sawmills at the lakeshore, sawed into lumber, and loaded aboard ships for Chicago, which grew to be the nation's largest lumber market. Although the rivers carrying the richest drives were the Menominee in the Green Bay lumbering region and the Manistee and Muskegon on the Michigan lower peninsula, most of the rivers that honeycombed the forests also delivered logs to the lakeside sawmills.

Small logging and milling operations serving local needs began on Lake Michigan in the 1830s. Large-scale commercial lumbering dates from the properous years of the 1850s, and the big cut came after the Civil War. By 1900 the heyday of lumbering on Lake Michigan had passed.

Lake Michigan's timber stands fell to axe and saw rapidly and wastefully because of their proximity to the growing cities and farmlands of the Midwest. During the late nineteenth century, the rapid development of the Mississippi River watershed, large sections of it treeless grassland, created a great demand for lumber. Chicago, so accessible to the source of timber supply, grew as the center of a railroad network that fanned out in all directions, creating a delivery system for inland lumber consuming communities.

From South Haven on Lake Michigan's eastern shore and Sheboygan on the western shore northward, the lumbering industry spawned sawdust towns that bustled to the sound of whining saws and the diverse languages of American-born and immigrant workers. Lumbermen of means wielded great influence over all phases of town life. In the great woods life revolved around lumber camps, where lumberjacks ate and slept while horses and oxen gathered strength for another day. Come daybreak the axe, saw, canthook, peavey, bobsled, big wheels, the shout of "timber," and the earth-shaking crash of great trees absorbed attention and energy. Lumber schooners and steam-powered vessels came into port with all manner of needed supplies and left with lumber cargoes destined for Chicago. In the late nineteenth century, logging locomotives puffed and whistled through the woods.

Who were Lake Michigan's lumbermen, lumberjacks, and millworkers? Some of the earliest and most influential lumbermen came fresh from their lumbering experiences in New Brunswick, Maine, Pennsylvania, and New York, moving westward into the rich upper Great Lakes pineries as profits and timber stands in the Northeast declined. They brought with them experience, capital, and skill. A late nineteenth-century historian of the upper midwestern lumbering industry believed that Maine had contributed more lumbermen to the region than any of the other older areas of the nation. Possibly considering Michigan, Wisconsin, and Minnesota as a whole he was right, but it would be a mistake to give Maine such weight in speaking of Lake Michigan's large lumbermen. Experienced Maine men were there, but far more numerous were ambitious young New Englanders, New Yorkers, and Pennsylvanians without direct connections to the northeastern lumbering industry, lured westward in search of business opportunities in a developing area. Many had only a few years of experience in small businesses. They were on the make. Some of Lake Michigan's very successful lumbermen were born in Michigan, Illinois, and Wisconsin, and some men of immigrant origin joined the ranks of leadership and wealth, men born in the Germanies, England, Ireland, Scotland, and French Canada. Some made great fortunes; many achieved modest business success; and some failed altogether in a rough and highly competitive business, the victims of widely fluctuating prices, market gluts, indebtedness, and a great variety of unfortunate business decisions.

As for the workers, the army of mackinaw-clad lumberjacks and the host of millworkers, they too came from diverse places for many reasons. Young men in search of the money to buy farms regularly worked as farm laborers until harvest time and then headed for the pineries during the winter months. Late in the nineteenth century, when the log harvest became virtually a year-round business, many of them worked continuously as millhands and lumberjacks for a time. But other farmers continued as seasonal employees throughout the lumbering era to help pay for land and improvements, turning over home responsibilities to wives and children at the end of harvest season. Newly arrived immigrants in search of work found it in the north woods. Germans, Swedes, Norwegians, Finns, Bohemians, Belgians, and French Canadians made up a significant part of the workforce.

Lumberjacks at work with a crosscut saw. Photo by E. Ammermann. From the Collections of the Michigan State Archives, Department of State. 10738

Lumber workers were a far more sober and industrious lot than the rowdy, gambling, wenching, hard-drinking, swearing, singing, storytelling lumberjacks of local legend.

There was a real contrast in life style and influence between the lumberjack and millworker and the large, successful lumberman. The workers lived on modest wages—some very modest indeed—in either simple houses or company-owned dormitories. The successful lumbermen lived in very comfortable homes and, if among the very successful, in spacious, well-appointed mansions staffed with servants. The Perry Hannah House in Traverse City, Michigan, the home of a lumberman turned banker and merchant, is an excellent example. Hannah capped his career by building in 1891 a beautiful Queen Anne mansion of perhaps forty rooms embellished with cut leaded glass windows, a great variety of fine woodwork (mahogany, cherry, bird's-eye maple, and birch), imported marble fireplaces, and expensive wallpaper. It overlooks the Boardman River, where the first Hannah sawmill stood (see site 132). Three mansions in Muskegon—the Charles R. Hackley, Thomas Hume, and John Torrent homes—also reflect the life style of highly successful Lake Michigan lumbermen (see site 156).

These men often dominated the political, social, and cultural affairs as well as the economies of their home communities. They were as much a part of the entrepreneurial spirit of the late 19th century as the better-known captains of industry like John D. Rockefeller and Andrew Carnegie. They assumed that government existed to help, and not to interfere with, their businesses. They believed that they performed a very valuable service to society by engaging in business, creating jobs, and producing needed products for the market. While not all did so, lumbermen like Perry Hannah, Charles R. Hackley, and Isaac Stephenson felt an obligation to use their wealth in the communities from which they derived it. They continued to live where they had made their fortunes even after lumbering declined and promoted community betterment by giving money for libraries, parks, schools, and even in Hackley's case, an art gallery. They were often the leading figures in establishing churches, which they liberally supported. While the public generally admired their success and hoped to emulate them, sawmill and lumber-camp workers did not always share these views. Strikes over hours and wages occurred but rarely succeeded. The lumbermen generally assumed a paternalistic attitude toward their workers and did their best to discourage unionization.

Without question the lumbermen used government to suit their ends. They pressed the federal government for river and harbor improvements to facilitate their businesses. They promoted local railroad lines and asked Congress for federal land grants to construct lines through timberland inaccessible by natural waterways. The Green Bay lumbermen sought and got a land grant to support the construction of the Sturgeon Bay Ship Canal to eliminate the treacherous water passage around the Door Peninsula (site 46). They fought with the railroad companies over rates. They solicited state legislatures for charters to construct dams and booms on the rivers to improve and control log delivery. They ran for and got elected to office at the local, state, and national levels. They tried to cooperate among themselves to control production, markets, access to pine stumpage, and lumber prices, but here they did not succeed. Lumbering on Lake Michigan was never a monopoly or a near monopoly; rather, it was a competitive industry with many small and medium producers and some very large businesses. The largest organized their businesses by purchasing pinelands, mills, transportation facilities and by developing their own market outlets.

Because the lumbermen lived in an age when the government and the public alike supported the development of what seemed to be almost unlimited natural resources, the more unscrupulous of Lake Michigan's lumbermen encountered little serious resistance when they bent laws to suit their purposes. Many examples might be cited, but a few will suffice. It was illegal, but not unusual, to steal timber from the public lands, of which Lake Michigan's timberlands were initially a part. It was not as though federal policies made timber land expensive, for stumpage sold for $1.25 per acre at the most, and there were legal methods of getting it for less. After the register of the Green Bay federal land office reported widespread timber thefts in 1849, an investigation ensued. It ended when local lumbermen successfully pressured their congressmen into having federal investigating agents removed.

Isaac Willard, appointed by the Secretary of the Interior in 1853 to bring a halt to timber theft from public lands in Michigan, found that about 50 million feet of lumber had been cut from federal lands lying between the Menominee and the Grand rivers—monumental thievery. His experiences in 1853 and 1854 read like a western thriller. At Manistee mob insurrection, bribery, arson, threats, beatings, and even murder stymied his efforts. Ultimately he got help from the U.S. Navy which assigned the *Michigan*, the Navy's first iron ship, to help him apprehend the lawbreakers. Political pressure by lumbermen on the Secretary of the Interior led to the dismissal of the commissioner of the General Land Office and all timber agents. That ended the federal government's attempts in the 1850s to enforce the law in Michigan. The task was assigned to local officers who, under local pressures, did little. As timber grew scarce, lumbermen cast covetous eyes upon Indian reservation timber stands and pressed the Bureau of Indian Affairs for permission to cut there as well. Sometimes they succeeded.

The great river drives of pine logs are perhaps the most colorful chapter in the history of lumbering around the shores of Lake Michigan. River delivery, the earliest method, continued as long as it was the most economical one, and most of Lake Michigan's lumber went to the Chicago market by ship. The last of the drives came down the Menominee River in 1917. Initially the lumbermen concentrated on harvesting the pines, especially white pine and red pine, for these durable and easily workable woods were much in demand for all kinds of construction. Following methods developed in the Northeast, lumbermen established camps in the woods for their workers with bunkhouses, cookhouses, stables, and sheds. Workmen cut the pine during the winter months, hauled it on oxen or horse-drawn bobsleds to stream and river banks, log marked it with branding irons, and piled it up. In spring, when the ice melted and the waters rose, the logs were sent on their way to the mills located at the lake edge. There, at scaling ponds, work crews sorted the logs belonging to different millowners and floated them into mill storage ponds.

Use of the same streams and rivers by many small and large competitors could and did produce chaos. Lake Michigan's larger lumbermen organized and chartered log boom companies designed to make improvements, such as dams, to control water flow and to introduce order and control in log delivery. In return for their investments and services, they assessed a delivery price per log. This technique, first used in the northeastern pineries, worked successfully in the until iron and steel virtually replaced it at the end of the nineteenth century.

Salt and chemical production, which also originated as a satellite to lumbering, proved to be a very long-lived industry. Michigan salt production, originally fostered by a state bounty, mushroomed once Michigan lumbermen came up with the idea of using sawmill refuse and the exhaust generated by steam-powered sawmills for the evaporation process. Using processes pioneered in the Saginaw Valley, lumbermen in Frankfort, Ludington, and Manistee sank wells, acting on the findings of the state geologist during the 1880s. At Manistee the Reitz lumber company began salt production in 1880. By 1899 its wells had produced almost 16 million bushels of salt, and Manistee styled itself "The Salt City of the Inland Seas." Michigan emerged as the leading national salt producer.

In the long run a chemical industry utilizing salt by-products far overshadowed the economic importance of salt production associated with lumbering. Dow Chemical Company of Midland, which grew directly from the salt wells sunk by the lumberman, operates a sizable plant at Ludington. Lake Michigan's hardwood forests fostered chemical industries in yet another way. Lumbermen found that the fumes from charcoal making could be converted to wood alcohol and acetates. A number of lumbering communities boasted chemical plants in the late nineteenth and early twentieth centuries.

The total dollar value derived from the products of Lake Michigan's forests—lumber, shingles, tanbark, cordwood, railroad ties, posts, and poles, plus the output of the satellite industries described above—defies calculation. It surely ran into the hundreds of billions of dollars. There are good estimates of lumber production. Considering only the timber harvest from the watersheds of Lake Michigan's major logging rivers, the volume reached staggering proportions by the end of the century. The western shore of the Michigan lower peninsula yielded a conservative 47 billion board feet, and the Green Bay watershed—that is, the western and northern shores, exclusive of the Door Peninsula—20 billion board feet. The Mackinac shore yielded 3 billion. George W. Hotchkiss, author of the voluminous *History of the Lumber and Forest Industry of the Northwest*, explained the 20 billion Green Bay figure quite graphically: "If the total cut of the Green Bay region was placed, each board at the end of another, it would form a walk one inch thick and one foot wide, nearly 357,000 miles in length, or fourteen times around the globe, and at five thousand feet to the acre denuding no less than 4,000,000 acres of land in its production." The lumbermen and their contemporaries were impressed with the magnitude of their accomplishments.

The environmental price of the big cut ran high. From the destruction of the forest cover, the people, the land, the wildlife, the streams, the rivers, and the lake suffered severely. Perhaps the first and most obvious damage came in the form of the devastating forest fires of 1870–1920. The combination of great heaps of slash on the forest floor, the influx of farmer-settlers into cutover land, and the extension of the railroads into the north woods led to spectacular holocausts, none more vividly publicized than the great fires of 1871. In Wisconsin these swept through the Fox River Valley, along the western shore of Green Bay, and through the Door Peninsula south of Sturgeon Bay, and in Michigan from large areas along Lake Michigan's eastern shore across the lower peninsula to Port Huron. In the annals of Great Lakes lumbering, the fires of 1871 are invariably linked with the disaster at Peshtigo because of the heavy loss of life there (see site 74) and the dramatic horror of the fire.

For many weeks in the fall of 1871 isolated fires had burned in the Green Bay woods and underground, sending a pall of smoke over the water and endangering navigation. For weeks frightened farmers, townspeople, sawmill owners, and railroad men had worked day and night to protect people and property, hauling water, plowing strips of land, building earthworks and ditches, and anxiously scanning the sky for rain. Many believed on Sunday, October 8 that the worst had passed. They were wrong. The worst came at 9:00 P.M., when a strong southwest wind whipped isolated slash fires, farm-clearing fires, and railroad construction campfires into a fury that one contemporary aptly labeled a fire storm. "The sky was brass. The earth was ashes." Peshtigo disappeared in a hurricane of fire. In panic people and animals rushed for the river, already filled with burning logs and bridge and building timber. Many died there, and many others perished before reaching the water. At least 800 died in the town, and unknown numbers on surrounding farms died huddled in plowed fields or in root cellars and wells, many from suffocation.

From Peshtigo the fire raced north and east toward Marinette and Menominee. Oconto (site 73) escaped its full fury and sustained only minor damage, and a line of sand hills between Peshtigo and Marinette deflected the major part of the tornado of flames west of these towns. Several mills and a church burned, and so did most of the village of Menekaunee. After jumping the Menominee River, the fire struck and destroyed the village of Birch Creek.

On Green Bay's eastern shore, at just about the time of the Peshtigo disaster, fires erupted on the Door Peninsula south of Sturgeon Bay. Afterward contemporaries suggested that the fire leaped the bay and set the peninsula ablaze. This is rather unlikely because of the northeasterly direction of the wind. Probably ignited from summer clearing fires, these conflagrations destroyed New Franken, Robinsonville, Williamsonville (see Tornado Memorial Park, site 64), Brussels, and Little Sturgeon. Estimates of fatalities ran as high as 105. A prominent leader in the Belgian community believed that the fire left at least 5,000 homeless and destitute. Given the ferocity and magnitude of the blaze, small wonder that many Peshtigo and Door Peninsula residents believed that the Day of Judgment had come. One conservative estimate of damage to the Lake Michigan western shore placed the destruction at a minimum of 1,152 lives and 1,280,000 acres despoiled, mostly forest land from which only a fraction of the burned and scorched softwoods could be salvaged.

Yet the devastation on the western shore was only part of the story. Michigan residents with a historical bent are annoyed by the emphasis on the Peshtigo fire, for Michigan's timber land suffered even more extensively

PROCLAMATION!

Our sister City of Holland is nearly destroyed by fire. More than two thousand people are left homeless and exposed to to the pittiless storm. Food and Clothing is the immediate want.

I, HENRY GRIFFIN, Mayor of the City of Grand Haven, do hereby call upon all good citizens to contribute to the relief of these sufferers.

For this purpose I have caused Subscription Papers to be opened at my office.

Any provisions, cooked or otherwise, and clothing, will be of comfort, and such donations taken to the Office of E. P. FERRY, will be there received and record kept of Donors.

HENRY GRIFFIN, Mayor.

Grand Haven. Oct. 10th, 1871.

Courtesy Michigan Historical Collections, Bentley Historical Library, University of Michigan.

on October 8, 1871. Along Lake Michigan's northern shore, forest fires raged on the Stonington Peninsula, in the Fayette district, and near Escanaba, all Green Bay communities on Little and Big Bays De Noc. To the south, in the lower peninsula, the devastation of forest lands assumed massive proportions. In all, probably at least 2.5 million acres of Michigan timber burned. Fire approached the town of Holland in mid-afternoon, and by the next morning most of the city lay in ashes. Miraculously—providentially, some believed—Van Vleck Hall at Hope College and Albertus Van Raalte's beautiful pillared 1856 Greek Revival church escaped (see site 160). Forest fires burned for hundreds of miles along the east coast. Manistee (site 147), a rough and bustling lumbering town 50 miles north of Holland, virtually burned to the ground. Fanned by strong winds out of the southwest, the fire raced northeast through the lower peninsula, threatening Lansing, and on into Thumb country all the way to Lake Huron. Port Huron escaped. Saginaw suffered damage but not destruction. Flames seared the forests of the Au Sable River and its tributaries as well as the woodlands in the Thunder Bay region. Fortunately, the loss of life in Michigan was small—10 persons or possibly a few more. Contemporaries hypothesized that the wind carried embers from the great Chicago fire of the same day to Michigan's forests, but it seems most probable that the combination of wind, drought, slash, and clearing and construction fires caused the conflagration. Ironically, destruction led to destruction. Lumbermen thereafter argued that the presence of farmers made it imperative to cut the timber before great fires ignited by small clearing fires could destroy it.

While contemporaries dwelt on the loss of human life and timber in forest fires, they seem to have ignored their impact on wildlife. Fires destroyed birds and animals and their natural habitat, and fish died from the heat and from the toxic runoff. The first complaint about the impact of lumbering on water quality apparently came from fisherman, who complained that log drives and the practice of dumping sawmill refuse into rivers and the lake decreased the catch and fouled spawning grounds. Another consequence of lumbering, farming on the cutover lands, produced further environmental and human problems. To many Americans, accustomed to the time-honored formula of removing trees and creating farms, it seemed logical that

From the Mines to the Blast Furnaces

United States Steel blast furnace at Gary, Indiana. Courtesy United States Steel Corporation.

For well over a century, since 1865, great shiploads of iron ore have sailed over Lake Michigan, bound first for the iron and steel-making cities of Lake Erie's south shore, since the 1870s for Chicago's steel mills, and after 1900 for the expanding Gary–Burns Harbor–East Chicago steel-manufacturing complex. In dollar value and in significance for the national economy, the lake's importance as an avenue for ore carriers is hard to estimate.

The rich iron resources in Michigan's Upper Peninsula and northern Wisconsin, the even greater riches in Minnesota, the plentiful Michigan limestone, and the coal resources of Pennsylvania, Ohio, Kentucky, and Illinois cast the Great Lakes in the role of a water highway for bringing together the heavy, bulky components of steel making. Without the lakes, the steel-making industry of the Midwest would probably have developed a very different geographic pattern, with blast furnaces located close to the sources of iron ore and limestone. As it was, industrialists chose to build steel plants on the southern Lake Erie and Lake Michigan shores. Ore and limestone came by water to points well served by railroads. Coal came by rail, and iron and steel products went to market by rail.

Until the enactment of restrictive immigration laws in the 1920s, labor to mine the ore, transport it, and man the steel mills was plentiful, cheap, and too poorly organized to challenge management. The national government used tariffs to protect its emerging iron and steel industry from foreign producers and aided entrepreneurs in their efforts to exploit ore deposits by generous land disposal policies, liberal land grants for the construction of canals and railroads, large appropriations for river and harbor improvements, and, in the twentieth century, funds for scientific research to solve the technical problems of mining. Similarly, the state governments encouraged the industry with favorable tax laws, bounties to ore producers, support for the exploration of potential ore lands and the development of new transportation systems, and funding for research and technical education.

The mines that produced the great shiploads of iron ore came into production between 1845 and 1892. The Marquette Range, lying in the Michigan Upper Peninsula, came into production first, followed by the Menominee and the Gogebic, shared by Michigan and Wisconsin. While conducting a linear and geological survey for the federal government, William A. Burt, inventor of the solar compass, found iron ore south of Teal Lake near Negaunee, Michigan, in September 1844. A year later Philo M. Everett of Jackson, Michigan, led a group of men into the Upper Peninsula in search of mineral wealth. His search team "rediscovered" it when he was not present. Everett formed the Jackson Mining Company, the first to mine the riches of the Marquette Range.

Burt and other mining pioneers in the Marquette tapped a source of ore that by 1980 had yielded more than 500 million long tons. The first ores from the Menominee came to market in 1877, and the first from the Gogebic in 1884. By 1980 the mined wealth of the Menominee Range totaled almost 330 million long tons. By 1967, when mining ceased in the Gogebic, the yield totaled over 320 million long tons. The Marquette and the Menominee are still producing, but the richest deposits are long since gone, and 97 percent of Michigan's ore now comes from leaner types that are refined into pellet concentrates before being shipped to the blast furnaces. The mineral wealth of these three ranges made Michigan the nation's leading producer of iron ore until 1900, when the fabulously endowed Mesabi Range of Minnesota gave that state the number one position that it retains and will retain far into the future.

The presence of iron ore in Minnesota came to public attention decades before mining began. The problem was to identify the most promising site for development. When the Minnesota Iron Company incorporated in 1882, the Vermilion Range seemed the most likely. Two years later carriers loaded with Vermilion ore set out from Two Harbors to make their first delivery to Lake Erie steel mills. The first Mesabi ore went to Duluth in October 1892, clear evidence of the efforts of the Merritt Brothers, the "Seven Iron Men," who were largely responsible for opening the Mesabi Range.

For pioneer producers in the iron ranges of Michigan, Wisconsin, and Minnesota, transportation constituted a major problem, for ore deposits lay miles inland from the Superior and Michigan lakeshores. Ultimately mine owners built railroads to bring ore to the lakeshore and docks to facilitate loading it into the ships that made the long journey south to the steel-making centers. Until the completion of the Sault Ste. Marie Canal in 1855, Marquette Range developers had to move ore by ship to the rapids, carry it overland around the rapids, and then reload it aboard ships bound for Lake

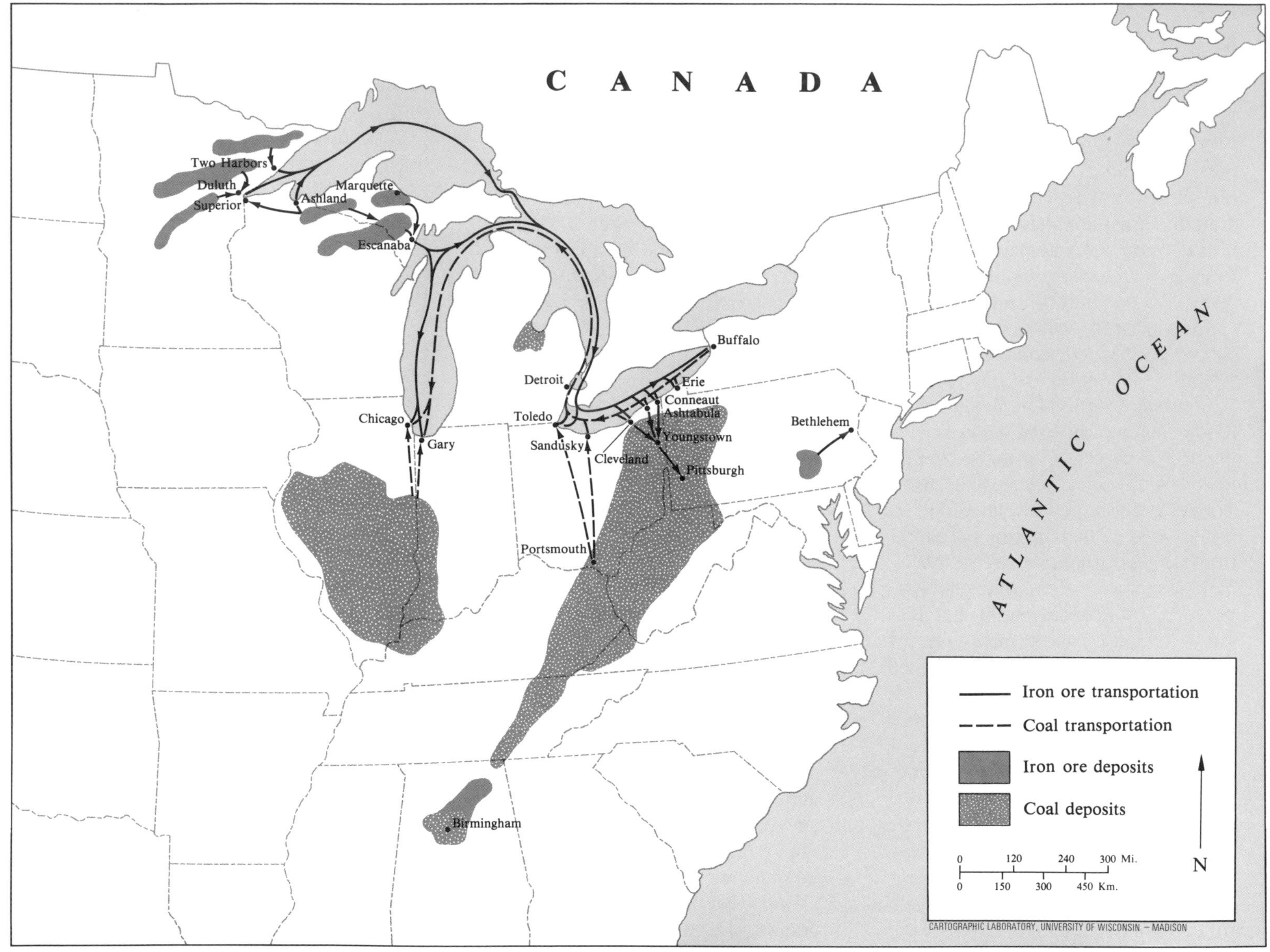

Iron Ore and Coal Transportation Pattern, 1935.

Erie. This expensive and time-consuming delivery system inspired the pioneer developers to ponder alternative ways of delivering their ore.

With the abundant limestone and vast hardwood forests of Michigan's Upper Peninsula at hand, it seemed logical to many that the ore should be turned into pigs of charcoal iron close to the mines and then marketed. Until 1854 charcoal smelting dominated pig iron production in the United States. Blacksmiths and small foundaries preferred the tough, malleable charcoal-smelted product to either anthracite- or coke-smelted iron. With improvements the coal-coke process would soon gain precedence, but for the first quarter-century of Marquette Range production, the market demand for charcoal iron justified local smelters. Moreover, transportation linkages by rail and water between the Upper

Peninsula and the great coal beds south of the lakes needed further testing and development to make it clearly advantageous to ship ore long distances.

While the charcoal blast furnace industry around Lake Michigan's northern shores is insignificant compared to the large-scale, long-term development of coal and coke smelting, it is well worth noting as an example of an industry dependent on local natural resources. The first of the Upper Peninsula forges, built at Carp River near Negaunee, Michigan, produced bar iron in 1848. Nine years later the Pioneer Iron Company built a blast furnace at Negaunee, the first on the Upper Peninsula. Over the next half-century, 25 more charcoal-fueled blast furnaces came into production on the Upper Penninsula, while others were located at Green Bay and De Pere, Wisconsin, and at Elk Rapids, Boyne City, Leland, Frankfort, and Grand Haven on the Lake Michigan side of the lower peninsula. On the Lake Michigan side of the Upper Peninsula, furnaces and forges fired by charcoal assumed an important, albeit temporary, place in the economies of Menominee, Escanaba, Gladstone, Fayette, Manistique, and St. Ignace.

While all of these smelters experienced a rather checkered business life, beset by fluctuations in pig iron prices, ever-increasing competition with the large-scale coke-fired iron and steel plants on the southern lakeshores, and dwindling charcoal supplies, their longevity varied considerably. Escanaba's furnace operated for perhaps three years, 1872–1875, before being dismantled and moved to Pittsburgh. Ten to twenty years of operation was not unusual.

The Elk Rapids iron-smelting business (see site 129) of the Dexter and Noble lumbering company, whose productive years extended from 1872 to World War I, was perhaps the longest-lived of these. Depletion of local hardwoods led to its closing, an inevitability that optimists of 1887 had expected sometime after 1937. The ruins of one of the blast furnaces remain at Elk Rapids as a reminder of the years when lumbering and iron smelting produced great prosperity for the town.

The remarkably productive Fayette furnaces of the Jackson Iron Company deserve special attention here, for at the site of the company town of Fayette, now a Michigan State Park (site 92), visitors can learn much about the operations of nineteenth-century Lake Michigan charcoal smelters. Unlike the Dexter and Nobel furnace, which was primarily an adjunct to a very successful lumbering business, the Fayette furnaces were an adjunct to iron mining. Directors of the Jackson Iron Company of Negaunee, Michigan, founded in 1845, decided that the railroad line opened between Negaunee and Escanaba in 1864 would make a smelting business near Escanaba profitable. The company chose land about 20 miles east of Escanaba, a beautiful location on Little Bay De Noc with a good harbor, plentiful hardwoods, and an abundance of limestone. The ore could be shipped from company mines to Escanaba by rail, loaded aboard barges, and towed to the company furnaces at Fayette. The first of these went into blast on Christmas Day, 1867, and a second was added in 1869.

The company built a town adjacent to the furnace for its employees, complete with a school, churches, opera house, company store, and residences. It forbade the sale of liquor in Fayette in an effort to maximize worker efficiency and preserve a good moral atmosphere in a very isolated community, a rule that led to the growth of saloons adjacent to company lands and to the arrival in harbor of floating bars and houses of prostitution on weekends and paydays. Fayette prospered from 1867 through the 1880s, but the hardwoods needed to make charcoal grew more and more scarce, and fuel costs rose. By 1887–1888 company workers were cutting hardwoods 15 to 20 miles from the furnaces to keep them in blast. The smelters literally denuded the Garden Peninsula. In December 1890, fuel costs having risen so high that operations did not pay, the Fayette furnaces produced their last pig iron. The second-largest charcoal iron producers in Michigan, the Fayette furnaces over the years smelted almost 230,000 tons, while all Upper Peninsula production totaled more than 1,500,000 tons. Harlan Hatcher estimates that the Upper Peninsula furnaces had consumed 330,000 acres of hardwood by 1900.

Although it was economical to produce pig iron close to the mines, smelting in a remote frontier area presented serious technical problems, and some companies shipped small quantities of ore to the smelting furnaces of western Pennsylvania and northeastern Ohio during the first decade of production. The opening of the Sault Ste. Marie Canal in 1855 helped to solve the problem of a water route for Marquette Range ores, and Marquette grew as an important ore-shipping port. By the outbreak of the Civil War, the lakes were earning a reputation as

In recent years the James R. Barker, *a one thousand foot self-unloading supercarrier, has carried taconite pellets over the lakes to Cleveland. Courtesy Lake Carriers Association, Cleveland.*

of a whaleback is the *Meteor*, formerly the *Frank Rockefeller*, now a floating museum at Superior, Wisconsin. The general design of the *Onoko* prevailed.

Innovations in ore carrier design and the volume of launchings followed the ups and downs of the business cycle and the demands of war. In the prosperous years of the early twentieth century, carrier capacity reached 10,700 tons. During World War I larger craft with 13,000-ton capacity joined the carrier fleet. During the twenties, when the new automobile industry and construction boomed, the *William G. Mather*, a carrier with a 13,500-ton capacity, came down the ways, destined, in Harlan Hatcher's words, to be "the last word in ship design, propulsion, navigation equipment and crew accommodations" for the next 17 years. The Great Depression of the 1930s deeply affected Great Lakes shipping, and very few new carriers were launched. World War II brought a frenzy of construction, as the campaign to modernize the Great Lakes fleet got underway, including the construction (subsidized by the Maritime Commission) of carriers with capacities of 15,000 to 17,500 tons.

In the prosperous years following World War II and through the 1960s, as the U.S. economy responded to the stimulus of defense contracts and a booming national and international market for producer and consumer goods, American shipyards produced bigger and better carriers. At mid-century much of the Great Lakes ore fleet was old and in need of replacement. The *Roger Blough*, 850 feet in length, wider and longer than the largest ore carrier in use, went into service in 1972. The *Stewart J. Cort*, 1,000 feet long, and the *Presque Isle*, of the same length but differently designed followed in quick succession. By 1980 the Great Lakes ore fleet included ten 1,000-foot self-unloading supercarriers.

A far cry in appearance from the brig *Columbia*, which passed through the Sault locks in 1855, these new vessels reflected the vast technological changes in loading and unloading methods that have accompanied improved ore carrier design over more than a century. Wheelbarrows and shovels have given way to highly sophisticated mechanical loading and unloading equipment. The turn-around time for ore-laden vessels is a matter of hours, and crew time ashore is very short. Ship crews tend to the highly skilled tasks of ship management and not to shoveling ore, as in the early years. Verse and ballad preserve the miseries of the past. Lake Michigan sailors disliked loading at Escanaba:

Some sailors took shovels, while others
got spades
And some took wheelbarrows—each
man to his trade,
We looked like red devils, our fingers
got sore,
We cursed Escanaba and that damned
iron ore.†

Cost studies show that the most effective use of the great new ships is in carrying ore exclusively, even if that means returning to Escanaba, Marquette, Duluth-Superior, and Two Harbors without cargo. From 1900 to 1950 ore boats commonly carried coal on the return voyage. The supercarriers operate more efficiently by discharging taconite pellets and returning, without waiting to load coal. Smaller, older freighters handle the coal trade. Ship power too has been revolutionized—from wind to coal-powered steam engines to diesel power. Speed, cost efficiency, and space have dictated these changes. Expansion of dock, harbor, river, and canal capacity went hand in hand with the growth in the size of carriers. The capacity of the Sault Ste. Marie canal locks, originally required by federal legislation to be at least 250 feet in length and 60 in width, measured 1,200 by 110 feet at the opening of the renovated Poe Lock in 1969.

The iron and steel industry made the United States an industrially powerful nation with a high living standard, but the American people have paid a high price in alteration of the natural environment. River and harbor improvements have seriously disturbed Lake Michigan fish and wildlife habitats. In building steel plants, large areas of sand dunes in the Gary–East Chicago–Burns Harbor area were leveled, and large areas of wetlands, natural strainers of runoff from lands adjacent to the lake, were filled in. The aesthetics of the shoreline suffered. Steel plants and their worker populations clustered at Gary and East Chicago, adding human and industrial pollutants to lake waters. Until recently, the ore carriers discharged garbage and human and fuel wastes as they plied Lake Michigan.

An excellent place to ponder the wisdom of it all is at the Indiana Dunes National Lakeshore in the Michigan City–Burns Harbor–Gary area (site 175). At Michigan City the little pocket of dune land supporting a variety of trees and flora includes a beautiful, if rather small, expanse of dune beach. At the lakeshore the recently built Michigan City power plant comes starkly into view, an abrupt reminder that Lake Michigan's waters are essential for power production. At the Burns Harbor and Gary segments of the lakeshore, peaceful natural islands in the midst of steel production, the sounds and smells of heavy industry keep twentieth-century realities in mind.

At Iron Mountain, (see site 85) heart of the Menominee Range, once so productive of high-grade iron ore, a scarred landscape of abandoned mines lies all around. The old mines have closed, and ore production now depends on lean ores that must be refined into concentrated pellets before shipment. The Gogebic ceased production in 1967, and the high-grade ores of the Mesabi have long since been exhausted. Refinement of the leaner taconite is the basis of the Minnesota iron-mining industry.

The great ore carriers make an impressive sight as they glide south through the Straits of Mackinac to the Indiana steel mills or sit docked for the winter in Milwaukee harbor. Unless the iron and steel industry experiences drastic changes, they will continue to do so for many decades. Blast furnaces close to the ore source, an idea that seemed so logical to early nineteenth-century Michigan mining companies, may once again be tried, using western coal shipped by unit trains. The posibility intrigues some of the industry's leaders.

Fayette State Park is an outstanding historical site on the Michigan Upper Peninsula for those interested in the northern shore's charcoal-fired blast furnaces (site 92). At Norway and Iron Mountain the reminders of the Menominee Range's most productive years are highly visible (sites 84–85). At Escanaba (site 81), ore carriers still load their cargoes. During the winter months the great carriers of the U.S. Steel Corporation are at dock in Milwaukee's inner harbor (see site 23). Although the steel plants in the Burns Harbor–Gary–East Chicago area do not permit visitors, one can get an excellent view of them from Interstate 90, the Indiana Toll Road.

†Reprinted by permission of the publishers from *Ballads and Songs of the Shanty-Boy* by Franz Rickaby, Cambridge, Mass.: Harvard University Press, copyright 1926 by the President and Fellows of Harvard College, © renewed 1954 by Lillian Rickaby Dykstra.

The Lake and the Fish

They sound like big fish stories, those observations of the seventeenth-century Jesuit priests. Instructed to record natural phenomena and all they could learn about Indian life and culture for the benefit of French officials, the black robes provided posterity with the best and largest remaining body of knowledge about the wilderness possessions of New France. From their writings Lake Michigan emerges as a clear, sparkling lake, abounding in fish, with unbelievably large specimens of whitefish, sturgeon, and trout. For the Indians, who fished with spears, nets, and weirs, the lake's bounty supplied a major part of their food. Explorers and fur traders also relied on lake fish. These early users made little impact on the fish population or on the fish habitat, for they were relatively few in number and the fish were legion.

Fishing station probably at Kenosha, Wisconsin, in the 1850s. Courtesy State Historical Society of Wisconsin. WHi(X3)11000

When the permanent settlers of the 1830s fell heir to Lake Michigan's wealth, some recognized the fisheries as a potential gold mine, provided that they could process and market salted fish. Consider the experiences of Captain J. V. Edwards and Jacob Conroe in 1836. A test seining between Two Rivers and Manitowoc, Wisconsin, netted 10 barrels of fish (2,000 pounds)—mostly whitefish. They enthusiastically decided to establish a fishing business at Two Rivers. John P. Clark of Detroit soon joined them. He used a ship to collect fish from a number of Lake Michigan stations and deliver them to the Detroit market. Edwards and Clark formed a partnership that for some years caught, salted, and packed 2,000 barrels of fish annually. Detroit did not long remain the major market for the Lake Michigan catch.

Once the depression of the late 1830s had run its course, the lower Lake Michigan region attracted settlers by the thousands (see "A Heterogeneous People"). During the 1850s a vastly expanded local market for fish stimulated commercial fishing along the southern and western lakeshores. Historians of this area stress the seemingly endless wealth of whitefish, the favored species for local consumption, and the importance of local fishing industries during the first few decades of development. In the 1860s and 1870s, fishermen sent more and more of their catches to wholesalers in Milwaukee and particularly Chicago, already the hub of an expanding railroad network. There, fish wholesalers did a lively business, sending Lake Michigan whitefish by rail to the growing communities in the Midwest. They handled about 7.5 million pounds in 1872. Three years later, according to the U.S. Commission of Fish and Fisheries, their wholesale receipts reached 12 million pounds, primarily from Lake Michigan fishing stations. Market demand far exceeded supply. Fishermen responded to that demand. In 1880 they took a recorded 23 million pounds from Lake Michigan, and there is good reason to believe that the figure is conservative. The abundant and highly prized whitefish accounted for more than half the catch. Sturgeon, herring, and trout stood in second, third, and fourth places.

Fortunately the need to redraft U.S.-Canadian fishing agreements led the U.S. Commissioner of Fish and Fisheries to call in 1885 for a careful study of the Great Lakes fisheries. They had grown tremendously, he noted, since 1880 in order to supply the needs of a rapidly expanding American population, particularly in the West. The number of people employed in the fisheries on Lake Michigan more than doubled between 1880 and 1885, reaching a total of 3,400 in the latter year. In that same five-year period, the value of equipment used in the fisheries more than tripled to nearly $1.8 million. The study, the first such "exhaustive investigation," provides a clear picture of Lake Michigan's fishing industry after 30 years of steadily intensifying commercial development.

Although the fisheries in 1885 were scattered all along the lakeshore, the most important and productive lay along the northern shores near the Beaver Islands and in Green Bay, in distinct contrast to the early decades, when fishermen operated mainly on the southern and western shores. The ethnic origins of the fishermen had also changed. Initially Indians and American-born whites were a majority. By 1885, the commissioner noted, the industry was practically in the hands of "foreigners." These were principally Germans, Scandinavians, Irish, and French Canadians, but Dutch and Poles also stood in the ranks of the fishermen.

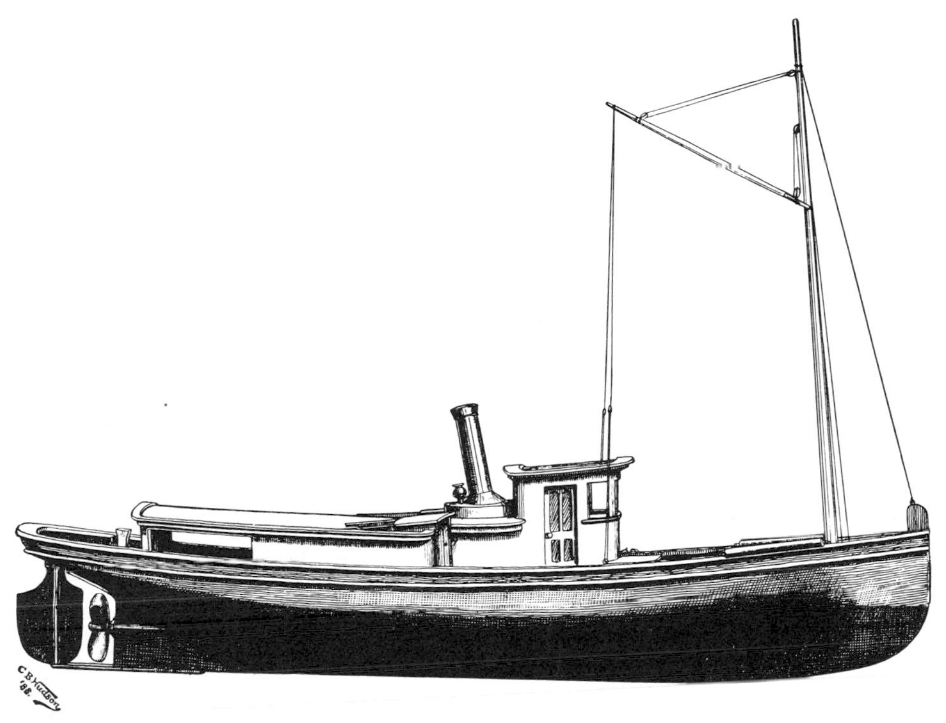

Gill Net Steamer from U.S. Commission of Fish and Fisheries, Report of the Commissioner for 1887.

Methods of fishing on Lake Michigan also showed a marked change from earlier decades, when fishermen using various types of nets and sailboats operated relatively close to shore. The first gill-net steamers came into use on Lake Michigan in 1869, when the *Kittie Gaylord* of Washington Island and the *Pottawattomie*, owned by a fisherman near Green Bay, began netting whitefish. Thirty steamers operated in 1880. Five years later the number stood at 82. While the average sailboat carried 60 to 100 gill nets, steamers fished with several times as many. The gill net, developed and used first by Indians, trapped fish by their gills when, after swimming into it, they tried to back out. The mesh size determined the size of the fish caught. In 1885 gill nets found more widespread use on Lake Michigan than anywhere else on the Great Lakes. The use of steamers to set and lift the nets greatly enhanced the fisherman's catch because of the quantity of nets the boats carried and their ability to operate farther from shore than sailing craft. The 1885 report noted that the nets set by fishermen on opposite sides "nearly meet at the center."

Lake Michigan's fishermen also used pound nets from the mid 1850s on. These were used first in Green Bay, whence they spread all around the lake. Useful relatively close to shore, the nets are set at 80 feet or less to lead fish into a crib or pot from which they have little chance of escaping. Poles driven into the lake bottom hold the nets in place.

Around much of the lake the fishing season lasted from spring through November, but for many years an extensive ice fishery made Green Bay virtually a year-round fishing ground. Prospering especially between 1860 and 1880, Green Bay's winter fishermen built hundreds of shanties on the ice and lived there most of the time. Fish dealers and merchants drove out to collect the catch and to sell supplies. By 1885, however, Green Bay's winter fishery was in decline.

Most of Lake Michigan's catch in 1885 went to Chicago wholesalers, who arranged with lake steamship lines and railroads for speedy delivery of the catch, 75 percent of which went to market fresh. Only fishermen remote from transportation salted or smoked it because fresh fish brought much higher prices. At Escanaba, Fairport, Sturgeon Bay, Petoskey, and Traverse City, refrigerator plants constructed to handle the surplus summer catch preserved the overage for marketing in winter, when prices justified doing so.

Although the screw-propelled gill-net steamers operating mainly out of Milwaukee, Sheboygan, Manistique, Frankfort, Charlevoix, Grand Haven, and St. Joseph made very large catches, they were a minority among Lake Michigan fishing craft in 1885.

All told, 1,402 fishing boats operated on Lake Michigan in that year. Of these, 1,320 were propelled by sail or oar. Wind-powered vessels operating gill nets included Mackinaw boats, Huron boats, and Norwegian boats. The last were a Lake Michigan adaptation of the fishing boats used in Norway, the favorite of Scandinavian fishermen but scorned by American fishermen, who found them too heavy, unwieldy, and hard to row in calm weather. Pound-net fishermen used other kinds of boats, different from the sailing craft that ventured far onto the lake. These included the pound-net sailboat for lifting and carrying the catch to shore, ore-propelled pound-net dinghies, and decked stake boats, used to install and remove the nets.

The marketing organization of the Lake Michigan fishing industry in 1885 encompassed both small local operators and large concerns based in Chicago and Detroit. Some of the latter were wholesalers who had expanded their original marketing operations to include fishing, collecting the catch from independent fishermen, and processing the catch. In 1885 A. Booth and Sons of Chicago had a substantial capital investment in gill-net steamers, nets, sailboats, express steamers to move the fresh catch swiftly to Chicago, and refrigeration plants along the northern shore to freeze portions of the summer catch for the winter market. At the same time, smaller dealers in Green Bay, Traverse City, Sturgeon Bay, and Milwaukee also collected and marketed fish.

Lake Michigan's fish and fish products found ready buyers throughout the East, Midwest, and West and even overseas. The sturgeon, once regarded as a trash fish that should be dumped on beaches to rot, came into its own, prized for caviar and as a source of isinglass. These products were marketed both in the United States and in Europe. On the local scene peddlers carried fresh fish through the streets of Milwaukee and Chicago and throughout the Wisconsin countryside. At the other extreme, railroad refrigerator cars transported the catch thousands of miles.

The Lake Michigan fisheries constituted a booming business in the 1880s, but even then, scarcely 30 years after the beginnings of intensive commercial fishing, all was not well. The whitefish population grew smaller and smaller. Once abundant in the southern part of the lake, the catch dwindled there and the great netloads came from the northern shores. Even there fishermen reported declines in Green Bay and at Washington Island. This downward trend, which had probably set in before 1885, continued steadily. Early on, fishermen had advocated stocking the lake to reverse the decline, and both state and federal fish commissions had responded. Lake Michigan received almost 69 million artificially propagated whitefish between 1875 and 1885 alone. Yet the whitefish catch continued to drop, from 6.5 million pounds in 1885 to less than three-quarters of a million pounds in 1940.

The whitefish problem in 1885 was just the tip of the iceberg. Nevertheless, very intensive commercial fishing continued. As the whitefish declined, trout and herring became the mainstays. The trout yield remained reasonably constant until 1940, but the herring catch fluctuated wildly, leading some observers to wonder if Lake Michigan was experiencing the same overfishing that had led to the collapse of the herring fishery on Lake Erie. The sturgeon catch declined sharply early in the twentieth century, dropped into the thousands of pounds by the 1920s, and vanished from the statistics in the 1930s.

In 1908 Lake Michigan's commercial

Gill nets drying in the sun at Fishtown, Leland, Michigan. Photo by Margaret Bogue.

catch surpassed all previous years of record—47 million pounds. Thereafter it gradually declined, averaging 23 million pounds from 1911 to 1946, and fishermen called for the application of their time-honored formula of accelerated stocking programs. Not until 1967 did Lake Michigan's fish yield surpass the 1908 record, when it reached 59 million pounds. The contrast in the quality of the catch between 1908 and 1967 was startling. In 1908 herring and trout dominated, with whitefish and sturgeon running a poor third and fourth. Alewives made up 70 percent of the 1967 catch, and chubs 15 percent. By then the lake's commercial fishing industry had undergone an utter transformation, passing through decline and virtual ruin from the sea lamprey into an era of strict regulation and massive efforts to save something from the debacle.

Why did decline and devastation occur? While it is impossible to determine the precise relative importance of the many reasons for the decline, the contributing factors are clear. They all fit under the general umbrella of human failure to use wisely the great natural resource the lake provided. Prevailing nineteenth- and twentieth-century attitudes toward natural resources, individual economic rights, and government regulation underlay that failure. Americans generally believed that nature's bounty should be used and that there was no danger of exhausting it. They could not foresee the population explosion of the mid-twentieth century; nor did they believe in governmental control of resource use. Rather, they subscribed to the idea that governments should adopt policies that helped people use natural wealth. Not until the turn of the twen-

declining fish populations were, he stated, overfishing, small nets that destroyed immature fish, the fishermen's deliberate efforts to exterminate rough fish, fishing in spawning grounds, and water pollution. He advocated uniform regulation of mesh size and net depth, limitation of the size of the catch, closing the spawning seasons, and the designation of closed areas.

Regulation of the Great Lakes fisheries presented enormous problems. Government control was unpopular. Moreover, if it was to be effective, all the states, the federal government, the province of Ontario, and the Canadian government needed to cooperate. The long-recognized need for cooperation led to conference after conference and voluminous reports and recommendations. Between 1883 and 1938 21 conferences and meetings convened for the specific purpose of addressing the problems of the Great Lakes fisheries, attended at times by representatives of the Great Lakes states, at times by federal and state officials, and at times by federal, state, and Ontario provincial representatives. All emphasized the need for uniform controls but could find no way to achieve this goal. An international treaty seemed to be the best method, but for one to be negotiated, the states would have to cede to the United States their sovereign rights to Great Lakes waters. That they would not do.

Interstate compacts emerged as another possibility. But compacts were not binding upon the states, and the states simply refused to cooperate with each other. As fishery problems became more critical in the 1920s and 1930s, conferences and meetings multiplied. They were held in all but three years between 1927 and 1938. Finally, in 1940, the governments of the United States and Canada appointed, for the third time (the first was in 1893 and the second in 1908), a joint body to study the problems of the Great Lakes fisheries and to make recommendations.

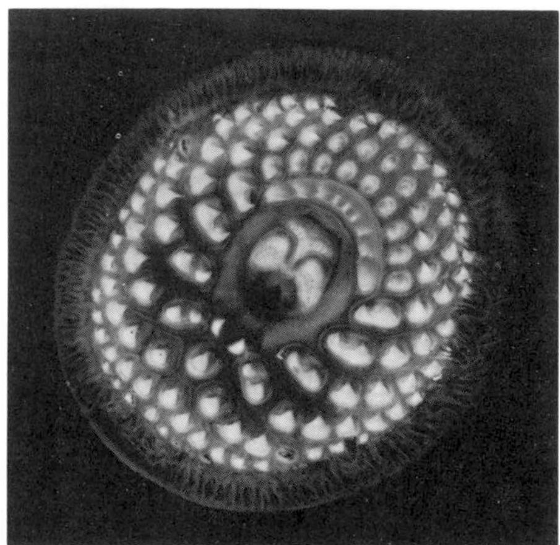

Lamprey mouth. Courtesy Wisconsin Department of Natural Resources.

Time was running out, for already the sea lamprey, long found in Lake Ontario, had made its way into Lake Huron (1932), Lake Michigan (1934), and Lake Superior (1938). Descended from species that date back about 250 million years, a jawless fish with an eel-like body and a mouth that is a sucking disc lined with teeth, the sea lamprey came into the Great Lakes either via the St. Lawrence River, Lake Ontario, and the Welland Canal, or via the Hudson River and Erie Canal. This parasitic fish eats by attaching itself to a fish and feeding at will on its blood. In Lake Michigan it first attacked the lake trout. The catch dropped from 5,500,000 pounds in 1945 to 53,700 pounds five years later. Between 1950 and 1955 the whitefish catch plummeted from 2,470,000 pounds to 391,000 pounds. All important commercial species fell prey to the lamprey. In the fall of 1953 their savage attack on the fish of Green Bay left dead and dying fish littering the surface of the water. Commercial fishing virtually ceased.

In the face of disaster, state, federal, and Canadian governmental officials cooperated as never before. The United States and Canada joined forces in forming the Great Lakes Sea Lamprey Committee in 1946 and the Great Lakes Fishery Commission in 1955. Scientists pooled their research efforts to establish accurate information on the lamprey life cycle and behavior and discover the best method of control. They eventually decided that the most vulnerable point in the life cycle was the time when lampreys spawned in streams.

Barriers, especially electromechanical barriers, proved somewhat effective, but a lamprecide, TFM (3-trifluormethyl-4-nitrophenol), proved the most successful treatment for spawning streams. After researchers had tried and eliminated some 6,000 other compounds, it was discovered in 1958 at the U.S. Fish and Wildlife Service's Hammond Bay Biological Station. Stream treatment began on Lake Superior, where the largest remaining trout populations lived. Successful in retarding the sea lamprey there, in 1960 the Great Lakes Fishery Commission began treatment of northern Lake Michigan. Thirteen years later almost all of Lake Michigan's streams had been treated once. The lamprey remains a menace, requiring constant vigilance and appropriate treatment.

The lamprey crisis forced the Great Lakes states to rethink fishery policies.

Salmon catch, Lake Michigan. Courtesy Wisconsin Department of Natural Resources.

In the absence of the trout, Lake Michigan's major natural predator fish, the alewife, a small, sardinelike fish used extensively for commercial pet food (see site 72), multiplied very rapidly. With the balance of species totally disturbed, the Great Lakes states acted. Already embarked on a trout restocking program, Michigan opted in 1965 to introduce salmon, another predator, and at the same time to manage the state fisheries primarily for the benefit of recreational fishermen. Coho stocking began in 1966; chinook stocking in 1967. Other salmon species were introduced as well. Quite by accident the pink salmon, intended for Hudson Bay, was introduced into Lake Superior in 1955.

Regulatory and stocking policies adopted by Michigan, Indiana, Illinois, and Wisconsin since 1965 have been a boon to sportsmen and something of a thorn in the side of commercial fishermen. Michigan restricted commercial fishing sharply, and so did Illinois. Indiana was less restrictive, and Wisconsin in the mid-1970s opted for a policy combining sport and commercial fishing. For commercial fishing, all four of the states utilize fish quotas, closure by species (salmon, for example, are reserved for sport fishing), limited entry, restrictions on fish length and on net types and mesh size, and geographic limitations. Commercial fishermen resisted, but were no match for the powerful sport-fishing lobbies. States opted for the type of fishing that they considered most productive of income to their residents.

Fishing regulations have led to many a court battle. Commercial fishermen complain that favoritism toward sport fishing deprives them of a living, and some who dislike state regulations break the law. In the fall of 1983, the Wisconsin Department of Natural Resources estimated that commercial fishermen illegally take about a million pounds of fish, chiefly trout, from Wisconsin's Lake Michigan waters every year. Recently, aggrieved Door County, Wisconsin, fishermen apprehended by the Department of Natural Resources found a champion in a local judge, who spoke of them as "good, God-fearing people. It's pretty hard to jump on people like that. They read their Bible and that's where they get their law from. They take it literally. They firmly believe in a God-given right to take the fish."

Fishing regulations fly in the face of the unlimited fishing rights guaranteed to Indian peoples forever in nineteenth-century treaties with the federal government. The courts have often upheld treaty rights, arousing the ire of non-Indian sport and commercial fishermen and departments of natural resources. Some of the latter have tried to negotiate special quotas with Indian groups to balance treaty rights and contemporary conservation goals.

One hundred and thirty years after J. V. Edwards and Jacob Conroe netted 2,000 pounds of fish, in a single test seining in 1836, Lake Michigan's commercial fishermen harvested 48,400,000 pounds, 80 percent of which consisted of alewives. But the whitefish, under careful management, made a comeback from the lamprey devastation. In 1976 commercial fishermen caught more than 4 million pounds of whitefish in Lake Michigan. The future of the fisheries depends on careful management with due regard for a balance of species, limited catches, and lamprey control. The health of the lake, the fish, and the people depends on very careful control of all forms of pollution, including the more recent containments—DDT, mercury, arsenic, PCBs, and dioxin.

All around Lake Michigan, marinas for sport-fishing craft are much in evidence. They make a strikingly beautiful sight, nowhere more so, perhaps, than the marina at Fish Creek, Wisconsin, on the Door Peninsula. Locations reflecting the history of commercial fishing include Fishtown at Leland, Michigan (see site 138), Rogers Street Fishing Village at Two Rivers, Wisconsin (see site 37), and the Fishing Village Museum at Washington Island (see site 55). To see how a family with a long tradition as Lake Michigan commercial fishermen has adapted to change, visit the Smith Brothers Restaurant in Port Washington, Wisconsin (site 26). In the wake of the decline of commercial fishing and the rise of sport fishing, the family has gone into the restaurant and motel industry.

To observe the work of fish hatcheries involved in restocking programs, visit the Thompson State Fish Hatchery, east of Manistique (site 94), the Charlevoix Great Lakes Fisheries Station (see site 126), or the Platte River State Anadromous Fish Hatchery near Benzonia, Michigan (site 145). To gain a fuller understanding of Michigan's Great Lakes fishery policies, visit the Interpretive Center at the Wolf Lake State Fish Hatchery (site 166).

Cities and Towns

Around the shores of Lake Michigan, from the bustling, heavily peopled, industrial southern shore to the quiet, wooded northern shores lie a host of cities, towns, and villages, each with its individual character and its particular reasons for being. These population centers are larger and more numerous along the southern third of the lakeshore. North beyond Milwaukee and Muskegon, the intervals of countryside and shoreline between them grow and their size diminishes irregularly until, in the great northern arc from Escanaba to Traverse City, no other cities are found the size of these two, each with approximately 15,000 people. In the 340-mile shoreline area lie only six cities with a population of more than 1,000.

On the southern and western shores, towns and cities are far more numerous and far larger than those on the northern and eastern sides of the lake. The difference stems in large measure from the size and kinds of markets—local, national, and international—they provide with goods and services. Western and southern Lake Michigan communities have far larger hinterlands; the northern and eastern shore communities have a smaller and less heavily populated land area at their back doors. They are lake-locked, the northern shore by Lake Superior and the lower peninsula by Lakes Huron, St. Clair, and Erie on the east.

Although the distribution of villages, towns, and cities does not fit into simple, tidy packages either geographically or numerically, nevertheless, regional city types are apparent. Lake Michigan's industrial area from Burns Harbor west to Chicago and north through Milwaukee is the most heavily populated segment of the lakeshore, an important part of the midwestern industrial region. Manufacturing is the dominant economic activity, with heavy emphasis on primary metals and fabricated metal products. Chicago, Waukegan, Racine, Kenosha, Milwaukee, and Hammond are the more venerable cities in the industrial core. With the exception of Hammond, they evolved into manufacturing centers over a considerable time span. By contrast, Cudahy, South Milwaukee, Whiting, East Chicago, and Gary are newer, dating from the late nineteenth and early twentieth centuries, when they were founded specifically as manufacturing centers. Burns Harbor, Indiana, and the city of Oak Creek, Wisconsin, also founded for industrial purposes, date from the 1950s.

Industry in Milwaukee's Menominee Valley from the 16th Street Bridge. Photo by Margaret Bogue.

Both Chicago and Milwaukee developed with adjacent industrial communities lying south of their metropolitan centers and with upper-middle- and upper-class suburbs lying to the north. The direction of industrial spread in large measure reflected the convenience and cost advantages of real estate and of lake, river, highway, and railroad transportation. The topography of the lakeshore, including harbor potential, also greatly influenced these thrusts. The development of commuter lines north from metropolitan centers spurred north shore suburban developments. Evanston, Wilmette, Kenilworth, Winnetka, Glencoe, Highland Park, and Lake Forest developed as Chicago's well-to-do residential suburbs; Shorewood, Whitefish Bay, Fox Point, and Bayside as Milwaukee's. A panorama of living environments varying according to income and occupation unfolds between Burns Harbor, Indiana, and Lake Forest, Illinois, and between Oak Creek and Bayside, Wisconsin. From south to north lie industrial plants and worker homes; next, the business and financial districts of these cities; and then the well-to-do north shore suburban residential communities, where professionals, managers, and business owners live.

Manufacturing plays an important role in the economy of many Lake Michigan towns other than those found in the industrial core. On the western shore, in every city from Port Washington north to Sturgeon Bay, and from the city of Green Bay to Escanaba, industry is quite significant for town and city vitality. Sheboygan, Kohler, Manitowoc, Two Rivers, Sturgeon Bay, Green Bay, Marinette, Menominee, and Escanaba are the most heavily industrialized. Manistique is the only city along the northern shore with a significant industrial component.

On the eastern shore, industry is prominent in most cities lying between Michigan City and Muskegon, where a wide variety of fabricated metal products and heavy equipment are produced. North of Muskegon, industry gradually declines in importance. Ludington, Manistee, Frankfort, Traverse City, Elk Rapids, Charlevoix, and Petoskey all have industry in varying degrees, but the shoreline from Petoskey to Manistique on the northern shore is virtually devoid of manufacturing establishments. Here, villages and towns depend heavily on recreation and tourism, based primarily on Lake Michigan's natural beauty and the opportunities it offers for sport fishing, boating, and swimming. Nor have northern Lake Michigan's towns neglected to emphasize the area's rich history. The accelerated development of historic sites at Mackinaw City, Mackinac Island, and St. Ignace grew out of the stimulus to tourist and vacation business given by the automobile, good roads, and the Mackinac bridge.

Lake Michigan fosters great extremes in community types, from Gary, an almost purely industrial city on the southern shore, to Fish Creek and Ephraim on the Door Peninsula of Wisconsin, two villages of almost exclusively recreational character. Most of its villages, cities, and towns rest on more diversified economic activity, however. Chicago (see site 1), population 2,997,000 in 1982, is the most complex city of all. Strategically located at the base of the lake's southern thrust, it is the hub of a national transportation system and serves as a center for distribution, trade, commerce, and finance and as home base for national and international corporations. It offers all manner of services. Its cultural and educational institutions, lakefront setting, and national accessibility attract convention groups and visitors in droves. The city's leaders over the years capitalized on its location by developing a beautiful lakefront with parks and architecturally impressive buildings. Nevertheless, manufacturing is the principal economic activity. Chicago serves a vast regional, national, and international market.

Milwaukee (see site 23), population 636,200, ranks as the second most complex of Lake Michigan's cities, a manufacturing city that performs most of the same trade, service, and educational and cultural functions as Chicago for a smaller regional, national, and international market. Green Bay, (see site 67) third-largest of the economically diversified Lake Michigan cities and considerably smaller (population 88,000) than the big two, is an industrial city, a county seat, a religious and educational center, and the focus of wholesale distribution, retail trade, and a wide range of services for northeastern Wisconsin and the Upper Peninsula.

Most of Lake Michigan's cities in the medium population category (5,000–50,000), from Michigan City northward on the eastern shore and from Port Washington north on the western shore, combine a variety of services, manufacturing, and trade with a lively recreation industry. The smaller villages, towns, and cities survive on a less complete roster of income-producing activities. The ways each have combined diversified economic functions over the years are described in the essays on each community that follow.

Most of Lake Michigan's villages, towns, and cities go back a century or more. More often than not the reasons for their beginnings and those for their continued existence are very

Lake Michigan's Cities and Towns showing development today in three categories: (1) heavily industrial, (2) industry prominent in the economy, and (3) recreation and tourism of primary importance.

The Moravian church at Ephraim symbolizes the aspirations of its Norwegian Moravian founders. Photo by Margaret Bogue.

from the desire of Presbyterians to find a suitable location for a denominational school. They founded the Lake Forest Association in 1856 and platted the community. (see site 9). John Alexander Dowie, a Scotsman from Australia, founded Zion, Illinois, in 1899 as a planned, church-owned, utopian community where the members of his Christian Catholic church could lead strictly supervised, godly lives (see site 14).

Change characterizes the history of Lake Michigan's cities, towns, and villages, from their beginnings as small clusters of settlement in frontier areas to the present, and it will continue to characterize their future. Like all cities and towns, they have either performed useful functions in the local, regional, national, and even international economy, or they have withered away. As the society and economy changed, they have had to adapt to meet new needs. Over the decades the area's residents and leaders have recognized the importance of keeping their communities abreast of change and have put much thought and effort into finding ways to make their towns and cities grow. Sharp debate, hard work, experimentation, vast amounts of money, and gallons of printers' ink went into their efforts. While each community's record of adaptation and growth is in some sense unique, certain attitudes, ideas, and patterns of action are common to many.

They all looked to county, state, and national governments for assistance with transportation to tie them into larger markets and for laws that would encourage population and business growth. The prevailing attitude was that government should promote development. These communities shared the common belief that Lake Michigan and the great store of natural resources in and around its waters should be used and altered to their advantage. They worried very little about environmental impact, believing nature's bounty to be virtually inexhaustible.

For a century and a half, lakeshore communities have regarded the lake, once almost their sole means of transportation, as an important artery of commerce, and especially as an economical carrier of domestic bulk cargoes. As early as the mid-nineteenth century, business leaders came to view the lake as a facilitator of trade with

Tourists on the beach at South Haven, Michigan. From the Collections of the Michigan State Archives, Department of State. 09721.

Canada and tried to promote workable reciprocity treaties between the two nations. After World War I, its potential as an avenue for overseas trade fired their imaginations, and Chicago's and Milwaukee's chambers of commerce worked to make the St. Lawrence Seaway a reality. For many decades they also regarded the lake as a ready-made source of drinking water and as a natural depository for all manner of waste, human and industrial. By the mid-twentieth century, water quality had so deteriorated that national and regional action was imperative.

Since the late nineteenth century, most communities have regarded the lake's aesthetic qualities and potential for recreation as a source of community income. In the late nineteenth century and especially in the twentieth, park and beach development along the lakeshore appealed to some civic leaders as a way of making communities attractive to residents and visitors; it was less appealing to the business interests that had appropriated the lakeshore for their establishments. Industrialization had pretty well spoiled or was threatening to spoil the aesthetics of lake frontage. The "city beautiful" idea gained widespread citizen support in community after community and slowly—with great effort and the expenditure of millions of dollars—found expression. Chicago, with its magnificent lakefront, is the prime example of such a city (see site 1).

A tourism industry based on the lake's natural beauty and potential for recreation spurred the building of resorts, pleasure parks, and city lakeside parks. At the turn of the century, Michigan City and Benton Harbor developed most attractive recreational and vacation facilities for the Chicagoans who went there in droves to escape the city's heat, noise, and dirt (see sites 168, 174). The lumbering towns of the northern lakeshore, desperate for new business, also looked to the lake to save them. Ever since, the tourism-resort-recreation potential of the lake has generated big business. From the crowded marina at Michigan City, now self-styled "Coho Capital" (see site 174), to the busy harbor at Mackinac Island, marinas filled with power boats, charter fishing craft, sailboats, and yachts testify to the lake's popularity.

Accessibility was also important to

Manistee, and Ludington now have larger populations than in the lumbering period. The transition has gone less well for Elk Rapids, Leland, Frankfort, and Pentwater.

Some lumbering communities withered away. Two Creeks and Pensaukee, Wisconsin, and Cedar River, Michigan, are good examples. Near Sturgeon Bay (site 46) the sawmill village of Horn's Pier, a bustling little lumber port in the late nineteenth century, is gone save for old building foundations, and Lake Michigan waves now wash the sand beach where it once stood. Gone too is the sawmill town of Singapore, buried in the sand near Saugatuck and Douglas, Michigan.

Particularly since World War II, smaller communities more distant from the lake's industrial core have succeeded in attracting industry. On the eastern shore, light industry now extends as far north as Petoskey. Lower labor costs in these communities have been an attraction to businessmen. Industry in some form is now more often present in Lake Michigan cities, towns, and villages than not, and the urban population for the lake as a whole has grown beyond the wildest dreams of the early town builders.

AROUND THE LAKESHORE

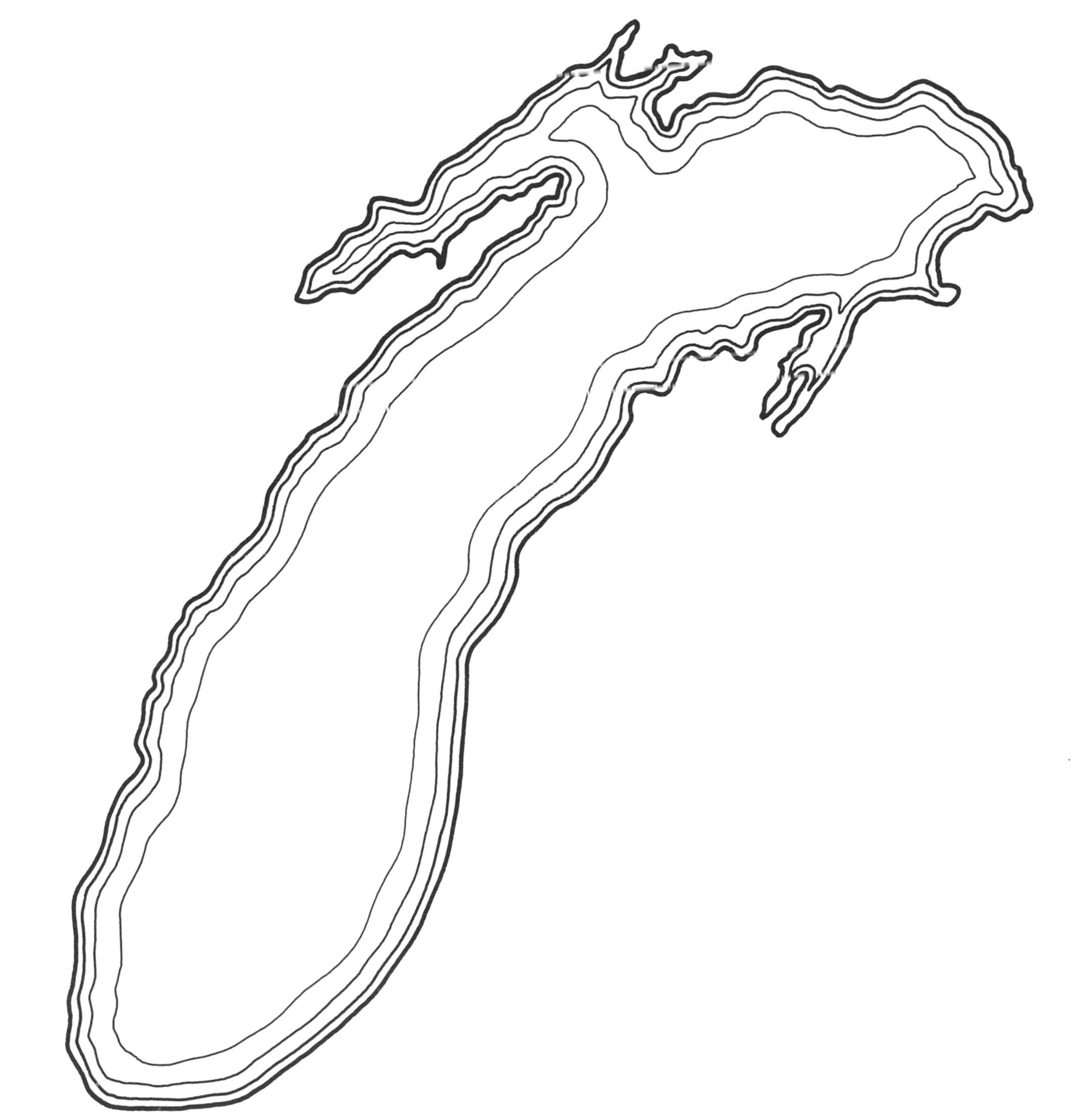

The Chicago Skyline. Photo by Kee Chang. Courtesy Chicago Association of Commerce and Industry.

Illinois

1. Chicago

Highways I-90 & I-94

From a trading post established in the late eighteenth century, Chicago has grown into the nation's third largest city, with a 1982 population of 2,997,000. Chicago's industrial metropolitan area ranks as the nation's largest producer of steel, consumer electrical goods, telephone and commercial equipment, metal products, and railroad engines and equipment. Chicago is the largest national furniture market, the home of the largest mail order businesses, and the nation's leading convention center. Forty percent of the national wholesale and retail trade takes place within a 500-mile radius of the Loop.

Chicago forms the hub of the national railroad network. Its ports handle more than 80 million tons of freight each year, making the city a major world port. It is the nation's largest trucking center and the focal point of a major oil pipeline system. Its metropolitan area contains the largest area of oil refineries in the country. O'Hare International is the world's busiest airport. Chicago's phenomenal growth over the last 150 years has transformed the low, marshy banks of the sluggish Chicago River and the adjacent shores of Lake Michigan into the heart of a wealthy, sprawling, industrial metropolis.

Location is the key to Chicago's remarkable growth and fortune. Louis Jolliet recognized the strategic importance of the mouth of the Chicago River in 1673. He, Jacques Marquette, and their companions found the Chicago-Des Plaines–Illinois–Mississippi river route to the Gulf of Mexico. A canal connecting the short portage between the Chicago and Des Plaines rivers, Jolliet observed, would create an all-water route from the Great Lakes to the gulf. The mouth of the Chicago River on Lake Michigan held the key to a continent.

While the Jesuits maintained a mission at the mouth of the Chicago for four years (1696–1700), the French did not fortify the location, nor did they succeed in colonizing the Illinois River Valley. Indian groups hostile to the French controlled the Des Plaines portage. At the mouth of the Chicago River about 1779, 16 years after the French lost New France to the British, Jean Baptiste Point Du Sable, a Santo Domingan of African and European parentage, built a log cabin and traded furs with the Indians, thereby becoming Chicago's first permanent settler.

Recognizing the location's strategic importance to the fur trade and the defense of the West, the United States built Fort Dearborn here in 1803. Following the outbreak of the War of 1812, the Americans, fearing an attack by Indian allies of the British, attempted to evacuate the post, only to be intercepted by a band of Indians. More than half of the 96 soldiers and civilians lost their lives, and the fort was burned. The Americans returned and built a new fort in 1816, and for the next 14 years, Chicago remained a squatter town where life centered on the fort, the fur trade, and treaty councils with the Indians.

Life at Chicago took on a new dimension in 1830 when Chicago was surveyed as the potential terminal of the Illinois-Michigan Canal. It became the seat of Cook County in 1831 and was incorporated as a town of about 350 in 1833. Once the canal opened in 1848, Chicago became a marketing and processing center for the agricultural produce of the Illinois prairies. Chicago's Lake Michigan location made it a transshipment and processing point for agricultural produce and a port for receiving finished goods and raw materials for local and regional use. The long-standing symbiotic relationship between hinterland and city was established.

Lying in the midst of a rich and developing agricultural area stretching from the Appalachians westward to the grasslands of the Great Plains, Chicago's trading and commercial position became much more advantageous with the development of a railroad network. As the Illinois and Michigan Canal neared completion in 1848, the first railroad line, the Galena and Chicago, reached the city. Lake Michigan's thrust 307 miles southward, cutting the lines of land transportation between the northeastern and the northwestern parts of the nation, played a key role in determining land transportation routes. The railway network built to serve a developing America during the last half of the nineteenth century ran from the East to Chicago and fanned out westward, northward, and south-

Woodcut engraving of the first Fort Dearborn, built in 1803 by the United States to strengthen its authority in what was then a remote frontier region. From Andreas, History of Chicago. *Courtesy Chicago Historical Society. ICHi-03037*

ward, giving the growing city a second delivery system to a very extensive agricultural hinterland. The railroads as well as the waterways provided excellent access to the rich resources of iron ore, timber, and limestone of the upper lakes and to the coal deposits of Pennsylvania and the lower Midwest.

Chicago has maintained and enhanced its position as a transportation hub during the twentieth century. The St. Lawrence Seaway makes it a very important international port. The construction of the Calumet Sag Channel and the Chicago Sanitary and Ship Canal greatly improved water transportation between Chicago and the Gulf of Mexico. O'Hare Airport serves as a focus for national and international flights. The interstate highway system funneling into Chicago provides yet another artery for the movement of freight shipments in an era when truck transportation has challenged the railroad lines.

The city has grown by leaps and bounds. From a little town of less than 350 in 1833, Chicago grew into a city of about 100,000 in 1860; more than 1,000,000 in 1890; more than 2,000,000 in 1910; more than 3,500,000 in 1950.

Marketing and commerce dominated Chicago's economic life in the early decades of the city's history. But well before 1860 manufacturing was contributing substantially to Chicago's economy. Its earliest industries served the needs of the agricultural hinterland and the town itself. Food processing, meat packing, leather and meat by-products, printing, textile, garment, and millinery manufacturing, and the building trades that produced lumber, sashes, doors and brick all flourished in the mid-1850s. In 1847 Cyrus H. McCormick established his reaper factory on the banks of the Chicago River to serve a growing midwestern market. The meat-packing industry had grown to such proportions by 1865 that railroads and packers joined to establish the Union Stock Yard.

In the two decades following the Civil War, manufacturing overtook trade and commerce as Chicago's chief economic function. Not even the Great Fire of 1871, which gutted four square miles of the downtown business area, did more than temporarily slow the city's growth. By 1875 traces of the fire's damage had all but disappeared. Five industries dominated production up until World War I: meat packing, farm machinery, railroad equipment, furniture, and men's clothing. Cudahy, Libby, Armour, Swift, McCormick, Deering, and Pullman—leading entrepreneurs in this industrial growth—became household names across America.

During the last half-century Chicago's economy has greatly diversified. The major industries of the pre–World War I years have declined in relative

This illustration from the 1885 catalogue of the McCormick Harvesting Machine Company shows the Chicago plant's molding floor. Courtesy State Historical Society of Wisconsin. WHi(X3)12294

importance. Steel, consumer electrical goods, telephone and commercial equipment, and metal products have risen to prominence. The combination of manufacturing with strong commercial, transportation, service, and government components gives Chicago a diversified and balanced economy. Industry continues to be the largest employer.

Along with the enormous physical growth of industry and business went Chicago's social and cultural growth. Because Chicago offered business opportunities and jobs, it attracted a large and diverse population. The lure of the dollar helped to produce a rich racial and ethnic mix and made Chicago home for many people from many different national origins. Although most of the city's first settlers came from New England, the Middle Atlantic states, Ohio, and Indiana, many European immigrants made their homes here as early as the 1840s. Before the Civil War they came chiefly from Ireland and the Germanies in search of a new and better life. By 1860 half of Chicago's population was foreign-born. In 1890 about 80 percent of the city's residents were either foreign-born or the sons and daughters of the foreign-born, many of them tracing their origins to the Scandinavian countries, Germany, and Ireland.

Between 1880 and 1920 southern and eastern European countries became a major source of workers for Chicago industry. Chief among these newer groups were people from Poland, Italy, Bohemia, Lithuania, Russia, Greece, Serbia, and Hungary. From necessity they congregated in ethnic enclaves in low-rent, substandard housing near the industrial areas of the city. Here they lived in a sink of bad health, low wages, poor food, overcrowded housing, liquor, and prostitution, vividly described by Upton Sinclair in his novel *The Jungle* (1904).

Jane Addams, who established Hull House in 1889, awakened Chicago's social conscience to the needs of these new Americans. The Hull House settlement addressed the social, economic, and educational needs of near west side immigrants. Under Addams's leadership it cooperated with existing city agencies to improve housing, sanitary, and health standards. The Hull House staff worked as well for reform legislation to limit working hours for women, to secure accident insurance for workers, and to eliminate child labor.

Following World War I the United States restricted immigration from abroad, and the streams of immigrants

A Black family just arrived in Chicago from the rural south. From The Chicago Commission on Race Relations, The Negro in Chicago. *Courtesy University of Chicago Press.*

from Europe to Chicago greatly diminished. Over time, new Americans living in the congested inner-city ghettos moved out into adjacent neighborhoods and the suburbs. European-born whites formed 27 percent of the city's population in 1927, but only 11 percent by 1970.

Industrial job opportunities attracted streams of migrants from other parts of the United States. Chicago had always had a Black population, but it was small until World War I, when thousands of southern agricultural workers, lured by wartime wages, sought jobs in Chicago industries. In succeeding decades Chicago's Black population has continued to grow, especially during and since World War II. By 1980 Blacks constituted 40 percent of the city's people.

Already economically and politically pressured into a ghetto existence by 1920, Blacks spread into many older areas of the South Side formerly occupied by immigrants. Most Blacks lived in the worst residential areas and held the lowest-paying jobs. Racial pressures tended to constrict the ghetto, creating incredible congestion and a long list of social problems including poor education, unemployment, substandard health, and crime. Yet, block by block, Black residential areas have expanded so that the Black community of 1920, which lay northeast and southeast of the stockyards, has grown into an L-shaped area stretching from the Loop west to Austin Avenue and south to Riverdale. Many of these areas were torn by racial violence during the 1960s.

Another segment of Chicago's population, the Spanish-speaking community, has grown substantially in the last decade. These residents, among them Mexicans, Cubans, and Puerto Ricans, numbered about 422,000, or 14 percent of the city's population in 1980. Like other in-migrants, they came in search of economic opportunity. The largest of the three groups, the Mexicans, first came into the Chicago area after the Mexican Revolution of 1910. Larger numbers followed during World Wars I and II and during the ensuing period of prosperity, when the majority found jobs in the steel mills. Living in barrios in manufacturing and commercial areas, they have suffered from the burdens of racism and the problems of adjusting to a new culture. Puerto Ricans have come to Chicago mainly since World War II. They too have experienced problems in finding a secure place in American society. The Cuban community, the smallest of the three, dates from the Cuban Revolution of the late 1950s.

Chicago's Spanish-speaking people are gradually moving into suburban areas, and the professionals among them into affluent communities. Most, however, have moved into industrial towns like Gary, Chicago Heights, and Waukegan.

Extensive industry and a large labor force have made the Chicago area a focal point for many bitter labor-management controversies during the past century. Chicago strikes have repeatedly made national headlines. The Railroad Strike of 1877, the McCormick Strike and the Haymarket Affair of 1886, the Pullman Strike of 1894 and the accompanying general railroad strike, and the 1937 "Memorial Day Massacre" at Republic Steel's South Chicago mill drew national attention. All were part of the struggle to establish the legality of unions, collective bargaining, and the strike as a counterforce to big management and big industry.

Against the backdrop of booming industry, dirt, stench, smoke, and its share of other urban problems, Chicago, "an overgrown gawk of a village" as Lincoln Steffens called it, developed a park system and many major cultural institutions in the nineteenth century. These included a public school system, the Chicago Historical Society, the University of Chicago, the Chicago Public Library, the Art Institute, the John Crerar Library, the Chicago Symphony Orchestra, the Newberry Library, and the Chicago Academy of Sciences. The fortunes of business and industrial leaders helped to make these possible. Chicago also pioneered in modern architecture. The skyscraper, a new urban architectural form, dramatically changed the skyline and placed Chicago in the forefront of architectural innovation. The Chicago School achieved international recognition. In 1893 Chicago hosted the World's Columbian Exposition at Jackson Park. Here a number of America's leading architects, ignoring the moderns, relied on antiquity and rendered the buildings in sparkling white. The exposition was a model of urban planning, yet it hardly squared with the realities lying all around in a dingy city suffering in the wake of a nationwide depression.

In the twentieth century Chicago's cultural institutions have greatly expanded to include 58 colleges and universities in the metropolitan area, a complex of museums and libraries, and a major opera company as well as a host of smaller companies, orchestras, and singing societies.

The Port of Chicago

Water transportation has always been important to Chicago's economy—at times all-important. The natural lake and river network converging at Chicago has repeatedly been improved since federal funds were first allocated to enhance the Chicago harbor in 1833. The Illinois and Michigan Canal was completed in 1848; the Chicago Sanitary and Ship Canal in 1900; the Calumet Sag Channel in 1922; and the St. Lawrence Seaway in 1959. These waterways have improved nature's links between Chicago, the Atlantic Ocean, and the Gulf of Mexico, making the city a major inland world port.

Canal and lake traffic carried most of Chicago's in- and outbound cargoes until the 1880s, when more than 26,000 vessels arrived and departed annually. Ships arrived from the upper lakes, with lumber, iron ore, limestone, passengers, and all manner of freight. They carried away industrial goods, farm produce, and passengers. Railroads overshadowed water traffic for the next half-century. For the growing bulk shipments of iron ore, coal, and limestone, however, ships and barges continued to be the cheapest mode of transportation. With the widening and deepening of the Chicago Sanitary and Ship Canal and the completion in 1922 of the Calumet Sag Channel, which improved the link to the Gulf of Mexico, water traffic revived. Barge traffic grew, and once the St. Lawrence Seaway was opened, so did international traffic. Railroads still dominate metropolitan Chicago's flow of freight traffic, while water transport accounts for about 12 percent of the total.

The facility at the mouth of the Chicago River used to be Chicago's major port; now it primarily handles newsprint. Navy Pier handles some general overseas cargo, and both the North and South branches of the Chicago River have some facilities for bulk traffic. The main port traffic shifted to the Calumet area in the late nineteenth century. The Calumet River, heavily industrialized and stretching from Lake Calumet to Lake Michigan, handles the greatest tonnage of any Chicago waterway. Lake Calumet Harbor is Chicago's major international port and is the most complete port facility on the Great Lakes for ocean, lake, and inland barges and ships.

Aerial view of the Chicago regional port district terminal. The Continental grain tower is on the left. Photo by Kee Chang. Courtesy Chicago Association of Commerce and Industry.

Chicago Lakefront

Highway US-41, Lake Shore Drive

Lake Shore Drive, running 124 blocks from the southern edge of Jackson Park at 67th Street to Hollywood Avenue at the northern edge of Lincoln Park, accentuates Chicago's finest natural asset, Lake Michigan. The development of the lakefront spans nine decades. Chicago has made lakefront improvement a priority item in city planning for 70 years. This was a courageous, expensive, long-term project. It rejected the familiar pattern of development in many Lake Michigan cities where business, manufacturing, shipping, and railroad facilities have laid claim to and held lake- and riverfront locations.

The first phase of the battle for lakefront development unfolded in the Grant Park area in 1890 when the city of Chicago announced plans to utilize the lakefront there for building a civic center with city hall, post office, police headquarters, and stables for the horses that drew city garbage wagons. The announcement angered Aaron Montgomery Ward, who owned Michigan Avenue property with a view of the lake. He argued that the lakeshore should be kept "open, clear, and free" between Randolph and Madison Streets, as noted on an early map and plat. He sued the city four times between 1890 and 1911 to clear the lakefront of buildings and to forbid its use except as public park. The Illinois Supreme Court upheld the lower court's decision in favor of Ward. Only two buildings were allowed to remain—the Chicago Public Library and the Art Institute.

Early in the twentieth century, lakefront development gained momentum when prominent citizens joined forces to sponsor a major plan to improve the physical character of the city. Their influence and concern led to the development of the Chicago Plan of 1909, popularly known as the Burnham Plan after its creator, Daniel H. Burnham, a leading Chicago architect and chief designer of the Columbian Exposition. Burnham determined "to take up the pressing needs of today," to develop a large master plan to meet those needs, and to produce a "well-ordered, convenient, and unified city." Along with other recommendations, the plan advocated that "everything possible should be done to enhance the attractiveness of the lake shore and

Looking north along the lakefront toward downtown. Photo by Kee Chang. Courtesy Chicago Association of Commerce and Industry.

to develop its natural beauties." Burnham saw the lakefront as a collection of beaches, lagoons, islands, and harbors available for the enjoyment of all. Adopted by the city in 1910, the Burnham Plan exerted great influence on city development for many decades. The dream of beaches and parks along the lakefront gradually materialized.

By 1930 Grant Park, still in the process of being landscaped, emerged as Chicago's lakeside front door, ringed with an exceptional cultural complex—the Public Library, the Art Institute, Orchestra Hall, the Fine Arts Building, and the Auditorium, plus three new cultural facilities, the Field Museum of Natural History, the Shedd Aquarium, and the Adler Planetarium.

Rescue and preservation of the natural beauty of the lakefront went forward following the adoption of the Lake Front Ordinance of 1919. Development thrust south from Grant Park, gradually transforming eight miles of shabby shoreline into parks and beaches. Daniel H. Burnham Park, lying between Grant and Jackson parks, honors the famous architect and planner. Lakefront improvement reached Hollywood Avenue at the northern edge of Lincoln Park after World War II.

Always expensive, always resisted by property owners, and always in danger of losing ground, Chicago's lakefront projects stand as a model of what a determined and publicly backed local government can do to enhance a city's natural assets. The 124 blocks of Lake Shore Drive seem like the fulfillment of Burnham's motto: "Make no little plans. They have no magic to stir men's blood. . . . Make big plans; aim high in hope and work, remembering that a noble logical diagram once recorded will never die but long after we are gone will be a living thing, asserting with growing intensity."

Chicago Sites of Interest

Chicago contains a wealth of cultural opportunities. The following locations reflect the city's architectural and artistic achievement, the philanthropy of its men of wealth, the success of its businesses, the role of immigrants and organized labor, and municipal development. This is only an introduction to the many attractions Chicago offers visitors. A full listing of places of interest may be found in *Illinois: A Descriptive and Historical Guide*, edited by Harry Hansen (New York: Hastings

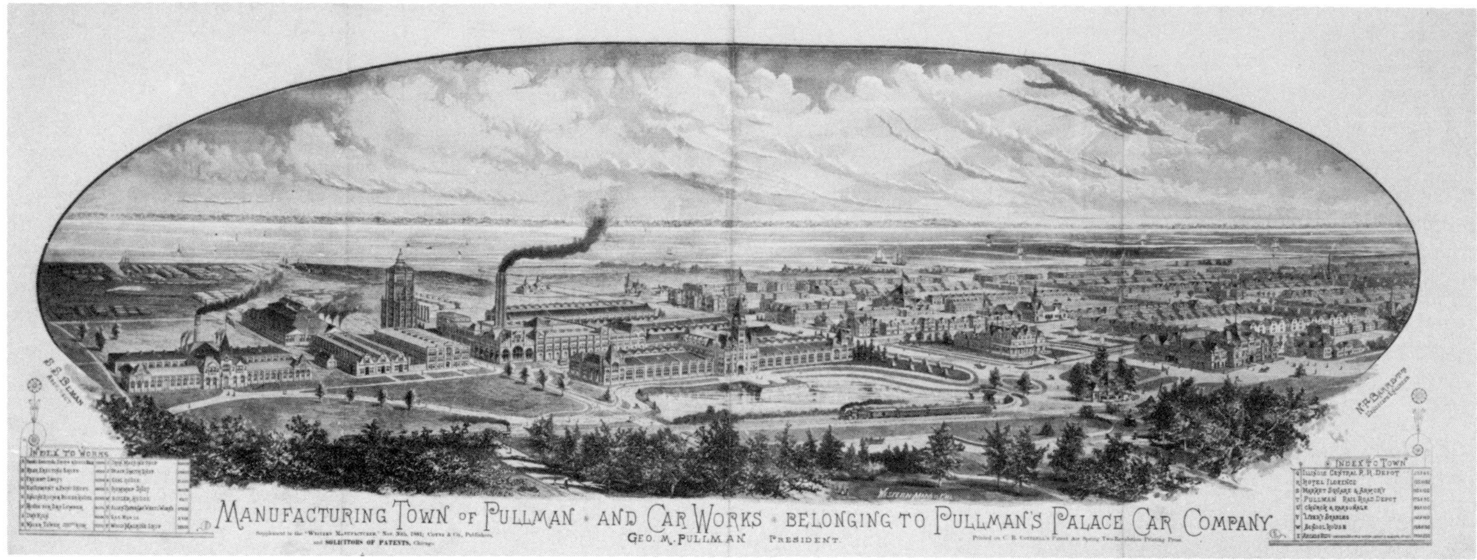

An 1881 bird's-eye view of George M. Pullman's company town. Courtesy Chicago Historical Society. ICHi-01918

House, 1974). Also useful to those who want to know Chicago better are Ira J. Bach, *Chicago on Foot: An Architectural Walking Tour* (Chicago: Follett, 1969); Norman Mark, *Norman Mark's Chicago: Walking, Bicycling, and Driving Tours of the City* (Chicago: Chicago Review Press, 1977); and Glen Holt and Dominic Pacyga, *Chicago: A Historical Guide to the Neighborhoods—The Loop and the South Side* (Chicago: Chicago Historical Society, 1979).

(1) Pullman Historic District*
Bounded on the north by 103rd Street, on the east by C.S.S. and S.B. Railroad tracks, on the south by 115th Street, and on the west by Cottage Grove Avenue

This famous experiment in town planning was the brainchild of George M. Pullman, who sought to create a self-contained community for workers employed at his Pullman Palace Car Company. In 1880 he commissioned an architect, Solon Spencer Beman, and a landscape engineer, Nathan F. Barrett, to design a town that would embody the latest thinking in town planning, with homes, shops, and facilities for recreation and culture. Visitors from all over the world came to Pullman to see the red brick row houses, duplexes, and single-family homes, the Greenstone Church, the school, market hall, and the huge Victorian Florence Hotel, named for Pullman's daughter.

Pullman's insistence that his community operate at a profit, even during the depression of 1893, created an intolerable situation for his workers, who were discouraged from living outside the company town. On May 11, 1894, after Pullman had cut wages and refused to lower rents, company workers struck. In an expression of support for the Pullman workers, Eugene V. Debs's American Railway Union workers at first refused to handle Pullman cars and later went on strike against the railroads.

George Pullman won the strike, but in 1898 the Illinois Supreme Court ordered the Pullman Company to sell all property not required for the manufacturing business and to cease all municipal functions. Pullman residents voted to become part of the City of Chicago, and the community ceased to be a company town.

Some of the original buildings in Pullman have been lost over the years because of fire or deterioration, but the efforts of its present residents to restore the remaining structures earned Pullman a place on the National Register of Historic Places and designation as a Chicago City Landmark. The Historic Pullman Foundation conducts walking tours of the community and has prepared a slide show on the community's history. The Historic Pullman Center, 614 East

113th Street, is open on the first Sunday of the month, May–October, 12:30–1:30 P.M. Group tours on request. $

(2) Jackson Park Historic Landscape District and Midway Plaisance,* and the University of Chicago

Bounded irregularly by 67th Street, Stony Island, 60th Street, Martin Luther King, Jr., Drive, 51st Street, Hyde Park Boulevard, Cottage Grove, and 56th Street

Many historians regard the World's Columbian Exposition as symbolic of the great changes in America that marked its passage from an agrarian to an urban, industrial nation. The Great White City occupied Jackson Park and the Midway Plaisance on Chicago's south side. While most of the fair buildings burned in 1894, or were torn down, or were moved elsewhere, the Art Palace escaped destruction. First it served as the Columbian Museum and after a major renovation in the 1920s, became the Museum of Science and Industry (see below). In 1893 the Midway Plaisance, a strip of land about 600 feet wide and one mile long, was developed as an exotic and festive Bazaar of Nations. It attracted crowds no matter what the weather was like. The Streets of Cairo, the Persian Palace of Eros, the Blarney Castle, and the German Village greatly impressed visitors. George W. G. Ferris' giant pleasure wheel delighted them. Now the Midway, still a pleasant place, is a park running through the University of Chicago Campus and connecting Jackson Park on the Lake and Washington Park, one mile to the west.

Jackson Park and the Midway Plaisance were added to the National Register of Historic Places in 1972 for a number of reasons other than having been the site of the Exposition. Frederick Law Olmsted, regarded as America's most prominent nineteeenth century landscape architect, developed many of Jackson Park's features and his sons used his plans in renovating the park after the Exposition. The Midway contains fine statuary. In Jackson Park, opposite 65th Street stands a replica of Daniel Chester French's statue, "Republic," that stood originally in the Court of Honor of the Columbian Exposition. The original was damaged beyond salvation.

View from the roof of the Manufacturers and Liberal Arts Building, World's Columbian Exposition, 1893. Courtesy Chicago Historical Society. ICHi-02525

For some years the Baptist church sponsored a university in Chicago, but financial problems led to its closing in 1886. The present University of Chicago dates from 1889, when John D. Rockefeller began his very large and consistent financial support to the institution. He and the institution's first president, William Rainey Harper, were largely responsible for the university's early, rapid growth and influence in higher education.

Today the University of Chicago lies on both sides of the Midway. Gothic-style architecture predominates on the north side of the Midway; contemporary buildings are found mostly on the south side.

Rated by many as a significant structure in modern architectural history, *Robie House** stands at 5757 South Woodlawn Avenue. Frank Lloyd Wright designed the home in 1908 for the family of Frederick C. Robie, a bicycle manufacturer. Extensively restored, it is used for the offices of the University of Chicago Alumni Association. Recognized today as a superb example of Wright's Prairie School style of architecture, it has been placed on the National Register of Historic Places and designated a Chicago City landmark. Open at noon, Monday–Saturday, all year. Free.

(3) Du Sable Museum of African American History

740 East 56th Place

Begun in 1961 and originally known as the Ebony Museum of Negro History and Art, the Du Sable Museum focuses its displays, collecting activities, publications, and educational programs on the heritage and achievements of Black Americans. Its objective is "to inspire black people and especially the youth to purposeful lives of achievement by acquainting them with the contributions of great Afro-Americans of the past and the worthwhile contributions of great Black Americans of the present." Its growing library includes books, periodicals, manuscripts, and pictures. The museum's name honors Jean Baptiste Point Du Sable, who established a trading post at the mouth of the Chicago River in the 1770s.

Open Monday–Friday, 9:00 A.M.–5:00 P.M.; weekends, noon–5:00 P.M. $

(4) Museum of Science and Industry

East 57th Street and South Lake Shore Drive

The New York architect David Atwood designed a Grecian-style building for the Palace of Fine Arts at the World's Columbian Exposition of 1893, but by 1923 it had become run-down, and city officials decided that it should be razed. However, women's club members rallied behind a movement to spare the building and influenced voters to approve a $5 million bond issue for its restoration. A generous contributor, Julius Rosenwald, president of Sears, Roebuck & Company, suggested that an industrial museum be created in the building, with technological and industrial exhibits similar to those he had seen in the Deutsches Museum in Munich. His contributions to the project eventually totaled more than $7 million.

In 1924 the building was reduced to its original steel skeleton, and the exterior was redone with permanent stone. The museum is a favorite with adults and children alike because its exhibits include many working models of machinery and effective audiovisual displays. Highlights include a full-size working coal mine, a captured German submarine, and a large exhibition on the petroleum industry.

Open all year, Monday–Friday, 9:30 A.M.–4:00 P.M.; weekends, 9:30 A.M.–5:30 P.M. Free.

(5) Chicago Portage National Historic Site*

South Harlem Avenue at Chicago Sanitary Ship Canal

The Chicago portage site includes the Cook County Forest Preserve, 91 wooded acres lying in the midst of residential and commercial development. At Portage Creek a boulder and a glass display case explain the importance of the location. A path leads from the boulder to the west channel of the Des Plaines River. The Chicago Portage, linking Lake Michigan and the Mississippi River via the south branch of the Chicago River, Mud Lake, Portage Creek, and the Des Plaines River, served for centuries as a major transportation, trade, and exploration route for the Indians, French, British, and Americans. Jacques Marquette and Louis Jolliet, the first recorded users of the route, utilized the portage on their return journey from the Mississippi in 1673. La Salle used it in 1682. Countless unknown Indians and whites used it for the fur trade. With the removal of the Indians, the decline in the fur trade, the influx of pioneer farmers, and the construction of the Illinois-Michigan Canal in 1836, the all-water route between Lake Michigan and the Mississippi, the portage became obsolete. After the diversion of the Des Plaines River in the late nineteenth century, the river and Portage Creek no longer joined. Mud Lake dried up, and the creek became stagnant.

(6) Stephen A. Douglas State Memorial*

East 35th Street and Cottage Grove Avenue

The Stephen A. Douglas State Memorial honors the prominent Democratic political leader who represented Illinois in the U.S. House of Representatives and the Senate from 1843 to 1861. Usually remembered as Lincoln's opponent in the Lincoln-Douglas debates and as an unsuccessful candidate for the presidency in 1860, Douglas deserves to be remembered for other accomplishments. Popularly known as "the Little Giant" because of his small stature and large head and shoulders, Douglas had a long and distinguished political career in Illinois and the nation during the turbulent years of the slavery controversy. Always a unionist, he supported the newly elected President Lincoln and renounced secession. Partly as a result of his strenuous activity on behalf of the union, he died at Chicago in 1861.

The 96-foot Douglas State Memorial, topped by a bronze statue of Douglas, contains his tomb. Leonard W. Volk, well known for his sculptures of Lincoln, designed the memorial. Completed in 1881, it cost over $90,000, financed mainly by the state of Illinois.

The small park where the memorial stands is a portion of the land Douglas purchased in 1849 for his estate, Oakenwald. Another part of this land Douglas gave to the first University of Chicago, while yet another portion became Camp Douglas during the Civil War. Initially a training center for Union troops, it later became a prison for Confederate soldiers. As well as being on the National Register of Historic Places, the memorial has been designated a Chicago City Landmark.

(7) Prairie Avenue Historic District* and Chicago Architecture Foundation

1800 South Prairie Avenue

Bounded by South Prairie and South Indiana Avenues and East 18th and Cullerton Streets, this historic district was once Chicago's most prestigious residential area. It contained the homes of a number of influential Chicago businessmen of the late nineteenth century, including George M. Pullman, Marshall Field, Philip D.

Armour, William W. Kimball, and John J. Glessner. Many of these luxurious dwellings have been razed, but others still stand. Four mansions were included in the district when it was added to the National Register of Historic Places in 1972.

The Chicago Architecture Foundation owns the most notable of these mansions,* designed by the Boston architect Henry Hobson Richardson for John J. Glessner, a farm-implement manufacturer, in 1886. It is an excellent example of Richardson's work and the last house he designed. Tours of the home are conducted by the foundation on a regular basis. Contact the foundation at (312) 326-1393 for times. $

The Henry B. Clarke House,* built about 1837, is believed to be the oldest in Chicago. It has been moved several times; its present location is in the 1800 block of South Indiana Avenue. In 1977 the Clarke House was added to the Prairie Avenue Historic District. It is in the Greek Revival style with a cupola and porch added in 1857. This restored structure, completely renovated and refurnished in the style of 1837–1857, is open to the public. $

Both the Glessner House and the Clarke House are official city landmarks.

Prairie Avenue and 18th Street was the location of the Fort Dearborn Massacre of 1812 (see above, p. 31), now marked by a bronze tablet.

(8) Adler Planetarium and Astronomical Museum

900 East Achsah Bond Drive

Erected on man-made Northerly Island, the Adler Planetarium opened to the public in 1931. Its directors proudly announced the installation of a two-ton Zeiss projector, the only such instrument in the United States at that time. In the upper-level Sky Theater, this complex projector reproduces the stars and planets on the planetarium's ceiling in daily sky shows.

Aerial View of the Field Museum, Shedd Aquarium, and Adler Planetarium, July 1947. Photo by Howard A. Wolf. Courtesy Chicago Historical Society. ICHi-00940

Museum displays on the lower levels include a fine collection of telescopes; navigational, mathematical, and engineering instruments; an exhibit on the space age; and another featuring the sun and stars. The Planetarium holds classes in astronomy and navigation for students of all ages. It has recently opened the Doane Observatory, where visitors may view the moon and planets with the aid of a television camera.

The Adler Planetarium is an unusual 12-sided building adorned with the signs of the zodiac. There are three tiers to the building, each stepped back, so that the top tier is only one-half the size of the bottom tier. Above the top tier is a copper cone rising 80 feet from the ground at the center.

Open daily throughout the year, Monday–Thursday, Saturday, and Sunday, 9:30 A.M.–4:30 P.M.; Friday, 9:30 A.M.–9:00 P.M. Museum free; Sky Show $.

(9) John G. Shedd Aquarium

1200 South Lake Shore Drive

When it was completed in 1929, the John G. Shedd Aquarium, designed by the architectural firm of Graham, Anderson, Probst, and White, housed the largest display of tropical and freshwater fish in the world. Funds were provided by Shedd, a Marshall Field and Company executive, whose support made it possible for the staff to visit overseas aquariums and select the most innovative features. A duplicate system of piping was installed to provide both fresh and sea water, which may be warm or cold as the fish require. A major attraction added in 1970 is a reef tank that displays a total marine community.

Open daily throughout the year. Winter hours are 10:00 A.M.–4:00 P.M. Open in summer 9:00 A.M.–5:00 P.M. $

(10) Field Museum of Natural History*

East Roosevelt Road at South Lake Shore Drive

Considered a leading museum of its kind, the Field Museum contains exhibits featuring all branches of natural history. Many of its older collections were acquired at the close of the World's Columbian Exposition of 1893, when displays brought to Chicago for the Exposition were gathered together in the former Fine Arts Hall for permanent exhibition. After Marshall Field contributed one million dollars to its endowment, the museum was named the Field Columbian Museum. Expeditions and purchases increased the collections beyond the original building's capacity. A Greek temple was the model for a new building in Grant Park, which opened to the public in 1921. Because the museum is considered an important educational resource for the city of Chicago, it contains not only the thousands of items on public display, but also extensive research collections in all aspects of natural history. One of the best-known exhibits in the museum is in Chauncy Keep Memorial Hall, where the sculptor Malvina Hoffman has created statues, busts, and heads representing the races of mankind in stone and bronze. Open daily year round, 9:00 A.M.–5:00 P.M. $

(11) Clarence Buckingham Memorial Fountain

Grant Park east of Congress Plaza

Although they may never have visited Chicago, thousands of Americans are familiar with the Buckingham Fountain in Grant Park, a favored subject for picture postcards. The French sculptor N. Marcel Loyau designed the fountain, modeling it in part on the Latona fountain at Versailles. Miss Kate Buckingham gave the fountain to the city in memory of her brother, Clarence Buckingham, a former director of the Art Institute. During the summer a 90-minute color display attracts crowds of tourists to the park after 9:00 P.M.

West of the fountain are the gardens designated as the Court of Presidents, originally intended to include statuary. Only "The Seated Lincoln" by Augustus Saint-Gaudens was ever acquired.

(12) The Art Institute of Chicago

South Michigan Avenue at East Adams Street

Five Chicago business leaders founded the Chicago Academy of the Fine Arts in 1879 for the purpose of establishing schools of art and design and maintaining exhibitions of art. The new Academy continued to grow with their support, and its name was changed in 1882 to the Art Institute of Chicago. Charles Hutchinson, the banker who served as its president for many years, persuaded the city of Chicago to turn over to the Art Institute a structure on the lakefront at Adams Street built to house the World's Congresses of the Columbian Exposition of 1893. Now the main unit of the Art Institute, the handsome building was designed in modified Italian Renaissance style by a Boston firm, Shepley, Rutan, and Coolidge.

The Art Institute of Chicago acquired Dutch masters, French impressionists, German and Oriental works, and the Thorne collection of miniature rooms, making it necessary to enlarge the structure many times. Auditoriums, lecture halls, an art library, and a library of architecture have been added. In 1977 the America Windows were installed by Marc Chagall. The bronze lions, given to the Institute by Mrs. Henry Field in 1895, still stand on the front steps, each bronze animal weighing three tons. On the south terrace stands Lorado Taft's fountain, "Spirit of the Great Lakes," completed in 1913.

Open all year, Monday–Wednesday and Friday, 10:30 A.M.–4:30 P.M.; Thursday, 10:30 A.M.–8:00 P.M.; weekends, 10:00 A.M.–5:00 P.M. $

(13) The ArchiCenter

310 South Michigan Avenue (2nd floor)

Visitors to Chicago who are interested in learning more about the city's architecture will want to visit the ArchiCenter, which was established as a Bicentennial project. The ArchiCenter stages frequent exhibits, lectures, and films and is the point of departure for walking and bus tours of Chicago architecture. These are scheduled at regular times throughout the year, and tours may be specially arranged for private groups. Erected in 1924, the building housing the center was designed by Graham, Anderson, Probst, and White, important Chicago architects, who took advantage of a new zoning law permitting heights of more than 400 feet in designing this 30-story, 475-foot structure.

Open Monday–Friday, 9:30 A.M.–5:00 P.M.; Saturday, 9:30 A.M.–3:00 P.M. Free.

Lorado Taft in studio with the fountain, "Spirit of the Great Lakes," in background. Courtesy Chicago Historical Society. DN# 76,522

(14) Chicago Public Library Cultural Center*
78 East Washington Street
The Chicago Public Library was recently converted into a cultural center for the city, thus sparing the structure designed by Shepley, Rutan, and Coolidge and built in 1893–1897. It stands on land that was once part of the Fort Dearborn Reservation. Initially the north half of the building served as the Grand Army of the Republic Memorial Hall and Museum because the land on which it was built had belonged to the Chicago Soldiers' Home. The rest of the building housed an extensive public library collection drawn together after the Chicago Fire of 1871.

The renovated library interior is "grandly designed and richly embellished" with marble and mosaics. Two glass domes, one in the Preston Bradley Room and another in the lobby of the GAR room, are probably Tiffany designs. A large portion of the building still serves as a library. Preston Bradley Hall is used for concerts and gatherings and as a reading room. In 1976 the structure was designated a Chicago Landmark.

(15) The Loop
Bounded by Lake, Van Buren, and Wells Streets and by Wabash Avenue, the Loop is the heart of Chicago's mercantile, financial, and governmental district, the area from which the village of Chicago expanded into a town and a city. Retail stores, banks, corporate offices, government office buildings, and a sprinkling of institutions of higher education, hotels, and churches lie within its bounds.

Readily identified against the skyline by its cluster of graceful skyscrapers, the Loop has an unusually high concentration of stores and offices within a small area. Three-quarters of a million workers and shoppers come and go daily. Nearly 352,000 motor vehicles add to the bustle and congestion on the streets, as well as to the large volume of Loop business transacted daily. Expressways and subways are recent remedies for the long-standing problem of traffic congestion in the Loop.

Applied to Chicago's downtown in the late nineteenth century, the name

An aerial view of the Chicago Loop. Photo by Kee Chang. Courtesy Chicago Association of Commerce and Industry.

"Loop" comes from the pattern of the public transportation system. When companies built mass transit lines to serve the needs of Chicago, they produced a fragmented system linking residential areas and downtown by horse-drawn street railway cars, then cablecars, and, at the end of the century, electric streetcars. The elevated railroad system began in Chicago in 1892 when the first el was built above the congested street traffic to carry people southward from the business district to the World's Columbian Exposition grounds. Thereafter the elevated system expanded rapidly as a faster alternative to streetcar travel. Both the streetcar and elevated systems made a swing or loop around the downtown area. The Loop today remains key to reaching outlying parts of the city by public transportation. The current goal is to remove the elevateds from the Loop and expand the subway system, which in 1980 totaled 21 miles of tracks.

Architecturally, artistically, and historically, the area is of prime importance. Within its bounds lie seven Chicago Landmark buildings dating from 1886 to 1930, illustrative of the efforts of earlier generations of Chicago architects to get the maximum use out of a limited land area with aesthetically pleasing functional structures. Near them stand more recent examples of the skyscraper. A few of the Loop's outstanding structures, well-known retail stores, and works of art are noted here (nos. [16]–[22]).

(16) Federal Center Plaza and Calder Stabile

South Clark and West Adams Streets

This complex includes three structures: the 27-story Dirksen Building, built by the General Services Administration in 1964 to house the federal courthouse and offices; a 45-story office tower; and a low-lying post office building. All were designed by Ludwig Mies van der Rohe.

The best-known works of Alexander Calder are his mobiles, but the term "stabile" was invented in 1932 to describe works like "Red Flamingo," which he created for the Federal Center Plaza in 1975. It is a 53-foot high figure of red steel.

(17) Chicago Board of Trade Building*

141 West Jackson Boulevard

Designed by Holabird and Root and completed in 1930, this impressive example of Art Deco architecture houses the largest grain exchange in the world. The structure fittingly symbolizes the importance of the commodities trade to Chicago since the founding of the board in 1848 to bring order to chaotic conditions in the city grain markets. Dramatically sited at the southern end of La Salle Street, the present structure is the second Board of Trade building at this location. The first, designed by W. W. Boyington, architect of the Water Tower (no. [27]) and dedicated in 1885, served the Board of Trade for 40 years before it became too small for board business and was torn down to make room for the present structure. The Board of Trade building is topped by a statue, "Ceres, Goddess of the Grain and Harvest," by John H. Stoors. Visitors will find the three-story Art Deco lobby impressive. From a special gallery they can observe shouting traders, hurrying messengers, bags of grain samples, and the quotations board. The structure was designated a Chicago Landmark in 1977.

(18) The Rookery*
209 South La Salle Street
The only survivor of a group of late nineteenth-century multistory commercial buildings in the La Salle Street financial district, the Rookery is named for a huge flock of pigeons that roosted on the water tank, City Hall, and the public library on the southeast corner of La Salle and Adams. The architects who designed the four-story office structure, Burnham and Root, included rooks in the carved ornamentation above the La Salle Street entrance. Built in 1885–1888, the Rookery is a remarkably beautiful building with an interior court designed to ensure light in inner offices, an unusual feature at that time and later widely imitated, and a fine spiral staircase enclosed in a cylindrical projection in the central court. The building combined a standard masonry system and iron-frame construction methods. Frank Lloyd Wright remodeled the lobby in 1905. The building is owned by Continental Illinois National Bank, whose deed of ownership contains a restrictive covenant designed to preserve its architectural integrity. Located in the heart of the Loop, its office space is prestigious. At one time both Burnham and Root and Frank Lloyd Wright had offices here. The Rookery was designated a Chicago Landmark in 1972.

(19) Carson Pirie Scott & Company Building*
One South State Street
Designed in 1899 by Louis H. Sullivan, a pioneer of modern architecture, and built in 1903–1904 with an addition in 1906 by D. H. Burnham and Company, the Carson Pirie Scott building is often regarded as Sullivan's finest commercial structure. It is notable both as an example of the steel building technology that Chicago architects developed in the late nineteenth century and as an example of Sullivan's skill with ornamentation. The structure gains additional importance from its place in Chicago's retail trade. Although it was originally built for Schlesinger and Mayer, one of Chicago's earliest department stores, Carson's has owned the structure since 1904. John Pirie and Samuel Carson, Belfast dry goods merchants, came from Ireland to La Salle, Illinois, in 1855 and there established a store. Within a decade they had entered the Chicago retail and wholesale markets. The present firm grew from these beginnings. State Street had emerged as the center of Chicago retail activity by 1869, largely due to the efforts of Potter Palmer, the "merchant prince of Chicago." The Carson Pirie Scott & Company Building was designated a Chicago Landmark in 1970.

(20) Chagall Mosaic
First National Bank Plaza, on Monroe between Dearborn and Clark Streets
C. F. Murphy Associates designed the First National Bank building in 1970. The multilevel plaza on which the building stands is a popular meeting place for Chicago citizens, especially during the warm summer months. The French artist Marc Chagall came to Chicago to supervise the installation of his mosaic, "The Four Seasons," a huge block 70 feet long, 14 feet high, and 10 feet deep, depicting dreamlike figures and objects executed in 350 hues and shades.

(21) Picasso Sculpture
Located on Washington Street at the Chicago Civic Center, bounded by Dearborn, Clark, Randolph, and Washington Streets
Picasso's sculpture, a gift to the people of Chicago, was unveiled in 1967. The 50-foot-high sculpture of rust brown Cor-ten steel, weighing 162 tons, was fabricated by workers of the U.S. Steel Corporation. It is expected that the special metal alloy will rust to the same color as the Civic Center building. The sculpture, which is five stories high, has evoked many comments from Chicago residents and visitors alike, particularly because it is untitled.

(22) Marshall Field and Company*
Marshall Field is on the block bounded by State, Washington, and Randolph Streets and Wabash Avenue
This nationally and internationally famous store has long played an important role in Chicago's economy,

both as a retail store and, until 1935, as a wholesale company serving a national market. Marshall Field began his Chicago business career in 1855 and through merchandising and shrewd investments in real estate acquired a fortune of $125 million by the time of his death in 1906. Marshall Field and Company was popular because of Field's liberal credit and return policies and an emphasis on comfort and convenience for customers. Fields was the first department store to include a restaurant for its customers. Marshall Field and Company is still well known for its fine line of merchandise attractively displayed. Field gave large gifts to the University of Chicago, the Field Museum of Natural History (no. [10]), and the Chicago Manual Training School. Designed for Marshall Field by the noted architect Daniel H. Burnham, this granite structure was built in four stages between 1892 and 1907. Measuring 340 by 385 feet, the building's exterior has been altered very little.

(23) Sears Tower Skydeck
South Wacker Drive at Jackson Boulevard
When Julius Rosenwald became president of Sears, Roebuck & Company in 1897, he wanted the various offices of the company gathered together under one roof. Therefore, he borrowed money to build the first Sears Tower building at the western edge of the city in 1904. Seventy years later, the mail-order business having outgrown this building, the company, owner of radio station WLS ("World's Largest Store"), commissioned the firm of Skidmore, Owings, and Merrill to design the world's tallest building for its headquarters. The Sears Tower stands 1,454 feet high with 110 stories. The fastest elevator in the world whisks visitors from the lobby to the Skydeck on the 103rd floor in 45 seconds for a magnificent view of the city. Open daily, 9:00 A.M.–midnight. $

(24) *U.S.S. Silversides**
Randolph Street and North Lake Shore Drive
Launched on August 28, 1941, at Mare Island Navy Yard in New York, the *U.S.S. Silversides* chalked up an enviable record in the Pacific theater during World War II, sinking 23 enemy ships and winning four presidential citations. Designated a Naval Reserve Training Vessel in 1962, the submarine was moved to Chicago. After eight years of service, the *U.S.S. Silversides* was retired as a training ship. Berthed at the Naval Armory at the foot of Randolph Street, the submarine has been restored as a memorial to the men of the submarine service. Open daily, Memorial Day–Labor Day, noon–6:00 P.M. $

(25) Jean Baptiste Du Sable Homesite* and site of Fort Dearborn
The Du Sable homesite is at 401 North Michigan Avenue and the Fort Dearborn site at the intersection of Michigan Avenue and Wacker Drive
On the north bank of the Chicago River, Jean Baptiste Du Sable, probably Chicago's first non-Indian permanent resident, built his home. Du Sable, whose father was French and whose mother was possibly a Black slave, was born in Haiti. Du Sable later migrated to Louisiana and then to the St. Louis area and had settled in Peoria by 1773. Before 1779 he established a fur-trading post and farm on the Chicago River. Du Sable lived here until 1800 except for a brief period during the Revolutionary War when the British held him prisoner at Mackinac. The site of the Du Sable cabin now lies partly in Pioneer Court Plaza, a 100,000-square-foot public open space developed by the Equitable Life and Chicago Tribune companies. The plaza fountain is inscribed with the names of Chicago pioneers and civic leaders.

In 1803 the federal government built Fort Dearborn on the south bank of the Chicago River near its mouth to protect the entrance to the strategic Lake Michigan–Mississippi River water route. Occupied until August 1812 and then evacuated (see p. 31), the original fort was burned by Indians. Rebuilt in 1816, the fort remained in this location for the next 40 years. Sidewalk markers at Michigan Avenue and Wacker Drive show the location of this Chicago Landmark.

(26) Navy Pier*
Grand Avenue and Lake Michigan at Streeter Drive
Daniel Burnham's 1909 plan for the city of Chicago urged the development of harbor facilities, calling for two long piers projecting into the lake on either side of the Chicago River. One pier materialized. Charles Sumner Frost's unique design combined commercial and recreational features in a 3,040-foot-long pier completed in 1916. On one side of the pier commercial shipping docked; on the other, passengers boarded excursion steamers for sightseeing cruises to Milwaukee or along the Chicago lakefront. A magnificent hall suitable for concerts, entertainment, and dancing and a restaurant were located at the

This 1913 photograph shows the east end of the Municipal Pier where a restaurant and dance hall–theater were located. Note the excursion boats which operated between the Pier and Jackson and Lincoln Parks. Courtesy Chicago Historical Society. Clark negative.

east end of the pier, served by a streetcar line.

Municipal Pier was renamed Navy Pier at the end of World War I to commemorate the naval dead. For a generation the pier served freight and passenger traffic as well as the recreational needs of Chicagoans. The U.S. Navy leased the entire pier for a naval training center at the beginning of World War II. After the war, the University of Illinois occupied the 34-acre space until its Chicago Circle campus opened in 1965. Following the removal of "Harvard on the Rocks," trade shows and expositions utilized the upper level of the pier. A promenade deck on the upper level is open to the public during the navigation season. Here visitors can observe the loading and unloading of some overseas cargo, much of which is newsprint. Chicago's major port facility, Calumet Harbor, lies to the south (see p. 101). The restoration of the recreational part of Navy Pier was undertaken as a Bicentennial project. Every August Navy Pier is the site of ChicagoFest. The pier has been designated a Chicago City Landmark.

(27) Old Chicago Water Tower District*

Chicago and Michigan Avenues

Designed by the Chicago architect William W. Boyington and built in 1866–1869, the castellated Gothic Water Tower and pumping station helped to meet Chicago's need for a clean water supply. The rapidly growing town developed serious drinking-water and sewage-disposal problems in the 1860s because the sewage emptied into the Chicago River contaminated drinking water drawn from a crib 200 feet off the Lake Michigan shore. The city chose Ellis S. Chesbrough, Boston's chief engineer, to solve the problem. Chesbrough planned and supervised the construction of a tunnel running two miles into Lake Michigan and lying 66 feet below the lakebed, a remarkable engineering feat that attracted international attention. The pumping station pumped water through the tunnel from its crib two miles offshore to provide a very adequate water supply for the city. Similar tunnels and cribs have since been added. The limestone Water Tower originally enclosed a stand pipe, which equalized water pressure for delivery through mains and pipes. New pumping equipment installed in 1906 made the stand pipe obsolete, and it was removed five years later.

This architect's drawing of the Old Water Tower and Pumping Station was probably done in 1865. Courtesy Chicago Historical Society.

But the pumping station still functions as part of Chicago's water system, and the Water Tower remains. The exteriors of the two buildings survived the fire of 1871. They stand not only as a monument to hydraulic engineering, but also as examples of the architecture found in this fashionable part of Chicago before the great fire. The Water Tower District is a Chicago Landmark.

The 74-story Water Tower Place, in the 800 block of North Michigan Avenue, just across the street from the Water Tower, was built in the early 1970s by subsidiaries of Marshall Field and Company and Aetna Life Insurance. This $130 million urban center houses a large Marshall Field store, the Ritz Carlton Hotel, condominiums, and four levels of underground parking.

(28) John Hancock Center
875 North Michigan Avenue

The Hancock Center Plaza is located in Streeterville, a historic section of Chicago named for George ("Cap") Wellington Streeter, a colorful circus owner, Civil War veteran, and steamboat captain. In 1886, en route to the Gulf of Mexico, his boat struck a sand bar about 450 feet offshore in Lake Michigan between Chicago Avenue and Oak Street. He and his wife, Maria, moved into the stranded boat, and through a combination of their efforts and the forces of nature surrounded the stricken boat with 186 acres of sand and municipal garbage. Cap declared the island a "District of Lake Michigan," subject only to the laws of God and the federal government. For the next 30 years, the Chicago government tried desperately to evict, jail, or sink the pair, while Streeter and his wife continued to live on their ship, selling sand bar lots at extravagant prices and occasionally opening gambling casinos and taverns. Big Bill Thompson, mayor in 1918, finally ousted them for the relatively minor offense of peddling liquor on a Sunday. From his new lakeshore houseboat, Cap continued to fight for his rights in the courts until his death in 1921.

The 100 stories of the multipurpose John Hancock Center accommodate housing, shops, offices, apartments, restaurants, and garages. Skidmore, Owings, and Merrill designed the center, which opened in 1969. The exterior is black anodized aluminum with tinted glass. The observation deck is open daily, 9:00 A.M.–midnight. $

(29) Chicago Historical Society
North Clark Street at the south end of Lincoln Park

Once the site of a cemetery, Lincoln Park, with its 1,200 acres of woodlands, lagoons, bridle paths, playgrounds, and golf courses, contains a zoo, a number of monuments to prominent persons, a conservatory, and museums.

Those interested in the history of Chicago will find the Chicago Historical Society well worth a visit. Organized in 1856, the society now occupies its fourth headquarters, the Georgian structure at the south end of Lincoln Park, built in 1932 and enlarged in 1972. The society's museum includes exhibits tracing Chicago's history and covering selected areas of American history; a gallery of Illinois pioneer life featuring daily craft demonstrations; presentations on Lincoln and the Civil War; and special exhibits highlighting the history of photography and print making, fashions, and the decorative arts. The society offers a number of other programs for the public, and its research library contains a wide variety of manuscripts, maps, graphics, and printed materials. Research collections are open for use Tuesday through Saturday (Monday through Friday during the summer) without charge. The museum is open daily, Monday–Saturday, 9:30 A.M.–4:30 P.M.; and Sunday noon–5:00 P.M. $

(30) Old Town Triangle District

This district is bounded by North Avenue, Lincoln Park, and the extension of Ogden Avenue north to Armitage Avenue.

In contrast to the upper-middle-class residential development pattern in suburban Oak Park, River Forest, and Riverside (see nos. [33] and [34]), the Old Town Triangle District developed as a working-class neighborhood. From the 1850s down to the fire of 1871, immigrants from many German principalities settled here and established the cultural character of the community. They built small frame homes known as Chicago cottages. They established St. Michael's parish in 1852, and in 1866 began construction of an impressive red brick sanctuary. They worked as shoemakers, garment makers, brewery employees, carpenters, railroad construction hands, and grain loaders.

The fire of October 8, 1871, virtually destroyed North Town, as Old Town was then called. Even the beautiful new St. Michael's Church was gutted, and only three double-brick exterior walls remained. Rebuilding began quickly. Within a year St. Michael's had been restored. Workers rebuilt frame Chicago cottages until 1874, when a city ordinance forbade wooden construction. Thereafter, brick became popular.

The last three decades of the century brought changes to North Town. The city developed Lincoln Park along the lakefront to the east of the neighborhood. To the working-class community came prosperous businessmen like brewer Frederick Wacker to build substantial homes. Developers constructed row houses. The German heritage remained, expressed in a Protestant and a Catholic church, with services in German; a variety of social, cultural, and recreational societies; and German restaurants and taverns.

Early in the twentieth century, North Town stopped growing and deteriorated somewhat under the impact of changes in the adjacent areas to the north, south, and west. The eastern part of North Town, moreover, dubbed "Old Town" after World War II, escaped substantial change. Thanks in large measure to the work of the Old Town Triangle Association, formed in 1948, North Town revived as a Chicago neighborhood with an interest in its historic past. The spirit of community again prevails.

Visitors to the Old Town Triangle District will note that St. Michael's still stands and its bells still peal. Examples of Chicago cottages still remain. The Wacker homes (the smaller of the two a converted carriage house) stand at 1836 and 1838 North Lincoln Park West. Examples of late nineteenth-century row houses are found in the 100 block of Eugenie Street. Five row houses designed by Louis Sullivan are located at 1826–1834 North Lincoln Park West. Daniel Crilly's row houses, built in 1885, are located on Crilly Court. The Old Town Triangle District was made a Chicago Landmark in 1977.

(31) Jane Addams's Hull House* and Dining Hall

800 South Halsted

This Chicago Landmark testifies to the ideals of Jane Addams and Ellen Gates Starr, who established Hull House in 1889 in an effort to meet the social needs of Chicago's vast immigrant population. On the near west side, they acquired the former home of a Chicago businessman, Charles Hull, built in 1856. It formed the hub of a growing neighborhood center that offered a host of social services.

Today Hull House is located on the Chicago Circle campus of the University of Illinois, developed in the 1960s on urban renewal land that included the Hull House Settlement complex of more than thirteen buildings. Because of their historical importance, the university agreed to restore and preserve the Charles Hull House as well as the Dining Hall (built in 1905) used by Hull House residents.

The reconstructed Hull House pres-

Children's art class in the Hull House neighborhood. Courtesy University of Illinois at Chicago, The Library, Jane Addams Memorial Collection.

ently includes a museum and research library. Many of Addams's personal furnishings may be seen in the sitting room–office on the first floor. Here also are restored double parlors. The reception room is now an exhibit area, as is the Octagon Room, which Charles Hull originally used as an office. The Dining Hall, which has been relocated a few feet south of the mansion, contains an ethnic museum of the immigrant neighborhood as Addams and her colleagues knew it.

The interpretative program at Hull House also includes slide tape presentations depicting Addams's work and the history of the surrounding neighborhood. Open daily year round, except holidays, Monday–Friday, 10:00 A.M.–4:00 P.M.; Sundays, noon–5:00 P.M., in the summer months. Free.

(32) Chicago's Immigrant Heritage

The growth and development of Chicago owe much to the hundreds of thousands of immigrants who settled in the city. They worked in factories and stockyards, helped build railroads and city transit systems, established shops and businesses, and served the city as policemen, firemen, and elected officials. Chicago has many visual reminders of its different national groups—churches, museums, art galleries, craft shops, restaurants, and neighborhoods. The following list is but a sampling. For other sites reflecting Chicago's ethnic history see Du Sable Museum of African American History (no. [3]); Old Town Triangle District (no. [30]); and Jane Addams's Hull House (no. [31]). Those interested in Chicago's wealth of churches and their ethnic origins should consult George Lane, *Chicago Churches and Synagogues: An Architectural Pilgrimage* (Chicago: Loyola University Press, 1981). The author has classified churches by national origin and by areas within the city in very useful indexes.

St. Stanislaus Kostka,
1351 West Evergreen Drive

Organized in 1867, St. Stanislaus Kostka is the oldest Polish parish within the city limits. At one time this beautiful structure, dedicated in 1881, had more than 30,000 communicants.

Church of the Five Holy Martyrs,
43rd and Richmond Streets

Five Holy Martyrs parish was founded in 1909 for the Polish community of Brighton Park. In 1969 and 1975 the parish hosted Cardinal Karol Wojtyla, who returned to the parish as Pope John Paul II. He celebrated an outdoor mass for the Polish community at the parish field on October 5, 1979. A crowd of 200,000 poured into Brighton Park to welcome the pope. To commemorate this event, the City Council of Chicago officially changed the name of a one-mile stretch of 43rd Street, from Western Avenue to Kedzie Avenue, to Pope John Paul II Drive.

Polish Museum of America,
984 North Milwaukee Avenue

Housed in facilities provided by the Polish Roman Catholic Union of America, the museum displays include the Paderewski Room, furnished with memorabilia of the famous pianist; a

Russian Orthodox community, Holy Trinity was consecrated in 1903. The task of designing the church was given to Sullivan after an earlier plan for a much grander structure had been discarded. Sullivan's design was similar to the Russian provincial churches known to the priest and his parishioners. The interior is lavishly decorated with examples of Russian ecclesiastical art. The church is a Chicago Historical and Architectural Landmark.

Swedish American Museum,
5248 North Clark Street

Dedicated by Carl XVI Gustaf, king of Sweden, in April 1976, the museum highlights Swedish culture and the achievements of Swedish Americans. Museum classes teach folk dancing, Swedish handicrafts, and cooking. Open Tuesday–Friday, 11:00 A.M.–2:00 P.M.; Saturday, 11:00 A.M.–3:00 P.M. Closed on Sunday and Monday. Donations accepted.

(33) Frank Lloyd Wright Prairie School of Architecture District* and River Forest Historic District*

Oak Park and River Forest

Because of the concentration of residential architecture designed by Frank Lloyd Wright and his Prairie School colleagues, students, and followers, portions of the village of Oak Park and its neighbor, River Forest, have been designated as historic districts on the National Register of Historic Places. These districts also include fine examples of other residential architectural styles dating from the 1850s through the 1920s.

The Wright Historic District in Oak Park is bounded approximately by Harlem Avenue and by Division, Ridgeland, and Lake Streets. The River Forest Historic District adjoins it, bounded by Harlem and Chicago Avenues, Lake Street, and the Des Plaines River.

Wright designed 25 Oak Park residences, plus Unity Temple, between 1889 and 1913. Over a hundred other structures designed by his contemporaries, associates, and students are also found here. They represent the work of the Prairie School of architecture, which emphasized open space, horizontal planes, and integrated use of natural materials like wood, brick, stone, and glass. Within the bounds of the River Forest District, 165 structures have been identified as having special architectural and/or historical importance, mainly Prairie school residences. Wright designed five of these homes and the River Forest Tennis Club.

The two districts offer those interested in Wright's architecture a unique opportunity to observe the evolution of his Prairie style between 1893 and 1909. Six of his structures have been separately identified on the National Register of Historic Places. As a young architect Wright built a home* in Oak Park in 1889, and in 1898 he added a studio* adjacent to it. The home and the studio, at 951 Chicago Avenue, are being restored to their appearance in 1909, the last year Wright lived and worked in them. At the southwest corner of Lake Street and Kenilworth Avenue stands Unity Temple,* designed by Wright in 1905 and completed in 1908 to replace the Oak Park Universalist Church, which had burned down. It has been called "the first monumentally expressed use of reinforced concrete in world architecture" and a "prime example of modern church architecture." The William H. Winslow House and Stable* are at 515 Auvergne Place, River Forest. Built in 1893, the house and stable were Wright's first independent commission. Also listed are the Walter Gale House* (1893), one of his bootleg houses (Wright moonlighted while working for Louis Sullivan); the Frank Thomas House,* his first Prairie house in Oak Park (1901); and the Mrs. Thomas Gale House* of 1909, which includes a cantilevered roof and balcony.

The history of the villages of Oak Park and River Forest goes back decades before the Wright years of residence. Although permanent white settlement in the area dates from the 1830s, substantial numbers of people chose to settle in the area only after the inauguration of regular railroad service from downtown Chicago in 1849. The Village of River Forest was incorporated in 1880, and the Village of Oak Park in 1901. With the establishment of good commuting service in the 1880s, both developed as pleasant villages attracting a good share of Chicago's more affluent businessmen and professionals, who preferred the environment of a spacious suburban town with shaded streets. Oak Park and River Forest developed cooperatively, sharing community facilities. Oak Park–River Forest is the designation today of the high school, the historical society, and the chamber of commerce. The Historical Society of Oak Park and River Forest is housed in the Farson-Mills House, which was designed by another Prairie architect, George Maher, in 1897. The collection includes memorabilia of another Oak Park notable, Ernest Hemingway.

Those interested in the architectural

main exhibit, which highlights folk and fine arts; the Kosciuszko collection; a marine exhibit; and an art gallery. The archives and library contain extensive collections on Polish and Polish American history. Open daily, noon–5:00 P.M. Donations welcome.

Lithuanian Plaza

This neighborhood, bounded by 67th Street, Rockwell Street, 71st Street, and California Avenue, includes a number of Lithuanian craft and gift shops.

Balzekas Museum of Lithuanian Culture, 4012 South Archer Avenue

The museum contains rich collections of Lithuanian art, stamps, coins, weaving, folk art, amber, armor, religious memorabilia, maps, clocks, and antique furniture. An extensive library includes theater and drama archives, Lithuanian genealogical materials, and collections of photographs and magazines. The museum conducts educational programs as well. Open daily 1:00–4:00 P.M. $

Chinatown South

A profusion of Chinese shops, restaurants, and grocery stores attracts tourists to the nine square blocks of Chinatown South, located on Wentworth Avenue from Cermak Road to 28th Street. The settlement of Chinese in the Wentworth Avenue and 22nd Street area began about 1905 when the most affluent of Chicago's Chinese purchased property here. Chinese moved from the west coast into Chicago after 1876 and lived initially in the area around South Clark and Van Buren Streets. Landlord exploitation there had much to do with the beginnings of Chinatown South.

Important public structures in Chinatown South include the Chinese Christian Union Church at Wentworth Avenue and West 23rd Street; St. Therese Catholic Mission on Alexander Street; the On Leong Tong building, often called the City Hall; and the Ling Long Museum, 2238 Wentworth Avenue.

Holy Trinity Russian Orthodox Cathedral. Courtesy Chicago Historical Society, ICHi-19263

Maurice Spertus Museum of Judaica, 618 South Michigan Avenue

The museum houses permanent collections of ceremonial objects, sculpture, paintings, graphic art, ethnographic materials, a Holocaust Memorial, and a special exhibit, "Room of the Generations," which places a Jewish family's experience in European and American historical perspective. Open Monday–Thursday, 10:00 A.M.–5:00 P.M.; Friday 10:00 A.M.–3:00 P.M.; and Sunday, 10:00 A.M.–4:00 P.M. $

Ukranian National Museum, 2453 West Chicago Avenue

The museum displays include a large collection of Ukranian folk a dolls, costumes, modern Ukranian folk instruments, and architectura historical exhibits. A library and a chive contain collections for those terested in Ukranian and Ukranian American research. Open Sunday, noon–3:00 P.M. Free.

Ukranian Institute of Modern Art, 2316 West Chicago Avenue

Open daily, noon–4:00 P.M., exc Monday. Donations accepted.

Holy Trinity Orthodox Cathedral a Rectory,* 1117–1127 North Leavitt Street

Designed by Louis Sullivan in 19 1901 to meet the needs of Chicago

Frank Lloyd Wright Home and Studio, Oak Park, Illinois. Courtesy The Frank Lloyd Wright Home and Studio Foundation.

riches of Oak Park and River Forest should begin their explorations at the Visitor Center at 158 Forest Avenue (one-half block north of Lake Street), open daily from March through November, 10:00 A.M.–5:00 P.M. Walking and bicycle tours of the area, offered at a modest fee and sponsored by the Frank Lloyd Wright Home and Studio Foundation, begin here. The center sells maps showing the location of architecturally significant structures and rents recorded walking-tour guides to the Wright buildings. For information on guided tours of the Frank Lloyd Wright Home and Studio and Unity Temple and visiting hours at the Farson-Mills House, call (312) 848–1978. To reach the Visitor Center by car, take the Eisenhower Expressway (I-290) to Harlem Avenue and exit north. Follow the brown and white signs to the historic district parking area at Lake Street and North Forest Avenue.

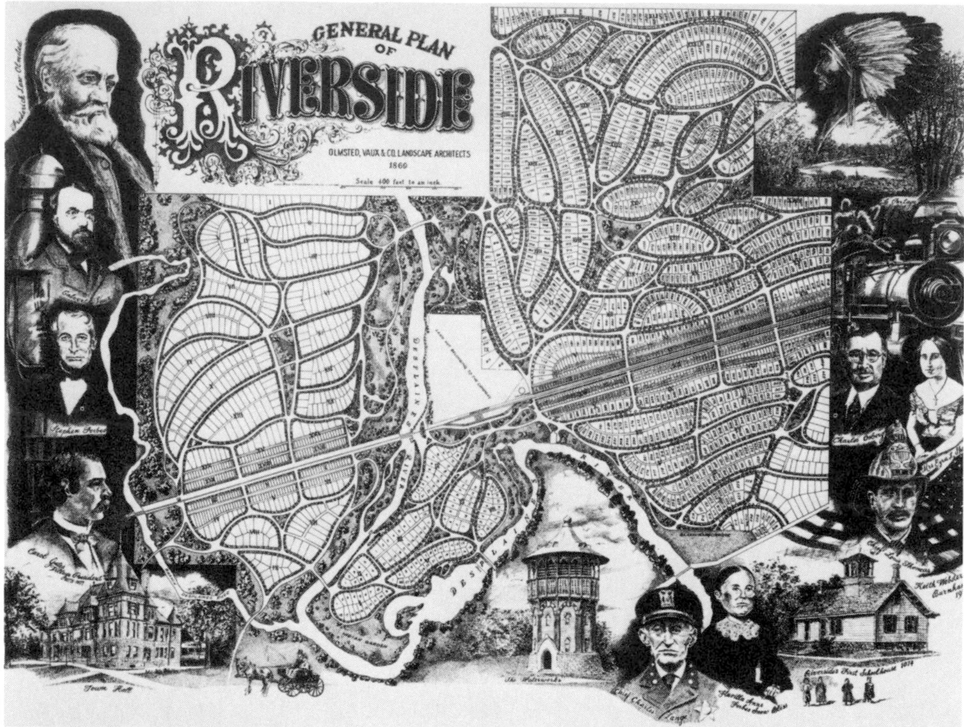

Keith Burnham, 1975. Riverside Historical Museum, Riverside, Illinois.

(34) Riverside Landscape Architecture District*

This district is bounded by 26th Street, Des Plaines Avenue, 31st Street, Forbes Road, the Des Plaines River, and Ogden and Harlem Avenues.

The Riverside Development Association was organized to promote a suburb that would be the first stop west of Chicago on the Chicago, Burlington and Quincy Railroad. The promoters envisioned homes for Chicago executives and their families in a pastoral setting, and in 1868 they commissioned the team of Frederick L. Olmsted and Calvert Vaux, designers of Central Park in New York City, to lay out the community.

The Olmsted-Vaux plan for Riverside broke with the established notions of American commuter suburb design. Rejecting the rectangular grid system popular with planners before 1868, Olmstead and Vaux chose instead to lay out streets so that they flow around the landscape's topography in harmony with the winding Des Plaines River. They recommended unfenced parks and recreation areas, clumped tree plantings along roadsides, large lots, restrictions on the distance between houses and roadways, and requirements that lot owners plant trees. The association agreed with these suggestions and energetically began to lay out roads, subdivide the land, lay water and gas mains, and construct a hotel, stores, a stone chapel, and spacious frame homes.

The depression of 1873 dampened expansion, and Riverside grew more slowly during the next half-century as a wealthy suburb with families of older American stock predominating. The 1920s brought change. Riverside experienced an influx of Bohemians and Poles and others of more recent European origin who came westward from Cicero, Berwyn, and Chicago's west side to build good, substantial homes. Apartment buildings cast their shadows over great old houses, and the grandeur of the old hotel dimmed. Streets were marked and houses numbered. The city had overtaken the suburb.

Nevertheless, 1,500 acres had been developed according to the Olmsted-Vaux plan, attracting many of Chicago's more affluent businessmen and professionals. This area has retained much of its early character. One hundred acres of the original tract, lying at the western edge of the historic district, did not follow the plan. The Chicago Zoological Park and two schools occupy part of it, and the balance fell to a developer who substituted tiny parks and small lots for the plan's generous ones in an effort to use all available land.

Of the buildings constructed in 1869–1871, a block of two-and-one-half-story red brick and stone stores and offices, a stone chapel, and a few frame residences remain. The district contains a few homes designed by William Le Baron Jenney, three by Frank Lloyd Wright, and two by Louis Sullivan. In the district are a representative sample of architectural styles from 1871 to 1969.

Those wishing to visit the Riverside Landscape District should go to the Riverside Historical Commission Museum, located in Centennial Square

Northwestern University Campus, 1907. Courtesy Northwestern University Archives.

in the heart of the village on Longcommon Road. The museum occupies a renovated water tower. Pamphlets are available here showing the location of structures of architectural and historical importance. Open on Saturday during the warm months.

2. Evanston

Sheridan Road

Evanston's early growth began with the founding of Northwestern University in 1851 by a group of Chicago Methodist leaders who were determined to establish "a university of the highest order of excellence." The town is named for one of them, Dr. John Evans. Incorporated as a town in 1863, Evanston grew substantially during the next three decades. Many Chicago merchants chose to build their homes in Evanston, a respectable and conservative town attractively located on Lake Michigan. Well served by commuter trains and a handsome lakeshore drive, Evanston grew as a satellite of Chicago, incorporating as a city in 1892.

Over the years many business, professional, insurance, and religious organizations selected Evanston as national headquarters. Industry began to develop in World War I and the 1920s. In 1979 Evanston's industries included 16 firms with more than 100 employees each. They produced a wide variety of products, including food, packaging materials, rust preventatives, cameras, and sheet steel. The two largest employers, with 500 workers each, produced hospital supplies and machinery.

This city of 73,700 has experienced an orderly growth, largely because of zoning and planning by a conservative government. Evanston retains open areas, parks, an attractive lakeshore, and wide, tree-lined streets, century-old characteristics of the university and residential town.

Evanston Sites of Interest

(1) Charles Gates Dawes House*
225 Greenwood Street
Built in 1894 for Dr. Robert D. Sheppard, treasurer and business manager of Northwestern University, this two-and-a-half story mansion, modeled on a French chateau, became the home of Charles G. Dawes in 1909. Dawes, a prominent financier and Republican, served as comptroller of the currency under William McKinley, director of the budget under Warren G. Harding, and vice president of the United States during the Coolidge administration. For his efforts to adjust German reparation payments for World War I, popularly known as the Dawes Plan, he received the Nobel Peace Prize for 1925. The Dawes family occupied the home until 1957, when Northwestern University took possession of the house under the terms of Dawes's will. Because of its national, state, and local significance, the Dawes House was designated a National Historic Landmark in 1976.

Since 1960 the Dawes House has served as the headquarters of the Evanston Historical Society, fulfilling Dawes's hope that his home would one day house the society's museum. It also serves as headquarters of the Junior League of Evanston. Five rooms on the first floor reflect the home as the Dawes family used it and contain exhibits of Dawes memorabilia and Evanston artifacts. Eight rooms on the second floor house displays of dolls and toys; the Historical Society office and meeting and research facilities; and Junior League quarters. A third floor was never completed and is not open to the public. It includes two servants' bedrooms, a stage, ballroom, and dressing room.

The Carriage House, built in 1892, originally accommodated horse-drawn vehicles but was adapted for automobiles and servants' quarters. The society plans to restore and open the ground floor as an exhibit area. Open Monday, Tuesday, Friday, and Saturday, 1:00–5:00 P.M. $

(2) Willard House*
1730 Chicago Avenue
At 1730 Chicago Avenue stand the headquarters of the Women's Christian Temperance Union, an organization working to restrict the use of alcohol. The WCTU and Frances Willard, its president from 1879–1898, made the town of Evanston well known both nationally and internationally. Willard, who had a distinguished teaching career, resigned as dean of women at Northwestern in 1874 to embark on a crusade for temperance and woman suffrage. Her social reform interests went far beyond these two issues. She worked for international peace and arbitration, labor reform, urban welfare, and prison reform. She dreamed of a unified women's social reform organization that would "do everything."

Rest Cottage, as the Willard family home is known today, stands on the WCTU grounds, a gabled Victorian Gothic structure built in 1865, with an addition in 1878. The house contains many original furnishings and personal possessions that reflect Willard's years of dedication to the temperance cause. Open Monday–Friday, 9:00 A.M.–noon and 1:00–4:00 P.M. Tour by appointment only. Call (312) 864-1397. Donation.

(3) Grosse Point Lighthouse*
2535 Sheridan Road
In response to requests from Evanston citizens, the federal government built Grosse Point Lighthouse in 1873 to prevent ships from foundering on the treacherous shoals of Grosse Point. A double home was built just a few steps away from the tower for the lighthouse keeper, his two assistants, and a laborer. The beehive-shaped lens for the Grosse Point light is a Civil War veteran. The reflector, sent from Paris to Louisiana during the war, failed to reach its destination and for a time lay buried in the sands of a Florida beach. Recovered and sent to Evanston, the lens still bears visible scratches from the sand. In 1935 the 60,000-candlepower light was converted to electricity and made automatic.

Today, the Evanston Environmental Association operates programs at the Lighthouse Nature Center to acquaint young and old with the beauties of nature along Lake Michigan's shore. There is a nature trail on the grounds, now part of the 10 acre Lighthouse Landing Park.

Plans are underway to restore the first floor of the assistant keeper's residence in the style of the 1880s. The Lighthouse Nature Center will be moved to the South Foghouse, and the North Foghouse will become a visitors' center showing an award-winning film on the Lighthouse produced for the Bicentennial.

Tours of the lighthouse are conducted on weekends from May to October, 1:30–4:30 P.M. Call (312) 328-6961 to make arrangements.

The federal government also built a lifesaving station on the lakeshore in 1876 in response to requests from Evanston citizens after the sinking of the *Lady Elgin* in 1860. Many Northwestern University students served as volunteer members of the crew. By the time the station was discontinued in 1916, these crews were credited with saving between 200 and 300 persons from drowning.

(4) Evanston Art Center
2603 Sheridan Road
The Evanston Art Center was organized in 1929 and in 1966 moved into its present quarters, a beautiful replica of a sixteenth-century English manor house, built for Harley Clarke, a utilities executive, in the 1920s. The Art Center has been successful in adapting the house to its new use without obscuring its basic beauty. Work areas for art students fill most of the house, and several fine galleries occupy the remainder.

The center is open daily, Monday–Friday, 9:00 A.M.–5:00 P.M.; Saturday, 9:00 A.M.–4:00 P.M.; and Sunday, 2:00–5:00 P.M. Free.

3. Wilmette
Sheridan Road

A residential community of 28,229, Wilmette is named for Archange Ouilmette, the Potawatomi Indian wife of Antoine Ouilmette, a French Canadian fur trader. The federal government awarded her two sections of land on Lake Michigan for herself and her children in the Treaty of Prairie du Chien in 1829. In 1869, 31 years after the Ouilmettes had departed for Council Bluffs, Iowa, the village was platted as a residential suburb of Chicago. Over the years about half of its working residents have commuted to Chicago jobs. The older tree-shaded residential sections of town near Lake Michigan are in distinct contrast to newer sections lying to the west and to the high-rise apartment complex developed on a newly incorporated strip of lakefront lying between Kenilworth and Wilmette.

Wilmette Sites of Interest

(1) Baha'i Temple*

100 Linden Avenue

Although the first Baha'i community in the United States was established in 1894, the world religion began in Persia earlier in the nineteenth century. Planning for a house of worship began as early as 1903, but it was not until 1953 that the shrine, designed by the French Canadian architect Louis Bourgeois, was dedicated. The building is one of the most beautiful and unusual edifices in Illinois. It is constructed of nine panels made from ground quartz and white cement, each panel incorporating a door and ornamental windows opening onto landscaped garden areas. On the interior of the approximately 190-foot-high dome are interwoven geometric forms and religious symbols. The House of Worship is open to visitors daily, May–October, 10:00 A.M.–10:00 P.M.; November–April, 10:00 A.M.–5:00 P.M. Free.

The *North Channel* of the Chicago Sanitary and Ship Canal begins just north of the Baha'i grounds. The canal runs through Evanston and joins the North Branch of the Chicago River within Chicago city limits.

The Baha'i Temple, September 1984. Photo by Margaret Bogue.

(2) Frank J. Baker House*
507 Lake Avenue
Frank Lloyd Wright designed this house in 1908 for a resident of Sewanee, Tennessee, and when the project did not materialize offered the design to Frank J. Baker in 1909. The magnificent two-story living room of this private residence projects toward the street.

(3) Chicago and North Western Railroad Depot*
1135–1141 Wilmette Avenue
The oldest surviving urban passenger station in the Chicago metropolitan area, the Wilmette depot played an important role in the town's development. Efforts to promote a town on this site failed until Wilmette's developers succeeded in persuading the Chicago and North Western Railroad to make their town site a railroad stop. They platted the first subdivision in 1869. The 1873 depot, more elaborate than many midwestern railroad stations, "was designed to receive, and impress, prospective land buyers from Chicago." In its next 20 years as a commuter suburb Wilamette's population grew from 300 to 3,000.

In 1897 the depot, sited on the wrong side of the tracks for passengers, was replaced by another passenger station. Moved to a new location, the 1873 depot served as a freight station until after World War II. It stood vacant from 1946 to 1974, when it was moved to its present location to prevent its destruction. The Wilmette Historical Society considers the depot the town's most historic building because of its age and its role in the town's growth.

(4) Wilmette Historical Museum
565 Hunter Road
The museum contains permanent exhibits on the history of the settlement of Wilmette and the Indian tribes of the area. It also houses the archives of Wilmette and a special room devoted to the history of costumes and clothing. Open Tuesday–Thursday, 9:30 A.M.-noon and 1:30 P.M.–4:00 P.M.; Saturday, 2:00–5:00 P.M.; the first Monday of the month, 7:30-9:30 P.M. Free.

4. Kenilworth
Sheridan Road

Having sold his interest in a successful lard-manufacturing business to Philip D. Armour, Joseph Sears, for nine years vice president of N. K. Fairbank and Company, applied his business expertise to the creation of a community north of Chicago for his fellow members of the Swedenborgian church. The 223 acres of level land he purchased in 1889 lay between Wilmette and Winnetka, east of the Chicago and North Western Railroad tracks.

With a group of friends, Sears formed the Kenilworth Company to develop and run the community until its incorporation as a village in 1896. The company laid out streets, operated the water works and gas supply system, and enforced deed restrictions to preserve the character of the community. The village ordinances prohibited alleys, required large lots, set building standards, and restricted lot sales to Caucasians.

The Kenilworth Company also named the streets and avenues. Sears chose the name Kenilworth after returning from a visit to England. Avenues were named after people or places in Sir Walter Scott's novel *Kenilworth*, while streets crossing Kenilworth Avenue were named for American authors.

Before moving to Kenilworth, Joseph Sears owned a home on Chicago's prestigious Prairie Avenue (site 1, no. [7]), built for him by Daniel Burnham. Burnham designed Sears's Kenilworth home and two other imposing residences in the village. Other well-known midwestern architects who designed homes and public buildings in Kenilworth include George W. Maher, John S. Van Bergen, Walter Burley Griffin, and Barry Byrne.

Kenilworth, with a current population of about 2,700, remains a high-income residential village. Most of its working population commutes to the Loop.

Kenilworth Sites of Interest

(1) George W. Maher House*
424 Warwick Road
Maher began working in the Chicago architectural firm of August Bauer and Henry Hill in 1878, while still a very young man. Before establishing his own practice in 1888, he worked as a draftsman along with Frank Lloyd Wright in the office of J. L. Silsbee. Maher was notably successful in designing houses for wealthy residents of the Chicago suburbs, and Kenilworth has the largest concentration of them. Here he also constructed his own home at 424 Warwick Road, picturesque in design, the Kenilworth Club, Kenilworth Assembly Hall, ravine bridges, and the Joseph Sears School. The Maher house built in 1893, is regarded by some architectural histo-

rians as an "excellent example of the earliest work of the Prairie School."

(2) Kenilworth Union Church
211 Kenilworth Avenue
The church was completed by the Kenilworth Company in 1892. Sears's five children gave the Swedenborgian window in memory of their parents. Pictured in the window are figures associated with the development of the Swedenborgian church, which was founded by followers of the Swedish scientist, philosopher, and theologian Emanuel Swedenborg in 1784.

(3) Episcopal Church of the Holy Comforter
Kenilworth Avenue and Warwick Road
In 1926, 20 years after this church was completed, the rector, Father Danforth, obtained permission to move the body of Eugene Field, children's poet, from Graceland Cemetery in Chicago to the garden of the Church of the Holy Comforter.

(4) Kenilworth Historical Society
415 Kenilworth Avenue
The society's museum includes photographic exhibits of Kenilworth's historic homes and buildings. Open Mondays, 1:00–3:00 P.M. Free.

5. Winnetka
Sheridan Road

Like Evanston, Wilmette, and Kenilworth, Winnetka is a residential suburb of Chicago, attractive to well-to-do Chicagoans for more than a century because of its beautiful lake location and its railroad connection, dating from 1854, with the central city. Winnetka, the name chosen by the wife of the town's founder, Charles E. Peck, has often been said to mean "beautiful land" in Potawatomi, but the meaning is apparently uncertain. Winnetka's site was long the home of the Potawatomi. Later it became a stopping place for travelers on the Chicago–Green Bay Trail. With the coming of the railroad, Charles Peck, a successful Chicago merchant, and Walter Gurnee, president of the Chicago and Milwaukee Railroad, laid out the town in 1854.

Six years after the founding of the town, on the morning of September 8, 1860, Winnetka residents awoke to find that a tragedy had occurred in Lake Michigan about 10 miles offshore during the stormy night. The *Lady Elgin*, an excursion sidewheeler carrying more than 300 passengers from Chicago to Milwaukee, had collided in the dark with an overloaded lumber schooner. More than 290 of the passengers drowned, many of them members of the Union Guards, an Irish American militia unit from Milwaukee. Those who survived owed their lives to the desperate efforts of lakeshore residents to save them. A mournful ballad, "Lost on the Lady Elgin," was sung around the parlor pianos for many years in memory of the tragedy.

Henry Demarest Lloyd, perhaps the best known of Winnetka's late nineteenth-century residents, moved to the village in 1878. He established his reputation as a critic of big business in the pages of the *Chicago Tribune* and became nationally prominent for his 1894 attack on the Standard Oil Company, *Wealth Against Commonwealth*.

The nationally famous Hadley School for the Blind, organized in 1921 by a Chicago educator, William A. Hadley, is located in Winnetka. The staff prepares Braille materials and recordings to enable students throughout the country to study at home. Visitors to the school are most welcome. With a 1980 population of about 12,800, the town retains its residential character.

Winnetka Sites of Interest

(1) Temporary Gravesite of *Lady Elgin* Victims
515 Sheridan Road
On the bluff behind the Artemis Carter house at 515 Sheridan Road, the victims of the *Lady Elgin* disaster were placed in temporary graves.

(2) Henry Demarest Lloyd House*
830 Sheridan Road
The Lloyd home, known as Wayside, became a popular place for visitors to Winnetka who had a penchant for discussing social and political issues. The Lloyds were also known for their hospitality to any hungry person who knocked on the door. The property has been preserved and restored in cooperation with the Landmarks Preservation Council of Illinois. The home is privately owned and not open to the public.

(3) Schmidt Cabin
1407 Tower Road
Believed to be the oldest remaining building in Cook County, the Schmidt cabin, built in 1820, has a porthole in the wall through which a gun could be pointed when strangers approached. The cabin belongs to the Anita Willetts Burnham family, who purchased it in 1919 and moved it to its present location. The structure

"Sinking of the Lady Elgin*" from the* New York Illustrated News*, Sept. 22, 1860. Courtesy Chicago Historical Society. ICHi-02055*

is privately owned and opened only by appointment with the owner.

(4) Crow Island School
1112 Willow Road
Designed by architects Lawrence Perkins and Eliel and Eero Saarinen, Crow Island School, completed in 1940, is the architectural expression of the educational ideas of Carleton W. Washburne, then superintendent of the Winnetka schools. Washburne believed that each student should progress at his or her own pace and that each should be respected as an individual. The building design includes individualized classrooms, each a separate unit with its own playground area, washroom, lab equipment, and drinking fountain. Each has its own outside courtyard. The auditorium, library, gym, shop, and art and music rooms are shared. The building is scaled for children. Crow Island is an unusual "island," a high area in the Skokie marsh covered with trees where crows perched. Crow Island is now Crow Island Woods, used by Crow Island School students for nature study and art classes.

The school building has received numerous architectural awards. Early in its history the American Institute of Architects designated it as "the school most advanced in elementary school design in the United States." AIA cited it in 1971 as "A landmark in design for education which demonstrates that an inspired educational philosophy can be translated into an architecture of continuing function and beauty."

(5) Village Hall
510 Green Bay Road
Inside the Village Hall are paintings by Winnetka artists. The structure was designed in 1925 by Edwin H. Clark and built with the money saved through

the operation of the municipal electric plant. Henry Demarest Lloyd championed public ownership of the town's utilities.

Visitors interested in exploring historic Winnetka will find a 1978 publication entitled "Ride the Historical Bicycle Trail: Winnetka" a useful guide. It is available at the Winnetka Chamber of Commerce, 841 Spruce Street.

6. Glencoe
Sheridan Road

Ten Chicago businessmen formed the Glencoe Company in 1867 and purchased a farm from former Chicago mayor Walter Gurnee, an early president of the Chicago and Milwaukee Railroad. The businessmen agreed that each would build a home here for himself and another to sell to a friend, thus forming the nucleus of a new suburb. In addition, the original ten agreed to support the new community by donating $500 annually for a church and school, $100 for roads, and $150 for the salaries of a pastor and teacher. The plan worked, and Glencoe, incorporated as a village in 1869, grew as a home for the well-to-do. With a current population of 9,200, most of Glencoe's workers commute to Chicago, and the balance work in north shore industry.

Glencoe Sites of Interest

(1) North Shore Congregation Israel
1185 Sheridan Road

North Shore Congregation Israel Synagogue, September 1984. Photo by Margaret Bogue.

This synagogue is a significant contribution to the distinguished architecture of the North Shore suburbs. Designed by the Michigan architect Minoru Yamasaki and completed in 1964, the building utilizes poured concrete, glass, and steel to create a structure that combines aesthetics with economy and function. Yamasaki's ideas for his design came from plant forms and result in a house of light. The natural landscaping of the grounds and its location on a bluff overlooking Lake Michigan enhance the synagogue's architectural beauty. Open Monday–Thursday, 8:30 A.M.–5:00 P.M.; Friday, 8:30 A.M.–4:30 P.M. Free.

(2) Botanic Garden
Lake-Cook Road, east of Edens Expressway (Highways I-94 and US-41)
The Forest Preserve of Cook County and the Chicago Horticultural Society jointly sponsor the educational and research activities offered at the Botanic Garden. There are 300 acres of grounds with demonstration and exhibition gardens, lakes, islands, a nature trail, and an education center housing exhibits, shops, meeting rooms, and greenhouses. Open daily, 9:00 A.M.–4:30 P.M. Parking fee.

7. Highland Park
Sheridan Road

Port Clinton and St. Johns, two small waterfront villages that supplied steamers with fuel, were the earliest white settlements in the present-day Highland Park area. They blossomed briefly after 1847, only to face a declining demand for their services once the railroad was extended north from Chicago. With the construction of the Chicago and Milwaukee Railroad along the north shore in 1854, Walter Gurnee, the company president, purchased land for town site promotions and named one of his purchases Highland Park. The depression of 1857 dampened development temporarily. In 1867 Gurnee sold a 12,000-acre tract to the Highland Park Building Company, which proceeded to lay out the town, promote lot sales, and expel all saloons.

Highland Park, with a current population of about 31,000, grew steadily as an affluent north shore suburb. By the end of the nineteenth century, Highland Park appealed to wealthy Chicagoans as an ideal place for a luxury summer home. The area east of the present-day Chicago and North Western Railroad developed into a particularly attractive, affluent residential area built on wooded bluffs and ravines along the lake. The portion of Highland Park immediately adjacent to Skokie Road has developed as an area of commerical and small industrial businesses. Most of its 70 manufacturers employ 10 or fewer workers. They produce a wide variety of light metal products and consumer goods. The seven largest, employing 50 or more workers each, produce electrical goods, television components, plastic cups and containers, vinyl house siding, and machine parts.

Highland Park Sites of Interest

(1) Yerkes Fountain

Sheridan Road and Forest Avenue

When the Sheridan Road from Chicago to Fort Sheridan was completed and dedicated in 1896, Charles G. Yerkes, the Chicago railway magnate, announced his gift of a fountain for thirsty horses, humans, dogs, and cats. The watering trough, restored by the Highland Park Garden Club in 1960, now holds flowers.

(2) Jean Butz James Museum and Walt Durbahn Tool Museum

326 Central Avenue

The James family presented this beautiful 10-room Victorian home to the Highland Park Historical Society in 1969 for use as a museum and headquarters. The home, one of the earliest in the town, was built by the Highland Park Building Company in 1871. The clay used for the bricks came from a pit nearby. The house contains collections depicting many facets of Highland Park's history.

The Historical Society converted a garage built adjacent to the house in 1910 into a museum to display the tool collection belonging to a former industrial arts teacher at Highland Park High School. Both museums are open all year, Tuesday–Saturday, 1:00 P.M.–5:00 P.M.; Sunday 2:00–4:00 P.M. Free.

(3) Francis Stupey Cabin

Laurel Park, between the Library and City Hall

The Highland Park Historical Society restored the Stupey cabin as a Highland Park Centennial project. Francis Stupey, an early settler whose family occupied the cabin at its original site for many years, built the structure of white-oak timbers in 1847. When the Stupey farm was purchased for a country club, the cabin was moved to its present location. The Highland Park Garden Club maintains a memorial rose garden next to the cabin. Open Sunday, 2:00–4:00 P.M., all year. Free.

(4) Ravinia Park

Enter from 400 block of Sheridan Road or from 200–300 block of Green Bay Road

The Chicago and Milwaukee Electric Railroad in 1902 purchased land crisscrossed with ravines and located south of Highland Park to develop an amusement park and thereby boost passenger traffic. When the railroad went into receivership in 1908, a group of North Shore residents moved to assume control of the park.

In 1911 the Ravinia Park Company, backed by Louis Eckstein, Julius Rosenwald, and Samuel Insull, all wealthy Chicago businessmen, purchased the park. Summer concerts became a great attraction at Ravinia. The programs were primarily symphonic until 1916, when Eckstein, an executive in a Chicago mail-order house, took over primary sponsorship. Opera then became the main fare. Because admission prices were kept low so that more could enjoy the performances, the season always ended with a deficit, which Eckstein paid. But in 1932, as the depression deepened and bills became larger and larger, Ravinia closed.

Four years later the Ravinia Festival Association reopened the park, and it became the summer home of the Chicago Symphony. Today the Ravinia Summer Music Festival includes everything from jazz to ballet to films, as well as symphony concerts. Two of the four original buildings remain: the Murray Theater and the Casino. Designed by Peter Weber, they were built in 1904. $

Duke Ellington concert at Ravinia Park, July 1, 1957. Courtesy Chicago Historical Society. ICHi-18279

(5) Frank Lloyd Wright Houses

Highland Park has three private residences designed by Frank Lloyd Wright: the home built for Ward W. Willitts in 1902 at 1445 Sheridan Road, six years before the Robie House in Chicago (see site 1, no. [2]); the home at 1923 Lake Avenue, built in 1905 for Mary M. W. Adams; and the home at 1689 Lake Avenue, built in 1906 for George Madison Millard.

(6) Brick Water Tower
near corner of Central Avenue and Green Bay Road
This unusual structure, built in 1930, is 126 feet high, 54 feet in diameter, and has a capacity of 500,000 gallons.

(7) Indian Trail Tree
174 Hazel Avenue
Indians bent this tree to make it grow crooked and serve as a trail marker. It is among the few such trees remaining on the North Shore.

(8) Original Elisha Gray House
461 Hazel Avenue
This Victorian structure, erected in 1871, was the home of Elisha Gray, believed by many to have invented the telephone before Alexander Graham Bell and to have been cheated out of the patent by questionable procedures in the U.S. Patent Office. Gray was a founder of the Graybar Electric and Western Electric companies.

(9) Ravinia Station of the Chicago and North Western Railroad
700 block of St. Johns Avenue at the tracks
Typical of the old wooden stations built around 1900, the Ravinia Station is one of the few of its type remaining in the Chicago area.

(10) House at 441 Cedar Avenue

Henry Dubin designed this International-style residence. Steel, white brick, and glass characterize the fireproof cubelike structure, built in 1930.

(11) Braeside Elementary School
150 Pierce Road
Designed by John Van Bergen, a student of Frank Lloyd Wright, and built in 1928, this Prairie School structure has unusually beautiful stonework. Following the advice of another eminent Highland Park resident, Jens Jensen, the internationally known landscape architect, the school was built in a park.

(12) Rosewood Park and Beach
700 block of Sheridan at Roger Williams Avenue
Located in the Ravinia area of Highland Park and now incorporated into the city park district, this 13-acre tract was part of the estate of Julius Rosenwald. Jens Jensen landscaped it. Rosenwald held top executive positions in Sears, Roebuck and Company for a number of years, serving as vice president from 1897–1910 and as president from 1910–1925. In 1925 he became chairman of the board of directors.

(13) Jens Jensen Memorial Park
Ravinia, at the intersection of St. Johns, Dean, and Roger Williams Avenues
Jens Jensen designed this park in 1924. Originally called Station Park, it was renamed in June 1980. When it was redesigned in 1930, Jensen's Indian Council Ring and a large boulder were added as a memorial to Mrs. Julius Rosenwald.

Henry X. Arenberg furnished the information about the Highland Park Sites of Interest on behalf of the board of the Highland Park Historical Society.

8. Fort Sheridan
Sheridan Road

In view of the tragic fire of 1871 and public fears of labor union activities, Chicago authorities wanted U.S. Army support close at hand. With the Haymarket Affair fresh in mind, the Chicago Commercial Club purchased wooded ravine land on Lake Michigan 28 miles north of Chicago and gave 599 acres to the federal government as a site for a military post.

Here the government established Camp Highwood in 1887. At first facilities consisted mainly of tents, but in 1889 construction began on the first structure of a 54-building complex. Most of the buildings were built of

Tent compound at Fort Sheridan, 1941. Courtesy Chicago Historical Society. C. R. Child's negative.

brick and stone quarried on the grounds. In 1888 Camp Highwood was renamed Fort Sheridan in honor of General Philip H. Sheridan, commander-in-chief of the army, who died August 5, 1888.

The Fort Sheridan motto is "Essential for Freedom Since 1887." With the country now at peace, Fort Sheridan serves as an administrative center for the regular army, the National Guard, the Army Reserve, and the Army ROTC. Visitors are encouraged to tour the grounds at any time during daylight hours and may visit the post exchange cafeteria any day except Sunday.

Fort Sheridan Sites of Interest

(1) Fort Sheridan Museum
Building No. 33, Lyster Road, Fort Sheridan
Since 1969 the former post stockade has housed Fort Sheridan's museum collection, valued at around $4 million. The building, designed by William Holabird and constructed of cream brick in 1890, had a capacity of 120 detainees. Exhibits reflect the participation of Fort Sheridan in every conflict since the Spanish-American War. The building is open daily, 10:00 A.M.–4:00 P.M. Free.

(2) Fort Sheridan Water Tower*
Building No. 49, Leonard Wood Avenue, Fort Sheridan
Another building designed by William Holabird is the 167-foot Water Tower building with a two-block-long administrative building attached. This building was originally used as barracks, and before Sheridan Road was rerouted, the tower was open at the base to allow traffic to pass through. The tower, completed in 1891, holds a 90,000-gallon water tank so that water will be available in case of fire. Shortened because of structural difficulties, it was originally 50 feet taller. The tower has become an unofficial symbol of Fort Sheridan and overlooks the former parade ground, now the golf course.

Among the other original buildings on the post are the officers' club on Leonard Wood Avenue, the post commander's residence on Logan Loop, the former post hospital (now library) on Bradley Loop, the infantry drill hall (now gym) on Whistler Road, and the residence of George S. Patton, Jr., during his first assignment after West Point (one of the officer's family quarters on Leonard Wood Avenue).

9. Lake Forest
Sheridan Road

Three ministers representing the interests of the First and Second Presbyterian churches of Chicago are largely responsible for selecting Lake Forest as the location for a Presbyterian college. After a number of exploratory trips in 1855, they took a train ride on the North Western railroad's newly finished line running north from Chicago, got off at the site of present-day Lake Forest, and liked what they found. With its beautiful view of Lake Michigan, a rich forest, the rolling terrain cut by deep ravines, and the steep bluffs rising 75 to 100 feet from the lake, the site appealed to them as the location for a college.

The Presbyterians organized the Lake Forest Association in 1856 and began purchasing 1,300 acres for a town site. The articles of association reserved 50 acres in the projected community for three educational institutions: a college, an academy for men, and a female seminary. In 1857 the Illinois legislature chartered Lind University, named to honor a Chicago Presbyterian layman who pledged real estate valued at $80,000 to establish a department of theology at the new college.

The association asked Olmsted and Vaux, New York landscape architects who had recently designed Central Park for the city of New York, to design Lake Forest. They in turn recommended Jed Hotchkiss, an engineer and landscape architect from St. Louis, to do the work. Laying out the city in park style, his plan called for curving streets to follow ravine lines and spacious residential lots. The plat reserved every other lot for the benefit of Lind University upon sale.

The association surveyed the site in 1857 and proceeded to sell lots, lay out streets, build bridges, and construct a hotel to accommodate potential lot buyers. Lake Forest Academy used the hotel for classrooms until its building was completed in 1859. The Young Ladies' Seminary began holding classes in 1860, but not until 1869, when Ferry Hall was completed, did the women's finishing school function as the association charter intended. It granted a terminal degree. The college was designated as for men only. That would soon change.

The financial panic of 1857 and the ensuing depression dampened Lake Forest's development. Lind lost much of his fortune and was unable to pay the $80,000 he had promised to the college. The Civil War years also brought hard times to Lake Forest. Not until the summer of 1876 did the college now known as Lake Forest, its name under the revised 1865 charter, become a permanent institution. The college's benefactor at that point in its history was Mrs. C. B. Farwell, a wealthy and well-educated Chicagoan, who gave the school substantial sums of money and succeeded in making it a coeducational institution. Classes convened in a large hotel built in 1870 until it burned down in 1877. The school's first building, College Hall, was completed in 1878.

In addition to its educational institutions and its beautiful natural setting, the railroad too helped Lake Forest to grow. Lake Forest attracted many Chicago industrialists, businessmen, and professionals, who built year-round and summer residences there because it was easy to commute to the Loop. The estates of the Swift, Cudahy, Armour, and McCormick families and others gave Lake Forest the reputation of being one of the wealthiest and most beautiful suburbs in America. Several well-known Chicago architects who built their homes in Lake Forest also designed buildings here. Among these was Howard Van Doren Shaw, who purchased a 50-acre estate, Ragdale,* in 1896 (see below).

To many of Lake Forest's 3,000 residents in 1915, it seemed that the town's business center projected a poor image. In 1916 Howard Shaw was commissioned to design a new civic center that would give visitors arriving on the railroad a good impression of the community. Today, Shaw's Market Square is regarded as an early shopping center, similar to those planned for the age of the automobile. Shaw's plan, which combined beauty with utility, called for buildings on three sides of a landscaped mall. The buildings, which have a medieval air, contain shops, offices, and apartments. There are two towers and a covered walkway connecting the shops. A flagpole at the west end of the mall commemorates the dead of World War I, and the Shaw Memorial Fountain is at the east end. The Young Men's Club Building, which is part of the Market Square plan, has served as a community recreation center for many years. Marshall Field's store occupies a building on the west side of the square that was originally built as the West Side Bank.

The North Western Railroad depot on the west side of McKinley Avenue at Market Square was designed in 1899 by the firm of Frost & Granger, who made a specialty of railroad station design. These architects, who were also Lake Forest residents, designed the City Hall at 220 East Deerpath Street in 1898. The Lake Forest Public Library occupied rooms on the second floor of the City Hall until 1931, when a new brick and white stone building, designed by Edwin H. Clark was erected. This building won the Craftsmen's Award from the Chicago Architect's Association. Charles Sumner Frost also designed the First Presbyterian Church at 700 North Sheridan Road, of which he was a member, in 1887.

Lake Forest College has grown to occupy a North Campus, Middle Campus, and South Campus, each separated from the others by a natural ravine. Frost and Granger designed

Lake Forest Market Square about 1930. Courtesy Chicago Historical Society. C. R. Child's negative.

Lois Durand Hall on the North Campus in 1897 and Reid Memorial Library and Lily Reid Holt Chapel on the Middle Campus in 1899. Howard Shaw designed Durand Commons on the Middle Campus in 1907. The Henry Durand Art Institute on the North Campus was designed in 1891 by Henry Ives Cobb, another Lake Forest resident. A second institution of higher learning was added to Lake Forest in 1904 when the Academy of the Sacred Heart (Barat College) was moved from Chicago, where it was founded in 1858.

In 1978 most of the original town, bounded by Western Avenue, Westleigh Road, Lake Michigan, and the northern city limit, was designated as the Lake Forest Historic District on the National Register of Historic Places. All of the structures and institutions cited above lie within its bounds. The large residences in the district, in contrast to those in Oak Park and River Forest, represent conservative ideas in late nineteenth-century and early twentieth-century suburban architecture. They are traditional, many of them in Tudor, Classical, and Gothic Styles. About a hundred of the district's 474 structures have been identified as having special historical and architectural importance.

There are no industries in Lake Forest. Now with a population of more than 15,000, Lake Forest, still a very prestigious North Shore suburb, is changing. Some of the large estates are being divided, and more modest housing is evident. Inflation, high real estate values, and taxes have had an impact on owners of undeveloped properties within the city limits.

Ragdale*
1230 North Green Bay Road
Howard Van Doren Shaw, a very prominent Chicago architect who opened his practice in 1893, chose Lake Forest for his summer residence, designing and building Ragdale in 1896–1897. Ragdale remains distinctive because the whole estate is well preserved, both the stucco house reflecting modern English taste and the grounds, which include a large garden, an early log cabin, an outdoor theater, a restored farmhouse and barn of about 1850, and three acres of virgin prairie. In addition to Market Square, Shaw designed more than 30 large residences in Lake Forest before 1925. Shortly before his death he was awarded the Gold Medal of the American Institute of Architects.

10. Great Lakes Naval Training Center
Sheridan Road

The naval site-selection board considered at least 27 sites in the Midwest for a Great Lakes training station before choosing a 172-acre tract just south of North Chicago. High real estate values deterred board members until the Merchants Club of Chicago, aided by the Chicago and North Western and Chicago and Milwaukee railroads, raised the money to buy the land.

When President William Howard Taft dedicated the new training station on October 28, 1911, 300 farm boys from throughout the Midwest became the first navel recruits to be trained here. World War I brought a spurt in activities and the beginnings of a naval aviation program that required student aviators to fly the mail to Chicago as part of their training. John Philip Sousa came out of retirement to take charge of the 14 regimental bands that added spark to the recruits' parades.

Aerial View of Great Lakes Naval Training Station.
Courtesy Chicago Historical Society. ICHi-17830

Activities at the Training Center were greatly curtailed after the armistice in 1918. Training ceased in 1922, and the center closed in 1933. Chambers of commerce of Chicago and towns in the center's immediate vicinity persuaded the government to reopen it in 1935, and soon World War II brought another period of rapid growth. America's large role in world affairs since 1945 has led to further improvement of the facilities.

Today Great Lakes is the largest naval training station in the world; the number of trainees each year reaches 30,000 with an additional 27,500 technical students. Programs added since the end of World War II include a volunteer ecology program and a steam-propulsion training facility.

To ensure that training programs proceed undisturbed, the Navy discourages unauthorized visitors. High school groups may arrange for conducted tours by contacting the center's Public Affairs Office.

11. North Chicago

Sheridan Road

The character of the Lake Michigan shoreline communities changes at North Chicago. From Evanston north through Lake Forest, they are primarily residential; from North Chicago to Milwaukee, they are primarily industrial.

Prior to 1891 the North Chicago area was strictly farmland. Then developers bought up the land and laid out a town that was called South Waukegan until 1909, stressing its advantages for manufacturing plants and making it off-limits for saloons.

Within the first year, the Chicago and North Western railroad built a depot, and three manufacturing companies began construction. The Washburn-Moen Manufacturing Company (later the U.S. Steel Corporation) erected a mill along the lakeshore. Then followed the Lanyon Zinc Oxide Company and the Morrow Brothers Harness Factory. By 1912, 14 more factories had located in North Chicago, making it an important manufacturing center.

The availability of jobs attracted Poles, Croatians, Slovaks, and Slovenians who built single-family houses on 25- to 125-foot lots. To preserve their heritage the Poles established their own church and cultural center; the Croatians, Slovaks, and Slovenians joined together to build theirs. In 1910 foreign-born residents constituted 40 percent of the city's 3,300 residents.

During the first quarter of the twentieth century, two major governmental institutions were built directly south of the city: the Great Lakes Naval Training Center, opened in 1911 (site 10), and the North Chicago Veterans' Administration Hospital, which opened in 1926. For its first 50 years, the hospital provided neuropsychiatric care for veterans. Thereafter its operation expanded to include general medical care and surgery, a development that led to its affiliation with the University of Health Sciences/Chicago Medical School. Its new campus opened in October 1980 adjacent to the Veterans' Hospital.

North Chicago experienced its

Abbott Laboratories, North Chicago's largest employer. Photo by Margaret Bogue.

greatest growth between 1950 and 1970. In 1950 the city's population was 8,600, virtually the same as in 1930. By 1960 it had expanded to almost 23,000 and by 1970 to more than 47,000. While most of the dramatic increase of the 1960s reflected the annexation of the Great Lakes Naval Training Center, some of the growth stemmed from industry. Industrial jobs attracted Black workers in the 1950s and 1960s, giving North Chicago a 17 percent Black population in 1970. Blacks were 27 percent of the population in 1980.

The city's expansion led to the formation of the city's own high school district and the construction of both a high school and a new city hall. Today North Chicago is an ethnically diversified community that retains its small-town character along with a strong industrial base. Over 40 industries produce a wide variety of products, including pharmaceuticals, corrugated fiberboard, beauty products, plastics, chemicals, industrial and automotive tools and equipment, cable and wire, refractory metals, and gourmet candy. North Chicago also derives considerable economic benefit from the business generated by the Great Lakes Naval Training Center and the Veterans' Hospital.

12. Waukegan
Sheridan Road

Waukegan's written history goes back to the late seventeenth century, when the French established a fur-trading post here, a stockade called Petite Fort. Although the river emptying into Lake Michigan at Petite Fort did not flow inland for any great distance, during high water it made a five-mile portage to the Des Plaines quite possible. Like many Lake Michigan towns of fur-trading origin, Little Fort retained some of its village population after the fur trade declined.

When northern Illinois began attracting permanent settlers in the 1840s, Little Fort took on new life, acquiring a U.S. post office and becoming a county seat and a lakeport of some importance. Little Fort, with its good harbor, supplied settlers in Lake, McHenry, and Boone counties with lumber and other essentials for pioneer farming and provided a market outlet for agricultural produce. Little Fort grew remarkably in the 1840s. Its population mushroomed from 150 in 1844 to more than 3,000 in 1850. Port traffic increased from 149 boats in 1845 to almost 1,100 in 1850. Little Fort incorporated as a village in 1849, adopting the name Waukegan, said to be derived from the Potawatomi word for "trading place." In 1859 it achieved city status.

Once the railroad connected Chicago and Milwaukee in the mid-1850s, port traffic began a gradual decline. Chicago and Milwaukee reaped the main benefits of trade with the developing agricultural mid-continent after the Civil War, and Waukegan languished. Its population declined between 1870 and 1880. The town had only small industries before the 1890s—lumber, flour milling, tanning, pork packing, and the manufacture of stoves and scales. The most prosperous of these was a brewery.

The modern industrial city took shape in the 1890s after the construction of the Waukegan and Southern Railroad in 1891 gave the town access to all rail connections in the Chicago area. Waukegan's population doubled within a decade. The first new industry, the forerunner of American Steel and Wire, opened in 1891, locating along the new railway. The 1903 Illinois factory inspectors' report listed 26 industries at Waukegan. The industrial section developed adjacent to the railroad lines on the lakeshore and the residential area on the bluff.

The city's population nearly doubled again between 1900 and 1920, when 19,200 people lived there. Its foreign-born population increased during those two decades as more immigrants made Waukegan their home, the majority from Germany, Russia, Austria, and Sweden, but with a liberal sprinkling from Armenia, Italy, Yugoslavia, Poland, England, Lithuania, and Denmark as well. In 1910, 69 percent of Waukegan's people were either foreign-born or had at least one foreign-born parent. Thereafter the percentage of foreign-born declined. The city's greatest growth occurred between 1950 and 1970, when the population expanded from about 39,000 to over 65,000. During the 1960s Waukegan's Black population grew from less than one percent to 12 percent and is now 20 percent of the city's 67,600 total.

Location has much to do with Waukegan's industrial growth. Good transportation connections by rail, highway, and lake, nearness to major markets and sources of raw materials, plus an adequate labor supply all attracted industry. Currently Waukegan's industries number about 100. They are very diversified, producing hospital supplies, components for the automotive and truck industry, printed matter, gypsum building products, outboard marine engines, chemicals, wire and wire products, and railroad freight car parts. The largest employers, with more than 1,000 persons on the payroll, include the Cherry Electrical Products Corporation, the Johns-Manville Corporation, and the Outboard Marine Corporation.

Joseph T. Bowen Country Club (Haines House) is located in Bowen Park. Photo by Margaret Bogue.

Waukegan Sites of Interest

(1) Joseph T. Bowen Country Club* (Haines House), Waukegan Historical Society
1917 North Sheridan Road
This lovely Victorian farmhouse was part of a 72-acre farm when the mayor of Chicago, John C. Haines, purchased it as a country retreat. The mayor of Waukegan, Fred Buck, owned the property from 1909 to 1911. In 1911 Jane Addams and Louise Bowen purchased the farm as a fresh-air vacation spot for underprivileged neighbors of Hull House in Chicago. Over 40,000 children and many adults enjoyed the Bowen Country Club, as it was called, until 1963, when the property was sold to the Waukegan Park District.

Waukegan Historical Society members leased the house in 1973 and began restoration work, aided by the diaries of the carpenters who had added rooms to the house in the 1870s. A restored Victorian parlor and a historical research library are on the first floor. Upstairs, the Lincoln Room has the bed in which Lincoln slept during a visit to Waukegan. The society is open year round, Wednesday and Friday, 10:00 A.M.–2:30 P.M., and on the first and third Sundays of the month, 1:00–3:00 P.M. Free. Group tours by appointment.

A special Christmas open house is held the first Sunday in December. The rooms are traditionally decorated, and free refreshments are offered. The society's Annual Tour of Historical Homes occurs the third Sunday in May.

(2) Near North Historic District*
Bounded roughly by Ash Street, the railroad tracks, Glen Flora Avenue, and City Hall
The Near North Historic District,

which grew slowly as a residential area, contains a wide variety of homes dating from the 1840s to 1928. Many architectural styles popular in the Midwest during those nine decades are represented: revivals (Greek, Gothic, Classical, Georgian, Renaissance, Tudor, Romanesque), Italianate, Queen Anne, Stick, Carpenter Gothic, and Prairie School. During every decade in the district's history, new structures were added. Here lived businessmen, tradesmen, professionals, and civic leaders, Waukegan's prominent and influential citizens. The district stands as an expression of their life styles, physically undisturbed by industrial growth except for the addition of homes for the town's newer business leaders. For a description of district structures, see *Waukegan's Legacy—Our Landmarks*, published by the Waukegan Historical Society, 1917 North Sheridan Road, Waukegan, Illinois 60085.

Dunes and dune grass at Illinois Beach State Park. Courtesy Illinois Department of Conservation. 1884-7

13. Illinois Beach State Park

Sheridan Road south of Zion (CHPS)

The only sand dunes in the state of Illinois are found on the 3.5 miles of shoreline at Illinois Beach State Park. The park was formed to guard the area from the encroachment of industry. Marsh and prairie land and pine and oak forests are included as well as sand dunes. During certain times of the year a pond is created by a sand bar that blocks the mouth of the Dead River and prevents its opening into Lake Michigan. Many interesting flora and fauna have been discovered in this pond. There are campgrounds for tents and trailers, hiking trails, scuba-diving facilities, swimming beaches, and a nature center in the park.

14. Zion

Sheridan Road

Today Zion may seem much like other cities along the shore of Lake Michigan north of Chicago, but it was founded as a theocracy. John Alexander Dowie used the term to describe his city, where the "rule of God would replace the rule of man." Dowie was a Scotsman from Australia whose activities as an evangelist and faith healer attracted attention in Chicago in the 1890s. He founded the Christian Catholic church in 1896 and won thousands of converts who believed in his healing powers.

Dowie was not content to confine his work to Chicago. He carefully laid plans to move with his followers to a church-owned utopian community where he could prove the superiority of theocracy and free his people from the contaminating influences of the city. In 1899 Dowie purchased a 1,100-acre site between Chicago and Milwaukee on Lake Michigan and there founded Zion City, appointing himself its General Overseer. In this capacity he intended to govern all facets of his people's lives—social, personal, and economic as well as religious.

He employed an experienced city planner to design the city with full water and sewer service, lighting, and rapid transit systems. Broad boulevards with biblical names radiated from the center of town, where stood the Zion Tabernacle, built to seat 6,000. Eager to make the community an economic success, Dowie had an industrial park developed east of the Chicago and North Western Railroad tracks with a lace factory, bakery, candy factory, and printing establishment. Specially recruited English artisans staffed the lace factory, but Dowie insisted on directing their operations too.

Enthusiasm for the experiment waned when Dowie's followers grew alarmed about his management of community funds and his 1901 announcement that he was the Old Testament prophet Elijah reborn. After it became apparent that Zion City industries were in financial trouble, Dowie's associates replaced him as General Overseer while he was in Mexico investigating the possibility of starting another community.

After a period of unrest, Wilbur Glenn Voliva succeeded Dowie. He began the first religious radio station in the country, Zion's WCED, in 1923. He also originated the presentation of an annual Passion Play, which was performed outdoors from 1935 through 1977 and is now presented in an auditorium. Write to the Christian Catholic Church, Dowie Memorial Drive, Zion, Illinois 60099, for details. Church ownership and control of property gradually eroded after 1907 and Zion's industries, lands, homes, and businesses passed into private ownership. The political influence of the Christian Catholic church weakened.

Elijah Hospice, the Zion Hotel, 1962. Photo by Robert Foote. Courtesy Chicago Historical Society. ICHi-07556

With a current population of about 17,900, Zion has over 20 relatively small industries providing a wide variety of products—from sporting goods to fig bars. The largest of these, employing over 200, produces industrial coatings. The two large nuclear power generators built by Commonwealth Edison in the early seventies have provided more jobs.

Zion Sites of Interest

(1) Shiloh House*

1300 Shiloh Boulevard

John Alexander Dowie commissioned the Swiss-born architect Paul Burkhardt to design a home for himself and his family. Completed in 1903 at a cost of $90,000, it resembles Swiss architecture only in its plaster and wood panels. The rare tiles on its colorful roof form designs possibly representing the Trinity or maybe lightning. The 25-room mansion was constructed with indoor plumbing, full electricity, and showers. Following Dowie's death the house had other occupants. It was purchased by the Zion Historical Society for $18,500 in 1967. The society has located and restored many of the original furnishings. The building now houses the society, a museum with exhibits on the history of Zion, and the Darms Memorial Library with extensive holdings of religious manuscripts, many on the subject of divine healing.

The museum is open Memorial Day–Labor Day, Saturday and Sunday, 2:00–5:00 P.M., or by appointment the rest of the year. $

(2) Zion Hotel*

2561 Sheridan Road

This important building was demolished in December 1979 despite the vigorous efforts of historic preservationists to save it and its site is now a bank parking lot. Its dome, 24 feet in diameter, now stands on land donated by the Zion State Bank at North Sheridan Road and 26th Street.

Zion Hotel (originally called Elijah Hospice) was believed to be the largest balloon-frame building in the United States. It was built in 1902 to house newly arrived heads of families while they constructed homes in Zion City. Five hundred men completed the massive edifice between May 3 and July 14, using more than 3 million feet of lumber. No nails were used in the building; each piece of wood was carefully pegged, usually in mahogany or oak. The three-story building had 350 rooms. It occupied an entire city block and surrounded a large inner courtyard. For many years it was used as a nursing home but closed when a modern building for that purpose was completed.

A huge bell hung in the Bell Tower over the main entrance and was rung twice a day as a signal for silent prayer. The 54-ton bell was removed from the weakened tower in 1943 and is preserved on the grounds of the Christian Catholic Church (see below).

(3) Christian Catholic Church

Dowie Memorial Drive

The first Zion Tabernacle was a 6,000-seat wooden temple, which burned down in 1937. The present structure, located on the original site, opened in 1961.

(4) Old Lace Factory Building

2700 Block, Deborah Avenue

This structure housed the lace factory that Dowie brought to Zion. Initially successful, the facility produced lace curtains, dresses, and so on. Marshall Field and Company purchased it in 1906 after it had gone bankrupt and used it for about 50 years. Various other firms—currently Whiteside Drapery and several small companies—have used it since.

(5) Zion Industries, Inc.

27th Street and Ebenezer Avenue

Part of the original economic development plan, Zion Baking Company, now Zion Industries, still produces fig bars.

(6) First House in Zion City

2802 Elizabeth Avenue

Houses similar to this one may be seen on Edina or Bethel Boulevards or Elisha Avenue.

(7) Lake Mound Cemetery

29th Street and Elizabeth Avenue

Here is the grave site of Alexander Dowie. He was buried after an elaborate Shiloh House funeral on March 14, 1907.

15. Kenosha
Highway W-32

Kenosha Harbor in 1871. Courtesy State Historical Society of Wisconsin. WHi(X3)31629

Swept up in the land boom of the 1830s and lured by glowing descriptions of farmlands and waterways in present-day southeastern Wisconsin, a group of Hannibal, New York, residents formed the Western Emigration Company in late 1834. In search of economic opportunities, the company's founders and stockholders decided to develop a settlement on Lake Michigan. They selected a location on Pike Creek, confident that a Lake Michigan harbor could be developed and that the agricultural hinterland would soon become a prosperous farming area.

The depression of 1837 dampened growth, but Pike Creek, with a population of about 340, incorporated as a village in 1840, using the name Southport, a more auspicious label for a settlement bent on getting federal aid for harbor improvement.

Southport is noted in Wisconsin history for its leadership in the free public school movement as well as other social reforms. At the urging of Michael Frank, editor of the *Southport Telegraph* and member of the territorial legislature, the legislators in 1845 authorized a free school in Southport. Four years later funds were raised to build and operate the school. Frank and other state leaders joined to support the free school idea, which became part of the state constitution of 1848.

By 1850 Southport's population, then including immigrants from the Germanies and the British Isles, as well as Yankees, had grown to about 3,400. It incorporated as a city, taking the name Kenosha. Southport/Kenosha repeatedly received federal funds and spent local tax dollars to develop the port, but ships after 1855 carried only part of the local passenger and freight traffic. The quality of the potential harbor and the cost of improvement were very serious problems. Railroads assumed major importance. The line from Chicago to Milwaukee, completed in 1855, carried passengers and essentials to and from Kenosha. The Kenosha and Rockford Railroad, completed in 1861, ran west from Kenosha, giving the town an important artery for transporting farm products.

County seat and trade and agricultural service center, Kenosha grew from the beginning in the shadow of Milwaukee and Chicago, cities that took precedence in many of the wholesale and retail trade functions in the intervening lakeshore communities. In the mid-nineteenth century, small industries like flour mills, tanneries, bakeries, and wagon works processed local farm produce and supplied some manufactured essentials. A small town, with only 1,000 employed in manufacturing in 1890, its major producers were the Bain Wagon Company, the Northwest Wire Mattress Company (Simmons), N. R. Allen and Son Tannery, Pettit Malting Company, and the Chicago Brass Company, all of which made products for more widespread distribution.

Kenosha grew rapidly as an industrial city between 1890 and 1920. Its population mushroomed from about 6,500 to 40,500. Laborers in manufacturing grew from 1,000 to 13,000; the value of manufactured products, from $2.5 million to $103.7 million. Automobile production accounted for much of the growth. Beginning in 1901 in an old bicycle factory, the T. B. Jeffrey Company produced Ramblers. The firm became the Nash Motor Company in 1916 and part of the American Motors Corporation in the 1950s. By 1920 the automobile plant ranked as Kenosha's largest employer and has remained so.

Kenosha has attracted manufacturing because of good transportation connections and proximity to important markets, sources of capital, and raw materials. The labor supply has been adequate. At the turn of the twentieth century, when American-born and northern European-born people made up about equal parts of the town's population, Kenosha received an influx of immigrants from southern and eastern Europe: Russians, Poles, Italians, Hungarians, Czechoslovaks, Yugoslavs, and Lithuanians. They supplied much of the labor for growing industry. While relatively small numbers of Black and Mexican American workers lived in Kenosha at that time, their numbers increased dramatically after World War II.

Currently, Kenosha's four chief industrial employers produce automobiles, copper and brass products, tools, electrical machines, and electronic controls. Although Kenosha, with a population of about 77,700, is mainly an industrial city, the lakeshore, once the site of industry, is in large part municipally owned and developed as parkland. Kenosha's municipal reformers of the early twentieth century strongly advocated lakefront parks, and Harland Bartholomew emphasized their importance in his 1925 plan for Kenosha development. The park development program was largely completed before World War II.

Kenosha Sites of Interest

(1) Kemper Hall* (Center)
6501 3rd Avenue
Located on seven acres of well-landscaped Lake Michigan shoreland, the Kemper Hall group of buildings in the Gothic revival style, constructed between 1871 and 1911, served for decades as an Episcopalian girls' preparatory school. The only exception to the Gothic Revival style is the oldest structure in the complex. Dating from 1861, the cream brick, Italianate two-and-a-half-story mansion was built for U.S. Senator Charles Durkee.

As an educational institution Kemper Hall dates from 1855, when the Kenosha Female Seminary was chartered. To house this school, the founders purchased the Durkee mansion in 1865. Additions thereafter produced a series of connected structures. The chapel, built out of light-colored stone and red and cream brick in 1875, is among the earliest surviving churches in Kenosha, a charming example of Gothic revival architecture.

Kemper Hall was named for Bishop Jackson Kemper, Episcopal missionary in territorial Wisconsin and Wisconsin's first Episcopal bishop. For 105 years Kemper Hall served as a girls' preparatory school. From 1970 to June 1975, it was a coeducational elementary school. Now Kemper Hall serves as a cultural center for Kenosha County.

(2) Kenosha County Historical Museum
6300 3rd Avenue
In 1899 George Yule, vice president of the Badger Manufacturing Company and superintendent of the Bain Wagon Company, built the beautiful residence now housing the museum displays of the Kenosha Historical Society. The first floor has been furnished in the style of an upper-middle-class home of about 1900; the second floor depicts nineteenth-century life in Kenosha County, including a law office, children's room, a display of Indian artifacts, a war memorial room, a barber shop, a Victorian bedroom, and an apothecary shop; the lower level includes a pioneer room, harness shop, buttery, country store, typewriter history room, and a room from the Burr Oak School. The structure also houses the society's research library. Open year round, Tuesdays and Thursdays, 2:00 P.M.–4:30 P.M. Free.

(3) Library Park
between 7th and 8th Avenues at 60th Street
The south half of Library Park was the site of the log home built by Charles

Durkee and his wife when they came to Southport in 1839. Later, as a U.S. Senator, Durkee presented the land to the city of Kenosha. The north half was the gift of George Kimball, a Massachusetts lawyer who came to Pike Creek in 1832.

In the center of Library Park is the *Gilbert M. Simmons Library.** Z. G. Simmons, a successful Kenosha mattress manufacturer, gave this library building as a memorial to his son, Gilbert M. Simmons. Designed by a prominent architect, Daniel Burnham of Chicago, the Neo-Classical building was completed and occupied in 1900.

Also in Library Park are the Winged Victory Monument to Civil War soldiers, given by Z. G. Simmons and dedicated on the same day as the library, and a statue of Abraham Lincoln, dedicated in 1909. Orla Calkins, a retired businessman, donated the Lincoln statue.

On the streets surrounding the park, leading nineteenth-century Kenosha businessmen, bankers, and professionals built their homes. Among them is the Edward Bain house at 6107 7th Avenue, built in 1860 for the president of a major Kenosha industry, the Bain Wagon Company.

(4) Kenosha Public Museum
5608 10th Avenue
The museum's holdings include displays on North and Central American Indians, world ethnology, the military history of World Wars I and II, regional birds and mammals, gems, minerals, and lake formation; collections of pressed glass and bottles, ivory, Oriental decorative arts, and twentieth-century lithographs; a diverse and quite complete collection of Wisconsin pottery; and Lorado Taft's dioramas on the history of western sculpture. The museum is housed in a building constructed in 1908 as a post office and moved to this site in 1932. Open Monday–Friday, 9:00 A.M.–noon, 1:00–5:00 P.M.; Saturday, 9:00 A.M.–noon; and Sunday, 1:00–4:00 P.M. Free.

(5) John McCaffary House*
5732 13th Court
This simple two-story cream brick structure, built in 1842, has historical importance because of its place in the movement to abolish capital punishment in the state of Wisconsin. John McCaffary, accused of drowning his wife in a cistern (possibly a partially buried hogshead) behind the house, was tried, found guilty of the murder, and in August 1851 executed amid a carnival atmosphere in a field south of Kenosha. The whole procedure so disgusted two members of the state legislature that they revitalized the movement to abolish capital punishment. The legislature outlawed execution in 1853.

(6) American Motors Corporation
5626 25th Avenue
Kenosha's largest employer, the American Motors Corporation, offers public tours of the automobile plant. Those interested in visiting should call (414) 658-6401 to find out tour times.

(7) Lighthouse and Keeper's Home
5117–19 4th Avenue
In 1844 the federal government appropriated funds for the development of a harbor at the mouth of Pike Creek. This lighthouse, built in 1866, replaced the original one. The living quarters for the lighthouse keeper and his family were in the adjoining house, which was probably built a few years later and in recent years has been used as a group home for minors.

Ramblers made in the American Motors plant being loaded for shipment overseas at Kenosha harbor. Courtesy State Historical Society of Wisconsin. WHi(X3)40549

(8) Ethnic Kenosha
During the nineteenth and early twentieth centuries, Kenosha developed distinctive ethnic neighborhoods. The Yankees located along the lakefront south of the Pike River; the Germans, originally, north of the river, near the lake; the Irish in between the Yankees and Germans; the Scandinavians, later arrivals, in the southwestern part of town. The newer immigrants from central and southern Europe located north of the river and in the vicinity of factories, wherever they could find low-cost housing within walking distance of work. A 1935 study of residential patterns identified northern and western Kenosha as the areas where the greatest numbers of foreign-born lived. Most of Kenosha's minorities live in the area behind the American Brass factory.

Many ethnic neighborhoods, characterized by their churches, small businesses, parochial schools, and benevolent and fraternal societies, have dispersed over time. Yet a number of structures remain that reflect Kenosha's ethnic history. A few are noted here.

Social, Benevolent, and Fraternal Organizations

These institutions provided security and cultural continuity for Kenosha's immigrants as they adapted to American society. When financially possible, they built substantial structures to house their activities. Three examples of these are noted here. The *Danish Brotherhood Building* at 22nd Avenue and 63rd Street, built in 1910, served as a social and cultural center. It originally contained space for stores, club rooms, and an auditorium. The *German-American Club* building, now the Christian Youth Center at 1715 52nd Street, was built in 1921, very late in the history of the Kenosha German community, which organized a host of cultural and fraternal societies during the last half of the nineteenth century. The *Italian-American Club*, 2215 52nd Street, built in 1926, remains a very active cultural and social center for Kenosha residents of Italian background.

Churches

Churches performed a key role in the lives of new Americans, offering much-needed spiritual guidance, social activity, and welfare. Churches stood at the heart of most ethnic communities. A few of Kenosha's original church structures still stand, and the congregations in some of the newer sanctuaries remember well their immigrant origins. *St. James's Catholic Church*, 5805 10th Avenue, first served the Irish and has since welcomed other national groups new to Kenosha. Constructed in 1883, St James's is the second church structure in Kenosha to house a Catholic congregation made up originally of Irish immigrants. St. Mark's built in 1845 was the first. The name of the parish was changed to St. James's at the time of the cornerstone laying for a new church in 1883. The church provided a home for Kenosha's earliest Italian immigrants in the late nineteenth century. In the 1970s St. James's furnished space for the Spanish Center established to facilitate work with Kenosha's Spanish-speaking community.

The history of both *Mount Carmel* and *Holy Rosary* Catholic parishes is closely linked with Kenosha's Italian community. Originally one parish served an Italian immigrant population that mushroomed from 102 in 1900 to 1,900 in 1920. A split in the congregation over the Americanization issue in 1921 produced the two parishes. Both parishes now occupy newer sanctuaries at locations other than their original ones. Our Lady of Mount Carmel is located at 1919 54th Street, and Our Lady of the Holy Rosary at 2224 45th Street.

A small group of Russian immigrants informally founded *St. Nicholas' Russian Orthodox Church*, now located at 4313 18th Avenue, in 1912 when they organized the St. Nicholas Orthodox Brotherhood Mutual Aid Society. The church structure was completed in 1930, and the parish was officially incorporated in 1935.

St. Mary's Lutheran Church, founded in 1874 by Danish immigrants, has moved several times and now occupies a building complex at 2001 80th Street that was dedicated in 1961. Services were held in Danish through World War I and then in both Danish and English until the late 1940s, when Danish was discontinued.

Second Baptist Church, located at 3925 32nd Avenue, was organized in 1919 to serve Kenosha'a Black population of about 100 as a Union Mission for both Methodists and Baptists. The congregation selected the present name in 1943. Another Baptist congregation, the Friendship Baptist Church, now also serves Baptists among Kenosha's greatly increased Black community.

Businesses

Kenosha's ethnic neighborhoods developed stores, shops, and small businesses founded by residents to serve their neighbors. *Hrupka's Quality Food*, 5022 6th Avenue, housed in an 1863 brick structure, had this origin. The Hrupka family came to Kenosha from Slovakia. They have owned the grocery store since the 1920s, when they opened it to cater to Kenosha's Slovak community, which at the time numbered 658.

Visitors wishing to learn more about Kenosha's historic buildings should consult *Kenosha Historical Sites*, published by the Kenosha Landmarks Commission in 1979, which gives a detailed description of historic structures in the Civic Center, Lakeshore, Library Park, and Northside areas. The Lakeshore community contains the homes of many of Kenosha's leading businessmen, professionals, and industrialists, dating from as early as the 1840s through the 1920s. *Kenosha's Historical Sites* lends itself readily to walking and riding tours.

16. Racine
Highway W-32

Racine's beginnings date from the "Wisconsin fever" of the early 1830s, which brought many New England and New York settlers to the western shores of Lake Michigan in search of new economic opportunities. Racine's founder, Gilbert Knapp, born and raised in Massachusetts, knew the western shore of Lake Michigan well before he ventured to found a town at the mouth of the Root River in 1834.

Knapp had served as a ship captain on Lake Michigan, a member of the U.S. government's Great Lakes Revenue Service, which helped to police the fur trade. After 10 years of service on the lakes, Knapp resigned in 1828 and went into a merchandise and shipping business on Lake Erie in New York State. The popular interest in Wisconsin that followed the Black Hawk War of 1832 encouraged him to return to the mouth of the Root River to promote a settlement. In November 1834, in partnership with a prominent Chicago businessman and a local fur trader, he founded Port Gilbert, popularly known as Root River. Surveyors platted the town in 1836, and it took the name of Racine.

While the depression of 1837 blighted its earliest growth, Racine soon expanded remarkably, from a population of about 300 at the beginning of the 1840s to nearly 7,000 at the end. In 1848 Racine, "the Belle City," officially became a city. Already the original New York–New England population had diversified with the influx of immigrants from the Germanies and the British Isles, approximately 40 percent of the Racine county population by 1850.

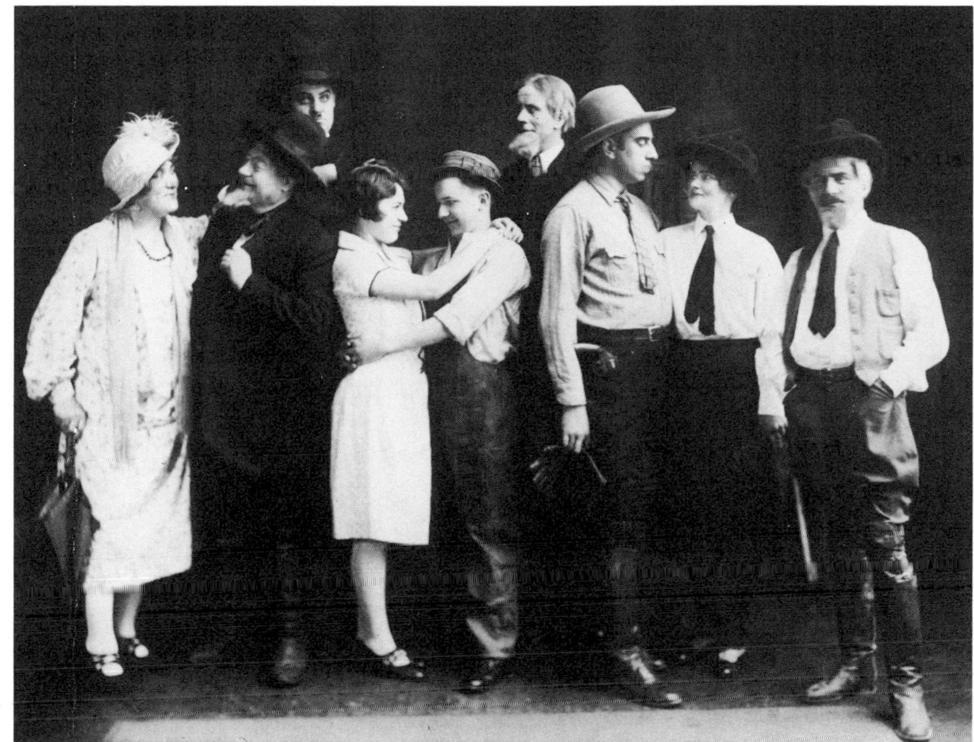

The Dania Dramatic Club, Racine, in 1929. The original of this photograph is in the collection of the Dania Society, Racine.
Courtesy State Historical Society of Wisconsin. WHi(X3)36977

Racine continued to draw people from many countries and from many parts of the United States. Until about 1900 its European immigrants came primarily from the British Isles, Scandinavia, Germany, and Bohemia, many of them recruited to work in Racine's agricultural implement and wagon industries. Danes and Germans especially appealed to these employers.

Between 1900 and 1921 immigrants from eastern and southern Europe—chiefly Austria, Russia, Italy, Hungry, and present-day Czechoslovakia—poured into Racine by the thousands to take blue-collar jobs in the city's expanding industries. During and after World War II, a third wave of in-migrants, Blacks and Mexican Americans, came in sizable numbers in search of better jobs.

While Racine has been called "the most Danish city in America" and "the Czech Bethlehem," its ethnic profile has been very diverse for more than a century. The city's churches, important institutions in the lives of its immigrants, mirror that diversity. Between 80 and 90 Racine churches established during the last 140 years had ethnic origins. They were founded to serve Afro-Americans, Armenians, Bohemians, Danes, Dutch, Germans, Greeks, Hungarians, Irish, Italians, Lithuanians, Mexican Americans, Norwegians, Poles, Russians, Serbs,

Slovaks, Swedes, and Welsh.

Racine developed initially with an economy geared to lake commerce and trade with its agricultural hinterland, serving as county seat, marketing and service center, and processing point for agricultural products. Grain elevators proliferated for a quarter-century after the town's founding. There is much truth in the saying that "wheat made Racine." By 1850 the town boasted a number of small industries, sawmills, a gristmill, several tanneries, an iron foundry, two wagon factories, and the J. I. Case agricultural machinery company. The last, established at Racine in 1847 to manufacture threshing machines, grew and adapted over the decades to become the longest-lived of Racine's industries and currently the town's largest employer.

Like neighboring Kenosha, Racine worked strenuously to develop transportation lines with the outside world. A good harbor was the first objective. Both federal funds and local money and labor improved the harbor. From the 1840s to the 1870s, Racine was a busy port, but railroads soon overshadowed its importance. Racine acquired both a north-south line and a connection with the farmlands lying to the west in the 1850s. Soon these rail lines carried most of Racine's freight and passenger traffic. In the long run the railroad network helped shift trading functions to Milwaukee and Chicago, and Racine lost ground as a trade center. At the same time, the railroad helped Racine to develop as a manufacturing town.

Industry grew steadily in the last half of the nineteenth century. Agricultural machinery and implement, carriage, and wagon factories produced Racine's most valuable products and were its largest industries through 1900. The city emerged as a national production center for farm wagons and machinery. It's manufacturing profile changed after 1900, however. The first 20 years of the new century, and especially the World War I years, were a period of remarkable growth. The number of workers in industry doubled; the value of manufactured products increased eightfold; the number of manufacturing plants grew from 135 to 230. The census figures for 1919 revealed a shift in industrial production. Agricultural implements, foundry and machine shop products, automobiles, bodies, and parts, and electrical machinery emerged as the four largest industries. Machinery and metal products dominated production as never before.

The production trends set by 1920 continued into the 1980s. Always diversified, Racine's industries now produce automobile products, wax, books, iron and steel castings, home appliances, electrical equipment, farm and construction equipment, and food.

Racine, with a population of 85,700 in 1980, ranks high on the list of Wisconsin's industrial cities. Its prominence comes from its location in the Chicago-Milwaukee corridor, where transportation, supplies of materials, services, and labor, and access to markets produce cost advantages for industry. Lake Michigan, so important as an avenue of transportation in the mid-nineteenth century, plays a minor role compared with rail and truck transport. Of eleven Wisconsin Lake Michigan ports, Racine ranks ninth in tonnage handled.

Racine Sites of Interest

(1) Racine College/DeKoven Foundation for Church Work*

600 21st Street

Racine College, founded in 1852 as an educational institution of the Episcopal church, functioned initially as a college and from 1881 to 1933 as a preparatory school. In 1935 it became the DeKoven Foundation for Church Work, serving as a retreat and conference center, a summer camp, and a center for Episcopal church activities. The eight buildings on 40 acres of land include Park Hall, Assembly Hall, the Dining Hall, Kemper Hall, Taylor Hall, a gymnasium, a gatehouse, and the centrally located St. John's Chapel, all constructed from the 1850s through the 1870s. The architect was possibly Lucas Bradley, Racine's most famous architect and builder in its formative years. The buildings are a fine example of a nineteenth-century college complex and for the most part have undergone little alteration. Especially fine is St. John's Chapel, built in 1864 along the lines of English Gothic parish churches. The original interior, with oak pews, trusses, and paneling and stained-glass windows, has been preserved.

(2) Johnson Wax Administration Building* and Research Tower*

1525 Howe Street

Having invented a wax product to care for parquet floors, Samuel Curtis Johnson in 1887 founded the industry that today also manufactures household products, personal care items, and insecticides. Frank Lloyd Wright designed the administration building, which was completed in 1939. It was one of the most advanced examples of

The S. C. Johnson and Sons, Inc., office building, designed by Frank Lloyd Wright, about 1948. Courtesy State Historical Society of Wisconsin. WHi(X3)54

business architecture in the country. In 1976 the American Institute of Architects chose the administration building and research tower (also designed by Wright) as two of the most significant architectural designs in the United States. Tours of the administration building are held regularly, Monday–Friday. Advance reservations are suggested. Call (414) 631-2154.

On the grounds of the Johnson Wax Company stands the Golden Rondelle Theatre. It was built in 1964 for the New York World's Fair to show the award-winning film "To Be Alive." At the close of the fair, the theater was moved to Racine, where the film is shown using specially designed multiple projectors and wide screens. Additional films have been produced for the theatre, including "The American Years," which commemorates the Bicentennial. The public is invited to view the films without charge at several showings daily, but reservations should be made in advance at 1525 Howe Street. Call (414) 631-2154.

(3) Southside Historic District*
Bounded roughly by Lake Michigan, DeKoven Avenue, Lake Avenue, and Southern and 8th Streets
The Southside Historic District reflects the architectural preferences and life style of Racine's successful manufacturers, businesssmen, professionals, and civic leaders from the mid-nineteenth century through 1920. In contrast to the upper-class residential areas in many industrial towns, Racine's Southside Historic District retains an unusually rich concentration of well-constructed Victorian houses in a wide array of architectural styles. More than 40 structures of primary historical and architectural significance have been identified in the district for the National Register of Historic Places. The following are a few of Racine's outstanding structures.

Henry Durand Residence, 1012 South Main Street

Now the property of the masonic order, this cream brick Italianate villa was built in 1856. Durand was one of the many New Englanders who came to Racine early in its history. He had a very successful career in banking, insurance, lumbering, transportation, and city planning.

Cooley House,* 1135 South Main Street (Racine Landmark)

Eli R. Cooley, a hardware merchant and the city's first mayor, had Lucas Bradley design this Greek Revival house for him. It was constructed between 1851 and 1854.

Chauncey Hall Residence,* 1235 South Main Street (Racine Landmark)

Chauncey Hall, a Racine tailor and banker, had this Gothic Revival home built in the late 1840s. It is among the earliest Gothic Revival houses built in Wisconsin and is believed to have been the first such house built in Racine.

Thomas P. Hardy House,*
1319 South Main Street

Frank Lloyd Wright designed this Prairie School residence for Racine attorney Thomas P. Hardy. It was built in 1905 against the bluff overlooking Lake Michigan.

Samuel Curtis Johnson Residence, 1737 South Wisconsin Avenue

Samuel Curtis Johnson, founder of S. C. Johnson and Son, had this Late Picturesque Gothic cottage built in 1903. Johnson came from Ohio to Racine in 1880 and worked for the Racine Hardware Company. In 1887 he established a parquet flooring business that evolved into the floor wax company. Johnson himself designed the house and laid its parquet floors.

St. Luke's Hospital School of Nursing Offices, 1301 College Avenue

Built in 1876, this Victorian Gothic structure was originally St. Luke's Hospital. Newer buildings have long since engulfed it, yet it remains a fine example of Victorian Gothic in cream and red brick.

Thomas Jones House, 1526 College Avenue

Built for an officer of a Racine lumber company in 1878, this large two-story cream brick home is High Victorian Italianate in style. Its second owner, Ernst J. Hueffner, purchased it in 1886. Hueffner, who came to Racine from Germany in 1849, became a business and civic leader, serving as mayor in 1879. He is representative of a social trend in the Southside District in the late nineteenth century, the very successful immigrant who became a resident after achieving wealth and recognition.

Charles Knoblock Home, 1119 Park Avenue

Charles Knoblock, president of the Racine Malleable Iron Company, had this two-and-a-half-story frame Queen Anne home built in 1892–1894. The house has unusual proportions and attractive detail, including a large Palladian window, a decorative frieze between the second and third stories, and a second-floor balcony.

Winslow School, 1325 Park Avenue

The old section of this structure, designed by Lucas Bradley, was built in 1856. It is one of the city's three original schools. In 1897 James G. Chandler rebuilt it, adding cream brick wings decorated with parapet gables.

(4) Racine County Historical Museum

701 Main Street

The museum occupies a former Carnegie Library building, constructed in 1904. The collections include local history, archives, natural history, and glass. A larger library built in 1963 houses historical exhibits. Open Tuesday–Saturday, 9:00 A.M.–5:00 P.M.; Sunday, 1:00 A.M.–5:00 P.M. Closed Monday. Free.

(5) First Presbyterian Church*

716 College Avenue

Designed by Racine architect Lucas Bradley, this fine specimen of simple Greek Revival architecture has repeatedly won the praise of architectural historians. It was constructed of cream brick in 1852 and is the oldest church building in Racine.

(6) Racine Harbor Lighthouse and Lifesaving Station*

North Pier at entrance to Racine Harbor

Built between 1863 and 1866, the Racine Harbor Lighthouse, a cream brick structure, was equipped with a fixed white light, which operated until 1903. In that year a 120-foot galvanized steel tower designed to display storm warnings, a two-story frame lifesaving station, and a boathouse were added to the site. The lifesaving station carried out search and rescue missions along 16 miles of shoreline between Milwaukee and Kenosha. Since the Coast Guard gave up service here in 1973, the County Water Safety Patrol has used the buildings.

(7) Charles A. Wustum Museum of Fine Arts

2519 Northwestern Avenue

Located in the Victorian Italianate home of Charles and Jennie Wustum, given to the city of Racine in 1941, the Museum of Fine Arts has an excellent permanent collection of paintings, graphics, and photographs by Wisconsin, midwestern, New York, and California artists working under the Works Progress Administration's Federal Arts Project of the 1930s. Its holdings include between 50 and 60 watercolors by Wisconsin artists. These, along with subsequent acquisitions, are presented to the public annually in about ten blocks of shows, each containing one to three exhibits. Several special group shows devoted to the work of Wisconsin artists are offered each year.

The Museum of Fine Arts offers guided tours and art classes for children and adults. Open daily, 1:00–5:00 P.M., and on Mondays and Thursdays, 1:00–9:00 P.M. Free.

(8) Northside Racine

Although Racine, lying to the north of the Root River, boasts no historic district on the National Register of Historic Places, its older buildings reflect the history of the city's early industrial and working-class neighborhood. Here immigrant workers lived in ethnic enclaves, built their churches, and organized their clubs and societies. Below are a few examples of characteristic northside structures.

Brick Cottages, Erie Street and Goold to Yout Streets

Built from the 1860s to 1900, modest cream brick cottages like these were the homes of German and middle-European immigrant workers who succeeded in becoming homeowners. The Erie Street cottages were built between the mid-1880s and 1900 from brick made on Racine's Northside.

St. Joseph's Church, Erie and St. Patrick Streets

St. Joseph's congregation, founded in 1875 by Northside German Catholics who wanted a neighborhood church, contributed much of the labor to construct this beautiful Gothic revival structure. It was dedicated in 1878.

Sokol Hall, 1313 Lincoln Street

Built as St. Anne's (German Lutheran) Zion Church, this structure became the home of the Czech Sokol Society in 1892. The Sokol movement was similar to the German Turnverein, a social and educational organization. Over time, most Czech lodges, societies, and organizations met here.

J. I. Case Company, 700 State Street

Racine's Danish community grew adjacent to factories making farm machinery and wagons. State Street was both the Northside shopping area and the center of the Danish community. The J. I. Case Company has been very important to Racine's economic life since Jerome Case opened his first factory here in 1847. The firm's administration building at 700 State was built in 1904. Its style is said to have been inspired by the Boston Public Library.

Pictured here are the members of the J. I. Case Company Engineering Department in 1884. Courtesy State Historical Society of Wisconsin. WHi(X3)32444

Dania Hall, 1015 State Street

Organized in 1867 to help Danish immigrants learn English and American mores, the Dania Society had this Classical Revival–style building constructed in 1905. The Danish community has migrated to the west side, but Dania Hall is still the social center for Racine's Danes. Here they held a reception for Queen Margrethe II and Prince Henrik of Denmark during their 1976 visit.

(9) Wingspread

33 East Four Mile Road, Wind Point

Encouraged by the enthusiastic reception of his design for the Johnson Wax administration building, Frank Lloyd Wright agreed to design an equally outstanding home for Herbert Johnson and his family. The result was Wingspread, built in 1937.

The long, low building has four wings radiating from the center—hence its name. Wingspread became the home in 1960 of the Johnson Foundation and functions as an educational conference center. The public may visit the grounds at any time, and visits to the inside of the home may be arranged if a conference is not in session.

(10) Wind Point Lighthouse*

Four Mile Road (County Trunk G), east off Hy W-32

Built in 1880, this beautiful 108-foot tower originally operated on kerosene lamps. Automated in 1964, the beacon is visible for 19 miles. When radar and depth finders became standard equipment on Great Lakes ships, the foghorn at the light was removed. The lighthouse, closed to the public, has long attracted visitors who enjoy the lake view and the graceful Italianate tower.

Preservation-Racine, a community organization committed to architectural and historical research and education, has published two booklets that give an excellent introduction to Racine's historic buildings: *Renewing Our Roots—A Guide to Racine, Wisconsin: Central City, Southside* and *Renewing Our Roots—The Northside: Racine, Wisconsin*. They are available from Preservation—Racine, P.O. Box 383, Racine, WI 53401.

(11) Industrial Tours
A number of Racine manufacturing plants offer tours for interested visitors, but they do not maintain a schedule of set dates and times. Contact the Chamber of Commerce to find out how to arrange visits.

Old World Wisconsin Side Trip

Those interested in the ethnic history of the Lake Michigan region will find it very worthwhile to make a side trip from Racine to Old World Wisconsin, the outdoor ethnic museum being developed by the State Historical Society of Wisconsin. The museum clearly reflects the heterogeneity of Lake Michigan's people.

Stump fence and Lantta Hay barn in the Finnish area at Old World Wisconsin. The Finnish farmstead complex, among the most well developed, preserves the rural architecture of one of Wisconsin's later (1880s–1920) arriving immigrant groups in rich detail. The barn was built with loose fitting logs to allow ventilation and slanted walls to promote rain runoff. The Finns farmed in the cutover lands of Douglas, Iron, and Bayfield Counties, Wisconsin. The Finns laboriously pulled stumps left by the lumbermen, often using them for fences such as the one pictured here. Photo by Margaret Bogue.

17. Old World Wisconsin

Via Highways W-20 & W-67 from Racine (Southern Unit, Kettle Moraine State Forest)

The outdoor museum at Old World Wisconsin features houses, farmstead outbuildings, a school, a church, and a town hall, all moved from their original locations throughout the state to this 576-acre site in the southern unit of the Kettle Moraine State Forest. The state's wealth of architectural styles, brought by the immigrant groups that settled in rural Wisconsin, have been preserved for the future at Old World Wisconsin.

Grouped according to ethnic origin, structures are spaced far enough apart to retain a rural atmosphere. Costumed guides carry out typical activities in the home and about the farmstead.

When Old World Wisconsin opened on July 4, 1976, Norwegian, Danish, and Finnish structures were represented, and the Pomeranian half-timbered Koepsel House* from Washington County was under construction. Queen Margrethe II of Denmark, who was visiting Wisconsin at that time, dedicated the Pedersen house, built originally by a Danish immigrant in Polk County, Wisconsin, in 1872. Now there are nine buildings in the Finnish farmsteads that are open to the public, four Norwegian buildings, and two Danish, with several more under construction. Four more buildings have joined the Koepsel House in the German area.

Two miles of roads and several nature trails connect the building clusters at Old World Wisconsin, so it is wise to wear stout walking shoes when you visit. An octagonal barn, illustrating a form of architecture used in Ozaukee County, has been transformed into a cafeteria on the museum grounds.

Old World Wisconsin is open daily from May 1 to October 31 as follows: May–June, September–October, Monday–Friday, 9:00 A.M.–4:00 P.M.; Saturday and Sunday, 10:00 A.M.–5:00 P.M. July–August hours are daily, 10:00 A.M.–5:00 P.M. $

Old World Wisconsin occupies only a small portion of the Southern Unit of Kettle Moraine State Forest. In 1939 the state purchased the first lands for the Southern Unit before urban sprawl made such acquisition impossible. A marked scenic drive about 20 miles in length follows a ridge of hills created by a glacier and ends near the Whitewater Lake Recreation Area. Facilities here and at the Ottawa Lake Recreation Area permit camping, picnicking, swimming, boating, fishing, and hiking. There are two major hiking trails, with one route set aside for horseback riders. The Scuppernong Hiking Trail winds through a pine forest, and the Emma Carlin Trail is especially beautiful in autumn.

18. Oak Creek

Highway W-32

The city of Oak Creek (not to be confused with the 1834 settlement at the mouth of Oak Creek) was incorporated in 1955 in response to the efforts of the city of Milwaukee to annex it. The history of permanent settlement in the area, however, goes back to the 1830s, when people from England, Massachusetts, and New York began occupying lands along the shores of Lake Michigan (see South Milwaukee, site 19). Industrial beginnings within the present Oak Creek corporate limits date from the turn of the century, when the U.S. Glue Company located a plant and housing for its employees at what was then known as Carrollville. In succeeding years four more plants located in the vicinity, but in the 1940s the area was more rural than urban. Its rural character was lost after 1951, when the Wisconsin Electric Power Company decided to locate a steam-generating plant at Carrollville. The power plant is often cited as the reason for Milwaukee's interest in annexation—an interest thwarted by local residents.

This largely industrial city has grown rapidly over the last 30 years, from less than 5,000 in the early 1950s to about 17,000 in 1980, but much of Oak Creek is as yet undeveloped by industry or housing. Its many industries produce a wide variety of goods, including catalytic converters for emission control, overhead cranes and hoists, adhesives, fertilizer, computers, and precast concrete products.

Oak Creek's Lake Michigan shoreline includes both industrial and recreational sites. The Wisconsin Natural Gas Company's storage area, the South Shore Sewage Treatment Plant, and the Oak Creek plant of the Wisconsin Electric Power Company are here. In a demonstration program, the Oak Creek Power Plant burns light combustible garbage from the city of Milwaukee to replace part of the coal used in producing electricity.

Oak Creek Sites of Interest

(1) Walter Bender Park
East Ryan Road and the lakeshore
The County Park Commission established Walter Bender Park on a 300-acre tract of shoreland in 1970. It was named for a long-time president of the commission who was particularly interested in preserving lakeshore land for recreation. The Southeastern Wisconsin Regional Planning Commission has suggested that parkland be obtained for a hiking trail along the lake from Walter Bender Park south two miles to Racine's Cliffside Park.

(2) Oak Creek Historical Society Pioneer Village
Forest Hill Road and East 15th Avenue
Located west of Forest Hill Memorial Park, the pioneer village includes a log cabin, pioneer chapel, depot, town hall, blacksmith shop, cobbler shop, and print shop. Open May 30–September 1, Sundays, 2:00 P.M.–4:00 P.M. Group tours by appointment. $

19. South Milwaukee
Highway W-32

Shortly after the organization of Milwaukee County in 1834, a group of men and women from Massachusetts, New York, and England settled at the mouth of Oak Creek. So named for the dense growth of white oaks along its banks, the stream appealed to them because it offered the possibility of a modest lakeport and water power for a gristmill and sawmill. In 1835 an inn was built for the comfort of travelers on the Chicago–Green Bay Road, who

The Bucyrus-Erie Company is a leading South Milwaukee employer today. Photo by Margaret Bogue.

passed through the Oak Creek settlement.

Oak Creek Town (township) remained largely rural with a small, slowly developing village at the mouth of the creek where saw and grist mills, a small wagon-making business, a brickyard, stores, churches, a school, and homes clustered together before 1860. A few new businesses were founded after the war. The best-known among them was the Fowle and Wells brickyard, begun in 1870 to produce cream brick for sale in Milwaukee, Chicago, and Michigan ports. Not until the South Milwaukee Company organized in 1891 to promote industrial growth did the rural character of Oak Creek Town change appreciably.

The entrepreneurs bought up land, platted lots and industrial sites, and offered real estate and money to encourage companies to locate in the newly named village of South Milwaukee. A building boom developed after the Bucyrus Steam Shovel and Dredge Company of Bucyrus, Ohio, decided to locate here early in 1892. Factories, sidewalks, streets, and homes mushroomed until the panic of 1893 temporarily dampened development. With the return of prosperity, South Milwaukee again built rapidly. It incorporated as a city in 1897. At the turn of the century the city boasted 29 manufacturing establishments with a combined capital investment of more than a million dollars and a labor force of almost 600.

Industrial jobs attracted immigrant workers of many nationalities, principally Poles, Germans, Hungarians, Slovaks, and Armenians. Churches, schools, and immigrant fraternal and social organizations proliferated to meet their particular needs, and South

Milwaukee took on a cosmopolitan flavor. As late as 1930, 20 percent of the city's population was foreign-born, and approximately one-third of its 10,700 residents were of Polish descent.

South Milwaukee's periods of great growth and expansion came in 1897–1914, during the postwar prosperity of the 1920s, and again in the 1950s. The city continues to be an important industrial suburb of Milwaukee, with a 1980 population of 21,000. The largest employer is Bucyrus-Erie, an early industry that has grown over the years as a national and international corporation. South Milwaukee's industries produce construction, mining, and earth-moving equipment and leather, electrical, and metal products for industry, as well as some finished consumer goods.

South Milwaukee's original Chicago and North Western Railroad Passenger Station, September 1984. Photo by Margaret Bogue.

South Milwaukee Sites of Interest

(1) South Milwaukee Historical Society Museum

717 Milwaukee Avenue

The collections of the South Milwaukee Historical Society are displayed in three rooms of a two-story brown house built in 1892. They include a wide assortment of pictures, furniture, clothing, and memorabilia. Open Memorial Day–Labor Day, Sunday afternoons, 2:00–4:00 P.M. Free.

(2) Delos Fowle Home

627 Hawthorne Avenue

The Fowle family, prominent in the early settlement of the Oak Creek area, came from England to America in the 1830s. John Fowle and his four sons all acquired land and farmed. John Fowle ran a gristmill and a saw mill as well. The house was built about 1850.

(3) Joseph Dibley Home

507 Hawthorne Avenue

Joseph Dibley and family were early settlers who came to the United States from England in company with the Fowles. The home Joseph Dibley built around 1850 has been restored and kept in excellent condition. Dibley was a carpenter and a farmer. From 1856 to 1859 he ran a brickyard.

(4) Horace Fowle Home

Grant Park

Built in 1892 as a home for Horace Fowle, son of John Fowle, the house was a very elegant residence until 1917. Then the land around it became part of the Milwaukee County Park system. A Milwaukee County Landmark, it is now known as the Grant Park Club House.

(5) The Mansfield House

1209 North Chicago Avenue

Fred Mansfield was a member of the group of businessmen who formed the South Milwaukee Company in 1891 and encouraged commercial and industrial development of the newly platted community. This house was built for Mansfield, who became the first president of the chartered village of South Milwaukee.

(6) South Milwaukee Passenger Station*

Milwaukee Avenue

The Chicago and North Western Railroad accepted the offer of the South Milwaukee Company to furnish a site worth $10,000 for a new depot, agreeing to invest a like amount in the

This bird's-eye view of Cudahy dating from the early 1890s clearly shows the stockyards and Cudahy packing houses. Courtesy State Historical Society of Wisconsin. WHi(X3)39850

to that of Andrew Carnegie or Frederick Weyerhaeuser. He came with his parents to the United States from Ireland as an infant in 1849 and in his youth worked at all sorts of humble occupations before getting into the meat-packing business along with his brothers, Philip, Edward, Michael, and John. The five played leading roles in the development of the meat-packing industry in the Midwest, especially at Chicago, Milwaukee, and Omaha. Patrick and John Cudahy organized the Cudahy Brothers Company in 1888, successor to the John Plankinton and Company meat-packing business of Milwaukee. Within four years they took steps to relocate the plant.

The Chicago and North Western Railroad made no more than a brief stop at a small settlement called Buckhorn until 1892, when Cudahy platted the present city of Cudahy there. Fearing passage of a Milwaukee city ordinance banning meat packing as an objectionable nuisance, Cudahy purchased the new 700-acre site about five miles south of Milwaukee. Lying between the railroad tracks and Lake Michigan, the location presented transportation advantages for the meat business. A streetcar line connecting Cudahy and Milwaukee began operation in 1895, a boon to local passenger traffic. As founder and promoter of the town, Cudahy chose street names to honor prominent midwestern meat packers: Swift, Armour, Plankinton, and Layton.

The Cudahy plant began operations in late 1893, and despite the dampening influence of a national depression upon all business and the Cudahy business in particular, the new community incorporated as a village in 1895. Eleven years later Cudahy became a city with a population of over 2,500.

During the first two decades of its development, Cudahy attracted good-sized industries and a sizable workforce. Thousands of workers born in Poland, Czechoslovakia, and Germany and smaller numbers from other central and southern European countries came to Cudahy to live and work. In 1930 a quarter of Cudahy's population was foreign-born, and more than 50 percent had either foreign or mixed parentage. Churches, schools, and social, fraternal, and cultural organizations proliferated to meet the needs of these immigrant groups. A survey of Cudahy civic and fraternal organizations made in 1956 showed five with an ethnic base (three Polish and two Slovak).

Cudahy experienced great periods of growth between 1895 and 1914, during the 1920s, and again during the 1950s. The town suffered particularly during the 1930s from the loss of a rubber products company that employed about 4,000 out of a total Cudahy workforce of 7,000. Its population in 1940 was slightly less than that of a decade before. Its diversified industries then included a tannery, a drop forge plant, a box factory, a vinegar distillery, a shoe factory, and a manufacturer of bottle-washing equipment, as well as the packing plant.

In 1980 this industrial city of 19,500 had 42 industrial establishments, which produced leather, meat products, and a wide variety of metal producer goods, including tools and dies, foundry products, drop forgings, bottle-washing equipment, and air compressors. The largest industry is the Ladish Company, one of three firms founded in Cudahy before World War I and still in business here.

Cudahy Sites of Interest

(1) North Western Railroad Depot
South Kinnickinnic Avenue and Plankinton Avenue
The Cudahy Historical Society purchased this structure and is restoring it to its 1892 appearance. It will be used as both museum and society headquarters. The depot, consisting of waiting room, freight shed, stationmaster's office, and lookout tower, was last used in 1973.

(2) Sheridan Park
Adjacent to Highway W-32 (Lake Avenue)
Public service and philanthropy as well as business were part of Patrick Cudahy's life. For a number of years he served on the Milwaukee County Park Board. Eight years after his death, the Cudahy family gave lakeshore land to the Milwaukee County Park Commission. It became the nucleus of Sheridan Park. In 1965 Michael Cudahy commissioned a Washington, D.C., sculptor, Felix de Weldon, to create a statue of Patrick Cudahy. It was placed at the east end of Layton Avenue in Sheridan Park. On the black granite base are plaques that depict Cudahy as founder of the city and as a longtime member of the County Park Commission.

(3) Pulaski Park
Bounded by East Adams, East Morris, South Hately, and South Swift Avenues
The park is named to honor the contribution of Cudahy's many Polish immigrants to the economic and cultural life of the town. In 1929 the newly organized Polish Central Association of Cudahy embarked on a fund-raising campaign to erect a monument to Casimir Pulaski, a Polish nobleman who fought on the side of the colonists during the American Revolution and was killed at Savannah, Georgia, in 1779. The 16-acre park, acquired by the city of Cudahy in 1926, was originally named Lindbergh Park. In 1929 it was renamed Pulaski Park. A bust of Pulaski by Joseph Aszlcar was unveiled here in 1932.

22. St. Francis
Highway W-32

Beautifully sited on Lake Michigan, this community originated as a center for the training of Catholic priests. St. Francis Seminary grew from the dream of John Martin Henni, first bishop of Wisconsin, to found a school for priests to serve Wisconsin's growing German Catholic immigrant population and from the determination of a small Franciscan community that came to Milwaukee in 1849. Two Bavarian priests and a dozen lay Franciscan men and women founded a mission community on a 36-acre site at present-day St. Francis with the goal of educating and helping candidates for the priesthood, teachers, and poor children. This society evolved into the Sisterhood of St. Francis of Assisi of Milwaukee and La Crosse.

Specific plans for the seminary took shape in 1853. After buying additional land, engaging in a strenuous fund-raising campaign, and directing the hard work of constructing the seminary building, the founding fathers opened the school in 1856. Since named Henni Hall* in honor of John Martin Henni, the original seminary building, designed by Victor Schulte in Italianate style, still stands. Recently it has been added to the National Register of Historic Places. Henni Hall housed the community's first chapel, classrooms, and living quarters for faculty and students. As St. Francis Seminary grew over the years, other buildings took over seminary functions originally sheltered by Henni Hall. The exterior of Henni Hall, a landmark in the religious and educational history of Wisconsin, now appears much as it did originally. The interior includes a notably fine chapel and a twin serpentine staircase in the main entrance foyer.

In the nineteenth century the St. Francis institutional complex included the convent for the sisters of St. Francis of Assisi, St. Aemilian's Orphan Asylum, both dating from the 1850s, and St. John's Institute for the Deaf, organized in 1876.

The village of St. Francis grew up around the Catholic institutions, attracting German Catholic immigrants in the nineteenth century. St. Francis was incorporated as a city in 1951. It attracted the attention of the engineering world in 1921 when the Wisconsin

Victor Schulte, who designed Henni Hall, was an important architect in Milwaukee in the mid-nineteenth century. He designed, as well, St. John's Roman Catholic Cathedral, Old St. Mary's, and Holy Trinity. Photo by Margaret Bogue.

Electric Power Company built its Lakeside Power Plant (now closed) to demonstrate the use of pulverized coal in the production of electric power. Here, in the 1934 strike against the Milwaukee Electric Railway and Light Company, a labor demonstration culminated in the death of a strike sympathizer.

Industry came to St. Francis in the post–World War II years. Currently, 21 jobbing, light manufacturing, and industrial service firms are located here. The largest employer, E Z Painter, makes paint brushes and rollers. The present population is about 10,000.

Those interested in visiting St. Francis Seminary should call and make arrangements for a tour.

23. Milwaukee

Highway I-94

Indian peoples early recognized the advantages of the site of modern Milwaukee at the juncture of the Menomonee, Kinnickinnic, and Milwaukee rivers near the Milwaukee's exit into Lake Michigan. Here, according to the French, they found the Fox, the Mascounten, and the Potawatomi in the seventeenth century. Here the French and the British and later the Americans engaged in the fur trade, but the Indian village on the Milwaukee River was always a minor trade center compared to Green Bay or Mackinac.

When Solomon Juneau arrived in 1819 to represent the interests of the American Fur Company, the Milwaukee River Indian trading post stood on the brink of rapid change. After the Black Hawk War in 1832 and

Solomon Juneau's trading post. Courtesy State Historical Society of Wisconsin. WHi(W6)20755

the 1831 and 1833 Indian cessions of Milwaukee-area land, it was swept up in the settlement and land-speculating boom of the 1830s. The shrewd promoters, mostly New York or New England Yankees, who roamed southern Wisconsin looking for prospective town sites fully appreciated the virtues of Solomon Juneau's trading post. Among them were Morgan L. Martin, Green Bay land speculator and promoter, and Byron Kilbourn, assistant to the surveyor general of Michigan.

These men and their business associates, along with George H. Walker, a Virginia fur trader, preempted land crucially located on the Milwaukee River and proceeded to promote town sites. In 1837 the Wisconsin territorial legislature authorized two separate towns: "the Town of Milwaukee" (Juneautown) and "the Town of Milwaukee on the West Side of the River" (Kilbourntown). A year later, in the depths of a nationwide depression, the two consolidated into the village of Milwaukee.

Milwaukee's promoters envisioned a town of commercial glory. They worked strenuously to make it the focal point of a transportation network, at first by the construction of a canal connecting the Milwaukee and Rock rivers and by harbor improvements, and later, in the 1840s, by promoting road and railroad construction.

Initially Milwaukee's trade centered on importing goods to serve villagers and those headed inland to develop farms. By the mid-1840s enough settlers had developed farms from Wisconsin's virgin lands to produce grain and livestock for export at Milwaukee. This was the beginning of Milwaukee's role as market outlet for agricultural produce from its hinterland, supplier of its imported needs, and port of entry for thousands of American-born and foreign-born migrants in search of new homes and better fortunes. Milwaukee's population grew from a mere 1,712 in 1840 to 20,061 in 1850. It assumed city status in 1846.

From the 1840s until the early 1870s, trade and commerce were Milwaukee's principal economic functions. City promoters succeeded in a campaign to secure railroads connecting the lake and the Mississippi River and to improve the harbor. Milwaukee became the leading wheat market of the world in 1862, the largest flour-milling city in the West in the mid-1860's, and fourth-largest national meat-packing center in 1870.

Commercial preeminence was short-lived. Milwaukee business leaders were always well aware that Chicago posed the greatest threat to Milwaukee's position as the leading commercial city of the Midwest. In the long run Chicago's superior geographic position and rail connections with a vast hinterland spelled the doom of Milwaukee's hopes. In the seventies it lost first place in the wheat trade. It lost first place in flour milling to St. Louis in 1871. Milwaukee business promoters generally came to recognize that commerce was not enough.

By 1872 between one-third and one-half of Milwaukee's labor force worked in industry. Four of its major industries—flour milling, tanning, meat packing, and brewing and distilling—processed agricultural products. Other major industries—producers of men's clothing, metal castings, machines, and engines—made essential goods for the consumption of the hinterland. Thereafter Milwaukee industry grew steadily, producing goods for an ever-wider market. It experienced a remarkable growth in the first

Sailing vessels unload tan bark at the Pfister and Vogel leather company. Courtesy Milwaukee County Historical Society.

decade of the twentieth century and again in the post–World War II period. The city emerged as a bustling industrial workshop, and most of its labor force was employed in the dominant iron and steel, machinery, and automotive equipment industries.

In 1979 Milwaukee's 25 largest industries produced a wide variety of metal products, ranging from motors, parts, and electrical and electronic controls to finished construction, mining, agricultural, and industrial equipment and consumer goods such as motorcycles. Twelve of these manufacturers employed over 2,000 persons. Among them were three major breweries. Thirteen employed between 900 and 2,000 workers.

If Milwaukee is known today as an industrial city of 636,212 people and an international port on the St. Lawrence Seaway, during the nineteenth century it was known as a city of immigrants. In the 1840s an influx of immigrants, principally from the Germanies and Ireland, greatly changed the character of the original Yankee population. In 1850, 64 percent of the town's population was foreign-born, and two-thirds of that number were from the Germanies. The Germans formed a self-conscious community in the northwestern part of the city and for economic and cultural reasons were initially slow to mix with the American-born population. Bohemians, Dutch, British, Poles, Austrians, Black Americans, and Norwegians were present in smaller numbers at the mid-century.

While German immigrants continued to arrive in large numbers in the late nineteenth century and to be the dominant foreign-born element, people from eastern and southern Europe added diversity to Milwaukee's population profile. Substantial numbers of Poles, Czechs, Slovaks, Hungarians, Italians, Greeks, and Russians sought a better life in Wisconsin's most industrial city, among them the young Golda Meir for whom the public school at 1542 North 4th Street was renamed in 1979. After immigration restriction began in 1921, the percentage of foreign-born residents declined rapidly. The figure stood at 30 percent in 1910 and at less than 15 percent in 1940, but more than 20 percent of Milwaukee's residents still spoke German, an indication of the longevity of German culture in the city.

Milwaukee's foreign-born newcomers experienced the same problems as Chicago's immigrants: low pay, congested living conditions, dirt, squalor, disease, and poor urban services. They clustered together in language or nationality groups and adapted slowly to the urban environment.

In the twentieth century two other

major groups of in-migrants—Blacks and Hispanics—have added further diversity to Milwaukee's population. Milwaukee had a small and slowly increasing Black population throughout the nineteenth century, which began to grow rapidly in the 1920s after immigration restriction and especially during and after World War II. By 1980 approximately 146,000 Blacks made up 23 percent of the city's population. They worked principally at unskilled, low-paying, blue-collar jobs and experienced great difficulty in moving into professional, clerical, and skilled positions. Hampered in their upward struggle by lack of education and skills, the same kinds of disabilities foreign-born immigrants of an earlier era had experienced, they bore the additional burden of racial discrimination. A high unemployment rate has been a constant problem. Black frustrations with unemployment, low wages, education, housing, health, and law enforcement burst forth during the Civil Rights Movement of the 1960s, though somewhat less dramatically than in some other midwestern industrial cities.

Although Milwaukee's Hispanic community dates from the 1920s, it has grown much more rapidly during the past 20 years. The 1980 census showed a Hispanic population of 26,111, 4.1 percent of Milwaukee's total. Half of them, mostly Mexican Americans, live on Milwaukee's Near South Side, and an additional 20 percent live on the North Side and the East Side. The East Side community is mainly Puerto Rican.

Hispanics too have experienced difficulty in finding jobs, are mainly blue-collar workers, and have a higher unemployment rate than the non-minority population. They experience discrimination, but to a lesser extent than Milwaukee's Blacks. Blacks and Hispanics have contributed to the city's cultural diversity and have reminded the city government that they are a political force with which it must reckon.

Urban jobs also attracted increasing numbers of American Indians to Milwaukee after World War II. The 1980 census showed about 5,800 living in Milwaukee County.

Possibly the two major benefits of Milwaukee's ethnic diversity are a tempering effect upon the political process and variety in cultural institutions. Every year Milwaukee honors that cultural diversity with an elaborate folk festival sponsored by the International Institute, organized in 1923 to develop leadership within ethnic groups and to promote public appreciation for and knowledge of their cultural contributions.

Milwaukee's Lake Michigan harbor has greatly influenced the city's fortunes. From the beginnings of the village to the present, Milwaukee's business leaders have tried to improve on nature's bounty. Despite strenuous efforts of Milwaukeeans in the 1830s, Congress failed to respond to requests for harbor improvements until 1843. Meanwhile villagers ran a fleet of small boats out to deep water to taxi passengers and goods to shore. One entrepreneur, Horatio G. Stevens, in 1842–1843 completed the first of a series of long, very substantial piers where vessels could dock and unload.

Two theories about early harbor improvement mustered support. One called for improving the natural outlet from the Milwaukee River into the lake; the other for making a straight cut from the Milwaukee River across a 300-foot strip of land dividing the river from the lake about 3,000 feet north of the natural outlet. Both the 1843 and the 1845 federal appropriations for Milwaukee harbor improvement were spent on the natural outlet, but in 1852 Congress designated funds for improvements at the straight cut. When completed, this harbor improvement cost $84,000 in federal money and $446,000 in local tax revenue. The cut created Jones Island.

At no time in Milwaukee's history was the port so crucial as in the years before the construction of the railroads. By the mid-1840s the docks bustled with inbound immigrants and Americans seeking homes in Wisconsin. Huge piles of imported merchandise lined the docks. Wagonloads of wheat rolled into town for export. Bullwhackers, colorfully clad in red shirts and rough trousers, drove their ox-drawn wagons laden with lead from the southwestern Wisconsin mines to Milwaukee for export.

By the late 1860s the port had felt the impact of the overland railroad network. Milwaukee lost its preeminence as exporter of wheat to Chicago, but lake transportation assumed an important new role. Milwaukee's growing factories needed coal. The cheapest way to get it from the eastern coalfields was by using lake freighters for part of the journey. Imports grew with industrial expansion until coal accounted for two-thirds of the city's waterborne commerce between 1910 and 1939. Water transport remains the most economical for a number of bulk items, such as grain, newsprint, limestone, and coal. Harbor promotion therefore continued to be a key feature of the campaign to improve Mil-

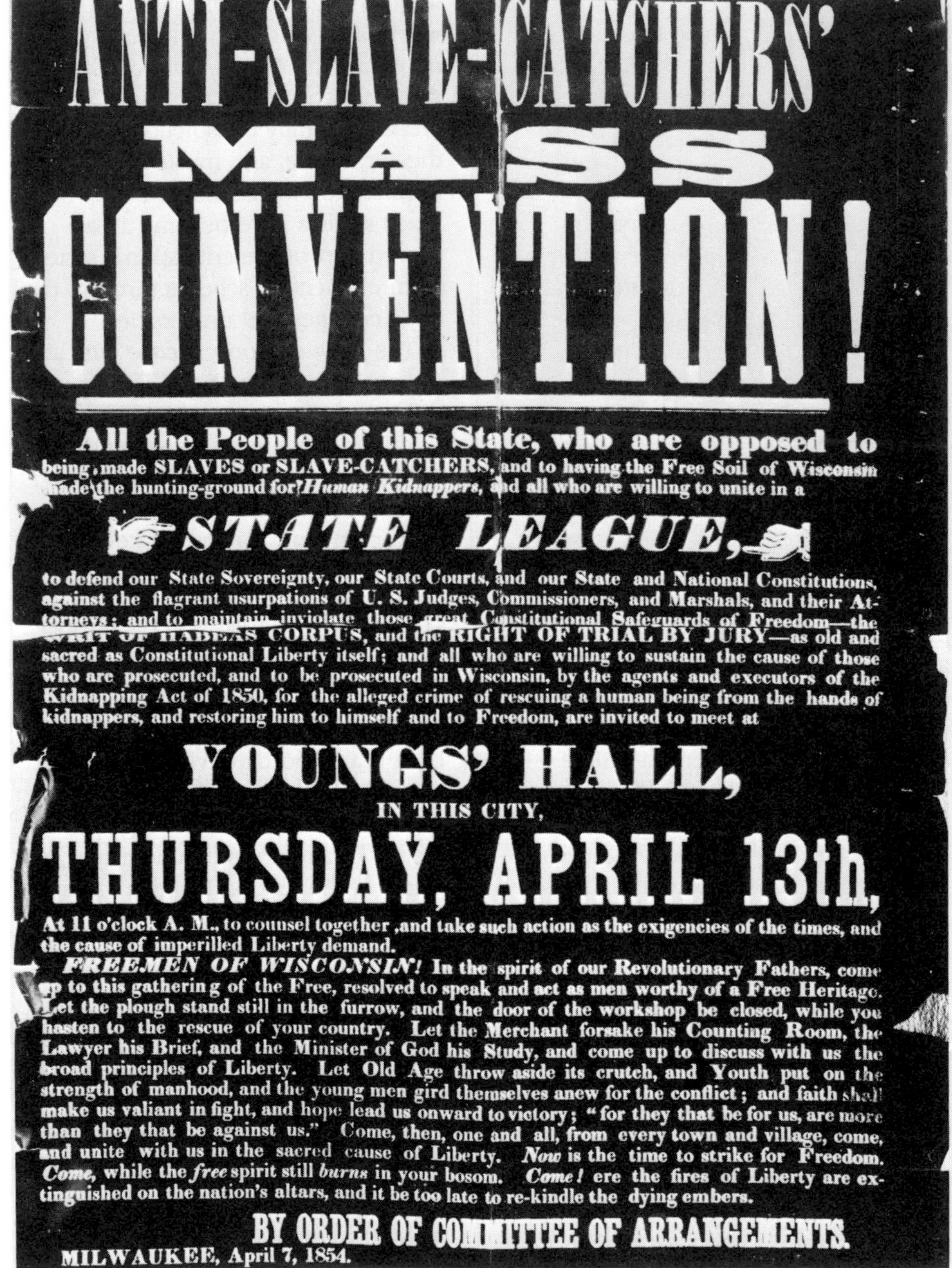

ANTI-SLAVE-CATCHERS'

MASS

CONVENTION!

All the People of this State, who are opposed to being made SLAVES or SLAVE-CATCHERS, and to having the Free Soil of Wisconsin made the hunting-ground for *Human Kidnappers*, and all who are willing to unite in a

STATE LEAGUE,

to defend our State Sovereignty, our State Courts, and our State and National Constitutions, against the flagrant usurpations of U. S. Judges, Commissioners, and Marshals, and their Attorneys; and to maintain inviolate those great Constitutional Safeguards of Freedom—the WRIT OF HABEAS CORPUS, and the RIGHT OF TRIAL BY JURY—as old and sacred as Constitutional Liberty itself; and all who are willing to sustain the cause of those who are prosecuted, and to be prosecuted in Wisconsin, by the agents and executors of the Kidnapping Act of 1850, for the alleged crime of rescuing a human being from the hands of kidnappers, and restoring him to himself and to Freedom, are invited to meet at

YOUNGS' HALL,

IN THIS CITY,

THURSDAY, APRIL 13th,

At 11 o'clock A. M., to counsel together, and take such action as the exigencies of the times, and the cause of imperilled Liberty demand.

FREEMEN OF WISCONSIN! In the spirit of our Revolutionary Fathers, come up to this gathering of the Free, resolved to speak and act as men worthy of a Free Heritage. Let the plough stand still in the furrow, and the door of the workshop be closed, while you hasten to the rescue of your country. Let the Merchant forsake his Counting Room, the Lawyer his Brief, and the Minister of God his Study, and come up to discuss with us the broad principles of Liberty. Let Old Age throw aside its crutch, and Youth put on the strength of manhood, and the young men gird themselves anew for the conflict; and faith shall make us valiant in fight, and hope lead us onward to victory; "for they that be for us, are more than they that be against us." Come, then, one and all, from every town and village, come, and unite with us in the sacred cause of Liberty. *Now* is the time to strike for Freedom. *Come,* while the *free* spirit still *burns* in your bosom. *Come!* ere the fires of Liberty are extinguished on the nation's altars, and it be too late to re-kindle the dying embers.

BY ORDER OF COMMITTEE OF ARRANGEMENTS.

MILWAUKEE, April 7, 1854.

The Glover incident inspired continued protest to the federal Fugitive Slave Act of 1850. Courtesy State Historical Society of Wisconsin. WHi(X3)2710

football field, tennis courts, and areas for roller skating as well as picnic facilities. The center's 46,000 square feet provide space for a wide range of programs, such as a well baby clinic, classes in arts and crafts, physical fitness, and photography. Included in the center are game rooms, a community branch of the city library system with a tutorial staff to assist students, and an auditorium suitable for the performing arts with a seating capacity of 240. During the summer months many of these programs are held in an outside amphitheater. Recreational programs run from 8:00 A.M. to 10:00 P.M. daily. The center has become a prototype for recreational programs throughout the United States. Built and staffed by the Milwaukee County Department of Parks, Recreation and Culture, the facility received partial funding from the Department of Housing and Urban Development on the understanding that minorities would be involved in the planning, construction, and operation of the center. The architectural firm of Atkins and Jackels of Minneapolis, working in cooperation with the University of Wisconsin–Milwaukee School of Architecture, designed the facility and park.

Designed by the Milwaukee architectural firm of Flad and Associates and completed in 1978, the *North Division Senior High School*, 1011 West Center Street, has a current enrollment of 1,250. Considered one of the most outstanding high school structures in the nation, the building stands in part on the site of St. Boniface's Church, Father James Groppi's church, which figured so prominently in the Civil Rights Movement of the 1960s. When St. Boniface's was razed to make room for the new school, many came to take a brick from the ruins as a memento of the work of Milwaukee's fiery young priest on behalf of the Black community. Planned with neighborhood advice and built using neighborhood labor, the school specializes in medical-dental education, training, for example, hygienists, nurses' aides, and medical transcribers. It also offers preparatory education for those planning to attend nursing, dental, and medical schools.

The *Columbia Savings and Loan Association*, 2000 West Fond du Lac Avenue, founded in October 1924 by Wilbur and Ardie Halyard, is Milwaukee's first Black-operated savings and loan institution. The Halyards came from Atlanta to Milwaukee via Beloit for the specific purpose of helping with Black housing problems. After considerable difficulty in securing a charter, they succeeded, as Mrs. Halyard puts it, "through political means." The new institution opened its doors on January 1, 1925, with a subscribed capital of $50,000, which grew over the years to more than $3.2 million in 1976. By making mortgage loans available to Blacks, who have had great difficulty securing credit, it has helped Blacks to become homeowners and to move out of the restrictive inner core.

The Halyards were for years very active members of Calvary Baptist Church and Chapters of the NAACP in Milwaukee, Racine, Kenosha, and elsewhere in Wisconsin. Among the many public honors received for their work was the naming of Halyard Street for Wilbur Halyard in 1965. It lies east of the north-south expressway.

The oldest Black Baptist congregation in Milwaukee, *Calvary Baptist Church*, 2959 North Teutonia Avenue, was founded as a mission in 1895. Then named Mt. Olive Baptist Church, it initially had a small membership but has grown over the years along with Milwaukee's population. Today there are about 1,200 members. Designed by William Wenzler and Associates to suggest the rich cultural background of Africa, the structure was completed in 1970. Calvary Baptist is concerned with the problems of daily life as well as purely spiritual matters. It offers family counseling, gives students scholarships, and participates in community improvement programs and projects. Recently Calvary Baptist built a 72-unit housing project for senior citizens adjoining the church at 1515 West Chambers Street.

The *Martin Luther King Library* is at 310 Locust Street. Built in 1971 to serve the Black community, this branch of the public library system houses a circulating collection of 6,400 volumes. It also offers educational programs in cooperation with various groups to meet community interests and needs. They range broadly over such subjects as children's art, home maintenance, Black history, and defensive driving and include films for young adults and reading programs. Monthly Black art exhibits focus generally, but not exclusively, on the work of Milwaukee artists. Hours vary, but the library is open year round in the afternoon, Monday–Saturday.

St. Mark's African Methodist Episcopal Church, 1616 West Atkinson Avenue, was organized in 1869 as the First African Methodist Episcopal Church of Milwaukee. The congregation at first made its home in the German Zion Evangelical church building. Renamed St. Mark's in 1886, the congregation occupied several locations before moving into the present structure, built in 1969. The church is especially meaningful in the history of the Milwaukee Black community because of its longevity. Moreover, among its founders was Ezekiel Gillespie, the Black Milwaukeean who, denied the vote at the polls in 1865, joined forces with Milwaukee lawyer Byron Paine to win the suffrage for Wisconsin's Black men in a case decided by the Wisconsin Supreme Court in 1866, four years before the Fifteenth Amendment to the U.S. Constitution sanctioned Negro suffrage. The church's fellowship hall is named for Gillespie.

Milwaukee has a number of successful Black businesses. Among them is the *Central Manufacturing Corporation*, 3901 North 2nd Street, a custom metal fabrication plant that provides cutting, welding, bending, consulting, and prototype services for the midwestern market. Organized in 1979, it employs 32 people, four of them engineers. Visitors are welcome, but those wishing to see the plant should call (414) 963-1108 a day in advance of the visit so that the firm's president, Irvine W. Palmer, can schedule a personally conducted tour.

Hispanic Neighborhoods

Although Milwaukee's 26,111 Hispanics live in widely scattered parts of the city, about 70 percent reside in three distinct neighborhoods. Half, largely Mexican-Americans, live on the near South Side in an area roughly bounded by Kinnickinnic Avenue and 1st Street on the east, the Menomonee River on the north, 35th and 31st Streets on the west, and West Cleveland and East Russell Avenues on the

This photo was taken on the south side in June of 1977. Courtesy Milwaukee Journal.

south. An additional 10 percent live on the North Side in an irregularly shaped area roughly bounded by the east-west freeway on the south, Center Street on the north, 20th and 27th Streets on the east, and 41st Street on the west. The East Side community, predominantly Puerto Rican, lies between Keefe Avenue on the north, Brady Street on the south, the Milwaukee River on the east, and North Palmer and 5th Streets on the west. This group constitutes about 9 percent of Milwaukee's Hispanic population.

Recruited to work in the tanneries, Mexicans came to Milwaukee in sizable numbers in the 1920s. In the depths of the depression, when unemployment was widespread and relief scarce, many of them were deported to their homeland on the grounds of irregular entry into the United States. During the past three decades, the Mexican American population has again grown. While the earlier migrants came directly from Mexico, the more recent ones are from both Mexico and the southwestern United States, principally Texas. Many of these people had been migratory harvest workers in the northern states. In Milwaukee they found jobs in the tanneries and foundries.

Milwaukee's Puerto Ricans are part of a sizable migration from the island to the mainland in the 1940s. Settling in large numbers in New York City and Chicago, Puerto Ricans by 1950 had moved to Milwaukee and formed a community. Many former sugar-cane workers found jobs in Milwaukee's tanneries and foundries.

The discontinuity in the Hispanic community produced by the forced return of Mexican workers in the 1930s, its relatively recent origin, and the racial prejudice that has complicated the efforts of Hispanics to earn a secure livelihood have kept the Hispanic community in Milwaukee from fully developing the cultural institutions and the architecture often associated with the older ethnic neighborhoods. Nevertheless, social and cultural institutions are at work.

Community centers, churches, and a number of special programs and projects sponsored by the federal government, private organizations, the public schools, and the University of Wisconsin–Milwaukee focus on educational needs. At least four churches offer religious services in Spanish: Holy Trinity–Our Lady of Guadalupe (see below), St. Michael's, St. Patrick's, and St. Rose's. A wide variety of social service organizations, some working exclusively with the Spanish-speaking community, have programs designed to serve Hispanics. They focus their work on many social needs, ranging from housing, employment, credit, and welfare to art and music appreciation, counseling on racial discrimination, parenting, legal assistance, and drug problems. The impressive list of social service organizations in Milwaukee might suggest that the needs of Hispanics are well met. In reality it testifies to the magnitude and scope of their needs.

Radio and television stations offer a limited number of programs for Hispanics. *La Guardia* and *Soy Yo* are newspapers published monthly in Spanish. The *Milwaukee Journal* runs a weekly column entitled "The Latin Corner."

*Holy Trinity-Our Lady of Guadalupe Roman Catholic Church,** 605 South 4th Street, offers services in Spanish (see no. [5] below).

The *South Side Community Health Clinic*, 1231 South 7th Street, offers general health care and dental service. *El Centro Hispano* (Council for the Spanish Speaking), 614 West National Avenue, provides educational programs, employment and training counseling, and translation to broaden the community's understanding of a wide spectrum of government-related rights and obligations; instruction for Hispanic prisoners at Waupun State Prison; tutoring for students from kindergarten through grade 12; and Christmas and Thanksgiving distributions to the needy. The Concerned Consumers' League and El Centro Credit Union have offices here.

The *Guadalupe Center (Council for Spanish Speaking)*, 239 West Washington Street, offers a broad spectrum of educational services, including art and music appreciation classes, preschool education, summer youth programs, parent education programs, arts and crafts instruction, and emergency assistance to the needy. The *Latin American Union for Civil Rights*, 621 West Mitchell Street, gives general legal help and assistance with problems related to housing, employment, and discrimination. *United Migrant Opportunity Services, Inc.*, 809 West Greenfield Avenue, assists migrant field workers during the harvest season and helps migrant workers find permanent homes and jobs through legal, educational, and social service programs. The *United Community Center (Centro de la Comunidad Unida)*, 1028 South 9th Street, offers a wide variety of services and programs to meet the social, recreational, and developmental needs of the Milwaukee Hispanic community. The *Santa Cruz Apartments*, 3029 West Wells Street, are a housing facility for Hispanic senior citizens.

Of Milwaukee's older ethnic neighborhoods, some are still identifiable, but time, urban renewal, and freeway construction have erased others completely. The churches, homes, and businesses of many older ethnic groups have moved farther west or north in the city or to one of the suburbs. Three examples of older neighborhoods and structures closely associated with their history, either in their original locations or transplanted, follow.

The German Neighborhood

Of Milwaukee's many nineteenth-century immigrant groups, the Germans were the most numerous. A few Germans lived in the village in the 1830s, and others began coming in very substantial numbers in the following decade, propelled to America by economic, political, and religious conditions in the Germanies and attracted by the hope of a better life, news and propaganda about New World opportunities, and the active solicitation of state-supported immigration agencies. In 1850 two-thirds of Milwaukee's population was foreign-born, with immigrants from the Germanies in an overwhelming majority. They lived in "German Town" in the northwestern part of the city, as Bayrd Still noted, a "self-contained and self-conscious" community of laborers, craftsmen, businessmen, and professionals.

The German community developed its own business districts and organizations paralleling those in the American community—churches, debating clubs, lodges, schools, musical societies, fire and military companies, and German newspapers. Milwaukee's German society had the flavor of the Fatherland. As early as the 1840s, the German presence was helping launch the brewery business that was ultimately to be important in Milwaukee's economy.

German Town continued to grow as more and more immigrants arrived. German-born residents made up a third of Milwaukee's population in 1870. In 1910 over one-half of Milwaukee's population claimed German background. The German cultural character of the city peaked in the last quarter of the nineteenth century, earning for Milwaukee a reputation as the "most German city in the United States," the Deutsch-Athen. During those 25 years, German music and drama, the German-language press, and German political clout reached their greatest development. These were the years when the Pabst, Miller, Blatz, Gettelman, and Schlitz breweries, all founded by German immigrants, rose to national prominence, the period when Captain Frederick Pabst built his opulent mansion, the Pabst theater, and an impressive downtown office building. So influential were the Milwaukee Turner societies (see Turner Hall below) that they hosted the Festival of the North American Turner Societies in 1893.

Clearly by 1900 the separation of German society from American was fading. Vigorous participation in politics, the forces of urban life, the growth of social classes in the Milwaukee German community, and par-

Christ Vetter's Band, Milwaukee, 1870, was one among dozens of German musical organizations. Courtesy Milwaukee County Historical Society.

ticularly the outstanding success of German businessmen tended to break down cultural barriers. The German press, theater, Turner societies, singing societies, and political influence were all on the wane, even before anti-German feelings engendered by World War I hastened the decline of a distinctly German geographical and cultural community in Milwaukee.

Some of the combined business and residential structures of German Town still remain along North 3d Street from Wisconsin Avenue north to Burleigh Street and on Green Bay Avenue.

The church, of central importance in the lives of German immigrants, served social and welfare as well as spiritual functions. Although the majority of Milwaukee's Germans were Protestants, sizable numbers from southern Germany were Catholic. Several churches built to serve German immigrants remain. *St. Mary's Church*, located at 836 North Broadway, was Milwaukee's first German Catholic church, built in 1846 and rebuilt in 1867. In the latter year large additions were made to the front and rear of the original structure, including the tower and steeple. Victor Schulte, the German-born architect who designed several Milwaukee churches and the original St. Francis Seminary building (see site 22), drew up the plans for the 1867 alterations. A painting of the Annunciation over the altar was given by King Ludwig I of Bavaria. *Holy Trinity–Our Lady of Guadalupe Roman Catholic Church** in the Walker's Point Historic District was also designed by Victor Schulte for a German parish (see no. [5]).

The second church structure to house the Trinity Evangelical Lutheran congregation, founded in 1847, stands at 1046 North 9th Street. Built in 1878, *Trinity Lutheran** has been called one of the state's finest examples of Victorian Gothic design. The beautiful brick structure with wood and limestone trim, carved woodwork, stained glass windows, and rare old altar paintings is unspoiled and in virtually original condition. Trinity Lutheran is the mother church of the Missouri Lutheran Synod in Wisconsin and founder of Concordia College.

*Turner Hall,** 1034 4th Street, built in 1882 and 1883, was one of a number of Turner halls built in Milwaukee. The Turners, subscribing to the ideas of free speech and assembly, tolerance, and reason, played a part in the unsuccessful German Revolution of 1848. Refugees from the revolution brought the organization to the United States, where it took root in midwestern towns and cities and became an important German social and cultural institution. The Milwaukee Turners practiced German gymnastics, held annual balls, and offered lectures and debates in German. They also formed a company of sharpshooters that served in the Union Army during the Civil War. The Milwaukee Turners' gymnastic team captured the world's Turner championship in 1880.

Richardsonian Romanesque in style, the brick structure contains a very German-looking pub, a gymnasium, and, on the second floor, an unusual ballroom and theater stage. A fire in 1933 damaged the second floor facilities beyond use, but there are plans for renovation.

Milwaukee's famous Breweries include the *Pabst Brewery*, 917 West Juneau Avenue, a Milwaukee City Landmark, and the *Miller Brewery*, 4251 West State Street. Thousands of Milwaukee visitors annually join the tours conducted by Milwaukee's two big breweries. The brewing industry has played an important part in Milwaukee's economy ever since the first brewery opened in 1840. At first the industry supplied the area's increasing German population. By 1852 hundreds of barrels of Milwaukee brew sold in other markets as well. In 1890 brewing ranked as Milwaukee's leading industry. Pabst, Miller, and Schlitz, because of keen competition, improved brewing methods, and skillful marketing and advertising, were the giants of the business. Beer made Milwaukee nationally known. All four of the large breweries were founded by German immigrants who brought their Old World brewing skills to Milwaukee with them.

Some of the buildings in the former Schlitz Brewing Company complex and many in the Pabst Brewing Company complex date from the late nineteenth century. The old brewhouse, built in 1886, is still among the Miller Brewing Company structures. The Frederick Miller Residence, built about 1884, stands nearby at 3713 West Miller Lane. Adjacent to it stood the Miller Beer Garden on a bluff overlooking the brewery.

Free brewery tours take place Monday–Friday throughout the year and on Saturday in summer. They conclude with a visit to the hospitality center, where visitors sample the brew.

The *Captain Frederick Pabst Mansion*,* 2000 West Wisconsin Avenue, is a Milwaukee City Landmark. The architectural firm of Ferry and Clas designed this home in the Flemish Renaissance style for Captain Frederick Pabst and his family in 1890. Frederick Pabst had been captain on a Great Lakes ship before he began his career in the brewing industry in 1864, when he became a partner in the Best Brewing Company, owned by his father-in-law, Phillip Best. Having succeeded to the presidency of the brewery in 1889, the captain changed its name to the Pabst Brewing company and made it the foremost producer of lager beer in the world.

An 1892 view of the Fred Miller Brewing Company, published in Milwaukee Real Estate Board, Milwaukee, 100 Photogravures, *1892. Courtesy State Historical Society of Wisconsin. WHi(X3)39849*

After Pabst's death in 1904, the house was sold to the Milwaukee Roman Catholic archdiocese as a home for the archbishop. The stable and carriage house were used as chancery offices. In May 1978 Wisconsin Heritages, Inc., a group of private citizens, decided to preserve the lovely old home from demolition. The group procured a grant from the U.S. Department of the Interior and a mortgage loan from the Savings and Loan Council of Milwaukee County. With additional proceeds from several fund-raising events, Wisconsin Heritages purchased the building. When the purchase was announced, many of the original furnishings were returned for display in a remarkably well-preserved interior. The mansion is used for lectures, concerts, and balls. Tours are conducted daily, including Sunday. Hours vary with the day and season. $

The *Pabst Theater*,* 144 East Wells Street, was designed by Otto Straack in a style variously described as opulent Victorian Baroque and Renaissance Revival by architectural historians. The theater was built between 1893 and 1895 for Captain Frederick Pabst at a cost of more than $300,000. In part the magnificent building reflects Pabst's efforts to capture city markets for his brew by creating fashionable outlets for sale and consumption in major cities across the country. To the lavishly built, furnished, and equipped Pabst Theater, a Pabst Theater Cafe was attached. What was more important was that the theater made Pabst a cultural leader in Milwaukee, a role often assumed by very successful late nineteenth-century businessmen.

From the 1890s until World War I, the Pabst was a German theater. With the growth of strong anti-German feeling in Wisconsin during World War I, German performances were dropped and productions became compatible with the Allied cause. The Historic American Buildings Survey comments on the theater's important role in Milwaukee's cultural life: "In 75 years of almost continuous use the Pabst has welcomed a dazzling array of talent."

The theater has been altered both on the exterior and in the interior over the years, but it retains most of its Victorian character and still serves performers and audiences well. It is the last of Milwaukee's nineteenth-century theaters. Tours available. $

The Germania (Brumder) Building at 135 West Wells Street reflects the era when German-language newspapers flourished. From a modest beginning—the founding of the *Wiskonsin-Banner*, a weekly, in 1844—the German press grew to include the *Volksfreund* and *Seebote* before the Civil War and the *Herold* and *Germania* thereafter. The combined circulation of German newspapers in Milwaukee in 1884 was twice as large as that of English-language papers.

The Germania Building, built in 1896 in Classical Revival style and topped by four hemispheric domes, represents the life work of George Brumder, publisher of the *Germania Abend-Post*, the *Milwaukee Herold* and the *Sonntag-Post*, the nation's foremost German-language newspaper and book publisher. Construction materials are granite, limestone, and pressed brick with terra-cotta trim.

Milwaukee's Polish Communities

Milwaukee's Polish communities developed in the late nineteenth century as thousands of Poles settled in the city, working in industry and as tailors, painters, plasterers, and saloon keepers. They came as part of the great migration of 2 to 3 million Poles to the United States between 1865 and 1920. Driven from their homeland by poverty, small land holdings, overpopulation, the military draft, and political oppression, the Poles came in search of a better life. About 30 Polish families settled in Milwaukee between 1848 and 1864. By 1920 the city's Polish-born population numbered about 23,000.

The Poles formed distinctive communities in the southeastern section of Milwaukee, including Mitchell Street, in the area between Brady Street and the Milwaukee River, and on Jones Island. They were almost exclusively Catholic, and much of their cultural life centered on the church. Seven Polish Catholic parishes had been organized by 1910.

The Poles participated vigorously in politics, becoming a political power that parties dared not ignore. They established Polish libraries, at least a hundred societies and organizations to further their social, cultural, economic, and political position, and five Polish newspapers. At the urging of the Polish community, the Milwaukee School Board agreed to introduce Polish into the elementary school curriculum in 1909.

Thrift, hard work, commitment to homeownership, and a strong sense of loyalty to church, family, and the mother country tended to keep the Poles a very conscious community as late as 1950. This was true despite the fact that the Polish community had developed an economic class structure and produced many successful businessmen and professionals and participated very actively in politics.

Examples of original Polish worker's homes built in the nineteenth and early twentieth centuries may be seen on East Locust Street between Humboldt Avenue and North Holton Street, and on 6th Street south of the expressway. Note the ground-level apartments in many of these homes. Designed to accommodate two families, these houses allowed the owner to rent out one level as a source of income.

St. Stanislaus' Roman Catholic Church, 1681 South 5th Street, built in 1872–1873, was the home of the city's first exclusively Polish parish, formed in 1863. Designed by Leonard Schmidtner and built at an original cost of $80,000, the church is constructed of cream brick trimmed with limestone. An extensive remodeling in 1962 replaced the copper domes on the twin towers with welded aluminum covered with gold leaf.

Very impressive is *St. Josaphat Basilica*,* located at 601 West Lincoln Avenue. The Polish parishioners of St. Josaphat's wanted to rebuild their church with more enduring materials after fire destroyed the frame sanctuary in 1889. While Erhard Brielmaier was preparing drawings for a new church, the pastor, Father Grutza, learned that the old Chicago Post Office was being razed. He purchased the marble, copper, wrought iron, carved stone, and paneled mahogany—500 freight-car loads—for the new church for $20,000. Brielmaier made new drawings, and construction began in 1897.

The structure is in the shape of a Latin cross with transept and a magnificent dome rising 250 feet above ground level. Interior decoration includes murals depicting St. Josaphat and events in Polish history. The stained glass windows were imported from Austria. St. Josaphat was designated a basilica in 1929, the first church built by Polish Americans to receive this status. Visitors may arrange for a guided tour of the basilica for a small fee. St. Josaphat is a Milwaukee City Landmark as well as a National Register site.

Three other distinguished south side church structures housed Polish parishioners. *St. Hyacinth's Roman Catholic Church*, located at West Becher Street and South 14th Street, was built in 1882–1883 after St. Stanislaus' congregation outgrew its church. When St. Hyacinth's congregation, in turn, outgrew its church, *St. Vincent de Paul*'s parish was formed in 1888. In 1900 the parish had Bernard Kolpacki, a Milwaukee Polish architect, design the present structure. An impressive 182-foot-tall building constructed of tan brick and limestone, the church has two copper-domed towers. The style is similar to German Renaissance. The church is at West Mitchell and South 21st Streets.

Ss. Cyril and Methodius Catholic Church, at the intersection of West

Interior of the St. Josaphat Basilica from a photograph entered in a 1951 contest by Vernon A. Boyd, Milwaukee. Courtesy State Historical Society of Wisconsin. WHi(X3)2628

Annunciation Greek Orthodox Church, May 1977. Photo by Allan Bogue.

Hayes Avenue, West Windlake Avenue, and South 15th Street, was also designed by Bernard Kolpacki for a Polish congregation. In contrast with St. Vincent's, the 1893 structure is in the Victorian Gothic style and built with cream-colored brick with orange terracotta and sheet copper trim. The parishioners came from St. Hyacinth's and St. Josaphat's parishes.

The Greek Neighborhood

Most of Milwaukee's Greek immigrants came to the city early in twentieth century, leaving adverse economic conditions in their homeland to search for a better livelihood. Congregating in the old Third Ward lying south of East Wisconsin Avenue and between the Milwaukee River and Lake Michigan, and in the Fourth Ward as well, Milwaukee's Greeks numbered between 4,000 and 5,000 in 1922. Most found jobs in Milwaukee's tanneries, in the iron and steel mills, in railroad construction, and in service occupations. Perhaps as many as 130 went into the confectionery, restaurant, coffee house, shoe shine, grocery, barber, floral, butchering, and saloon businesses.

Of the many Greek institutions transplanted to Milwaukee, probably the Greek Orthodox church was the most important. The Church of the Annunciation of the Milwaukee Hellenic Community was formally organized in 1906. In 1914 the community completed a church at Broadway and Knapp Streets. A second parish, Ss. Constantine and Helen, was constituted in 1922 as a result of political divisions in the Greek community. Since World War II, as a result of the movement of Milwaukee's Greeks away from the downtown area, new churches have been built in Wauwatosa.

Frank Lloyd Wright designed the new *Annunciation Greek Orthodox Church** at 9400 West Congress Street. Completed in 1961, the $1.5 million building has excited interest and admiration ever since. The blue-tiled dome, which rises 45 feet above the main building, is 104 feet in diameter. The building is in the form of a Greek cross. Traditional Byzantine colors of gold and blue have been used throughout the interior. Recent memorial gifts made possible the addition of stained glass windows beneath the dome and on the entrance doors. As well as being on the National Register of Historic Places, Annunciation Greek Orthodox Church is a Milwaukee County Landmark.

Visitors are welcome at services on Sunday. Groups of 20 or more may take guided tours for a small fee.

Built in 1969, the church currently housing the *Ss. Constantine and Helen* congregation is located at 2160 Wauwatosa Avenue in Wauwatosa. While the original downtown Greek neighborhood is gone, these churches symbolize the success of Milwaukee's Greek immigrants in adapting to American life and the great importance of the church in their lives.

(3) Milwaukee County Zoo
10001 West Bluemound Road
The Milwaukee County Zoo successfully creates the illusion that one is seeing animals in their natural surroundings. Animals from all over the world are grouped by continents. Native Wisconsin fish and wildlife have not been forgotten. Visitors can see small animals in a woodland setting from the interior and exterior windows of a split-fieldstone building. In the Reptile House is a miniature Lake Wisconsin, home for native Wisconsin fish species. The Bird House is de-

signed to allow visitors to walk among the birds.

When Milwaukee's Zoo, which dates from the 1890s, reached capacity in the early 1960s, the present facility was constructed. A children's area was opened in 1971. Two small passenger trains carry visitors around the grounds, giving them an overview of the entire zoo collection. A Zoomobile provides shorter rides along paths between exhibits. There is a cafeteria in the entrance building. Open daily at 9:00 A.M. Closing hours vary. In fall and winter 4:30 P.M. is closing time; in summer, it is 5:00 P.M. Monday–Saturday, and 6:00 P.M. on Sunday. $

(4) Mitchell Park Horticultural Conservatory

524 South Layton Boulevard

Three aluminum- and glass-sheathed precast concrete domes were completed between 1964 and 1967 to house the Mitchell Park Conservatory. Each of the 87-foot domes has its own climate, yet the three are linked into one complex. From the entrance foyer visitors may choose to enter the arid environment of the Southwest, a tropical rain forest, or a frequently changed seasonal display. Humidities and temperatures vary considerably, but circulating fans keep the atmosphere comfortable.

The present Mitchell Park Conservatory replaces one built in the park in 1898. It is located in one of the earliest parks laid out in the city of Milwaukee and overlooks the once-busy industrial Menomonee Valley. John Lendrum Mitchell gave part and sold part of the parkland to the city. Mitchell was a U.S. senator for Wisconsin and the son of Alexander Mitchell, a prominent Milwaukee banker, financier, and railroad magnate. Open year round, Monday–Friday, 9:00 A.M.–5:00 P.M.; Saturday and Sunday, 9:00 A.M.–8:00 P.M. $

(5) Walker's Point Historic District*

Roughly bounded by the freeway, Menomonee Canal, and Scott, 2nd, and West Virginia Streets

Walker's Point was one of Milwaukee's three earliest-platted settlements. It was named for George H. Walker, who in 1834 built a small trading post on a point of land jutting into the Menomonee River. When ratification of Indian treaties made the land available for white settlers, Walker platted the area still known as Walker's Point. It was joined with former Juneautown and Kilbourntown as part of the City of Milwaukee in 1846.

This neighborhood was named to the National Register of Historic Places in 1978 because many of its buildings reflect nineteenth-century history. German and Scandinavian immigrants lived here, followed by people from Slavic countries at the turn of the century and by Spanish-speaking residents today. Architectural styles vary from the Greek Revival structures of the 1850s to the Victorian Gothic homes built some years later.

Holy Trinity–Our Lady of Guadalupe Roman Catholic Church* was built at 605 South 4th Street for a German-speaking congregation in 1849. In 1965 Spanish-speaking members of the Our Lady of Guadalupe congregation merged with Holy Trinity, and the combined congregations now occupy the 1849 brick and stone building, which is listed on the National Register of Historic Places. Designed by a Milwaukee architect, Victor Schulte, the building is Romanesque in style. The octagon steeple was added in 1862.

Historic Milwaukee offers tours of the architecture of the older parts of the city, including Walker's Point. Its headquarters are located in the Tivoli Palm Garden Building, 504 West National Avenue, recently restored on the exterior as a Schlitz Brewery facility and housing also the Milwaukee Ballet Company. Arrangements for tours may be made at 504 National Avenue during the summer months. The mailing address is P.O. Box 2132, Milwaukee, WI 53201. $

(6) Daniel Webster Hoan Memorial Bridge and Port of Milwaukee

Highway I-794

The Hoan Memorial Bridge spans Jones Island, the location of Milwaukee's outer harbor and the harbor entrance. Beneath this bridge pass ocean-going vessels from all over the world and Great Lakes carriers during the shipping season. The harbor facilities include cargo terminal buildings, rail and truck connections, and some of the largest heavy-lift cranes on the Great Lakes. A municipal car ferry terminal, built in 1929, served the Chesapeake & Ohio Railway Company for many years. Also located on Jones Island is a sewage treatment plant completed in 1925.

Between the Jones Island peninsula and the mainland originally lay a swampy area, which was dredged in 1933 for the use of larger lake freighters. During the winter more than 30 ships moor here, including the Great Lakes fleet of the U.S. Steel Corporation.

During the 1920s, Milwaukee's long-

Biking by the Milwaukee River under the center span of the Daniel Webster Hoan Memorial Bridge. Courtesy Milwaukee County Historical Society.

time Socialist mayor, Daniel Webster Hoan, often called visitors' attention to the beauty of Milwaukee's bay, which he called more lovely than the famed Bay of Naples. For this reason his name has been given to the bridge that spans the harbor entrance and speeds traffic from the south side to downtown Milwaukee. Although the value of such a bridge had been discussed in Milwaukee's common council since the 1930s, it opened for traffic for the first time in November 1977. The day before vehicle traffic began, pedestrians flocked across the bridge to enjoy the marvelous view that drivers, in the interest of safety, have to forego.

(7) Milwaukee County War Memorial Center and Milwaukee Art Museum

750 North Lincoln Memorial Drive

In 1957 Eero Saarinen, the Finnish-born Detroit architect, designed the Milwaukee County War Memorial and Art Museum. These were among the last buildings in his distinguished career. The idea of a war memorial in the form of a community and cultural center had been publicly discussed as early as 1944. Saarinen's design combined facilities for veterans' services and a much-needed art museum in one structure. On the west side is the Wisconsin artist Edmund Lewandowski's mosaic depicting in roman numerals the dates of World War II and the Korean War. The names of Milwaukee's war dead are inscribed on black granite blocks around a reflecting pool in the open court. David Kahler designed a 1975 addition to the original building that quadrupled gallery space. Mrs. Harry Lynde Bradley gave hundreds of modern European and American works to the center's collections and $1 million toward the construction of the new wing.

The museum's collections range chronologically from ancient Egyptian to contemporary American works, with great strength in nineteenth- and twentieth-century European and American art. Open Tuesday, Wednesday, Friday, Saturday, 10:00 A.M.–5:00 P.M.; Thursday, noon–9:00 P.M.; Sunday, 1:00–6:00 P.M. Closed Mondays. $

North of the Milwaukee County War Memorial Center is Juneau Park lagoon, where in winter generations of Milwaukee children have delighted in feeding the ducks that collect on its open water. The lagoon froze over every winter until a Milwaukee industrialist contributed an aerating device that keeps ice from forming. In summer the Milwaukee County Park Commission's McKinley Marina, north of the lagoon, provides berths for the vessels of the city's many boating enthusiasts. The sight of hundreds of white sails offshore during a weekend sailboat race delights lakefront watchers.

(8) Milwaukee County Historical Center*

910 North 3rd Street

The Milwaukee County Historical Center, a City Landmark, occupies a former bank building, built of limestone in modified French Renaissance style between 1911 and 1913 for the Second Ward Savings Bank. Decades after the bank's merger with the First Wisconsin National Bank, the building was donated to Milwaukee County for use by the Historial Society for its headquarters, research library, and museum exhibits of Milwaukee history. Although the vaults no longer hold money, they are full of valuable documents of Milwaukee's past. Special exhibits include a panorama painters' display, a transportation hall, and displays of women's fashions and early firefighting and military equipment. One area is restored to its original appearance as part of the bank, and another is a recreation of Alfred Uihlen's parlor from his home near the Schlitz Brewery. Open Monday–Friday, 9:30 A.M.–5:00 P.M.; Saturday, 10:00 A.M.–5:00 P.M.; and Sunday, 1:00–5:00 P.M. Guided tours may be arranged. Free.

(9) Pere Marquette Park

West Kilbourn Avenue to West State

Milwaukee County Historical Center. Courtesy Milwaukee County Historical Society.

Street at the Milwaukee River
Lying between the Milwaukee County Historical Center and the Milwaukee River, Pere Marquette Park provides a beautiful open green space between the Historical Center and the Performing Arts Center directly across the river. The park is named for Father Jacques Marquette, who may have camped on this site from November 23 to November 27, 1674. Marquette and his two assistants, Pierre and Jacques, were traveling south to found a mission for the Illinois Indians at Kaskaskia, Illinois. Marquette's health forced him to cut short his visit to the Illinois, and he died in May 1675 on the eastern shore of Lake Michigan while en route to Sault Ste. Marie (see pp. 281–282). The park is a Milwaukee City Landmark and a Wisconsin Registered Landmark.

(10) MacArthur Square and Milwaukee Public Museum

800 West Wells Street
Surrounded by city, county, and state governmental buildings, MacArthur Square is an open space with landscaped gardens. The square covers an underground parking structure, constructed in 1967 after many years of planning. From the square the visitor has access to the Milwaukee County Courthouse, the Milwaukee Public Safety Building, and the Police Administration Building. The Wisconsin State Office Building is across the street to the east, and farther east stands City Hall with its imposing tower. On the south lawn is Robert Dean's bronze statue of General Douglas MacArthur, facing north. Although born in Arkansas, MacArthur often referred to Milwaukee as his hometown because his father and grandfather had lived here and he himself was living here at the time of his appointment to West Point by a Milwaukee congressman.

The Milwaukee Public Museum, operated by the county, is housed in a $6.5 million structure completed in 1963. It specializes in natural history and history. Displays are skillfully and creatively organized to unify these fields and to introduce the visitor to the human experience in the natural environment.

Those interested in Lake Michigan history will enjoy especially The Streets of Old Milwaukee display and the museum's extensive collection on Woodland Indians and North American Indians found in various parts of the museum.

The museum began with a natural history collection of 19,000 specimens made by Peter Engelmann, a nineteenth-century schoolmaster. In 1881 the Natural History Society of Wisconsin gave the collection to the city of Milwaukee on the understanding that it would furnish a free public museum for its display. The Milwaukee Public Museum opened in 1884.

The museum developed rapidly, not only in size but also in innovative display techniques and services offered to the public. Its officially stated objectives are "the collection and preservation of collections, and the interpretation of those collections

pany was organized in the late nineteenth century to utilize limestone in the bed of the Milwaukee River, but its owners found by 1909 that they could not compete with producers of Portland cement. The Park Commission purchased the cement company's land with the intention of creating a park. Development took place in the 1930s.

Kilbourntown House, also known as the Benjamin Church House,* stands on Estabrook Park Drive and is accessible from either Capitol Drive or Hampton Avenue. This beautiful Greek Revival structure, built in 1844, originally stood on North 4th Street in downtown Milwaukee. In the late 1930s, when the house was threatened with destruction, the WPA moved it for Milwaukee County to Estabrook Park. The National Society of Colonial Dames in Wisconsin furnished the house in the style of the 1840s. While not all of the furnishings are original to the house, they are all authentic to the period before 1865. Because the house originally stood in the Kilbourntown area of Milwaukee, it is called Kilbourntown House. Operated by the Milwaukee County Historical Society, the site is open for visitors from the end of June to Labor Day, Tuesdays, Thursdays, and Saturdays, 10:00 A.M.–5:00 P.M.; Sundays, 1:00–5:00 P.M. Free.

Captain Frederick Pabst's Whitefish Bay Resort, one of many fashionable dining and drinking establishments he had built in the late nineteenth century to publicize his brew. Courtesy Milwaukee County Historical Society.

Whitefish Bay

Realtors conceived of the Whitefish Bay area as an ideal location for a residential suburb and began platting a development in the 1880s. Rumors that a railroad repair shop would locate there in 1892 triggered a hasty promotional effort and the incorporation of the village. Several miles of sidewalk were laid before the financial panic of 1893 slowed development plans.

Resorts rather than residential sites first attracted many Milwaukeeans to Whitefish Bay. Famous among them was Captain Frederick Pabst's resort established in 1889. Developed as an 18-acre park with an ornate pavilion, a bandstand, shooting gallery, and Ferris wheel, Pabst's resort became a high-class beer garden. Milwaukeeans biked there or rode in horse-drawn buggies over a graveled toll road to enjoy the unspoiled lakeshore and a planked whitefish dinner. Others boarded the *Bloomer Girl* at a Milwaukee dock for a short cruise to Whitefish Bay, or took the steam railway. The resort closed in 1914, and nothing remains.

Named for the whitefish once so plentiful here, the popular resort of the early twentieth century became a wealthy residential suburb in the 1920s. Prominent among the Milwaukee industrialists who built mansions in Whitefish Bay in the post–World War I period was Herman Uihlein of the Schlitz Brewing Company. The Italian Renaissance *Uihlein Residence*, built in 1918, stands at 5270 North Lake Drive.

Development during the 1920s swelled Whitefish Bay's population from 880 to about 5,000 in 1930. In 1940 only about 40 percent of the residential suburb had been built up. During the post–World War II prosperity, Whitefish Bay expanded rapidly. The current population is about 15,000. Village government carefully restricted development to preserve the town's residential character,

to control business activity, and to promote aesthetic qualities. Whitefish Bay's voters early displayed their ability to control their environment when, in the late twenties, they forced the Chicago and North Western Railroad to remove tracks that ran through the center of the village. The railroad right-of-way became Marlborough Drive. Park development is further evidence of civic pride and attention to aesthetics. In *Old School Park*, adjacent to Marlborough Drive, the village maintains lovely flower gardens. Two parks—Big Bay Park and Klode Park—front on Lake Michigan. Both are accessible from Hy W-32.

Fox Point

Now an upper-class residential community of about 7,600, Fox Point goes back well over a century. Within the present limits of the town, Dutch immigrant families settled on small farms in the 1840s. They established the Bethlehem Dutch Reformed Church, school, and cemetery. Although the Dutch settlement did not grow and develop as did Cedar Grove (see site 29), Oostburg, and Gibbsville, some of the settlers and their descendants remained for many decades. Meanwhile, pioneer farmers of other nationalities, principally Germans, also settled in the area.

But it was not until the 1920s that Fox Point's beautiful lakefront appealed to wealthy merchants, manufacturers, and financiers from Milwaukee as a prime location for fine homes. Fox Point organized as a village in 1926. A 1941 publication described it as "a long, wooded village set among gardens and trees along the lake; many a 'Private Road' sign lists in gilt letters the names of those who live behind the fences and hedges that shield their houses from the road." It was then still small, with a population of less than 500. Its greatest growth has come since World War II.

Fox Point Sites of Interest

Doctor's Park, turn east off Hy W-32 onto Dean Road

In 1928 Dr. Joseph Schneider, a well-known eye specialist, died and left his land to Milwaukee County for a park and nature preserve so that city dwellers could enjoy the natural landscape with its flowers and trees. The memorial gateway to Doctor's Park was dedicated in 1936.

Dutch Pioneer Cemetery, adjacent to Doctor's Park on Fox Lane

The cemetery where Fox Point's Dutch immigrants buried their dead adjoins Doctor's Park on the south. Descendants of these pioneers restored the long-neglected burial ground in 1928 and erected a monument honoring them. The cemetery is a Wisconsin Registered Landmark.

Bayside

The newest of Milwaukee's northern lakeshore suburbs, Bayside was incorporated in 1953, including land in both Milwaukee and Ozaukee Counties. Originally restricted to permit single-family dwellings only, Bayside has since sanctioned multifamily units. Eighty percent of Bayside's adult male workers are employed in white-collar jobs. Bayside passed an open housing ordinance in 1967. Its 1980 population was about 4,700.

Bayside Site of Interest

Schlitz Audubon Center, 1111 East Brown Deer Road

The Schlitz Foundation presented over a hundred acres of land to the Audubon Society in 1971 for a nature education center. The Uihlein family, owners of the Schlitz Brewing Company in Milwaukee, had purchased the land in the 1880s to provide pasture for tired brewery horses and a picnic site for the family. The Uihleins dubbed it "Nine Mile Farm" because it was located nine miles from the brewery.

Now the water tower that was used to provide water for the horses is almost the only reminder of the old farm. It has been turned into an environmental education facility. A cedar and glass interpretive center for classes and meetings opened in 1973. Three miles of hiking trails lead to ponds, deep ravines, and the beach. Wavecut terraces, probably formed at least 7,000 years ago, rise 15 feet above the present shoreline of Lake Michigan here. In winter cross-country skiers use the trails. Films and other nature programs are presented in the center's buildings on Saturday afternoons.

Open Tuesday–Sunday, 9:00 A.M.–5:00 P.M. Audubon members free; nonmembers $.

25. Port Ulao

Highway I-43 to exit 20, east on Ulao Road

Port Ulao flourished briefly as a refueling point for lake steamers plying Lake Michigan's waters between Chicago

and the upper Great Lakes. In 1847, as settlers in the Port Washington area were busily clearing timber from lakeshore lands, James T. Gifford, a resident of Elgin, Illinois, and former Illinois state legislator, founded a cordwood business at Port Ulao. Buying felled trees from neighboring farmers, Gifford milled them into cordwood and delivered them from bluff to beach by a system of chutes. Steamboats loaded the cordwood from a pier built out into the lake. Gifford's business served both Chicago-bound and northbound traffic.

Foreseeing the time when local wood supplies would dwindle, Gifford in 1847 secured a charter from the territorial legislature to construct a road west from Port Ulao to the Wisconsin River. He planned to tap the supply of northern Wisconsin pine logs regularly floated downstream. Wagons would haul them to the port.

For unknown reasons, Gifford left Port Ulao in 1850 when only three miles of the road had been built, having sold the business to John Randolph Howe, a Great Lakes ship captain. The road was never completed as originally planned, and when the local cordwood supply was exhausted after the Civil War, Port Ulao declined.

The town is perhaps best known in history as the boyhood home of Charles Guiteau, assassin of President James A Garfield, and as the port where troops landed to quell the riot in Port Washington in 1862 (see site 26).

Port Ulao has almost vanished. Now farmland and empty beach lie where the town and cordwood business once flourished. Ghost Town Tavern stands east of Hy I-43 on Ulao Road. About a mile and a half farther east, on the bluff overlooking Lake Michigan, the remains of the wagon road to the beach can be detected in spring, when apple trees and lilac bushes planted along the road are in bloom.

26. Port Washington
Highway W-32

A group of Yankee land speculators, headed by Wooster Harrison, an experienced town site promoter with real estate interests in Walker's Point and elsewhere, established a town site at the mouth of Sauk Creek in 1835. First known as Wisconsin City and later as Sauk Washington, the village was officially named Port Washington in 1844. The little settlement, beautifully sited on Lake Michigan and apparently blessed with the potential for a man-made harbor, boomed until the panic of 1837, languished, and then revived in the 1840s.

Thereafter Port Washington grew as a trade and service center for a developing agricultural hinterland. Until the 1870s, when two railroad lines paralleling the lake were built through Ozaukee County, farmers hauled their produce to town by wagon. Lake steamers and sailing vessels carried it to market. From the 1840s through the 1870s, Ozaukee County residents depended more completely on the lake than ever before or since. In those years Port Washingtonians built a pier out to deep water, acquired a lighthouse, pressed Congress for harbor improvements, and with federal and local money began to create an artificial harbor. The port hummed with daily arrivals and departures.

After the organization of Ozaukee County in 1853, Port Washington became the county seat. During these formative years a small fishing industry developed along with small industries that processed the products of Ozaukee County's prosperous farms and produced manufactured goods for local consumption. Saw and grist mills, a brickyard, tannery, brewery, a cheese factory, and a company manufacturing agricultural machinery prospered. In the early 1870s Port Washington acquired its first iron foundry. In 1882 it incorporated as a city.

The industry that made Port Washington famous for many decades, the Wisconsin Chair Company, was founded in 1888 and went out of business in 1954. A 1917 gazetteer called it "the largest chair factory in the world." It stood on the lakefront at the foot of East Pier Street and extended south to Grand Avenue.

Port Washington and Ozaukee County's earliest settlers came from the eastern United States. Beginning in the 1840s, immigrants from the Germanies and from Luxembourg moved into the area to develop farms. By 1860 Germans and Luxembourgers made up over half the county population. Sturdy and hardworking, they made a marked and impressive contribution to local economic and cultural development. They gained national attention in the fall of 1862 when they staged a mass protest against the Civil War draft.

The local draft commissioner, a German Protestant and a Democrat, attempted at that time to draw names to fill Ozaukee County's quota of Union troops. Luxembourgers and a handful of German farmers, supported by an angry mob of 1,000 draft pro-

In this etching made sometime between 1896 and 1936, Paul Hammersmith of Milwaukee captured the beauty of a fishing tug in the Port Washington Harbor. Courtesy State Historical Society of Wisconsin. WHi(X3)40321

testers, assailed Commissioner William A. Pors, beat him up, and destroyed the draft box before going on a spree of wrecking and plundering the town. Pors escaped to Milwaukee and summoned federal help. Over 750 heavily armed officers and men of the 28th Wisconsin Volunteers set sail for Port Ulao and landed there, four miles south of Port Washington. They marched overland, surrounded the rebellious town, and rounded up the rioters. The Civil War draft, generally unpopular but especially so with new Americans of Catholic-Democratic allegiance, led to similar disturbances in several other Wisconsin communities. One newspaper reporter stated that parts of Port Washington looked as if a tornado had struck them.

The directions of Port Washington's early economic development have continued in modified form to the present. The harbor is still used commercially, now mainly for inbound cargoes of coal. For more than a hundred years, efforts to make the harbor safe failed. High winds continued to smash boats against the shoreline as they did the *Toledo* in 1856. However, extensive 1980 harbor improvements seem to have resolved the problem. Pleasure craft fill the harbor in the warm months. The commercial fishing industry has diminished, but sport fishing for chinook, coho, and lake trout grows.

Industry has survived, changed, and increased over 125 years. Metal industries predominate, producing foundry products; road construction, outdoor power, foundry, and water clarification equipment; and synthetics. Port Washington industries now produce for a national rather than a local or regional market as they did a century ago. A Wisconsin Electric Power Company plant serving southern Wisconsin is sited here. Port Washington, "The Little City of Seven Hills," population 8,600, remains the seat of county government.

Port Washington Sites of Interest

(1) St. Mary's Roman Catholic Church*

430 North Johnson Street

The origins of St. Mary's Catholic parish go back to the German-speaking Catholic immigrants from Luxembourg

St. Mary's Roman Catholic Church at Port Washington stands atop the highest hill. It has long been a landmark to guide lake craft. The beautiful interior is well worth visiting. Photo by Margaret Bogue.

and the Germanies who made Ozaukee County and Port Washington their home. Three families gathered to hold services in a private home in 1847. Two years later 20 families who needed a house of worship built a small frame church on Lighthouse Bluff, the highest hill in Port Washington, on land donated by Hiram Johnson, one of Port Washington's early settlers. In 1853 St. Mary's received a resident priest. In 1860 the growing congregation undertook construction of a handsome stone church. Soon it was too small. The present structure, a simple Gothic Revival edifice constructed from local limestone with a richly decorated interior, dates from 1881–1884. It was designed by a Milwaukee architect, Henry Messmer, to serve over 200 families in the parish. This beautiful structure dominates Port Washington's profile. The three bells in the tower are from the second church on this site.

(2) Ozaukee County Courthouse*
109 West Main Street
Port Washington has been the county seat of Ozaukee County since 1854. When its first courthouse, a far less imposing building than the present one, proved inadequate, the county board authorized plans for a new structure. In 1902 the Richardsonian Romanesque structure, designed by the Milwaukee architect Frederick A. Graf, was built of blue-gray limestone from the nearby Cedarburg quarry. The imposing oak staircase and oak wainscotting are notable features of the interior. Above the five-story-high clocktower perches a golden eagle, embellished with gold leaf. A modern addition was made to the building in 1969.

(3) Dodge House (Pebble House)*
146 South Wisconsin Street
Edward Dodge, a young blacksmith, built this one-and-a-half story Greek Revival house in 1848 on the south bank of Sauk Creek. Dodge brought the idea for his Wisconsin home with him from his native New York State, where cobblestone houses of this type were built between 1835 and 1845. It became fashionable in that decade to use beach stones from the shores of Lake Ontario selected for uniformity of size and color.

The pebbles forming the exterior walls of Dodge House came from the creek and Lake Michigan. Workmen matched them for size and color and laid the walls with a banded effect. Architectural historians consider the house an outstanding example of Wisconsin cobblestone architecture. The Wisconsin Electric Power Company moved the house to its present location in 1931 for use as a gatehouse. It is not open to the public.

(4) U.S. Coast Guard Station
311 East Johnson Street
Solon Johnson donated land on North Bluff to the federal government for the purpose of establishing a lighthouse in 1849. The first lighthouse was a wooden structure, replaced in 1860 with this more substantial brick building. The basement served as keeper's quarters and the light stood atop the roof. Although the light has long since been removed to the government breakwater, the Coast Guard still uses the building.

(5) Sites Relating to the *Toledo* Sinking
Smith Brothers Restaurant and Union Cemetery
The Port Washington harbor has proven an untrustworthy haven in storms. Its original deficiencies were well demonstrated in October 1856, when the *Toledo*, one of the larger propeller steamboats on the lakes, lay at anchor at Port Washington. A sudden storm literally crushed the boat to pieces on the shore, with the loss of at least 40 and perhaps 55 lives. Three persons survived the disaster. The bodies recovered from this tragedy are buried in Union Cemetery. Close by stands the original anchor from the *Toledo* as a memorial to the dead. In

the parking lot of Smith Brothers Restaurant at the harbor is another anchor, similar to the *Toledo*'s, displayed along with a brass plaque describing the *Toledo* disaster.

(6) Eghart House
316 Grand Avenue
Leopold Eghart, an Austrian immigrant, admired the view from this spot when he arrived in Port Washington in 1849. In 1872 he purchased the home built here by Byron Teed. Eghart served as a judge in the Ozaukee County court from 1878 to 1901. The Eghart family occupied this frame Victorian home until the death of daughter Elsa in 1969. The home now belongs to the W. J. Niederkorn Museum, which has furnished it with items that belonged to the Eghart family and other Port Washington residents between 1850 and 1900.

Open Sundays from mid-May through October, 1:00–4:00 P.M. Group tours may be arranged. $

Blacksmith Shop, Ozaukee County Pioneer Village. Photo By Margaret Bogue.

27. Side Trip to Ozaukee County Pioneer Village

From Port Washington take Hy W-33 west and County Trunk I north to Hawthorne Hills County Park to visit "Pioneer Village," a well-developed historical site owned and operated by the Ozaukee County Historical Society. Here the society has assembled a group of 15 buildings reflecting Ozaukee County's nineteenth-century history that would have been torn down if left in their original locations. The process began in 1961 when the society rescued an 1850 log house from destruction and moved it to this site. Included in the structures are an 1848 trading post, barns, sheds, carpenter and blacksmith shops, a schoolhouse, and frame, log, and German half-timber houses. Open from the first Sunday in June through the second Sunday in October, Wednesdays, Saturdays, and Sundays, noon–5:00 P.M. Group tours may be arranged. $

28. Harrington Beach State Park

Highway W-32 and County Trunk D, 2 miles east of Belgium (FHPS)

This park, designed for day use only, was named for the first superintendent of the state park board, C. L. Harrington. Here, between 1894 and 1925, the Northwest Stone Company quarried limestone and company workers lived. The 23-acre quarry is now a picturesque little lake surrounded by white cedar trees and sumac. While the company operated, loads of crushed rock were hauled to the shore and loaded onto ships for transportation to Milwaukee or Chicago. The company burned some of the limestone in kilns on the property to make commercial lime. One of the old pot kilns remains. Nature and hiking trails lie around Quarry Lake and along the Lake Michigan shore. $

29. Cedar Grove

Highway I-43

Hard times and religious frictions in the Netherlands led to the migration of hundreds of Dutch families to American Midwest in the 1840s. Sheboygan County became one focal point of settlement. Dutch immigrants began arriving in the Cedar Grove area from New York State or directly from Holland in 1845. In 1847 the man who became spiritual leader for many of the settlers, Dominie Pieter Zonne, came first to Milwaukee and then to Sheboygan County, where a number of Dutch families had migrated earlier.

Cedar Grove and nearby Oostburg developed gradually as rural villages, centers for business and social life. The village of Amsterdam on the Lake Michigan shore competed with them for a time. There Dutch settlers developed a thriving fishery and built a pier into the lake, from which they shipped cordwood and lumber. But the fisheries declined rapidly, and the timber supply was soon exhausted. After a north-south railroad line was built through Cedar Grove and Oostburg in 1872, Amsterdam's fate was sealed. It declined while Cedar Grove, Oostburg, and Gibbsville (founded after the Civil War) prospered.

"De Visch." Photo by Margaret Bogue.

Most new settlements have their calamities, and so did the Dutch settlements in Holland Township, Sheboygan County. At least 127 Dutch immigrants died early Sunday morning on November 21, 1847, when their steamship, the *Phoenix*, caught fire within five miles of the Sheboygan harbor. About 25 survived the tragedy. An official Wisconsin marker north of Cedar Grove commemorates the disaster.

At Cedar Grove an annual Holland Festival, held on the last Friday and Saturday of July, commemorates the early Dutch settlers and the community's principal ethnic heritage. The program includes a parade, street scrubbing, and dances performed by Cedar Grove residents dressed in colorful Dutch costumes.

Cedar Grove Sites of Interest

(1) "De Visch"

The Cedar Grove Boosters Club presented this replica of a South Holland gristmill to the city in 1968. Serving as a decorative and symbolic information center, "De Visch" stands in a small park on Main Street.

(2) Het Museum

Main Street

Located in a blacksmith shop of the 1880s, the museum, a Cedar Grove Bicentennial Project, contains Dutch artifacts and memorabilia of the Cedar Grove area. The back room has displays of farm implements, tools, and a blacksmith's forge. Open June–Labor Day, Wednesday and Friday evenings, 7:00–9:00 P.M. $

30. Terry Andrae and John Michael Kohler State Park

Accessible from Highway I-43 and County Trunk KK (CFHS)

Terry Andrae and his wife experimented with the growth of vegetation in sandy soil at their summer home, Pine Dunes, built in 1924. Hoping to preserve the sand dunes, the Andraes set out many pine trees along the lakeshore. After Terry Andrae died in 1927, Mrs. Andrae presented 112 acres of land to the state to be used for a park. The park became so popular that it was necessary to add more land.

An adjacent second park development grew from the 221 acres presented to Wisconsin in 1965 by the

At the turn of the century and until 1930 the Sheboygan harbor was busy with passenger-freight steam boats. In the foreground the tug Peter Reiss *bears the name of one of Sheboygan's prominent businessmen. Courtesy State Historical Society of Wisconsin. WHi(X3)40550*

Kohler Foundation of Sheboygan. The two parks are administered as a single unit. There are two miles of beach with interesting sand dune formations, forests including white pines, oaks, elms, beeches, and sugar maples, and a wide variety of flora and fauna. The naturalist program at the parks includes guided nature hikes, evening programs during the summer months, and a new nature center–museum. $

31. Sheboygan

Highway I-43

A favored fishing location for Indians, the site of a North West Company fur trader's post in 1795 and of an independent American trader's cabin in 1820, the mouth of the Sheboygan River caught the attention of land speculators in the 1830s. In 1835 and 1836 a group of Yankees—"alien speculators," as one local historian has called them—platted the village and offered Sheboygan lots for sale in Chicago. Sheboygan grew to a village of 15 to 20 buildings before the panic of 1837. Real growth followed in the 1840s as American-born settlers and, after 1846, thousands of immigrants, many from the Germanies and the Netherlands, landed at Sheboygan's piers. They came in search of farmlands, attracted by the forests of beech, sugar maple, basswood, and oak that covered the Sheboygan River watershed.

Over the next two decades, as virgin forests were turned into wheat fields, Sheboygan grew. It served as the seat of local government, the trade and service center for a developing agricultural community, and focal point of lake passenger traffic and freight shipments. The lake served as the main artery of transportation until the building of north-south railroad lines in the 1870s. From the developing hinterland came pork, wheat, wool, lumber, shingles, and cordwood for export. A prosperous fishing industry produced whitefish for export. Into port came boatloads of pioneer settlers and essential food and manufactured goods not locally produced.

Sheboygan's initial prosperity depended upon the successful development of the lakeport. Residents succeeded in securing a federally constructed lighthouse in 1840 but did not persuade Congress to fund the first in a long series of harbor improvements until 1852. A U.S. lifesaving station was established in 1876.

In the mid-1840s shipbuilding emerged as a Sheboygan industry and remained an important one until the end of the nineteenth century. The year 1906 was the last time that *Polk's Wisconsin State Gazetteer* listed a shipyard and floating drydock among Sheboygan's businesses.

Sheboygan changed from being primarily a shipping point and trading center into a manufacturing city as well in the last half of the nineteenth century. Until the 1870s products of its cooperages, breweries, mills, tanneries, wagon and carriage factories, and agricultural machinery and furniture plants met the needs of the immediate area. Yet some of Sheboygan's manufactured products had always found their way beyond local markets.

After 1870 more and more were marketed nationally.

The production of chairs, tannery products, and furniture grew substantially after 1870 to assume a position of dominance among Sheboygan's diversified industries by the end of the century. Wooden chair and furniture plants employed 60 percent of Sheboygan's 5,300 wage earners in 1900. During the late nineteenth century, two new businesses developed that were destined ultimately to make metal industries more important than woodworking ones in Sheboygan's economy. German-born J. J. Vollrath and Austrian-born John M. Kohler founded iron enameled ware plants. At the turn of the century, Kohler established a large new factory four miles west of town (see site 32).

Notable also in Sheboygan's late nineteenth-century business development was the change in the character of exported agricultural products. Long a collecting and transshipment point for farm products from the surrounding countryside, Sheboygan became known as the "cheese city" as well as the "chair city." Sheboygan County farms had shifted from grain and mixed agricultural production to dairying.

Polk's Wisconsin State Gazetteer and Business Directory for 1917 characterized Sheboygan as "the liveliest manufacturing city of the west shore" aside from Chicago and Milwaukee. "Its six mammoth chair factories supply every civilized country in the world with chairs, and its enameling works are amongst the largest in the country. It has the largest excelsior factory in the state, several of the largest tanneries in the country, the largest coal and salt docks on the lakes and feeds the world with cheese." Annual manufacturing output was valued at $13 million.

As Wisconsin's hardwood supply diminished, so did the manufacture of wooden furniture. During Sheboygan's great industrial growth of the 1920s, the metal industries almost overtook furniture, and during World War II they did. The 1970 census showed the metal industries as the largest employers, with furniture, machinery, food, and construction ranking second through fifth.

Members of families prominent for decades in Sheboygan's industries—Vollrath, Jung, and Kohler, to mention conspicuous examples—still live in the city. The largest employer, the Kohler Company, manufacturers of plumbing fixtures, had 5,000 workers on the payroll in 1979. Twenty-three other manufacturers employ 100 or more workers each. They make a variety of products, including orthodontic equipment, furniture, industrial machinery, leather goods, dairy products, motor vehicle parts and accessories, plastics, stainless steel products, and clothing.

Sheboygan's manufacturing success owed much to a plentiful labor supply. Until World War I immigrants—principally from the Germanies—furnished much of that labor. They settled in Sheboygan by the thousands during the last half of the nineteenth century. After 1880 the city took on a German character: German-speaking immigrants occupied positions of leadership in some industries, German drama was performed often, and German actors and artists frequented nearby resorts. Singing societies, a symphony orchestra, aid societies and lodges, a political club, and the Turnverein had predominantly German memberships. Three German-language newspapers served the community. Sheboygan's German workers formed the backbone of the city's small, struggling labor unions at the turn of the century. A pre–World War I influx of immigrants from Lithuania, Russia (descendants of Germans colonized in the Volga River Valley in the eighteenth century), Slovenia and Croatia (now part of Yugoslavia), and Greece modified all this, and so did time. Yet adjectives like "neat," "orderly," "home-loving," and "homeowning," conventionally associated with German influence, were readily applied to Sheboygan in the late 1930s. In the 1960s and 1970s, an influx of Hispanic workers from Texas and Mexico joined the labor force in Sheboygan's metal industries. In 1980, 767 persons of Hispanic (primarily Mexican) origin lived in the city.

Lake Michigan's role in the industrial success of Sheboygan, now a city of about 48,000, has changed greatly over the last 140 years. At the outset the lake served as the main artery of trade and commerce. Now carriers of bulk cargoes, such as coal, are the main ships docking at the harbor. Other freight passes overland by truck and rail. The fishing industry, which employed 35 to 40 persons as late as the 1930s, is greatly diminished. Yet the lake still offers industrial Sheboygan a recreational resource for boating and sport fishing.

Sheboygan Sites of Interest

A combined driving and walking circuit through downtown Sheboygan provides a look at older structures that reflect many facets of the city's history.

Now the Vollrath Company makes a wide variety of stainless steel products. This illustration shows the enameling room when enameled ware was a major product. Courtesy State Historical Society of Wisconsin. WHi(W6)1185

Businesses, fishing shanties, industrial buildings, churches, residences, and public buildings illustrate the city's economic and social history during the late nineteenth and early twentieth centuries. A sampling rather than an exhaustive list of old structures is offered here. The sites are arranged with driving and walking convenience in mind. Those interested in a fuller list should consult *Prospects for the Past: A Study of Notable Architecture, Sheboygan Renewal Area, 1972*, prepared by the Redevelopment Authority of Sheboygan, and *Heritage Walk in Old Sheboygan*, prepared by Sheboygan County Landmarks, Ltd., in 1972. Both are available at the Mead Library on the 7th Street Mall.

(1) Trinity Evangelical Lutheran Church
824 Wisconsin Avenue
Sheboygan's large German-born population was affiliated with a number of religious groups: German Methodist Episcopal, Baptist, Evangelical, Reformed, and, most particularly, Lutheran and Roman Catholic. A 1910 local history identified 10 sizable and prosperous Sheboygan churches with distinctly German origins and predominantly German membership. They were important institutions in the German community as centers for spiritual guidance, education, charity, mutual aid, and social and cultural activities.

The Missouri Synod of the Evangelical Lutheran Church sent Reverend Selle on a journey through Wisconsin in 1848 to find out how well the spiritual needs of Lutherans were being served. He found no Lutheran church in Sheboygan. "The inhabitants," he reported, "are very industrious. For spiritual matters they show little concern." Five years later the Missouri Synod organized the Trinity Evangelical Lutheran congregation. Initially the Trinity congregation used a former Presbyterian church structure, but as more and more Germans arrived in Sheboygan, larger quarters became necessary. After fire destroyed the small church, the congregation voted to build a larger sanctuary. The cornerstone of the cream brick Gothic Revival structure at 824 Wisconsin Avenue was laid in 1869. Enlarged and altered over the years, the 1869 church is still used.

Trinity Evangelical Lutheran was the parent congregation for Bethlehem Lutheran, organized in 1889 to serve the growing number of southside German Lutherans. Construction began on the beautiful Gothic brick structure, located on the southwest corner of South 12th Street and Georgia Avenue, in 1889. One year later a second congregation, Immanuel Lutheran, organized and built a fine Gothic brick sanctuary at South 17th Street and Illinois Avenue. As a result of the establishment of these new congregations, Trinity lost 500 families and 400 parochial school students. The continued influx of German Lutherans into Sheboygan enabled Trinity to withstand the loss and to help establish St. Paul's Lutheran congregation on the north side in 1905.

For many decades German was the principal language used in Trinity Lutheran services. In 1922 the congregation decided to have regular English services as well.

(2) Commercial Buildings
500 and 600 blocks of North 8th Street
On 8th Street, Sheboygan's main business street during the nineteenth century, stand several older commercial buildings that record the architectural tastes of the city's German businessmen. The cream brick *Zaegel Building** at 632 North 8th has ornate brickwork, varied in pattern, texture, and color. It was built in 1886 by Max R. Zaegel, a pharmacist. Charles and Jacob Imig built the Italianate *Imig Block* (625–629 North 8th Street) in 1881–1882 to house their clothing and shoe stores as well as the Muhlendorf drugstore. John and Martin A. Bodenstein, sons of an early Sheboygan tailor, built the Romanesque sandstone commercial structure at 520 North 8th Street in 1893 as a clothing store.

(3) Jung Carriage Factory*
829–835 Pennsylvania Avenue
Jacob Jung, a German immigrant, came to Sheboygan in 1854 to find work as a wagonmaker. Hired by Brothers and John, a small wagon company, Jung soon found himself its proprietor when financial problems forced Brothers and John to deed their shop to him in compensation for back pay. His small business grew and prospered in the 1860s and 1870s.

About 1885 Jung built this brick structure with its interesting façade to house his wagon shop. Here he and later his sons, William and Jacob, Jr., produced high-grade, custom-made carriages, wagons, and sleighs. The business was always a small one, never engaging in mass production. Quality, craftsmanship, and individuality of product were their trademarks. At the Wesley W. Jung Carriage Museum at Greenbush, restored vehicles made in the Jung Carriage Factory are on display (see site 34).

(4) Jung Shoe Company
620 South 8th Street
Henry Jung, son of Jacob Jung, founder of the carriage factory, was a very successful manufacturer and banker. Jung founded the Jung Shoe Company in 1892 and was among the incorporators of the Sheboygan Shoe Company in 1909. These businesses are illustrative of the importance of the leather goods industry in Sheboygan's economy. The 1912 history of Sheboygan County eulogized him, one of its patrons, as displaying the "sterling characteristics of his German ancestry," "wide awake" and "alert." The Jung Shoe Company building complex includes three attractive industrial structures built in 1906, 1909, and 1916 to house the growing business.

(5) Ss. Cyril and Methodius' Church
820 New Jersey Avenue

Saints Cyril and Methodius, September 1984. Photo by Margaret Bogue.

The Catholic church adopted the policy of founding new parishes to accommodate the desire of different national groups for churches where priests could minister to them in their native languages. The German, Slavic, and Lithuanian Catholic parishes in Sheboygan clearly illustrate this policy.

In 1910 over 1,000 persons of Slovenian and Croatian origin lived in Sheboygan and worked in its factories. Many of them came from copper- and iron-mining communities in Michigan and Minnesota, where as immigrants they had initially sought jobs.

Ss. Cyril and Methodius' parish was organized in 1910 to meet the needs of the city's growing Slovenian and Croatian Catholics, who did not feel at home in German-speaking churches. Dedicated in 1911, this impressive stone Romanesque church, topped by a dome and cross that give it an eastern European character, overlooks the Sheboygan River. The architect was Frank Geib, who also designed the adjacent school, built in 1918.

(6) Immanuel Evangelical Lutheran Church
1634 Illinois Avenue
See no. (1).

(7) St. Peter Claver Catholic Church
Clara Avenue and South 11th Street
St. Peter Claver parish was organized on the south side in 1886 as an offshoot of Holy Name parish (see no. [13]), which had grown very large over the years in serving the Catholic German population, principally immigrants from southern Germany. The church's first pastor, Rev. J. P. Van Treeck, was born in Geldern in the German Rhineland. The growing parish constructed an imposing buff brick sanctuary, priest's home, and school in 1907 and 1908. The church structure has been somewhat modified over the years. One addition obscures the beautiful Romanesque arches of the original entrance.

(8) St. Spyridon's Greek Orthodox Church
1425 South 10th Street
The 1910 federal census showed 336 persons of Greek birth living in Sheboygan. Although only a small part of the city's 8,660 foreign-born residents (33 percent of the total population), the Greek community was close-knit and already had its own church. Sheboygan's earliest emigrants from Greece came in the late 1890s and were followed by several hundred more before 1914. A large proportion of them were men, single and married without their families, from the southern Greek provinces of Arcadia and Messinia. They came looking for work and planned to remain only long enough to accumulate money to take back to Greece and thus improve their economic status.

Sheboygan's Greeks lived on Indiana Avenue between South 7th and 14th Streets, a partially developed area of the city. Many found jobs in tanneries and furniture factories and with the railroads, while others launched small businesses, confectioneries, groceries, saloons, barbershops, bakeries, and tailoring shops. This tight-knit Greek-speaking community developed its own social life and its own governing council.

In 1904 its residents decided to organize a congregation, St. Spyridon's Greek Orthodox Community. They built the simple cream brick church in 1906 and added the tower in 1916. Built at a time when Sheboygan's Greeks were unpopular with some other residents, who criticized their overcrowded housing, poverty, competition with American labor, and "foreign" ways, the original church remains as a monument to the struggles of the early Greek immigrants and to the continued presence of Greek Orthodox communicants in Sheboygan 75 years later. St. Spyridon's proudly celebrated its seventy-fifth anniversary in the fall of 1981.

(9) Latin Pentecostal Holiness Church
South 10th Street and High Avenue
Organized in 1974, the Latin Pentecostal Holiness Church serves a small minority of the Spanish-speaking community. Membership numbered 36 in 1981. The church building was formerly used by the Assembly of God church.

The majority of Sheboygan Hispanics with church affiliations are Catholic. Mass is said in Spanish at *St. Clement's Parish Center*, 506 New York Avenue. The major social service agency for Hispanics in Sheboygan is United Migrant Opportunity Services.

(10) Croatian Hall
8th Street and Broadway
Croatian Hall, built in 1924, included a large meeting hall and smaller rooms for club and group gatherings. The plain tan brick structure served as a social and civic center for Croatian families dedicated to keeping Croatian culture alive. The Croatians organized sickness and death benefit (insurance) societies and in 1924 founded the Croatian Home, Inc. These, along with Ss. Cyril and Methodius' Church, were the major social institutions of the early twentieth-century immigrant community.

(11) Fishing Shanties
On the north bank of the Sheboygan River, east of the 8th Street bridge, stand fishing shanties that have been in use throughout the past half-century. Originally the fishing village lay west of the bridge. Now greatly diminished, as is all Lake Michigan commercial fishing, Sheboygan's fishing industry was an important part of the local economy from the mid-nineteenth century until the 1930s.

(12) Homes of Sheboygan's Business Leaders

*Friendship House,**
721 Ontario Avenue

Believed to have been built about 1870 for the owner of the Park Hotel, John Pfieler, this attractive two-story brick and masonry house in the Italian Villa style is very well maintained. Early in the twentieth century the Home for the Friendless, Inc. acquired it. Friendship House is now used as a group home for dependent boys.

Henry Jung Home,
503 Ontario Avenue

Henry Jung (see no. [4]) built this home in 1900–1901 in the Neo-Classical–late Victorian style. It symbolizes his business success and prominence in the community. With only minor exterior alterations, the house has been adapted for use as a halfway house by Sheboygan County Halfway House, Inc.

T. M. Blackstock House,
507 Washington Court

Thomas M. Blockstock, who built this Italian Villa home in 1864, came to the United States from Ireland in 1849. Prominent in Sheboygan business and government, he helped organize the Phoenix Chair Company and later became its president. He served in the Wisconsin State Assembly and as mayor of Sheboygan.

John M. Kohler Home,
608 New York Avenue

John Michael Kohler built this cream brick Italianate home for his family in 1882. At that time he ranked as one of Sheboygan's most successful industrial leaders, but the Kohler business was then small compared with what it became in later years. Kohler, an Austrian-born immigrant, purchased an interest in the Vollrath Foundry in 1873. Six years later he and two new partners formed a company that produced ornamental ironwork at first and later cast-iron plumbing fixtures.

The John Michael Kohler Arts Center during a special summer event in 1978. Photo by Margaret Bogue.

The Kohler home was deeded to the non-profit Sheboygan Arts Foundation in 1966. The foundation maintains the home as a year-round performing arts center, offers classes, and manages permanent and changing exhibits. Open daily, noon–5:00 P.M. Free.

Peter Reiss Home,
1227 North 7th Street

The Reiss home, a massive red sandstone structure reflecting both Richardsonian Romanesque and Gothic architectural styles, was built in 1905–1906. Alfred C. Clas of Milwaukee was the architect. Members of the Reiss family are well known in Sheboygan as founders and owners of the Reiss Coal Company.

A. P. Lyman House,
1126 North 6th Street

Probably built in the 1870s and owned by a succession of prominent Sheboygan businessmen, the Lyman house was originally the cream brick Italianate home of Asahel P. Lyman, pioneer merchant, owner of Great Lakes sailing ships, and advocate of railroad and harbor improvements for Sheboygan. Altered in appearance by successive owners, the house belonged for a time to an official of the Reiss Coal Company and later to the president of the Sheboygan Falls Machine Company. It was converted to an apartment building in the 1940s.

(13) Holy Name Catholic Church
8th and Huron Avenue
In the summer of 1845 a visiting priest said mass in a private home for Sheboygan's few Catholic residents. With the coming of southern German Catholics in substantial numbers, She-

boygan received a permanent pastor, Reverend F. X. Etschmann, in 1850, the first in a long succession of German-speaking priests to serve the Holy Name parish. The foundation of the present church structure was laid in 1867, and in 1872 the Bishop John Martin Henni of Milwaukee dedicated the building. Holy Name was the parent church of St. Peter Claver (no. [7]). Holy Name parishioners were described as "polyglot" in character in 1912, with those of German birth or descent in a majority.

(14) David Taylor House* and Sheboygan County Museum
3110 Erie Avenue
A modest and distinctive example of the Italian Villa style, the David Taylor house, built of cream brick in the 1850s and overlooking the Sheboygan River, now houses the Sheboygan County Historical Society museum. David A. Taylor, a lawyer, moved from New York State to Sheboygan in the 1840s and served in the State Assembly and Senate and on the state Supreme Court. During his legal career he prepared two revisions of the Statutes of Wisconsin. The Sheboygan County Historical Society received a 99-year lease of the house for use as a museum in 1948. The grounds have been landscaped by a garden club with appropriate nineteenth-century plants.

The museum exhibits include an 1862 log cabin built by the Weinhold family southeast of Adell. The society recently saved it from destruction, moved it to the museum site, and restored it. Rooms in Taylor House are devoted to medicine, music, and Indian artifacts; a parlor and a bedroom are furnished with nineteenth-century

The Indian Mound Park near Sheboygan, May 1982. The park, a beautiful and restful place, has a number of signs and a burial mound display to help visitors learn about the Effigy Mound culture. Photo by Margaret Bogue.

pieces. The house is a Sheboygan County Landmark. Open April 1–October 1, Tuesday–Saturday, 10:00 A.M.–5:00 P.M.; Sunday, 1:00–5:00 P.M. $

(15) Indian Mound Park
Near intersection of County Trunks KK and EE
Those interested in the Indian peoples who lived in the Sheboygan area before white settlement will find it worthwhile to make a short trip south of Sheboygan to visit Indian Mound Park. The park is owned by the city of Sheboygan but lies beyond the city limits in the township of Wilson. Take County Trunk KK south of Sheboygan to the intersection with County Trunk EE. One-quarter mile beyond the intersection turn east on Panther Avenue. Make a right turn onto South 9th Street.

This beautifully sited 15-acre park on the Black River preserves 18 prehistoric Indian burial mounds, which were explored by the Wisconsin Archaeological Society in the 1920s and excavated by the Milwaukee Public Museum in 1927. One of the mounds is open to display the method of burial and some of the artifacts found here. Because of recent vandalism, only reproductions of artifacts are now on display.

The mounds were constructed by the Effigy Mound Indians approximately 700 A.D. (see pp. 7, 9). Notable among them are five deer and two panther mounds. Nature trails, markers, and the exposed burial at Mound 19 help visitors understand what little is known about the Effigy Mound Indians, a Late Woodland culture concentrated mainly in the area from Green Bay to just south of the Wisconsin-Illinois border. The Sheboygan Area Garden Clubs are largely responsible for saving the 18 mounds (of an original 33). Opened to the public on June 25, 1966, the park is dedicated to "those oldest peoples of Wisconsin whose love for their homeland kept it green and beautiful and rich in nature's bounty. May we learn to preserve it half as well."

Kohler Residences on Church Street in West I, the first of the village units, as they look today. Photo by Margaret Bogue.

32. Kohler Village

Highways W-23 or W-28 west of Sheboygan

In 1898, two years before his death, John M. Kohler decided to buy land for a new plant four miles west of Sheboygan, a location with plenty of room for growth. Nearby workers built their homes in Riverside, a small unincorporated village. Walter J. Kohler, Sr., son of John M. Kohler, decided that instead of an architectural hodgepodge at its front door, the Kohler Company should develop a model industrial village, well planned and attractive.

Accordingly he visited industrial communities in the United States and abroad and in 1916 hired Werner Hegemann, a German-born planner, to prepare a master plan for the village of Kohler. Despite disagreements between Kohler and Hegemann that eventually led to the latter's resignation, development of the first unit of Kohler Village, West I, was nearly completed by 1924. Imitative of the English garden city idea, with houses simulating English cottages, West I included two large structures, the American Club, opened in 1918 (see below), and a two-story commercial building. The Milwaukee architect Richard Philipp designed most of the West I structures. Two more areas, South I and West II, were completed before the depression of the 1930s halted construction. The Olmsted Brothers of Brookline, Massachusetts, served as consultants to Kohler in the second planning phase, which began in the mid-1920s.

Until 1934 both the Kohler factory and the planned industrial village received a great deal of favorable publicity. Kohler was hailed as Wisconsin's most beautiful village and Walter Kohler, governor of the state from 1929 to 1931, as an industrialist who gave conspicuous service to humanity. All that changed abruptly when, in the summer of 1934, a bitter and violent strike of Kohler workers attracted national attention. The village police force and its deputies opened fire on a group of strikers and strike sympathizers on July 27, 1934, killing two men and wounding 47 people. A prolonged strike between 1954 and 1960, involving union recognition as well as other issues, created profound divisions in the surrounding community and tarnished Kohler's image as a model industrial village.

In more recent years management-labor relations have followed a smoother course. Construction began anew in 1962 with the development of West III. In 1975 the Kohler Company assigned the task of developing a master plan for the future to the Frank Lloyd Wright Foundation. There is much evidence to suggest that those who live in Kohler, a growing number of them not Kohler employees, regard the village as an extremely attractive and well-planned community.

Kohler Village's history brings to mind the Pullman story (see site 1, no. [1]). Although George Pullman and Walter Kohler, Sr., had many ideas in common, the two cases are not really parallel, for Kohler preferred individual ownership of homes to company ownership.

Kohler Sites of Interest

(1) American Club*
Kohler Memorial Drive
In 1918 the American Club, a large Tudor-style red brick structure, was built to provide rooms for single male workers at the Kohler Company plant. Many of these workers were recent immigrants from Germany, Russia, and elsewhere. In addition to dormitory rooms, the club included recreational facilities, reading rooms, a dining hall, and baths. One of the club's major purposes was to teach immigrants American ways through language and citizenship classes. The original furnishings included portraits of American presidents and an abundance of American flags. Walter Kohler's desire to Americanize immigrants reflected a vigorous national movement for 100 percent Americanization during World War I. Now the American Club is operated by the Kohler Company as a clubhouse for employees and as a residential hotel. In the summer of 1980, the company began a two-year renovation program to convert it to a motel.

(2) Waelderhaus
off Highway W-28 via Riverside Drive
Planned as a memorial to John Michael Kohler, Waelderhaus is a replica of his home in Austria. An architect and sculptor came from Austria in 1929 to design and supervise its construction and furnishing. Waelderhaus is open to the public daily without charge.

(3) Kohler Company Tours
Tour headquarters, High Street
Visitors to the Kohler Company can see the production of vitreous china and enameled cast iron plumbing fixtures and learn about the company's history. Kohler products for the bath, powder room, and kitchen are displayed in the showroom. The Kohler Com pany also produces gasoline engines. Call (414) 457-4441, extension 2243, to make tour appointments. Tours are available Monday–Friday after 9:00 A.M. all year. Reservation needed.

(4) Riverbend*
Lower Falls Road
Riverbend, the Kohler family estate, was the home of two presidents of the Kohler Company, Walter Kohler, Sr., and Walter Kohler, Jr. Conservative Republicans in politics, both served as governors of Wisconsin, the former from January 1929 to January 1931, and the latter from January 1951 to January 1957.

Designed and built for Walter Kohler, Sr., between 1921 and 1923, the estate buildings include an impressive Tudor-style residence, a greenhouse, a chauffeur's cottage, and a garage. Richard Philipp of Milwaukee designed these structures as well as most of the buildings in the West I unit of Kohler Village. The brick Kohler home is trimmed in Bedford limestone. With its gable-roofed units, it is considered one of Wisconsin's outstanding private homes. The beautiful wooded setting at a bend of the Sheboygan River was landscaped by the Olmsted Brothers of Brookline, Massachusetts, who also planned portions of Kohler Village. This is a private residence not open to the public.

33. Kettle Moraine State Forest, Northern Unit

West of Sheboygan via Highway W-23 (BCFHPS)

The Northern Unit of Kettle Moraine State Forest was created in 1937 when the state of Wisconsin acquired 800 acres of wilderness from the Isaak Walton League. Over the last 40 years, the state has added 27,000 of a projected 30,000 acres to the forest. Picnic and swimming facilities are found at Seven Lakes, and camping is permitted at both Mauthe Lake and Long Lake recreation areas. A 120-mile scenic drive connects the Northern and Southern Units of the forest.

The Kettle Moraine Forest takes its name from glacial potholes made by slowly melting ice left by glaciers more than 10,000 years ago. In addition to kettles, visitors to the forest can see kames (cones of sand and gravel left by melting ice), eskers (narrow ridges of gravel deposited by glacial streams), and moraines (gravelly hills deposited at the edge of the glacier's advance).

In 1970 the first section of a proposed 600-mile Ice Age Trail running north and south through the forest was opened. When completed, the trail will take hikers through nine units in the Ice Age National Scientific Reserve, which is scattered across the state of Wisconsin. Land included in the reserve has been placed under federal and state protection to preserve the physiographical features formed during the Ice Age (see site 41).

Maps of the Ice Age Trail, as well as other hiking trails in the forest, may be obtained from forest headquarters at Mauthe Lake.

The original of this fine drawing of Wade House at Greenbush, possibly showing it as it was about 1870, hangs in the American Club at Kohler, Wisconsin. Courtesy State Historical Society of Wisconsin. WHi(X3)1959

34. Old Wade House State Park

Greenbush, Highway W-23 west of Sheboygan (P)

Old Wade House,* a stagecoach inn built between 1847 and 1851 and the Wesley W. Jung Carriage Museum, both located in this state park, capture much of the history of horse-drawn transportation in nineteenth-century America. Sylvanus Wade, a skilled blacksmith and ambitious businessman, came to Wisconsin from Massachusetts after extended intermediate stops in Pennsylvania and Illinois, finally settling at Greenbush in 1844. He hoped to found a busy village midway between the growing towns of Fond du Lac and Sheboygan. From the beginning he operated an inn in his home, but by the late 1840s the road between the two towns was so well traveled that Wade decided to build a real inn to accommodate stagecoach travelers. The organization of the Sheboygan and Fond du Lac Plank Road Company in 1848 made increased travel through Greenbush a sure thing. Wade's son-in-law, Charles Robinson, a carpenter and proprietor of a sawmill at Greenbush, helped design and build Wade House, a beautiful Greek Revival structure. Soon afterward Robinson built *Butternut House* for his family, another Greek Revival structure. Much of its interior woodwork was made from local butternut.

The plank road was completed in 1852, and business boomed at Wade House. But prosperity faded quickly after the construction of an east-west railroad line out of Sheboygan, designed to connect with a line between Chicago and Fond du Lac. The railroad ran through Glenbeulah, bypassing Greenbush. The first train arrived at Glenbeulah in 1860. Greenbush village and Wade House business declined. The stagecoach gave way to the railroad, and decade after decade the house deteriorated. In 1950 the Kohler Foundation embarked on a massive, painstaking restoration of both Wade House and Butternut House. They were presented to the State Historical Society of Wisconsin, which now operates them as public museums. The State Department of Natural Resources created park and picnic grounds around the buildings.

The *Wesley W. Jung Carriage Museum* on the grounds at Old Wade House State Park was opened in 1968. The museum contains a very fine collection of wagons and carriages, most of them built at the Jacob Jung Carriage Factory in Sheboygan in the late nineteenth and early twentieth centuries (see site 31, no. [3]). Wesley W. Jung, grandson of Jacob Jung, restored most of these beautiful old vehicles. Old Wade House, Butternut House, and the Jung Carriage Museum are open May 1–October 31. Hours in

May, June, September, and October are Monday–Friday, 9:00 A.M.–4:00 P.M.; Saturday and Sunday, 10:00 A.M.–5:00 P.M. July and August hours are Monday–Sunday, 10:00 A.M.–5:00 P.M. $

35. St. Nazianz

Intersection of County Trunks A and C, south of Highway US-151

St. Nazianz, a small rural town with a population of about 700, lies southwest of Manitowoc in a rich farming area. With one major industry, a producer of agricultural supplies and equipment, employing 60 workers, the town is primarily an agricultural service and educational center. Many of its residents work in neighboring industrial towns.

For over a century St. Nazianz was a very special place for religious reasons. The town's early history is unique, for here in 1854 a group of 113 Catholic German immigrants from the Grand Duchy of Baden established a communal religious settlement, naming the colony for their patron, St. Gregory of Nazianz. Contemporaries gave several reasons for the group's decision to come to the New World: overpopulation in the homeland, a succession of poor harvests from small landholdings, political turmoil following the Revolution of 1848, and a feeling of uncertainty about the future of Catholicism in view of the government's desire to secularize the church. Their leader, Father Ambrose Oschwald, a local priest whose unorthodox views placed him in disfavor with church authorities, had but one motive. He wanted to establish an ideal religious community, a model for others to follow.

The group formed an association with written statutes that set forth a system of theocratic government, standards of conduct, and rules of social and economic organization. Membership cost a specified amount of cash or labor. Association funds were earmarked for transportation to America and for the purchase of land to be held in common. "The mode of living will be in common as much as possible," said section 14 of the statutes of the association. Yet the association was more flexible than some nineteenth-century American religious collectives, for it recognized the right to obtain private property, provided for reimbursement to those who left the community, and sanctioned both married life and celibacy among its membership.

Although the statutes entrusted government to the Ephorate, made up of 12 elders and the parish priest, this system was not used. In practice Father Oschwald and his able assistant, Anton Stoll, were the governing authorities. They guarded the public morality, managed public affairs, admitted and dismissed association members, provided for public education, assigned tasks to members, and settled disagreements. Obedience to the colony's laws and to superiors was a condition of membership. The final section of the laws specified: "There must be charity, harmony, true Christian fraternal love and real Christianity . . . which was our purpose in working together and coming to America." The association's laws established a system of social welfare for the group.

With the funds it collected, the association paid for its members' passage to New York and retained enough to make a downpayment on land. Apparently attracted to Wisconsin because of its large German population, the group left New York, the port of debarkation, for Milwaukee. Father Oschwald contracted for 3,800 acres of heavily timbered Manitowoc County land. The long struggle to establish the St. Nazianz community began in the late summer of 1854. Hard work, sickness, death, and money shortages plagued the pioneers for the next few years, but they persevered and ultimately prospered.

By the time of Father Oschwald's death in 1873, the colony had a handsome stone church (St. Gregory's), convent, monastery, school, orphanage, hospital, seminary, numerous cottages for families, a central kitchen, and farm structures as well as a tannery, mills, and shops to provide lumber, flour, shoes, cloth, and clothing, primarily for association members.

Communal ownership continued without major protests until 1873. Just after the founder's death, discontented members, discovering that the association had never been incorporated under Wisconsin law, contested Father Oschwald's will and demanded to separate from the association, taking with them the money they had contributed originally and compensation for their work over the years. A long period of legal warfare weakened the colony, many withdrew, and association membership declined.

In 1896 the lay brothers and sisters of the association, many of them advanced in years, petitioned to be unified with the Salvatorians, the Society of the Divine Savior, as a way of continuing Father Oschwald's work. The Salvatorians agreed and for a half-century pursued a program of building and expansion. They constructed St. Ambrose's Church (1898), assumed responsibility for St. Gregory's parish, enlarged the monastery, and converted the facilities into the first Salvatorian seminary in the United States. From time to time the seminary was called St. Mary's College. The development of the seminary and the assistance that the Salvatorians rendered St. Gregory's parish added much vitality to the town. In 1968 the seminary was converted into an innovative coeducational school, the John F. Kennedy Preparatory School. Because of financial problems, it closed in January 1982.

St. Nazianz Sites of Interest

Although most of the original colony structures are gone, some dating from Father Oschwald's time remain, and the Salvatorian period is well represented.

(1) Oschwald Burial Site
Father Oschwald is buried in a mausoleum on the hill near the Loretto Chapel, built under his direction in 1870 and 1872 to house the shrine of Our Lady of Loretto.

(2) Loretto Shrine Chapel*
One-half mile west of County Trunk A behind the John F. Kennedy Preparatory School
Constructed in 1870 and 1872, the Loretto Shrine Chapel is a small one-story stucco structure with a gable roof and bell tower. Father Oschwald had erected the colony's first shrine to Our Lady of Loretto in a tree niche in the very early years of the settlement and replaced it with a glass-encased

St. Gregory's Church now without its steeple stands on a hill overlooking the town. Around it is the graveyard with burials dating back more than a century. Both the church inside and out and the graveyard are well worth a visit. Photo by Margaret Bogue.

pedestal in 1863. Storm damage to both of these early shrines led him to begin work on the Loretto Shrine Chapel in 1870. Loretto Hill had long since become an important place of pilgrimage.

(3) St. Gregory's Church*
212 Church Street
The fine stone church built between 1864 and 1868 under the direction of Father Oschwald is still in use, now serving St. Gregory's parish of approximately 500 families. The wooden steeple burned down in 1957, but the exterior of the stone and concrete building, styled in the Country Church Gothic tradition is basically unaltered. The interior was extensively remodeled in 1958. The site of the first St. Gregory's church, a frame structure erected in the early days of the settlement, is marked with a memorial altar.

(4) St. Mary's Convent*
300 South 2nd Avenue
Constructed in 1865 and 1866 for use as an orphanage and hospital, the building is a combination of mortar and rock construction on the lower floors and stucco above. Both the hospital and the orphanage were projects of central importance to Father Ambrose Oschwald. Section 7 of the statutes of the association, which he authored, committed the membership to provide care for the poor, invalids, and orphans "so that the poor shall receive the same care as the rich." The structure was named St. Mary's Convent in 1896 when the Sisters of the Divine Savior became its owners.

(5) St. Ambrose's Church and Seminary Buildings
The religious community of Salvatorians, now numbering about 30 permanent residents, continues to reside at St. Nazianz. The seminary building and many of the associated structures were converted for the use of the John F. Kennedy Preparatory School, a majority of whose students were boarders. With the retirement of the Sisters of the Divine Savior, their residence was converted for the use of residential faculty. The once-busy publishing department buildings served as a boys' dormitory. The original gymnasium became a theater, and a new

gymnasium was built. The recent closing of the school leaves the future use of these facilities undecided. The large and imposing St. Ambrose's Church is used on special occasions.

36. Manitowoc

Highway US-151 and I-43

Located on the shores of Lake Michigan at the mouth of the Manitowoc River, the city of Manitowoc is now known for its metal and machinery industries. Because of the fine schooners built in its shipyards, it used to be known as "The Clipper City." Growth, change, and successful economic adjustment have characterized Manitowoc's 150-year history.

The town dates from the boom years of the 1830s, when Chicago land speculators platted Manitowoc (meaning "home of the great spirit"), hastily erected buildings, and pushed lot sales, only to have their hopes dashed by the financial panic of 1837. In the mid-1840s the settlement revived and grew remarkably from a village with 20 or 30 buildings, a pier, and a lighthouse in 1844 to a town of almost 2,200 in 1855. Among the newcomers were a large number of German immigrants and some Irish, Norwegian, and Bohemian families. In the 1860s Polish immigrants added to Manitowoc's ethnic diversity.

Manitowoc in the early years played second fiddle to Manitowoc Rapids, located upriver with excellent water power for saw and grist mills. But by 1853, when Manitowoc took the county seat away from Manitowoc Rapids, the lakeside village clearly had the advantage. Lake commerce, steam-powered sawmilling, fishing, and shipbuilding lay at the heart of Manitowoc's early prosperity. Not until the early 1870s did Manitowoc have railroad connections to the south and the west. Meanwhile the lake was vital for passenger and freight traffic. Local resources of timber and fish provided the major exports.

Manitowoc harbor pictured here in 1887 was crowded and busy. The photo shows eight steamers, a tug, seven schooners, and two scows. Courtesy State Historical Society of Wisconsin. WHi(X3)30632

Recognizing that a good harbor was essential for growth, Manitowoc business leaders pushed for harbor improvements from the very beginning. In the 1830s they sought federal money to remove sand bars and to dredge. They also promoted the idea of building a canal to connect Manitowoc to Lake Winnebago. Although it received a lighthouse in 1840, Manitowoc's other appeals for federal aid failed until 1852, when Congress appropriated a few thousand dollars for harbor improvements. A more generous appropriation of $52,000 was made in 1866. Meanwhile Manitowoc used bond issues to raise much of the necessary capital to clear the harbor of shifting sand bars and deepen it.

Once railroad connections to Manitowoc were established in the early 1870s, the port became less essential for freight and passenger traffic. Yet in other ways the railroads increased that traffic. In the late 1880s the Flint and Pere Marquette Railroad opened a line of break bulk freighters between Ludington and Manitowoc. This was part of the east-west railroads' strategy for bridging the gap created by the lake, thereby saving the mileage, time, and expense involved in going around the lakeshore via Chicago. In 1896, when the Wisconsin Central built a line to Manitowoc, the railroad's improvement plans greatly benefited the port city. Grain elevators, coal docks, and a car ferry connection with Ludington increased port business. In the early twentieth century, coal accounted for much of Manitowoc's inbound tonnage as it does now. Car ferry service to Ludington was suspended in January, 1982.

Manitowoc, now primarily industrial, has a venerable manufacturing and maritime history. Commercial fishing ranked as a very important industry in the early years. In the summer of 1837, John P. Clark of Detroit discovered the rich resources of whitefish and trout in Manitowoc lake waters. By the late 1850s the annual exported catch amounted to 2,250 barrels. Eight or nine fishing enterprises operated out of Manitowoc in the 1860s. The industry continued to be an important one but was plagued with problems and a long-term decline in catch.

For decades shipbuilding was among Manitowoc's main industries. The first schooner, the 60-ton *Citizen*, slid from the ways in 1847. Manitowoc shipbuilders launched 24 more schooners in the 1850s. By 1900 the yards had built 112 schooners, earning for Manitowoc the name "The Clipper City." Thirty-nine steamers and 36 tugs were launched here before 1900. One local historian boasted that Manitowoc clipper ships were unequaled in sailing qualities. Another considered the best work of the yards up to 1910 to be the "magnificent" passenger steamers built for the Goodrich Transport Company of Chicago.

Shipbuilding at Manitowoc finally ceased in the late 1960s because the Manitowoc River was not large enough to handle launchings of the huge new bulk carriers. The yards of the city's major builder, the Manitowoc Company, were moved to Sturgeon Bay between 1968 and 1972. But between the founding of that company in 1902 and the cessation of shipbuilding at Manitowoc, it produced a wide variety of ships for industry and government. Before 1914 the company both repaired wooden ships and built steel passenger and freight vessels on order. During World War I the company expanded fourfold to produce under government contract 33 freighters with 3,500-ton capacity for war use. The yards turned out car ferries, oil tankers, and the company's first self-unloading freighter between World Wars I and II. During World War II the Manitowoc Company produced submarines and landing craft. From 1945 until the removal of the yard to Sturgeon Bay, the company built large self-unloading bulk carriers (the largest of these was 730 feet long), converted and modernized older vessels, and constructed a number of smaller crane-mounted vessels. Currently one construction firm, the Burger Boat Company, builds aluminum pleasure craft at Manitowoc.

Industrial activity other than fishing and shipbuilding has always been important to Manitowoc's economy. As long as the original forests lasted, Manitowoc exported tanned leather produced with local hemlock bark, staves, cordwood, and millions of shingles and board feet of lumber. Brewing, malt production, and brick making were old and long-lived industries. Manitowoc city fathers worked strenuously to attract new industries as its four lumber mills and its tanneries closed. By the early twentieth century, they had met with a measure of success. The city had acquired a nucleus of metal industries, including iron and aluminum foundries, a steam boiler works, and an aluminum goods factory. Shipbuilding received a shot in the arm early in the century when Chicago shipbuilders consolidated and expanded the longstanding Manitowoc industry. Newer businesses included a knitting mill and four canning and pickle factories.

Now Manitowoc has 20 industries employing 100 or more workers and 2 very large firms with at least 3,000 each on the payroll: the Manitowoc Company (manufacturers of cranes, excavators, ice-cube makers, and debarking equipment) and the Mirro Corporation (makers of aluminum products). Metal industries predominate, turning out a wide variety of aluminum products from cookware to castings. Other firms produce metal office equipment, hose couplings, machine tools, ice-cube-making machines, and refrigeration equipment. Food (dairy products, sausages, baked goods, canned vegetables) and wood and ceramic products are also on the roster of manufactured goods. In 1970 manufacturing plants employed about 40 percent of the city's total workforce. The city population in 1980 was 32,500.

Manitowoc Sites of Interest

(1) Manitowoc County Court House*
8th Street at Washington Street
An excellent example of the monumental Neo-Classical public

Launching a Goodrich Transportation Company vessel built in Manitowoc in 1889, City of Racine. *Photo by H. J. Packard. Courtesy State Historical Society of Wisconsin. WHi(X3)36985*

Ship's anchor and Manitowoc Maritime Museum, 1984. The museum's fine displays have grown so rapidly in recent years that the staff is concerned about a possible move where more space will permit continued expansion. Photo by Margaret Bogue.

architecture of the turn of the century, the Manitowoc County Court House was designed by a locally prominent architect, Christ H. Tegen, and built in 1906. The structure stands on the site of the courthouse built in Manitowoc in 1861, eight years after the growing Lake Michigan port city captured the county seat from Manitowoc Rapids. Well preserved and maintained, the courthouse is very prominent in the city's profile. The high, copper-covered dome and open lantern rise well above surrounding structures and are visible for a considerable distance. Much of the interior is, like the exterior, original and well worth seeing, especially the large, square, open lobby rising to the cupola, the cast iron stairway with its ornamental cast iron balustrade, the tile floors, oak woodwork, and marble wainscot. The exterior is faced with dressed Indiana limestone. The building has served as the focus of county government for 78 years and should serve far into the future.

(2) Manitowoc Maritime Museum
809 South 8th Street
Here well-designed museum displays depict the history of Manitowoc as a shipbuilding center with emphasis on the shipbuilders, on the Goodrich Transportation Company, largest of the passenger and freight steamship companies on Lake Michigan, and on the life of the nineteenth-century mariner. In the spring of 1983, the museum opened a new permanent exhibit, "The Wooden Ship Era," focusing on the period from 1850 to 1900. Outstanding in the new exhibit is a full-scale reproduction of the midsection of the schooner *Clipper City*, a 185-ton lumber vessel built at Manitowoc in 1854 by William Bates. Bates's design, an innovation in Great Lakes wooden ship construction, permitted the schooner to pass through the very shallow harbor entrances with narrow channels that were typical of many Great Lakes ports in 1850.

Across the street from the museum in the Manitowoc River is the *U.S.S. Cobia*, the International Submariners Memorial. During World War II, 28 submarines and landing craft were built here, and although this submarine was not built in Manitowoc, it is a distinguished veteran of the war. As visitors progress through the submarine from stern to bow, they hear the recorded sounds of an actual submarine dive and may examine the engine, control, and forward torpedo rooms. The museum is open daily all year, 9:00 A.M.–5:00 P.M. The submarine is open to visitors from mid-April through Labor Day. $

(3) Joseph Vilas, Jr., House (Vilas-Rahr House)*

Rahr-West Center, 610 North 8th Street
Designed by the Milwaukee architectural firm of Ferry and Clas and built in 1891–1893 for Joseph Vilas, Jr., the Vilas-Rahr house incorporates the Queen Anne and Shingle styles of the late Victorian period. Both owners of the home were very prominent in the Manitowoc business community. Joseph Vilas, Jr., helped promote the construction of the Milwaukee, Lake Shore and Western Railroad, was for a time president of the company, and served as mayor of Manitowoc in 1893–1895. In 1863 and 1864 he held the office of state senator. Reinhardt Rahr purchased the house in 1910. His business interests included the William Rahr Sons malt house and brewery, the Cereal Products Company, the Manitowoc State Bank, and other enterprises. In 1941 Rahr's widow and his son, Guido Rahr, transferred ownership of the house to the city for use as a civic center. The house and a modern addition built with funds donated by Mr. and Mrs. John West contain art and historical displays. The Rahr Parlor and a permanent collection of prehistoric Indian artifacts are outstanding. Open daily except Mondays, 9:00 A.M.–4:30 P.M. Open in winter on Sundays, noon–4:30 P.M. Open May 1–Oct. 31 on Saturdays and Sundays, 1:00–4:00 P.M. Free.

(4) Manitowoc's Nineteenth-Century Immigrant Churches

Some of the many beautiful churches built by immigrant groups in Manitowoc during the nineteenth century remain in use. Although these churches have largely lost their original ethnic character, the buildings are reminders of the importance of the church as a central institution in the lives of the newly arrived Americans who built them.

St. Boniface's Catholic Church,
1110 South 10th Street

Although St. Boniface's parish was not established until 1857, St. Boniface's church dates from 1853, when the German Catholics of Manitowoc raised funds to erect their first house of worship. St. Boniface's served Polish Catholics as well until 1870, when they organized their own parish, St. Mary's, one of four parishes that had their origins in St. Boniface's. St. Boniface's itself included about 1,000 families by 1900.

In 1884, to meet the needs of its growing congregation, St. Boniface's embarked on a building program. The beautiful Gothic church in current use was consecrated in 1886.

First German Evangelical Lutheran Church, 1033 South 8th Street

Sizable numbers of Protestant as well as Catholic Germans settled in Manitowoc early in its development. The First German Evangelical Lutheran congregation was organized in 1855 and built its first church the next year. This structure was used for the next 17 years. Membership grew rapidly as more immigrants arrived until in 1866 the congregation included 184 families and its parochial school 193 children. The Gothic church now in use was built in 1873. The congregation first introduced a service in English in 1912 and began in 1922 to hold services every Sunday in both German and English. In 1955 the English service was the preference of the congregation by a ratio of about seven to one. Proud of the historic sanctuary, the congregation has maintained it well, celebrating its fiftieth and one hundredth anniversaries with special services in 1923 and 1973.

St. Mary's Catholic Church,
1114 South 21st Street

Organized as a separate parish to meet the needs of the Polish communicants of St. Boniface's in 1870, St. Mary's parishioners in 1873 purchased a frame church previously occupied by a German Lutheran congregation. St. Mary's gradually grew in numbers and financial strength until in 1888 its members decided to build a costly new sanctuary. Construction proceeded slowly. The cornerstone of this cream brick Gothic church was laid in 1894. Dedication ceremonies took place in 1899.

Who were St. Mary's parishioners? Manitowoc's earliest Polish settler arrived in 1858 and settled in what is now the southwest corner of the city, then a beautiful pine-covered hill, which became known as Polish Hill. Others arrived from Poland in the 1860s, and between 1867 and 1875 a number of Milwaukee Poles joined them. Those emigrating directly from

Poland preferred farming and logging, while many of the Milwaukee Poles found city jobs. By the end of the century, with the growth of Manitowoc industry and increased demand for labor, many residents of Polish Hill found jobs on the docks, in the factories, on lake boats, at grain elevators, and with the railroads. Polish Hill was incorporated into the city in 1891 and soon became the Seventh Ward. Here Polish remained the chief language until after World War I. In the 1920s one out of every six Manitowoc residents was of Polish background.

Former First Lutheran Church, 8th and State Streets, *and Former St. Paul's Norwegian Lutheran Church,* North 10th and St. Claire Streets

When the First Lutheran Church of Manitowoc prepared a centennial history of the congregation in 1950, pride in its Norwegian origins led the authors of the commemorative pamphlet to begin with an account of the Norwegian migration to America. Because Norwegian settlers of the 1850s in the Manitowoc area congregated in relatively small numbers at Gjerpen, Valders, and Manitowoc, they joined in organizing the Norwegian Lutheran Congregation of Manitowoc and vicinity in 1859 and in calling a pastor.

The Manitowoc Norwegians at first met in a small public school house. In 1866 they began work on a new sanctuary, dedicated in 1869. In 1871 the Manitowoc congregation separated from the Gjerpen and Valders congregations and called its own pastor, incorporating as the Norwegian Evangelical Lutheran Congregation of Manitowoc. Two years later the congregation split over doctrinal differences. St. Paul's Norwegian Lutheran Church was organized, and its members constructed a separate house of worship. The two groups continued on their separate ways, and at the end of the century both built modified Gothic brick sanctuaries, somewhat similar in appearance.

First Lutheran Church (the name adopted in 1924 by the Norwegian Evangelical Lutheran Congregation of Manitowoc) built its new church at 8th and State Streets in 1899–1900. The building remains, now used as a synagogue. The First Lutheran congregation now occupies a new church at 521 North 8th Street. The St. Paul's Norwegian Lutheran congregation built its sanctuary in 1898–1899 at North 10th and St. Claire Streets. That structure is now used by the Twin City Baptist Church, and St. Paul's congregation has relocated in a new sanctuary at 2601 South 10th Street. For many years these churches belonged to different Lutheran synods. Both are now members of the American Lutheran Church.

(5) Pinecrest Historical Village of Manitowoc County

off County Trunk JJ, about 5 miles west of Manitowoc

From various locations in Manitowoc County, the Manitowoc County Historical Society has gathered a dozen structures illustrative of the area's nineteenth-century history. Renovated and restored to their original appearance, they are grouped together as an outdoor museum on a 40-acre tract of land donated by Mr. and Mrs. Hugo Vetting. Included are three distinctly different log cabins dating from 1846 through the late 1850s, built by Norwegian, German, and Austrian pioneer farmers. A board and batten farmhouse built by a German immigrant in 1866, a barn containing a display of agricultural implements, a sawmill, the Collins Railroad Depot (built in 1896), an early twentieth-century lawyer's office, an early twentieth-century Valders meat market, now developed as a harness and shoe shop, an 1872 wooden clapboard school, and a Presbyterian mission church built in 1864 are included in the village. Open June 1–Labor Day, Tuesday–Sunday, 10:00 A.M.–4:00 P.M. Open by special appointment for groups. $

(6) Woodland Dunes Nature Center

off Memorial Drive at Woodland Drive and Goodland Road

The nature center is situated between two natural regions. Both northern and southern species of plants and birds are found here. The wooded ridges from which the center receives its name mark the level reached by a preglacial lake. There are no facilities for picnics or camping, but visitors are welcome to hike, sketch, or take photographs. Trails are open all year, Monday–Saturday. $

37. Two Rivers

Highway W-42

Lake Michigan's Indians often established their villages at locations with a natural abundance of food and avenues for canoe travel. The lakeshore from Two Rivers north to within a mile of Two Creeks, where whitefish were unusually abundant, was one such ideal site. Archaeological evidence dug from the beach sands indicates that prehistoric Indians chose

The fishing docks at Two Rivers remained in use until the toll of the sea lamprey in the 1940s depressed all Lake Michigan fishing severely. Here Paul Hammersmith's etching pictures the fishing shanties and boats sometime between 1900 and 1936. The fishing sheds are now part of the Rogers Street Fishing Village Museum. Courtesy State Historical Society of Wisconsin. WHi(X3)40322

this location for their villages. In the nineteenth century Ottawas, Potawatomis, and Chippewas lived here, using the whitefish as a major source of food. The Chippewas called the site Neshoto, meaning "twins."

Until permanent white settlers began to appear in the 1830s, fur traders found the Two Rivers area an advantageous place to trade. The rich forest resources near the juncture of the Mishicot (now called East Twin) and Neshoto (now called West Twin) rivers, as well as the plentiful fisheries, attracted Green Bay, Milwaukee, and Fond du Lac land speculators and developers in the mid-1830s. A sawmill was erected in 1837, but the tiny village languished until the next decade, when economic times improved. Then it attracted hundreds of settlers—New Englanders, French Canadians, and Germans—and was incorporated as a village in 1858.

In the four decades following 1836, the prosperity of Two Rivers was largely based on lumbering and fishing. Mills at Two Rivers cut pine and hemlock logs into lumber and turned out millions of shingles. A chair factory and a pail factory opened in the mid-1850s. At least four tanneries (the first opened in 1851) utilized local supplies of hemlock bark to tan hides shipped in from Milwaukee and Chicago. By the 1880s, with the local bark supply exhausted, the last of the tanneries had closed.

Captain J. V. Edwards of Green Bay launched a commercial fishing business at Two Rivers, the first in Manitowoc County, in 1837 after testing the waters between Manitowoc and Two Rivers with seines. Local legend tells us that his initial test produced ten barrels of fish. Seemingly inexhaustible supplies of whitefish attracted other commercial fishing companies, most notably John P. Clark and Company of Detroit. In the late 1840s Clark and Company operated at Two Rivers and Whitefish Bay with fishing crews and several sailing vessels that made periodic trips to pick up the barreled, salted catch and market it in Detroit. Clark is said to have made a fortune from the business. Unrestricted use of seines and nets soon took its toll of the fish population. Within 25 years whitefish at Two Rivers and Manitowoc were in obvious decline. The wasteful practice of dumping unsalable live fish on the beach and the fishermen's war on the sturgeon, which they considered an unmarketable pest, altered the fish habitat. Nor did the refuse dumped into the rivers and lake by lumbering and tanning operations help matters.

Shipbuilding was yet another dimension of Two Rivers' early economy. From 1852 to 1875 several yards at Two Rivers turned out canal boats, scows, tugs, and schooners. Hanson and Scove, the main yard, moved its operations to Manitowoc in 1875. Not until the 1950s did the industry revive; then Schwartz Marine moved from Manitowoc to Two Rivers and began producing aluminum and steel boats 30 to 70 feet long.

With the lumbering era past, Two Rivers developed a number of successful industries that relied on locational advantages, special skills, and a plentiful labor supply. The Hamilton Manufacturing Company, established in 1880, specialized in the manufacture of wood type and printer's furniture, a business that grew and diversified over the years. At the turn of the century, the city boasted two aluminum factories, a pail and tub factory, a cannery, a chair factory, a veneer mill, a marine gasoline engine works, an art glass company, a knitting mill, two gristmills, one sawmill, and a brewery.

Two Rivers, with a 1980 population of 13,350, remains an industrial town as well as a service and distribution center. Metal industries are the largest employers. Electrical equipment, furniture, and machinery manufacturers rank second, third, and fourth. In 1980 Hamilton Industries employed about 1,700 people to make hospital, medical, dental, and scientific equipment and furniture, specialized tables, and wood type for graphic arts industries.

The other very large employer, with 1,000 workers on the payroll in 1980, is Paragon Electric, which makes electric time controls. The third-largest industrial employer, Eggers Plywood Company, a Two Rivers business since 1884, employed 200 workers in 1980. Twenty smaller firms produce a wide variety of products from fish nets to woolen goods to small household appliances. Three-fifths of the city's workforce is employed in manufacturing.

Two Rivers Sites of Interest

(1) St. Luke's Catholic Church
1814 Jefferson Street

(2) St. John's Evangelical Lutheran Church
17th and East Park Street
As you drive through Two Rivers on route W-42, two striking nineteenth-century churches stand out among the buildings of the downtown area: St. Luke's Catholic Church and St. John's Evangelical Lutheran Church. Both are monuments to the faith of the city's nineteenth-century foreign-born residents, principally Germans, but also French Canadians, Poles, and Bohemians.

French Canadians who came to Two Rivers in the late 1840s to fish the bountiful lake waters and Catholic Germans attracted to jobs in the city's lumbering industries combined to found St. Luke's parish in 1851. To this predominantly German-speaking congregation an influx of Poles and Bohemians added further language and national diversity during the 1880s. In 1889, when St. Luke's membership numbered almost 1,500, 35 Polish families separated to form a new parish, Sacred Heart, and a Polish priest was assigned to serve them. The German, French, Bohemian, and English-speaking Catholics remained at St. Luke's. The parish had outgrown the church and parochial school buildings at the time of the split. The modified Gothic sanctuary still serving the congregation was completed in 1892, with parishioners contributing much of the work. The congregation decided in 1919 that all sermons should be in English.

St. John's Evangelical Lutheran Church, Two Rivers, September 1984. Photo by Margaret Bogue.

The German-speaking congregation that built St. Johns' Evangelical Lutheran Church, a beautiful, modified Gothic, cream brick structure, had its roots in the tannery industry that developed on the East Twin River in the 1850s. A Manitowoc Lutheran pastor established a preaching station for the German Lutheran immigrants who came to work in the tanneries, and at first Two Rivers Lutherans attended services in this industrial woodland setting three miles up river. St. Johns' congregation was organized in 1863 and used a remodeled Episcopal church in Two Rivers for services until the growth of the congregation in the 1880s made new facilities necessary. Jobs in wood-working plants attracted a substantial number of Protestant Germans to Two Rivers in that decade. The present church was built in 1889–1890. A half-century after the founding of St. John's, the congregation agreed to have one service in English. Not until 1958 were German services discontinued.

(3) Rogers Street Fishing Village Museum
East end of East Twin River Bridge, Highway W-42
The Two Rivers Historical Society developed this old commercial fishing village located on the banks of the East Twin River as a museum. An old engine shed contains exhibits of photographs, drawings, and other memorabilia of early Two Rivers. The old 1883 lighthouse stands in the village museum, a gift of the U.S. Coast Guard to the Two Rivers Historical Society after a steel structure replaced it in 1970.

The Engine Room, formerly a fishing shanty, contains artifacts of the commercial fishing industry and a 5,000-pound two-cylinder Kahlenberg diesel engine in perfect condition. The engine is a local product, built in 1924 and used in two boats over a 25-year period. Also featured are objects from the sunken *Vernon* (1887) and the "Christman Tree Ship," the *Rouse Simons* (1912). Both vessels sank approximately 12 miles northeast of Two Rivers. A fishing boat, the *Buddy O*, built in 1936, is on display. One building features paintings and wood carvings by a local artist. Open daily, June–August, 10:00 A.M.–4:00 P.M. Free.

38. Point Beach State Forest

Hys W-42 and W-177, 6 miles north of Two Rivers (CFHPS)

Today Point Beach is one of eight forests owned by the state of Wisconsin. It consists of 2,700 acres of forest and six miles of the widest sand-ridged beach on the western shore of Lake Michigan. Acquisition of the forest began in 1937 when the state secured 80 acres from the federal government, formerly part of the U.S. Coast Guard reservation at Rawley Point.

The Point, named for Peter Rawley, the area's first white settler, presented serious problems for shipping. Hidden shoals accounted for at least 10 recorded shipwrecks in the 1850s and 1860s. The government ultimately responded to local appeals for help. While the earliest lighthouse at Rawley Point dates from 1853, apparently it was not under federal jurisdiction until 1873 when the U.S. Lighthouse Service had plans drawn for a more substantial brick structure. The present beautiful steel tower was built in 1894, a reconstruction and enlargement of a lighthouse from the Chicago River entrance to Lake Michigan. The old brick

Rawley Point Lighthouse is among the more graceful and beautiful lighthouses on Lake Michigan. A display of the remains of an unidentified shipwreck near Rawley Point located at the entrance to the state forest testifies to the hazards of navigation along this stretch of the shoreline. Photo by Margaret Bogue.

tower was cut down to the level of the keeper's house. Both structures are now being considered for addition to the National Register of Historic Places. A fog signal, once part of the lighthouse services, was discontinued after the lighthouse became a radio beacon transmitting station in 1969. Visitors may tour Rawley Point Lighthouse on Friday afternoons in summer.

The state forest contains both scientific and archaeological riches in an extensive area of relatively undisturbed parallel beach ridges. These were formed about 3500–1500 B.C. as Glacial lake Nipissing receded. The Wisconsin Department of Natural Resources designated 183 acres of the Point Beach ridges as a State Scientific Area. Because of the archaeological importance of the beach ridges, the area has been nominated to the National Register of Historic Places as the Point Beach Archaeological District.

Here for the last 80 years archaeologists have been finding in the shifting sands fragmentary evidence of prehistoric and historic Indian villages. A thorough and systematic study of this beach area remains to be made. Such a study could reveal the nature of Indian coastal settlements from several thousand years B.C., or even earlier, through 1850 A.D.

39. Energy Information Center, Point Beach Nuclear Power Plant

off Hy W-42, 13 miles north of Two Rivers

The Wisconsin Electric Power Company and the Wisconsin-Michigan Power Company jointly operate this plant, which produces electric power through the controlled fission of uranium fuel. Visitors will find the subject of power production, now and in the future, explained in audiovisual displays at the information center. A half-mile nature trail has been laid out on the center grounds, and there is an observation tower for a good view of Lake Michigan.

Groups may have a guided tour of

the center or use its meeting facilities for programs on area history, the environment, or energy.

Open daily, 8:30 A.M.–5:00 P.M., except holidays. Free.

40. Two Creeks
Hy W-42

Today the site of the old village of Two Creeks is little more than a sandy ruin on Lake Michigan's shore. Subdivided and set off from Two Creeks Township in 1859, the village first bore the name of Rawley, honoring Peter Rawley, first white settler in the township. By petition, residents of the little fishing village changed the name to Two Creeks two years later. The settlement took on new life in 1862, when Guido Pfister, a successful Milwaukee tanner and leather goods merchant, purchased several hundred acres of land around the village and established a tannery to utilize local supplies of hemlock bark. Pfister's company built a sawmill, a pier, tannery buildings, and homes for employee families, many of them German, Bohemian, and Polish immigrants. Within 20 years the local hemlock was gone, and Pfister closed the Two Creeks plant. Many of its employees moved away.

Thereafter the village served as a shopping and service center for the surrounding countryside and a stopping place for stages running between Two Rivers and Kewaunee. In 1889 Two Creeks, population 140, boasted two hotels, a wagonmaker, a pier builder, a shoemaker, a veterinarian, three cheese factories, a blacksmith, a farm implement dealer, a creamery,

Guido Pfister, a very successful German-born Milwaukee entrepreneur. Courtesy Milwaukee County Historical Society.

and two general stores. After the construction of a rail line from Kewaunee to Green Bay in 1891, the village declined rapidly. The population by 1901 was only 40 persons.

Two Creeks, now located inland from its original site, is a small rural community on Hy W-42.

41. Buried Forest Unit, Ice Age National Scientific Reserve
Hy W-42 and County Trunk BB

When the geographer Jonathan Goldsmith studied the Lake Michigan shoreline for the Wisconsin Geographical Survey in 1905, he discovered the fossilized remains of trees and logs in the soil of the lake bluff near here. Scientists continue to be interested in these soil deposits, which must be at least 12,000 years old. They reveal vast changes in the climate and ecology of the lake shoreline during the Ice Age. They also present a picture of glacial action. In 1964 federal legislation designated nine areas across the state of Wisconsin notably affected by glacial action as units of the Ice Age National Scientific Reserve. Wisconsin now owns 25 acres in the Buried Forest Unit. Future plans call for interpretive facilities at the sites and a hiking trail linking the nine units. (See site 33.)

42. Kewaunee
Hy W-42

Long the home of Potawatomi Indians, the site of present-day Kewaunee is believed to have been frequented by French explorers, fur traders, and missionaries. Kewauneeans often cite a visit by Father Jacques Marquette in 1674 as the earliest recorded event in local history. Fur traders, including a representative of the North West Company, established posts at Kewaunee in the late eighteenth century.

Permanent white settlement here, as along much of Wisconsin's Lake Michigan shoreline, dates from the 1830s. Then wealthy land speculators, including John Jacob Astor of the American Fur Company and James Duane Doty, a prominent political figure in Wisconsin's territorial history, observed that Kewaunee's fine natural harbor could make it an important lakeport. The village was platted in 1836, and lots were sold in Chicago. Reports of the discovery of gold in the swampy lands near the Kewaunee River mouth sent land values skyrocketing to as much as $500 per acre before the panic of 1837 silenced the sawmill and dampened all activity.

A revival came in the 1840s and Kewaunee began to grow as a lumbering town. In the 1860s a cedar post and lumber trade centered at Kewaunee. Logs cut upstream and floated to Kewaunee sawmills clogged the river in springtime. Hundreds of settlers from the German and Belgian settlements of Brown, Kewaunee, and Door counties hauled loads of ties and posts to town. One local historian noted, "The streets are lively with teams of oxen and sleds emerging from the woods at all times of the day, carrying shingles and cord wood." From the busy harbor ships carried products of the forest to Milwaukee and Chicago markets.

Excitement other than the bustle of the lumber business marked Kewaunee's history in 1862. One fall day a body of more than a hundred settlers marched from Red River, armed with clubs and guns, to protest against the drawing of names for military service. They accused the local draft commissioner, W. S. Finlay, of unfairness and partiality. Finlay fled to a steamboat in the harbor while his wife and a store clerk placated the mob with food. Finlay went to Milwaukee and returned with federal troops, who remained during the fall to help enforce the Civil War draft. (See also site 26.)

During the village's early years, Kewauneeans developed the rich Lake Michigan fisheries and launched a number of lake schooners. Nevertheless, lumbering remained for many years the major business. As late as 1889 two sawmills and two planing mills still operated, but the town's economy was shifting to serve the growing agricultural community. A fanning-mill factory, a plaster and feed mill, a grain elevator, a boot and shoe factory, two breweries, a large flour mill, and a foundry and machine shop were on the 1889 business roster.

Workers and interior of the Leyse Aluminum Company plant in 1922. Courtesy State Historical Society of Wisconsin. WHi(X3)24556

Kewaunee businesses very clearly reflected the transition from lumbering to agriculture at the turn of the century. Canning factories and plants that produced farm equipment—stump pullers, feed cutters, plows, pea-harvesting and shelling equipment, whey separators, and cheese boxes—added to the volume of the city's business. Woodworking plants that made laboratory and church furniture were firmly established, and in 1905 an aluminum products plant was located at Kewaunee. The whine of the sawmills had ceased.

At the end of the century, the Kewaunee harbor, always a great asset to the town's economy, took on new importance. In 1891 the completion of the Kewaunee, Green Bay and Western Railroad gave the city a westward connection, and one year later the Toledo, Ann Arbor and Northern Michigan inaugurated car ferry and passenger service betwen Frankfort, Michigan, and Kewaunee. A combination of private and federal funds financed major improvements in the harbor facilities.

The city, long dependent upon stagelines and Lake Michigan sail and steam boats, acquired the potential for railroad passenger and freight traffic east and west. Kewaunee became an east-west transshipment point as well as the seat of county government, a trade and sevice center, a processor of agricultural produce, and a manufacturing town. It had achieved the status of incorporated village in 1873 and moved on to city status in 1883.

Kewaunee industry still includes three firms with long histories in the community: Svaboda Industires, dating from 1881 and now specializing in grandfather clocks and church furniture, its original product; Leyse Aluminum, organized in 1903; and the Frank Hamachek Machine Company, established in 1924. In 1980 the largest employer, Kewaunee Engineering, with about 1,200 workers on the payroll, produced heavy steel machinery components. Leyse Aluminum, the second-largest firm, employed approximately 600–800 workers, and Hamachek, the third-largest, 200–300. Industry, transportation, recreation, tourism, and farming are all important components of Kewaunee's present economy. With a population of about 2,700, Kewaunee is larger today than at the height of the lumbering boom.

Kewaunee Sites of Interest

(1) Kewaunee County Jail Museum

Courthouse Square

The cells for prisoners in Kewaunee's jail, built in 1876, became a county history exhibit in 1969. The sheriff's office and living quarters have been converted into a museum, several rooms of which are furnished in the style of the nineteenth century. The Kewaunee County Historical Society's collection of rare books and documents, which formerly belonged to Edward Decker, are housed here as well. Decker, a pioneer resident, was a banker, newspaper owner, and manager of the Ahnapee and Western Railroad. Also in the museum is a model of the *U.S.S. Pueblo*. The Kewaunee Engineering Company built the original at Kewaunee in 1944. North Koreans captured it in 1968. In addition, there are lifelike carved basswood figures of Father Marquette and the Indians who greeted his landing here. The artist was Luis Shrovnal. The large hand-carved sculpture depicting Custer's Last Stand was produced in 1904–1910 by two master carvers and donated to the museum by Svaboda Industries.

Open Memorial Day–Labor Day, Thursday–Sunday, 12:30 P.M.–4:00 P.M. $

(2) Svaboda Industries

303 Park Street

Svaboda Industries, founded in 1881, was based on the artistry and craftsmanship of Joseph Svaboda, Sr., born in Bohemia and trained in artistic woodworking, carving, architecture, and design in Vienna. He came from Vienna to Kewaunee County and for a time farmed. Encouraged to use his wood-carving skills by the Reverend Adalbert Cipin, he helped build the altars for old St. Mary's Church in Algoma (see site 43, no. [3]). In 1881 he started a modest wood-carving business and retail furniture store in Kewaunee. From this grew the Svaboda Church Furniture Company, today known as Svaboda Industries. While there are no plant tours, Svaboda Industries has a showroom for visitors where examples of current products, including grandfather clocks, and a collection of old wood carvings are on display. Open year round, Monday–Saturday 9:00 A.M.–5:00 P.M.; Sunday, 10:00 A.M.–5:00 P.M.

Car ferries docked at the Kewaunee slip. Photo by George M. Frisbie. Courtesy State Historical Society of Wisconsin. WHi(X3)40554

(3) Railroad Car and Auto Ferry Pier

Kewaunee Harbor

Those interested in crossing the lake from Kewaunee to Ludington, Michigan, should inquire at the ferry office for sailing times.

(4) Kewaunee Nuclear Power Plant

Hy W-42

Located about six miles south of the city on the lakeshore, the plant is owned by Wisconsin Power and Light

Company, Madison Gas and Electric, and the Wisconsin Public Service Corporation and has been operated by the last-named company since it went into commercial operation in June 1974. Not open to the public.

43. Algoma

Hy W-42

Like Kewaunee, Algoma developed as a lumbering town. Originally the village was called Wolf River; later it was renamed Ahnapee; in 1896 it adopted the name Algoma. Located at the mouth of the Ahnapee River, with a fine natural harbor, the site appealed to the imaginations of town promoters in the 1830s. Not until the 1850s, however, did sawmills and settlers make Ahnapee a genuine town.

Kewaunee and Ahnapee were rivals in the lumber trade, for the seat of county govenment, and for local influence. That spirit of rivalry led residents of Ahnapee to call Kewaunee "Sawdustville, inhabited by Bohemians and fleas." Kewaunee villagers prayed for "south winds to keep the smell of sauerkraut from Wolf River within its own confines." Both communities had numerous immigrant settlers from the same European sources, but plainly Ahnapee was considered more German and Kewaunee more Bohemian at the height of the lumber boom.

When lumbering was in its heyday in the late 1860s, Ahnapee, like other Kewaunee and Door County sawmill towns, caught the Great Lakes boatbuilding fever. In the winter of 1866–67, woodsmen scoured the woods for shipbuilding timber. Keels for several vessels were laid at Ahnapee. The first sizable vessel built in Kewaunee County, the *Ahnapee of Chicago*, a lumber schooner, was launched four miles from town in 1868.

Commercial fishing in the early decades also provided a living for a number of families who caught, salted, and exported thousands of barrels of whitefish and trout to Milwaukee, Chicago, and other distribution points.

Ahnapee's lumber boom was at its height when the devastating forest fires of 1871 severely damaged timber stands in the Ahnapee River Valley. The three sawmills still operating in the town in 1879 disappeared from the roster of local industries a decade later. The population declined from 1,500 to 1,000 during that 10-year period.

Algoma made a successful transition from lumbering to other forms of economic activity. As farmers turned the cutover lands to grain and dairy production, Algoma became the marketplace and supply center for the surrounding countryside. The town also developed industry to serve the farms. By 1890 Algoma boasted a wagon, carriage, and sleigh factory of some years standing, a foundry and machine shop capable of repairing machinery, a cheese-box factory, a large flour mill, and a fly net factory that supplied local needs and made life more bearable for Chicago horses. At least one important woodworking establishment remained in 1890, a manufacturer of sashes, doors, and blinds.

Convinced that a railroad connection would further Algoma's prosperity, the town fathers in 1891 worked strenuously to get local support for construction of a line to Sturgeon Bay. A successful petition campaign in both Kewaunee and Door counties led to the construction of the Ahnapee and Western from Algoma to Sturgeon Bay. That line connected with another, which gave access to Green Bay and Kewaunee. By 1894 freight and passenger service operated all the way from Green Bay to Sturgeon Bay via Kewaunee and Algoma. Farmers relied on the railroad rather than exclusively on ships, their only freight carriers for many years. The railroad ceased freight service in 1968 because it could no longer compete with truck transportation.

Algoma's economic life today still revolves around the lake, the fields, and the woodlands. Two companies, each employing over 200 workers, produce hardwood products. Another corporation produces farm machinery. Yet another, Algoma Net, successor to the fly net company of the late nineteenth century, makes hammocks, handbags, and other net products. A newer industry that processes apples and cherries, the Von Stiehl Winery, opened in 1968 (below). The tourist, recreation, vacation, and summer home businesses are very important to Algoma's economy. The beautiful Lake Michigan environment attracts thousands. Algoma, population 3,650, styles itself the "Trout and Salmon Capital of Wisconsin."

Algoma has a number of attractive new public buildings. City Hall, the police station, the elementary school, the large library serving Kewaunee and Door counties, and the city hospital on Fremont Street are contemporary in style and built of Lannon stone. A new high school stands at the south end of town and a youth club along the lakeshore.

Fishing boats at the dock in Algoma. Photo by Paul Vanderbilt (May 5, 1963). Both commercial and sport fishing continue at present-day Algoma; the catch is now far different than in the nineteenth century when trout and whitefish were abundant. Trout is a species closed to commercial fishing in Wisconsin's Lake Michigan waters while the Department of Natural Resources tries to mend the devastation of the lamprey. Courtesy State Historical Society of Wisconsin. WHi(X2)13977

Algoma Sites of Interest

(1) Von Stiehl Winery
115 Navarino Street
In 1967 Dr. C. W. Stiehl purchased this old brewery building for use as a winery. For 20 years the sturcture housed a brewing business founded by Bohemian immigrants, Wojta Stransky and Francis Swatz, in 1866. The Von Stiehl Winery makes cherry and apple wines. Open daily, May–October, 9:00 A.M.–5:00 P.M. Free tours.

(2) St. Paul's Evangelical Lutheran Church
4th and State Streets
In December 1862 German-born Protestants in Algoma organized St. Paul's Evangelical Lutheran Church. Two church structures served their needs before the congregation voted in 1895 to build the beautiful brick Gothic sanctuary currently in use.

For decades St. Paul's served Kewaunee's German-born Lutherans as a center for social, educational, and cultural as well as spiritual activities. Pastors preached in German; the congregation sang in German. Until 1881 pastors had the responsibility for educating the children of the congregation. In that year the church built a Christian day school and hired a German-speaking teacher to teach in it. Not until 1904 was the pastor given permission to preach an occasional English sermon. Seven years later the congregation agreed that children should be instructed in English when and where they didn't understand German. When the church celebrated its Diamond Jubilee in 1937, two services were held in English and one in Ger-

In July, along Hy 42 near Kewaunee and Algoma, lie cherry orchards with fruit laden trees like this one. The Von Stiehl Winery is one of three wineries on the Door Peninsula that use locally produced fruit. Photo by Margaret Bogue.

man. In 1956 German services were permanently dropped. On October 14, 1962, St. Paul's celebrated its Centennial Jubilee with three special services and a church dinner attended by more than a thousand persons.

(3) St. Mary's Church
118 Church Street
Although Algoma's Bohemian Hall, built in the 1870s, is no longer standing, St. Mary's Church, which owes its existence in large measure to Czech-speaking Bohemians, is a reminder of their importance in Algoma's early history. The congregation of the Immaculate Conception of the Blessed Virgin Mary was organized about 1860. It built a small frame church in 1863 and received its first resident priest in 1868. During the next 10 years, the parish, served by nine different priests, made only modest gains, apparently because it could not find a priest satisfactory to its communicants. The most notable achievements of the decade were the building of a new sanctuary in 1872, a handsome, white frame Gothic structure, and the establishment of a small parochial school. When Father Adalbert Cipin, a Bohemian-speaking priest, began his 16 years of service to St. Mary's in 1878, the parish entered a new era of growth.

During the first half-century, St. Mary's played an important role in the lives of Algoma's Bohemians. Bohemian-speaking priests, whom the congregation repeatedly requested, helped to foster a cultural and spiritual sense of community by involving parishioners directly in the work of the church. St. Mary's parochial school grew to meet the educational needs of the children. Nor were worldly needs neglected. St. Mary's organized benevolent societies that provided sickness benefits and assistance to families whose main wage earner had died.

The congregation that decided to build a more substantial church early in the twentieth century was considerably more diverse. Communicants of German and French Canadian origin were well represented. Here and there Irish names appeared on the parish roster. The third St. Mary's church was built in 1905 and 1906. A Green Bay architect, W. E. Reynolds, designed the beautiful brick Gothic structure that still serves the parish. Both interior and exterior have been altered. The major external change, an entrance built in 1949–1950 to enclose the front steps, diminishes the beauty of the original structure.

44. Ahnapee State Park Trail
(BFHP)

An abandoned railroad right-of-way following the Ahnapee River now serves as a 15-mile hiking and biking route from Algoma to Sturgeon Bay. The Ahnapee and Western Railway, organized in the 1890s to provide rail connections for Algoma, discontinued freight service in the 1960s. The state Department of Natural Resources then acquired land for the trail, which opened in 1971. It passes open farmland, cedar swamps, the Ahnapee Wildlife Area, and the Forestville Millpond.

The southern end of the trail is at County Trunk M at the limits of Algoma, and the northern at Nelson Road at the limits of Sturgeon Bay. The old mill dam at Forestville provides an attractive spot to rest or fish.

45. Robert La Salle County Park
County Trunk U, south of Sturgeon Bay (P)

Separated from food and supplies and lost in a storm, René-Robert Cavelier de La Salle and his men struggled ashore in 1679 at a site generally believed to have been in this vicinity. The French explorer was canoeing along the Wisconsin shoreline with his party when the storm overtook them. Legend has it that they were saved from starvation by the generosity of Potawatomi Indians.

La Salle's 1679 journey to the Door Peninsula was part of a fur-trading venture. His sailing ship, the *Griffon*, built above the falls of the Niagara, sailed, it is believed, to the islands at the tip of the Door Peninsula, took on a load of furs, and started for Niagara in the fall of 1679. It never reached Niagara, and its fate has never been learned.

Robert La Salle County Park was established by the Door County Park Commission in 1929.

46. Sturgeon Bay
Hys W-42 and W-57

The site of Sturgeon Bay at a portage between the head of the bay and Lake Michigan has a venerable history. Here Indians, explorers, missionaries, fur

Bird's-eye view of Sturgeon Bay in 1880. Note the two lumber mills, center and right with sawed lumber on the dock ready for shipment. In the background (right of center) is the Door County Courthouse (9) below, built in 1878. Courtesy State Historical Society of Wisconsin. WHi(X3)40694

traders, and later settlers came and went by the hundreds in their travels between Green Bay and Lake Michigan proper, avoiding the long and dangerous journey by water around the peninsula. The procession included many notable people, among them Father Jacques Marquette in 1674 and a few years later Father Claude Allouez, the first traveler to record the name of the overland stretch: "La Portage des Esturgeons." Fur traders lived here off and on until 1835, but not until 1850 did Oliver P. Graham build the first house in the beautiful virgin white pine forest that covered the site of present-day Sturgeon Bay. One year later some of the Norwegian Moravian followers of Rev. Andreas M. Iverson (see site 59) settled in the area, despite their leader's dim view of pine forest as potential farmland.

Upper New York State developers who felt very optimistic about the future demand for Sturgeon Bay lumber in Chicago markets arrived in the boom years of the 1850s. Before the panic of 1857, three sawmills operated about a half-mile apart, each with its boarding house, primitive shanties, and seasonal population of itinerant mill hands of many nationalities. The panic closed the mills, but after the Civil War all went into operation again.

Although Sturgeon Bay was the county seat of Door County and a lumbering town, it was small and was incorporated as a village only in 1874, more than two decades after the beginning of settlement. Overshadowed until 1875, by Little Sturgeon Bay, where a local businessman operated lumber and grist mills and a shipbuilding yard, Sturgeon Bay nevertheless had staunch supporters who dreamed of great future development. Central in their dreams was the idea of building a canal to open a water route between Green Bay and Lake Michigan.

Joseph Harris, Jr. (see no. [8]), spearheaded Sturgeon Bay's efforts to secure a federal land grant to help finance canal construction and to interest private capital in the venture. Congress in 1866 approved legislation granting 200,000 acres of public domain for support of the canal, but refused Harris' later request for an additional 200,000 acres. Construction work finally began in 1873, and five years later the waters of Lake Michigan and Green Bay met in an opening wide enough for a rowboat to pass through. The canal opened to general navigation in 1882–100 feet wide, 7,400 feet long, and deep enough for vessels with a 13-foot draft. The federal government assumed responsibility for the canal in 1893.

Canal traffic brought business to the community. As well as serving Green Bay shippers, principally the lumbermen of the western shore, the canal route to Milwaukee and Chicago proved advantageous for Sturgeon Bay lumbermen and the developers of

Leathem D. Smith Stone Company at Sturgeon Bay. Courtesy State Historical Society of Wisconsin. WHi(A6)3936

commercial stone quarries, which grew in importance after 1880, supplying tons of stone to improve Lake Michigan harbors. The canal also made it very convenient for Lake Michigan passenger boats to bring vacationers and tourists to Sturgeon Bay. The town fathers envisioned a thriving resort industry, and they were not disappointed.

Commercial fishing continued as an important part of the local economy. Always a part of local industry, shipbuilding grew in the late nineteenth and early twentieth centuries. A well-known twentieth-century firm, the Sturgeon Bay Shipbuilding and Dry Dock Corporation, originated at Sturgeon Bay in 1896 as Rieboldt and Wolter's Shipyard, specializing in vessel overhauling and repair and in dry-dock construction. The company had operated at Sheboygan for more than a decade prior to the move to Sturgeon Bay. In 1917 it was the largest single business in Door County. Early in the twentieth century the Leathem D. Smith Shipbuilding Corporation organized as a successor to the Leathem and Smith Towing and Wrecking Company. The successors to both of these companies became part of the Bay Shipbuilding Corporation in the early 1970s. Two other shipbuilding businesses founded early in the twentieth century still survive as separate firms: Peterson Builders, founded in 1907, and Palmer Johnson, founded in 1918. Shipbuilding, repair, and maintenance is now Sturgeon Bay's largest industry, and the Bay Shipbuilding Corporation is the town's largest employer. The company, organized as a subsidiary of the Manitowoc Company, combines a long history of shipbuilding at Manitowoc with similar efforts at Sturgeon Bay. Manitowoc harbor facilities weren't adequate to permit the launching of the large bulk carriers needed to replace a fleet of aging Great Lakes freighters. The move from Manitowoc to Sturgeon Bay came in 1972.

Sturgeon Bay grew more rapidly between 1940 and 1950 than ever before in its history. The town's population increased by almost 2,000, and in 1950 it had more than 7,000 residents. The town boomed during World War II as government contracts stimulated shipbuilding. Its yards turned out patrol boats (PT boats), cargo boats, and barges for the Navy and a wide variety of craft for the Army Transportation Corps.

While the shipbuilding and resort industries are the most obvious ways in which Sturgeon Bay's economy compensated for the loss of lumbering at the end of the nineteenth century, farming on the cutover lands of the Door Peninsula also contributed to economic growth. This county seat became the trade, banking, and distribution center for the upper Door Peninsula, where both dairying and fruit farming have prospered for many decades on the rocky limestone soils of the Door.

Joseph Zettel, a native of Switzerland who established commercial apple orchards on the Door Peninsula in the Sturgeon Bay vicinity, is generally regarded as the founder of commercial fruit farming in the area. But others deserve mention in the roster of pioneer fruit growers. Dr. E. M. Thorpe planted a 20-acre vineyard on Strawberry Island in 1865. Probably in 1862, the same year Zettel set out apple trees, Robert Laurie of Sturgeon Bay (see no. [6]) planted an orchard. Zettel's persistence and success attracted the attention of Emmett S. Goff of the University of Wisconsin and Arthur L. Hatch, an orchardist. They planted an experimental acreage of cherries, apples, pears, and plums in 1893. Commercial production of red tart cherries dates from 1896, when a few of the more adventurous planted small acreages. National recognition of Door County as a producer of red tart cherries came in 1908–1910, and commercial success led to a veritable red tart cherry boom. Door County's cherry orchards covered about 3,300 acres in 1917. Sturgeon Bay became a shipping, packing, and processing center for cherries.

Now Sturgeon Bay has more industry than ever before in its history. In 1980 three companies employed more than 500 workers each. The largest of these, employing 1,900 in 1980 is the Bay Shipbuilding Corporation, which builds ocean and Great Lakes carriers and does ship maintenance work. The second-largest, employing 650 workers in 1980, Doerr Electric, produces electric motors. Peterson Builders with 626 full-time workers in 1980, produces a wide variety of wood, steel, aluminum, and fiberglass vessels. Three firms with 100–200 employees in 1980 produce yachts, men's work shoes and boots, and commercial electrical kitchen equipment. Almost a dozen smaller firms produce various metal products. Two firms process fruit from Door County orchards. The town's current population is about 8,800. Long known as the gateway to the beautiful vacationland of the Door Peninsula and the land of apple and cherry blossoms, Sturgeon Bay, the industrial-shipbuilding town, is very evident at the old highway bridge across the Sturgeon Bay Canal.

Construction in progress at Peterson Builders, Sturgeon Bay, 1980. Photo by Margaret Bogue.

Sturgeon Bay Sites of Interest

(1) Shipbuilding Yards

Two locations offer good views of shipbuilding operations. The view north from City Hys W-42 and W-57 at the canal crossing offers a panorama of ship construction. From North 3rd Avenue and Florida Street there is an impressive view of construction from a much closer range. These are the yards of Bay Shipbuilding Corporation.

(2) Sturgeon Bay Marine Museum

North 3rd Avenue and Florida Street in Sunset Park

Located in the former office of a steamship company adjacent to the Bay Shipbuilding Corporation, the museum contains exhibits on Sturgeon Bay's shipbuilding industry. Open daily, Memorial Day–Labor Day, 10:00 A.M.–noon; 1:30–4:00 P.M.

(3) Door County Historical Museum

4th Avenue and Michigan Street

Housed in a building constructed of local limestone by the Door County Historical Society in 1938, the museum contains over 5,000 items illustrating Door County history. The museum is well worth a visit. The first curator of the museum did much of the work on the structure and supplied the motto carved over the huge fireplace: "Past, present, and future cannot be separated." Open May 15–October 15, Tuesday–Saturday, 10:00 A.M.–noon; 1:00–5:00 P.M. Open daily at these times in July and August. Donation.

(4) Miller Art Center
4th Avenue and Nebraska Street
Door County painter Gerhard C. F. Miller and his wife contributed substantially to the Miller Art Center, which is located in the Door County Public Library building. The center offers approximately six special exhibits per year, ranging from the works of local artists of all ages to those of nationally and internationally known artists. Summer hours are Monday–Saturday, 10:00A.M.–noon, 1:00–5:00 P.M.; and Monday, Wednesday, and Friday evenings, 7:00–9:00 P.M. Free.

(5) Door County Library
4th Avenue and Nebraska Street
In addition to its general collections of books, newspapers, magazines, films, filmstrips, records, slides, and cassettes, the library's Laurie Room has a special collection dealing with local and Wisconsin history. Open year round, Monday–Friday, 10:00 A.M.–9:00 P.M.; Saturday, 10:00 A.M.–5:00 P.M.

(6) Robert Laurie House
4635 Bay Shore Drive (North 3rd Avenue extended)
Robert Laurie built this fine eight-room house out of local stone for his family in 1866–1870. A Scotsman born in Glasgow, Laurie became a ship's carpenter and sailed the seven seas before coming to Buffalo with his family in 1852. Three years later, he and his brother built a boat and set out on the Great Lakes in search of a new location with plentiful timber near the water. They chose the Sturgeon Bay area. Farmers at first, the Lauries also built boats and developed a small trading business with early Door County settlers, sailing from port to port with their wares. Robert Laurie prospered. In 1862 he planted an apple orchard, which produced the 13 varieties of apples he exhibited at the Door County Fair in 1869. Sometime after 1865 he built lime kilns and began to produce commercial lime. In 1880 he and his son John opened a stone quarry. The business had proven very successful at the time of Robert Laurie's death in 1889.

The house reflects Laurie's prosperity as a pioneer shipbuilder, merchant, orchardist, and developer of the Sturgeon Bay lime and stone industry. It is privately owned and not open to the public.

(7) Turner House
4369 Bay Shore Drive (North 3rd Avenue extended)
In 1886 Alexander Laurie, son of Robert Laurie, built this house, distinguished by carefully cut and faced stone construction. Laurie was a Great Lakes ship captain who began his career sailing his father's boats. In 1880 he became a registered steamboat captain. Laurie and his wife occupied the house only until 1904. It has since had several owners. The interior is completely changed, but the exterior is much like the original. The house is privately owned and not open to the public.

(8) Joseph Harris, Jr., House
201 West Maple Street
Joseph Harris, Jr., was an important figure in the early history of Sturgeon Bay. An Englishman by birth, he came to New York State in 1850 and to Sturgeon Bay in 1855, where he helped organize Door County government and founded the *Door County Advocate* in 1862. He served as the first register of deeds, the first treasurer, and the first county clerk. In 1864 Harris was elected to represent Door County in the Wisconsin Senate. He worked strenuously to secure federal aid for the construction of the Sturgeon Bay Ship Canal. In 1876 Harris built this Milwaukee cream brick residence, Victorian Picturesque in style, the first brick house in Sturgeon Bay. Both the exterior and the nine original rooms have been altered. The house is privately owned and not open to the public.

(9) Door County Courthouse
138 South 4th Avenue
Built in 1878, this is the second Door County courthouse, built to replace a two-story frame structure that stood at the southeast corner of 2nd and Michigan Streets. H. C. Koch and G. A. Graebert, Milwaukee architects, designed the structure in Italianate style with a square tower. In 1953, when an addition was built, the tower was removed. Most of the original woodwork and the attractive pressed sheet steel ceiling remain, but the building does not have the impressive quality it once had as the only building on a full city block.

Those interested in looking at more of Sturgeon Bay's historic buildings will find John Kahlert and Albert Quinlan, *Early Door County Buildings and the People Who Built Them, 1849–1910* (Baileys Harbor: Meadow Lane Publishers, 1976) a very helpful guide.

Sturgeon Bay Canal lighthouse. Photo by Margaret Bogue.

(10) U.S. Coast Guard Station
East End of Sturgeon Bay Ship Canal
The grounds of the station are open to visitors daily. The Sturgeon Bay Canal lighthouse is also located here. Built as an experiment in 1899 with a 78-foot cylindrical iron tower supported by lattice, triangular buttresses, and guy wires, the structure failed to withstand wind stress. It now stands as redesigned in 1903, with a 98-foot cylindrical stair tower, a new skeletal steel framework, and enlarged buttresses. In June 1980 the lighthouse was declared eligible for the National Register of Historic Places.

The U.S. Coast Guard cutter *Mobile Bay*, berthed at Sturgeon Bay, is open to visitors on Sunday afternoons in summer. The easiest access to the station is from Hys W-42 and W-57, which bypass the downtown area. A U.S. Coast Guard Station sign marks the turn-off point.

(11) University of Wisconsin Agricultural Experiment Station
Hy W-42
Established in 1922 to help the fruit growers of the Door Peninsula, the 120-acre experimental station is located adjacent to the site of Joseph Zettel's orchard. Visitors may obtain maps for a self-guided tour of experimental plots where fruits and vegetables are growing. Open year round, Monday–Friday, 8:00 A.M.–5:00 P.M. Free.

47. Whitefish Dunes State Park

Hy W-57, Clark Lake Road (HPS)

Landscape architect Jens Jensen of Chicago and Ellison Bay (see site 57, no. [1]) and the State Conservation Commission recommended that the Whitefish Dunes area be preserved as public parkland in 1937, 30 years before the state authorized purchase of 821 acres. Only recently has this popular park been open to the public. Visitors may swim, picnic, hike, and enjoy the beautiful dunes along Lake Michigan. Vegetation has stabilized the tallest of the dunes, but the smaller ones are active under the influence of wind and wave. Behind the dunes is Clark Lake, formed when Lake Michigan waves and currents deposited sand and gravel across a deep indentation in the shoreline. There are two other coastal lakes on the eastern shore of Door County: Kangaroo Lake south of Baileys Harbor and Europe Lake near the tip of the peninsula. $

48. Cave Point County Park

Cave Point Drive off Hy W-57, just east of Valmy (HP)

Waves have hollowed out many caves in the limestone ledges at the shoreline here. One is 40 feet deep. Visitors who stand near the shore and see and hear the waves crashing into this cave feel the ground tremble under their feet because the bedrock forming the shoreline is actually the roof of the cave. This cave may be the opening of a passage running under the entire Door Peninsula to Green Bay.

At least 25 caves lie on the Green Bay side of the peninsula. Discovered near Egg Harbor in 1879, the longest cave in the Niagara Escarpment is believed to be hundreds of feet deep. Visitors should not attempt exploration of caves on either shore. The risk of drowning is great.

49. Jacksonport

Hy W-57

The forests and the fisheries attracted developers and settlers to the site of present-day Jacksonport. A few settlers made the region their home in the 1850s and early 1860s, but not until after the Civil War did developers decide to exploit its lumber resources. The three organizers of the land company that sought to develop Jacksonport were an interesting crew. They were Colonel C. L. Harris, a Green Bay businessman; Andrew Jackson, a federal official in the U.S. Land Office at Menasha; and John Reynolds, a Madison real estate dealer. They bought land in the area, and in February 1867

Lake Michigan shore near Jacksonport. Photo by Paul Vanderbilt. Courtesy State Historical Society of Wisconsin. WHi(X2)13983

sent out a work crew of 37 untrained lumberjacks under the supervision of a Maine woodsman. The combination of a capital shortage, inexperienced labor, poor production, and a skunk's invasion of the boarding house soon led the company into bankruptcy. Eventually Charles Reynolds, a Green Bay merchant and brother of John Reynolds, acquired the property, moved to Jacksonport, and in the mid-1870s established a successful store and lumbering business. Among the settlers who came to Jacksonport in the 1870s was a Canadian, Joseph Smith, whose extensive production of cedar posts earned him the title of Cedar King of Door County. With the depletion of the timber, farming on the cutover lands gradually developed.

Like the stands of virgin timber, the great untapped fisheries of Lake Michigan invited early exploitation. Hundreds of barrels of salted whitefish and trout were shipped from Jacksonport in the 1860s and 1870s. Some were marketed fresh and some (in wintertime) frozen. In the 1880s local fishermen shifted to herring because the preferred species had been fished out. By 1917 commercial fishing was in sharp decline.

Jacksonport and the surrounding countryside attracted immigrants from many areas, especially from Germany, in the 1880s. They helped carve farms from cutover lands and left a community heritage that is still commemorated with a May Festival.

50. Baileys Harbor
Hy W-57

In the late 1840s in the midst of a storm that threatened to wreck his schooner, Captain Justice Bailey sailed into the harbor that bears his name. He was on a return trip to Milwaukee from Buffalo with a boatload of immigrants in search of new homes. Both Captain Bailey and his passengers were charmed with what they found. Bailey saw great possibilities in the local stone and stands of timber, for too many Milwaukee-bound ships from Buffalo sailed short of cargo. The immigrants, tired of the monotonous ship's diet, feasted on the excellent raspberries found on shore.

Captain Bailey reported his find to his fellow captains. The owner of the line and a well-known speculator, Alanson Sweet, purchased land at the site of present-day Baileys Harbor in 1849, built a pier and a sawmill, and opened a stone quarry. At his urging the federal government built a lighthouse for the harbor in 1852. Largely through his efforts, the state legislature created Door County and made Baileys Harbor the county seat. Within a few years Sweet withdrew from the Baileys Harbor development. Another developer, A. K. Lee, in 1857 saw great possibilities in the Baileys Harbor location. He built a substantial home and six lime kilns. After one year, Lee abandoned the project, but one of his Irish workers stayed and farmed. He encouraged other Irish families to join him during and immediately after the Civil War.

The beginnings of a permanent village date from 1861, when Moses Kilgore built the first permanent pier. For the next 40 years, Baileys Harbor thrived as Door County's major shipping point for cedar poles, ties, and cordwood. During the navigation season schooners arrived daily to carry away products of the forest, and steamboats sailing between Chicago and Buffalo stopped regularly to fuel.

Wood-cutting jobs created by the lumbering industry attracted Finns, Germans, and Poles to Baileys Harbor. Many of them stayed to develop farms on the cutover lands. The Germans were in the majority.

As timber supplies dwindled at the turn of the century, farming and fishing became the major ways of making a living, and life in the village assumed a more leisurely pace. Now Baileys Harbor relies mainly on tourism, recreation, and summer homes for economic vitality. Lake Michigan, as in the past, still holds the key to the village's well-being.

Baileys Harbor Sites of Interest

(1) Bjorklunden Chapel

Chapel Lane south of Baileys Harbor

As you come into Baileys Harbor from the south, take a right turn off Hy W-57 onto Lake Shore Drive and follow it to Chapel Lane, where signs point the way to Bjorklunden Chapel.

Before 1939 Mr. and Mrs. Donald Boynton of Highland Park, Illinois, enjoyed many happy summers here on their estate. Then world events scattered their family, and the Boyntons embarked on a project to symbolize memories of past summers spent at Baileys Harbor.

On their travels they had admired a wooden *stavkirke*, or chapel, at Lillehammer, Norway, and decided to construct a similar chapel on their estate. Many years were spent planning and building the chapel. The Boyntons executed interior and exterior wood carvings for it. Mrs. Boynton, in addition, painted 41 murals, symbolizing religious thought through the ages, in the chapel. The structure was dedicated in 1949.

After the deaths of both Boyntons, their 360-acre estate, Bjorklunden Vid Sjon, meaning "birch forest by the water," was bequeathed to Lawrence University. Following the wishes of the Boyntons, Lawrence University shares the peace and beauty of the chapel and estate with others. University students act as guides in the chapel. Open mid-June through August, Monday–Wednesday, 1:00–3:30 P.M. $

(2) St. Mary of the Lake

Hy W-57

Before 1874 traveling priests said mass in private homes to meet the needs of Baileys Harbor Catholics. In that year St. Mary of the Lake parish built a white frame church overlooking Lake Michigan. The present church, a simple and beautiful Door County limestone structure, was built in 1936 with money that Michael W. McArdle had bequeathed for that specific purpose. McArdle was born and raised on the family farm on the outskirts of Baileys Harbor. After teaching school for four years at Sister Bay and Ellison Bay, he attended Oshkosh Normal School and the University of Wisconsin. In 1901 he earned a law degree in Madison and thereafter practiced law in a number of locations before moving to Chicago and embarking on a business career. McArdle became a very successful industrialist, president of the Chicago Flexible Shaft Company and of Flexible Shaft Co., Ltd., Toronto.

Five or six years before his death, he developed the Maxwelton Braes resort adjacent to his boyhood home at Baileys Harbor and ultimately purchased the home property as well. Perhaps he was making retirement plans, but cancer cut them short. He died in 1935, leaving a will that provided for the construction of St. Mary's church and rectory, as well as the Baileys Harbor town hall and library building. Michael McArdle also left substantial sums to the University of Wisconsin for cancer research.

(3) Toft House

Hy W-57 in the center of Baileys Harbor

A home built by Miles Carrington, a Baileys Harbor settler from Ohio, originally stood on this site. It burned down in the 1860s or early 1870s, and Joel Carrington built this New England clapboard salt-box structure to replace it. The Toft family purchased the house in 1900. In recent years Emma Toft, a distinguished Wisconsin conservationist (see no. [7]), lived here. John Kahlert, a student of Door County architecture, regards it as "one of a very few" early Door County buildings with New England architectural antecedents.

(4) Globe Hotel*

8090 Main Street (Hy W-57)

The old Globe Hotel building, constructed in 1867, served first as a store; then, in 1875, a native of Providence,

Stovewood log barn located about 4 miles northwest of Baileys Harbor on County Trunk F. Photo by Margaret Bogue.

Rhode Island, adapted it for use as a hotel. The exterior is virtually unaltered.

(5) Proposed Rural Stovewood Structure Historic District

In the 1970s preservationists suggested adding the many stovewood structures in the Baileys Harbor Area to the National Register of Historic Places. Characteristic of this interesting and practical form of construction are walls made from stove-length pieces of wood mortared together to form a thick, solid wall. Many of the stovewood structures in Door County are a version of the half-timber style and were probably built by German immigrant settlers.

An excellent example of a stovewood and half-timber barn can be seen on County Trunk F, about four miles northwest of Baileys Harbor. The A. Zahn residence and the adjacent blacksmith shop, located on Hy W-57 in Baileys Harbor, are of stovewood construction covered with clapboard. The sign "Zahn's Aprons and Gifts" in front of the two-story residence easily identifies it. The two Baileys Harbor structures were built about 1900 by German immigrants.

(6) Baileys Harbor Range Lights

County Trunk Q off Hy W-57

Through the efforts of Alanson Sweet, a Milwaukee entrepreneur, Baileys Harbor acquired a lighthouse in 1852. In 1870 Cana Island Light (see site 51) and two separate beacons, the Baileys Harbor Range Lights, replaced it. The beacons are located on the property of the Ridges Sanctuary, one in the old range-light residence and the other in a small wooden tower. One beacon is higher than the other. Ship captains knew that they would have a safe passage if they maneuvered their ships until one beacon was directly above the other and then followed these aligned lights into port.

(7) Ridges Sanctuary–Toft's Point–Mud Lake Wildlife Area

County Trunk Q off Hy W-57, one-half mile north of Baileys Harbor

In 1967 the U.S. Department of the Interior designated the 800-acre Ridges Sanctuary as a Natural Landmark. It is named for the 16 sand ridges that lie inland from the shoreline, part of the lake bottom formed in the postglacial Lake Nippising stage. Boreal forest grows on the ridges, and in between them bogs support various species. This great botanical diversity enables visitors to observe a succession of vegetation from open water to climax boreal forest. Most of the usual Wisconsin plant species, plus many rare ones, are here, among them 25 kinds of orchids, Arctic primroses, and fringed gentians. The Ridges Sanctuary, Inc., organized in the 1930s, is responsible for the preservation of this natural area and for planning and presenting educational programs for the public.

In the 1930s the federal government gave the land on which the Ridges Sanctuary is located to Door County for a park. It was originally part of the lighthouse property. Different plans for the park immediately surfaced. Bread-and-butter-minded people in the midst of the Great Depression argued for a trailer park, an income producer. Some members of the Door County Park Commission and others of naturalist and conservationist frame

Miss Emma Toft seldom was photographed, but here Roy Lukes, chief Naturalist at the Ridges Sanctuary and Miss Toft's close friend, captured the spirit of her dedication to preserving nature. Courtesy Roy Lukes.

of mind, from the area and elsewhere, argued for a natural sanctuary. The determined action of the Door County Women's Club in organizing a public protest against the trailer park development helped preserve its natural state.

There is a self-guided nature trail for visitors; naturalists offer guided tours. One nature trail is specifically designed for the blind. Evening programs are held at the center in summer. The Ridges Sanctuary is recommended only for those who are seriously interested in nature study. Open May 30–September 1, Monday–Saturday, 9:00 A.M.–5:00 P.M.; Sunday, 1:00–5:00 P.M. $

Immediately adjacent to the Ridges lies Toft's Point, 340 acres in an almost virgin state, including a fine mixed stand of large red and white pines, hemlock, and northern hardwoods. It includes as well a spruce-tamarack bog, white cedar and spruce lowlands, and aquatic vegetation along the shore of the bay. Emma Toft, daughter of Thomas Toft, a Danish immigrant who worked in the pineries of Michigan and Wisconsin before coming to Baileys Harbor, devoted her life to preserving this natural area and the adjacent Ridges. Toft was born here in 1891, left her home for a few years to teach school and to train as a nurse in Chicago, and then returned in 1917 to care for her parents.

For over 40 years she lived alone on the point and ran a small family hotel for students of nature. She worked hard to fulfill her parents' dream of preserving the point for future generations. In 1968 she gave it to the University of Wisconsin–Green Bay on the understanding that it would remain a nature preserve. Before her death in 1982, Toft received many honors and awards for her conservation work. She and Jens Jensen were good friends (see site 57).

Mud Lake Wildlife Area, 960 acres, includes a muckbottomed lake lying over limestone and a freshwater marsh dominated by cattails. Here are diverse flora and abundant wildlife. Duck hunting is permitted.

In 1974 these three areas—the Ridges Sanctuary, Toft's Point, and the Mud Lake Wildlife Area—were combined as a single Natural Landmark.

Cana Island Lighthouse. Photo by Lynn Frederick. Courtesy Lynn Frederick.

51. Cana Island

4 miles north of Baileys Harbor: take County Trunk Q and Cana Island Road

A rocky causeway joins Cana Island with the mainland when the water level is low, as it usually is in late summer and autumn. When it is deeper, the nine-acre island is completely separated from the mainland. On this island the federal government in 1869 constructed an 88-foot lighthouse* of yellow brick, located between two good harbors, Moonlight Bay and North Bay, both places of refuge from storms. In 1901 the brick tower was encased in sheet steel and painted white. Now an automated electric beacon, the light operated for many years on lard, whale oil, and kerosene.

Lighthouses such as this one became absolutely essential once lumbering in the Green Bay area took on major proportions in the mid-nineteenth century. Not until 1882, when the Sturgeon Bay Canal made it possible to avoid the perilous journey around the peninsula and through Death's Door (see site 54), could lumber schooners avoid the risks of a long voyage through dangerous reefs, headlands, and hidden shoals. The traffic was very sizable: over 7,300 vessels passed up and down the bay annually, between 1868 and 1870, according to the count of one lighthouse keeper.

52. Newport State Park

Newport Drive south of Hy W-42 (CHPS)

Loggers created the village of Newport in the 1870s. Here lake boats stopped frequently to pick up cordwood for fuel. With the timber gone, the village rapidly lost population. In 1966 the state of Wisconsin purchased the site of Newport to create a park. Originally called Europe Lake Park, its name was changed to commemorate the lumbering village. Newport homes once stood at the picnic area. Nine miles of Lake Michigan shoreline offer opportunities for hiking and swimming, and there are about 28 miles of marked trails for hiking and skiing. The Newport Conifer-Hardwoods Scientific Area is on the south edge of the park, where ancient dunes support a hardwood forest. $

The Bounty II *at dock and loading for Washington Island. Photo by Margaret Bogue.*

53. Gills Rock

Hy W-42

Formerly known as Hedgehog Harbor, Gills Rock was named for Elias Gill, a local nineteenth-century landowner. It lies at the very tip of Door County's "thumb." The village cluster of resorts, cottages, and docks is the place to catch the auto ferry to cross Porte des Morts Strait to Washington Island. Steel ferry boats make as many as 15 round trips daily between island and mainland in the summer. They run less frequently in winter.

Door County Maritime Museum
Gills Rock Memorial Park, Wisconsin Bay Road
Museum exhibits include a picture display of boats built at Sturgeon Bay, marine engines, and artifacts of shipwrecks and commercial fishing. Open daily in July and August, 10:00 A.M.–4:00 P.M., and at those hours on weekends only in June and September. $

54. Death's Door (Porte des Morts Strait) and Grand Traverse Islands State Park (proposed)

terminus of Hy W-42

The strait lying between the tip of the Door Peninsula and Washington Island is appropriately named Death's Door, or Porte des Morts Strait. Treacherous currents, winds, and rocky shorelines have taken many a human life. Who named the strait? Some trace the name to the loss of an Indian war party caught in a sudden storm and crushed against the rocky shores. Others sug-

Paul Hammersmith of Milwaukee depicted commercial fishing on Washington Island in this etching dated August 23, 1902. Courtesy State Historical Society of Wisconsin. WHi(X3)40320

gest that the French are responsible. Whatever its origin, the name is appropriate.

Nineteenth-century sailors feared the waters, and rightly so. One lighthouse keeper recorded two shipwrecks per week at that point between 1872 and 1889. Sailing vessels stopped at Pilot Island to pick up a pilot to guide them through the channel.

To assist navigation through the Porte des Morts passage, the U.S. government built the Plum Island Range Lights in 1897. The front range-light tower was replaced in 1964, but the 65-foot-tall rear light dates from 1897, an iron skeletal structure with an iron watchroom topped by an octagonal lantern. It is a proposed National Register site.

People using the ferry today may feel that the name "Death's Door" is a joke because the crossing is so routine and uneventful most of the time. The sailors of the past, however, did not have diesel-powered engines or modern navigational equipment.

The Grand Traverse Islands, consisting of Rock, Detroit, Pilot, Plum, and Fish islands, have been proposed for a new state park. Rock Island is already available to the public for camping, but not the other islands, which are either owned privately or owned by the federal government. If and when the state acquires them, some areas will be reserved for wildlife. Pilot Island will be reserved as a nesting site for water birds. Wherever the waters of the islands are spawning grounds, they too will be protected.

Porte des Morts Site (Archaeological)*

On the far northeast coast of the Door Peninsula, archaeologists have discovered evidence of Indian occupation from 100 A.D. to the historical period. Identified Indian cultures include the Middle and Late Woodland and the Mississippian with one or more Oneota components. Some of the artifacts discovered may be evidence that La Salle's 1679 expedition took refuge here from a violent storm in the strait.

55. Washington Island

The sturdy steel ferry loaded with people, cars, campers, perhaps a bus, and a gasoline tanker truck pulls away from Gills Rock headed for Detroit Harbor, Washington Island. The tree-topped layered limestone cliffs at the tip of the Door slip by, and the ferry passes smoothly through the crosscurrents, choppy waters, and contrary winds of Death's Door, once the demise of many a sail- and steam-powered ship. On past the Plum Island range lights, past Detroit Island, the ferry moves to the Detroit Harbor dock and discharges its passengers and cargo. The seven-mile, 40-minute ride is over, but the brief taste of Green Bay, a deep sparkling blue on a sunny day, lingers. Ahead lies the exploration of 36-mile-square Washington Island, whose 550 permanent residents gladly talk about the island's past and present, where 100 miles of good roads lead to West Harbor, Washington Harbor, Jackson Harbor, and through the island interior, and where a beautiful shoreline offers many places to enjoy the bay and the lake. Washington Island, named for a U.S. Army vessel that stopped here en route to Green Bay in 1816, occupies a venerable place in Lake Michigan history.

Attracted by its excellent fisheries and natural protection, for unknown centuries Indians found Washington Island a good place to live. Before the Americans renamed it, the Indians called Washington and the surrounding islands the Huron or Potawatomi Islands, in honor of some of the groups who lived there.

This Norse mythological figure carved in wood on a chair for Thordarson's library may represent Thor, the most widely worshiped God in Iceland. The beautifully carved chairs, each with a different mythological figure, are no longer in the old Great Hall-Library. Photo by Paul Vanderbilt (about 1966). Courtesy State Historical Society of Wisconsin. WHi(X2)20104

The Thordarson Great Hall, September 1982. Photo by Margaret Bogue.

purchased it from the Thordarson estate and began developing a state park with primitive and backpacking campsites and 10.5 miles of hiking trails. The beauty of Lake Michigan, the woods, the sand and stone beaches, and the 140-foot cliff at Potawatomi Point make this roughly one-mile-square island ideal for nature lovers. Over 200 species of birds frequent the island. Deer, foxes, coyotes, and rabbits live here. The sounds of the wind in the trees and the waves on the beach create a peaceful, reflective mood on a sunny summer day. Choose the 6.5-mile Thordarson Loop Trail around the island, the 1.5-mile Fernwood Trail and Hauamal Trails across the island, or the 1-mile Algonquin Nature Trail for hiking.

Evidence of Rock Island's inhabitants in the distant past lies along these trails. In the primitive camping-swimming beach area, the island's historic district,* Lawrence University archaeologists have verified the presence of Indian peoples from the early centuries A.D. to the French and Indian War (1756–1763). Digs have identified the presence of the Potawatomi over long periods, and probably the presence of the Fox, Winnebago, and Menominee as well. Quite possibly the Hurons and Ottawa took refuge on Rock Island when in 1650–1652 they fled westward from the wrath of the Iroquois (see pp. 20–21).

Ronald J. Mason, professor of anthropology at Lawrence University and one of the archaeologists in charge of the Rock Island research, thinks that findings there may document the presence on the island of La Salle's trading post and the point from which the *Griffon* sailed to its doom in 1679. He regards the Rock Island Historical District* as having "unique historic importance" and as "a goldmine of information on the early French Empire in the western Great Lakes."

As the westward tide of American settlement began to utilize the Great Lakes water route into the midcontinent, safe navigation made a lighthouse on Rock Island imperative. *Pottawatomie Light** at the northwest point of Rock Island, built in 1839, is one of the older lights on the U.S. shoreline of the Great Lakes. It stood 137 feet above the lake level, marking the channel of navigation into Green Bay. After the original lighthouse washed away, the present building, constructed of coursed rubble (gray limestone), was built in 1858. Its automated light still warns Green Bay ship traffic away from its shores. Use the Thordarson Loop Trail to visit the lighthouse grounds. The building is not open to the public.

A group of seven trappers and fishermen from the Island of St. Helena in the Straits of Mackinac made the first permanent white American settlement on Rock Island in 1835 and 1836. Others, collectively known as the Illinois colony, joined them 1844–1847 to share the island with a hundred or more Chippewa Indians.

For a brief period Rock Island's community flourished. Its 169 inhabitants in 1850 were mostly fishermen, but the colony included coopers, a chairmaker, a blacksmith, a shoemaker, and a physician. Isolated and off the beaten path of the growing lake traffic, Rock Island families began moving away in the 1850s and 1860s. Many went to Washington Island. The cabins of the fishing village that dotted the eastern shore rotted, but two cemeteries are reminders of the pioneer fishermen. Both are marked and are accessible from the Thordarson Loop.

For a half-century the lighthouse keeper and his family were virtually the only residents of the island. In 1910, with the Thordarson purchase, a new chapter in island history began.

Ferry service to Rock Island is available at the Jackson Harbor Dock on Washington Island every hour from 10:00 A.M. to 4:00 P.M. in July and August (see site 55). Cars and motorized vehicles are prohibited on the island.

57. Ellison Bay

Hy W-42

A Danish immigrant, John Eliasen, founded the village of Ellison Bay in 1872 when he built a store and a large pier for a cordwood, cedar post, and telegraph pole business. Eliasen had settled at Ephraim (site 59) in 1854 and farmed 40 poor stony acres before embarking on this ambitious enterprise. Succeeding in his efforts to attract settlers, he prospered at Ellison Bay. Lumbering and fishing were the major means of livelihood in the small community until the early twentieth century, when fruit farming and tourism strengthened the local economy. Cherry and apple orchards date from 1908 when during Door County's fruit-growing boom, the Ellison Bay Orchard Company planted 210 acres. Tourism, now the mainstay of the community, began to develop in the twentieth century and blossomed in the 1920s with the advent of the widespread use of the automobile.

The Clearing*

Garret Bay Road

Located on a wooded 125-acre tract on the limestone cliffs overlooking Green Bay north of Ellison Bay, The Clearing was originally the summer home of Jens Jensen, prominent American landscape architect. Jensen was born and raised in Denmark and came to the United States in 1884 at the age of 24. During his first period of employment by the West Park Commission of Chicago, from 1886 to 1900, Jensen developed his theory of prairie landscape, a theory that he applied in private practice from 1900 to 1907 after being dismissed from his Park Commission job for political reasons. Again from 1907 to 1920 he worked for the city of Chicago, this time as superintendent of the West Parks and as landscape architect, redesigning three parks and completely designing Columbus Park, considered to be among his major works.

Main Lodge at The Clearing, Ellison Bay. Courtesy Donald S. Bucholz.

In 1920 Jensen, weary of Chicago politics, left the West Parks position and returned to private practice. During the next 15 years he landscaped several estates in the north shore suburbs, undertook many projects for the Ford family in Detroit, landscaped the Ford Motor Car Company's exhibit at the Chicago Fair in 1933, and accepted commissions for large and small projects in many cities in the Midwest. He continued to accept public work. The Lincoln Memorial Gardens in Springfield, Illinois, are a beautiful example of his later public projects.

Jensen has been called "the last great exponent of the tradition of romantic landscape architecture." He rejected formalism and placed great importance on the use of local plant materials and a use of space, rock, and water sensitive to nature.

Jensen began buying Door County land in 1919, but not until 1936 did he retire to northern Wisconsin to found a school, "The Clearing," where his students were encouraged to contemplate nature and pursue their skills and crafts. He believed that nature was capable of both restoring and inspiring the individual. Hence the school's name, which referred to the process of clearing the mind and putting oneself in contact with nature. After the first school Jensen built on the Ellison Bay property burned down in 1937, he rebuilt it using local stone and wood to blend with the natural environment. Jensen died in 1951, and for 18 years his longtime secretary, Mertha Fulkerson, ran the school, emphasizing Jensen's educational philosophy. The property is now owned and operated by the Wisconsin Farm Bureau. Visitors on Sundays only, 1:00–4:00 P.M. Free.

58. Sister Bay

Hys W-42 and W-57

Andrew Seaquist, one of a number of Swedish immigrant woodcutters who came into the area in the 1860s, is generally regarded as the founder of Sister Bay. By 1870, following the construction of a pier, a large sawmill, a gristmill, several stores, and a hotel, Sister Bay had emerged as a lumber port of some importance. During the next 15 to 20 years it exported cordwood, cedar poles, railroad ties, and hemlock bark. Like other Door County villages, Sister Bay also drew its vitality from fishing and farming. Around the turn of the century, summer tourists began coming to the Sister Bay area, but initially they patronized neighboring Liberty Park. Now Sister Bay is an important shopping center for northern Door County and a large resort community.

Sister Bay Sites of Interest

(1) Little Log School, Sister Bay Visitors' Information Center
intersection, Hys W-42 and W-57, Gateway Park
Built in 1865 by Hans Gunnerson, a Norwegian immigrant, the school originally stood near the intersection of old Stage Road and County Trunk Z. It was used as a school until 1881. The building was then moved several times and put to various uses. In 1960 the Door County Historical Society acquired it, moved it to its present location, and restored it at a cost of $8,000. Its original cost was $100.

(2) Sister Islands
Located northwest of Sister Bay, the Sister Islands, from which the town takes its name, are gull nesting areas maintained by the Wisconsin Department of Natural Resources. They are an official scientific area of the state.

(3) Larson Orchards
Hy W-42, north of village
Formerly known as the Roen Orchards, the Larson Orchards since 1971 have been producing apples, apple cider, and cherry juice. Visitors can pick their own apples and see packing and pressing operations.

59. Ephraim

Hy W-42

The desire of a group of Scandinavian Moravians to establish a religious community led to the founding of Ephraim. Rev. Andreas M. Iverson, a Norwegian Moravian, led his flock to Ephraim (meaning "the very fruitful") in the spring of 1853, just four years after his arrival in America. Years of hard work, worry, and discord lay behind the establishment of this religious community.

Iverson began his ministry in Milwaukee and soon discovered that his congregation wanted to escape the distractions, dirt, and poverty of the city. When Nils Otto Tank, a wealthy retired Norwegian Moravian missionary, offered to help the group set up an agricultural community, Iverson and his congregation gladly accepted. Purchasing a substantial acreage near Fort Howard (on the west side of the city of Green Bay), Tank provided the settlers with land, homes, a church, and a school for a communal religious settlement. Soon Iverson and a fellow Moravian minister began to question Tank's motives and to insist that individual rather than collective ownership of property was desirable (see site 67, no. [7]). When Tank refused to deed the land to the members of the community, Iverson led most of the group to Ephraim, a decision that he seems to have regretted in later years.

The Ephraim settlement quickly encountered serious problems. The scouting party that selected the location had tested the soil and felt satisfied that it was good for farming. Iverson later remarked: "Least of all did we dream of that layer of limestone which lay only a few feet under the surface." Moreover, the settlers were desperately poor, and Iverson found it essential to travel and solicit donations to help with land purchases, building construction, and the necessities of life. Meanwhile, the group bravely felled trees, built cabins, cleared land, and planted crops. Soon the Ephraim colonists, like other Door

County settlers, found that the best way to make a living was by a combination of selling timber products, fishing, and farming. The settlers built a school in 1857 and began a church that was completed two years later. In 1858 Aslag Anderson built a long dock out into the bay so that ships could load lumber and cordwood, and he opened a store. The financial panic of 1857 added to the colony's woes, but with the return of better times in 1859, Ephraim began to grow. The period of greatest hardship and struggle had passed when, in 1864, Rev. Iverson was assigned to Moravian communities in Illinois.

Ephraim's beauty, fine harbor, and many recreational opportunities attracted both an artists' colony and tourists in the twentieth century. Visitors may still see a number of original buildings associated with the Moravian colony.

Goodleston Cabin, Ephraim. Photo by Margaret Bogue.

Ephraim Sites of Interest

(1) Anderson's Dock and Store

Hy W-42

Built in 1858, the dock, warehouse, and store remain historic landmarks commemorating the early years of the Ephraim settlement. The wooden dock and frame warehouse, partially burned in 1880, were rebuilt and have remained in use. Yachts still moor at the dock. The warehouse, now the Hardy Gallery, is used for exhibits of the Peninsula Arts Association in July and August.

The store, built by Aslag Anderson in 1858, remained a family business until the 1950s. Now owned by the Ephraim Foundation, it has been restored and stocked with the kinds of items Anderson sold to settlers and sailors in pioneer days. Open in July and August, Monday–Saturday, 10:00 A.M.–1:00 P.M., 2:00–5:00 P.M.

(2) Goodleston Cabin

Moravia Street

In this early Ephraim log home, the Moravian congregation met before the colony had a church. Now owned and operated by the Ephraim Foundation, as is the schoolhouse (see below), it serves as a museum to display the furnishings collected from local homes. Open Monday–Saturday in summer, 10:00 A.M.–noon, 1:00–4:00 P.M. Donation.

(3) Pioneer Schoolhouse

Moravia Street adjacent to Goodleston Cabin

Ephraim's second schoolhouse, built in 1869, now houses a collection of pioneer school furnishings and equipment, and it also serves as an art gallery and headquarters for the summer Music Festival of the Peninsula Arts Association.

Ephraim's first schoolhouse was built in 1857, a small log structure located on land donated by Rev. Iverson. By 1869 school-age children in Ephraim were so numerous that a larger building was needed. This second school remained in use for 70 years, at times with as many as 64 children in attendance. Open in July and August, Monday–Saturday, 2:00–4:30 P.M. Donation.

(4) Iverson Parsonage

Moravia Street (County Trunk Q)

Andreas M. Iverson was born in Christiansand, Norway, in 1823. Before migrating to America in 1849, he acquired the skills of farmer, carpenter, and shipbuilder. He attended the Mission Institute at Stavanger from 1844 to 1848 and was ordained a Moravian minister in 1850.

As leader of the Ephraim settlement he built his house, a more elaborate home than most in the pioneer community, in 1853 and 1854. It measures 36 feet by 24 feet and has a central hallway with two rooms on either side on the first floor. The second-story loft originally had a finished fifth room and a hay loft. A two-stall stable was hewn into the rocky hillside beneath the house. The walls of the house are flat-hewn logs covered with wide vertical siding. The interior was plastered and the home whitewashed inside and out. For a short time the Moravian congregation met in the Iverson home. The solid building still stands, with only minor alterations. It is privately owned and not open to the public.

(5) Moravian Church
Moravia Street
This frame church is a substantial enlargement of the colony's first church, built in 1857–1859 by the struggling settlers. It was moved from its original location on the shore.

60. Peninsula State Park
Hy W-42 (BCHPS)

Peninsula State Park is one of the first parks established by the state of Wisconsin. Created in 1907 "to preserve, protect and appropriately improve the many places of uncommon beauty in the state," the Wisconsin State Park Board immediately felt pressures from advocates of various sites. Residents of Baraboo and Madison argued for the creation of a state park at Devil's Lake.

Caves in bluffs at Peninsula State Park. Courtesy Wisconsin Department of Natural Resources.

Thomas Reynolds, assemblyman from Door County, secured a pledge of $25,000 from U.S. Senator Isaac Stephenson to match state funds and countered with a proposal to create a state park in Door County. After considering three potential Door County sites, the State Park Board and John Nolen, a nationally prominent landscape architect, unanimously agreed that the land lying between Fish Creek and Ephraim, with its deep green woods, cliffs, and sandy beaches was the finest site in Wisconsin for a state park. Taking a slap at Stephenson, Robert M. La Follette, Sr.'s Progressives who dominated the Wisconsin legislature refused the gift and the idea of naming the park for him. The state began buying land for Peninsula State Park in 1910 and added more gradually. Now it contains 3,800 acres.

Some owners did not wish to sell immediately. Fishermen occupying shanties on Shanty Bay, now known as Nicolet Bay, at first refused state offers to buy their homes. Sven Anderson, "a gentle minded old bachelor" whose home stood atop what is now known as "Sven's Bluff," wanted to stay where he could see "the most beautiful view in America." The state acquired the land after the death of the old fisherman. The park's golf course occupies the site of a large cherry orchard. The village of Fish Creek still owns cemetery land now within park borders.

Door County residents call Peninsula State Park the "paradise of Wisconsin" because of its great natural beauty. Besides Sven's Bluff, there are Eagle Bluff, where cliffs drop 180 feet to the water level, and Norway Bluff, which is one quarter-mile back from the shoreline. Two 75-foot observation towers at Eagle Bluff and Sven's Bluff provide an even better view. Park naturalists conduct nature hikes from the White Cedar Nature Center and present evening campfire programs. There are many miles of hiking trails through the dense woods. At one time an old cooper's furnace stood along the shore road. Here coopers made barrels for shipping fish to urban markets. $

Peninsula State Park Sites of Interest

(1) Indian Monument

Peninsula State Park Golf Course

On the Peninsula State Park Golf Course stands a 30-foot pole, a memorial to the Potawatomi and Menominee Indians. Hjalmar R. Holand, president of the Door County Historical Society, developed the idea for the pole in 1926 to honor the Potawatomis, who established themselves in Door County in the seventeenth century. (In fact Wisconsin Indians did not erect poles. This idea for the memorial is borrowed from the traditions of Indians of the northwest coast.) An artist carved the pole with scenes representing events in Potawatomi history. At the dedication ceremony in 1927, Chief Simon Kahquados unveiled the monument. After his death four years later, Chief Kahquados was buried beneath a glacial boulder a few feet north of the memorial pole, as he had requested.

By the late 1960s weathering had rotted the original pole. The sculptor Adlai Stevenson Hardin duplicated the original carvings on it and added additional bands representing the Menominee Indians, since they too had once lived in Door County. Hardin

Chief Simon Kahquados of the Potawatomi. Courtesy State Historical Society of Wisconsin. WHi(X3)33204

worked on the carving for almost two years prior to its raising on July 14, 1970.

(2) Eagle Bluff Lighthouse*

Shore Road

The lighthouse was built in 1868, a square brick light tower attached to the keeper's house and diagonally oriented to it. One of the early keepers of the light, William Duclon, occupied the house with his wife and seven sons for almost 40 years. With so much assistance, the keeper regularly won a U.S. Lighthouse Service award for well-maintained grounds. The light is now automatic. In 1961 the Door County Historical Society undertook the project of restoring the house to its nineteenth-century appearance and filling it with period furnishings. The museum and the restoration of the lighthouse are exceptionally well done. Open daily, mid-June to Labor Day, 9:30 A.M.–5:00 P.M. $

61. Fish Creek
Hy W-42, and
Chambers Island
5 miles Offshore

Pleasure craft at the marina in Fish Creek. Photo by Margaret Bogue.

Named by Increase Claflin, the first settler in the area in 1842, Fish Creek owes its early development to Asa Thorp, a New York Yankee who preempted land there in 1845 with the idea of building a pier and supplying cordwood to passing steamboats. There was not a single pier or cordwood business from Washington Harbor to the head of the bay, and steamboats often ran out of fuel. Eight years later when Thorp built his pier and opened a cordwood business, Fish Creek developed into a busy village. Lumbering and milling were very important to Fish Creek's prosperity for the next four decades, and so was fishing. The village emerged as the major fishing center on the Door. As Hjalmar R. Holand noted in *Old Peninsula Days*: "Nearly every man in the village was a fisherman, and north and south of the village the shore was lined with fishermen's homes and nets."

By the close of the century, forests and fisheries afforded a livelihood to fewer and fewer people, and Fish Creek began a transition to resort town where city dwellers could enjoy relatively pollen-free air and the beauties of Lake Michigan. Pioneer resort businesses included those of Edgar Thorp, son of Asa Thorp, who in 1895 enlarged his house to accommodate vacationers from Milwaukee and St. Louis, and Dr. Herman Weckler of Milwaukee, who first tried his hand at raising trotting horses at Fish Creek, failed at that, and then went into the hotel business. By 1917 these summer hotels, the largest in Door County, served 300 guests. From this modest beginning, Fish Creek's current major industry, tourism, has grown to serve thousands each year.

Fish Creek Sites of Interest

(1) Thorp Cabin
Founder's Square
Located in the center of Fish Creek, Founder's Square includes buildings that Edgar Thorp used as part of his resort hotel. In one corner stands the Asa Thorp log cabin, where the Thorps lived after coming to Fish Creek. The crude structure was built, possibly in 1849, by an unknown person. It is believed to be among the oldest remaining structures in Door County.

(2) Noble House
southeast corner Hy W-42
at Main Street
According to John Kahlert, a student of early Door County buildings, the Noble House is the oldest home in Fish Creek other than the Thorp Cabin. Alexander Noble, a farmer and blacksmith, built it in 1868. The two-story, 10 room frame house is much the same as when it was built, except for the porch and pillars, which were added later. This private residence was

still occupied by a member of the family in 1976.

(3) Church of the Atonement
Main Street
Episcopalians who wanted a house of worship converted a fishermen's home into this simple Gothic frame structure in 1878.

(4) Peninsula Players Theater in a Garden
Hy W-42, 3 miles south of Fish Creek
Since they began quite modestly in Fish Creek in 1935, the Peninsula Players have become a major summer cultural attraction in Door County. In 1981, in their forty-seventh season, this professional resident summer theater included productions of Broadway hits performed by an acting company made up of professionals from New York, Chicago, and the West Coast and from regional theaters and television studios. Performances are staged in an all-weather pavilion seating 500 in a garden setting. For information and reservations call (414) 868-3287.

(5) Peninsula Music Festival
Gibraltar Auditorium, Fish Creek
The year 1981 marked the twenty-ninth Annual Peninsula Music Festival, a program of classical chamber music with instrumental and vocal soloists at each performance. Three concerts were performed weekly for two weeks in August. The conductor of the festival orchestra in 1981 was Michael Charry, conductor of the Nashville Symphony. The musicians came from major symphony orchestras and conservatories throughout the country. For information on the concert season, write Peninsula Music Festival, Ephraim, WI 54211.

Chambers Island

The island was named for Talbot Chambers, one of four officers on the sailing vessels carrying troops from Fort Mackinac to establish an American fort at Green Bay in August 1816. Fishermen, shipbuilders, and lumbermen came to the island in the mid-nineteenth century to use its bountiful natural resources.

Hjalmar R. Holand has called Captain David Clow of Chambers Island "the most interesting boat builder of Door County." He built a number of boats and ships at Chambers Island, including the 285-ton *Sarah Clow*, launched in 1862. Captain Clow and his wife felled the trees, cut the lumber, and built the boat that the captain named after her.

The Wisconsin Chair Company of Port Washington cut the oak and hemlock in the 1890s and then retained the island for the company owner's summer home until the mid-1920s. A resort development of the 1920s failed. Currently the island is privately owned and partially developed.

Chambers Island Lighthouse*
Constructed of buff brick in 1868 and resembling Eagle Bluff Lighthouse in design (see site 60, no. [2]), Chambers Island Light is now the property of the township of Gibraltar. Nearby a new automated light mounted on a metal tower marks the west passage of Green Bay. Around the lighthouse is a park with facilities for hiking and picnicking, Memorial Day through Labor Day. Campfires are not allowed.

62. Egg Harbor
Hy W-42

Egg Harbor's name has had many explanations, ranging from the shape of the bay to the abundance of gull and duck eggs found there in pioneer days. Most fun of all is Elizabeth Fisher Baird's story. She and her husband, a prominent Green Bay attorney, took passage to Mackinac in June 1825 with Joseph Rolette in one of several large canoes laden with furs and bound for John Jacob Astor's fur-trading headquarters. As the boats neared Egg Harbor on the second day of the journey, the crews of two boats got into a paddling contest to see which would reach shore first. Paddling gave way to egg throwing after Mrs. Baird had been carefully protected by a tarpaulin. The battle continued on land until all the eggs were smashed. "To this rude frolic," Baird concluded, "may be attributed the origin of the name of this town in Door County."

Levi and Jacob, brothers of Asa Thorp, the founder of Fish Creek, settled at Egg Harbor in the 1850s, built a pier, and went into the business of selling cedar posts and cordwood. Levi became a very successful businessman. In 1880 he owned the largest farm in Door County. In 1894 he planted a commercial apple orchard, one of the earliest in northern Door County. Among his other businesses was a general merchandise store in Egg Harbor. In 1871 he built Cupola House, an impressive home in its day, symbolic of his status in the community (see below).

Although Egg Harbor's history as a resort town dates from the turn of the century, tourism assumed great im-

Cupola House. Photo by Margaret Bogue.

portance in the 1920s. It is now the major business of this village of fewer than 200 permanent residents.

Egg Harbor Sites of Interest

(1) Cupola House*
7836 Egg Harbor Road
Built by Levi Thorp in 1871 after years of careful planning, this clapboard house in the Victorian Italianate style stands on high ground. It now, with a recently refurbished exterior, serves as a gift shop. The home contains 14 rooms, including a ballroom and servants' quarters at the rear of the second floor.

(2) St. John the Baptist Catholic Church
Hy W-42, south of the village
The parish of St. John the Baptist was organized in the 1870s. The present church, built in 1909–1910 of native limestone and glacial rocks, is well worth seeing. A solid and beautiful structure, it is an impressive sanctuary for a congregation of about 60 families to have built.

63. Potawatomi State Park
Hy W-42 (BCFHP)

This 1,200-acre park was established in 1928 at the site of Government Bluff Quarry, where the federal government quarried limestone from 1835 to 1885 to make federally funded harbor improvements on Lake Michigan. For a time the federal government considered establishing a naval training center here, but picked the Lake Forest, Illinois, site instead (see site 9). In 1928, when the federal government offered the site to Wisconsin at $1.25 per acre on the understanding that it would be used for a park, Wisconsin accepted.

The bluff overlooks Green Bay and Sawyer's Harbor, two or more miles of shoreline, islands, bays, inlets, meadows, and a large cherry orchard on a slope across Sturgeon Bay. From the 75-foot observation tower, on a clear day there is even a view of Lake Michigan in the distance. Deer, raccoons, and at least 60 species of songbirds are found in the park. Island View and Hemlock trails provide ample opportunities to see the park's dense woodlands and many species of wildflowers. $

Sherwood Point Lighthouse is close to the park, accessible from County Trunk M. Built by the federal government in 1881, the brick tower with keeper's home attached marks the Green Bay entrance to Sturgeon Bay. The lighthouse has been suggested as a National Register site.

64. The Belgian Settlements: Brussels, Namur, Dyckesville, and Tornado Memorial Park
Hy W-57

Along Highway W-57, running south from Sturgeon Bay to Green Bay, lie three villages—Brussels, Namur, and Dyckesville—that are at the heart of the peninsula's nineteenth-century Belgian settlements. Belgians came to live in the forested lands of Green Bay in the seven years before the Civil War because they believed that greater opportunity lay in America than in their densely populated homeland, because the availability of cheap farmland in America was well publicized, and because Antwerp shipowners carried on a very effective campaign of recruiting emigrant passengers. Small farmers, laborers, and mechanics had serious doubts about their economic prospects in the homeland after 1830. Some may have decided to emigrate for religious reasons. Protestants, always a minority in Belgium, were among the 10 families that left for America in 1853 to form the first of the Belgian settlements on the Door Peninsula.

The immigrants of 1853 might well have settled near present-day Kaukauna had the new arrivals not chanced to meet a Belgian priest, Father Edward Daems, who persuaded them to locate at the Bay Settlement 10 miles northeast of Green Bay. They selected lands 4 miles south of Dyckesville. By no means wealthy and in no sense prepared for the rigors of clearing heavily forested land, they endured all kinds of physical hardships, including a cholera epidemic. In 1857 hard times magnified their problems. Some of the men sought work in Green Bay, Milwaukee, and Chicago to earn money to improve their lands. They found a better solution close at hand, utilizing their stands of pine to make shingles acceptable to storekeepers in Green Bay and Kewaunee as payment for supplies, tools, and food. The Belgian colony grew to an estimated 800 settlers in Brown, Kewaunee, and Door counties by 1860.

After the Civil War came a six-year period of substantial prosperity. More and more settlers joined the original group. Homes, schools, and churches proliferated, and the Belgians took an active part in politics. Better times came in large measure from the opening of saw and shingle mills, especially the enterprises of B. F. Gardner at Little Sturgeon, which gave supplemental employment to the struggling farmers. By then they had cleared more land for cultivation.

Disaster struck when the great fire of 1871 spread ruin over much of the peninsula from Green Bay to Sturgeon Bay. The *Door County Advocate* printed a roster of county losses 18 days after the fire. In Brussels Township 53 died, and 64 farm families had all or part of their homes, barns, crops, livestock, and farming implements destroyed. At Williamsonville, now the site of Tornado Memorial Park (Hy W-57, northeast of Brussels), fire destroyed all the buildings and killed 60. Xavier Martin, a leader in the Belgian communities, estimated that the great fire left 5,000 homeless and destitute.

With the aid of relief organizations, the persistent Belgians rebuilt, often with stone and brick, and turned their cutover and burned-over lands into prosperous farms that produced grain, livestock, wool, butter, and cheese. Brussels, Namur, and Dyckesville developed as villages serving the surrounding farms.

Religion played an important part in the lives of the Belgian immigrants, both socially and spiritually. While the great majority were Catholic, the minority displayed considerable religious diversity. The Protestants among them formed several small French-speaking Presbyterian congregations. Jean Baptiste Everts, a Belgian convert to spiritualism, established a church in Gardner that as late as 1917 served 50 families. An enterprising French-speaking priest, Joseph René Vilatte, an ordained Old Catholic, established a church at Gardner in 1885 and recruited a substantial congregation, which prospered for about a decade. The Catholic bishop of Green Bay was concerned over the loss of communicants to the Old Catholics—Catholics who denied the dogma of papal infallibility, proclaimed by the pope in 1870. He requested assistance from the Norbertine order, which responded by sending several priests to serve the Belgian community in 1893.

Shortly after the establishment of the Belgian settlements, events in the Belgian Catholic community created some concern for the local priests. These stemmed from the religious experience of Adele Brice, who at the age of 24 came from Belgium with her family and settled in the Robinsonville area. She claimed that she had seen Mary, the Mother of Jesus, upon several occasions in 1859 and that the vision directed her to teach salvation to the children of the wilderness. Despite initial opposition from the local Catholic priests, she devoted her life to teaching children the catechism. Her father built a small chapel, La Chapelle, at the location of the visions, and afterward Adele Brice established a convent and school nearby. There she continued to teach until her death in 1896. At the site of La Chapelle (a half-mile east of Champion) stands a red brick Gothic chapel built in 1941. Nearby is the grave of Sister Adele. Sister Adele's example had a great impact upon the Belgian Catholic community. In the late nineteenth century,

The August 15, 1943, procession, Feast of the Assumption of the Blessed Virgin Mary at Robinsonville. Courtesy State Historical Society of Wisconsin. WHi(X3)40497

a flood of pilgrims made their way to La Chapelle each May, and on August 15 a large procession assembled at the church.

Catholics of the early Belgian communities in Brown, Door, and Kewaunee counties built at least 15 churches. Most of these have been replaced by newer structures, but 3 late nineteenth-century churches still in use in the Dyckesville area are St. Louis's in Dyckesville (built in 1888), St. Martin's at Tonet (1879), and St. Pierre's at Lincoln (1883). The Presbyterian church at Robinsonville (a half-mile west of Champion), a white clapboard structure, although altered somewhat also dates from the nineteenth century.

For decades life in the Belgian communities clearly reflected the culture of the homeland in many ways other than religion. The food, drink, songs, dances, games, language (the settlers were mainly French-speaking Walloons), and celebrations of the Old World were very evident. Traditional festivals included a special procession on Ascension Day, the Maypole Dance, and Kermiss, a three-day harvest festival that featured mass, feasting, dancing, and games. These gradually passed into disuse, but descendants of the Belgian settlers remain, and so do some of the late nineteenth-century structures they built.

Belgian Settlements Sites of Interest

(1) DuBois House
Hy W-57, between Brussels and Namur
Built by Marcelin Baudhuin about 1895, this red brick structure contains five bedrooms, a kitchen, and a dining room. Many Belgian farm families built red brick houses after the disastrous fire of 1871. This house is unusual because of its front porch and the bull's-eye in the front gable, believed to be the builder's trademark. The house is owned by Donald DuBois, the grandson of Baudhuin.

(2) Baudhuin House
Hy W-57, between Brussels and Namur
Jean Joseph Baudhuin, who emigrated from Belgium in 1869, built this impressive two-story stone house in 1880. The first floor contained six rooms. The second floor was used as a granary and the full basement as a root cellar. On the right side of the house stands a summer kitchen and a brick bake oven. The walls are two feet thick. The home is now owned by Baudhuin's great-grandson, James Baudhuin. Note also the log barn on the property.

(3) Log structure
Hy W-57, left-hand side just beyond Bauduin House
Typical of the log structures built for pioneer Belgian farms, this building is now used for storage. On side roads in the Dyckesville, Namur, and Brussels area, many such examples can be found.

65. Red Banks Wayside

Hy W-57, 12 miles north of Green Bay

To commemorate the landing of the French fur trader and explorer Jean Nicollet (see pp. 11, 13) somewhere along the shore in this general vicinity in 1634, the State Historical Society of Wisconsin has erected a marker at the Red Banks wayside. A bronze statue of Nicollet stands nearby. Explanations of the reasons for Nicollet's journey vary. Some historians stress the role of Samuel de Champlain, governor of New France, and specifically his desire to find a northwest passage and to form alliances with the "people of the sea." More recently historians have emphasized the role of the Huron Indians in initiating the journey as part of an effort to strengthen their trading empire.

66. Green Bay

Stretching from the city of Green Bay in a northeasterly direction for about 120 miles, Green Bay, named La Baye Vert by the French because its shoreline turns green in spring before Mackinac's, is the second-largest bay on the Great Lakes. Ranging from 10 to 20 miles in width and averaging 100 feet in depth, the bay is bordered by the Door Peninsula on the east and by the Wisconsin and Michigan shoreline on the west and north. In its island-strewn mouth lie Plum, Detroit, Washington, Rock, St. Martin, Poverty, and Summer islands. The Garden Peninsula divides it from Lake Michigan on the north. The bay's beautiful irregular cliff and beach shoreline stretches for hundreds of miles. Long since gone are the transparent waters that Henry R. Schoolcraft noted in 1820.

Historically Green Bay is one of the most important water routes in North America. The Fox River, emptying into the bay at its southwestern extremity, enabled canoes to pass from Lake Michigan to the Mississippi River via Lake Winnebago and the Wisconsin River. Marquette and Jolliet used the Fox River–Lake Winnebago–Wisconsin River route on their expolorations in 1673. Long before and long after, the route offered Indians, explorers, missionaries, and fur traders access to vast areas of the mid-continent.

Throughout recorded history, Green Bay has been noted for its bountiful fish and today is the source of half the fish caught in Lake Michigan. Over the centuries the catch has changed. Before 1900 fishermen found a profusion of whitefish, trout, herring, chubs, and sturgeon in the bay's waters. At the turn of the century, they recorded catches of perch. Expanded activity and improved technology in commercial fishing took a heavy toll of the fish population. At the same time, lumbering, paper mills, farming, and industrial growth affected the fish habitat. During the twentieth century pronounced decreases in the catch, changes in fish species, and the sea lamprey problem have been the major concerns of Green Bay fishermen. Currently the largest and least valuable commercial catch is the alewife; there are also smaller and more valuable catches of perch and whitefish.

University of Wisconsin and Lawrence University scientists are studying methods of predator control, fish habitats, reproduction, feeding, and growth as well as the relationships between fish species. The Wisconsin Department of Natural Resources searches for constructive stocking and regulatory policies. Scientists and policymakers alike seek a common goal: the growth of the bay's commercial and game fish populations.

For centuries, people have enjoyed the beauty of the bay waters and the forests, beaches, and cliffs of the shoreline. Since the late nineteenth century, the bay has attracted vacationers and summer residents. Although the southern portions of Green Bay had lost much of their potential for recreational use by the mid-twentieth century, now, with cleaner water and greater opportunities for swimming and sport fishing, their popularity is growing.

67. City of Green Bay

Hys W-57, US-141, US-41, I-43

Green Bay ranks as a place of major importance in the annals of Lake Michigan history. Its location on the lake at the mouth of the Fox River had special geographic, trade, and ethnopolitical advantages, recognized first by the French and later by the British and Americans. All three nations maintained fortified fur-trading posts here at the entrance to a system of waterways that led into the mid-continent. The Fox and Wisconsin rivers, separated by only a short overland portage, connected Lake Michigan with the Mississippi River.

During the French régime, explorers, fur traders, and missionaries—prominent among them Jacques Marquette, Louis Jolliet, Nicolas Perrot, and Daniel Greysolon, Sieur Du Lhut—used the Fox-Wisconsin route, long known to the Indians. French fur traders found the Green Bay location advantageous in the late 1660s, and by 1680 it had emerged as an outpost of fur trade and mission activity. From La Baye, as the French called it, French expeditions marched to wrest control of the Fox-Wisconsin route from the hostile Fox Indians in 1716, 1728, and 1733. After the outbreak of the French and Indian War, French traders and soldiers departed, and Fort La Baye (formally named Fort St. Francis) stood deserted.

Occupying British troops found a dilapidated Fort St. Francis in 1761, which the commandant promptly repaired and named Fort Edward Augustus. The fur trade and life in the French village, with its farms stretching back from the river in a ribbonlike

Fort Howard, from Francis (Comte) de Castelnau, Vues et Souvenirs de l'Amerique du Nord *(Paris, 1842). Courtesy State Historical Society of Wisconsin. WHi(X3)32689*

pattern, continued under British control until the War of 1812.

When the Americans took possession of Green Bay in 1816, they found a village of 40 to 45 families all claiming to be British subjects, impoverished by their support for the British war effort, and generally inhospitable toward their new masters. The Americans promptly built Fort Howard.

The United States applied to Green Bay the general system of government-managed trading factories designed to ensure fair trade with the Indians. John Jacob Astor's American Fur Company and other traders were so opposed to regulation, however, that Congress abolished the system in 1822. Thereafter Astor's firm and the enterprising Daniel Whitney rose to a position of dominance in the Green

Bay trade. The trade changed greatly in characer, relying more and more on fox, raccoon, muskrat, deer, wolf, and other species as the beaver population declined. Conditions essential to successful fur trading—plentiful pelts, a friendly Indian population, and a wilderness setting—were soon threatened. Cession of Indian lands to the United States was well under way in 1834, the year in which the federal government first offered surveyed portions of the public lands in Wisconsin for sale. By then the tide of settlement was spreading toward the western shore of Lake Michigan.

Reading the handwriting of the wall, Green Bay fur traders utilized eastern capital to embark on town site promotion in the 1830s. They hoped to develop Green Bay as the major port city of Lake Michigan. Not only did the financial panic of 1837 frustrate their efforts, but so did the successful bids of Milwaukee and Chicago in succeeding decades for federal funds for harbor improvement. Both of these budding towns had greater natural potential as major ports, given their physical assets and advantageous locations as trade centers for the rich, developing farmlands nearby.

Green Bay lay in a heavily forested region north of the mainstream of settlement and development in the midcontinent from 1840 to 1880 and at the southern end of the bay, making a hazardous passage around Porte des Morts essential to ship access until 1882. It grew more slowly than its rivals. Aware of the need to develop avenues of transportation, Green Bay's village promoters and city fathers alike displayed considerable imagination over the years in promoting harbor, river, canal, and railroad projects. In the 1830s they championed the Fox-Wisconsin waterway, a plan to improve the Fox River and to build a canal at Portage, thus establishing an all-water route from Lake Michigan to the Mississippi. Although the scheme never lived up to its promise, improvements to the lower Fox brought a substantial amount of river trade to the lakeport. Green Bay promoters repeatedly pressed upon the federal government their case for harbor improvements. They were enthusiastic about the construction of the Sturgeon Bay Ship Canal, which was opened to traffic in 1882. They supported the construction of railroads to connect Green Bay with Milwaukee, Chicago, and Minneapolis and with the pineries and the iron mines of the Michigan Upper Peninsula. Green Bay received excellent railroad connections between 1862 and the close of the century.

Murphy Lumber Company sawmill at Green Bay in the late nineteenth century. Courtesy Neville Public Museum of Brown County. 10,386

Meanwhile, from its fur-trading and military post beginnings, Green Bay emerged in the mid-nineteenth century as a lumber port and a trade and immigrant-outfitting center for northeastern Wisconsin. Incorporated as a city in 1854, Green Bay succeeded in capturing the seat of Brown County government from De Pere in the same year. In the boom years of the 1850s, the rapid growth of Milwaukee and Chicago and the thrust of settlement into Illinois and Wisconsin farmlands created an enormous demand for lumber. Brown County turned into a beehive of logging activity, and Green Bay flourished as a supply center for lumber camps and mills as well as a milling center and port where schooners could load lumber destined for Chicago and Milwaukee. Brown County boasted 35 sawmills in the mid-1850s, 4 of them at Green Bay.

Although the financial panic of 1857 devastated many Green Bay lumbermen and slowed the milling boom, good times returned in 1862, and the sawmills once more ran at full steam. Shingle making, once a home industry, became a commercial business as shingle mills proliferated. In 1870 Green Bay claimed the title of the world's largest shingle market, exporting 500 million shingles that year.

The great forest fires of 1871 hastened the end of the lumbering era. Scant snowfall during the winter, followed by an unusually hot, dry summer in 1871, turned the slashings left by lumbermen in Michigan and Wisconsin woodlands into a tinder box. Fires burned for weeks in the woods around Green Bay before the fateful day of October 8. Smoke hung over the waters of the bay, and dense smoke and ashes filled the air in Green Bay and Fort Howard. More than once during the early fall, flames entered the city limits of both, yet both escaped the savage fury of destruction on October 8, the day Peshtigo burned (see site 74). According to one local observer, the burned district, where about a third of the standing timber was totally destroyed, extended 50 miles west and 70 miles north of the head of the bay, up the Door Peninsula as far as Sturgeon Bay, and south from Green Bay to Lake Winnebago in a strip 10 to 20 miles wide. Green Bay and Fort Howard became havens for fire victims from the surrounding countryside who flocked there seeking medical aid, food, and shelter.

Symptoms of decline had appeared in the Brown County lumbering industry well before the fires of 1871. Lumbermen had long since harvested the pines and had begun cutting hardwoods. A number of Green Bay establishments made a variey of finished wood products. In 1866–1870 De Pere, Green Bay, and Fort Howard all became iron-smelting centers. Blast furnaces built along the Fox River utilized charcoal made from local hardwoods, local limestone, and Upper Peninsula ore to produce pig iron. The last of the furnaces closed in 1893.

A livelihood for some early Green Bay residents came from the exploitation of yet another natural resource, Lake Michigan's bountiful fish. Indians fished with net and spear in both the bay and the river. In the Fox River rapids at De Pere they used weirs. Settlers at De Pere adopted this Indian technique to catch enormous numbers of pike, whitefish, herring, and sturgeon. Between 1850 and 1870 catches here were said to have numbered in the hundreds of thousands of fish. When the railroad connected Green Bay and De Pere with Chicago, the fish were loaded into railroad cars and covered with ice for delivery to markets.

In 1854 Green Bay exported 2,236 barrels of fish. The take for all of Brown County in 1888 amounted to over 700 tons. The catch at Green Bay still numbered over a million fish in 1912, but more efficient nets, an increase in the number of fishermen, and wasteful methods had begun taking their toll in the late nineteenth century. Fishermen often caught more fish than they could market profitably. They selected the best and left the balance to rot on the beach or disposed of them for fertilizer. The sturgeon disappeared, and the whitefish yields declined. Well before the turn of the century, fishing interests persuaded the state to go into the business of restocking the lake with millions of fry annually.

During 1880–1920 Lake Michigan's bounty furnished the raw materials for yet another big business. Green Bay, like many another Wisconsin lake and river town, developed an ice trade. In the 1880s and 1890s, Green Bay supplied 100,000 to 300,000 tons of ice a year to Chicago, the nation's railroad hub, which required ice for shipping meat. The business continued until about 1920, when perfected artifical ice-making methods caused its collapse. Shipbuilding, begun at Green Bay in the Civil War years, was yet another lake-oriented industry destined to prosper for many decades.

After lumbering languished, the city's business interests, like those in many Lake Michigan lumber ports, mounted a vigorous campaign to attract industry. In 1882 the business community, infused with new blood, organized a Business Men's Association. It worked not only to attract new businesses but also to improve the harbor and to secure rail connections with Minneapolis in hopes of capturing part of the wheat trade. The association published an *Exposition* to lure new investors, parading all of Green Bay's conceivable advantages: its fine harbor and railroad connections, healthful climate, mineral springs, fine schools and churches, low indebtedness and taxes, available labor supply, nearness to timber and iron ore, and potential as a wholesale distribution point and as a service, market,·processing, and manufacturing center for northeastern Wisconsin's developing farms.

The campaign met with some im-

The paper industry in its infancy at the turn of the century ranked as the city's largest employer eighty years later. This aerial view of the Northern Paper Mills at Green Bay was made in 1948. Courtesy State Historical Society of Wisconsin. WHi(X3)39832

mediate success, and by 1910 Green Bay boasted almost a hundred small, diversified manufacturing businesses, some completely new. The breweries, flour mills, market gardens, fish-packing enterprises, stave and cooperage mills, brickyards, and shipyards, the wagon and carriage company, and the firms that bottled waters of mineral springs were businesses of long standing. Firms making wood products had long been a part of the Green Bay scene, but new firms with new lines of wood products appeared. The city's two large sawmills were busy and very specialized in output compared with their production 50 years earlier. New were the company William Larson founded in 1890 to can peas, the three paper mills founded around the turn of the century, a wood-working machine firm, and a gasoline engine company.

Green Bay's role as a wholesale and distribution center for a wide area was hardly new, but it assumed new proportions at the close of the nineteenth century, when the city became the central distributing point for three large railroads. Its harbor too was very busy, despite the loss of much freight business to the railroads. Bulk cargoes of coal and wheat accounted for most of the 1902 import and export total of 1,230,000 tons. Package freighters, fishing boats, passenger steamers, and pleasure craft as well kept the city's five miles of wharves busy.

By World War I the directions of future development of the new commercial-manufacturing Green Bay were visible. Paper milling would grow, and so would the metal industry. The processing of food produced on farmlands that once nurtured fine stands of pine and hardwood would grow in succeeding decades to include enormous quantities of meat, cheese, and cannery crops. Green Bay's role as wholesale distribution, retail trade, service, and financial center for northeastern Wisconsin and the Upper Peninsula too appeared well established.

City population figures reflected the economic transition. From a total of 4,666 residents in 1870, Green Bay grew to 9,000 in 1890. Twenty years later the population was more than 25,000. From the era of the fur trade to the disruption of European immigration in 1914, Green Bay attracted people from many nations. Families with French Canadian backgrounds lingered after the United States assumed control at Fort Howard, and in the 1830s Green Bay attracted easterners with town-building ambitions. Before the close of the next decade, German and Irish immigrants arrived, and Dutch, Belgians, and Norwegians increased Green Bay's ethnic diversity by 1860. The town's first permanent Polish residents came in 1864. A decade later at least 38 Polish families lived in Green Bay, and at the turn of the century there were more than double that number. A substantial number of Danes came in the late nineteenth century.

The foreign-born came to Green Bay by choice and direction, not by accident. Shipping, railroad, and real estate interests deliberately sought them, and so did some industries. Letters from families and friends describing life in the Green Bay area also influenced those in search of better economic opportunities. In 1870 almost 40 percent of Green Bay's population was foreign-born. Although that percentage had declined to 11.5 by 1920, persons of foreign-born stock (the foreign-born and people with one or both foreign-born parents) were then still a majority, 53 percent of the city's population. The largest national groups were German, Belgian, Polish, and Irish, but none was large enough to dominate Green Bay's ethnic character. In addition to these larger groups, the early twentieth-century city was home for Austrians, French and British Canadians, Danes, Finns, French, Dutch, Hungarians, Italians, Russians, Scots, Swedes, Swiss, Turks, and Welsh.

In the mid-nineteenth century, lumbering-related and road, harbor, canal, and railroad construction jobs provided work for unskilled immigrant labor. Others with skills found employment as tradesmen and mechanics, and some established a variety of small businesses. Thanks to Green Bay's industrial development at the turn of the century, paper mills, foundries, canneries, cheese factories, and packing plants required a large labor force, which immigrant labor helped to supply.

Expanding industry in the twentieth century has supported Green Bay's growing population. In 1980 this busy commercial-industrial city of 88,000 persons had 32 firms employing 100 or more workers each. Among them, the manufacturers of paper and paper products employed the largest number. Fort Howard Paper Company and Procter and Gamble Paper Products Company were the biggest employers, each with more than 2,000 on the payroll. Eleven companies each employed more than 100 in preparing, processing, and packing foods. The largest of these firms was Packerland Packing Company, producers of beef and meat products. Nine machinery and metal product companies, each with a payroll of more than 100, were noted in the 1980 Green Bay Chamber of Commerce listing. The biggest employer among them was the Paper Converting Machine Company, with more than 900 employees. Green Bay's major educational institutions, including the University of Wisconsin–Green Bay and Northeast Wisconsin Technical Institute, are also large employers.

Most Americans identify Green Bay with the Green Bay Packers professional football team, a member of the National Football League. Earl Louis (Curly) Lambeau founded the team in 1919 with a $500 contribution for sweaters and stockings from his employer, the Indian Packing Company, a short-lived meat-canning firm. Later Lambeau reminisced: "All they wanted was the name 'Indian Packing Co.' on the sweaters." The press promptly dubbed the team "the Green Bay Packers," a name that Lambeau tried to get rid of once the company folded. He failed and later commented: "It's a great name. But we didn't realize it then."

From a very modest beginning, the team grew in national prominence, reaching its greatest success under the management and coaching of Vincent Lombardi. In the decade after 1959, Lombardi led the Packers to five National Football League championships, six titles in the Western Division, and Super Bowl victories over the American Football League champions in 1967 and 1968. Lombardi Avenue (Hy W-32) in front of Lambeau Field commemorates his contribution to the Packers and the city of Green Bay.

Green Bay Sites of Interest

(1) Northern Voyageurs and Loggers Sculptures

201 North Monroe Avenue

These striking steel sculptures, located in front of the First Northern Savings and Loan building, stand as memorials to the fur trade and lumbering eras. The sculptor, Lyndon Pomeroy, completed "First Northern Voyageurs" in 1975 and "First Northern Loggers" in 1980, using more than six tons of steel.

(2) Brown County Courthouse*
100 South Jefferson Street
Built 1908–1910 to replace Green Bay's 1854 courthouse, the present building is an excellent example of Beaux-Arts architecture. Because the money allocated for its construction was not completely spent, the balance was used for artwork. Franz Rohrbeck, a German-born panorama painter of San Francisco and Milwaukee, did the murals on the walls and ceiling of the courthouse. He depicted figures and events in Green Bay history. For the dome he used the themes of justice, agriculture, commerce, and industry.

On the southeast corner of Courthouse Square stands an imposing statue, "Spirit of the North West," by Sidney Bedore, a student of Lorado Taft. The three figures represent Nicolas Perrot, Claude Allouez, and an Indian.

(3) The Neville Public Museum of Brown County
210 Museum Place
For many decades housed in cramped quarters in the Neville Public Library, the museum now occupies spacious new quarters. An exceptionally fine display, "On the Edge of the Inland Sea," traces the history of northeastern Wisconsin from the ice age to the present utilizing 7,200 square feet of space to depict the region's history. The main art gallery and space for traveling exhibits occupy the first floor. Science, history, and art are the focuses of five galleries on the second. Open year round, Monday, Tuesday, Friday, and Saturday, 9:00 A.M.–5:00 P.M.; Wednesday and Thursday, 9:00 A.M.–9:00 P.M.; Sunday, noon–5:00 P.M. Free.

(4) Astor Historic District*
The Astor Historic District is a 39-block area bounded roughly by the Fox River on the west, East Mason Street on the north, South Van Buren Street and South Webster Avenue on the east, and Emilie and Grignon streets on the south. It lies in what was originally the town of Astor, laid out in 1835 by agents of the American Fur Company as a town site speculation. Historically known as "The Hill," this part of present-day Green Bay became the main residential area of the town's economic and political leaders from the time of settlement well into the twentieth century.

The district's influential residents included Charles de Langlade, an officer in the French and later the British armies, skilled in marshalling Indian support; Pierre Grignon, Sr., a French fur trader; Jacob Franks and John Lawe, English entrepreneurs; and Morgan L. Martin, an American prominent in Wisconsin's political life in the territorial period (see no. [5]). Between the Civil War and the 1890s, the businessmen who shaped Green Bay's economic development chose the Astor District for their fine homes. Many members of the Green Bay Business Men's Association (above) lived here, as did the pioneer paper mill owners of the turn of the century. Other influential residents represented industry, commerce, shipbuilding, business, politics, the professions, and finance.

Visitors who would like to sample the architechtural richness of the district will find a concentration of interesting structures in the 900 block of South Madison, the 600–1100 blocks of South Monroe, and the 600–900 blocks of South Quincy.

(5) Hazelwood*
1008 South Monroe Avenue (Hy W-57)
The Neville Public Museum assumed responsibility for the home of Morgan L. Martin after the death of the last Martin family member. Hazelwood is both a lovely home and a structure of historical importance for both Green Bay and the state of Wisconsin. Morgan L. Martin was a member of the Wisconsin Territorial Council, the territory's representative in Congress, and president of the second State Constitutional Convention in 1847–1848. Later he served as a state senator and Brown County judge. Many of the original Martin family furnishings may be seen in Hazelwood. The house was built about 1837 in the Greek Revival style and is restored to the period 1830–1870. Open May through September, Wednesday–Sunday, 1:00–5:00 P.M., and the balance of the year Tuesday–Saturday during those hours. $

(6) Green Bay Churches with Distinctive National Origins
Largely because of the variety of national groups in Green Bay in the nineteenth and early twentieth centuries, the city blossomed with handsome churches. Six Catholic churches had distinct national origins: French, German, Dutch, Irish, Polish, and Belgian. The Lutheran churches of Green Bay served German, Norwegian, and Danish national groups. French-speaking Belgians organized one of the city's Presbyterian congregations. The two Moravian congregations in Green Bay were Norwegian and German in origin. There were, in addition, a German and a Norwegian-Danish Methodist-Episcopal church and one German Reformed church on the city roster in 1906. Fearing that

Hazelwood, beautifully preserved, ranks among Wisconsin's finer and more significant historic homes. The Neville Public Museum of Brown County staff conducts high quality tours. Photo by Margaret Bogue.

their English-speaking children would lose the faith, concerned Green Bay Lutherans organized Grace Lutheran in 1909 as an English-speaking congregation; at the time, not one of the three Lutheran congregations in the city conducted services in English. As for the nineteenth century American-born Protestants, they belonged mainly to Episcopal, Presbyterian, Methodist, and Baptist churches.

St. Mary of the Angels Catholic Church, 645 South Irwin Avenue

For almost a quarter-century before the construction of St. Mary of the Angels, the Polish Catholics of Green Bay struggled to establish a separate parish served by a Polish-speaking priest. The first permanent Polish settlers in Green Bay date from 1864, and Poles arrived in sufficient numbers during the seventies to attempt organization of a separate parish. In the panic year of 1873, the newly organized Polish parish of at least 38 families began gathering funds to build St. Stanislaus Kostka church. The frame structure, completed and dedicated in 1875, served its Polish congregation very briefly, for hard times made it impossible to pay the church debt. Sold at public auction to satisfy a mechanic's lien, the building was repurchased by the bishop of Green Bay and sold to the Poles of Pine Grove, a small, rural Polish community southeast of Green Bay. They dismantled, moved, and rebuilt it there, and it served their needs for many years.

Until 1898 the Polish people of Green Bay worshiped at St. Francis Xavier Cathedral. Then, with the encouragement of the Franciscan Fathers at Pulaski (site 71), they made a second atttempt at establishing a separate parish and church. As a result, the stone Gothic Revival Franciscan Monastery and St. Mary of the Angels Church were built in 1901–1903. The parish then comprised 80 families, 76 of them Polish and the balance Bohemian, German, and French. Not all of Green Bay's estimated 100 Polish families chose to worship there. Although the parish has lost much of its original ethnic character, as late as 1954, 48 percent of the membership was of Polish or partly Polish descent.

Grace Presbyterian Church, 612 Stuart Street

Organized in 1873, with 31 charter members, as the French Presbyterian Church, this French-speaking Belgian congregation occupied several sanctuaries before building a church at Stuart and Monroe Streets in 1910. That structure remains in use, along with a 1929 addition that presently serves as the sancturary. While the congregation has grown over the years, about 90 percent of Grace Presbyterian's current members are descendants of the Protestant Belgians who came to Green Bay and the Door Peninsula in the nineteenth century. The congregation is a rarity among Presbyterian churches because its members are mostly blue-collar workers employed in Green Bay industry. The businessmen and professionals so prominent in most Presbyterian congregations are absent.

St. John the Evangelist Catholic Church, 413 St. John Street

The original St. John the Evangelist Church, built in 1832 at Shantytown, a settlement on the Fox River between De Pere and Green Bay, was designed by Father Samuel Mazzuchelli, a Dominican missionary generally associated with the lead-mining region of Wisconsin, Illinios, and Iowa. Initially the congregation was mainly French, but by the 1840s immigrants from Ireland and Germany also worshiped at St. John's. The Mazzuchelli church burned down in 1847, and St. John's relocated in a small frame structure, formerly used by the Methodists, very near the site of the present church. The congregation built a beautiful twin-towered red brick Gothic Revival structure to meet the needs of the growing parish in 1873. After fire completely destroyed it, construction began in 1912 on the brick Romanesque sancturary currently used by St. John's parishioners. St. John's is the mother church of Green Bay's Catholic parishes. The Germans, Dutch, and Flemish in St. John's congregation were the first to depart to form their own churches (see below).

St. Francis Xavier Cathedral,
139 South Madison Street

The history of the cathedral is closely connected with the numerous German Catholics who settled in the Green Bay area in the mid-nineteenth century. Initially members of St. John the Evangelist parish, they experienced such language difficulties that they began planning for a church and parochial school headed by a German-speaking priest. In 1851, 65 German families established a new parish, the Annunciation of the Blessed Virgin Mary. They built Old St. Mary's, as it was popularly known, and a parochial school on South Madison Street.

In 1868, when the diocese of Green Bay was created, its first bishop selected Old St. Mary's as his procathedral. His successor, Francis Xavier Krautbauer, who became the second bishop in 1875, set about replacing St. Mary's "a wooden building shaken by every storm, of which every peasant congregation . . . would be ashamed." He drew up plans for a new cathedral patterned after St. Ludwig's in the Bavarian city of Munich.

St. Francis Xavier Cathedral, July 1984. Photo by Margaret Bogue.

The cornerstone for this beautiful red brick Romanesque church was laid in 1876, and the structure was consecrated in 1881. Two years earlier it had been named St. Francis Xavier in honor of the patron saint of the first Catholic mission established in the Green Bay area in 1671–1672. The towers, initially finished only to the belfry section, were completed in 1903. Some original interior ornamentation remains. Of special merit are stained glass windows from Innsbruck, Austria, and a mural, "The Crucifixion," painted by Johann Schmitt, an emigrant to the United States from the Duchy of Baden who had studied painting in Munich and Vienna.

Over the years the interior and the exterior of the cathedral have been modified somewhat. Murals were added. Marble replaced the simulated marble of the sanctuary. Gold leaf was restored. New front entrances were added. A sacristy addition was built in 1917. These have on the whole complemented the original structure.

St. Willebrord's Catholic Church,
209 Adams Street

In 1864 the Dutch and Flemish Catholics of Green Bay organized their own parish, adapting a frame building formerly used as a school, town hall, and courthouse for their church. After conversion, the small Greek Revival structure served as a place of worship until 1889, when the congregation of 200 families began construction of a much larger church on the same site. The cornerstone for St. Willebrord's present church was laid in 1891. The handsome brick Gothic Revival structure has served the parish, with changes and alterations, for 90 years.

First Evangelical Lutheran Church
(original), Cherry and Van Buren Streets

For 94 years, from 1863 to 1957, the First Evangelical Lutheran congregation met for worship on Cherry Street in a church building that has now been adapted for commercial use. The German Lutherans of Green Bay organized as a congregation in 1862 after almost a decade of meeting as the Lutheran Society in the East Moravian Church. The original church structure, built in 1863, was enlarged and modified over the years, evolving into a white clapboard structure, eclectic in style, with a beautiful steeple and stained glass windows. The congregation established a Christian day school in 1869.

German continued to be used exclusively in the church until 1917, when English services began to be held every other Sunday. German was dropped completely in 1948. When the congregation moved to its new church in 1957, the sanctuary on Cherry Street became the Central Assembly of God Church. In 1981, after the Central Assembly built a new church, old First Lutheran was adapted for use as a bridal chapel.

Ss. Peter and Paul Catholic Church,
710 North Baird Street

In the spring of 1875, the Belgian and German families living on what was then the eastern boundary of Green Bay received permission to organize a parish and build their own church. By 1876 the congregation of 150 families, having done much of the work with their own hands, completed the church and attended dedication services. But at the end of that year, because of misunderstandings between the parishioners and the church authorities, the church was closed. Reopened in 1892, it served until 1910, when a new, larger church, Romanesque Revival in style, was completed to meet the needs of more than 250 families. The original parochial school was built in 1901.

Trinity Lutheran,
333 South Chestnut Avenue

At Fort Howard in January, 1867, a group of 34 Norwegians organized Den Norske Evangeliske Lutheran Menighed congregation. Among them were two shipbuilders, a Great Lakes sea captain, and a merchant. While information about the founders is scanty, they were apparently persons of some substance, for they immediately raised money to build a modest frame church. Enlarged, moved, and modified over the years, it served Green Bay's growing Norwegian-speaking congregation until 1915, when plans for a new church required its removal. By then the original church had evolved into a modified Gothic clapboard structure with an unusual steeple and stained glass windows. In the sanctuary hung a model of a three-masted ship, a memorial to the Norwegian sailors and shipbuilders who had helped found the congregation.

The cornerstone for the new sanctuary, a modified Gothic stone structure, was laid in 1916, and the building was completed and dedicated the next year. The present church is an enlargement of the 1916 structure with substantial exterior and interior alterations.

For more than four decades after 1867, services were held in Norwegian, and the church served as a social and cultural as well as a spiritual association for Green Bay's first-generation Norwegian Americans. By the early twentieth century, change became essential, and language became a major issue. Because many children spoke English but not Norwegian, some families had left in search of an English-speaking church. In 1911 English was sanctioned for two services per month, and a decade later for three. With the introduction of English, persons of different national backgrounds joined the congregation, an important factor in the 1917 decision to change the church name to Trinity Lutheran. Debates over the razing of the old church, the language question, and the new church name all signaled the diminishing Norwegian character of the congregation. Yet 100 years after its founding, a high proportion of Trinity Lutheran members had Norwegian names.

St. Patrick's Catholic Church,
211 North Maple Avenue

The Irish of Fort Howard (a separate town until its incorporation into Green Bay in 1895) decided in 1864 that they needed a parish of their own on the west bank of the Fox River. They set about raising funds to build St. Patrick's Church, a white frame clapboard structure that was completed in 1866 except for the steeple, which was added later. St. Patrick's was the smallest of the Green Bay parishes. It limped along in the late nineteenth century, not really fulfilling the hope that it would serve the English-speaking Catholic population of both Green Bay and Fort Howard. The majority of its parishioners were members of Irish families living in Fort Howard where many found jobs with the railroads. Unlike Green Bay's other Catholic parishes, St. Patrick's remained too poor to provide a parochial school.

When St. Patrick's acquired an energetic new priest in 1893, he found an "old and rickety church building," unattractive for worship, and a congregation with "very little enthusiasm." That year marked a turning point in St. Patrick's history. A new sanctuary was given high priority. The present St. Patrick's dates from 1893, when work began on an imposing Gothic Revival brick church. A parochial school was added in 1906.

East Moravian Church (see no. [7])

(7) Heritage Hill State Park
off Hy W-57 at 2640 South Webster Avenue
Heritage Hill State Park contains a group of historic Green Bay buildings moved here to ensure their preservation, maintenance, and accessibility to the public. Replicas of other pioneer buildings have been added to the outdoor museum complex. The 43-acre site was the location of Camp Smith in 1820–1822 and years later became a truck garden operated by the Wisconsin State Reformatory. In 1971 the land was transferred to the Wisconsin Department of Natural Resources. The Brown County Historical Society began the process of moving the historic buildings to the park, which opened in 1977. Facilities for camping are planned for the future. Open Memorial Day–Labor Day, Tuesday–Sunday, 10:00 A.M.–5:00 P.M.; May 1–Memorial Day and in September after Labor Day, weekends, 10:00 A.M.–5:00 P.M. $

Roi-Porlier-Tank Cottage

Believed to be the oldest extant building constructed in the state of Wisconsin (the Dudley J. Godrey, Jr., Home in Milwaukee, moved there from New Hampshire, is older), the original portion of the cottage was built in 1776 by Joseph Le Roi, a French fur trader. Later covered with clapboard, its original construction was wattle and daub, a method in which boughs and twigs are woven between upright supports and plastered over with mud and clay. Judge Jacques Porlier, a justice of the peace in Green Bay and reputedly Wisconsin's first schoolteacher, purchased the one-and-a-half-story cottage in 1805 and lived here until 1850.

Roi-Porlier-Tank Cottage. Photo by Margaret Bogue.

At that time Nils Otto Tank bought it. Tank, a retired Moravian missionary, led a Scandinavian Moravian group to Green Bay in order to establish a communal colony. Calling themselves the "Ephraim" congregation, which means "the very fruitful," the group soon became disenchanted with Tank's management. With their spiritual advisor, Rev. Andreas M. Iverson, the Ephraim congregation left Green Bay to begin anew in Door County (see site 59), leaving Tank and his family alone in their cottage. Tank added one-story wings at each end of the building, one to be used as kitchen and dining room and the other for Moravian church services.

After the deaths of Mr. and Mrs. Tank, the cottage was donated to the city of Green Bay in 1909 and moved to Union Park, southwest of the cottage's original location on the west bank of the Fox River. The city in turn donated it to Heritage Hill. At the park, a small bake oven has been attached to a corner of the left wing of the cottage, although it was not originally part of it.

*Fort Howard Buildings**

Because the place where the Fox River enters into Green Bay had strategic advantages, the French and British built fortified fur-trading posts there. When the Americans took possession, they chose the same location on which to build Fort Howard in 1816. The regional need for federal troops no longer existed in 1863, when the fort was abandoned and sold for a railroad yard. Most of the fort buldings were razed, but at least two of them have survived because they were moved several blocks away and used as residences. A rear wing detached from the Fort Howard hospital building has been restored to suggest its original use as a hospital and ward. The kitchen formerly attached to the commanding officer's quarters has been moved to the park and furnished as the quarters for Fort Howard officers. A replica of the Fort Howard school is included in the fort complex.

*Baird Law Office**

When Henry Baird acquired this building for his law office in 1841, he had it moved across Main Street to a site near his home. Samuel W. Beall had built the one-story Greek Revival building in 1835 for the federal land office. Baird, who has been called the "father of the Wisconsin bar," was the first lawyer to practice in territorial Wisconsin and its first attorney general. He used the building as a law office until his retirement in 1865. It was moved a few blocks away and used as a residence until Brown County moved it in 1953 to the courthouse lawn. Fire regulations, however, made it necessary to remove the frame building from the downtown area. So it was moved again, this time to the grounds of the Cotton House, and opened to the public. With the development of Heritage Hill State Park, the little law office became part of a streetscape on the park's north edge.

*Cotton House**

When the site for Heritage Hill was chosen, the Brown County Historical Society rejoiced that the Cotton House would not have to be moved again. Judge Joseph P. Arndt had the house built for his daughter, Mary, and his son-in-law, Lt. John Cotton, about 1849 roughly a mile north of its present site. Cotton spent some time at Fort Howard, and at other frontier forts, during his career with the U.S. Army and returned to Green Bay upon his retirement. When his beautiful Greek Revival home was about to be razed in 1938, the Brown County Historical Society bought it, moved it to its present location, and opened it to the public, long before Heritage Hill was planned.

*East Moravian Church**

Members of the Scandinavian Moravian group who came to Green Bay under the leadership of Nils Otto Tank and Rev. Andreas M. Iverson built this beautiful white frame church in 1851–1852. It is considered a fine example of the blending of Greek Revival and Gothic styles. Historically it is an impressive reminder of the efforts of Scandinavian Moravians to develop an ideal community based on common ownership of property under the philanthropic leadership of Tank, a retired Moravian missionary. When the experiment failed and many of the group left to settle at Ephraim and Sturgeon Bay (see site 59), some Moravians remained at Green Bay and others joined them. For years the congregation used this sanctuary. In 1981 the structure was moved from 518 Moravian Street to Heritage Hill State Park.

Also in the park are a replica of Wisconsin's first courthouse, Allouez Town Hall, a blacksmith shop, a general store, a firehouse, a fur trader's cabin, and Green Bay's first Young Men's Christian Association building.

(8) National Railroad Museum

2285 South Broadway

Although the railroads have experienced serious economic problems in the face of competition from trucks and airlines, visitors at the National Railroad Museum can enjoy railroading's past. The museum opened in 1958 with a collection donated by a railroad buff. Now there are more than 60 pieces on display. Among them are steam locomotives, passenger coaches, freight cars, and other specialized railroad cars. A train ride around the 11-acre site is a memorable experience. At the old railroad depot, now a visitors' center, railroad memorabilia are on display. Tape-recorded, self-guided tours are planned for individuals in the future, but groups may arrange for guides. Open daily, May 1–October 1, 9:00 A.M.–5:00 P.M. $

(9) Green Bay Packer Hall of Fame

1901 South Oneida Street, off Hy W-32

The economy of Green Bay has benefited greatly from the Green Bay Packers, an NFL professional football team organized in 1919. Each year during the football season, win or lose, fans fill the Packer stadium (Lambeau Field). In season or out, the Green Bay Packer Hall of Fame attracts fans. Although the team's memorabilia have been displayed informally since 1968, a permanent display was opened in 1976 at ceremonies attended by President Gerald Ford. A wide-screen presentation on nine projectors tells the story of the founding of the Packers. In the Playing Field the visitor may learn more about professional playing techniques and attempt to kick a winning field goal. The Hall of Fame itself displays many team trophies earned throught the years.

The Green Bay Packer Hall of Fame is open year round, 10:00 A.M.–5:00 P.M. $

This silver Perrot ostensorium given by Nicolas Perrot to the St. Francis Xavier Mission in 1686 is now on display in The Neville Public Museum of Brown County at Green Bay. Courtesy Neville Public Museum.

68. De Pere

Hy W-57

De Pere, like Green Bay, is one of Wisconsin's very old settlements. Here, at a series of rapids in the Fox River, Father Claude Allouez in 1671–1672 established the first Jesuit mission on the river, the mission of St. Francis Xavier, as a base for his work among the Indians. French soldiers sent to guard the missionaries and fur traders called the site "*les rapides des pères,*" and from this the city has taken its name. The Fox Indians burned the mission in 1687. The Jesuits rebuilt it and remained at this location until 1717, when, in the face of protracted warfare between the French and the Fox, they moved closer to the protection of Fort La Baye. A tablet at the eastern end of the Claude Allouez Bridge memorializes the work of the pioneer Jesuit missionaries. (See pp. 17–18.)

In the decades following the abandonment of the Jesuit mission, the rapids remained a favored place for Indians and fur traders. The Indians, using weirs, harvested the bountiful fish of the Fox River. By 1830 settlement was about to change all this. Prospects for the village of De Pere looked bright in the 1830s for the planned Fox-Wisconsin waterway seemed to place it in a very strategic position for trade and commerce. Construction on the first federally built dam in the project began at the De Pere rapids in 1836, and to the ire of Green Bay residents, in 1837 De Pere became the county seat of Brown County, an honor it retained until 1854. But the speculative excesses of investors, the financial panic beginning in the fall of 1837, and the destruction of the dam in 1847 slowed the community's development. A new dam, built in 1849, and the return of better times ushered in a period of moderate growth. The De Pere population in 1860 was about 500 persons. Separate towns developed on the east and west banks of the Fox River (West De Pere became an incorporated village in 1870) but finally consolidated in 1890 to form a town with a population of 3,600.

Like Green Bay, De Pere prospered during the lumbering boom of the 1850s and 1860s. The town acquired a gristmill, sawmills, and lath and shingle mills. The millions of feet of lumber sawed annually found ready markets in Milwaukee and Chicago. Fishing emerged as an important industry (see p. 240). So did iron smelting, from the late 1860s until the last blast furnace closed at De Pere in 1893.

The town experienced all the difficulties of other lumbering centers in making a transition to new ways of life once the timber was gone. De Pere's water power continued to be one of its major assets as an industrial location. So did its access to the outside world. In the 1870s two railroad lines and the Fox River served as avenues of delivery for local products. Industrial development in the late nineteenth century reflected De Pere's growing ties with the developing farmlands that surrounded it and the transition from lumber, shingle, and stave production to paper making. Early in the twentieth century, the roster of local industries included grain elevators, a flour mill, creameries, a hay press and warehouse, and a cannery. *Polk's Wisconsin Gazetteer* for 1901–1902 claimed for De Pere "one of the largest writing paper mills in the world." Its metal industries—an iron and steel mill and a boiler works—then held a modest place in the roster of De Pere manufacturing establishments, but by 1929 they had expanded to include gas and gasoline engines, power transmission machinery, and hardware-producing plants. De Pere grew modestly from a town of 3,625 in 1890 to one of about 5,500 in 1929.

The importance of paper and paper-related industries, agribusiness, and metal-based manufacturing clearly apparent in the 1920s has continued to the present. The city's greatest population growth came between World War

II and 1970, when the number of people living in De Pere more than doubled, from 6,300 to 13,300. The 1980 census showed a population of almost 14,900.

De Pere's 1980 industries produced a wide variety of paper, metal, and food products. Metal- and wood-related industries are the most numerous and the largest employers. Six companies have more than 100 persons each on the payroll. The largest among them, employing 400, is Nicolet Paper, which markets a wide variety of paper products; the second-largest is TEC Systems, employer of 350, which makes dryers for printing, paper, and converting industries and air-pollution-control systems.

De Pere Sites of Interest

(1) St. Norbert College and St. Norbert Abbey

A striking part of the city's profile at the Fox River Bridge, St. Norbert College reminds visitors of De Pere's religious beginnings. Well over two centuries after the coming of the Jesuit fathers, Norbertine missionaries came to Green Bay from Holland in 1893, at the invitation of the bishop of Green Bay, to do missionary work among the Belgian Catholics under his care. The Premonstratensians, or "white canons," as the Norbertines were called because of their distinctive white habits, agreed to serve Brown County parishes if an abbey was established for them. The decision to train students for the priesthood, resulted in the founding in 1898 of St. Norbert College, now a liberal arts college with an enrollment of about 1,500 students. At St. Norbert Abbey, a few miles north of De Pere on Highway W-57, there are six large bells, cast in Holland, in the carillon.

(2) White Pillars

*403 North Broadway, and North Broadway Street Historic District**

Built in 1836 as the office of the De Pere Hydraulic Company, White Pillars houses the museum and research center of the De Pere Historical Society. During its long history it has served as a school, store, church, warehouse, and residence. In 1973 the Fort Howard Paper Company donated it to the historical society. Originally White Pillars was a far simpler example of Greek Revival architecture. Both the present pediment and columns replaced the simpler originals when it was converted into a residence in 1913.

The society's extensive collection includes maps from the early French period to the present, government records, newspapers, photographs, military equipment, and many other tangible reminders of the area's long history. Open March–January, Monday–Saturday, 2:00–5:00 P.M., and in February at those hours, Monday and Thursday. Free.

White Pillars lies within the *North Broadway Street Historic District*, a five-block area of North Broadway Street extending from Cass Street to several blocks north of Randall Avenue. It includes 54 buildings, primarily residences. Here business, professional, civic, and social leaders of the community of the late nineteenth and early twentieth centuries built their homes. While many are altered from their original appearance, many are not, and North Broadway still reflects the atmosphere of a prestigious residential neighborhood.

Eleazer Williams, from a pencil sketch of the original portrait by J. Stewart of Hartford, 1806. Courtesy State Historical Society of Wisconsin. WHi(X3)1226

69. Lost Dauphin State Park (now closed)

5 miles south of De Pere on County Trunk D

Lost Dauphin State Park, recently closed by the Wisconsin Department of Natural Resources, is named for a colorful and controversial man who lived on the park site. Eleazer Williams, a man of British, French, and St. Regis Indian lineage, was born at Sault St. Louis, Quebec, received training for missionary work in Massachusetts, studied at Dartmouth College, and after the War of 1812 went into Episcopal mission work among the Oneida Indians of New York as schoolmaster, catechist, and lay reader.

When the idea of removing the New

York Indians westward was noised about in 1818-1820, Williams championed it. In 1821 he came west with a delegation of Oneidas and members of other tribes to plan a settlement and perhaps an Indian empire west of Lake Michigan. Williams continued his missionary work, may have become an ordained Episcopal priest, married one of his students, and settled on the west bank of the Fox River. Many of his Indian followers held him in high esteem, but many came to regard him as an opportunist and traitor. Once he became convinced that he was the lost son of King Louis XVI of France, Williams became a stormcenter of controversy. Most who heard him speak on the subject scoffed at his claim, and Williams died in 1858, alone and impoverished, in a small town in New York State. Honor came to him in 1947 when, in recognition of his work with the Oneidas, his remains were reburied in the churchyard of Holy Apostles Episcopal church at Oneida, Wisconsin.

When the land on which the original Eleazer Williams cabin stood became a state park, a replica of it was constructed. Recently, because of budgetary problems and vandalism, the Department of Natural Resources closed the park. It may become part of the Brown County park system. Although there are no facilities for visitors, it is worthwhile to climb the hillside from County Trunk D and look at the historical marker. The view of the Fox River is beautiful.

Iroquois longhouse, Oneida Indian Museum. Photo by Margaret Bogue.

70. Oneida Indian Reservation

Hy W-54, west of Green Bay

Approximately 1,980 Oneida Indians lived on or near the 2,580-acre reservation west of Green Bay in 1972. They are the descendants of the Oneidas famous in American colonial history as one of the Five (later Six) Nations of the powerful League of the Iroquois living in what is now upper New York State. Allies of the British in the fur trade and in their struggles against New France, the Iroquois divided in their loyalties during the American Revolution. Afterward part of the Iroquois remained in the United States, and part, intensely loyal to the British cause, moved to Canada, among them some of the Oneidas.

Immediately after the War of 1812, pressures for settlement and development of the New York lands of the Iroquois led such American officials as President James Monroe and Secretary of War John C. Calhoun to advocate the removal of the Indians far to the west. Eleazer Williams (see site 69) led the first group of New York Indians westward to the Green Bay area in 1821. A long series of negotiations with the Menominee for lands for the Oneida and other tribes began in 1821 and continued in 1827 and in 1833. The treaty ratified in 1838 established an Oneida reservation of 65,000 acres, much of it richly timbered with hardwoods. Over time the Oneidas lost much of this land through the sale of allotments by individual Inidan owners, often pressured and cheated by the unscrupulous and land-hungry. By 1934 their holdings had dwindled to less then 1,000 acres. Under the Indian Reorganization Act of 1934, the tribe reorganized and has since purchased some additional land.

Oneida Sites of Interest

(1) Holy Apostles Episcopal Church

This lovely stone church, built in 1886, is a lineal descendant of the log church built under the direction of Eleazer Williams, missionary to the Oneidas, in 1825. In 1938 a stone from the tribal altar of the Iroquois Confederation in New York was presented to the Wisconsin Oneidas to use as part of their church altar. Eleazer Williams' grave is beside the church.

(2) Oneida Indian Museum

5 miles southwest of Oneida at the intersection of Outagamie County Trunks E and EE

Near the village of Oneida the Oneida tribe has developed an excellent museum that displays the history and cutlure of the Iroquois. A museum building, stockaded grounds, and long house portray the formation of the League of the Iroquois, Oneida culture, the move westward with Eleazer Williams, the establishment of the reservation, the loss of reservation land, and twentieth-century efforts to increase tribal holdings.

Open all year, Tuesday–Friday, 9:00 A.M.–5:00 P.M.; Saturday, 10:00 A.M.–5:00 P.M. Also open on Sundays, Memorial Day–Labor Day, 10:00 A.M.–5:00 P.M. $

71. Pulaski

Hys W-29 and W-32
from Green Bay

Northwest of Green Bay lies a prosperous farming area distinguished by dairy herds and well-kept fields. The farmers are descendants of Polish settlers who came to the area in the late nineteenth century.

The settlements grew from the promotional efforts of the J. J. Hof Land Company, which dealt extensively in Wisconsin cutover lands. To attract Polish immigrants to the area, Hof helped secure the establishment of a Franciscan monastery at Pulaski. He advertised the farmlands in glowing terms in the national press. Polish settlers came in the 1880s and 1890s from many American cities: Milwaukee, Chicago, Denver, San Francisco, and Pittsburgh. By 1905, 650 Polish families had settled on Hof's land.

Zachow, Krakow, Kunesh, Sobieski, and Angelica are other towns in this district. At Pulaski visitors find the town's profile dominated by the Church of the Assumption of the Blessed Virgin Mary, completed in 1923. Modified Romanesque in style, with twin towers and gold-leaf domes, the red brick church has fine stained glass windows and a small shrine to the Virgin Mary. Adjacent is the Franciscan monastery. This church is the heart of the Polish farming community.

Take County Trunk B just south of Pulaski, following it east to Hy US-41. As you travel this road, you will see many fine farms. Watch for shrines adjacent to farmhouses.

The Church of the Assumption of the Blessed Virgin Mary. Photo by Margaret Bogue.

72. Pensaukee River and the Village of Pensaukee

Hy US-41

Four rivers on the Wisconsin western shore of Green Bay—the Pensaukee, the Oconto, the Peshtigo, and the Menominee—served as main arteries for the delivery of logs and lumber to Green Bay's shoreline in the late nineteenth century. All four flowed through fine stands of white pine. The most extensive were the pineries of the Menominee River's 4,000-square-mile watershed. On all four rivers, lumbering companies developed extensive sawmilling operations. Pensaukee, Oconto, Peshtigo, Marinette, and Memonimee grew as busy lumber

Holt sawmill at Oconto, probably about 1900. Courtesy State Historical
y of Wisconsin. WHi(W6)13623

, only a few of which are listed
v.

nto Sites of Interest

St. Peter's Catholic Church*
Brazeau Avenue
beautiful red brick Romanesque ch, erected in 1899, is the second uary built in Oconto to serve the ch community. The first, a frame ding, was erected in 1857. Algh Oconto's ethnic differences ess obvious today than in the teenth century, when they caused cleavages in its Catholic popula- St. Peter's French origins are obvious from the inscriptions below its stained glass windows and on the entry plaque.

(2) Allouez Cross
Brazeau Avenue (Hy US-41) near intersection with Mill Street
The cross commemorates Father Claude Allouez, S. J., who landed at the site of Oconto in 1669. (See pp. 17–18.)

(3) Copper Culture State Park*
take Hy W-22 off Hy US-41 (Brazeau Avenue) and turn left on Mill Street
The park is the site of a cemetery of Old Copper Culture people, who lived in the northern Midwest about 2500 B.C. Discovered in 1952 by Donald Baldwin, a 13-year-old who was digging in an old gravel pit, the site drew the attention of both the Oconto County Historical Society and the Milwaukee Public Museum staffs, who proceeded to investigate it. The site had already been partially destroyed by the gravel quarry, but digs revealed 21 remaining burial pits. As many as 200 persons may have been buried here. The contents of the graves helped archaeologists learn more about the Old Copper Culture people. Artifacts from these digs are on display at the Oconto County Historical Society's Museum (see no. [8]).

The park, owned by the state of Wisconsin, is a quiet and beautiful site. It includes a small, brick Belgian-styled house built in the 1920s, where visitors may see small displays of Copper Culture and Woodland Indian artifacts.

(4) First Church of Christ, Scientist*
102 Chicago Street
Built in 1886, this Carpenter Gothic structure with board and batten siding was the first church built specifically to serve a Christian Science congregation. The building has been restored to its original appearance.

The church stands close to the homes of James and Henry Sargent, who were lumber merchants and landowners. Laura and Victoria Adams Sargent, their wives, deeply interested in the teachings of Mary Baker Eddy, helped to organize the Christian Science congregation in Oconto in 1886. Henry and Victoria Adams Sargent donated the land and plans for the church. Laura Adams Sargent later served as Mary Baker Eddy's secretary-companion.

ports, their harbors crowded with lake vessels that carried lumber to markets lying to the south.

Of these five lumbering centers, Pensaukee suffered the greatest loss of population and the greatest economic decline at the end of the lumbering era. A sawmill village with a population of about 360 in 1860, it weathered two natural disasters in the 1870s. The great fire of 1871 consumed all the lumbering camps in the township. In 1877 a tornado left the town a heap of ruins. The Gardner House, a three-story brick hotel, "well-planned, modern and elegant, the show place of Oconto County," a sawmill, planing mill, flour mill, boarding house, school, depot, 25 dwellings and barns, and several hundred thousand feet of sawed lumber were destroyed. Pensaukee rebuilt and continued to produce lumber and shingles until the late 1880s when milling ceased.

In 1892 *Polk's Wisconsin Gazetteer* reported that the village population had dropped to 150 from the 1886 high of 400. Thereafter, commercial fishing assumed new importance in village life. Eight commercial fishermen lived at Pensaukee in 1896, and 15 in 1928. Until the early 1950s herring were the major catch at Pensaukee, then perch, and now alewives. Millions of pounds are caught and processd into pet food and fish meal annually. A dozen commercial fishermen operated from the port of Pensaukee in 1981. The village population is 150 persons, most of whom commute to work in Green Bay and Oconto.

73. Oconto

Hy US-41

Long before the days of its lumbering glory, Oconto was the site of a Menominee Indian village and a Jesuit mission founded by Father Claude Allouez in 1669. Frequented by French fur traders in the mid-seventeenth century and the location of a trading post of the American Fur Company in the 1820s, Oconto began to develop as a town in the 1840s.

It grew into a town of some consequence because of its location on the Oconto River near the place where it empties into Green Bay. The river provided a ready-made avenue for delivering logs from the rich virgin timber stands along its banks. Lake Michigan provided a natural avenue for low-cost delivery of lumber to rapidly growing communities farther south. Oconto served as a processing and shipping point for the log harvest.

From one mill in 1849, the town's capacity to saw the logs from the surrounding pineries grew to 14 mills in the 1870s. Oconto became the county seat in 1851 and a chartered city in 1869. More fortunate than Peshtigo, Oconto escaped the ravages of the fire of 1871 except for minor damage at the northern edge of town. The city's most prosperous period occurred in the 1880s and 1890s, when lumbering was at its height.

Lumbering was a diminished but still important industry in 1915. Thereafter it dwindled rapidly, and business leaders faced the problem of how to keep the town alive. Oconto has gradually made a transition, becoming more a rural residential town than an industrial one. Commercial fishing, a venerable industry at Oconto, con-

tinued for a
brewery ope
The Oconto
founded in 1
able new lin
the Bond Pic
remains an i
almost 100 o
other busine
forces, three
War II: a crui
company, a m
machines, anc
The fifth, Gre
60, dates from
Oconto's work
mute to jobs e
population wa

Oconto's eth
varied. Norweg
cial fishermen.
mans, Irish, an
labor for the p
along with an a
born workers.

The glories c
still very obviou
fine nineteenth-
town includes t
Schofield, (no. [
lumber baron g
Other architectu
boom years are
Library, a forme
office, and the cl
meet the needs
many nationalitie

Visitors to Occ
the Tourist Infor
US-41 or at the C
ical Museum and
Park Avenue and
Era Oconto Tour
by the Committee
of Historic Ocont
guide to the many

The F
Socie

tow
belo

Oc

(1)
516
This
chu
sanc
Fre
bui
tho
are
nin
rea
tion

The Beyer Home. Photo by Margaret Bogue.

The reading room is open on Monday, Wednesday, and Friday during the summer, 2:00–5:00 P.M. Notice the hand-hewn stone horse-watering fountain in the little triangular park in front of the church. The Oconto Women's Club erected it in 1916.

(5) West Main Street Historic District*

400 and 500 blocks of Main Street

The 21 houses and one church in the West Main Street Historic District date mainly from 1860 to 1905. In the heyday of Oconto's lumbering boom, Main Street became an upper-middle-class residential district where lumbermen, professionals, and merchants lived in relatively high style. A variety of Victorian architectural styles are represented. The district includes two structures on the national Register of Historic Places: the First Church of Christ, Scientist, noted above, and the Governor Edward Scofield House, described below. West Main Street, although not as plush as in its heyday, remains a very impressive reminder of Oconto's lumbering days. A walk along the 400 and 500 blocks is worthwhile.

(6) Governor Edward Scofield House*

610 Main Street

Built about 1868, this buff brick Italianate house served as Edward Scofield's home from 1883 to 1925. The structure is now much the same as then except for the removal of a wrap-around veranda that extended across the front and partially along both sides. Scofield was prominent in both the business and the political life of nineteenth-century Wisconsin. A Civil War veteran, he came to Oconto in the late 1860s and rose from foreman in a local lumber company to partner in the Scofield and Arnold Manufacturing Company, a very successful lumbering business. He served as state senator from 1887 to 1890 and as governor of Wisconsin, from 1897 to 1901.

(7) Nicolas Perrot Monument

intersection of Main and Congress Streets

The stone monument in the form of an Indian tepee honors Nicolas Perrot, the French fur trader and explorer, who passed through the Oconto area in 1668. (See p. 17.)

(8) Beyer Home Museum* and Museum Annex

917 Park Avenue

Captain Cyrus Hart, builder of the red brick Beyer home, made his livelihood from a variety of businesses, among them the Hart Steam Boat Line and the Oconto *Reporter*. George Beyer, a later owner, did a flourishing business in land, lumber, banking, and insurance. Originally Italianate when built in 1868, the house was changed to Queen Ann style in the 1890s. The home is furnished in the Victorian style of the middle-to-late nineteenth century. The Museum Annex has excellent displays relating to the Old Copper Culture people, the fur trade, lumbering, and a nineteenth-century "main street." The Oconto County Historical Society owns and operates the home and museum. Open daily, May 31–Labor Day, 9:00 A.M.–5:00 P.M. $

(9) St. Joseph's Catholic Church*
705 Park Avenue
St. Joseph's congregation was an offshoot from St. Peter's (see no. (1)) in 1869. The story of its formation is a very familiar one in many American cities where Catholic immigrants of different nationalities settled. St. Peter's congregation used French in its services. When Irish, German, Dutch, and Bohemian immigrants later came to Oconto to work in the lumber mills and camps, they did not feel at home in the French congregation. In 1869 a German priest established a new church, St. Joseph's, where sermons were delivered in English, Dutch, German, and Bohemian according to an established schedule. High Victorian Gothic in style, this strikingly beautiful church initially catches the eye because of its red and cream brickwork. The structure was built in 1870 and altered in 1895. Its stained glass window inscriptions reflect the German, Irish, and Bohemian origins of the people it served.

(10) Holt-Balcom Lumber Company Office*
106 Superior Avenue
The Holt-Balcom Lumber Company Office is the only office remaining of the 14 lumber companies that operated at Oconto during the lumber boom years of the late nineteenth century. Built in 1854 by Samuel B. Gilkey, in 1863 this frame building became the branch office of the Holt-Balcom Lumber Company, which was organized in 1862 with headquarters in Chicago. The business grew to be very important, with hundreds of thousands of dollars invested in Oconto and Marinette County pinelands, mills, farms, boarding houses, ships, and logging camps. Two of its subsidiaries were the Oconto River Improvement Company and the Oconto Electric Company. The company ceased business in 1938.

74. Peshtigo
Hy US-41

Like Oconto, Peshtigo grew and prospered because of its river and port location in the richly timbered northern Lake Michigan country. The town developed as a sawmill center for the logs delivered downstream by the river's extensive, meandering waters. Lumber schooners filled their holds for delivery points downlake.

By 1871 the town boasted a population of 1,700, a woodenware factory owned and operated by a Chicago millionaire, William G. Ogden, a sawmill, a sash, door, and blind factory, stores, hotels, homes, a school, and two churches.

The town's history dramatically illustrates the wasteful, destructive impact of the lumbering industry at its worst. Peshtigo burned to the ground on the night of October 8, 1871, in a vast conflagration that consumed 2,400 square miles of timberland along the western and eastern shores of Green Bay. The great fire resulted from the indiscriminate cutting, which left heaps of slash on the forest floor, and the carelessness of hunters, lumberjacks, farmers, and railroad workers. The season had been extremely dry, and a northeasterly storm with high winds fanned small fires into a holocaust. The great forest fire has been called the Peshtigo Fire because there the fire seems to have been most intense and to have caused the greatest loss of human life.

At least 800 perished at Peshtigo, and the town virtually disappeared in a roaring inferno. Only a few structures survived. Father Peter Pernin, who along with many others survived by rushing into the river upstream from the Highway US-41 bridge, wrote a vivid account of the "tempest," "the strange and terrible noise," "the neighing of horses, falling of chimneys, crashing of uprooted trees, roaring and whistling of the wind, crackling of fire," and the people struck dumb with terror.

The town rebuilt rapidly, woodenware factory and all. Lumbering continued to be the major industry in the late nineteenth century, but the end of the big cut was close at hand. Peshtigo adapted by becoming a town that served the market needs of farmers struggling to tame the cutover. Wood products, however, continued to a lesser degree to be important in Peshtigo's economy.

In 1979 three firms together employed more than 650 people to produce paper products, store fixtures, and laminated wood beams. The largest employer was Badger Paper Mills. Another sizable business, employing over 100, made fiberglass boats. Peshtigo, with a 1980 population of approximately 2,800, is a far quieter town than in the days when the sawmills whined, the sawdust burners trailed smoke, and the lumber schooners made port.

"The Burning of Peshtigo" published in Harper's Weekly, *November 25, 1871. Courtesy State Historical Society of Wisconsin. WHi(X3)96*

Peshtigo Sites of Interest

(1) Peshtigo Fire Cemetery*
off Hy US-41
The cemetery lies near Hy US-41 in the town of Peshtigo and is designated by a Wisconsin Historical Marker. Many of those who died lie buried here, including 350 people burned beyond recognition. The latter are interred in a mass grave.

(2) Peshtigo Fire Museum
off Hy US-41
Adjacent to the cemetery stands the Fire Museum, housed in the old Congregational Church built shortly after the fire. Some of the museum displays, including a series of murals, relate to the fire. Other displays include a wide variety of artifacts illustrating life at Peshtigo in the nineteenth and twentieth centuries. Open daily, June–September, 9:00 A.M.–5:00 P.M. Free.

75. Marinette–Menominee
Hy US-41

The Menominee Indians, the Menominee River, Lake Michigan, the fur trade, the fisheries, and the great stands of virgin timber unified the history of the twin cities of Marinette, Wisconsin, and Menominee, Michigan, from the seventeenth through the early twentieth centuries. The earliest

The log-filled Menominee River at Marinette-Menominee as pictured in Marinette and Menominee Illustrated, *published in 1887. Courtesy State Historical Society of Wisconsin. WHi(X3)40495*

activities of the French explorers in the Menominee River area are shrouded in obscurity. French fur traders frequented the Menominee River beginning in the mid-seventeenth century in order to trade at a large Menominee Indian village located at the juncture of the river with Green Bay.

Stanislaus Chaput, also known as Louis Chappee, is usually regarded as Menominee's first non-Indian resident. He established a fur-trading post at the mouth of the Menominee River in the early 1800s, where he exchanged furs and traded goods with the Menominee Indians on behalf of John Jacob Astor's American Fur Company. Caught in trade rivalries, Chappee decided to abandon his original location and move upstream to the foot of the rapids of the Menominee. Here he continued to live and trade with the Menominees until his death in 1852.

Marinette, like Menominee, is associated by its name with the Indian past. Marinette, the granddaughter of a Chippewa chief, lived at the site of the town from the early 1820s until her death in 1865. Three-quarters Chippewa and one-quarter Menominee, a handsome and able woman, she was successively the wife of two fur traders. For years a respected citizen, she managed a trading post and acquired considerable real estate in the town.

Fur trading and commercial fishing were the earliest forms of economic activity in the twin villages. They began a remarkable transformation into busy towns when the white pine of the Menominee River and its tributaries came into demand in the post–Civil War years. The few sawmills at Menominee and Marinette that supplied local needs in the 1840s were a mere prelude to the sawmill expansion of the next four decades, when lumbering companies backed by Chicago, Milwaukee, and eastern capital reaped the harvest of white pine.

The ensuing scramble for pine stumpage and the right to send log drives down the Menominee quickly created competitive chaos. Isaac Stephenson, who had become a partner in the Nelson Ludington Company lumber business in 1858, applied knowledge acquired in Maine logging and lumbering operations to organize the Menominee River delivery system. He and his brothers, Samuel and Robert, along with Harrison and Nelson Ludington, organized the Menominee River Manufacturing Company in 1867. Subsequently renamed the Menominee River Boom Company, it bought up existing dams and improvements on the river, developed others, organized the log drives systematically, and assessed the cost of log delivery down river against owners. A complete traffic-control system involving thousands of square miles of stumpage along the Menominee and its tributaries sent an estimated 10.5 billion

Lumber mills, their refuse burners, and a lumber schooner along the Menominee River bank pictured in Marinette and Menominee Illustrated, *published in 1887. Courtesy State Historical Society of Wisconsin. WHi(X3)40496*

board feet to the Menominee-Marinette sawmills from 1867 through 1917, the year of the last drive. The colorful drives involved log marks, company scalers who counted logs at landings, peavey men, polers to man the bateaux, cooks, watchmen, time keepers, messengers, teamsters, blacksmiths, foremen, superintendents, and crews for the wanigans, boats that carried food and camping gear.

Marinette and Menominee escaped the total devastation experienced at Peshtigo in the fire of 1871. The fire forked before reaching these towns and destroyed much of the village of Menekaunee at the mouth of the Menominee River on the Wisconsin side and the Menominee River Lumber Company's mill as well. It destroyed one Menominee sawmill on the Green Bay shoreline. In Marinette a mill and a sash, door, and blind factory burned down, but the town's three largest sawmills escaped the blaze. One fork of the fire jumped the river before reaching Marinette and passed northward into Michigan destroying the settlement of Birch Creek before burning itself out.

The white pine harvest peaked in the late 1880s, when approximately 20 sawmills in Menominee and Marinette turned logs into lumber and shingles to be loaded aboard waiting ships or freight cars and sent to market. Near Menominee pig-iron production became an important lumber-related industry, utilizing locally made charcoal, limestone, and Menominee Range iron ore.

Menominee and Marinette attained their greatest prosperity and maximum populations during the white pine lumber boom. Marinette's population stood at almost 16,200 in 1900, and Menominee's at 12,800. Much of the late nineteenth-century population growth came from an influx of French Canadians, Swedes, and Germans in search of work in the sawmills and lumber camps. About half the population of both towns in 1900 was foreign-born. Marinette-Menominee workers lived adjacent to the sawmills along the riverbank.

Isaac Stephenson accumulated the best-known fortune in the Menominee lumbering business, leaving a $22 million estate in 1918, but a number of other residents of the towns also belonged to the ranks of the lumber barons. Architectural reminders of the lumber boom are abundant. Stephenson family homes and commercial buildings may still be seen. Memories of the immigrant workers who felled the trees and manned the sawmills remain in the Catholic and Protestant churches built to serve the Germans, Swedes, Poles, Bohemians, Danes, and Norwegians.

As the white pine stands disapeared, the twin cities began a difficult transition to other forms of economic activity. The lumber industry turned to harvesting hardwoods and prolonged the lumbering era to 1931, when the last of the large hardwood mills in Menominee closed. Paper making became an established industry well before the turn of the century. The first paper mill dates from the 1880s. A second began operation in 1893. Paper making has remained a viable industry to the present, and both Menominee Paper and Scott Paper at Marinette are large and important employers. Despite the organized efforts of local businessmen, such other turn-of-the-century alternatives as an agricultural implement factory, an iron works, flour mills, and sash, door, and interior woodwork mills were short-lived.

The populations of Marinette and Menominee dwindled by 24 percent between 1900 and 1920. Yet, over time, especially in the post–World War II years, their economies have adjusted, and population has grown modestly in recent years. Marinette's 1980 population was 12,000, and Menominee's was 10,000. Among the successful newer industries is Marinette Marine, founded in 1942 as a wartime industry. It produces landing craft, patrol boats, barges, tugs, and workboats for the U.S. Navy and an increasing number of vessels for the commercial market. In each of the two cities in 1979 there were 13 firms employing more than 100 workers each. The workforce engaged in industry totaled about 9,000. The 13 largest industries produced helicopters, chemicals, castings, pressure vessels, paper, twine and netting, boats and ships, automotive parts, funiture, small motors, and electrical appliances.

As in most communities, industrialization has created environmental problems. The most publicized of these are arsenic residues in the Menominee riverbed, serious enough to discourage dredging to improve the harbor. University of Wisconsin water chemists are studying the effects of arsenic runoff into Green Bay on water quality and fish populations.

Marinette Sites of Interest

(1) Stephenson Business Buildings

on Hall Street (Hy US-41) adjacent to the Marinette County Courthouse

These red brick structures, erected in the late nineteenth century to serve the needs of the Stephenson business interests, include the Stephenson Building, the Stephenson Bank, and the Stephenson Block.

(2) Stephenson Public Library

intersection of Hall Street and Riverside Avenue

Isaac Stephenson, sometimes criticized for being stingy, made a number of gifts to Marinette. He gave lots and money for churches, the land for a courthouse, and $10,000 for an opera house and, after 1900, donated the Stephenson Library to the town.

(3) Riverside Avenue Mansions

Riverside Avenue between Hall and Hattie Streets

In this block, fronting on the Menominee River, some of the homes of Marinette's business leaders of the lumbering era still stand. Senator Isaac Stephenson presented the house at 1919 Riverside Avenue, built in 1885, to his daughter as a wedding present. The Victorian house at 1931 Riverside Avenue, built in the 1880s, was a wedding present for another daughter. The Isaac W. Stephenson mansion, an impressive Second Empire brick structure with a four-story tower, originally stood at 1947 Riverside, now the site of the Presbyterian church. Across Riveside Avenue on the bank of the Menominee River stands a statue of Isaac Stephenson, recalling the days when from his home he could survey the log-choked Menominee River. A classical structure, the pillared A. J. Lauerman house at 1975 Riverside dates from 1910. Lauerman operated a large and successful general merchandise store in Marinette and was associated with the Stephenson enterprises.

(4) Marinette County Logging Museum

Stephenson Island, accessible from the Interstate Bridge (Hy US-41)

The museum contains displays on the lumbering era, including a miniature logging camp constructed with meticulous accuracy by John B. Mayer, a veteran woodsman and riverman of Marinette. The Marinette County Historical Society operates the museum, which is open June 1 through the first weekend in October, Monday–Saturday, 10:00 A.M.–4:30 P.M.; Sunday, 9:00 A.M.–4:00 P.M. $

(5) Scott Paper Company Tour

3120 Riverside Avenue

The Scott Paper Company gives public tours of its plant at 3:00 P.M. on workdays for persons over 12 years of age Memorial Day–Labor Day. Arrangements must be made ahead of time. Free. For other possible industrial tours contact the Marinette and Menominee chambers of commerce.

The Alvin Clark. *Photo by Margaret Bogue.*

Menominee Sites of Interest

(1) *Alvin Clark* ("Mystery Ship") Marine Museum*

accessible from Hy US-41 at 10th Street and 10th Avenue

Here the visitor may board the *Alvin Clark*, a Great Lakes cargo vessel built near Detroit, Michigan, in 1846 for John P. Clark, a Detroit fisherman, businessman, and shipbuilder. A 220-ton ship, 113 feet long, the *Alvin Clark* carried salt, grain, coal, and rough lumber from port to port on the upper Great Lakes until June 29, 1864. On that day, with a crew of only five, empty of cargo and heading for Oconto under full sail, the boat capsized and sank during a summer squall. In July 1969 Frank Hoffman and a group of volunteer workers, using equipment funished by Marinette Marine, raised the *Alvin Clark* from a depth of 100 feet off Chambers Island in Green Bay. Subsequently taken to Menominee for exhibition, the ship was designated a State of Michigan Historical Site and added to the National Register of Historic Places. Frank Hoffman has not gotten the support needed to preserve the *Alvin Clark*, and the ship is deteriorating. The museum building contains displays on the ship's raising, its history, and its artifacts. Open daily, mid-June–mid-October, 9:00 A.M.–6:00 P.M. $

(2) Menominee County Historical Society Museum

9th Street and 11 Avenue, accessible from Hy US-41 as marked

In 1976 the Menominee County Historical Society purchased St John's Catholic Church, erected in 1921, from the Roman Catholic diocese of Marquette to house its extensive collections of artifacts and its research library. The church ceased to be used for worship when the Catholic parishes of Menominee were reorganized to conform to current needs.

The museum collections stress the lumbering era, pioneer life, military weapons, Indian artifacts, and life in late nineteenth-century Menominee County. Of special interest are examples of the business records of the Menominee River Boom Company. Open daily, May–early October, 9:00 A.M.–5:00 P.M. Donation.

(3) Menominee County Courthouse*

10th Avenue between 8th and 10th Streets

Completed in 1875, the Menominee County courthouse, a cube-shaped three-story brick and stone structure in classical style, stands on two acres of wooded parkland in downtown Menominee. The board of supervisors chose the plans and specifications of a Chicago architect, G. P. Randall, from the eight responses to their advertisement. The new structure reflected and complemented the town's growing success as a lumbering center. Shortly after Marinette County was created in 1879, Marinette also acquired a courthouse, taller, larger, and more expensive than Menominee's, but that structure is no longer standing. Over the years other buildings have been added to house Menominee County government offices, but the exterior of the 1875 structure remains much the same as when it was built. Menominee preservationists have strongly encouraged the county to retain the structure and to adopt plans for sensitive interior and exterior renovations.

(4) Main Street Historic District*

Today it is difficult to find a Lake Michigan town that was a major lumbering center in the late nineteenth century with its old business district intact. Most such districts have been destroyed as town economies have changed. The Menominee Main Street District, where the buildings of the lumbering era remain, some in use and some vacant, is an exception. Bounded by 10th Avenue, the Green Bay shoreline, 4th Avenue, and 2nd Street, it includes more than 40 commercial and civic buildings and some residences. Many of the structures designed and built of red sandstone and brick by Menominee architects and builders are local adaptations of styles popular in the

Midwest between 1880 and 1910. Others, designed by Chicago, Minneapolis, and Green Bay architects, are Beaux-Arts in style; see, for example, the Spies Public Library, described below. Running parallel to Green Bay, 1st Street (formally Main Street) is the focal point of the district. A drive or walk along this street from 10th Avenue to 4th Avenue is a good way to get an impression of the district. Below are some of the older structures well worth noticing.

Menominee Abstract Company, 945 1st Street

Built in 1903, this red sandstone structure is representative of commercial architecture in the Michigan Upper Peninsula at the turn of the century. Two Menominee architects, Derrick Hubert and William M. Brown, designed the building in a regional adaptation of the Richardsonian Romanesque style.

Spies Public Library, 940 1st Street

August Spies was a very successful Menominee businessman. For a number of years he operated a grocery and butcher shop; then, in 1880, he founded the A. Spies Lumber and Cedar Company in partnership with Henry Martin. Acting in the philanthropic tradition of many successful late nineteenth-century American businessmen, Spies gave the library to the city as a memorial to his business success. Constructed in 1903, the building is in the Beaux-Arts style.

Victory Park, on 1st Street between Spies Public Library and 8th Avenue

Located on the site where a sawmill once stood, the park fronts on Green Bay. The bandstand in the center of the park is used for summer concerts. The marina accommodates pleasure craft.

Schale Building, 601 1st Street

Designed by a Menominee architect, Charles W. Maass, this office block was built in 1895 using cream-colored brick and Lake Superior red sandstone quarried in the Keweenaw Peninsula near the Portage entry to the Keweenaw Waterway. Attractive to contemporaries because of its varied shape and color, the building was described by the *Menominee Democrat* as "one of the handsomest in the city, occupying as it does, the most prominent corner in the business center." For many decades, its corner tower has been a landmark for sailors bound for the Menominee harbor.

Ludington, Wells and Van Schaick Company General Store, 501 1st Street

Now vacant, this brick building was constructed in the 1870s as the company store for one of Menominee's largest lumber companies. The company was founded by wealthy businessmen who, like the owners of many Menominee lumbering businesses, lived in Milwaukee and Chicago, where the wholesale and retail ends of their enterprises were located. The large companies maintained sizable merchandise stores in Menominee to supply their workers and the townspeople as well.

Menominee Opera House, 5th Avenue between 1st and 2nd Streets

Built in 1902 to add to the town's cultural life, this brick structure, designed by the Chicago architect G. O. Garnsey, is taking a new lease on life. The exterior is currently being restored, and the Menominee Arts Council hopes soon to restore the fire-damaged interior so that it can be used for the performing arts. The opera house was a familiar feature of prosperous late nineteenth-century towns, providing facilities for traveling speakers and music and drama groups.

Isaac Stephenson House, 400 1st Street

Built in the 1880s for Isaac Stephenson, nephew of Isaac Stephenson of Marinette and son of Robert Stephenson, who was associated with the Ludington, Wells and Van Schaick Lumber Company, this spacious cream brick home with classical detail stands at the southeast corner of the Main Street Historic District with grounds that extend to Green Bay.

(5) Chappee Historical Marker

River Road, 5 miles north of city limits

This memorial marker stands near the site of Louis Chappee's fur-trading post.

76. Stephenson Charcoal Kilns
Hy US-41

Those interested in lumbering and iron smelting will find it worthwhile to make a brief trip from Menominee north on Hy US-41 to Stephenson. The village took its name from two large timberland owners in the township, Samuel and Robert Stephenson, brothers of Isaac Stephenson (see site 75). It began as a sawmilling center in the 1870s. To supply the fuel needs of its blast furnace, located just north of Menominee, the Menominee Furnace Company built a group of charcoal kilns at Stephenson, 20 miles north of the furnace on the Chicago and North Western Railroad line. The furnace operated from 1872 to 1883. Five of the kilns, located on private property off County Road 352, east of Hy US-41, are well preserved.

77. Scenic Green Bay Drive
Hy M-35

From Menominee to Escanaba, Hy M-35 follows closely the western shoreline of Green Bay. This beautiful drive offers lots of opportunities to see the waters of the bay and to enjoy the woods along the shore.

Camping at J. W. Wells State park. Both beach and wooded sites are beautiful, but campers will find the mosquitos less pestiferous on the beach. Photo by Margaret Bogue.

78. J. W. Wells State Park
Hy M-35 (BCFHPS)

Named for a prominent Menominee lumberman, this densely wooded 974-acre park includes three miles of frontage on Green Bay and 1,400 feet of frontage on the Big Cedar River. A varied, undulating topography includes low parallel ridges marking old lakeshore and a long chain of irregular hills which were formed by ancient glaciers. Visitors to the park will find a wide variety of trees: maple, beech, hemlock, basswood, pine, cedar, birch, spruce, and elm. Well-marked foot trails offer opportunities to see the many species of wildflowers, wild berries, birds, and wild animals, especially deer. $

79. Cedar River
Hy M-35

Cedar River in the late nineteenth century was a bustling sawmill village and busy Green Bay port where barges were loaded with lumber for the Chicago market. After fire destroyed the

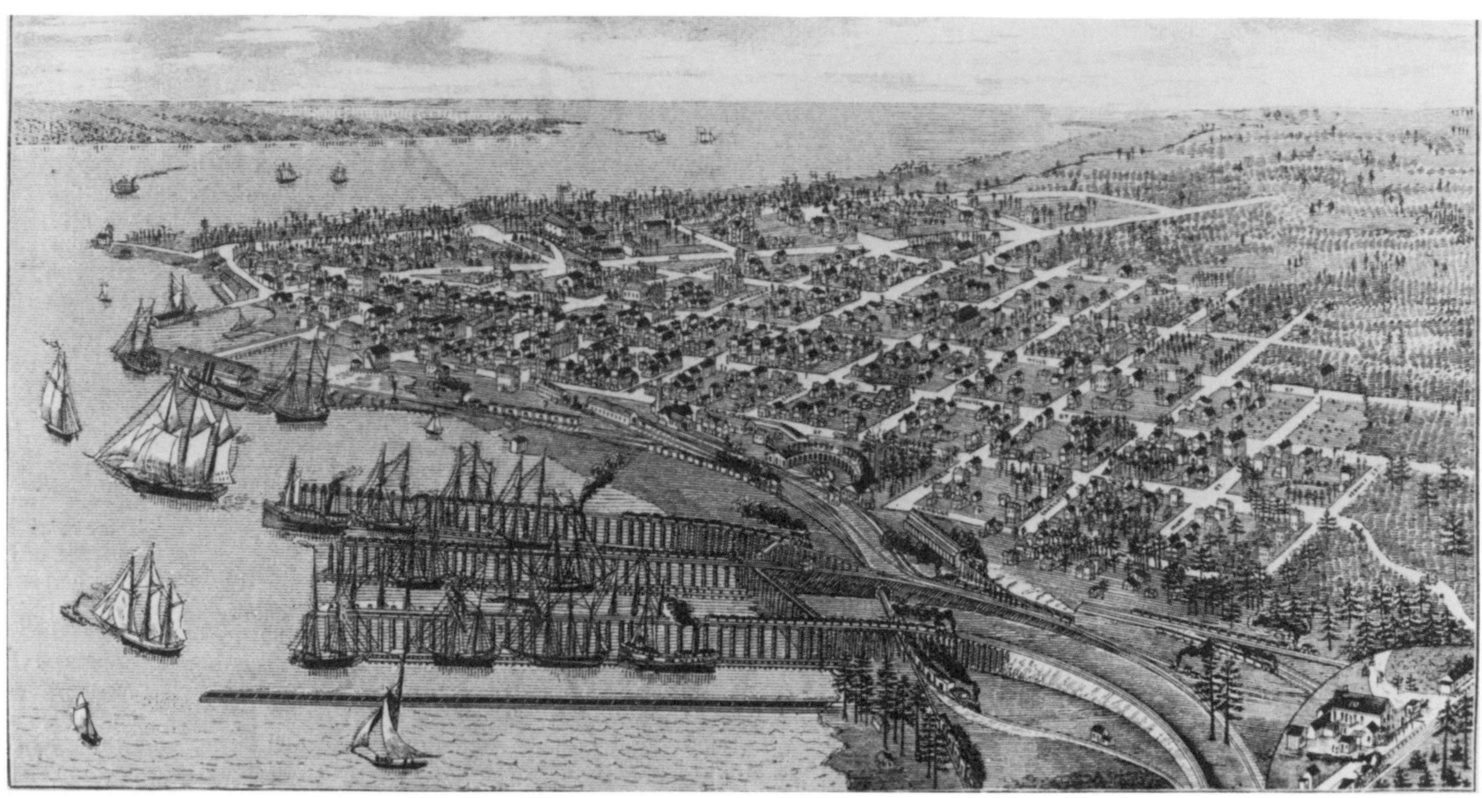

The ore docks at Escanaba in the era when sailing vessels and small steamboats carried the red iron ore. Courtesy Michigan Historical Collections, Bentley Historical Library, University of Michigan.

mill, the village lost much of its population. Adjacent to the highway stands the Catholic Church of the Sacred Heart, built in 1887, and the Mission Chapel, dating from 1889.

80. Ford River

Hy M-35

The village of Ford River reached its greatest prosperity in the lumbering days of the late nineteenth century, when its population totaled 1,000. In those days its sawmills turned out 50 million board feet of lumber annually, which was shipped downlake from seven docks.

81. Escanaba

Hys M-35, US-41, and US-2

Located on lands originally occupied by the Noke or Noquet band of Chippewa Indians, the town of Escanaba grew from the lumbering enterprises of the Nelson Ludington Company of Marinette. Lumbermen had long recognized the high quality of the white pine in the area when the company decided to survey and plat Escanaba in 1862. The earliest sawmill dated from the mid-1830s, but the big cut began in the 1860s when the Ludington Company found it advantageous to supplement its extensive timber stands farther south on Green Bay with Little Bay De Noc stumpage.

Escanaba emerged as a frontier lumber village with a small wintertime population servicing the needs of the surrounding lumber camps. In spring, with the log harvest dispatched downriver, the village took on new life as the lumberjacks and rivermen hit town with their winter wages. Commercial fishing and sawmilling were also important parts of Escanaba's early industry.

The iron mines of the Marquette and Menominee ranges contributed substantially to Escanaba's early growth and prosperity. Spurred during the 1860s by the Union's wartime needs for iron ore, railroad builders laid plans to connect the iron mines at Negaunee with Escanaba. They reasoned that Escanaba's deep harbor would make an excellent Lake Michigan outlet for Marquette Range ores. The completed rail line carried its first ore shipments to Escanaba in 1864.

Already a busy transshipment point for iron ore in the 1870s, Escanaba benefited greatly from the Chicago and North Western's branch line to the Menominee Range. The connection between Quinnesec and Escanaba was completed in 1877. Three years later the line reached Iron Mountain. Between 1864 and 1964 more than 340 million tons of iron ore reached Escanaba for shipment southward by ore carriers.

By 1890 Escanaba claimed to be "the iron port of the world," and boasted a total outbound vessel tonnage of over 8 million. The port bustled with the comings and goings of steamships of 14 lines that made Escanaba a regular stop. A local marine historian tells us that 8 to 10 freight and passenger steamers docked at Escanaba every day, often with four or five large vessels in port at the same time.

Under the stimulus of railroad building, the lumber and iron ore trade, and commercial fishing, Escanaba grew steadily. It was incorporated as a village in 1866 and as a city in 1883. The population numbered 1,370, about one-third of them foreign-born, in 1870. At the turn of the century, the figure stood at 9,500. In 1940 its population total approached 15,000. The 1980 census reported 14,355 residents. This could have never been the case had the town failed to make a transition from the era of the great extractive industries into more diversified economic activity. Gone are the great sawmills, which employed thousands of workmen as late as 1900. Gone are the days of the great catches of whitefish, lake trout, and sturgeon from Little Bay De Noc waters.

Now Escanaba thrives as a service center, as a county seat, and as a home for newer industry. A large paper mill, a wood specialty manufacturing company, and a wood veneer business still utilize forest resources. An automotive and machine company and a truck crane plant are more recent additions to the city's employers. Escanaba is a distribution point for oil and coal brought to port by lake carriers. A chemical plant, a metal fabrication company, and a woodenware business failed in the transitional years.

Much physical evidence of the heyday of extractive industry remains. Stephenson Street, Ludington Street, and Ludington Park preserve the big names of the lumbering boom. From ore dock No. 6, built by the North Western Railroad in 1903, about 12 million tons of ore pellets from the Marquette and Menominee ranges are shipped annually in times of economic prosperity.

Escanaba Sites of Interest

Many of Escanaba's points of historical interest are located on the waterfront on Little Bay De Noc in Ludington Park. As you enter town on Ludington Street, follow it to the waterfront to see the following sites.

(1) Delta County Historical Museum
Ludington Park, adjacent to Coast Guard Station
This small but expanding museum contains displays on iron mining, lumbering, and railroads. Open afternoons, May 15–Labor Day. Free.

(2) Historical Markers
Ludington Park
Two markers headed "Little Bay De Noc" and "Centennial of Iron Ore Shipping" make informative reading.

(3) Ludington Park
Escanaba has done a beautiful job of developing the Little Bay De Noc waterfront. The park area includes picnic tables, a swimming beach and bathhouse, a marina, and other recreational facilities, such as tennis courts.

(4) Escanaba Chamber of Commerce
corner of North 3rd and Ludington Streets
This office provides visitors with maps, brief digests of Delta county history, and assistance in finding points of interest in Delta County.

82. Hannahville Potawatomi Reservation

west of Hy M-35, access from Hy US-41

The history of the Hannahville Reservation illustrates many of the hardships that grew out of the early nineteenth-century federal policy of removing Indians from their tribal lands east of the Mississippi to a "permanent" Indian Territory west of the river, away from the incoming tide of white settlement. Lake Michigan's Indian tribes pressured into removal before 1848 included the Sac and Fox, Chippewa, Winnebago, Ottawa, Menominee, and Potawatomi. The Chippewa and Menominee were the most successful in defeating wholesale removal, ultimately acquiring reservations on ceded tribal lands.

After cessions of their tribal lands in Michigan, Indiana, Illinois, and Wisconsin beginning in 1807, the Potawatomi relinquished the last of their claims to land east of the Mississippi in 1833. Removals characterized by force, resistance, misery, death, and official profiteering dragged on for the next seven years. By 1840 most of the Potawatomi had been removed from their homelands, but not all. Some—exactly how many is unknown—fled to Canada. Others—an estimated 300, according to the U.S. Court of Claims—fled into northern Wisconsin and Michigan, where they established small, scattered settlements along the shore of Lake Michigan. They were joined by some of the Potawatomi who had been removed to Iowa and Kansas and had returned, dissatisfied with the new homes assigned them by the U.S. government.

These Indians, known as the Wisconsin band of Potawatomi, did not receive their proportion of tribal payments guaranteed under the terms of treaties with the United States. They owned no land and for decades lived miserable lives, roaming from one place to another, picking berries, digging ginseng, and seeking day labor. They congregated briefly in squatter settlements in Winnebago, Washington, Fond du Lac, Milwaukee, Door, Kewaunee, Shawano, Vilas, Manitowoc, and Sheboygan counties in Wisconsin and in Menominee, Delta, and Schoolcraft counties in Michigan, drifting ever northward, away from the main body of the white population.

In the 1890s some of the Wisconsin band of Potawatomi settled in Forest County, Wisconsin, squatting on cutover land owned by lumber companies. A few of them homesteaded under the terms of the Indian Homestead Act. Most of them might well have remained landless had it not been for the efforts of Rev. Erik O. Morstad, a Lutheran missionary who settled among the Forest County group in 1901 and decided to undertake a legal battle to secure for the Wisconsin band the federal treaty payments to which they were entitled. Morstad corresponded with the Office of Indian Affairs in Washington and secured legal help to validate their claims.

Along with an agent of the Office of Indian Affairs and Charles Kisheck, a Potawatomi chief who served as interpreter, Morstad visited the Potawatomi camps in the summer of 1907 in order to provide the government with a tribal census. The three traveled through northern Wisconsin, Michigan, and Canada from the eastern end of Lake Superior and along the Lake Huron shoreline from Georgian Bay to the southeastern shore of Lake Huron, visiting Potawatomi settlements and constructing an accurate tribal roll. They found these people impoverished, demoralized, sullen, and suspicious, a people who considered themselves refugees, still fearful that they would be forcibly collected and moved to Kansas, and fearful as well that their children would be taken from them and sent to U.S. Indian boarding schools.

Potawatomi women of the Harris and Bark River area, about 1900–1910. Courtesy State Historical Society of Wisconsin. WHi(X3)18847

At Harris and Bark River, about 17 miles west of Escanaba, Michigan, Morstad and his companions found a settlement of Potawatomi living on privately owned lands in log houses. Their settlement included a school and a church. Peter Marksman, a Methodist misssionary, had led these people to the Harris location from Cedar River, 20 miles south, about 1883. He had chosen the land and lent them funds to start their community. They had land under cultivation, but they did not own it.

The work of Rev. Erik Morstad resulted in legislation in 1913 establishing a federal reservation for the Potawatomi of Forest County, Wisconsin, and Menominee County, Michigan. The United States purchased 3,360 acres for the latter group, which

Wisconsin Land and Lumber Company employees pose for a formal picture at Hermansville. From the Collections of the Michigan State Archives, Department of State. 00138

named the reservation Hannahville to honor Peter Marksman's wife, Hannah, and express their appreciation for the missionary's assistance in establishing the community. The reservation lands in the Harris-Wilson area are scattered and are alloted to individual Indians.

Side Trip to Iron Mountain

While at Escanaba, visitors who are interested in lumbering and in the history of iron mining in the Menominee Range will find it well worthwhile to make a side trip on Hy US-2 to Hermansville, Vulcan, Norway, Quinnesec, and Iron Mountain. The towns of Bark River, Harris, Wilson, Spaulding, Hermansville, Cunard, and Waucedah had their origins in the lumbering industry. Loretto, located on the rim of the Menominee Iron Range, Vulcan, Norway, Quinnesec, and Iron Mountain owed their greatest prosperity to iron mining. As you pass through Vulcan and Norway, the view of the Menominee Range is excellent. The best remaining evidence of the lumbering industry on this route is at Hermansville.

83. Hermansville
Hy US-2

The Wisconsin Land and Lumber Company built Hermansville as a company town. C. J. L. Meyer, a German immigrant, founded the parent company in Fond du Lac, Wisconsin, shortly after the Civil War to produce pine sashes, doors, and blinds. By 1878 Meyer had decided to buy Michigan pineland to supply the needs of his mill. In the same year he dismantled his Fond du Lac sawmill and moved it to the site of Hermansville. Early in 1879 he started operations, using Michigan logs.

Hermansville, named for his son, grew around the mill operations with company housing, store, school, and church. Within a decade Meyer's 50,000 acres of pine were exhausted. Foreseeing the depletion of softwoods, in 1882 Meyer built a hardwood sawmill. His company pioneered in producing high quality hardwood flooring under the trademark "IXL."

Over the years the company expanded its operations to include 250,000 acres of timberland, three railroads, and three villages. Between 1910 and 1930 the plant shipped 12 carloads of wood products to market daily. The plant long ago ceased to manufacture hardwood flooring, but the main portion of the IXL factory still stands, as does the company office building.

The Office Building of the Wisconsin Land and Lumber Company
Built in 1882–1883, this building is much the same as it was in the 1920s. A grandson of C. J. L. Meyer, Dr. George Washington Earle, has developed a family museum that preserves artifacts of the lumbering era. The museum, located on the village main street is often open to visitors in the mornings during the summer months.

84. Norway

Hy US-2

Test pits at Norway in 1877 showed extremely rich deposits of iron ore. This once-busy mining village, at times endangered by cave-ins, no longer has active mines, but evidence of past iron mining is quite apparent.

Norway Sites of Interest

(1) Iron Mountain Iron Mine
Hy US-2, east of Norway
Opened in the 1870s, the Iron Mountain Iron Mine, part of the Penn Iron Mines, produced over 22 million tons of ore during its 68-year production history (1877–1945). The tour of this mine, developed commercially to illustrate iron-mining techniques, takes visitors through 2,600 feet of underground drifts and tunnels where methods of timbering are explained, the geology of the mine is elaborated, and mining technology—from the picks and shovels of the early days to modern water liner drills—is demonstrated.

Curry Mine Shaft at Norway, August 1980. Photo by Allan Bogue.

Open daily all year, 9:00 A.M.–5:00 P.M. $

(2) Curry Mine Shaft
This shaft is visible on the right as you enter town westbound on Hy US-2. To get a good look at it, turn right on Walnut Street and proceed one block north to the corner of Walnut and Railroad Avenue.

(3) Norway Spring
Just to the west of town on Hy US-2 lies Norway Spring, identified by a Michigan Historic Site marker. The spring is a result of a 1,094-foot hole drilled in 1902 by the Oliver Mining Company, which was in search of iron ore. Earlier the spring's location was the site of a sawmill.

85. Iron Mountain

Hy US-2

Long before the iron-mining boom and the founding of the town, the lumbering operations of Menominee's timber barons reached the Iron Mountain area. In the mid-1850s timber cruisers located the stands of white pine on the upper Menominee River. Cutting began, and by 1880 the best of the white pine had been sent downriver to the sawmills at Marinette-Menominee.

The earliest sawmills in the Iron Mountain area dated from the mining boom of the late 1870s. Then hardwoods, left by the lumbermen because such wood does not float well for long distances, were harvested for use in mine construction. Lumbering continued as an important industry until well into the twentieth century, but on a much smaller scale than in the last half of the nineteenth.

The iron ore of the Menominee Range proved a far more lucrative natural resource than timber. While geologists as early as 1848 reported the existence of iron ore in the Iron Mountain area, Menominee Range mining required railroad connections to bring in essential supplies and equipment and to carry the ore to market. Serious interest in mining dated from the late 1870s, after the railroad connected Iron Mountain with Escanaba, where the ore was transferred to lake carriers bound for steel mills.

Workable deposits of high-grade iron ore in the Vulcan-Norway-Quinnesec area east of Iron Mountain were discovered before the panic of 1873. Development came after the depression eased. The North Western Railway reached Quinnesec in 1877, and the village grew as the mining center of the Menominee range.

Quinnesec quickly slipped to second place. In 1879 Nelson Powell Hulst of the Menominee Mining Company discovered the Chapin Mine at the site of present-day Iron Mountain. Hulst, a graduate of Yale and the Sheffield Scientific School with special training in geology, chemistry, and metallurgy played an important role in the discovery of Menominee Range mines and in the supervision and development of mining at Iron Mountain.

Because the Chapin Mine was located on the property of Henry Chapin of Niles (see site 170), the developers had to lease the land and pay the owner royalties for the ore mined. The mine presented unusual challenges because the richest of its ore deposits lay on swampy land beneath quicksand. Hulst and his associates developed a freezing process that made it possible to sink the shaft.

The Chapin Mine developers induced the North Western Railroad to build its line to Iron Mountain in 1879. The first shipment of the Chapin ore went to market in 1880. The Chapin Mine established itself as the giant of the Menominee, the mine with the greatest output and the largest workforce. It employed 1,800, almost half of Iron Mountain's mineworkers in 1890. Between 1880 and 1932, when the Chapin Mine closed, at least 25 million tons of iron ore came up its shafts. In 1901 this mine became a subsidiary of U.S. Steel.

Chapin Mine workers, probably in 1880. Courtesy Menominee Range Historical Foundation Archives, Iron Mountain, Michigan.

Iron Mountain was platted in the fall of 1879 by Isaac Stephenson and his Marinette-Menominee business associates. The town mushroomed from a few tents, shacks, and boarding houses to a village of more than a thousand a few years later. It incorporated as a village in 1887 and as a city the following year. It continued to grow very rapidly until 1893, when it had a population of over 8,500.

With the opening of the Menominee mines, a flood of immigrant workers poured in seeking jobs. New York and Boston mineowners sought skilled Cornish miners for underground work. Swedes, French Canadians, Hungarians, Russians, Finns, Poles, Germans, and Italians swelled the labor force. One local historian has estimated that one-third of the mineworkers were Cornish and one-third Swedish.

Cosmopolitan Iron Mountain developed as a rough and ready mining and lumbering town, complete with saloons, gambling houses, brothels, and a high incidence of rowdy behavior. Mining accidents and deaths and abortive attempts by mineworkers to organize and strike characterized the developmental years. So did the ethnic frictions depicted in Vivian La Jeunesse Parsons' novel, *Not without Honor*.

90. Peninsula Point Lighthouse*

County Road 513, Stonington Road off Hy US-2 (P)

For the venturesome traveler, the 30-minute ride on County Road 513 to Peninsula Point Lighthouse is well worthwhile. The road is partly blacktopped and partly graveled, and it becomes increasingly narrow as you approach the tip of Peninsula Point. Along the way you will notice old log structures on some of the farms. Peninsula Point Lighthouse, located at the end of the road, lies in a beautiful and well-kept park with picnic tables. The lighthouse, built in 1865, warned ships away from "The Devil's Ten Acres"—a "trap with teeth of rocks set in a series of treacherous shoals" near the entrance to Little Bay De Noc. The light was automated in 1922 but ceased operation in 1936, when the Minneapolis Shoal lighthouse was built. Restored by the Stonington Grange, the tower, with its iron spiral stairway, is open to visitors. The building and grounds are cared for by the Hiawatha National Forest staff. Free.

91. Hiawatha National Forest

Hy US-2 (BCFHPS)

The Hiawatha National Forest was formally established in 1931 at a time when the ravages of heavy logging and forest fires remained all too apparent. This 860,000-acre tract, now covered with cedars, pines, and sugar maples, is a forest of dense tree stands, wetlands, and scattered rolling hills with miles of streams and lakes. The forest lies in two segments, divided by state forest lands. The western portion extends roughly from Gladstone to Manistique; the eastern from Brevort well to the east of St. Ignace.

White-tail deer and black bears are very abundant. The forest has plenty of snowshoe hares, beavers, squirrels, porcupines, coyotes, red foxes, weasels, and raccoons. The pine marten, previously extinct in the area, has been reintroduced. Grouse, woodcock, a variety of waterfowl, and songbird species are abundant. In the streams and lakes, fishermen will find trout, bass, perch, walleye and northern pike, coho salmon, smelt, and steelhead.

In addition to its recreational use, the Hiawatha National Forest produces wood for local industry. Controlled cuts yield approximately 18,000 cords of pulpwood and 2 million board feet of lumber annually.

In the West Unit lie a number of areas of special interest: Ogontz Natureway, Bay Furnace, Bay De Noc-Grand Island Hiking Trail (site 89), and Peninsula Point (site 90). Information is available both at the Rapid River Ranger Station and at the Ogontz roadside information station.

Areas of special interest in the East Unit include Point aux Chenes, Round Island, Government Island, Point Iroquois Lighthouse, and several fish hatcheries. Stop at Point aux Chenes visitor information station for more details.

92. Fayette State Park*

off Hy US-2 on County Road 483

As you drive the 17 miles down the Garden Peninsula from Hy US-2 to Fayette State Park, you will pass through the village of Garden, the first white settlement on the Garden Peninsula. Notice the lovely little Catholic church and the nineteenth-century fire engine on display in the center of the village.

The Garden Peninsula attracted white settlers in the mid-nineteenth century because of its potential for fishing and lumbering. Here the newcomers found Indians cultivating the rich gardens that gave the peninsula its name.

Historic Fayette Townsite, part of the Michigan State Park system, preserves the Jackson Iron Company's town. Laid out in 1866, Fayette developed into a very profitable iron-smelting venture between 1867 and 1890. The Jackson Mine at Negaunee, 75 miles northwest of Fayette, produced iron ore and shipped it downlake to iron- and steel-making centers in the Cleveland and Chicago areas. The company developed Fayette to convert the ore into iron pigs and cut transportation costs. Fayette offered great locational advantages: it was on the way to market; it had a fine, deep, protected harbor. Nearby were abundant stands of hardwoods for making the charcoal needed for iron smelting. High-quality limestone was also in good supply here.

At the site the visitor will see the remains of Fayette, which was virtually abandoned in 1890 when the smelting operation ceased. Hardwood had become more and more scarce, and the

Ruins of the big furnace, Fayette State Park, rear view. Photo by Margaret Bogue.

charcoal furnaces could no longer compete with coke-fired smelters.

The production side of this company town lives on in the big furnace, lime kilns, charcoal kilns, sawmill site, and service buildings. The flavor of life here is preserved in the homes of laborers and supervisors, the company doctor and the superintendent, the company store, the hotel, the boarding house, the opera house, and the jail. Fayette State Park is administered jointly by the Parks Division of the Michigan Department of Natural Resources and the History Division of the Michigan Department of State. $ (See also p. 71.)

93. Summer Island*

at the tip of the Garden Peninsula

Ceramic and stone artifacts found here, as well as evidence of a pole dwelling, indicate that there were at least three distinctive cultural groups of people living here in the third, thirteenth, and seventeenth centuries A.D.

94. Thompson State Fish Hatchery

north on Hy M-149 from Hy US-2

The two units of this Department of Natural Resources fish hatchery propagate brook, brown, and rainbow trout, coho salmon, muskies, northern pike, walleyes, and suckers. The hatchery is open to the public Monday–Friday, 8:00 A.M.–4:30 P.M.; Saturday and Sunday, 8:00 A.M.–4:00 P.M.

95. Palms Book State Park

11 miles north of Hy US-2 via Hy M-149 (P)

This park preserves for the enjoyment of visitors the largest spring in the state of Michigan. Kitch-iti-ki-pi, or "big spring," as it was called by the Indians, is 200 feet in diameter and 42 feet deep. From observation windows in a platform raft, visitors look down into the constantly bubbling depth of the spring, where 10,000 gallons of water per minute flow from cracks in limestone bedrock. The spring, considered sacred by the Indians, has puzzled geologists for many years. They believe that it may have been caused by the slumping of rock strata or perhaps by the downward movement of surface waters, enlarging cracks in limestone outcroppings.

The park dates from 1929, when the Palms Book Land Company of Detroit gave the state 89 acres of land including the spring with the provision that there be no camping on the property. $

The platform raft at Kitch-iti-ki-pi. Photo by Margaret Bogue.

96. Indian Lake State Park

County Road 455, adjacent to Palms Book Park (BCHPS)

In 1932, in the depths of the Great Depression, the state of Michigan purchased land to develop Indian Lake State Park. The site's advantages included a fine sand beach along the lake, good fishing, and a location central to much fine Upper Peninsula natural scenery.

Containing 320 acres, Indian Lake Park is divided into two units, one on the southern and one on the western shore, both with camping facilities. The park area is heavily wooded, and the lake, fed by the waters of Kitch-iti-ki-pi, is attractive for swimmers.

On the eastern shore of Indian Lake is a small outdoor shrine and a plaque marking the site of a log and bark chapel. Construction of this small chapel began in 1832, when Indians in the area learned that Father Frederic Baraga was to pay them a visit. Arriving before the chapel had been completed, Father Baraga assisted in its completion. This was the first of many chapels he built during his service to the Chippewas in the Upper Peninsula. A few feet north of the site is an abandoned Indian cemetery. $

97. Manistique

Hy US-2

The name of this town and its river comes from an Indian word meaning "vermilion" or "red ocher," for the Manistique River has a distinctive color, acquired as it flows through the bog ore district of Upper Michigan. Possessed of a fine lake harbor that does not freeze in winter and ample water power from the Manistique and Indian rivers, and surrounded by great stands of white pine, the town began as a lumbering center.

Some cutting and milling operations date from the 1850s, but real development came with the activites of the Chicago Lumbering Company in the 1870s. The company built houses, stores, docks, and mills and organized a company-owned town. It purchased its own stumpage and its own fleet of boats to deliver lumber to the growing cities of southern Lake Michigan. In its heyday the firm manufactured 10 to 20 million board feet of lumber per month. Other lumber businesses also grew up at Manistique and in the surrounding area. By the early twentieth century, the timber boom was over.

Manistique ceased to be a company-owned town in 1912, when two businessmen purchased both the Chicago Lumbering Company and its affiliate, the Weston Lumber Company. Company-owned homes and businesses were offered for sale to the public. The transition to pulp and paper making began in 1916, when W. J. Murphy, owner and publisher of the *Minneapolis Tribune*, organized the Manistique Pulp and Paper Company. Now owned by Field Enterprises of Chicago, the company is a major employer.

Inland Lime and Stone Company's piles of limestone ready to be loaded aboard ship at Port Inland, 1972. Courtesy Inland Steel Company, Indiana Harbor Works Photographic Services.

Of great importance in Manistique's present economy, the Inland Lime and Stone Company dates from 1928. In that year Inland Steel of East Chicago (see site 179), in search of a supply of high-quality limestone for its steel mills, decided to locate its quarry and plant on Seul Choix Point near Manistique. From a modest initial production of 1 million tons in 1931, the output has risen to 4 million annually. The third major industry in Manistique is tourism. The current population of this county seat town is 3,962, about 2,400 less than at its high point in 1920.

Manistique Sites of Interest

(1) Imogene Herbert Historical Museum

near the Water Tower and the Siphon Bridge on Hy US-2

This small museum is operated by the Pioneer Historical Society of Schoolcraft County. Housed in the Imogene Herbert House, one of the older houses in Manistique, the museum contains artifacts on nineteenth century life here. Open daily in summer months, 9:00 A.M.–5:00 P.M. Donation.

The society plans to develop its two-and-a-half-acre park area further by adding a log building that was once a part of the Hiawatha Colony, located 13 miles north of Manistique. Founded by the American socialist Walter Thomas Mills and Abe Byers, a Populist leader, in the 1890s, this agricultural colony built 20 structures to house 225 persons. The group pooled their land and resources, worked together, and shared the profits. The colony flourished briefly and was abandoned in 1896.

(2) Siphon Bridge and Water Tower

Hy US-2

After the *Minneapolis Tribune* secured water rights on the Manistique River in 1916, the company built the Manistique Pulp and Paper Company to supply its needs for newsprint. To furnish the plant with water, the company constructed a dam and a reinforced concrete flume paralleling the river in 1918–1920. This 3,300-foot-long flume has the ability to deliver 8,000 cubic feet of water per second. Later, when Hy US-2 was built through Manistique, engineers decided to construct the highway bridge through the upper part of the flume, with the roadway running four feet below water level. Local residents named the structure "The Siphon Bridge."

Manistique's most outstanding landmark is the Water Tower, an octagonal brick building 200 feet high adjacent to the Siphon Bridge. It was completed in 1922. No longer used as part of the water supply system, currently the tower houses the Manistique Chamber of Commerce, where visitors will find literature on the area's history and information about local businesses and recreation.

(3) Manistique Papers, Incorporated

Hy US-2

From Hy US-2 the traveler gets two good views of Manistique Papers, Inc.:

This interior view at Manistique Papers, Inc., shows winding paper onto the "Reel," the last step at the dry end of the paper machine prior to converting it to rolls of specific size for the customer at the rewinder. Courtesy Brian J. Nelson of Manistique Papers, Inc.

one coming into town from the west, and the other near the Siphon Bridge. At the latter point the great storage yard filled with logs comes into clear view.

(4) Manistique Light House
Hy US-2
On a sunny day, the brilliant red of this lighthouse against the blue lake waters catches the eye as you drive into Manistique eastbound. The best viewing point is from Lakeview Park, just off Hy US-2 on the eastern edge of town.

(5) Wyman State Nursery
The easiest access to the nursery is from Hy US-2, coming into Manistique from the west. Turn left on Deer Street, right on M-94, and right on the nursery access road just before 94 crosses Indian River. On the 55-acre nursery tract, the Department of Natural Resources produces about 2 million trees annually for planting on state land and for public sale at cost for reforesting vacant land. The nursery is open during daylight hours. Tours may be arranged with the superintendent.

98. Lime Kilns
Hy US-2, 4 miles east of Schoolcraft County Airport

As you drive east from Manistique, you will notice old stone kilns on the left-hand side of the road four miles beyond the Schoolcraft County Airport. These are the ruins of the lime kilns of the White Marble Lime Company, founded at Manistique in 1889 as a satellite of the lumbering industry. The company made quicklime, utilizing lumber wastes and local limestone. The state of Michigan plans to preserve the site.

99. Seul Choix Point Lighthouse
County Roads 432 and 431 off Hy US-2

Take County Road 432 south off Hy US-2 for 4.3 miles, and turn right on County Road 431 to Mueller Township Park to find Seul Choix Point Lighthouse, a handsome structure built in

Seul Choix Point Lighthouse is one of a number built on the Great Lakes and elsewhere by the federal government in the late nineteenth century using the same architectural design. Note the Italianate bracketry and curved window design at the upper level. Photo by Margaret Bogue.

1892. Although the lighthouse is not generally open to the public, visitors are welcome to view the grounds. Seul Choix Point was so named because it was the only place where boats could take refuge from rough lake waters for some distance along the shoreline. Here French Canadian families settled during the nineteenth century and established a fishing village.

100. Port Inland

County Road 432 south off Hy US-2

Port Inland is the location of the Inland Lime and Stone Company's plant (see site 97). Both the plant and the business offices are located at the termination of County Road 432. The plant is not open to the public.

101. Blaney Park

Hy US-2

Blaney Park originated from the efforts of the Wisconsin Land and Lumber Company (see site 83) to develop a 22,000-acre tract of its cutover land as a tourist resort in the 1920s. Groups of cottages were built, and old logging roads were converted to hiking and riding trails. The Celibeth cabin and the golf course are still in use. Here also is a hunting preserve and bird sanctuary.

Bobcat. Courtesy State Historical Society of Wisconsin. WHi(X18)12351

102. Seney National Wildlife Refuge

Hy M-77 north from Hy US-2 at Blaney Park (FHP)

The federal government established this 95,455-acre wildlife refuge in 1935 under the Fish and Wildlife Service of the U.S. Department of the Interior upon the recommendation of the Michigan Conservation Department. Its creation was part of a larger effort during the 1930s to restore cutover lands. Michigan's Upper Peninsula pine forests fell to axe and saw in the late nineteenth century, and Seney developed into a lumber boom town in the 1880s. Following the big cut, fires burned uncontrolled over the area, making it impossible for nature to produce a new forest. Land companies promoted farming, but farming led to failures, foreclosures, and tax-delinquent lands. During the 1930s the federal government used Civilian Conservation Corps workers to construct a system of ditches and pools suitable for waterfowl.

The refuge now contains 7,000 acres of open water in 21 open pools that support a nesting flock of Canada Geese and several species of ducks. More than 200 bird species find the refuge attractive, including sandhill cranes, bald eagles, and pileated woodpeckers. Beavers, white-tailed deer, black bears, otters, coyotes, foxes, minks, muskrats, bobcats, and even wolves inhabit the refuge.

Exhibits and environmental information may be found in the visitors' center. A 7-mile, self-guided Marshland Wildlife Drive, a 1.4-mile nature trail for hikers, and two picnic areas are available for use. The visitors' center is open mid-May–September 30, 9:00 A.M.–4:00 P.M. In summer, movie and slide programs are shown here.

103. Naubinway

Hy US-2

French fishermen settled here in 1880. Shortly afterward lumbermen began operations in the vicinity. As lumbering and fishing expanded, Naubinway's population grew to 1,500. The sawmill employed nearly 600, and the fishermen operated 34 fishing boats. Population declined greatly when the lumber mill closed in 1896. Commercial fishing declined dramatically with the lamprey infestation in Lake Michigan in the 1940s. Today it is primarily a village of summer homes and resorts.

104. Scenic Lake Michigan Drive from Naubinway to St. Ignace

Highway US-2 from Naubinway to St. Ingnace offers exceptionally beautiful views of Lake Michigan and a number of state roadside parks and turnouts. Here travelers can pull off the road to fully enjoy the scenery, the sandy beaches, the surf, and the lake waters. On warm, sunny days many take advantage of fine wading and swimming opportunities. The road at times runs very close to the beach and at others runs high above Lake Michigan's waters. The scenery is especially fine at Epoufette and Cut River Bridge. As you near St. Ignace, there are a number of turnouts with good views of the Straits of Mackinac, the Mackinac Bridge, and the lower peninsula. Lake Michigan reaches its northernmost point two miles east of Naubinway.

105. Epoufette

Hy US-2

It is believed that Father Jacques Marquette used the harbor here as the first stop an a journey from St. Ignace into Lake Michigan. French fishermen established the village in 1859, and in the 1880s Epoufette attracted lumbermen.

106. Brevort

Hy US-2

Named for Henry Brevort, Jr., a surveyor, the town was originally known

as "The Warehouse." Here in 1875 the Mackinaw Lumber Company built a depot for supplies brought in by ship. Commercial fishing followed lumbering. The village holds an annual Swedish summer festival, honoring the Swedish immigrants who came here to work in the lumbering camps. Travelers will notice an attractive church on the right of the highway, Trinity Lutheran, built in 1922.

107. Pointe aux Chenes
Hy US-2

Named by the French for its natural oak forest, Pointe aux Chenes was long the site of an Indian settlement.

108. Gros Cap Cemetery*
Hy US-2

The archaeologist George I. Quimby dates the early use of the Gros Cap Cemetery to the years 1710–1760. Here lie buried Ottawa, Illinois, Miami, Sauk, Fox, and Potawatomi Indians and a number of nineteenth-century settlers. Because many old burial places in Moran Township were becoming obscured by shifting sands and deteriorating markers, in 1889 the township established Gros Cap Cemetery (formerly known as Western Cemetery). Some of the more recent graves were moved to Gros Cap at that time. Pioneer children, among them victims of diphtheria and smallpox, lie here, as do adults who died in lumbering and drowning accidents. The cemetery still serves the community.

"In memory of Josephine. May her soul rest in peace. Amen." Grave marker in Gros Cap Cemetery, west of St. Ignace. Photo by Margaret Bogue.

109. Gros Cap and St. Helena Island

At the mouth of the Moran River, a village of 1,500 Ottawa Indians lived in the late seventeenth century. Moran River and Moran Bay at Gros Cap are named for a French fur trader who established a post here. French Canadian fishermen came to Gros Cap in the nineteenth century, settling on the mainland and on St. Helena Island. During the last half of that century, Archie and Wilson Newton established a successful fishing and shipping business on the island.

110. The Straits of Mackinac

In the late seventeenth century, French explorers and missionaries found Chippewa, Huron, and Ottawa Indians living near the Straits of Mackinac, many of them fugitives from the powerful Iroquois. The advantages of the location were many. It was a strategic point in the water routes linking Lakes Michigan and Huron, and the waters around Mackinac Island abounded in fish. Father Claude Dablon described it in 1670: "This spot is the most noted in all these regions for its abundance of fish. . . . In fact, besides the fish common to all the other Nations, as the herring, carp, pike, golden fish, whitefish, and sturgeon, there are here found three kinds of trout: one, the common kind; the second, larger, being three feet in length and one in width; and the third, monstrous, for no other word expresses it."

The straits had special strategic importance for the French and the British in their pursuit of empire and the fur trade. The struggle to control the straits led to conflicts between them and later between the British and the Americans. At the straits the French built two forts and the British one. Once under U.S. management, Mackinac Island served again as a major rendezvous and transshipment point for fur traders.

Jean Nicollet passed through the straits in 1634. La Salle's *Griffon* sailed its waters in 1679. For centuries boats plied the straits between Mackinac Island and the Upper and lower peninsulas. The Mackinac Bridge opened in 1957, ushering in a new era of automobile traffic for the Upper Peninsula.

With increased tourism, the work of historic preservation at St. Ignace, Mackinaw City, and Mackinac Island took on new urgency. Today visitors to the straits will find a wealth of living history to help them recall the Indians, the explorers, the missionaries, the fur traders, the *voyageurs*, the soldiers, the lumbermen, and the fishermen whose lives were so closely tied to the waters of Michilimackinac.

What are the origin and meaning of the name Mackinac? Many explanations have been offered over the centuries. Early French records speak of the "Isle of Missilimackinac," where an Indian tribe with that name lived. Cadillac said that it meant "island of the tortoise." One authority on Indian languages suggested that it meant "big turtle clan." An eighteenth-century French writer traced the name to an Indian belief that a supernatural friend lived there. Other explanations relate to physical features: the island's arch rock, the conical rock formations on the island and near St. Ignace, and the deep land crevice near St. Ignace. Whatever their origin and meaning, Michilimackinac and Mackinac are both pronounced as though the "ac" ending were spelled "aw."

111. St. Ignace
Hy US-2 and I-75

Father Jacques Marquette founded the settlement at St. Ignace in 1671 when he arrived with a group of Huron Indians. He named his mission St. Ignace de Michilimackinac in honor of St. Ignatius of Loyola, founder of the Jesuit order. This remarkable Jesuit missionary-explorer spent only two years at the mission. In 1673 he departed with Louis Jolliet for the famous journey down the Mississippi. Marquette died on the return journey, but the work of the mission continued until 1705.

The Marquette Memorial—a simple, modest, and beautiful structure—overlooks the Straits of Mackinac. Photo by Margaret Bogue.

Meanwhile, in 1677 the Jesuits erected a second chapel near St. Ignace, named for St. Francis Borgia and intended to serve the Ottawa. Later, in the 1680s, the French built at St. Ignace the first of their two forts in the straits area, Fort de Buade, designed as a fur-trading post and a protective outpost for the water route between Lake Superior and Montreal. The fort became an important governmental and civil center. In the 1690s a sizable French and Indian settlement centered here. The French village contained 60 houses, the mission, and an Indian population of 7,000.

Its importance faded rapidly as the French scheme of fur trade and defense changed. The change had something to do with frictions at St. Ignace. The French commandant at Fort de Buade, Antoine de la Mothe Cadillac, quarreled with the Jesuits, who wanted military posts and fur traders removed from the western country. Jesuit objections, coupled with a slump in fur prices in the late seventeenth century, led the crown to curtail the trade.

Cadillac countered by pleading for the establishment of a strong fort at Detroit that could become the center of French influence. His wish was granted. The garrison left Fort de Buade in 1698, and Detroit was founded in 1701. Many of the Indians accepted Cadillac's invitation to come to Detroit. Most of the fur traders departed. The Jesuits burned the mission

Inside the Marquette Memorial, looking up. Photo by Margaret Bogue.

in 1706 and left. When the French reestablished a fort at the straits in 1715, they built Fort Michilimackinac on the lower peninsula.

St. Ignace did not develop substantially again until the late nineteenth century. Lumbering and iron making assumed temporary importance, but fishing remained important for a long time. In 1882 St. Ignace became the county seat. The town survived the decline of lumbering and grew, first as a port of entry for the Upper Peninsula and then, in the late nineteenth century, as a tourist center. Since 1957, with the completion of the bridge, its tourism industry has greatly expanded. The 1980 population was 2,632.

St. Ignace Sites of Interest

(1) Father Marquette Memorial
off Hy US-2 on the west side of town
This beautiful memorial park has been established with money appropriated by Congress and the state of Michigan. The memorial is only partially completed. The finished portion is a contemporary open structure that contains a bronze plaque mounted on stone outlining the main facts of Marquette's life. A fine museum portrays Marquette's missionary labors in New France and broadly interprets Indian life and the environment. A 16-minute film shown in the museum auditorium depicts the final months of Marquette's mission work. The park, operated by the state of Michigan, overlooks the straits and the Mackinac Bridge. Open daily, May 15–Labor Day, 9:00 A.M.–5:30 P.M. Free.

(2) Michilimackinac Historical Society Museum
Spring Street between North State and Church Streets
Housed in the former Michigan Bell Telephone Building, this museum has well-orgainized and attractively displayed artifacts relating to the history of St. Ignace. Permanent exhibits deal with lumbering, commercial fishing, the building of the Mackinac Bridge, the geology of the straits, and many other subjects. Open daily, May 15–Labor Day, 9:00 A.M.–5:00 P.M. Free.

(3) Old Mission Church*
Marquette Park at North State and North Marquette streets (Hy I-75)
Located very close to what is believed to be the site of the Marquette mission of 1671, this structure was built in 1837 at Moran Bay. Used for services until 1904, it was later moved to Marquette Park and now serves as a museum. Its collections contain some materials relating to mission activity and a miscellaneous collection of nineteenth-century artifacts. Open daily, May 15–Labor Day, 9:00 A.M.–5:00 P.M. Free.

(4) Father Marquette Statue
Marquette Park, at North State and North Marquette streets, (Hy I-75)
Beside the Mission Church stands a statue of Father Marquette, erected in 1954.

(5) Marquette Grave
Marquette Park, at North State and North Marquette streets (Hy I-75)
At the north side of the Mission Church stands a monument marking what many believe to be the second burial place of the remains of Father Marquette. Marquette died in 1675 on

his return journey from Illinois country and was buried somewhere on the eastern shore of Lake Michigan, probably near Ludington. Father Pierre François Xavier de Charlevoix, writing in 1721, states that a year after Marquette's death, one of his companions returned to the burial site and brought the remains to St. Ignace, where they were buried under the chapel altar in 1677. A grave believed to be Marquette's was discovered in 1877. The citizens of St. Ignace in 1882 erected this monument on the place where the remains were found. The chains around the monument represent the walls of the original mission chapel. Some of the bone fragments from the 1877 excavation were given to the Jesuits when they founded Marquette University in Milwaukee.

(6) Archaeological Site
Mission Church area, North State Street
In the summer of 1983, the St. Ignace Downtown Development Association funded a dig in cooperation with the Department of Anthropology at Michigan State University. The goal is to learn about the Huron and Ottawa Indian sites associated with the Marquette mission. The team discovered evidence of Huron refuse pits, a long house, and a palisade during the first summer's work.

(7) Fort de Buade Museum
335 North State Street
Here are fine collections of Indian beadwork, guns, relics of the French and British periods, and paintings of Great Lakes Indians. Open daily, mid-May–mid-October, 9:00 A.M.–5:00 P.M. Free.

(8) Walk-Drive Tour of St. Ignace
The St. Ignace Area Chamber of Commerce, located on the State Street water front, offers a walk-drive tour pamphlet and map to help visitors find many points of historical interest. Use this as a guide to the outdoor displays in the city parks, which include boats and artifacts of early sailing history.

(9) Ferry to Mackinac Island
North State Street
Three companies—Arnold Transit, Star Line Boats, and Shepler's Mackinac Island Ferry—run ferries to Mackinac Island, with scheduled service from May through December.

112. Straits State Park
from Hy US-2 (CHPS)

This beautiful wooded park on a high bluff overlooking Mackinac Bridge is divided into two parts. The Father Marquette unit contains a memorial to the missionary (site 111, no. [1]). The other unit, located east of the bridge, contains park headquarters, two camping areas, and a fine beach. $

113. Mackinac Island
accessible by ferry from St. Ignace or Mackinaw City

The island has a very long history, beginning with the ancient Indians who lived there and used it as a burial ground. The Jesuit missionary Claude Dablon wintered on the island in 1670–1671. Father Jacques Marquette also visited the island before deciding to establish his mission on the mainland.

The island became a key fortification for the British in 1780–1781 when they moved there from Fort Michilimackinac on the southern side of the Straits of Mackinac, believing that the new location would be more defensible against American revolutionary attack. Stone-walled Fort Mackinac stood on the hill overlooking the harbor, out of range of bombardment from American ships and in a position to rain heavy cannon fire on enemy vessels that dared to enter the harbor.

Although the 1783 treaty of peace awarded the island to the United States, the British continued to occupy this post until the summer of 1796. Below the fort grew a village of British fur traders and Indians, for Mackinac Island served as a supply depot and a great rendezvous point in the fur trade. When the United States took control, it established a government fur trade warehouse.

Early in the War of 1812, a small party of British regulars, bolstered by *voyageurs* and Indian allies, captured Fort Mackinac. The Americans did not succeed in recapturing the fort, but it was surrendered to them at the end of the war.

After 1815 John Jacob Astor's American Fur Company made Mackinac Island the headquarters for its Great Lakes fur-trading business. By 1830, as the trade dwindled, Mackinac Island had already begun to attract tourists. Its natural beauty made it a popular summering place throughout the nineteenth century. In 1887 the Grand Rapids and Indiana Railroad, the Michigan Central Railroad, and the Detroit and Cleveland Navigation Company built the Grand Hotel, reputedly

Mackinac Island in 1813. A print drawn by Richard Dillon, Jr., engraved by Thomas Hall, and inscribed to the "Governor General and Commander in Chief of all his Majesty's Forces in British America." Courtesy McCord Museum, McGill University, Montreal. 173954

the world's largest summer hotel.

The desire to conserve the island's natural beauty for future generations led the federal government in 1875 to withdraw the public lands on Mackinac Island from sale and make it a national park. In 1895 both the park and the fort were turned over to the state of Michigan. For decades the Mackinac Island State Park Commission had a very difficult time securing enough state money to do necessary repairs, let alone restoration work.

All this changed in the 1950s. With increased tourism, the opening of the Mackinac Bridge, and the example of the successful restoration of two sites on the island by private organizations, the Park Commission renewed its search for funds. A revenue bond issue proved to be the key to restoration and development of an interpretive historical program. Now, more than two decades later, the results of the Park Commission's work at both Fort Mackinac and Fort Michilimackinac offer visitors a fine visual understanding of the history of the strategic straits.

Mackinac Island Sites of Interest

The Mackinac Island State Park Commission has prepared an inexpensive book, *Historic Guidebook: Mackinac Island*, available at the Visitor Center. It contains descriptions of the island's many sites of interest, 51 in all, both historical and natural. The book also suggests a number of walking and bicycling tours.

(1) State Park Visitor Center
on Huron Street near boat docks
This is the best place to begin a visit to the island. Displays and printed materials give a good idea of the many points of historical interest. Here tickets are sold for admission to all state-park owned sites. If you are planning on visiting both the island and Fort Michilimackinac, a single ticket at a reduced rate is available. No automobiles are allowed on the island. Horse-drawn carriages and bicycles are available.

(2) Marquette Park
below the fort on Huron Street
Formerly the location of the fort gardens and stables, Marquette Park, established in 1904, commemorates the work of Father Marquette (see site 111). The statue of Marquette in the center of the park was dedicated in 1909.

(3) Bark Chapel
Fort Street
This reconstructed bark chapel commemorates the work of the seventeenth-century Jesuit missionaries. It is probably much like the one Father

Fort Mackinac, North Blockhouse built in 1798. Photo by Margaret Bogue.

Claude Dablon built on the island when he wintered here in 1670–71. Displays inside show Dablon ministering to two Indians.

(4) Fort Mackinac

Of the 15 structures at the fort, the stone ramparts, the south sally port, and the officers' stone quarters are part of the original fort, dating from the 1780s. The other buildings, including the commissary, post headquarters, quartermaster's storehouse, soldiers' barracks, schoolhouse, blockhouses, commandant's house, hospital, officers' wooden quarters, guardhouse, bathhouse, and north sally port, date from the 1790s to 1885.

The buildings include interpretive museum displays explaining the history of the area and the fort. The main museum is in the soldiers' barracks. The officers stone quarters contains the Fort Tea Room, where you may sit at tables on the piazza, have refreshments, and look out over the harbor below busy with pleasure craft and ferry boats. Costumed soldiers and demonstrations of cannon and musket firing give the flavor of life at the fort. Open daily, mid-May–mid-June and after Labor Day to October 14, 10:00 A.M.–4:00 P.M.; June 15–Labor Day, 9:00 A.M.–6:00 P.M. $

(5) Beaumont Memorial

Market Street

In 1954 the Michigan State Medical Society completed the Beaumont Memorial. It is in the reconstructed American Fur Company store. Displays commemorate the work on the digestive system done by Dr. William Beaumont, fort surgeon. For a discussion of Dr. Beaumont's work (see p. 33). Open daily, May 30–Labor Day, 11:00 A.M.–5:00 P.M.

(6) Agency House and Astor Warehouse

Market Street

These two buildings are the remaining original buildings of John Jacob Astor's American Fur Trading Company. Following the decline of the fur trade, the Agency House, the fur warehouse, and a clerk's quarters were combined into one structure to form a hotel known as the Astor House. The connective structure has since been torn away. Agency House, also known as Stuart House, was built in 1817 to house the company agents, Robert Stuart and Ramsey Crooks, and their clerks. Operated by the city as a museum, it contains displays on the fur trade and nineteenth-century home furnishings. Open Mother's Day–October, Monday–Saturday, 9:00 A.M.–5:00 P.M.; Sunday, 11:00 A.M.–5:00 P.M. $

(7) County Courthouse

Market Street

This structure, now the city hall, served as the Mackinac County Courthouse from 1839 to 1882. In the latter year, St. Ignace became the county seat.

(8) Biddle House

Market Street

Biddle House is probably the oldest house on the island. Portions of it date from the 1780s. During the 1820s it was the home of Edward Biddle, a fur trader. In 1959 the Michigan Society of Architects and Michigan builders spent $75,000 restoring this Quebec rural style house. The frame, filler logs, interior trim, living room mantle, and some of the window glass are original.

(9) Benjamin Blacksmith Shop

Market Street

The Mackinac Island State Park Commission has built a replica of the Benjamin blacksmith shop that houses the tools and equipment of the original. For 80 years the shop was an active business. It is open for inspection during the summer months.

(10) Grand Hotel

West Bluff Road

Built in 1887, the Grand Hotel is one of the few monumental resort structures in the Great Lakes area that survived the era of the lake excursion boats. Built of white pine, the hotel has a pillared porch over 800 feet in length. It stands as a memorial to the gracious living of the 1890s and the early decades of the twentieth century.

(11) Governor's Mansion
Fort Street
In 1945 the state of Michigan purchased this Victorian summer home (built in 1901) for the official summer residence of the governor. Michigan governors have spent the summer months on Mackinac Island since 1888.

(12) Indian Dormitory
Huron Street
The Treaty of Washington of 1836, whereby the Chippewa and Ottawa ceded their claims to vast portions of the Michigan lower and Upper peninsulas to the United States, provided for the construction of a dormitory for Indians visiting Fort Mackinac. Henry R. Schoolcraft, a principal author of the treaty and noted American Indian agent (he worked among the Chippewa), designed the structure. For a decade it served as an Indian dormitory and then as a customs house and school. The Mackinac Island State Park Commission purchased and restored the building in 1966.

(13) Mission Church
Huron Street
The congregation of Rev. William M. Ferry, a Presbyterian missionary, built this structure in 1829 and 1830 to complement the activites of the nearby Indian mission. This structure, along with the bark chapel (no. [3]) and St. Anne's Church (no. [14]), reflect the efforts of the Christian churches to make Indian converts. It is now a nondemoninational chapel. Visitors are welcome daily, June 15–Labor Day, 11:00 A.M.–4:00 P.M.

(14) St. Anne's Church
Huron Street
A beautiful and more imposing structure just a little way down the street, St. Anne's, was constructed in the 1870s to serve the island's Catholic population. This structure replaced Old St. Anne's Mission Church, moved here across the straits from Fort Michilimackinac in the 1780s.

(15) Fort Holmes
Fort Holmes Road
At the island's highest point, the British built a fort in 1814 to help them repulse the expected American attack. They named it Fort George. The Americans did not succeed in capturing the island in 1814, thanks, at least in part, to this new fortification. After Mackinac Island was returned to the United States in 1815, the post was renamed Fort Holmes, but was not garrisoned. The blockhouse at the site today is a replica of the original.

Mackinac Bridge spanning the Straits viewed from Fort Michilimackinac
Photo by Allan Bogue

114. Mackinac Bridge, St. Ignace to Mackinaw City
Hy I-75

The people of Michigan had long wanted a bridge across the Straits of Mackinac to join the Upper and lower peninsulas for automobile traffic. Ferries could not adequately accommodate summer traffic. Engineers doubted the possibility of building a structure strong enough to withstand the terrible storms and high winds that accompany winter at the straits. David B. Steinman, however, after conducting extensive tests, became convinced that a safe bridge was possible and that he could build it. Despite the dire predictions of others, the bridge opened to traffic in November 1957. Dedication ceremonies, put off until better weather, were held in June 1958.

Mr. Steinman described his creation as "a symphony in steel and stone, a poem stretched across the Straits." The symmetry of the three bridge spans and the soaring towers is indeed artistic. The spans and cables are painted foliage green and the towers ivory. Lights originally hung along the cables to permit night construction were allowed to remain because many admired the effect, resembling pearls on a necklace. Although Steinman designed 400 bridges in all parts of the world, he considered the Mackinac Bridge the culmination of his career. He died a few years after its completion. On Labor Day each year, two lanes of the bridge are closed to traffic and opened to pedestrians, who walk across the bridge 148 feet above the water to obtain an unforgettable view in all directions. As many as 25,000 persons have participated in the annual "Bridge Walk."

Palisade and water gate entrance to restored Fort Michilimackinac. Photo by Margaret Bogue.

115. Mackinaw City
Hy I-75

The early history of Mackinaw City revolves around the Fort Michilimackinac, built here about 1715 by the French. The French decision to refortify the Straits of Mackinac came after a period when no French soldiers occupied this strategic location. Fort de Buade at St. Ignace had been evacuated in 1698 (see site 111). The French in 1715 faced a very real British threat to their empire and fur trade. Two years before they had given up all claim to the Hudson Bay area. To preserve their deteriorating position, the French needed to build strategic fortifications, to woo Indian allies, and to chasten rebellious tribes.

Fort Michilimackinac was part of this larger plan. It became a center for the French fur trade and a launching point for expeditions against the rebellious Sauk and Fox tribes. In 1755 an Indian war party assembled here under the leadership of Charles Langlade to participate in the defeat of British General Braddock. Braddock had been sent to capture Fort Duquesne, the French outpost near present-day Pittsburgh. This was an early incident in the French and Indian War, which concluded with France's loss of its North American possessions.

In 1761 Fort Michilimackinac became a British fort. The former Indian allies of the French, rejecting British allegiance, rose up in rebellion under the leadership of Pontiac in 1763. Heartened by Pontiac's success at Detroit, but acting on their own, Indians managed to seize Fort Michilimackinac under dramatic circumstances. In June 1763 a group of Chippewa played lacrosse outside the fort while British soldiers relaxed and watched. Suddenly the Indians rushed the open gates and either killed or captured most of the occupants. The British did not reoccupy the fort for a year.

Between 1766 and 1768 Major Robert Rogers, the most famous commandant of the fort, assumed control of affairs and from here launched an expedition to find the long-sought northwest passage to the Pacific. With the coming of the American Revolution, Fort Michilimackinac served as a launching place for Indian war parties against American outposts in the west. Concluding that the fort would be difficult to defend against American attack, the British built Fort Mackinac on Mackinac Island in 1780–1781, using some of the materials from the mainland site for the new fortification (see site 113).

To a considerable extent the fortunes of Mackinaw City (population 820) are still bound up with the old fort. In 1959 the Mackinac Island State Park Commission began a reconstruction of it. Built almost entirely of wood and the victim of rot and fire, the original structure had long since disappeared. Eugene T. Petersen, director of the Park Commission, tells us: "Only a badly deteriorated stockade wall put up in 1936 and a bronze plaque were visible reminders of the days of Fort Michilimackinac." To complete the reconstruction, knowledge of the original fort was essential. Research in historical archives in Canada, the United States, and Europe revealed the necessary information. Archaeologists working at the site unearthed much material confirming the written record and adding to formally recorded knowledge. Reconstruction was well under way by the mid-1960s. With restoration came hundreds of thousands of visitors annually to capture a sense of the lives of the eighteenth-century soldiers, traders, priests, *voyageurs*, and Indians who frequented Fort Michilimackinac.

Fort Michilimackinac Historic Park

Off Hy I-75

(1) Fort Michilimackinac

The visitors' orientation center, where tickets are available, contains a wide variety of literature for sale and displays that put the history of Forts Michilimackinac and Mackinac in historical context. The restored fort complex includes the stockade and block houses, water and land gates, the commanding officer's house, soldiers' barracks, the guardhouse, the king's storehouse, British and French traders' houses, St. Anne's Church, the priest's house, a blacksmith shop, and the powder magazine. Modern museum displays, period furnishings, costumed mannequins, live demonstrations of weapons, costumed guides, and a sound and light program in the church enhance the fort's living history. Outside the stockade near the land gate stands an exhibit of eighteenth-century devices for military punishment. Summer visitors can view the continuing archaeological work. Open daily mid-May–mid-June and after Labor Day to October 14, 9:00 A.M.–5:00 P.M.; June 15–Labor Day, 9:00 A.M.–7:00 P.M. $

(2) Mackinac Marine Park

This marine park forms the second component of the Historic Park. It is accessible from the visitors' orientation center. Opened in 1972, the park includes Old Mackinac Point Lighthouse,* which contains a fine maritime museum, an aquarium, the Shay steam yacht (see site 119, no. [3]), the LaWay schooner, a birchbark canoe, and examples of Mackinaw boats.

The Marine Park's Bicentennial project was reconstruction of the *Welcome*. Owned by John Askin, a British trader, the ship was taken over by the British Navy in 1779 and used to carry parts of Fort Michilimackinac to Mackinac Island for use in building Fort Mackinac. The boat sank in a storm in 1781. The reconstructed *Welcome* was launched May 30, 1980, and is open to the public. It is anchored near the ferry dock in Mackinaw City. $

The Welcome *at anchor at the Mackinaw City docks. Photo by Margaret Bogue.*

(3) Ferry Service to Mackinac Island

At the Mackinaw City docks, several transport companies offer ferry service to Mackinac Island with scheduled departures from May through December.

116. Old Mill Creek State Historic Park

Hy US-23

The Straits of Mackinac's newest historic attraction, Old Mill Creek State Historic Park, opened June 15, 1984. A 1790 working water powered sawmill, a mill dam, a museum, an interpretive

The Mill and mill stream. Courtesy Michigan Department of Natural Resources.

White-tailed deer. A Wisconsin Conservation Department Photo. Courtesy State Historical Society of Wisconsin. WHi(X3)33659

program, and craft demonstrations introduce visitors to a little known dimension of the area's history during the years 1780–1820. After British authorities refused to authorize construction of a sawmill, a private individual apparently built the original mill in 1780 to supply British troops with the sawed lumber essential to build Fort Mackinac on the Island. The mill continued to operate after the Americans took possession of the fort in 1796, supplying the military with essential building materials. Open daily, June 15–Labor Day, 10:00 A.M.–6:00 P.M. $

117. Wilderness State Park

11 miles west of Mackinaw City, Hy US-31, or follow exit signs from I-75 at Mackinaw City (BCFHPS)

Located on the Straits of Mackinac, this 7,000-acre park offers visitors great natural beauty. Wilderness State Park, created from tax-delinquent cutover land, is a tribute to the ideal of conservation and the healing power of nature.

Evergreen forests, a wildlife refuge, natural beaches, and miles of rocky shoreline on Waugoshance Point and Waugoshance Island make the name "wilderness" appropriate. The park has a good representation of native Michigan orchids. Wildlife includes white-tailed deer, beavers, otters, black bears, ruffed grouse, water fowl, and small-mouth bass. More than 115 species of birds have been sighted in the park, making it an excellent place for bird watchers. The red pine and hemlock interpretive nature trails are self-guiding.

In addition to 210 campsites, camping facilites include four rustic trail cabins available year round. $

118. Cross Village

County Road 66 from Hy US-31 or from I-75 (also accessible from Wilderness State Park)

The Cross Village–Harbor Springs area was known to the French Jesuits as

L'Arbre Croche, "crooked tree," named for a tall, crooked pine on the lake shore, a landmark for passing canoes. Steeped in Ottawa and Chippewa history, the area also had a long record of missionary activity. Jesuits ministered to the Ottawa Indians who moved to L'Arbre Croche from the village of St. Ignace in the 1740s. The principal Indian villages in the area were Cross Village, Middle Village, Seven Mile Point, and Harbor Springs. A few families settled at Petoskey. Father Samuel Mazzuchelli noted in his memoirs that five churches served the L'Arbre Croche area in 1831.

Father John B. Weikamp established the Society of St. Francis at Cross Village in 1855. It operated a 2,000-acre farm, saw and grist mills, a convent, school, church, and cemetery. The convent was abandoned in 1896, and the buildings burned down 10 years later. A cross stands on the bluff overlooking the lake, a replica of a cross placed here by Jesuit missionaries.

By 1825 commercial fishermen fished the waters of the Cross Village–Arbre Croche coast, marketing their catch at Mackinac. The first permanent white settlers came to Cross Village in 1840 and built a sawmill and cooper shop. A lumbering industry flourished here between 1880 and 1911, employing as many as 500 of the local Indian residents.

The view of Lake Michigan from the steep bluff at Cross Village which rises 100 feet above the lake, is very fine. On a clear day three lighthouses are visible, Isle aux Galets, Gray's Reef, and White Shoals.

Ottawa Indian family. Photo by Albert Greene Heath, Courtesy State Historical Society of Wisconsin. WHi(H38)20

119. Harbor Springs

Hy M-131

The road from Cross Village to Harbor Springs is an unusually beautiful winding drive, much of it heavily wooded but permitting occasional glimpses of Lake Michigan.

Harbor Springs has long been a place of human settlement. Indians lived in the beautiful region long before recorded history. The French passed this way before 1700. Ottawa Indians relocating from the St. Ignace area in the eighteenth century settled nearby and all along the Arbre Croche coast north to Cross Village. Many of their descendants remain. Missionaries, fur traders, and fishermen frequented Harbor Springs long before it developed into a town.

Here the federal government in 1836 established a temporary Indian reservation that included a sizable part of Emmet County. Not until the early 1870s were all of the former reservation lands offered for sale to the general public. This sale, plus the construction of the Grand Rapids and Indiana Railroad as far as Petoskey in 1874, marked the begining of the lumbering era and of agricultural development in the Harbor Springs–Petoskey area. Rail connections between Petoskey and Mackinaw City in 1882 further spurred the logging industry. Immigrants from French Canada, Germany, Ireland, and Poland came to work in the lumbering camps.

By the 1920s the logging era was over, the mills closed, and workers departed. The heyday of lumbering left in its wake stumps and slash, the tinder for the forest fires that followed. The lumber companies sold what cutover lands they could for farming. Some of this land supported very productive fruit farms. Much of what was left reverted to the state for taxes and is now held as state forest.

Currently much of Harbor Springs' prosperity comes from a large year-round resort and recreation business. Harbor Springs is a very exclusive summer resort area. The 1980 population was 1,567.

In addition to the work of itinerant Jesuits in the eighteenth century, Catholic mission activity at Harbor Springs spans the nineteenth and twentieth centuries. Father Pierre Déjean is credited with founding an Indian school here in 1829, but its origins may well be somewhat earlier. Now known as the Holy Childhood of Jesus School, this mission to the Ottawa began with a log church, originally called St. Peter's, and a log school. Over its 155-year history, the school has been both a boarding and a day school. The initial enrollment of 63 Indian boys and girls included 25 boarders. They learned vocational skills, reading, writing, and arithmetic in French.

Father Frederic Baraga began his remarkable missionary labors here in 1831. The Franciscan Fathers and the School Sisters of Notre Dame took over the work in the 1880s and continue it at the present time.

Holy Childhood of Jesus Church, Harbor Springs. Photo by Margaret Bogue.

Harbor Springs Sites of Interest

(1) Holy Childhood of Jesus Church and School

West Main Street

The present structures of both church and school are a far cry from the original log buildings, but they serve the same purposes. The school's current enrollment is about 50 day students and 50 boarding students, both Indian and non-Indian.

(2) Chief Andrew J. Blackbird Museum*

360 East Main Street

Andrew J. Blackbird was an Ottawa Indian scholar and author of several books on Indian language and legends. For some years he was the postmaster at Harbor Springs. The Michigan Indian Foundation purchased Blackbird's home, which served as the town's first post office, and made it into a museum now operated by the city of Harbor Springs. The bulk of the collection consists of Ottawa artifacts. Open May 15–September 15, Monday–Saturday, 10:00 A.M.–5:00 P.M. $

(3) The Hexagon*

373 Main Street

Built for Ephraim Shay, a local inventor, this six-sided house, now a dress shop, was Shay's home from 1888 until his death in 1916. The Hexagon was built with a central core and six wings extending from it. The walls are made of pressed steel sheets with a brick design stamped on the exterior. The City Fire Hall,* just across the street from the Hexagon, was originally the Shay workshop.

Shay is best known for the logging locomotive he patented in 1881. It had great traction and could operate well on tight curves. Manufactured in Lima, Ohio, the locomotives were used by the thousands for mining and logging in many parts of the world.

Shay also invented a steel boat and a hose cart. When he found an artesian well on his property, he built the Harbor Springs waterworks to supply the whole village and a narrow-gauge railroad, the Hemlock Central, to carry timber to be used as fuel in the waterworks. Shay's grave in Lake View Cemetery is marked by a meteorite found on his Harbor Springs property.

The Little Traverse Regional Historical Society at Petoskey has a display on the Shay logging locomotive (site 123, no. [1]). The Mackinac Marine Park has the Shay steam yacht, *Aha*, built about 1891 for the inventor's personal use (site 115, no. [2]).

120. Crooked Lake

County Road 68 east off
Hy M-131

A marker erected by the state of Michigan at the Oden State Fish Hatchery on Crooked Lake commemorates the now extinct passenger pigeon. Passenger pigeons by the hundreds of thousands nested in Michigan during the nineteenth century. At Crooked Lake the 1878 nesting extended over a 90 square mile area.

Popularly regarded as pests, the pigeons became a commercial food item. At Petoskey they were slaughtered, packed, and shipped to Chicago and other lakeports. Between 1875 and 1880 two boats regularly plied the lake between Petoskey and Chicago carrying cages of passenger pigeons to supply shoot clubs throughout the Midwest. Indiscriminate slaughter of the birds made them extinct by 1914.

The Little Traverse Regional Historical Society at Petoskey has a display on the passenger pigeon (see site 123, no. [1]).

121. Petoskey State Park

Hy US-31, 4 miles northeast of
Petoskey (CFHPS)

The most outstanding features of this 300-acre park are the sand dunes and an excellent swimming beach on Little Traverse Bay. Of several hiking trails, the Old Baldy and Portage trails are the longest. $

122. Bay View*

Hy US-31

As you enter Bay View, the neat, well-kept Victorian houses that line Hy US-31 will catch the eye. So will the sign that reads, "Bay View Association—A Historic Place on the National Register." Methodists founded the association in 1875 and made Bay View their summer campground. They received financial assistance from both the residents of Petoskey and the Grand Rapids and Indiana Railroad Company to buy the land on which Bay View is located.

By the 1880s the association had graduated from tents into substantial cottages, built from Victorian carpenters' pattern books with liberal use of cupolas, towers, and gingerbread. "Cottages" hardly seems the appropriate term, for the houses are large, built to hold whole families gathered for the summer months. The architecture here is similar to that of summer resorts originating in the Chautauqua movement. The Bay View Assembly, providing summer programs modeled after the Chautauqua program in New York, was the central focus of this Methodist settlement. Association programs are conducted today under the auspices of Albion College, a Methodist school.

Later structures built between 1895 and 1936 according to the plans of E. H. Meade are more formal than the original cottages, with sloping roofs, inset porches, and window pane designs. The architecture of both eras, recognized by the association for its historical value, has a good chance of surviving the changes that have come to so many communities. The association lots are leased, not owned; membership is restricted; building or renovation has to be approved by the association committee.

The Bay View Association's summer programs include worship, special movies, and musical and theatrical events. The public is welcome to participate. The Bay View Historical Museum is open July–August 23, Tuesday and Thursday, 2:30–4:30 P.M. Free.

123. Petoskey

Hy US-131 and Hy US-31

As is true of Harbor Springs, much of the early history of Petoskey revolves around the Ottawa and Chippewa Indians, missionaries, fur traders, and fishermen. The land on which Petoskey is located was part of a Chippewa-Ottawa Indian Reservation created by the federal government under the terms of an 1836 treaty with these tribes. Here both Protestant and Catholic missions labored to Christianize the Indians. In 1852 Andrew Porter, a Presbyterian missionary, established an Indian school that operated along with federally established reservation schools for Indians. In 1871 the Porter mission closed for lack of funds. In 1859 Father Frederic Baraga founded a Catholic Indian mission at Petoskey, the St. Francis Solanus Mission.

When the federal lands in the Petoskey area were opened for purchase and settlement in the 1870s (see site 119), the village of Petoskey took shape. It is named for Ignatius Pe-to-se-ga, a Chippewa who lived on the site and owned much of the land that is now part of the city. Railroad construction in the 1870s opened the area to homesteaders and lumbermen. For

This beautiful statue depicting Father Frederic Baraga's founding of the mission stands at the St. Francis Solanus Indian Mission church. Frederic Baraga was among the outstanding missionaries to the Indians of the upper great lakes in the nineteenth century. A memorial honoring his work, "The Shrine of the Snow Shoe Priest," is located at L'Anse, Michigan. Photo by Margaret Bogue.

about a half-century, lumbering was the major economic activity. Limestone quarrying on the the cliffs on the south side of Little Traverse Bay was also an important industry in the late nineteenth century and remains so today. This limestone, rich in fossils, is the source of Petoskey stones. The Petoskey stone is the Michigan state stone.

Almost simultaneously with the beginnings of lumbering, Petoskey established its reputation as an outstanding resort area. Its villagers were eager to assist the Bay View Association in establishing a summer camp nearby. In 1882 the Western Hay Fever Association made Petoskey its headquarters, designating the village as "the most favorable resort for hay fever sufferers." Summer homes and resorts and winter recreation form a very significant part of the town's present economy. The downtown gas-light shopping area includes a number of fine, exclusive shops reminiscent of the best found in Miami Beach and Scottsdale, Arizona.

Incorporated as a city in 1895, Petoskey became the county seat of Emmet County in 1902. The town now serves as a distribution and service center for the surrounding farming community. Major products of its industries are limestone, tools, wire products, chrome plating, casting, and wood products. The Penn-Dixie plant made Portland cement, one of the city's most important products, for many years until it was closed in 1981, putting 200 workers out of jobs. The 1980 population was 6,097.

Petoskey Sites of Interest

(1) Little Traverse Regional Historical Society Museum*

1 Waterfront Park

The museum is located in an 1892 railroad passenger station, which has been designated a National Historic Site. The museum contains many fine exhibits, including one on Ernest Hemingway, who spent many summers in Petoskey. There is a special display honoring Bruce Catton, the American Civil War historian, who was born here. Other exhibits of special importance are the Pailthorp collection of quill and grass baskets made by local Indians and displays on the Shay locomotive and the passenger pigeon. Open May 1–November, Monday–Saturday, 9:00 A.M.–5:00 P.M. Donation.

(2) St. Francis Solanus Indian Mission*
500 block of East Lake Street off Hy US-31
Believed to be the oldest building in Petoskey, the St. Francis Solanus Indian Mission expresses the concern of Father Frederic Baraga for the Indians. Although he assumed the duties of a bishop in 1853, he continued to closely supervise Indian mission work. The efforts of Catholics to open a mission at Petoskey aroused the determined opposition of Protestant missionaries. Without Father Baraga's intervention to work out a compromise, St. Francis Solanus might never have been built. Constructed in 1859–1860 and blessed by Father Baraga on July 23, 1860, the chapel was used for services until 1896. It was repaired and rededicated in 1931. Adjacent to the mission is an Indian cemetery.

(3) Underwater Park, Little Traverse Bay
Marked off by buoys in the Petoskey harbor lies an underwater skin divers' park. It contains a large crucifix of marble and black walnut.

Greensky Hill Mission stands in a beautifully wooded and peaceful setting. Photo by Margaret Bogue.

(4) Ernest Hemingway Cottage (Windemere)*
The Hemingway cottage is located at Walloon Lake near Petoskey, between the north shore of Walloon Lake and Lake Grove Road. It is not open to the public.

124. Young State Park

Hy US-131, Hy M-75, and County Road 56 from Petoskey (BCFHPS)

Young State Park, beautifully located on Lake Charlevoix, is noted chiefly for its fine beach. Covering nearly a square mile, the park has four miles of hiking trails and 293 camp sites. $

125. Greensky Hill Mission*

County Road 56 off Hy US-31, 4 miles east of Charlevoix

Although a little difficult to find, the Greensky Hill Mission site is well worth visiting. When traveling south toward Charlevoix on Hy US-31, turn left on Boyne City Road (County Road 56), and then left on Old US-31. The Greensky Hill Misssion turnoff is plainly marked on Old US-31. On this quiet, wooded hilltop, Peter Greensky established a Methodist mission to the Chippewa Indians in the 1840s. The first mission church was built of boughs and bark. In the 1850s the Indians built the old log church that is still in use.

Local legend says that Greensky Hill

served as the meeting place for Indian peoples from the Traverse area. Here, at one meeting, 30 Indian chiefs each planted a maple tree, promising to remain at peace with the other tribes as long as the trees lived. They bent and tied each tree with a basswood thong. The newly planted trees represent the trees of the original council circle.

126. Charlevoix

Hy US-31

Lumber schooners in Round Lake. From the Collections of the Michigan State Archives, Department of State. 13063

The bountiful fishing in Lake Michigan's waters near Pine River attracted Indians and whites to the present site of Charlevoix long before the town began. The first permanent white settlers came in the 1850s to begin farming in the otherwise unbroken forests stretching along the lakeshore from Pine River to Elk Rapids. Surveyors platted Charlevoix in 1866. It is named in honor of the French Jesuit explorer and historian, Pierre François Xavier de Charlevoix.

For half a century Charlevoix grew and prospered from its abundant natural wealth of timber, fish, and limestone. Although transportation problems made the development of large-scale lumbering at Charlevoix slower than it was in other areas of Michigan's lower peninsula, by the mid 1880s it too was a sawdust city.

Round Lake provided an excellent natural harbor, but its entrance from Lake Michigan was shallow and narrow. Two channels, one completed in 1873 and another in 1882, made the town accessible to large lake craft. Improvements in the latter year gave access from Round Lake to Lake Charlevoix as well. A lumbering boom ensued. The completion of a railroad connection to Charlevoix in 1892 speeded the cut. Two other major industries dependent upon plentiful timber supplies developed near Charlevoix as well. One was an iron smelter at Ironton on the south arm of Lake Charlevoix, which utilized locally made charcoal, iron ore from Michigan's Upper Peninsula, and local limestone. The other was the production of lime in kilns fired by charcoal. All of these industries depended upon cheap water transportation, provided by ships plying Lake Michigan from sources of supply to market.

By 1915 the timber was gone and the town faced a difficult transition to other forms of economic activity. Commercial fishing continued as an important industry until well into the twentieth century. Since the onslaught of the sea lamprey, the industry has been largely replaced by sport fishing.

Tourism and the resort business have been a constant feature of the local economy since the 1870s. As early as 1874 and 1880, Charlevoix attracted two religious groups that established colonies. Currently the lake environment's natural beauty attracts city dwellers in search of summer homes and tourists in search of recreation.

A number of light industries have also been attracted to the town. In 1979 they employed over 500 workers. A sizable cement plant, Medusa Cement Company, utilizes local limestone. Round Lake, as late as 1910 crowded with ships to carry away lumber, pig iron, and fish, is now crowded with pleasure craft and ferry boats bound for Beaver Island. In 1980 the population was 3,296.

Charlevoix Sites of Interest

(1) Charlevoix Great Lakes Fisheries Station
Grant Street
The Michigan Department of Natural Resources raises steelhead, brown, rainbow, and brook trout to stock Michigan's lakes with game fish. Adjacent to the fish hatchery is the waterway connecting Lake Michigan and Round Lake. The beach at the fishing station is an excellent place to observe the large lake boats coming and going from the cement plant. The Fisheries Station is open to visitors Monday–Friday, 8:00 A.M.–noon and 1:00–5:00 P.M.

(2) Beaver Island Ferry
At the main dock on Round Lake, visitors may board the ferry for Beaver Island. It operates daily from mid-June through August and less frequently in May and from September to December. $

127. Beaver Island
(BCFHPS)

Originally occupied by mound-building Indians and later by Chippewa and Ottawa, visited by *voyageurs* and fur traders, Beaver Island has served as home and haven for many thousands of years. The American Fur Company established a post here in 1831. Boats and ships caught in Lake Michigan's storms found safety in its harbors. Steam-propelled vessels found it a convenient fueling place. Fishermen, both Indian and white, earned their livelihood from the bountiful catches in the waters of the Beaver Island group, often regarded as

Strang's residence on Beaver Island, a pen drawing. Courtesy State Historical Society of Wisconsin. WHi(X3)39603

the finest fishery on Lake Michigan.

Perhaps the most famous episode in Beaver Island's history arose from the establishment of a Mormon colony in 1847. Led by James J. Strang, who had split off from the followers of Brigham Young, a group of Mormons settled on Beaver Island, hoping to find isolation from the mainstream of American society and to build a temple and found a kingdom on earth according to their beliefs. In 1850 Strang proclaimed himself king of his followers. He was crowned in a partially built tabernacle on the shores of Paradise Bay.

The history of the Mormons at Beaver Bay Island and on the adjacent mainland was brief and stormy. For ideological and economic reasons, their nine-year stay created friction with their neighbors. Mormon fishermen competed with a colony of Irish fishermen on Beaver Island. The Irish and the Mormons clashed over the liquor issue, and the Mormons' protective attitude toward the Indians stood in sharp contrast with the hostility of other local settlers. Perhaps most galling of all to the gentiles, the Mormons organized the original county government in the Charlevoix area, locating the county seat at St. James on Beaver Island.

This fact of political life led to the so-called Battle of Pine River in 1853. Trouble arose when Strang's followers tried to summon three gentiles from the fishing settlement at Pine River to appear in the island court. The Mormons were routed.

Frictions within the colony led two of Strang's followers to murder him in 1856. Shortly afterward, most of the Mormons were driven off Beaver Island by the mainlanders. Many of them moved to the western shore of Lake Michigan and settled at Voree, Wisconsin. Some remained in the Charlevoix area, downplaying their religious convictions.

The Irish fishermen who had settled on the island continued to pursue profitable commercial fishing. At its peak, the Beaver Island fisheries produced tons of whitefish and trout annually for midwestern and eastern markets. Charlie Martin, son of an Irish immigrant fisherman, recalls that his father's fishing business involved a steamboat, eight miles of staked nets, and a work crew of seven. One summer their catch included six tons of whitefish and lake trout. While commercial fishing has declined greatly, three commercial fishermen operated out of St. James, the island's main harbor, in 1978.

For a time lumbering became a major commercial enterprise, attracting as many as 1,800 residents to the island. With its decline, tourism has become the main source of revenue. About 200 people live on Beaver Island year round. Its population swells to over 1,000 during the summer.

Unlike Mackinac Island, Beaver Island allows cars. Visitors can bring their cars on the ferry from Charlevoix or rent vehicles to drive the island roads. The ferry operates from May to December. There are resort facilities and plenty of opportunities for camping, hiking, swimming, fishing, picnicking, and boating. About one-third of the island is designated as a state forest and hunting ground.

Beaver Island Sites of Interest

(1) Beaver Island Historical Museum
This museum is located at St. James in the stone print shop* built by the Mormons in 1848. Here Strang published his newspaper, the *Northern Islander*, and also wrote *Some Remarks on the Nautral History of Beaver Island*. It was published by the Smithsonian Institution in 1853. The building houses a collection of artifacts reflecting the island's history. Open in the summer months. $

(2) Marine Museum
Also at St. James, this museum has displays illustrating the history of commercial fishing at Beaver Island.

(3) American Fur Company Post Site
This site, at St. James Bay, is identified by a historical marker.

(4) Mormon Temple Site
King's Highway
The temple was burned when the Mormons were driven out of Beaver Island. This site is identified by a marker.

(5) Feodar Protar's Cabin* and Grave
Dr. Feodar Protar, a Russian political refugee, is said to have come upon Beaver Island by chance. In 1894 he landed on the island, liked the location, and made a cabin constructed in 1858 his home. It is now open to visitors. For 30 years he served the medical needs of Beaver Islanders. He died in 1926. His imposing tomb, provided by island fishermen, contains a bronze plaque that reads, "To our heaven-sent friend in need, Feodar Protar, who never failed us, in imperishable gratitude, his people of Beaver Island."

(6) Beaver Island Light*
Located at the southern tip of the island, this lighthouse dates back to 1851. A decade ago the 138-foot, red and white, horizontally banded skeleton tower was added.

(7) St. James Harbor Light
This white cylindrical tower, rising 38 feet above the water, is also a historic lighthouse, readily viewable at St. James Harbor. It dates from 1856 and 1870.

128. Fisherman's Island State Park
accessible from Hy US-31
(CFHPS)

A long stretch of natural, underdeveloped Lake Michigan beach is Fisherman's Island State Park's most outstanding natural feature. In the park's 2,608 acres are 90 rustic campsites and ample opportunities to enjoy the natural environment. $

129. Elk Rapids
Hy US-31

Like Charlevoix (site 126) and Fayette (site 92), Elk Rapids achieved its greatest prosperity from lumbering and iron smelting. Lumbering began at Elk Rapids in 1853. The business partnership that dominated the economic life of Antrim County for more than a half-century was formed in 1855 when Wirt Dexter and Henry Noble purchased the sawmill at Elk Rapids. The mill's strategic location at the mouth of the Elk River enabled its owners to control Lake Michigan's access for logs harvested along the lakes and streams of most of Antrim County. The Elk was the only river in the county that exited into Lake Michigan. What had already grown to be a very sizable logging and sawmilling business took on new dimensions when Dexter and Noble built an iron-smelting furnace at Elk Rapids in 1872. The furnace was 47 feet high and 12 feet in diameter. Iron production began in 1873 and continued into World War I, when timber supplies were exhausted.

During the 1870s the furnace was among the nation's major producers of charcoal iron. Like the smelting operations at Fayette and Charlevoix, the Elk Rapids furnace utilized local hardwood for charcoal, local limestone, and iron ore brought by lake freighters from Escanaba. Often as many as four ships loaded with ore would be in the harbor at once. Later a chemical plant built south of the blast furnace converted the gas and acrid smoke from the charcoal kilns into wood alcohol and acetate of lime.

O. F. Jordan, an outside entrepreneur, organized yet another local industry based on Elk Rapids' natural resources. The Elk Portland Cement Company was founded in 1899. The firm drained Petobego Lake and used its marl bed to make cement. When the marl was exhausted in 1911, the plant ceased operations.

By that date all of Elk Rapids' original industries based on natural resources were living on borrowed time, for in a few years the timber was gone and the furnace and sawmill had shut down.

In its flush years Elk Rapids developed as a company town, with a company flour mill and a company store where workers' credit was good. Life revolved around the Dexter and Noble Lumbering Company. Immigrants and local Indians formed a large part of the labor force. Until 1879 Elk Rapids was the county seat of Antrim County.

Small now by comparison with the late nineteenth-century town, Elk Rapids has a population of 1,504. Light industry, summer homes for city dwellers, resorts, and tourism are of major importance to its economic vitality.

To the left of Hy US-31 lies the section of town where the iron company workers lived. To the right lies the business section, with the old residences of the prosperous businessmen and professionals of the nineteenth century and fine nineteenth-century Catholic, Presbyterian, Methodist, and Episcopal churches as well. Those interested in the town's past will find it worthwhile to drive around and see these.

St. Paul's Episcopal Church is probably the finest building architecturally in Elk Rapids. Photo by Margaret Bogue.

Elk Rapids Sites of Interest

(1) Elk Rapids Iron Company Marker

A Michigan Historic Site marker at the intersection of Hy US-31 and the main street into town marks the location of the hearth of the Elk Rapids Iron Company.

(2) St. Paul's Episcopal Church

This fine American Gothic structure, built in 1873, stands at Spruce and Traverse Streets. This is the church to which the Noble family belonged.

(3) Town Hall

Located on Spruce Street near the public library, the town hall, built of cream brick in 1883, has been restored by the Elk Rapids community and the local historical society. This was originally the Elk Rapids Opera House, where summer stock companies offered a smorgasbord of entertainment in the late nineteenth century.

(4) Public Library

Located off Main Street on an island near the boat dock and facing Lake Michigan, the public library was once the home of the Noble family.

130. Old Mission Peninsula

Hy M-37 from Hy US-31

Old Mission Peninsula stretches north from the southern shore of Grand Traverse Bay, dividing the bay into the East Arm and the West Arm. Grand Traverse Bay is the second-largest bay on Lake Michigan. Much smaller than Green Bay, Grand Traverse is approximately 13 miles across at its widest point and about 30 in length. The Frenchmen who named Little Traverse Bay at Petoskey and Big Traverse Bay were referring to the water crossing at their mouths.

The drive from Traverse City up the Old Mission Peninsula is extremely beautiful. Cherry orchards and vineyards lie on either side of the road. Fine old maples line much of Hy M-37. The deep blue waters of Grand Traverse Bay on sunny days may be seen a good deal of the way to the lighthouse (see no. [3]).

(1) Old Mission Church

Hy M-37

The church, a replica of the original

between 1885 and 1919 except for the central portion, which was built in 1963.

The hospital is the third-oldest institution established in Michigan for the care of mental patients. The first asylum, completed in 1859, is at Kalamazoo; the second, at Pontiac, was constructd in 1878. Perry Hannah, as a member of the state site-selection commission, was instrumental in securing the facility for Traverse City. It was known as the Northern Michigan Asylum until 1911. Gordon W. Lloyd of Detroit designed the original building, No. 50, following the ideas developed by Thomas S. Kirkbride, director of the Pennsylvania Hospital for the Insane. Kirkbride was very concerned about building design, for he believed that appropriate physical environment was essential to patient recovery. His ideas were widely adopted throughout America in the nineteenth century. The early structures in the hospital complex reflect not only the architecture of the nineteenth-century mental hospitals, but also many nineteenth-century ideas about the appropriate care and treatment of mental patients.

Early in the twentieth century, when medical thought shifted to favor outpatient treatment whenever possible, the patient population of Traverse City State Hospital began to decline. At one time the hosptial housed as many as 3,000 patients; currently it houses between 400 and 500.

(10) Cherry Canning Plants
These plants are open to visitors at certain times. Inquire at the Chamber of Commerce, Hy US-31 at Cass Street, for visiting times and locations.

(11) Historic Trees
In the Grand Traverse Area, 16 fine old trees will interest those who appreciate the natural heritage. Among the species represented are basswood, birch, cedar, chestnut, dogwood, elder, elm, ironwood, juniper, maple, and willow. For a complete listing and directions on how to find them, consult the Chamber of Commerce, Hy US-31 at Cass Street.

133. Interlochen National Music Camp and Interlochen Arts Academy
Hy US-31 and M-137

Located 14 miles south of Traverse City, the National Music Camp each summer brings together several hundred high school music students to study with outstanding musicians. During the normal school year, the Interlochen Arts Academy offers a full high school program. Located in one of the region's few remaining stands of original pine, the National Music Camp offers daily concerts Tuesday through Sunday in June, July, and August.

The National Music Camp is an outgrowth of Camp Interlochen, established for girls by the state of Michigan in 1922. In 1928 it became the National High School Orchestra Camp, and then, after remarkable growth, it became the National Music Camp in 1931. In 1942 the camp affiliated with the University of Michigan. The Arts Academy was chartered in 1960.

Visitors at Interlochen State Park will find giant white pines like the ones pictured here interspersed in the woods. Photo by Louis A. Maier. Courtesy State Historical Society of Wisconsin. WHi(X3)26186

134. Interlochen State Park
Hys US-31 and M-137 from Traverse City (BCFHPS)

This 187-acre park lies adjacent to the National Music Camp in a virgin pine stand and includes 550 campsites. Although most of the original white pine in the area was logged in the late nineteenth century, this stand between Green Lake and Duck Lake was left. The state of Michigan purchased the land in 1917 and made it into one of its first state parks. $

135. Suttons Bay

Hy M-22 north from Traverse City

When passing through Suttons Bay, a town of some importance in the heyday of lumbering, you will want to notice St. Michael's Catholic Church on the corner of Broadway and Elm Street, a late nineteenth-century structure of buff cream brick.

136. Omena

Hy M-22 from Traverse City

The early history of Omena is closely tied to the missionary efforts of Peter Dougherty, the Presbyterian sent by U.S. Indian Agent Henry Schoolcraft to work among the Indians of the Grand Traverse Bay area. When Dougherty found that his mission on Old Mission Peninsula (see site 130) was losing its Indian parishioners, he decided to move it to the present site of Omena. The exodus of Indians was a direct consequence of the transfer of Indian lands to the federal government. Many departed to Canada and to Wisconsin.

Dougherty encouraged the Indians to save portions of their annual government payments to buy land, and some of them did so in the vicinity of Omena. Dougherty moved the mission in 1852, building a two-story structure to serve as church, school, and community center. In 1858 the Grove Hill New Mission Church* was dedicated. It is one of the few remaining buildings of those constructed by Dougherty during his 30-years of service to the Indians of the Grand Traverse Bay area.

Dougherty's work at the new location continued for 19 years before a decline in the Indian population led to the closing of the mission school. In 1871 the mission ceased its work. In recent years only summer services have been held in the structure. The construction is of white clapboard on a fieldstone foundation. The portico and steeple were added in later years. The bell is the original one.

137. Leelanau State Park

Hys M-22 and M-201 from Traverse City (CPS)

Beautifully situated at the tip of the Leelanau Peninsula, this 784-acre park contains 42 rustic camping sites and a fine swimming beach. $

Nearby stands the *Grand Traverse Light*, erected in 1852.

138. Leland

Hy M-22

From modest beginnings as a lumbering village in 1853, when Antoine Manseau and his son erected a sawmill at the confluence of the Carp River and Lake Michigan, Leland grew by 1867 to a town of 200 and boasted two sawmills, a gristmill, and three docks. In 1870 Leland acquired another important industry, the Leland Lake Superior Iron Company. It operated a smelter at the harbor's edge until 1884, when local stands of hardwood timber for making charcoal were exhausted.

Fishing too was vital to the life of the village from the 1870s until well into the twentieth century, and at the beginning of the century Leland boasted eight full-scale operations. Leland's history in many ways is like that of Elk Rapids, Charlevoix, and Fayette, yet the village's survivals of the past are different, for they include fishing shanties built when commercial fishing flourished, a rarity in Lake Michigan communities. Fishing on a much reduced scale continues to furnish a livelihood for some. The recreation and tourism industries have grown in importance, and picturesque Leland remains the seat of Leelanau County government. From the harbor, improved repeatedly over the past century, ferry boats carrying mail and passengers sail daily to North and South Manitou Islands (see site 140).

Leland Sites of Interest

(1) Fishtown*
On the Leland waterfront where the Carp River flows into Lake Michigan stands a group of gray, weathered shanties constructed by fishermen to house their equipment, repair their nets, and store ice. Built betwen 1900 and the 1930s, they remain to a large extent unchanged. Some are still used for commercial fishing and others for gift shops. Here the visitor sees nets drying on racks, fishing boats, and all manner of fishing equipment. Often fresh fish are offered for sale. Although fishermen's shanties were once commonplace along the shores of Lake Michigan, most of them have disappeared. Fishtown preserves the flavor of the period from 1890 to 1930, when commercial fishing was an important occupation around the northern shores of Lake Michigan. The area is included in the Leland Historic District.*

The fishing docks and old fishing shanties at Leland's Fishtown. Photo by Margaret Bogue.

(2) Leland Lake Superior Iron Company Marker
In the harbor park area stands a marker on a slag heap. It is the last visible reminder of the industry that from 1870 to 1884 dominated the town's economy.

(3) Harbor House*
This building in Leland's commercial district is included in the Leland Historical District. Its first story serves as a general store and the second as a meeting hall. It is the largest building in the district.

(4) *Leelanau Enterprise* Print Shop*
This is another of the older structures in the business district. Built in 1880 and originally called the "coffee house," it served Leland Lake Superior Iron Company workers as a restaurant.

(5) Leelanau County Historical Museum
111 Chandler Street
Housed in a red brick structure built in 1901 from bricks made in the kilns of the Old Leland Iron Works, the museum served until 1959 as the county jail. The museum collection contains Indian artifacts and relics of the lumbering era in the Great Lakes region. Open Memorial Day–Labor Day, Monday–Saturday, 10:00 A.M.–4:00 P.M. $

139. Drive from Leland to Sleeping Bear Dunes National Lakeshore

Hy M-22 and Hy M-109

As you travel south from Leland on Hy M-22 to the Sleeping Bear Dunes National Lakeshore, you pass through logged-over land. A number of features are worth noting. Sugar Loaf Mountain Road, left off Hy M-22 before Glen Arbor, offers an excellent view. Shortly beyond the turn-off for Sugar Loaf Mountain on Hy M-22, on the right, stands an old schoolhouse painted bright red as part of Leelanau County's effort to call attention to its remaining old structures during the Bicentennial.

Continue for a few more miles on Hy M-22. On the left stands the Cleveland Township Hall, a well-preserved and well-used older structure with Greek Revival architectural details.

As you approach Glen Arbor, an old lumbering town, note a structure walled off with yellow concrete. Located near the intersection of Hy M-22 and Bay Road, this is a privately owned old mill dating back to the logging era.

At Glen Arbor, leave Hy M-22 and take M-109 to the National Lakeshore.

The dunes and the lake. Photo by Richard Frear. Courtesy The Sleeping Bear Dunes National Lakeshore, National Park Service, U.S. Department of the Interior.

140. Sleeping Bear Dunes National Lakeshore

Hy M-22 and M-109 from Leland (BCFHPS)

Stretching from Goodharbor Bay south of Leland nearly to Point Betsie near Frankfort, the Sleeping Bear Dunes National Lakeshore will ultimately include 63,000 acres, or approximately 100 square miles, of scenic shoreline and North and South Manitou Islands. A great portion of this National Lakeshore is already in the possession of the National Park Service of the U.S. Department of the Interior.

Here those interested in geology, ecology, and animal and plant life find excellent opportunities to study them and to enjoy the beauty of Lake Michigan's shoreline.

Sleeping Bear Dune, the most striking of the lakeshore dunes, geologists say, developed from the action of southwest winds against the glacial shoreline. Ever changing and moving through the action of wind and water, it is believed to be the largest live dune in the United States.

Chippewa legend describes its origin differently. A mother bear and her cubs tried to swim across Lake Michigan long ago. The mother made it to shore, but the exhausted cubs did not. The mother climbed the bluff to await the cubs. For her the solitary Sleeping Bear Dune is named. The Great Manitou raised the cubs from the water. They are North and South Manitou Islands.

Indians apparently made very little use of the Manitou Islands. When the first few settlers established a fueling station for boats on South Manitou in the 1830s, they found virgin forests of pine, cedar, and hemlock. Much of the original forest on both North and South Manitou disappeared, cut to supply cordwood fuel for steamboats, to make way for farms for late nineteenth-century settlers, and to supply lumber. Yet South Manitou still has some elegant old trees. In the Valley of the Giants stands some original white cedar that escaped the axe. Second growth includes sugar maples, white ash, basswood, beech, common elder, oak, hemlock, and birch. Here too stand jack pines, unusual for islands in this part of the state.

A great variety of plant life and 24 species of birds add to South Manitou's natural attractions. At Gull Point, herring and ringbilled gulls nest. Visitors may view the nesting ground from a distance by using a trail to the north side of the island. On the west side of the island, dunes rise more than 350 feet above the lake. Using designated paths only, visitors may walk the dunes.

On the south side of the island lies the wreck of the *Francisco Morizon*, which ran aground in a heavy November storm in 1960. It is but one of numerous shipwrecks off the South Manitou shore. Nearby stands a lighthouse, the second structure built on South Manitou to assist navigation. The federal government appropriated funds to build the first structure, which was completed in 1840. It was literally a house with a light on top. Replaced in 1871 with the graceful 100-foot tower, the light was tended by keepers until 1958 when it was closed. Automated warning lights installed elsewhere now function in place of it. Close to the lighthouse is the South Manitou Island Visitor Center.

South Manitou is accessible by boat from Leland for camping, fishing, hiking, swimming, and nature study. North Manitou may be used for primitive camping and hiking.

Visitors at the Sleeping Bear Dunes National Lakeshore will find rewarding scenes like this one by hiking in the dunes. Courtesy Sleeping Bear Dunes National Lakeshore, National Park Service, U.S. Department of the Interior.

Special features of the mainland portion of the Sleeping Bear Dunes National Lakeshore include the Pierce Stocking Scenic Drive, more than seven miles across the dunes with scenic overlooks and markers explaining the historical and natural features of special interest. It is named for its developer who operated the drive as a private toll road until 1977 when the U.S. government bought the property from him. The dune climb at Sleeping Bear adjacent to Glen Lake rewards the energetic visitor with a fine view of dune country and an invitation to hike on to high overlooks 330 feet above the lake.

Interpretive programs offered from mid-June through Labor Day help visitors learn about the park. Conducted walks, self-guiding trails, and evening campfire programs stress the natural and cultural history of the area.

The Lakeshore Visitor Center, the best place to begin an exploration of the National Lakeshore, contains a museum of geologic and maritime history and offers for sale a number of publications relating to the dune country. At Glen Haven in 1984 the Lakeshore opened a Marine Museum in the U.S. Coast Guard buildings unused since 1942. Rescue work and Great Lakes shipping are well depicted. Both the Platte River and the D. H. Day campgrounds offer access to the beach. Thirty miles of marked cross-country ski trails provide winter enjoyment of the lakeshore.

The D. H. Day Campground is named for the first chairman of the Michigan State Park Commission, which was created in 1919.

Future developments planned for the Sleeping Bear Dunes National

Point Betsie Lighthouse. Photo by Margaret Bogue.

Lakeshore include a 30-mile scenic corridor drive. Now the Pierce Stocking Scenic Drive provides one of the best vantage points along the entire western Michigan shoreline from which to view Lake Michigan.

Administrative headquarters for the lakeshore are located at Frankfort.

141. Point Betsie Lighthouse

Hy M-22

To find Point Betsie Lighthouse, turn off Hy M-22 at the U.S. Coast Guard Station sign just north of Frankfort. It was erected in 1858. "Betsie" may be derived from *bec scie*, French for "saw bill," referring to the merganser ducks that were so abundant in the area during the period of French exploration and fur trading.

142. Frankfort

Hy M-22

Father Jacques Marquette may have been the first European to visit the forested shoreline of Lake Michigan at the mouth of the Betsie River in 1675. Some believe that Frankfort was the original burial place of this eminent Jesuit priest. Long a matter of controversy, the Frankfort claim was both bolstered and denied during the 1960s. Without question Frenchmen

The Frankfort Harbor about 1875 is the central focus. Note as well the upper left inset of South Frankfort, later renamed Elberta. The oval inset stakes Frankfort's claim to being the place where Jacques Marquette died. The Ludington versus Frankfort controversy still continues. Courtesy State Historical Society of Wisconsin. WHi(X3)40553

visited the area, lured to the Betsie River by the fur trade. For a time an Indian village stood on the north bank of the Betsie about a mile from its entrance into Lake Michigan. The Frankfort region's abundant game made it an important hunting ground.

The virtues of the site of present-day Frankfort were not lost on the federal surveyors who in 1838 worked in the area. One noted that it "would make a commodious harbor for lake vessels should the mouth of the river be improved. On the north side of the lake is a beautiful situation for a small town." A few permanent settlers came in the early 1850s, and in the following decade, particularly after the Civil War, settlement in the Frankfort area began in earnest. Federal appropriations for harbor improvements helped the town grow as a lumbering center.

In the 1870s large steam-powered sawmills suitable for commercial production were built. While the Betsie River watershed did not have the stands of white pine that lumbermen prized so highly, it did have fine stands of hardwoods, aspen, hemlock, and fir. Lumbering at Frankfort utilized these timber stands until about 1920, when the forests became so depleted that commercial lumbering no longer paid.

Frankfort developed two important satellite industries of lumbering: iron smelting and salt making. Hardwoods provided raw materials for the local iron smelter. Like Leland to the north, Frankfort had the charcoal supply, the good harbor facilities, and the local limestone essential for pig iron production utilizing ore shipped by lake boats from the Upper Peninsula. Salt making also grew in importance. Wells at Frankfort produced a brine that could be evaporated with exhaust steam from the sawmills and by using leftover scrap wood. Commercial fishing also figured prominently in Frankfort's economy from the late nineteenth century until the 1930s.

At the turn of the century, the Toledo, Ann Arbor, and Northern Michigan Railroad brought a thriving summer resort business to Frankfort. In 1901, 11 years after the Ann Arbor Road first carried passengers to Frankfort, the company built the Royal Frontenac summer hotel on the waterfront. Trains carried wealthy Ohioans to spend their vacations on the shores of Lake Michigan, using the fine accommodations the Royal Frontenac offered. It was an impressive structure, 500 feet long and three stories high. Chicagoans also came by boat to enjoy luxurious summer living. To the distress of the Frankfort townspeople, the Royal Frontenac burned down in 1912 and was not rebuilt.

The Ann Arbor Railroad contributed to Frankfort's prosperity in many ways, and especially by developing a car ferry service in 1892 to carry loaded freight cars across Lake Michigan to Kewaunee, Wisconsin, and to Menominee and Manistique, Michigan. Eight ferries were commissioned. None remain in service.

The timber resources of the Betsie River watershed, the mainstay of Frankfort's initial prosperity, were obviously showing signs of depletion by the turn of the century. Frankfort's future worried many of the town fathers, for with the timber gone, both milling and iron smelting were doomed. Fruit farming on cutover lands emerged as a successful local industry. The town tried to attract other new industries, with only modest success.

Frankfort also tried to become the permanent seat of government for Benzie County. From 1869 to 1872 it had been the county seat. It recaptured this honor temporarily from 1908 to 1916 in a county that has had no fewer than four county seats in 110 years.

Today, with a population of about 1,600, Frankfort services the surrounding fruit-producing area and has some small light industry. Tourism, recreation, and summer homes are also important to its economy.

Frankfort Sites of Interest

(1) Father Marquette Historical Marker and Cross

The marker for the burial site of Father Marquette, erected by authorization of the Michigan Historical Commission, and a simple cross stand at the Frankfort harbor waterfront adjacent to the U.S. Coast Guard Station. They mark what some scholars believe to be the original burial place of Father Marquette in 1675. Marquette and two French companions were on the return journey to St. Ignace from a mission to the Kaskaskia Indians when Marquette died. After his initial burial, his remains were removed and reburied at St. Ignace, many believe. On this same site the Ann Arbor Railroad built the Royal Frontenac summer resort hotel in 1901 after leveling the hill that stood here.

(2) Lighthouse

The Frankfort harbor lighthouse, manned by the U.S. Coast Guard, stands on the site of the first lighthouse structure, built in 1873.

(3) Drive Around Frankfort

Those interested in the visible reminders of old Frankfort should notice the late nineteenth- and early twentieth-century storefronts on Main Street. At Forest Avenue and 5th Street stands a handsome nineteenth-century Congregational Church. On Forest and Leelanau Avenues are many of the homes of Frankfort's successful nineteenth-century business leaders and professionals.

143. Elberta
Hy M-22

Michigan's Shore to Shore Hiking and Riding Trail begins at the Lake Michigan shore at Elberta and crosses 210 miles to Tawas City on Lake Huron. Boy Scouts assisted in its contruction and hike the trail frequently.

At Elberta, formerly known as South Frankfort, stood the Frankfort Iron Smelting Furnace. The stone building on the road to the Ann Arbor Boat Docks in Elberta is what remains of the iron works.

Although the Ann Arbor Railroad always listed Frankfort as the terminus of its car ferries across Lake Michigan to Wisconsin, the ferries actually departed from docks on the south side of Lake Betsie, opposite Frankfort, in Elberta. The village of Elberta in 1956 was supported by the Michigan Supreme Court in its contention that the car ferry docks were within the village limits, but the Ann Arbor Railroad continued to ignore Elberta in its advertisements for the ferry service.

144. Benzonia
Hy M-115 from Frankfort

The town of Benzonia grew from the aspirations of Rev. Charles E. Bailey, a Congregational pastor and graduate of Oberlin College. He wanted to found a colony, church, and college in a frontier area to serve the needs of pioneer settlers. He selected the wilderness east of present-day Frankfort and led a small group of settlers to Benzonia in 1858.

His dream of founding another Oberlin fell short of the goal. Thanks to his efforts, however, Grand Traverse College opened in 1863, and the first college building was completed in 1869. Renamed Benzonia College in 1891, for nine years the college had the support of the Congregational church. From 1900 to 1918 it was known as Benzonia Academy. In the latter year it closed. One of its best-known graduates was Bruce Catton, the American Civil War historian. Two structures associated with the college remain: the former Mills Cottage and the Congregational Church, both located adjacent to Benzonia Village Park.

Benzonia Sites of Interest

(1) Mills Community House*
Built in 1909 as a girls' dormitory for Benzonia Academy, Mills Cottage, now Mills Community House, serves the village of Benzonia as a public library, auditorium, and hall for community dinners.

(2) Benzie Area Historical Museum
Located in the 1887 Congregational Church just across the park from Mills Community House, the museum stresses the history of the area, highlighting lumbering, shipping, commercial fishing, farming, education, religion, and artifacts of nineteenth-century life. Open Memorial Day–mid-October, Monday–Saturday, 1:30 A.M.–5:00 P.M. Free.

(3) Benzie County Lumber Mills
Several sawmills and other survivals of the lumbering era may be seen at scattered locations in Benzie County. Inquire at the Benzie Area Historical Museum for locations and directions on how to find them.

The work of fish hatcheries like the Platte River, Michigan hatchery make happy Lake Michigan fishermen like these. Photo by Lynn Frederick. Courtesy Lynn Frederick.

145. Platte River State Anadromous Fish Hatchery
Hy US-31

Located east of Honor, this Fish Hatchery is Michigan's largest and most modern. It was constructed between 1969 and 1974 at a cost of $6 million, provided by the state of Michigan, the U.S. Department of the Interior, and the Great Lakes Regional Commission.

It is devoted to the hatching of anadromous fish—that is, fish that spend most of their lives in large lakes or oceans, but return to rivers to spawn. The hatchery produces about 350,000 pounds a year of steelhead, coho salmon, and chinook salmon, literally millions of fingerlings to stock the Great Lakes. An interpretive facility in the administration building is the best place to start a self-guided tour of the hatchery complex. Visitors are welcome daily, 8:00 A.M.–4:30 P.M.

146. Orchard Beach State Park

Hys US-31 and M-110 (CFHPS)

Located on a bluff overlooking Lake Michigan just north of Manistee, Orchard Beach State Park has an attractive camping ground with 210 campsites on its 175 acres and a beach for swimming. A historical marker erected by the state of Michigan tells the story of the great fire of 1871. On the same day as the famous Chicago Fire and the terrible forest fire that destroyed Peshtigo, Wisconsin, the eastern coast of Lake Michigan experienced similar conflagrations that destroyed most of Holland and Manistee. The fire swept across the Michigan lower peninsula all the way to Lake Huron, destroying more than 2 million acres of timberland, killing many, and leaving thousands homeless.

Orchard Beach State park was originally part of a fruit farm whose owner, General George A. Hart, decided in the 1890s to develop a "pleasure resort"—"a first class summer resort"—among his fruit orchards. A theater with a seating capacity of 700 and a dancing pavilion were among its major attractions. An electric railway made the park only a 20-minute ride from Manistee. The pleasure resort promotion was part of an effort of Manistee businessmen to develop new industries to compensate for the decline in lumbering. $

147. Manistee

Hy US-31

Manistee's beginnings and its early prosperity stemmed from the development of two bountiful natural resources; the timberlands of the Manistee River watershed and natural salt deposits. The first permanent white settlers, John and Adam Stronach, built a sawmill on the banks of the Manistee in 1841. When in 1849 the Chippewa relinquished their reservation at the site of present-day Manistee and the federal government offered the lands for sale to the public, settlement and lumbering proceeded, helped along by the first in a series of habor improvements in 1854.

At the close of the Civil War, Manistee, a typical lumbering town where Sunday was more a day for drinking and revelry than for religious worship, boasted a population of 1,100, 10 sawmills, a tannery, a sash and door factory, several lath and picket mills, and nine docks. In 1866, 60 million board feet of lumber left Manistee's docks.

A veritable boom, stimulated by high prices for lumber, trebled the city's population by 1870. Although the great forest fire of 1871 virtually leveled the town, Manistee rapidly rebuilt and continued to grow. The first salt well, drilled in 1879, added a new dimension to Manistee's business life. So did railroad connections to the north, the south, and the east in the last two decades of the century.

The winds and waves of Lake Michigan greatly enhanced Manistee's natural potential as a lumbering port. They created sand dunes along the shore, which dammed up river waters to form a lake. Lake Manistee furnished excellent industrial sites accessible to ships carrying the products of booming lumber and salt businesses. Similar dune, river, and lake formations at Charleviox, Elk Rapids, Leland, Frankfort, Pentwater, Montague-Whitehall, and Muskegon greatly enhanced port potential at those sites. This geographic feature of Lake Michigan's eastern lakeshore is unique among Great Lakes shorelines.

By 1899 Lake Manistee, as one local historian has noted, was "a scene of bustle and activity, as the entire distance around its shores is dotted with saw mills, salt blocks, lumber piles, docks, ship-yard, tannery, etc." Into its busy harbor in 1898 came 589 steam and 367 sailing vessels carrying food, feed, stone, bricks, and merchandise. On departure they were laden with lumber, shingles, bark, slabs, cordwood, and fruit. At the turn of the century, 24 salt wells produced 1,850,000 barrels of salt, and 15 sawmills 167 million board feet of lumber, in addition to very sizable outputs of lath and shingles. Manistee, "The Salt City of the Inland Seas," also had three foundries, a wagon factory, and a furniture-making business.

Late nineteenth-century Manistee's population had a high percentage of foreign-born. Immigrants from Germany, Ireland, Poland, Sweden, Nor-

Louis Sands lower mill, Manistee Lake about 1900. From the Collections of the Michigan State Archives, Department of State. 00562

way, and Denmark came to work in the lumber and salt-making industries. Churches proliferated to meet their needs for traditional services, and for the social life that church societies generated. By 1900 the town had 16 churches, many of which remain in use today.

Although lumbering was still very important at the turn of the century, signs of change in the economy and concern about the future were much in evidence. Some worried about the cutover lands and the need for reforestation. Others advocated experimentation with agricultural crops. Fruit growing had already been recognized as well suited to the soils and mild temperatures adjacent to the lake. Already the fruit belt from Big Traverse Bay south to the Michigan-Indiana line had taken shape. So also had the pattern of summer resorts and tourism.

In the transition, Manistee has lost some of its population. The 1900 census reported a population of 14,260. Manistee today has a city population of 7,566. Yet it remains important as a service center for the surrounding fruit-growing area, the site of 30 light manufacturing companies that together employ over 3,000, the focus of a tourist and recreation industry, and the county seat of Manistee County.

Manistee Sites of Interest

(1) 300 and 400 Blocks of River Street

The city of Manistee has in recent years made a special effort—known as "Project Facelift"—to enhance the appearance of the nineteenth-century commercial buildings on River Street. Those interested in historic preservation will want to take a walk on River Street especially in the 300 and 400 blocks, to see the results of this effort. Note particularly the *Ramsdell Building* at the corner of River and Maple, built before 1900 and combining red brick, gray stone, and lovely tile ornaments.

(2) Late Nineteenth-Century Homes

400 and 500 blocks of Maple and Oak Streets

A walk on Maple and Oak Streets in the 400 and 500 blocks will give the visitor a good idea of the kinds of large, elegant homes built by Manistee's successful businessmen and professionals in the late nineteenth century.

(3) Guardian Angels Church

5th and Sycamore Streets

Irish and German parishioners of St. Mary's, Manistee's original Catholic church, felt that the congregation was too large to suit their needs. They left St. Mary's and built this beautiful structure in 1890. It has fine stained glass windows, icons, and a traditional altar. Carved guardian angels stand at either side of the front entrance. Both exterior and interior are well worth viewing. The style combines Gothic and Romanesque details.

(4) Ramsdell Theater*

101 Maple Street

Built in 1903 of masonry and red brick by Thomas J. Ramsdell, a lawyer prominent in Manistee as early as 1860,

Guardian Angels Church is as beautiful inside as out. Note the guardian angels on either side of the entrance. Photo by Margaret Bogue.

the theater at first offered live stage performances. It was used during the 1920s for silent movies, later for summer stock productions, and beginning in 1963 for productions of the Manistee Drama Association. Currently the Manistee Civic Theater offers plays here. The building is typical of turn-of-the-century theaters.

(5) Our Savior's Evangelical Lutheran Church*
300 Walnut Street
Constructed 1868–1870 to serve the needs of a group of Danish, Norwegian, and Swedish immigrants, this modest frame building originally was named the Scandinavian Evangelical Lutheran Church. The structure was one of the few buildings in Manistee to come through the fire of 1871 undamaged. In 1874 Manistee's Danish population had grown large enough, and the influence of the Church Mission Society of the Danish Evangelical Lutheran Church in America strong enough, for Manistee's Danish Lutherans to have their own congregation. When the Swedish and Norwegian members left to form their own church, the Danes rechristened this church the Danish Lutheran Church. The building is believed to be the oldest existing Danish Lutheran church in the United States. The present name, Our Savior's Evangelical Lutheran Church, was adopted in 1924.

(6) First Congregational Church*
412 South 4th Street
This massive red brick structure, measuring 128 by 74 feet, was designed by the Chicago architects William Le Baron Jenney and William Otis. Construction began in 1888 and was completed in 1892. The building

The one display building of the Manistee County Historical Society is among the older structures on River Street that were part of "Project Facelift" (see (1) above). Photo by Margaret Bogue.

was large for its congregation, which for several decades included in its membership the lumber, shipping, and salt entrepreneurs of Manistee. An excellent example of Romanesque design, the structure has several stained glass windows, two of which are Tiffany windows.

(7) Manistee County Historical Museum
425 River Street
Part of the museum is housed in the A. H. Lyman building, built in 1883 as a retail store. It is in the heart of the portion of Water Street refurbished as part of Project Facelift. Museum collections include Victorian rooms, a general store, a drug store, and costumes. A second portion of the museum is housed in the Holly Water Works Building at 1st and Cedar streets. Marine, logging, and railroad exhibits are maintained in this 1881 structure. Open March 1–October 15, Tuesday–Saturday 10:00 A.M.–5:00 P.M., and June 1–October 1 on Monday as well, at the same hours. Free.

148. Manistee National Forest
Hy M-55

During the late nineteenth and early twentieth centuries, lumber companies, railroads, and the Western Michigan Development Bureau, headquartered at Traverse City, made strenuous efforts to encourage farming in the cutover lands of the present-day Manistee National Forest. Advertising it as a cutover Canaan, the best place in the country to make a home, a "Land of Fruit and Fortune," the promoters met with dismal failure. People left the area, and many of the lands reverted to the state for tax delinquency. The federal government during the 1930s began purchasing this submarginal farmland for reforestation.

"Manistee" is a Chippewa word meaning "spirit of the forest." The Manistee National Forest, established in 1938, covers almost half a million acres and stretches from Manistee south to Muskegon and east to Cadillac and Big Rapids. It includes pine, spruce, oak, and other tree species. Deer, bears, wild turkeys, and foxes are found among the forest's wildlife. The excesses of nineteenth- and early twentieth-century lumbering caused sand blowouts along the shoreline. The U.S. Forest Service is trying to halt the resulting erosion by replanting the Lake Michigan Recreation Area between Manistee and Ludington. Headquarters for the Manistee National Forest are at Cadillac, Michigan.

Ruffled grouse in the Manistee National Forest. Courtesy of the Manistee National Forest, U.S. Forest Service, U.S. Department of Agriculture.

149. Ludington State Park

Hy M 116, 8 miles north of Ludington (BCFHPS)

The village of Hamlin a century ago was a logging community on the shore of Hamlin Lake, developed by Charles Mears, Chicago shipping entrepreneur and timber baron of Mason, Oceana, and Muskegon counties. Logs were floated across the lake to the village mill. But in 1888 the mill brought tragedy to the village when the dam burst and destroyed Hamlin. Today, only the cemetery remains to tell the tale, and the village site is now a 150-acre state park. The park's 398 campsites and two beaches usually attract more campers each year than any other state park in Michigan. Fishermen have discovered that Hamlin Lake holds bass, pike, and walleyes. Hikers may choose from 8 hiking trails in the park, totaling 18 miles in length. Some of the trails follow the dune ridges, while others lead to Point Sable Lighthouse. The nature center contains displays on the area's flora and fauna and offers visual programs about the park and its wildlife. $

150. Ludington

Hy US-31

Ludington's greatest claim to a niche in American history lies in the life work of the French Jesuit missionary, Jacques Marquette. Many scholars are convinced that Marquette was buried on a pine-covered hill at Ludington on a day in May 1675. The river at Ludington bears his name.

Almost two centuries passed before the town of Ludington was founded. Meanwhile, Indians, fur traders, and fishermen came and went. In the late 1840s two settlers built a sawmill at the site of Ludington, an excellent choice of location. In the watershed of the Pere Marquette stood vast acreages of virgin white pine. The little settlement was called Pere Marquette.

The depression of the 1850s intervened, and the sawmill fell to James Ludington of Milwaukee by mortgage foreclosure. He leased the mill a few years later to Charles Mears, a substantial Chicago entrepreneur who was accumulating vast acreages of pinelands and harbor facilities between Manistee and Muskegon. Mears undertook essential harbor improvements almost immediately, the first in a whole series during the late nineteenth century that turned the harbor into an excellent facility for large vessels.

In 1867 James Ludington, member of a prominent Milwaukee mercantile, lumber, land, and banking family, laid out the town, succeeded in having it renamed, and plunged into the sawmilling business in style. In ill health, two years later he organized the Pere Marquette Lumbering Company, retained a part interest in it, and thereafter played a small role in the town's development.

During the late nineteenth century, Ludington grew into an important sawmilling town and supply base for lumbering. Business and cultural leadership fell to an influx of New Englanders who were experienced in lumbering. Immigrant workers from French Canada, Finland, and Germany cut the white pines and manned the mills. Eight sawmills came into operation, reaching their peak production of 146 million board feet in 1891.

In 1885 salt manufacturing became an adjunct to lumbering just as it had at Manistee. The development of salt wells came in part as the result of lumbermen's fears that the great stands of white pine would soon disappear. Already lumbermen had begun their onslaught on Mason County's hardwoods. Several factories were established at Ludington to turn out everything from broom handles to furniture. But what would become of Ludington when the hardwoods were gone?

The 1890s were indeed a gloomy decade. Commercial fishing, a livelihood for about 50 families, began to decline. The nearby sawmill town of Lincoln had already become a ghost town. Another mill in Ludington burned down. The bank failed. A Citizens Development Company, founded to attract new business, failed along with three factories that it had

Bird's-eye view of Ludington about 1880. The Pere Marquette Lumber Company's three saw mills are pictured around the harbor. From the Collections of the Michigan State Archives, Department of State. 06467

managed to attract to Ludington. The transition away from lumbering was painfully evident.

Business leaders tried to attract a tourist industry without notable initial success, although a youth organization of the Methodist Episcopal church did establish a colony at nearby Epworth in 1894. Some centered their hopes for the future on a transition to fruit farming and the utilization of Ludington's excellent harbor. Both of these ideas had real long-term merit.

The harbor developed a sizable freight transshipment business in 1874, when the Flint and Pere Marquette Railroad reached Ludington. Boats took aboard the freight destined for Lake Michigan's western shore. With the agricultural development of the hinterland, Ludington became an important fruit and vegetable shipping point. The railroad built its own fleet of boats to handle the growing traffic in freight and passengers between Ludington, Manistee, and Milwaukee.

Occasional work stoppages and the expense involved in the transfer of freight from train to boat led to the introduction of the car ferry. The first steel vessel, the *Pere Marquette No. 15*, went into service at Ludington in 1897, bound for Manitowoc, Wisconsin. The ferry connection grew to include Kewaunee and Milwaukee. Over the next 50 years the Pere Marquette line used 12 car ferries and has been described as operating "the most outstanding business of various Lake Michigan ferries." As a part of the Chesapeake and Ohio Railway system, these car ferries handled 32 loaded freight cars and 150 automoblies at a time. Trucking so successfully challenged the car ferries, however, that in January 1982 the ferry service to Manitowoc ceased. Service continues to Kewaunee, Wisconsin.

Rollaway, Pere Marquette River, with denuded forest land in background. The Pere Marquette's rich pine stands fed the mills in Ludington harbor. From the Collections of the Michigan State Archives, Department of State. 01579

Fruit growing, recreation, summer residences, and tourism grew in importance in the twentieth century and remains significant in Ludington's present economy. Over the years Ludington has succeeded in attracting industry. Currently it has about a dozen plants that employ from 100 to 325 workers each. Chemicals and metal products ranging from watchcases to iron castings, dies, tools, industrial equipment, wire, and tubing are very important to the economy, as are automobile interiors and a wide variety of finished consumer products.

Ludington has been the county seat since 1873, when it succeeded in wresting the honor from Charles Mears's mill village, Lincoln. The current population is is 8,937.

Ludington Sites of Interest

(1) Stearns Park on the Lake
Here two Michigan Historic Site markers stand as testimony to the hazards of navigation on Lake Michigan. One recounts the damage to ships and loss of life during the storm of November 11, 1940, considered one of the worst in the lake's history. The other tells about the sinking of the *Pere Marquette No. 18* of the Ludington car ferry fleet in September 1910, with the loss of all officers and many of the crew and passengers. Adjacent to the park stands the U.S. Coast Guard Station.

(2) Car Ferry Dock
Those interested in crossing Lake Michigan to Kewaunee, Wisconsin, should inquire at the ferry office. The ferry carries passengers, automobiles, and freight cars.

(3) Mason County Courthouse
Hy US-10 at the corner of Ludington Avenue and Delia Street
Built in 1893, a year of financial panic and general gloom in Ludington, the courthouse is a fine example of Richardsonian Romanesque architecture.

(4) Rose Hawley Museum
305 East Filer Street
The museum collections include Indian artifacts, lumbering and farming tools, nineteenth-century household items, a marine exhibit, and a typical Victorian apartment of the 1890s, as well as a collection of manuscripts and

published marerials on local history. Open Memorial Day–Labor Day, Monday–Saturday, noon–5:00 P.M. Free.

(5) White Pine Village
1687 South Lakeshore Road
The village is accessible from Highway US-31 south of Ludington. Turn right immediately after crossing the second bridge over the Pere Marquette River. The village is located three miles east of Hy US-31.

This outdoor museum is a community of historic buildings located on the site of the area's first non-Indian home, which was built in 1849. The village includes a working replica of a blacksmith shop; a fire barn, housing a collection of fire-fighting equipment; a general store, housed in an original Mason County split-log pioneer home; a combined post office and home, built about 1850; the home that served as Mason County's first courthouse; two museum buildings, one of which houses artifacts of the lumbering industry; the original Pere Marquette Township Hall; a one-room schoolhouse; and a chapel replica illustrating various architectural features of rural Mason County churches. Open daily, Memorial Day–Labor Day, 11:00 A.M.–5:00 P.M. Free.

(6) Father Marquette Memorial
South Lakeshore Drive north of the White Pine Village
Here a cross and an official Michigan Historic Site marker commemorate the death of Father Marquette on May 18, 1675, and his burial somewhere along the Lake Michigan shore.

(7) Ludington's Historic Homes
Many residences of the successful men of the lumbering era remain. For example, the three-story house at 702 East Ludington Avenue was built by James Foley, a prominent lumberman and shipper. Those interested in the town's impressive late nineteenth-century architecture may purchase *Historic Homes of Ludington* at the Rose Hawley Museum. It contains a listing of 41 locations, descriptive paragraphs on each, and a map to help you take a walking or a driving tour.

James Foley, Ludington lumberman, built this Victorian home, three stories with ballroom, about 1898 after thirty-two years in the lumber business. He came from Ontario County, New York, to Ludington in 1866. The house is now divided into apartments. Photo by Margaret Bogue.

151. Charles Mears State Park
Hy US-31 (BCFP)

Named for the Chicago businessman who was the area's most prominent lumbering and shipping entrepreneur, this 50-acre park has an excellent Lake Michigan swimming beach. $

152. Pentwater
Hy US-31

Located on Lake Michigan at the mouth of Pentwater Lake and the Pentwater River, Pentwater had all the attributes of a fine site for lumbering. The Pentwater River Watershed boasted fine stands of timber. The river, Pentwater Lake, and Lake Michigan provided a good avenue of transportation to market.

Charles Mears, for whom the nearby state park is named, was the Chicago entrepreneur who developed the harbor and engaged extensively in lumbering, shipping, and general merchandising in the late nineteenth century. Mears built his own fleet of ships for carrying passengers, livestock, and goods from Chicago into the Pentwater pinelands and for transporting lumber to Chicago. At the height of the lumbering boom, the entire north shore of Pentwater Lake was lined with saw, shingle, planing, and grist mills.

By 1882 lumbering in Oceana County had declined sharply, and worried businessmen sought industries to replace it. One early transitional industry was furniture manufacturing, and another was canning. Early efforts at developing a resort trade failed.

Today Pentwater (population 1,165) is much smaller than it was in the flush times of lumbering. Summer homes, tourism, and resort trade form an important part of its current economy. The town has a little light industry.

The nineteenth-century storefronts, houses, and churches reflect the town's past. So do two lighthouses: *Little Sable*, built in 1874 and lying 10 miles to the south of town, and *Big Sable*, built in 1867 several miles to the north. Both were erected to warn vessels of dangerous currents near the shore. Neither of these lighthouses is accessible by car.

Big Trees of Oceana and Mason Counties

The Pentwater Garden Club and Pentwater Environmental Protective Association have prepared a folder describing the big trees of Oceana and Mason counties. It describes 32 outstanding examples of different species and includes a keyed map to help the motorist locate these unusual and fine old trees. Those who enjoy the area's natural heritage will find it worthwhile to secure this guide from the tourist information booth in Pentwater or Hart.

153. Silver Lake State Park

accessible from US-31, 7 miles west of Hart (BCFHPS)

The most outstanding features of this beautiful 2,600-acre park are the wide, sandy Lake Michigan beaches and the sand dunes. Dune rides are available. The park includes 250 campsites. $

The pier at the White Lake entrance to Lake Michigan. Note the debris from lumber mills along the shore, a familiar sight on Lake Michigan's eastern shore in the late nineteenth century. Courtesy Michigan Historical Collections, Bentley Historical Library, University of Michigan.

154. Montague–Whitehall

Hy US-31

Both of these towns originated as lumbering centers in the nineteenth century. Charles Mears is largely responsible for the early development of the lumbering industry in the White River watershed. He established a residence at Whitehall in 1861. Today the towns' main economic activities are tourism, recreation, and summer homes for city dwellers.

White River Light Station Marine Museum

Visitors should stop in Whitehall and seek directions to this museum. Although it is a little difficult to locate, the museum is worth the effort. Owned and operated by Fruitlands Township, the museum is located in the old White River lighthouse, built in 1872. It stands at the opening of White Lake into Lake Michigan. The structure is itself a very interesting one, apparently a twin to the lighthouse built at Peninsula Point in 1865 (site 90).

The museum contains pictures, paintings, and artifacts of Great Lakes shipping. Open June–August, Tuesday–Friday, 10:00 A.M.–5:00 P.M.; Saturday and Sunday, 2:00–8:00 P.M. In May and September, open Saturday and Sunday 2:00–8:00 P.M. Free.

Hackley Public Library.
Photo by Margaret Bogue.

granite with brownstone trim. The building was dedicated in October 1890 with an elaborate ceremony. The interior is as interesting as the exterior. Visitors are welcome to view it and to browse in its fine collections. The library contains a marble bust of Hackley, donated by Muskegon's citizens.

St. Paul's Episcopal Church,
3rd Street and Clay Avenue

This grayish greenstone structure of Gothic design was erected in 1892, just two years after the dedication of the adjacent Hackley Library. Thomas Hume, Hackley's business partner, contributed heavily to the cost of construction. The interior design utilizes fine stained glass, marble, mosaics, and wood carving. Alois Lang, a wood carver of the Oberammergau group, crafted the lectern and litany desk.

Muskegon Museum of Art,
296 Webster Avenue

This Classical Revival structure, designed by S. S. Beman of Chicago, was completed and opened to the public in 1912. Hackley, who had long wanted to contribute an art museum to Muskegon, died in 1905 before its erection. He left a bequest of $150,000 to the Board of Education for the puchase of "pictures of the best kind" for Muskegon. Paintings acquired with these funds were temporarily housed in the public library. Most of the permanent collection was acquired with Hackley's bequest.

It is especially strong in American painting and includes works by Whistler, Homer, Wyeth, Curry, West, Ryder, Blakelock, Bellows, Burchfield, and Hopper. The L. C. Walker Collection of graphics includes prints by Durer, Rembrandt, Toulouse-Lautrec, Matisse, Renoir, Picasso, and others. Paintings by major European artists and an eastern collection give its holdings considerable breadth. It has been described as one of the finest of the smaller art museums in the United States. Open all year, Tuesday–Saturday, 10:00 A.M.–4:00 P.M. Free.

John Torrent Residence,
3rd Street and Webster Avenue

This magnificent stone house was built in 1892. Its owner, John Torrent, came to Muskegon in the late 1850s, soon established a shingle mill, and emerged a millionaire in the lumbering business. Torrent built the 30-room granite home, it is said, to outdo his business rival, Hackley. The structure now houses the Red Cross.

Hackley Central School,
3rd Street and Webster Avenue

A Grand Rapids building firm erected this structure in 1892 to replace the central school building that had burned down in 1890. Charles H. Hackley donated the funds for the school's construction. Romanesque in style, the building is now used as a school administration building for the Muskegon School System.

Hackley Park,
between Clay and Webster Avenues and 3rd and 4th Streets

The park lies in the center of the Historic District. Both the lands and the statues in the park were donated to the city by Charles H. Hackley. The park memorializes Union leaders, soldiers, and sailors of the Civil War. The Soldiers and Sailors Monument, by Joseph Carabelli, stands in the center of the park. Statues of Abraham Lincoln, David Farragut, Ulysses S. Grant, and William T. Sherman stand at the park's corners.

Hackley House and Hume House,**
West Webster Avenue and 6th Street

Charles H. Hackley built this spacious Victorian residence for himself, the adjacent Hume House for his business partner, Thomas Hume, and the shared Carriage House between the two in 1887. The Hackley House is currently being restored by the Hackley Heritage Association, Inc. Elaborate hand-carved woodwork, stenciled walls and ceilings, stained glass windows, and original furniture are among the Hackley House's outstanding features. The association plans restoration of the Hume House and the shared Carriage House in the future. Hackley House is open to the public Memorial Day–September 30, Wednesday, Saturday, and Sunday, 2:00–4:00 P.M.; and for six days in December to interpret an 1890s Christmas. $

(3) Muskegon County Museum
30 West Muskegon Avenue
The museum has good collections on lumbering from 1840 to 1890, the Indians, the fur trade, and the life and work of early settlers. Among the Indian artifacts is a dugout canoe found on the White River. Open all year, Tuesday–Friday, noon–5:00 P.M.; Saturday and Sunday, 2:00–5:00 P.M. $

(4) Grave of Jonathan Walker
inside entrance to Evergreen Cemetery, Pine and Irwin Streets
A 10-foot monument marks the grave of Jonathan Walker, a sea captain who attempted to help seven slaves escape from bondage in Florida by taking them to British islands in the Caribbean in 1844. Walker was captured, and a Florida federal court convicted him of violating the federal Fugitive Slave Law. His sentence included a fine, months of imprisonment, an hour in the pillory, and the branding of "S. S." (for "Slave Stealer") on the palm of his right hand. After his release he joined the ranks of abolitionist lecturers.

In the 1860s Walker purchased a small fruit farm at Lake Harbor, Michigan. Here he lived until his death in 1877. After his burial in Evergreen Cemetery, William Lloyd Garrison and other abolitionists raised funds to have the momument erected. Walker's branding led John Greenleaf Whittier, poet of the anti-slavery movement, to write "The Man with the Branded Hand." One verse of that poem is inscribed on one side of the Walker Monument, and on the other an open hand is carved showing the letters "S. S."

The Genevieve Gillette Nature Center, Michigan's Sand Dune Interpretive Center. Courtesy Michigan Department of Natural Resources.

157. P. J. Hoffmaster State Park

Hy US-31 (CFHPS)

The outstanding features of Hoffmaster Park are two and a half miles of Lake Michigan shoreline with forest-covered dunes. Sandy beaches run the entire length of the 1,000-acre park. Over 10 miles of natural hiking trails provide ample opportunites for nature study. Upland, shoreline, and waterbirds are plentiful. A Dune Climb Stairway leads to the top of a high sand dune, from

This view of Grand Haven shows both the Cutler House on the left and the Mineral Springs which catered to those who came to "take the waters." Courtesy Michigan Historical Collections, Bentley Historical Library, University of Michigan.

which the view is excellent. The park contains 333 campsites, a bridle path, and the Genevieve Gillette Nature Center, named for one of the state's leading conservationists.

The new building, dedicated in 1976, contains exceptionally fine exhibits explaining dune formation and ecology. In the theater multi-image slide shows portray dune ecology and the natural beauty of the Great Lakes. In the summer months the Nature Center offers lectures and guided hikes. The center is open to the general public throughout the summer seven days a week and in the winter on weekends and afternoons except Monday. $

158. Grand Haven
Hy US-31

Grand Haven evolved in the same pattern as many Lake Michigan towns lying north of the Grand River: Indian village, fur trading center, thriving sawmill town, county seat, shipbuilding and commercial fishing port, resort center, and industrial town. Both the lake and the Grand River, which flows into Lake Michigan at Grand Haven, have played major roles in shaping the town's development.

The Indian peoples and fur traders used the Grand River as a route between Lake Huron and Lake Michigan. The portage between the headwaters of the Grand and the Saginaw rivers was the one overland link where canoes and cargo had to be carried. The Ottawa, Chippewa, and Potawatomi built villages at the site of present-day Grand Haven, an excellent fishing location. French and British fur traders, and later John Jacob Astor's American Fur Company, established posts at the mouth of the Grand River and developed a lucrative trade with the local Indian tribes.

Permanent white settlers arrived in 1834 and the next year Grand Haven was platted. Its first sawmill began operations in 1836, and in 1837 the first lumber rafts came down the Grand River. This marked the beginning of the exploitation of the fine stands of white and cork pine, oak, beech, maple, and hemlock lying in the river's watershed.

Serious commercial logging began in the early 1850s in response to the demand for Michigan lumber for the developing homes, farms, cities, and factories in the Midwest. In 1856, 45 million board feet of lumber were shiped from the port of Grand Haven. By 1876 the town boasted eight saw and shingle mills. Already numerous federal appropriations had been made to improve the harbor.

Boat building developed as an important adjuct to lumbering. During the late nineteenth century five shipyards in the Grand Haven area turned out a wide variety of sail- and steam-powered vessels. Other satellite industries included tanneries, furniture manufacturing, salt refining, and iron ore smelting. Commercial fishing grew into a substantial business between the mid-1850s and 1910. It continued until the 1940s, when sea lampreys decimated the fish population.

The lumbering boom reached a climax in the early 1880s with annual production figures of 191 million board feet, but the industry dwindled in the next decade. As mill after mill closed, the town lost population, and businessmen scrambled to attract new industry.

Already the town entrepreneurs had discovered Grand Haven's potential for tourism and resorts. In 1870 a mill owner drilling for salt discovered magnetic mineral water at a depth of 200 feet. Several elaborate health resorts or "sanitariums" were built to cater to the hundreds of visitors who came annually to bathe and drink the magnetic waters. Grand Haven styled itself the Saratoga Springs of the West. Nor were the advantages of Grand Haven's beautiful white sand beach and surrounding lakes and streams lost on the developers.

The transition from cutover land to fruit farming was well under way before the turn of the century. Apples, pears, plums, and cherries found a ready market in Lake Michigan's large cities.

Grand Haven's excellent port facilities helped with the transition. During lumbering days Grand Haven was an extremely busy port, but lumbering products were only part of the outtraffic. Agricultural produce became more and more important as forest lands were turned to farming. The town became a transshipment point for passengers and freight for the Detroit and Milwaukee Railroad, which reached Grand Haven in 1858. This transshipment function continued to be important after lumbering declined. In 1903 railroad car ferries began operating between Grand Haven and Milwaukee and continued until the 1930s, when the car ferry service was transferred to Muskegon.

Grand Haven's water and rail transportation and labor supply, and its relative proximitiy to major markets, helped induce industries to locate here. Many have come and gone over the years, but the transition from an economy based on the original natural resources of lumber and fish has been very successful. Currently Grand Haven has 16 industries employing 100 or more. Some of the major products include metal and plastic components for consumer products such as automobiles and television sets, finished consumer goods, foundry products, and industrial machinery.

Grand Haven continues to be the Ottawa County seat, a center for recreation, resorts, and summer homes, and a service center for the surrounding fruit farms. The current population of about 12,000 is twice as large as that at the height of the lumbering boom.

Grand Haven Sites of Interest

(1) Tri-Cities Historical Society Museum

1 North Harbor Drive

Housed in the old depot of the Grand Trunk Railroad, the museum includes displays on Indian and pioneer life in the area, shipping, lumbering, and railroads. Open June–Labor Day, Wednesday–Sunday, 2:00–10:00 P.M. $

(2) U.S. Coast Guard Station

North Shore Road

U.S. Coast Guard Station personnel welcome visitors and appreciate calls in advance of the visit (the number is [616] 842-2510) so that the staff will be ready to explain the facilities and the station's work in enforcing maritime regulations and conducting search and rescue work, utilizing 41- and 25-foot craft.

(3) U.S. Coast Guard Festival

Held during the first week of August, the festival attracts many visitors. The festivities are designed to honor the work of the Coast Guard over many decades.

(4) The Lake Front and the Grand River

In addition to the U.S. Coast Guard Station, both Grand Haven State Park and the city park, located south of the Grand River's exit into Lake Michigan, afford ample opportunities for public enjoyment of the beautiful sand beach that has attracted tourists and vacationers since the late nineteenth century. The state park includes 170 campsites, a swimming beach, and a fishing pier. A trolley line connects the beach with the downtown shopping area of extensive and varied specialty shops. A paddlewheel harbor steamer, boarded near Waterfront Stadium on Harbor Avenue in the downtown area, offers rides on the river and along the lakeshore. Grand Haven also boasts a musical water and light show from Memorial Day through Labor Day. The Musical Fountain, located on the north bank of the Grand River across from the Chamber of Commerce and the Tri-Cities Historical Museum, is huge. Completed in 1963, it pumps 4,000 gallons of water per minute in varying patterns.

159. Zeeland

Hy I-196 and US-31

A town of 4,764, Zeeland is the location of one of western Michigan's early Dutch settlements. The town is named for the Netherlands province from which Cornelius Vander Meulen led his congregation to the New World in 1847. Of the various farming villages founded by Dutch immigrants around Holland (site 160), Zeeland has made the greatest growth. Graafschap, Overisel, Drenthe, and Vriesland remain small farming villages, but Zeeland has succeeded in attracting industries, among them a furniture plant and a clock-making company.

Many of the descendants of the original 457 colonists still live in Zeeland. Here visitors will also meet more recently arrived Spanish-speaking people.

Monument to the pioneers. Photo by Margaret Bogue.

Zeeland Sites of Interest

(1) Pioneer Square
southeast corner of Church and Central streets
This park is the site of the town's first log church and its first schoolhouse. Here colonists who died in the early years of the colony lie buried. The monument, erected in 1887, commemorates the town's pioneers.

(2) First Reformed Church
southwest corner of Church and Central streets
The church building was erected in 1866 and covered with bricks in 1929. It stands on the site of Zeeland's second log church, which was built in 1849 to accommodate a growing congregation.

(3) Dekker Huis and Zeeland Historical Museum
37 East Main Street
The museum collections recall Dutch family life in the Zeeland area from 1876 to 1920 and the history of the Zeeland colonization. Book, manuscript, and photograph collections are a resource for Zeeland history. Open April–September, Friday and Saturday, 10:00 A.M. to noon and 1:00–4:00 P.M. Donation.

Zeeland's Nineteenth-Century Homes
Zeeland retains a number of its historic nineteenth-century homes. The Zeeland Historical Society has prepared a pamphlet, "A Walking Tour of Architectural and Historic Sites," which is available at the museum. The structures, built between 1850 and 1900, represent a wide range of architectural styles, predominantly Victorian, Gothic Revival, and Queen Anne.

160. Holland

Hys US-31, I-196

The early history of Holland, Michigan, reads much like that of the Massachusetts Bay Colony. Here, in 1847, at the mouth of the Black River (later renamed Macatawa River), a small group of Dutch immigrants decided to make a new home for themselves. Seceders from the established Dutch church and refugees from Holland's potato famine, the original group of 47 people came under the leadership of Rev. Albertus Van Raalte, a courageous, able, and strong-willed leader. After much careful study, Van Raalte selected the Black River site, purchased several thousand acres of land, and proceeded to build a "city upon a hill," a model Christian community. His dreams for a theocracy failed to materialize, mainly because of physical hardships, individualism, and religious disputation. Yet a sizable Dutch community did take shape, and Dutch church leaders greatly influenced community development.

Hundreds of new settlers followed the founders—farmers, artisans, and mechanics used to the ways of the Old World but innocent of the stern realities of pioneering in a wooded wilderness. Theirs was a sobering experience. There was much suffering, hard work, and loss of life from malaria and cholera in the early years. Yet the Dutch settlers stuck together, built homes, and started farms and businesses. In 1851, largely because of Van Raalte's guidance, Hope College was founded to help meet the educational needs of the growing community.

As more and more immigrants came to the Holland area, migrating as individuals, families, and whole congregations, they established a number of separate settlements nearby. Among them were Overisel, Zeeland, Vriesland, Drenthe, and Graafschap. Although the Dutch preferred living in their own ethnic communities, some departed for nearby Yankee towns where they could readily find jobs. At Grand Rapids, Kalamazoo, Grand Haven, and Muskegon, they established their own neighborhoods.

Anxious to make the colony at Holland succeed, Van Raalte encouraged the development of businesses that would provide basic needs. A sawmill, a gristmill, a brickyard, an ashery, a shingle mill, and a stave factory were among the village's earliest industries. Also essential to success were harbor improvements, for the Black River's sand-clogged channel prevented the entrance of Lake Michigan vessels into Black Lake (later renamed Lake Macatawa). When an initial request for federal harbor-improvement money was turned down, the Dutch colonists began widening the channel themselves. The state of Michigan provided them with funds to build a wharf and to construct roads connecting Holland with surrounding towns.

Albertus Van Raalte. From the Collections of the Michigan State Archives, Department of State. 03735

In 1867 the village, with a population of about 2,000, incorporated as a city. Four years later disaster struck. Most of the town burned to the ground in 1871 as a result of massive forest fires, which had been burning for weeks in the surrounding swamps and woods. Both Van Vleck Hall at Hope College and Van Raalte's beautiful Greek Revival Pillar Church escaped the blaze (see nos. [5] and [6]).

The determined Dutch rebuilt the town. Slow growth characterized the city's late nineteenth-century years. A few industries flourished, including a leather-making company, several furniture factories, at least two woodworking mills, and, in 1892, a Heinz pickle factory. A tourist trade catering to Chicago and Grand Rapids residents was well established by the turn of the century at Ottawa Beach and Macatawa Park on Lake Michigan.

In the twentieth century Holland's business activity gradually changed from serving the surrounding farms and making wood products to an economy based mainly on heavy metal and technological industries. Currently Holland has more than 150 small industries employing 12,000 persons to produce a wide variety of products ranging from electrical appliances to pickles. At the time of the 1871 fire, Holland had a population of about 2,300 people. The 1980 census showed a population of 26,300.

The annual tulip festival, a promotional effort highlighting Holland's Dutch origins, dates from 1929. It attracts hundreds of thousands of visitors every May. Visitors especially interested in the history of Dutch settlements in the Holland area should talk with the staff at the Netherlands Museum for suggestions about other points of interest in Holland's adjacent villages.

Although many people of Dutch origin live in the Holland area, the ethnic composition of the population has become somewhat more diversified. Visitors will note a substantial number of Spanish-speaking people. Many of them came from Texas during World War II as migratory agricultural workers and settled here permanently.

Holland Sites of Interest

(1) The Netherlands Museum

8 East 12th Street at Central Avenue

Housed in a cut-stone and brick structure built in 1889 for Dr. Henry Kremers, physician and early mayor of Holland, the museum is the best place to begin a visit to the city's historic sites. The museum contains exceptionally fine collections relating to the Old World and the New World Dutch heritage, including many gifts from the Dutch government. Furniture crafted by Dutch cabinetmakers, Delft pottery and pewter, Leerdam glassware, handmade art glass churches, rooms furnished in the best of the old World tradition, and displays depicting the Dutch settlements in western Michigan are included. Open all year as follows: March–December except holidays, Monday–Saturday, 9:00 A.M.–5:00 P.M.; open on Sundays as well, 11:30 A.M.–5:00 P.M., May–Labor Day. In January and February, open Tuesday–Saturday, 10:00 A.M.–4:00 P.M. $

(2) Windmill Island Municipal Park

8th Street at Lincoln Avenue

In this 36-acre park stands "De Zwann," a 200-year-old Dutch windmill brought from Holland and reconstructed in 1964. It is still operating. Guides are on hand to explain its workings to visitors. The park has tulip displays in the spring and a Dutch patio with food, entertainment, and shops. Open May–Labor Day, Monday–Saturday, A.M. and P.M., and on Sunday afternoons. $

(3) The Baker Furniture Museum

6th Street and Columbia Avenue

Baker furniture, manufacturers of furniture at Holland and Grand Rapids since 1893, has in its museum collections old woodworking tools, representative period furniture designs, a print collection illustrating antique furniture, and a special collection of antique and modern chairs. Open mid-May–mid-October. $

(4) Third Reformed Church of Holland*

110 West 12th Street

Built in 1873–1874 and designed by John R. Kleyn, one of Holland's pioneer settlers, this vertical board and batten structure, Carpenter's Gothic in style, housed part of the congregation of Rev. Albertus Van Raalte, founder of the Holland colony. It was the third major structure to house his followers. The first on this site, built in 1867–1868 to take care of the overflow congregation of the Pillar Church, was burned in the Holland fire of 1871. Although altered somewhat over the years, the church in 1966 underwent a major renovation that restored the original interior color scheme and used cedar shingles to cover the roof as in the original design.

(5) The Pillar Church

9th Street and College Avenue

The beautiful example of Greek Revival architecture, with its massive Doric columns, was built in 1856 and housed Rev. Van Raalte's First Reformed Church congregation. In 1882 a controversy over whether or not it was appropriate for church members to belong to the Masonic Lodge split the congregation. Most of its members

Van Raalte's Pillar Church. Photo by Margaret Bogue.

split from the Reformed Church and joined the Christian Reformed Church. A bitter dispute arose over occupancy of the church structure. It is now called the Ninth Street Christian Reformed Church. A plaque at the front of the sancutary commemorates Van Raalte's ministry to the Dutch settlers from 1847 to 1867.

(6) Van Vleck Hall, Hope College

near East 10th Street and College Avenue

Van Vleck Hall is the oldest Hope College building. Erected in 1857, it was used as the Pioneer School and then as the Holland Academy. In 1866 the institution was chartered as Hope Academy. The college, established to meet the educational needs of the original settlers, continues to serve as a college of arts and sciences. Its name comes from Rev. Van Raalte's dedication address: "This is my anchor of Hope for this people in the future."

(7) Western Theological Seminary
12th Street between College and Columbia Avenues
In 1866 theological training began here, using the facilities and faculty of Hope College. In 1885 the school was officially designated the Western Theological Seminary of the Reformed Church in America. The seminary trains men and women for the ministry.

(8) Cappon House
9th Street and Washington Boulevard
This home was built in 1874 as a residence for Holland's first mayor, a partner in the Cappon Bertsch Tannery. It is now owned by the city of Holland and is maintained as a historic house. Tours are available to groups only, except during the Tulip Festival in May, when it is open to the general public. $

(9) Holland Harbor Lighthouse*
adjacent to Lake Michigan at entrance to Lake Macatawa
Built in 1907 and now considered obsolete as a lighthouse, this structure has been painted and repaired by the U.S. Coast Guard and turned over to the Holland Harbor Lighthouse Historical Commission for maintenance. The lens was given to the Netherlands Museum. Ask for directions to the lighthouse at the museum.

161. Holland State Park
accessible from Hy US-31
(CFPS)

The special attractions of this beautiful 143-acre park are impressive Lake Michigan sand dunes, a fine beach, and perch fishing. The park includes 342 campsites. With an annual attendance of over 1,300,000, Holland State Park is the most popular of Michigan's state parks. $

162. Saugatuck–Douglas
Hys I-196 and US 31

The beautiful woodlands lying at the mouth of the Kalamazoo River appealed to the Potawatomi and Ottawa Indians as an especially fine place to live. Bountiful fisheries and the river's natural avenue of transportation from Lake Michigan to the interior of the lower peninsula induced these tribes to establish villages here. Later, fur traders also recognized the location's advantages. In the 1830s white settlers began to arrive. They regarded the location as excellent for town site promotion especially in view of the superb stands of virgin timber in the Kalamazoo River watershed.

The first major town in the vicinity of Saugatuck–Douglas was Singapore, now one of Michigan's ghost towns. The New York and Michigan Company platted the town in 1838 with the idea of developing a sawmilling enterprise of major proportions. The original developers chose well, but a little too soon. In the 1860s and early 1870s the sawmills whined at Singapore, producing hundreds of millions of board feet of lumber. When the timber was gone, the town's residents moved south to Saugatuck, and the winds and waters of Lake Michigan buried Singapore beneath the sand.

Meanwhile both Saugatuck and Douglas had developed as sawmill and tannery towns producing millions of board feet of lumber, shingles, laths, and staves at the height of the lumber boom in the early 1870s. With the depletion of the forests, peach orchards planted on cutover land provided a very important source of income. Basket making also prospered. Commercial fishing was another important source of income for local residents, and Saugatuck developed an important boat-building industry as well. Almost 200 craft, tugs, schooners, and steamers were launched here, most of them in the last three decades of the nineteenth century.

Now Saugatuck, with a population of about 1,000 and Douglas, population 948, are primiarly centers for recreation, tourism, and summer homes.

Saugatuck Sites of Interest

A drive down Butler Street is rewarding for those who enjoy nineteenth-century architecture. The Village Hall, with a Michigan Historic Site marker commemorating the days of Singapore in front, the old storefronts, and the large, fine Greek Revival residence at 607 Butler Street are especially worthy of note. All Saint's Episcopal Church, at the corner of Hoffman and Grand Streets, three blocks from the downtown area, was built in 1873 and is a fine example of the Gothic style employed by Gordon W. Lloyd, one of the leading church architects of the

The S.S. Keewatin. *Photo by Margaret Bogue.*

late nineteenth century. A number of the older residences are restored and owned by artists. Saugatuck-Douglas have long been popular places of residence for landscape painters. The Ox-Bow Art School, founded in 1910, is one of the best-known summer art schools in the Midwest.

(1) Kalamazoo River Cruise
650 Water Street
A stern-wheeler, the *Queen of Saugatuck*, offers scenic Kalamazoo River cruises beginning in May. $

(2) Dune Rides
use exit 41 off Hy I-196
Dune "schooners" take visitors to the sand dune area of Lake Michigan's shoreline for 30–45 minute rides. May 1–Labor Day, Monday–Saturday, from 9:00 A.M.; Sundays from noon. $

Douglas Sites of Interest

(1) S.S. Keewatin
moored near Tower Marine, off the Blue Star Memorial Highway
The *S.S. Keewatin*, a luxury Great Lakes passenger liner built in Glasgow, Scotland, in 1907 for the Canadian Pacific Railroad, lies at anchor in the Kalamazoo River. From 1908 to 1965 it carried passengers and cargo between Port McNicoll on Georgian Bay and Thunder Bay on Lake Superior. Now a floating marine museum, the *S.S. Keewatin*, with its polished carved mahogany woodwork, shining brass, and red carpets, reflects the era when a cruise on the Great Lakes was a leisurely part of a transcontinental railroad travel. The luxury of such a cruise is still very evident to visitors. The vessel is 350 feet in length, almost 44 feet wide, and has a gross tonnage of 3,856. Guided tours take you to all decks, much of the interior, and the bridge. Tours daily, Memorial Day–Labor Day, 10:30 A.M.–4:30 P.M. $

(2) Boat Cruise
Tower Marine
A cruise service down the Kalamazoo River to Lake Michigan and Macatawa Bay is available. Daily, May–October. $

163. Allegan State Game Preserve

Hy M-89 off Hys I-196 and US-31 (BCFHP)

To reach the Allegan State Game Preserve take the Fennville exits off Hys I-196 and US-31, using Hy M-89 eastbound. The Michigan Department of Natural Resources created the game preserve in 1964 by combining the Allegan State Forest, the Swamp Creek Wildlife Experment Station, and the Fennville State Game Area. The game preserve, comprising 45,000 acres, offers a number of opportunites for recreation and nature study. Four camping areas, hiking trails, two swimming sites, and trails for snowmobiling, dog sledding, and cross-country skiing are designated. Those interested in nature study will enjoy bird watching, studying plants, trees, and wildflowers, and observing animal life. Public hunting is permitted under special restrictions. The wildlife refuge area along the Kalamazoo River must be respected by all visitors. A good place to begin your visit is the headquarters, located at 46th Street and 118th Avenue in the game preserve.

164. South Haven

Hys I-196 and US-31

While the first white settler arrived at the site of present day South Haven in 1831, not until the 1850s did an optimistic real estate promoter plat the village and not until 1869 was it formally incorporated. During the first fifty years of growth, South Haven developed with an economic life derived from its lake location and bountiful natural resources. The village grew as a sawmill town where logs floated down the Black River were sawed into lumber and loaded aboard ships bound for market. George Hannahs whose sawmill built in 1866 stood near the mouth of the river was the village's leading developer and lumberman. His mill and several others turned out millions of board feet of sawed lumber in the late nineteenth century.

Fishing in the lake's bountiful waters provided a living for some families. Ship building and shipping businesses formed another important part of the local economy. Initially shipbuilders launched lumber schooners and later steamers from the banks of the Black River. At the turn of the century the port bustled with vessels sailing between South Haven, Chicago, Milwaukee, and the ports along Lake Michigan's eastern shore carrying passengers and a wide variety of freight.

In the 1880s South Haven's residents discovered that Chicagoans enjoyed vacationing in the village with its beautiful stretch of lake beach and its surrounding fruit orchards where city dwellers could pick peaches. By the early 1900s, thousands came to stay in both large resort hotels and in residences turned into guest houses. The resort business boomed through the 1920s, dependent in large measure on comfortable and frequently scheduled passenger boat service with Chicago. South Haven achieved city status in 1902.

Meanwhile, the community earned a regional and national reputation for the fine fruit, especially peaches, shipped from its docks to Illinois and Wisconsin city markets, and by rail to more distant markets. A. S. Dykman is credited with planting the first commercial orchard before the Civil War. As lumbermen cleared more and more of the sandy land in the South Haven area, the fruit growing industry spread. Farmers of Van Buren County learned by 1850 that peaches did well relatively close to the lake, but winter-killed badly inland. Over the years fruit growing has expanded in importance, and so has South Haven's role in the growth of the Michigan fruit industry.

In the years 1924 through 1963, Michigan State University's Experiment Station located here led in the development of the Haven varieties of peaches so well adapted to the sandy soils of Michigan's fruit belt. These excellent commercial varieties of yellow free stone peaches ripen over a seven-week period in contrast to the usual three-week harvest period for peaches prior to development of the Haven varieties. The Experiment Station has also pioneered in the development of highbush blueberry varieties, the basis for Michigan's important blueberry growing industry. South Haven has a national blueberry festival every year in July.

Over the years the town has attracted industry. Two companies established in the late nineteenth century served the needs of fruit growers, one producing packaging for fruit, the other a cannery. Two piano factories, a woodworking plant, and several foundries opened business early in the twentieth century. Considerable industrial growth followed World War II. Currently South Haven's wide variety of industrial products includes pianos, gun stocks, agricultural machinery, chemicals, auto and truck motor castings and parts, and electronic coils. The 1980 population was 5,943.

South Haven Sites of Interest

(1) Liberty Hyde Bailey Memorial Museum

903 Bailey Avenue

South Haven is the birthplace of an internationally known botanist and horticulturist, Liberty Hyde Bailey. The home in which he was born in 1858 now houses the Bailey Memorial Museum. Bailey grew up in South Haven when the town was experiencing the lumbering boom. He received a degree from Michigan Agricultural College in 1882, later returned to its faculty, and then went to Cornell University as a professor of horticulture. Between 1903 and 1913 he served as dean of the New York State College of Agriculture at Cornell. He chaired Theodore Roosevelt's Country Life Commission. An author with 63 books to his credit, teacher, editor, and administrator, he gave national leadership to agricultural education and the improvement of farm life. This energetic son of South Haven died at the age of 96 in 1954.

The Bailey home. Photo by Margaret Bogue.

The house, built in the 1850s, is a state historic site containing a collection of Bailey's books on horticulture, many of the original Bailey household articles, collections of Indian artifacts, and nineteenth-century home furnishings and tools. Open year round, Tuesday and Friday, 2:00 P.M.–4:00 P.M. Closed on holidays. Free.

(2) Fruit Farms

Some fruit farms in the South Haven area welcome visitors. If you are interested in peach, blueberry, and apple production, the South Haven Chamber of Commerce at 535 Quaker Street will direct you to farms open to visitors.

The *National Blueberry Festival*, held each July, includes a wide variety of activities. Tours of blueberry farms are part of the program. Blueberry-harvesting and crop-dusting demonstrations are included.

(3) Scott Club

Phoenix and Pearl Streets

The Women's Literary Club, an organization similar to many such women's clubs in late nineteenth-century America, had this structure built in 1883 for the organization's meetings. It continues to be used for this purpose.

165. Van Buren State Park

County Road A2, Blue Star Memorial Highway from South Haven (CPS)

Although you can use Hy I-196 to drive from South Haven to Van Buren State Park, the Blue Star Memorial Highway is a more scenic route. The park is beautifully wooded, with sand dunes, a sandy Lake Michigan beach, and 205 campsites scattered over the 320-acre tract. $

Side Trip to Wolf Lake State Fish Hatchery and Paw Paw

Two important features of Lake Michigan's economic development are very well illustrated at the Wolf Lake State Fish Hatchery and at Paw Paw: fishing and fruit growing. Therefore, here a diversion inland from the shoreline is suggested.

166. Wolf Lake State Fish Hatchery

Hy M-43

Located three miles east of Armstrong Corners (intersection of Hys M-40 and M-43), the Interpretive Center at the Wolf Lake State Fish Hatchery is Michigan's best developed educational facility for people who want to learn about state fisheries' policies and management. The center contains displays on sport fishing, fish species in their underwater habitats, the history of commercial fishing, and the evolution of Michigan's fisheries management program. In the auditorium audio-visual programs explain the work of the hatchery and the routines of fish management.

The hatchery, with facilities capable of producing up to 150,000 pounds of trout and salmon and 50,000 pounds of warmwater fish, principally northern pike and tiger muskellunge, is a key facility in Michigan's efforts to revitalize stream and lake fisheries.

Inside the Michigan Fisheries Interpretive Center at Wolf Lake State Fish Hatchery. Courtesy Michigan Department of Natural Resources.

Vineyards in the Paw Paw area. Photo by Margaret Bogue.

While the building of the new facility at Wolf Lake began in 1980, the Wolf Lake Hatchery dates back to 1927 when the local chapter of the Isaac Walton League purchased 78 acres of land and donated it to the state of Michigan for a hatchery. Open year round, Wednesday–Friday, 9:00 A.M.–4:00 P.M.; Saturday, 9:00 A.M.–5:00 P.M.; Sunday, noon to 5:00 P.M. Free.

167. Paw Paw

Hy M-40

Either highways M-43 and M-40 from South Haven or highways I-94 and M-40 from St. Joseph and Benton Harbor will take you to Paw Paw, a village of 3,211 persons located about 25 miles inland from Lake Michigan. This village, in the very heart of Michigan's wine-producing region, is surrounded by well-tended vineyards. Because of the moderating influence of Lake Michigan and market demand, by 1899 the state of Michigan had emerged as the fifth-largest grape-growing state in the nation. At the time Van Buren and Berrien counties, the southernmost Michigan counties adjacent to the lake, produced over 60 precent of the state's grapes, and Van Buren, in which Paw Paw is located, far surpassed all Michigan counties in vines planted. By 1978 Van Buren and Berrien vineyards produced 92 percent of Michigan's grapes—108,740,520 pounds—approximately four times as many as in 1899. Michigan then ranked as the fourth-largest grape-producing state. Much of the grape harvest goes to local wineries. Paw Paw wineries welcome visitors to sample and buy their products.

168. St. Joseph and Benton Harbor

Hy US-33 and Business Route I-94

The geography of the St. Joseph River explains its long record of human use. It winds inland more than halfway across the Michigan lower peninsula, linking a vast hinterland with Lake Michigan. It also provides an entree into the Mississsippi River system via a short portage to the Kankakee River. The St. Joseph River formed part of a ready-made avenue for moving people and goods through thousands of miles of the mid-continent.

Prehistoric Indian peoples lived in the St. Joseph River Valley long before the coming of the French. The early explorers found the Miami and Potawatomi living near the mouth of the river, the site of present-day St. Joseph and Benton Harbor. An impressive list of Jesuit missionaries and French explorers frequented the St. Joseph, including Claude Allouez, Claude Dablon, and Jacques Marquette. La Salle waited here in vain for the first ship on the upper lakes, the *Griffon*, to appear with supplies in 1679. Here he erected Fort Miami.

Settlement of the village of St. Joseph began in the early 1830s. The village on the hill prospered as a transshipment point, especially after Congress began harbor improvements in 1835. It had served in this role during the era of the fur trade, but with the rapid movement of settlers into the upper Great Lakes, that role grew in importance. Incorportated as a village in 1834, St. Joseph became a busy port, receiving wheat, flour, pork, cranberries, wines, whiskey, lumber, and shingles from upstream for transfer onto lake boats bound for Chicago and elsewhere. Through St. Joseph's harbor passed necessities destined for the growing population centers of Kalamazoo, Niles, South Bend, and Elkhart. At the lakeport they were loaded onto river steamers, keel boats, and scows and moved upstream. Boat building, flour milling, and sawmilling were all businesses of early importance.

The opening of the territorial road from Detroit to St. Joseph in 1834 enhanced the volume of business at the port town. Many westward-bound immigrants used the road to get to St. Joseph, where they boarded boats for Chicago.

The commerical boom was short-lived, for in 1846 the Michigan legislature sold the Michigan Central Railroad to private interests that made New Buffalo the lake terminus. When the railroad was completed three years later, St. Joseph languished as a commercial center and New Buffalo boomed.

Sawmilling continued. Between the 1840s and 1880, sawmills at the mouth of the St. Joseph River turned out millions of board feet of lumber as well as shingles and thousands of railroad ties. Black walnut was one of the most valued products of southern Michigan's forests. One of the largest of the land and logging businesses was located on the site of present-day Benton Harbor.

For many years after the founding of St. Joseph on the hill, the site of Benton Harbor, low and swampy and lying across the river, boasted little more than a very successful tavern and hotel business catering to the territorial road traffic and a company store owned by the Britain lumber company. The village of Brunson Harbor was surveyed and platted in 1860 in the midst of a squabble between residents of opposite sides of the St. Joseph River over bridge building. Brunson Harbor (renamed Benton Harbor in 1865) resolved the problem by building a canal that gave the struggling swamp- and dune-logged town its own outlet into the St. Joseph River. Sawmilling constituted a major business at Benton Harbor until the mid-1880s, and it grew as a rowdy lumbertown and a shipping point for locally grown fruit.

The twin cities both benefited from the development of fruit growing on cutover land adjacent to Lake Michigan. Recognized throughout the settlement period as an area with a lake-tempered climate and soils well adapted to fruit growing, St. Joseph and Benton Harbor emerged in the late nineteenth century as a major national center for fruit production. Shipments of peaches, apples, pears, berries, and grapes in 1871 were already sizable. Fruit came downriver by boat and was transferred to lake boats bound for Chicago, Milwaukee, and other Lake Michigan ports. Over 1.5 million bushels of fruit went out of the St. Joseph–Benton Harbor port in 1916.

During the late nineteenth century, business leaders in both towns worked to attract new businesses as sawmills and woodenware factories closed. One of Benton Harbor's founders put his capital into a lake passenger and freight-shipping line. Another discovered mineral waters at a depth of 1,500 feet and developed a hotel and health spa. St. Joseph managed to attract a knitting mill in 1878 and in

1894 to recapture the county seat, which it had lost to Berrien Springs in 1838. The transition to industrial activity went slowly during the late nineteenth and early twentieth centuries, but made more rapid strides during World War I and the 1920s.

Meanwhile the towns developed a reputation as excellent vacation spots. They flourished on vacation and tourist trade in the early 1900s, attracting Chicagoans who paid a modest 50 cents for a round trip on a lake steamer. When Benjamin Purnell established the House of David religious community at Benton Harbor in 1903, he became the town benefactor. Purnell had a keen eye for business and developed a miniature railroad and amusement park, plus a long-haired baseball team, which brought hundreds of thousands of tourist dollars to the town.

Today St. Joseph and Benton Harbor are still known for their vineyards, orchards, and berry fields and their annual blossom festival, but they are predominantly industrial towns. The twin cities have 24 industrial plants employing more than 100 people each and four plants employing more than 900 workers each. The largest plants produce earth-moving equipment, automobile parts, and major home appliances. Metal castings, electronic products, plastics, industrial components, canned goods, metal cans, and a wide variety of finished consumer goods are also important products of twin-city industry. Benton Harbor is the more heavily industrialized of the two towns. In 1980 St. Joseph's population was 9,622, and Benton Harbor's 14,707.

Relations between St. Joseph and Benton Harbor have changed remarkably over the years. The fist fights, the free-for-alls at baseball games, the rough-and-tumble fights between ice skaters on the St. Joseph, the quarrels over bridges, canals, and river channel improvements, have all subsided. St. Joseph's citizens no longer refer to Benton Harbor as "Bungtown." Cooperation has replaced rivalry.

The two cities present a marked contrast in physical appearance. St. Joseph looks reasonably prosperous, while Benton Harbor's downtown area is empty and characterized by run-down, boarded-up buildings. In immediately adjacent residential areas, fine old houses are deteriorating.

House of David Baseball Players. From the Collections of the Michigan State Archives, Department of State 05228

Benton Harbor Sites of Interest

(1) Shiloh House*

Britain Road

Shiloh House serves as the administration building and dormitory for members of the House of David colony. The structure was built in 1910 from concrete blocks produced by colony workers. Benjamin Purnell founded the House of David in 1903 as a communal religious group in the tradition of the teachings of its founder, Joanna Southcott, an Englishwoman who attracted a following of 100,000 before her death in 1814. Of the seven angelic messengers recognized by the cult, Benjamin Purnell was the seventh, the king of the Israelites. Purnell was a very controversial leader with good business judgment and the ability to attract a devoted and loyal following. He chose a tract of farmland outside Benton Harbor as the site for his colony. Here the group, holding all property in common, developed a farm, an amusement park, a very successful, unique baseball team, and a band. When Purnell died in 1927, in the midst of a sensational court case involving the colony's sex mores, the group split into two factions but both remained at Benton Harbor. They ceased to go out and make converts, as they had in Purnell's day. Consequently their numbers have dwindled over the years. In 1973 there were still 99 members, but their ranks are currently far fewer.

(2) Morton House
501 Territorial Road
Built in 1849 by Eleazar Morton, the enterprising New Englander who had earlier built a log tavern on the territorial road below the hill, this historic house is now the property of the Benton Harbor Federation of Women's Clubs and a Michigan Historic Site. The Morton family occupied the home until 1936. Although the building has been radically changed since its erection in 1849, the original heavy oak timber frame and many of the wide, heavy planks used originally continue to make it a very sturdy structure. At the owner's invitation, Potawatomi Indians often slept on the porch when they traveled to St. Joseph to sell baskets. The barn, a heavy oak-framed structure built in 1840, was moved three times before coming to rest at its present location. The house is now the museum of the Fort Miami Heritage Society. Open mid-April–October, Thursday, 1:00–4:00 P.M., and Sunday, 2:00–4:00 P.M.

(3) Sarett Nature Center
2300 Benton Center Road
This 300-acre wildlife sanctuary, with a two-mile frontage on the Paw Paw River, contains rolling meadows, woodland, a swamp forest, a remnant bog, and a sedge meadow. A variety of small mammals, 180 species of birds, and many varieties of plants, including several protected species, are among its natural assets. Three miles of raised trails with observation platforms and a self-guiding loop trail pass through lowland and upland communites. The Nature Center's interpretive building overlooks the marsh. Here specially scheduled classes, films, slide shows, lectures, and workshops are offered, often on Saturdays and Sundays. Open Tuesday–Saturday, 10:00 A.M.–5:00 P.M.; Sunday, 1:00–5:00 P.M. Public program at 2:00 P.M. every Sunday. Naturalist-led tours by appointment. Closed December 22–January 2. Otherwise open year round. Donation.

(4) The Fruit Market
1891 Territorial Road
The surrounding fruit farms have been of great importance to Benton Harbor's economic life for more than a century. The market, once located downtown, is now situated two miles east of town. It serves small growers primarily, since larger growers now sell directly from the farm. Benton Harbor's fruit Market grew from the times of wagons, buggies, oxcarts, and sailing vessels through the era of steamships, railroads, and finally truck transportation. By the 1940s the market had earned the reputation of being the largest cash-to-grower market in the United States. Sales at the market in 1974 grossed over $7 million. At nearby Sodus millions of pounds of fruit are processed and shipped annually.

St. Joseph Sites of Interest

(1) Lake Boulevard Park Area fronting on Lake Michigan
Here, in this well-kept park overlooking Lake Michigan, the St. Joseph River, and many of St. Joseph's and Benton Harbor's industrial plants, stand a number of monuments to the past.

La Salle Marker
A simple stone, with a bronze plaque, reminds the reader of the La Salle expedition, which reached the mouth of the St. Joseph River in 1679.

Fort Miami Marker
The marker recounts the experience of La Salle, who waited here in the late fall of 1679 for the *Griffon* to arrive with its supplies and reinforcements. He had Fort Miami erected more than a decade before the construction of Fort St. Joseph upstream near Niles.

"Maids of the Mist" Fountain
The fountain stands near the Fort Miami marker and reflects another era in St. Joseph's history—the 1890s. St. Joseph received a city charter in 1892 after a prolonged battle in the state legislature over whether there should be one charter for St. Joseph and Benton Harbor or two separate ones. This romantic Victorian fountain dates from

"Maids of the Mist" fountain. Photo by Margaret Bogue.

1892 and reflects civic pride in St. Joseph's city status. It was restored and dedicated July 4, 1974, by the city of St. Joseph and the Fort Miami Heritage Society.

(2) Burnett's Post Site
Miller Drive and Langley Avenue
Here a Michigan Historic Site marker calls the viewer's attention to the career of William Burnett, an American fur trader who erected a trading post on the St. Joseph River during the years of the American Revolution. Some local histories cite Burnett as the first settler at St. Joseph.

(3) St. Joseph Business District
Broad and State Streets
Those who are interested in historic preservation will enjoy looking at the older buildings in the St. Joseph business district. One interesting example is the Troost Brothers Furniture and Carpet store at Broad and State streets, which is housed in a very well maintained turn-of-the-century structure.

169. Berrien Springs
Hys I-94, US-31, and US-33

The town of Berrien Springs dates from the 1830s, when settlers pressed into lower Michigan via the Erie Canal, Lake Erie, and recently established federal roads. They came in search of greater opportunity in a newly opened region. At Berrien Springs three early comers decided they had found it and platted the village in 1831. Lying on a territorial road from Niles to St. Joseph and on the St. Joseph River, Berrien Springs prospered initially because of its transportation advantages. Keelboats and steamers frequented its dock, and stagecoaches and assorted vehicles of westbound migrants rumbled into town. Berrien Springs managed to wrest the county seat from St. Joseph in 1838. In 1839 a beautiful Greek Revival courthouse was completed.

Berrien Springs' great expectations for the future were dampened when main transportation routes passed it by. Once the Michigan Central Railroad was completed, terminating at New Buffalo in 1849, the road and river traffic diminished. The town received no railroad connection until 1880. It functioned mainly as an agricultural service center and seat of county government.

Here a group of Shakers purchased a farm in 1860 and developed a commercial seed business. In 1894 Berrien Springs lost the county seat to St. Joseph, but a few years later, in 1901, the town rejoiced in the decision of the Seventh Day Adventists to move their college here from Battle Creek. The institution has grown over the years, reconstituting itself as Andrews University in 1960. It has been important to the town's economic life.

With the spread of the urban-industrial complex on Lake Michigan's southern shore, Berrien Springs has attracted some small industry. In the late 1970s three firms employed more than 100 workers each: a casting corporation, a wire-manufacturing plant, and the wooden household-furniture enterprise of Andrews University. The current population is about 2,000.

Berrien Springs' lively interest in preserving its past is expressed in the effort to restore the County Courthouse and surrounding buildings as a historical complex.

Berrien Springs Sites of Interest

(1) Old Berrien County Courthouse*
Gilbert Avery, a local master builder, designed this Greek Revival structure in 1838. It is now used as a museum. On the first floor are exhibits interpreting local history from the era of the fur trade through nineteenth-century pioneering. The courtroom on the second floor has been restored to its 1839 appearance. The Berrien County Historical Association, which administers the site, is in the process of restoring an

adjacent log cabin, built in the 1830s by Francis Murdock, the first practicing lawyer in Berrien County. Official Michigan Historic Site markers are found in front of the courthouse. Open all year, Tuesday–Friday, 9:00 A.M.–4:00 P.M.; Saturday and Sunday, 1:00–5:00 P.M. Free.

(2) Andrews University
When the Seventh Day Adventist College at Battle Creek decided to relocate at Berrien Springs to make room for its expanding student population, the people of Berrien Springs were delighted. The school's first year at the new location created a bustle of activity as the old courthouse and all the other county buildings were turned over for the use of the newly named Emmanuel Missionary College. Students and faculty boarded around town and in an old hotel that was floated down the St. Joseph River and fitted up for living quarters. From this lively beginning the school grew, developing its own campus, which now extends over 1,300 acres. In 1960 the Graduate School and the Adventists' Theological Seminary were moved to Emmanuel from Washington, D.C., and the name of the institution was changed to Andrews University in honor of a pioneer in the Adventist movement. A Michigan Historical Site marker stands on the campus.

170. Niles

Hys US-31 and US-33, 10 miles beyond Berrien Springs

The site of present-day Niles held great importance for the Indian peoples of the upper Great Lakes and for the French, the British, and the Americans who came afterward. At this site on the St. Joseph River, Indian trails of major importance converged. One was the Sauk trail, running from Detroit to Chicago. Another, the Kankakee trail, led south to a portage between the St. Joseph and Kankakee rivers. That route connected the St. Joseph River with the Mississsippi via the Kankakee and the Illinois. The site of Niles lay at the convergence of major east-west and north-south water and land routes at the southern end of Lake Michigan.

Because of its strategic location, the site of Niles played an important role in the plans of the French missionaries, explorers, and fur traders. La Salle chose the mouth of the St. Joseph River as a site for a fort in 1679, but that site was soon abandoned. In 1691 the French, seeking to establish their authority among the Miami and the Potawatomi and to control the fur trade, chose another location 25 miles upstream. There they erected Fort St. Joseph at the site of present-day Niles. Here, for the next 70 years, save for two brief periods when the fort was not officially garrisoned, the French sought to further the cause of empire and the fur trade. The Jesuits had established a mission in the same vicinity in the 1680s. Claude Allouez is often cited as its founder. As late as 1773 Jesuit priests carried on their work among the Indians from the mission at Fort St. Joseph.

In 1761, at the end of the French and Indian War, Fort St. Joseph was occupied by the British. Indians participating in Pontiac's rebellion against British authority in 1763 captured the fort and held it for two years. Ungarrisoned at the outbreak of the American Revolution, Fort St. Joseph became the object of thrusts and counterthrusts. Apparently uncertain of their loyalties, the British removed most of the resident civilian population to Mackinac. A French raiding party and later a Spanish raiding party made Fort St. Joseph their objective in 1780 and 1781. The Spanish flag flew over the fort for a few hours. Here lies the origin of Nile's nickname, "the city of four flags."

Fur trading continued at this location throughout the revolutionary period and well into the nineteenth century. Although the area became American territory in 1783 under the Treaty of Paris, some British fur traders stayed. Strife between British and American traders in the St. Joseph River Valley was very pronounced until after the War of 1812. Missionary activity also continued. Catholic missionaries frequented the Niles area, and in 1822 Isaac McCoy, a Baptist, opened a mission to the Potawatomi.

The village of Niles took shape in the 1820s as a few settlers filtered in from the east and settled near McCoy's mission (known as the Carey mission). By 1829, sensing that the time was right for town site speculation, several of the early comers platted Niles, naming it for Hezekiah Niles, Baltimore editor of the nationally prominent *Niles Weekly Register*. On a major overland trail and a navigable river with the only fording point for some miles, Niles's prospects looked good.

In the land and settlement boom of the 1830s, Niles grew as an important stop on the newly built Chicago Road, which linked Detroit with Chicago. The Michigan Central Railroad from Detroit reached Niles in 1848, and by 1853 had connected it with Chicago.

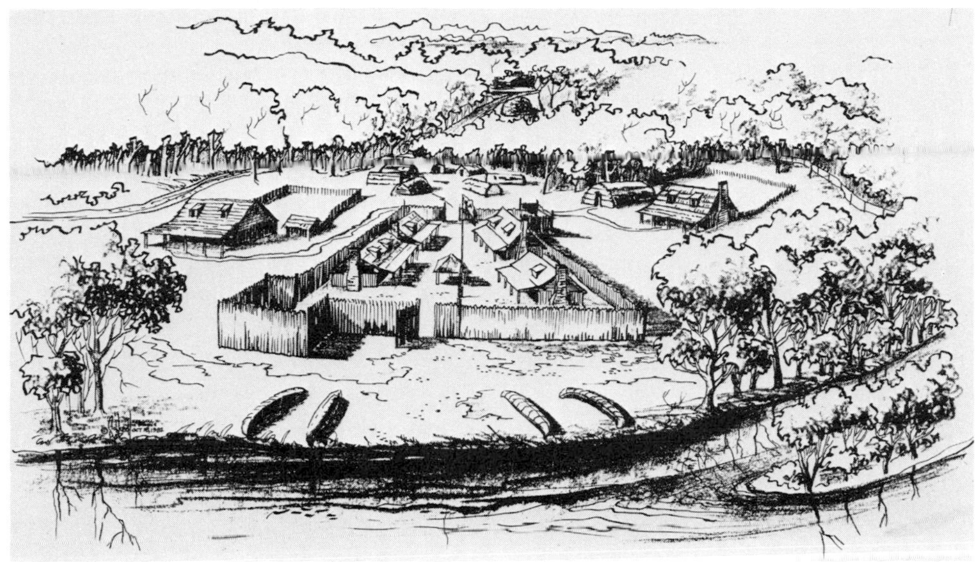

This drawing of what Fort St. Joseph must have looked like was prepared in 1982 to accompany a plan to replicate the original. The site of the old French fort now lies in the St. Joseph River bed. Plans call for construction on a site adjacent to the original location. The artist is G. N. Schlundt. Courtesy G. N. Schlundt, Dowagiac, Michigan.

Niles still lay on a major transportation route.

During the nineteenth century Niles remained a trading and service center for the surrounding farm community with a wide variety of small manufacturing establishments. One of the earliest was boat building, which utilized local timber resources. Here lake schooners were built and floated down the St. Joseph River for service on Lake Michigan. Grain milling grew to importance in the late nineteenth century. In 1872 the Michigan Wood Pulp Company began operations. It is the predecessor of the present-day French Paper Company. Furniture manufacturing also became an important Niles industry.

But try as the town's businessmen did to attract new industry, Niles lost poulation between 1870 and 1910. Since World War I, Niles has had better luck in attracting new business, and the town has grown. Now over 50 firms manufacture products from frozen foods to tools and dies. While most of these firms employ less than 100 people, the two largest companies have over 900 workers each. One produces specialized wire and machinery, and the other paper dress patterns. The current population of the Niles is about 13,000.

Niles is conscious of the famous people associated with it. These nationally prominent sons include Aaron Montgomery Ward, the Dodge Brothers (John and Horace), and Ring Lardner, the early twentieth-century journalist and humorist. Niles is also conscious of its history and shows an increasing interest in historic preservation.

Niles Sites of Interest

The best place to begin your tour of Niles is at the Fort St. Joseph Museum, described below. Here you can get a good overview of the area's history from many excellent displays. The museum also has a number of inexpensive publications about Niles history. Especially useful is the Heritage Tour Committee's driving tour guide, "19th Century Architecture of Niles, Michigan," prepared for use during the annual Four Flags Area Apple Festival. Illustrated, the booklet has annotated entries on 50 locations and a keyed map to help find them. It is more than a record of nineteenth-century architecture, for it includes most sites of historical interest for all periods.

(1) Fort St. Joseph Museum

508 East Main Street

The museum building is a carriage house and boiler house built in 1882 for the use of the Chapin family who lived in the lavish adjacent Victorian structure (now the Niles City Hall). The museum, a Michigan Historic Site, contains displays on the French fur traders and missionaries and the Potawatomi Indians, most of the artifacts recovered from Fort St. Joseph, a large collection of Sioux Indian beadwork,

The Henry A. Chapin home, now Niles City Hall. Photo by Margaret Bogue.

some unusual Sioux pictography, and artifacts of the early settlers who came to Niles from New England and New York. Open all year, Tuesday–Saturday, 10:00 A.M.–4:00 P.M.; Sunday, 1:00–4:00 P.M. Free.

(2) Niles City Hall
adjacent to museum
This unusual Queen Anne–style home was designed by Wheelock and Clay, Chicago architects, as the home of Henry A. Chapin and was built in 1882 and 1883. Chapin was an extremely successful businessman who had come to Niles in the late 1830s and opened a dry goods store. His successful career in banking, industry, insurance, and real estate received a boost when he acquired a piece of wild, undeveloped property in the Michigan Upper Peninsula at present-day Iron Mountain. Ultimately the property became the site of the Chapin Mine, a very large and productive iron mine (see site 85).

The Chapin family home became the property of the city of Niles in 1932. Since 1933 it has been used as the city administrative building. The interior is lavishly decorated with carved woodwork, French plate-glass mirrors, leaded stained glass, and stenciled ceilings. City Hall is open Monday–Friday, and visitors interested in the home's architecture and history are welcome.

(3) Trinity Church
4th and Broadway
Trinity Church is the oldest remaining church building in Niles. The church was constructed in 1858 in rural English Gothic style replacing a frame structure built in 1836. It served a parish in the Episcopal Diocese of Western Michigan. The parish was organized in 1834 when Niles was still a small village.

(4) Site of Fort St. Joseph* and Grave of Father Claude Allouez
Fort and Bond Streets
On the banks of the St. Joseph River is a stone marker indicating what is believed to be the original site of Fort St. Joseph, built in 1691. Plans have been developed for a million-dollar replication of Fort St. Joseph. Stairs to the right of the boulder lead to what many believe to be the grave of Father Claude Allouez in the Jesuit mission cemetery. The stone cross was erected in 1918 in memory of his pioneer mission work. He died in 1689.

(5) Riding Tour of Niles Historic Homes
The city of Niles contains many fine nineteenth-century homes, churches, business, and public buildings illustrating a variety of architectural styles. Greek Revival is well represented, as are Italianate, Gothic, and Queen Anne. To fully appreciate this architectural wealth, secure a copy of "19th Century Architecture of Niles, Michigan" (see above) and take the tour. Some of the highlights are listed below.

At 552 Grant Street is a stone house in the Italian Villa style. It was built in 1851. At 553 Grant Street is a board and batten Gothic house, built of tulipwood in 1851. The George H. Rough Home (2685 Chicago Road), a Victorian Italianate structure made of brick, was built in 1875 as the farm dwelling of a country gentleman. At 1509 Bond Street is a white clapboard Greek Revival house built in 1847.

The Ring Lardner House* (519 Bond Street) was built by an early Niles banker. This is where Lardner grew up. The original front veranda has been removed. It is believed to be the the first Gothic Revival house in Niles.

The Paine Bank* (1008 Oak Street) has been cited as a fine example of commercial Greek Revival architecture. The building was nearly destroyed in 1961 to make way for a parking lot. Mrs. Virgil Sherer, a Niles resident deeply interested in historic preservation, paid to have the structure moved here from its original location at Main and 3rd streets.

171. Bridgman

Hy I-94

Beginning in the 1850s and continuing until about 1870, lumbering businesses developed along the Lake Michigan shoreline from Bridgman south to Union Pier. Largest of all was the Charlotteville Lumber Company at Bridgman. Two miles south were the mill and pier of the Painterville Lumber Company. Two piers were built at Warren Dunes Park, where a horse-drawn railway hauled lumber from nearby mills to lake boats. The nearby town of Sawyer is named for Silas Sawyer, who developed it as a mill town. Lakeside and Union Pier both had 600-foot piers that furnished lumber and cordwood to Chicago-bound schooners.

Flagstone terrace facing Lake Michigan, Donald C. Cook Nuclear Center. Photo by Margaret Bogue.

The town of Bridgman was platted in 1870 by George Bridgman, one of the owners of the Charlotteville Lumber Company. The town grew very slowly until the 1920s. By 1949 it qualified as a city. The building of the Donald C. Cook Nuclear plant in 1968 brought another surge of growth. Currently it has 14 manufacturing plants that produce a variety of products, including metal die castings, engine parts, and specialized machinery. The two largest employers have between 200 and 300 persons on the payroll. The city's population is about 2,200.

Donald C. Cook Nuclear Center
Located on a high bluff overlooking Lake Michigan, the Nuclear Center is an educational facility that explains the nuclear plant owned and operated by the Indiana and Michigan Electric Company. Three theaters offer audiovisual programs that (1) trace the history of energy use from early times to the nuclear age; (2) explain how the nuclear plant generates electrical power using a scale model; and (3) relate energy use to the environment. The theaters are housed in an attractive modern visitors' center that provides outdoor picnic facilites as well. Closed for reasons of economy in 1982, it reopened in 1984. The approximate visitors' schedule is as follows; January–May, Monday–Friday, 10:00 A.M.–5:00 P.M.; June–September, Wednesday–Saturday, 10:00 A.M.–5:00

Dunegrass at Warren Dunes State Park. Photo by Margaret Bogue.

P.M., and Sundays, 11:00 A.M.–5:00 P.M.; October–November, Monday–Friday, 10:00 A.M.–5:00 P.M. Closed in December and on holidays. Free.

172. Warren Dunes State Park

Hy I-94 (CHPS)

Scenic wooded dunes, a sandy Lake Michigan beach, and over 190 campsites are among the special features of this 1,500-acre park. Next to Holland State Park, it is the most heavily used of all of Michigan's state parks.

Those interested in Michigan's natural heritage will want to visit the adjacent Warren Woods, which is under the jurisdiction of the park ranger. The Warren Woods is a 200-acre stand of virgin timber that has been designated a Registered Natural Landmark by the U.S. Department of the Interior. Some of the trees are 5 feet in diameter and 125 feet tall. Here stands the largest known beech tree in the United States. For directions to the Warren Woods, inquire at Warren Dunes State Park.

173. New Buffalo

Hy I-94 or Red Arrow Highway and Hy US-12

If on your way to New Buffalo you would like to get a close look at a vineyard, leave Hy I-94 at the Sawyer exit (exit 12) and follow the Red Arrow Highway south. Just north of Harbert you will see vinyards very close to the road. This is a good place to visit a winery if you are interested in learning about wine production. There is one at the Lakeside Vineyard.

The promoters of New Buffalo hoped that their town site would be exactly what its name said when they platted the town in the midst of the financial boom and the land-speculating mania of the 1830s. They even dreamed that it would become a great lakeport, greater than Chicago. The village was organized in 1836, but during the panic of 1837 it was virtually deserted.

When the Michigan Central Railroad completed its line to New Buffalo in 1849, the town took on new life. For three years it bustled with activity as westward-bound Michigan Central passengers boarded company-operated ships here for the last leg of their trip to Chicago. When in 1853 the Michigan Central acquired rail access to Chicago, New Buffalo again became a very quiet village. It remained small until about the turn of the century, when Chicago residents wanting to get out of the city in the hot summer months began building summer cottages and summer camps in the New Buffalo area. A similar development took place in this area all the way from Michiana to Union Pier. At New Buffalo the Pere Marquette Railroad built a 56-room luxury hotel in the 1920s.

The town grew especially after World War II. Currently, New Buffalo has a dozen industries, the two largest of which employ between 100 and 200 workers each and produce metal castings and molded plastic products. The harbor was developed during the 1970s as a refuge harbor. Much of the town's business activity relates to tourism, recreation, and summer homes. The 1980 population was 2,820.

174. Michigan City

Hy US-12

Michigan City originated from Indiana's desire for a commercial port on Lake Michigan. The state legislature had a port city in mind when in 1828 it laid plans to construct the Michigan Road. Designed to run from the Ohio River north to the Lake Michigan shore, the road's northern terminus was chosen after a search of the shoreline for the best harbor. The legislature's selection of the site of Michigan City marked the beginning of the town.

Laid out by a town site speculator in 1832, one year before completion of the Michigan Road to the lake, Michigan City developed as a commercial center during the boom years of the 1830s, spurred on by a federal appropriation for harbor improvements. Boosters presented a town lot to Daniel Webster, who appeared, spoke, and never returned. The town grew as a point of export for farm produce, especially wheat, as a supply center for the surrounding countryside, and as a stopping place for westbound travelers.

When the panic of 1837 slowed Michigan City's growth, the town did not collapse and disappear as did many towns of the decade. It grew slowly in the 1840s, continuing in the role of commercial center for the area. Lake boats brought necessities not made locally and took aboard corn, wheat, pork, beef, and fish bound for markets east and west. The town's population in the 1840s was about 1,000.

In Michigan City's formative years, the bountiful fish in Lake Michigan's waters provided a living for many families. Although commercial fishing remained important throughout the nineteenth century, the whitefish harvest here was greatest in 1856 and 1857.

The pattern of lake trade established in the 1840s changed dramatically with the coming of the railroads in the 1850s. The Michigan Central Railroad built a line to Michigan City in 1850, and soon thereafter the Monon (named for the Indiana town of its origins) reached town, providing a north-south connection. Thereafter, trains carried goods to Michigan City and hauled most local produce. Boat traffic at the port declined.

The economic life of Michigan City also changed. Manufacturing began to develop in the 1850s and grew in importance during the balance of the nineteenth century. The industry that dominated the town, the construction of freight cars, was founded here in 1852. At the end of the Civil War, the company produced two cars per day; by 1908 output had reached 15,000 cars per year. In 1922 the multimillion-dollar business merged with the Pullman Palace Car Company.

Meanwhile smaller manufacturing establishments producing a wide range of products developed at Michigan City. Factories turned out wire, agricultural implements, clothing, bricks, beer, engines, and wood products in the late nineteeth century. Factory jobs attracted immigrant workers, who changed Michigan City from a Yankee town into a town of ethnic diversity. Germans, Swedes, and Norwegians settled here, and by the turn of the century, many immigrants from eastern Europe, especially Poland, had swelled the labor force. Much of the late nineteenth-century industrial success of Michigan City stemmed from the fact that in 1858 the town became the site of the Northern Indiana Prison. Some of the new industries used prison labor under contract with the state for a great saving in labor costs.

By the turn of the century, Michigan City had become a resort as well as a manufacturing center. Chicago residents came by the boatload to stay at cottages and hotels and to enjoy the Lake Michigan beach.

Today diversified industries remain the key to the city's economy. Eighteen of the city's plants employ more than 100 workers each. They produce finished consumer goods, automobile components, plumbing and drainage products, instruments and equipment for industrial use, and concrete anchors. Tourism and recreation are also important. The town's official bumper sticker reads, "Coho Capital." Even a casual look at the extensive fleet of pleasure craft in the harbor reveals the local importance of sport fishing and boating on Lake Michigan. The 1980 population was 36,850.

One prominent natural landmark at Michigan City, the Hoosier Slide, a

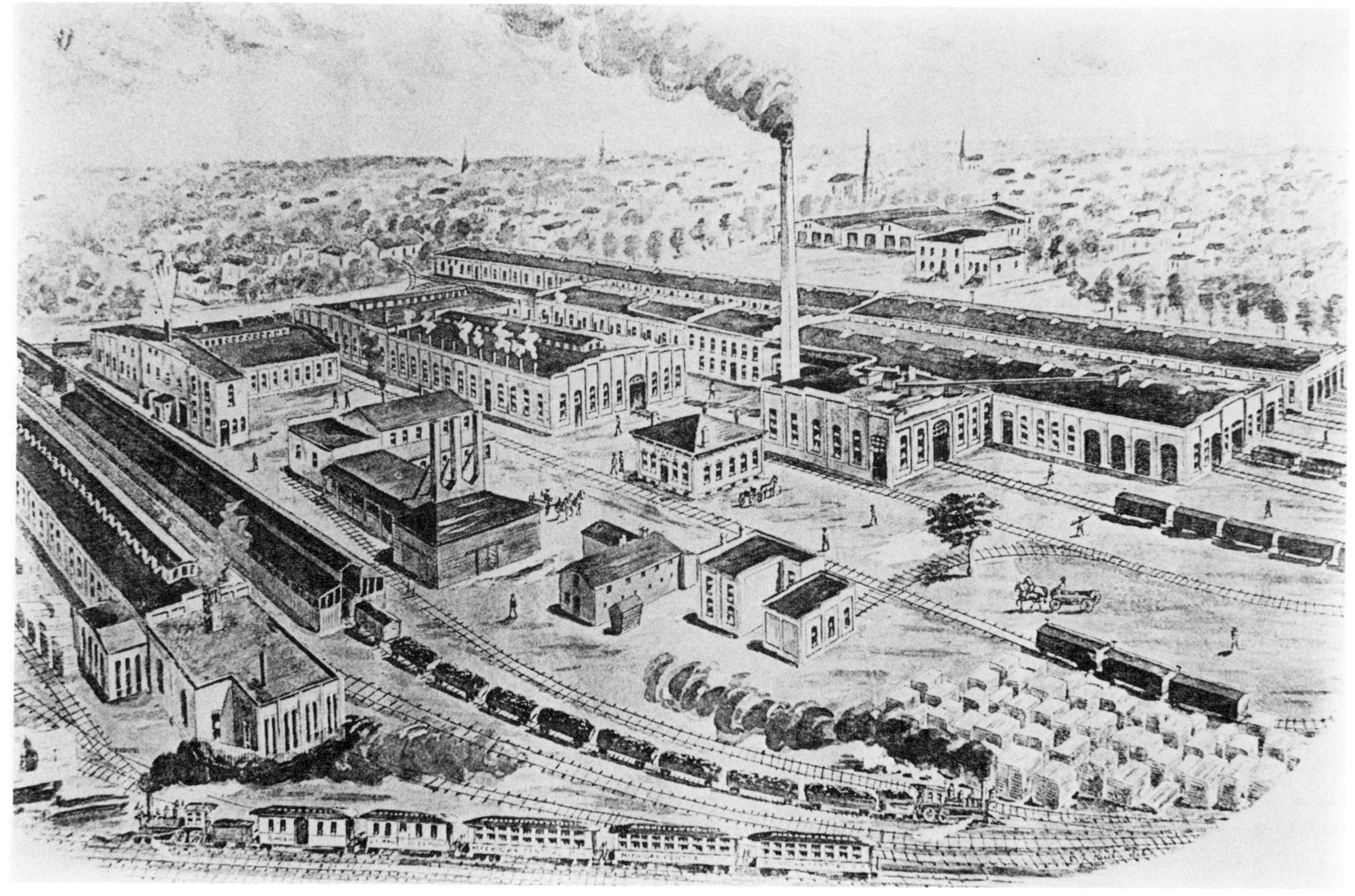

The Haskell and Barker Car Company, for many years Michigan City's most important industry. Courtesy of the CETA History Project and The News Dispatch *of Michigan City, Indiana.*

very large dune that always attracted the attention of visitors, has disappeared. It was leveled for industrial purposes. It used to stand where the Northern Indiana Public Serivce Company (NIPSCO) utility tower, the dominant feature of the city skyline, now stands.

Michigan City Sites of Interest

(1) Old Lighthouse* and Washington Park

off Hy US-12

In Washington Park, fronting on Lake Michigan, stands the Old Lighthouse, built by the federal government in 1858. The structure was remodeled in 1904, electrified in 1933, and retired from use in 1960. Harriet E. Colfax was tender of the light from 1853 to 1904. Now maintained by the Old Lighthouse Museum Historical Society, the museum contains displays on the history of the lighthouse and Michigan City. The keeper's living room and bedroom are furnished. Maritime displays include stories of local shipwrecks, shipbuilding tools, and on the outside grounds, a number of maritime artifacts. Open all year

The Old Lighthouse. Photo by Margaret Bogue.

Tuesdays–Sundays, 1:00–4:00 P.M. Closed Mondays and Holidays. $

While visiting the museum, take a stroll to the adjacent harbor and see the extensive fleet of pleasure craft nearby. The marina is a city-owned facility.

The memorial at the entrance to Washington Park is a monument to Civil War soldiers. The 90-acre park includes Lake Michigan beaches, a wooded picnic area, a small zoo, and a bandshell.

(2) First Congregational Church
6th and Washington Streets
Michigan City has a number of fine old churches. Among them is the First Congregational Church, built in 1881 in Gothic style. A fire in 1907 destroyed much of the interior, but the exterior has had only minor alterations. The bell is believed to be the bell placed in Michigan City's Congregational Mission Church in 1843. The Congregationalists were the third denomination to organize in Michigan City during the 1830s.

(3) The Barker Civic Center–John H. Barker Mansion*
631 Washington Street
This impressive residence was completed in 1905 for John H. Barker, Jr., a Michigan City industrialist who for years headed the Haskell and Barker Company, which manufactured railroad freight cars. The Barker family had invested in the firm in the 1850s and played an increasingly important role in its affairs in the late nineteenth century. John H. Barker, Jr., became general manager of the company in 1869 and president in 1883.

At the turn of the century, he decided to enlarge his residence with the help of a Chicago architect, Frederick Perkins. Perkins' design, inspired by an English manor house, included a very lavish interior. Imported furniture, art objects, hand-carved marble fireplaces, and teak, walnut, and mahogany woodwork enhance the foyer, library, drawing room, and dining room on the first floor. On the second are bedrooms, a morning room, and bathrooms. The third floor contained a ballroom, the Barker daughter's schoolroom, and her governess's quarters. Catherine Barker Hickox, daughter of John H. Barker, Jr., presented the mansion to the city in 1968, properly restored and containing most of its original furnishings. The home contains 38 rooms, 7 fireplaces, and 10 bathrooms. Outside is a walled Italianate formal garden. Now used as a civic center, the mansion is open for tours year round, Monday–Friday, 10:00 A.M.–3:00 P.M.; also open on Saturday and Sunday, noon–2:00 P.M., June 1–October 31. $

(4) Franklin Square Mall Area
9th and Franklin Streets
Michigan City contains a wealth of older buildings, many constructed of local red brick. A visit to the Franklin Square Mall area is a good way to see some of these. St. Paul's Lutheran Church, at the corner of 9th and Franklin streets, underwent restoration in 1979. An impressive Gothic structure built in 1875–1876, it served one of the two downtown Lutheran congregations. St. Paul's was organized in 1875 as a result of a split in the congregation of the Union Evangelical Lutheran Church over doctrinal matters.

On the corner diagonally across the street stands what used to be St. John's Evangelical Lutheran Church, built in 1867. Now minus the steeple, it serves as a community theater, the Canterbury. At the rear of the theater, a nineteenth-century red brick Italianate structure, built in 1882 as a parochial school for St. John's German-speaking congregation, has been adapted for use as a restaurant.

A leisurely drive through the city streets adjacent to the downtown area reveals many nineteenth-century residences. They range from workers' very modest homes to the spacious and elegant homes of the town's successful industrialists, businessmen, and professionals.

(5) St. Stanislaus Kostka Catholic Church

Ann and Washington Streets

The cornerstone for this muted red brick, stone-trimmed Romanesque church was laid in 1916. The church was built to serve the spiritual needs of Michigan City's immigrant Polish population. The Poles came to Michigan City early in the twentieth century in search of industrial jobs. They formed their own church, separate from St. Mary's, the cosmopolitan Catholic church founded at Michigan City in 1836 as a mission. The church is named for the courageous eleventh-century bishop of Cracow who excommunicated his prince. In retaliation, Prince Boleslaus II murdered the bishop during the celebration of the mass.

175. Indiana Dunes National Lakeshore and Indiana Dunes State Park

Hy US-12

The sand dunes lying between Michigan City and Gary formed part of Indiana's last area to attract population, the Calumet region. (For an overview of the Calumet's history, see p. 349). In the early twentieth century, industry at Gary on the west and at Michigan City on the east hemmed in these dunes. The remaining island of untamed wilderness seemed destined to disappear into the growing urban-industrial complex. Given its proximity to Chicago, to the lake, and to railroad lines, the dune country offered an ideal location for further industrial expansion. But conservationists and nature lovers interceded to prevent all of it from being leveled for industrial sites.

The Prairie Club of Chicago, an organization of nature lovers that included Jane Addams, Jens Jensen, and Carl Sandburg, spearheaded efforts to arouse public interest in conserving the dunes in 1913. A National Dunes Park Association was organized in 1916 to prevent sand companies from leveling some of the best of the dunes to obtain fill for Chicago. At a spectacular meeting that included three trainloads of concerned Chicagoans, the group organized at Waverly Beach. The membership proposed to purchase land and turn it over to the federal government for a national park.

The National Dunes Park Association interested the Department of the Interior in the project, but unfortunately opposition developed locally from business interests fearing that this project would end industrial development in the region. Some locals resisted because they predicted the loss of tax revenue.

At this point, in 1917, the Prairie Club of Chicago staged an elaborate historical pageant near Waverly Beach, "The Dunes Under Four Flags." The effort helped the cause, but local opposition and America's entrance into World War I stalled the national park idea. Conservationist forces turned to the idea of a state park.

Fearing that Hy US-12, the Dunes Highway from Gary to Michigan City, completed in 1923, would spoil chances for a park, park advocates increased pressure on the state legislature. A 1923 law imposed a state tax to raise funds to buy three miles of lakeshore dune land for a state park. The project got enough financial help from citizen contributions to make the land purchase in 1927. Large donors included Elbert H. Gary of the U.S. Steel Corporation, Julius Rosenwald of Sears and Roebuck, and Samuel Insull, Jr., the public utilities magnate who controlled the South Shore Line, which today runs through the dune area. The land for the 3.5-square-mile Indiana Dunes State Park cost about a million dollars.

After a half-century of agitation and persuasion by conservationists, Congress officially authorized the 8,000-acre Indiana Dunes National Lakeshore in 1966. Because of the delay, the National Lakeshore is as yet very limited in size. The acquisition process has been complicated and difficult. The lakeshore is divided into four separate units, which are interspersed with privately owned property.

These segments of the new and developing national park and the state park are listed in the order in which they are found when traveling from east to west on Highway US-12, the Dunes Highway.

Lakeshore and State Park Sites of Interest

(1) Mount Baldy Area of the National Lakeshore

Hy US-12 just outside Michigan City

Mount Baldy, a living dune that shifts and changes, rises 135 feet above the lake. Wind and water action cause this dune to move southward at the rate of about four feet per year. From atop Mount Baldy there is a fine view of Lake Michigan and an excellent perspective on the dune country. To the east, Michigan City's power plant stands in full view. To the west you see the steel mills at Burns Harbor and Gary. Mount Baldy is accessible by paths from the 25-car parking lot adjacent to Hy US-12. Open daily, 6:00 A.M.–10:00 P.M.

(2) Indiana Dunes State Park

Hys US-12 and IN-49 (CHPS)

This beautiful 2,200-acre park is largely wooded and has a fine Lake Michigan sand beach and complete bathhouse facilities. Ten hiking trails lead to Mt. Tom, Mt. Jackson, and Mt. Holden, all very large dunes with an elevation of more than 175 feet above the lake; to marsh areas; and to blowouts, where wind action has created a kind of natural sand saucer or bowl. The park has a naturalist whose services are available to visitors.

The park has historical as well as natural interest. The French established Petite Fort at the entrance of Fort Creek into Lake Michigan in 1750. It was a minor stockade built to enhance the fur trade. The British occupied the fort briefly and abandoned it in 1779. In December, 1780 the French and British skirmished here when the British overtook a French party that had raided Fort St. Joseph (see site 170).

During the land boom of the 1830s, the mouth of Fort Creek again attracted attention when a group of town site promoters built a hotel, tavern, blacksmith shop, sawmill, and store there. The development, begun in the panic year of 1837, quickly failed, and people moved away. $

The view to the east from Mount Baldy with the Michigan City power plant in the background. Photo by Margaret Bogue.

(3) Furnessville-Tremont Area of the National Lakeshore

Hy US-12, 6 miles west of Mount Baldy

The Furnessville-Tremont area contains the Indiana Dunes National Lakeshore Visitor Center. Here the visitor finds excellent displays and a seven-minute slide show explaining the natural features of the lakeshore. Rangers supply full information about scheduled walks with the park naturalists, who explain the flora and fauna and physical features of the various units in the park. The center offers scheduled lectures and movies as well. Pamphlets and books describing each segment of the Lakeshore are also available. Open daily, 8:00 A.M.–5:00 P.M., in winter; 8:00 A.M.–8:00 P.M. in summer. Free, as are all units of the National Lakeshore.

Hairy puccoon growing near the Lakeshore Visitor Center. Photo by Margaret Bogue.

The area contains two oak-covered dune ridges that are accessible by horseback and hiking trails. The Ly-Co-Ki-We horse trail is an especially good place to see dune wildflowers. Open 8:00 A.M.–dusk.

(4) Bailly Area of the National Lakeshore
south off Hy US-12 at Mineral Springs Road, 4.5 miles west of Visitor Center
The Bailly area contains the Chellburg and Bailly homesteads, which are being restored to reflect nineteenth-century rural life in the dunelands. The Chellburg farm site includes a red brick farmhouse, barn, pumphouse, chickenhouse, and other out-buildings. It is being restored to its condition of about 1900. The Bailly Homestead* was the home of a French fur trader, Joseph Bailly, member of a prominent Quebec French family. Bailly participated in the Mackinac fur trade and then expanded his operations into the Michigan lower peninsula. By 1805 his far-flung trade extended into the Kankakee River Valley as well. In 1822 he established his post at the Bailly Homestead site, adjacent to an Indian trail and a Potawatomi village. Here he engaged in the Little Calumet River fur trade from 1822 to 1833.

Today at the site stands a replica of a log warehouse, a chapel, the Bailly home, and a freestanding red brick structure built about 1875 or 1876. Altogether they represent building and remodeling over the span of more than a century. When completely restored, all of these buildings will be open to the public. Now they may be viewed from the outside. Informational displays in front of the struc tures help make this a very rewarding self-guided tour. The Bailly family cemetery is also found at this site.

(5) Cowles Bog Area of the National Lakeshore

turn north from Hy US-12 at Mineral Springs Road

This wetland zone is a National Registered Natural Landmark. Visitors may follow the trail to see bog, sedge, prairie, wetland woods, wooded dunes, and a bog-edge forest. It is named for Dr. Henry Chandler Cowles, a pioneer in plant ecology at the University of Chicago. He formulated theories of succession on the basis of his work in the Indiana Dunes area.

(6) West Beach of the National Lakeshore

Hy US-12 and County Line Road

Hiking trails lead to shoreline dunes, ponds among the dunes, prairie areas, and Long Lake. At Long Lake hikers may see great blue Herons, red-tail hawks, belted kingfishers, and many species of ducks. Foxes, muskrats, raccoons, skunks, deer, and ground hogs live in the Long Lake area. Three vegetation zones are observable: prairie, southern deciduous hardwoods, and northern conifers. It is difficult to believe that close by lie the great steel mills of Burns Harbor and Gary. Open 9:00 A.M.–8:00 P.M.

Hiking, picnicking, and swimming facilites are available at the Indiana Dunes National Lakeshore. The many educational features of the National Lakeshore program described above give people interested in ecology, plants, animals, and geology an opportunity to learn about the dunes environment.

(7) Hoosier Prairie

Within a 30-minute drive of the West Beach unit lies Hoosier Prairie, a 300-acre tract, the largest remaining prairie tract in Indiana. Those seriously interested in seeing the native plant life there should contact the Indiana Department of Natural Resources, Division of State Nature Preserves, 601 State Office Building, Indianapolis, IN 46204, for permission to do so. The prairie lies southwest of the West Beach unit. Take Hy I-80/94 west to Hy US-41 south. Turn east on Main Street toward Griffith.

Indiana's Industrial Duneland: Burns Harbor, Gary, Hammond, Whiting, and East Chicago

Hy US-12

Powell A. Moore, historian of the dunelands of the Calumet region, referred to the sandy northwestern area of Indiana lying on the Lake Michigan shoreline as "Indiana's last frontier." By the definition of the federal census it was indeed a frontier, with not less than two nor more than six persons per square mile until the coming of the railroads in the 1850s. Its geographic features long made it unattractive to permanent settlers.

Used by Indian peoples as a hunting ground and a fine source of wild rice and berries, crisscrossed by many Indian trails, the Calumet apparently had no permanent Indian villages. French fur traders were familiar with it and had one very minor trading post at the mouth of Fort Creek, but no major forts or trading centers. The streams and rivers of the Calumet area flowed into Lake Michigan but provided no good access route into the interior. Slow-moving, filled with reeds and wild rice, and clogged with sand at their mouths, they were more swamps than streams.

The federal government acquired title to these lands from the Indians late and surveyed them late. Here town site promoters tried and failed to make a killing in the land boom of the 1830s. The first settlements of any consequence developed with the construction of the railroads. Then the small villages of Hammond, Miller, Pine, and Whiting grew up as railroad workers' settlements.

In the late nineteenth century, the pine and cedar timber of the Calumet dunes attracted timber thieves, who cut the trees for firewood and lumber to supply the growing town of Chicago. Sportsmen's clubs found the dunes very attractive.

In 1869 the dunelands of the Calumet began to experience the impact of the industrial revolution when George W. Hammond established a meat-packing plant on the Grand Calumet River. The promotion of East Chicago as a choice industrial location began in 1887, 14 years before Inland Steel started construction of a huge plant there. At Whiting, Standard Oil began construction of a major refinery in 1889. U.S. Steel developed a steel mill at Gary between 1905 and 1908. Bethlehem Steel began development of its Burns Harbor plant in 1957.

In the 1920s Indiana's industrial dunelands contained the world's largest power plant (State Line), steel mill (U.S. Steel at Gary), cement plant (a subsidiary of U.S. Steel at Buffington), and oil refinery (Standard of Indiana at Whiting).

Historic sites in Gary, Hammond, Whiting, and East Chicago date for the most part from the early twentieth century. Already much of the physical evidence of the recent past has vanished before the bulldozer as industrial expansion has claimed more and more of the area occupied by the original towns.

Much of the information about sites 176–180 is drawn from the excellent work of Powell A. Moore, *The Calumet Region, Indiana's Last Frontier*. See bibliography for complete citation.

Aerial view, looking east, shows all production facilities at Bethlehem Steel's Burns Harbor plant. Courtesy Bethlehem Steel Corporation. 68661A-4

176. Burns Harbor–Port of Indiana

Hy US-12

Burns Harbor and the Port of Indiana grew out of the efforts of industrial developers to solve the problems of geography that the Calumet region presented to them. The present-day Port of Indiana at Burns Harbor originated in 1908 when Randall W. Burns of Chicago, owner of 1,200 acres of Little Calumet River swamp land, proposed to reclaim it by building a ditch. To do this, cuts had to be made through huge sand barriers lying between the Little Calumet and Lake Michigan. The proposed ditch would divert the waters of the Little Calumet and its tributary, Deep River, directly into Lake Michigan.

The proposal caused an uproar among local farmers, who feared tax increases, and among the railroad companies, who knew that the project meant new bridge building for them. Nevertheless, the ditch was eventually completed in 1926. Twenty thousand acres of land were reclaimed, and Gary rejoiced, for the periodic floods of the Little Calumet ceased.

In 1930, at the onset of the depression, the Midwest Steel Company purchased a tract of land east of Burns Ditch and planned a $30 million plant that was never built. In 1957 Bethlehem Steel bought 3,500 acres near Burns Ditch and announced that it would build a steel plant. Operations began in 1964. In 1979 Bethlehem Steel was the largest employer in Porter County, with a workforce of 6,000. The plant does not offer tours to the public.

Federal improvements to the Burns Ditch outlet to Lake Michigan created the Port of Indiana facility directly east of the steel plant. Dedicated as a deep-water port in 1970, the Port of Indiana has special equipment to accommodate self-unloading ore carriers. It is closed to the public.

177. Gary
Hy US-12

In its search for a new plant site, the U.S. Steel corporation chose a relatively uninhabited stretch of duneland lying between Buffington Harbor and the village of Miller just after the turn of the century. The decision came after careful consideration of the possibility of expanding its Illinois Steel Company mills in South Chicago and after studying the site possibilities at Waukegan. The company ruled out both South Chicago and Waukegan as too crowded for future growth. The Gary site had the advantages of moderately priced land, good prospects for a deep harbor on Lake Michigan for ore boats, proximity to Chicago's abundant labor supply, railroad connections, and room for expansion.

In 1905 U.S. Steel began purchasing 9,000 acres, which included seven miles of lakefront stretching south to the Wabash Railroad tracks. The Indiana Steel Company was organized in 1906 as a subsidiary of U.S. Steel to build and operate the mills. The Gary Land Company, a subsidiary of Indiana Steel, was created to lay out the town and build streets and water and sewer facilities.

U.S. Steel originally had no plans to construct, rent, or sell homes for workers. With the problems at Pullman fresh in mind (see site 1, no. [1]), company officials shied away from the company town idea. Housing, except for part of the managerial staff, would be left to private builders.

Elaborate preparations for the mill site began in 1906. Land had to be leveled and drained. Three railroads had to be rearranged, an operation involving 51 miles of tracks. The Grand

Grading and leveling in preparation for construction of the U.S. Steel plant. Courtesy U.S. Steel Corporation.

Calumet River had to be rechanneled. A harbor and a railroad switching yard had to be built. The plant's first blast furnace went into operation in 1908. In the same year the first ore ship from Lake Superior, the *Elbert H. Gary*, carrying 10,000 tons of ore, with great fanfare docked at the Gary Harbor works.

As for Gary, the town incorporated in 1906. It was named for Judge Elbert H. Gary, chairman of the board of directors of the U.S. Steel Corporation. Friction between the town government and the steel mill marked Gary's early years. The chief issues were related to expansion. The steel company favored an east-west expansion, while leaders in town government favored expansion southward.

Growth characterized Gary's early history. Soon the town had annexed all the land to the west as far as Hammond and East Chicago's city limits; later it annexed Miller, lying to the east, and spread southward as well. Population grew by leaps and bounds, from 16,800 in 1910 to 175,500 in 1970, making it the largest of Indiana's industrial duneland cities. Its growth reflects the success of the U.S. Steel plant.

During the first two decades of their operations, the steel mills attracted skilled American workers from Pittsburgh, Youngstown, and elsewhere. Immigrants—chiefly Poles, Czechs, Slovaks, Yugoslavs, Greeks, Italians, and Russians—came to Gary and took jobs as unskilled mill workers. Almost 50 percent of Gary's population in 1910 was foreign-born, and 70 percent of its residents had at least one parent born outside of the United States.

Gary developed as two towns. The

American-born, who were the skilled workers, the professionals, and the businessmen, lived in the part of Gary laid out systematically by the Gary Land Company. The new Americans lived south of the tracks in sprawling, disorderly "Hunkeytown," crowded together in cheap, flimsy, wooden houses. Gary's saloons, gambling houses, and brothels congregated in Hunkeytown. Over both Garys the steel mills belched out smoke and dirt. The steel company made one try at providing housing for unskilled immigrant laborers and gave up.

New elements were added to Gary's ethnic mix when immigration declined during World War I. Blacks, recruited in sizable numbers by industry in the Chicago-Gary area, filled unskilled industrial jobs. In 1916, 3,000 Blacks lived in Gary. During the 1920s and especially during World War II, Gary's Black population grew. In 1979 Blacks constituted 70 percent of the town's total population of 151,950. During World War I Mexican laborers came into the industrial cities of the Calumet region chiefly as railroad workers. More were recruited and brought to the steel mills during the 1919 steel strike. Gary's Mexican population in 1930 was roughly 3,500, about one-third as large as its population of Spanish origins in 1980. While Gary's ethnic diversity is less now than in the 1920s, it remains discernible in the accents of older workers and in the city's churches. About 3 percent of Gary's residents in 1970 were foreign-born.

Over the years U.S. Steel greatly expanded its Gary plant and organized a number of subidiaries. In 1909 the American Bridge Company and the American Sheet and Tin Plate Company were authorized by the corporation, and in 1922 the National Tube Company. Universal Atlas Cement is a division of U.S. Steel. Employing thousands of workers, U.S. Steel remains the city's largest employer. Most of Gary's other industry is metal-related. The early twentieth-century saying, "As go the steel mills, so goes Gary," still holds.

An aerial photo of the U.S. Steel plant at Gary taken about 1979. Courtesy U.S. Steel Corporation.

At times the steel business has not gone well. Serious labor troubles erupted at Gary in 1919. The unions failed to gain recognition and lost the strike. In 1937, without the drama of a strike, U.S. Steel negotiated with and recognized the Steel Workers Organizing Committee of the Congress of Industrial Organizations. Organized as the United States Steelworkers of America in 1942, the union has been very successful. Although strikes have periodically occurred in succeeding decades, none has produced the drama and ill feeling of the 1919 strike, which involved workers, strike breakers, townspeople, company officials, the state militia, and federal troops.

Gary Sites of Interest

(1) Marquette Park

This beautiful park is located on Gary's East Side and accessible from Hy US-12 via Lake and Miller avenues and Grand Boulevard. (Westbound travelers should turn right off Hy US-12 onto Lake, right on Miller, and left onto Grand Boulevard.) It represents the culmination of the efforts of Gary residents to find a Lake Michigan beach. Until 1918 residents of Gary had no beach access to the lake. The U.S. Steel company plant occupied the lakefront, and within the city limits no recreational frontage existed. Miller, a separate town lying east of Gary, seemed to offer the best possibility, for here a beautiful, nonindustrialized site on the lakeshore had long attracted bathers. But Miller could not be expected to develop a beach for Gary residents. Furthermore, land values were very high.

In 1918 Gary annexed Miller and the portion of Hobart Township lying on the lake. The Gary Park Board promptly condemned 179 acres for a park. Legal snarls ensued. Finally U.S. Steel purchased 120 acres of Miller lake frontage and gave it to the city for a park.

Jens Jensen, the Chicago landscape architect, designed the park. Landscaping of the park site began immediately. In 1922 a bathing pavilion was added, and in 1923 a restaurant and recreation building were. Known as Lake Front Park until 1930, it was then renamed Marquette Park. In the park stands an imposing bronze statue of Father Jacques Marquette, who passed this way in 1675.

Visitors to Marquette Park will find a marker south of the pavilion. It commemorates Octave Chanute's experimental glider flights at Miller dunes in 1896. Chanute, a successful civil engineer who designed railroads and railroad bridges, late in life became interested in aviation. At the Miller dunes he thought he had the right combination of privacy, adequate wind currents, and a soft crash site. Here he conducted a series of glider experiments that contributed much to solving the problems of control and equilibrium. His findings were of great help to the Wright brothers, with whom he maintained a lively correspondence.

Privacy for his experiments he did not find. Newspaper reporters found his camp shortly after he took his equipment off the train at Miller. A few weeks later he tried to set up camp secretly a few miles east of the town. This time, he came in by boat from Chicago. When a storm wrecked his equipment, he sent for more to be delivered by rail. The reporters came too.

(2) Miller Town Hall*

Intersection of Grand Boulevard, Old Hobart Road and Miller Street

This attractive, well-kept red brick structure, built in 1907, served as the seat of government for the village of Miller until Miller became part of Gary in 1918. Thereafter it was used as a firehouse until 1975, and since has been utilized for community purposes.

The town of Miller developed in the 1850s as a residential village for railroad maintenance workers. It was named for the railroad foreman. During the late nineteenth century, Miller supplied sand for construction fill for Chicago and ice for refrigerator cars. Here a sizable lake fishing industry developed. Professional fishermen operating at Miller as early as 1882 netted sturgeon and whitefish for the Chicago market.

Gary statue at City Hall. Photo by Margaret Bogue.

Nearby the Miami Powder Company of Xenia, Ohio, developed an explosives plant in 1881. Unpopular with the residents of Miller and Gary, who feared explosions, the plant confirmed their fears in 1914 when an explosion killed a number of workers and allegedly cracked every window in Gary. Residents heaved a sigh of relief in 1919 when, at the end of World War I, the plant closed.

(3) Gateway Park and Municipal Buildings

Hy US-12 at the intersection of Broadway and 4th Avenue

In an effort to give Gary a better public image, the U.S. Steel Corporation donated to the city an area of vacant lots and run-down buildings lying adjacent to 5th Avenue and the railroad station. Here Gary developed a municipal park adjacent to Hy US-12, the main thoroughfare for east-west traffic through the city. Just across the street from the park, the city erected a city hall, dedicated in 1928, and a county building, dedicated in 1929. Between the two buildings, facing Broadway, stands a bronze statue of Elbert H. Gary, who died in 1927. The inscription reads, "Lawyer, Industrialist, Benefactor, Founder of the City of Gary."

(4) Indiana Room, Public Library
220 West 5th Avenue
The fine collection of books about the Calumet region found here will be of interest to visitors who want to delve further into Gary's history.

(5) Gary Hotel
Broadway and 6th Avenue
Built in 1926, the Gary Hotel was once the place for fine food, entertainment, and overnight lodging. Long unused, its twin towers with their decorative stone and brick work stood empty. It is currently being renovated for a senior citizens' residential center.

(6) City Methodist Church
6th Avenue and Washington Street
This Gothic sructure, built of Indiana limestone, was dedicated in 1926. The principal benefactor of the church, originally known as the First Methodist Church, was Judge Elbert H. Gary of the U.S. Steel Corporation.

When in 1916 the First Methodist church received a new pastor, William Grant Seaman, the congregation was destined to build a new church to replace the structure completed and dedicated only four years earlier. Pastor Seaman believed that the church should be a combination of sanctuary and community house. After he enlisted Judge Gary's aid, the U.S. Steel Corporation's board of directors donated six city lots for the structure and agreed to match dollar for dollar the contributions of the Methodists for the new building. The original cost of the church was $800,000.

(7) Holy Angels Church
7th Avenue and Tyler Street
This modified English Gothic cathedral, an impressive and beautiful structure, is relatively new. The cornerstone was laid in 1947. The church is built of Wisconsin Lannon stone with Indiana limestone trim. The building dimensions are 60 by 177 feet. The structure replaced the original Holy Angels Church built in 1908–1909 to serve the many immigrant workers who came to Gary in search of work in the steel mills.

(8) Gary-Hobart Water Tower
7th Avenue and Madison Street
The water tower, built in 1908–1909, is part of the original water utility system that was planned and built by the Gary Land Company. Its architect received an award for design from the Waterworks Association of America.

(9) American Bridge Company
1 North Bridge Street
The American Bridge Company's original main building, a red brick structure with white stone trim, is plainly visible from the throughway to those who travel Hy I-90. Built in 1909–1910, in the western part of Gary, it is a beautiful example of early twentieth-century industrial architecture. U.S. Steel began construction of the American Bridge Company plant in 1909. It was designed to produce structural steel for bridges and buildings. The area around the plant became known as the Ambridge section of Gary. The Gary Land Company built houses near the plant for rent or sale to employees. The American Steel Bridge Company closed in 1980, and the structure may be razed. Among the many notable structures fabricated here were the San Francisco–Oakland Bay Bridge and the Mackinac Bridge.

(10) The Steel Mills
Hy I-90, the Indiana toll road, skirts the southern edge of the steel mills located on Lake Michigan. From the throughway travelers can get an excellent panoramic view of what some have styled America's Ruhr.

178. Hammond
Hy US-12

George H. Hammond's desire to establish a large meat-packing plant to supply a national and international market led to the development of Hammond. Only a few families lived in the area when in 1869 Hammond began the construction of his plant on the Grand Calumet River. At that time he owned a successful Detroit meat business and was pioneering the development of improved refrigerator cars. Before they chose the Hammond plant site, he and his partner, Marcus M. Towle, had already financed the development of a refrigerator car that preserved fresh meat at marketable quality.

At the Hammond site the Grand Calumet River supplied the ice and the Michigan Central Railroad the necessary rail connections. The site lay at the eastern edge of the region of beef cattle production. The plant was in operation by the fall of 1869 and proved to be very successful. In 1891 it employed about 1,000 workmen engaged in slaughtering cattle, sheep, and hogs and in the manufacture of oleomargarine. George Hammond rose in the ranks of late nineteenth-century entrepreneurs. His net worth stood at $6.4 million in 1890, the year of his death. He ranked among the Big Four of the meat-packing industry along with Swift, Morris, and Armour.

Hammond lived in Detroit, took little interest in the unattractive, smelly meat-packing town on the Grand Calumet, and concerned himself more with profits than with working conditions. His partner, Marcus Towle, and his brother, Thomas Hammond, both lived at the plant site and displayed a real interest in making the growing settlement an attractive place to live.

Towle platted the town of Hammond in 1875, but not until 1883 did Hammond become an incorporated community with a town government. It grew from 699 residents to a city of almost 12,400 in 1900.

In its early years Hammond was a very German town. A few Germans had already settled in the area before the building of the packing plant. The meat-packing industry attracted more with butchering and sausage-making skills. In 1910 the national origin of 30 percent of the population was either German of Austrian. Before the anti-German hysteria of World War I submerged Hammond's German culture, German-language newspapers, German Catholic and Lutheran churches, German singing and cultural societies, all flourished. The National German-American Alliance had 1,200 Hammond members in 1914. By then sizable numbers of Slavic immigrants had also settled in the city.

The G. H. Hammond packing plant in 1900. Courtesy The Hammond Historical Society, Hammond, Indiana.

The meat-packing plant burned to the ground in 1901 and was not rebuilt. With its major industry gone, Hammond went through a very difficult period of adustment. The town's leaders had been working well before 1901 to attract new industries and to secure access to Lake Michigan. They secured lake frontage but failed to develop either a harbor or a navigable waterway. They did succeed in attracting at least six minor industries before the turn of the century. Largest and most important among the new industries were the W. B. Conkey Printing and Bookbinding Company and the Simplex Railway Appliance Company.

A drive to attract new plants early in the twentieth century proved quite successful. The Standard Steel Car Company became a major employer. The location of a Shell Refinery at Hammond in 1926 and a Lever Brothers plant in 1930 helped the city continue to grow with a more diversified industrial base than in its early years.

Hammond has since continued to grow on the basis of diversified industry. In the 1970s the city had well over 20 manufacturing plants, which turned out a wide variety of metal products, chemicals, and foods; a major publishing house; and about 20 suppliers of services to business and industry, each of which employed more than 100 workers. The three largest manufacturers, each with 800 to 1,400 employees, produced soaps, detergents, food, corn products, and freight car parts.

Hammond's population has grown from 12,400 in 1900 to 93,700 in 1980. Over the years its ethnic composition has changed. The great influx of southern and eastern Europeans between the turn of the century and the imposition of national immigration quotas in the 1920s substantially altered the town's ethnic mix. In 1920, when foreign-born persons and those of foreign parentage made up 58 percent of the city's population, persons of Polish birth constituted the largest national group among the foreign-born. Germans ranked second, Austrians third, Russians fourth, and Hungarians fifth. Unlike Gary and Michigan City, Hammond industry did not attract substantial numbers of Blacks and Mexican migrants during the two world wars, but by 1980, 6.0 percent of the city's people were Blacks and 8.0 percent were of Hispanic origin.

Hammond is a relatively new city characterized by rapid industrial growth. Sites of historical importance have often given way to housing and industrial pressures, the bane of historical preservationists. Nevertheless, a number of sites relating to Hammond history remain and are worth visiting.

The Hammond Division of City Planning is currently making a survey of Hammond's historic structures. In the future, their planners will seek nomination to the National Register of Historic Places for the Glendale Parkway Mansions area, the Forest Avenue District, and the Ogden Street area, where the M. M. Towle house is located.

Hammond Sites of Interest

(1) G. H. Hammond Meat Packing Plant Site
Wilcox Street west of Hohman Avenue and south of the Grand Calumet River
This was the location of Hammond's meat-packing plant, chosen because of the accessibility to a plentiful water supply, ice, and railroad connections.

(2) St. Joseph's Roman Catholic Church
southwest corner of Hohman Avenue and Russell Street
Built in 1879, St. Joseph's Roman Catholic church served the Catholic German and Austrian immigrant workers of Hammond. The oldest church in the Calumet region, the structure was built of tan pressed brick and Indiana limestone. Italian marble altars, stained glass windows designed in Munich, Germany, and mosaics by Venetian artisans are outstanding features of the interior.

(3) Marcus M. Towle House
229 Ogden Street
Marcus M. Towle, business partner of G. H. Hammond, had this brick home and carriage house built about 1880. Towle was Hammond's first mayor. The YWCA now owns the building.

(4) "Man of Steel" Sculpture
northwest corner of Hohman Avenue and Waltham Street in Harrison Park
Herman Gurfinkel designed and executed the "Man of Steel" in 1976 to honor the steel industry and steel workers of the Calumet region.

(5) Glendale Parkway Mansions
Glendale Parkway west of Hohman Avenue
On narrow, circular Glendale Parkway stand several large brick and stone homes built in the 1920s and characterized by leaded glass windows and high pitched roofs. Spacious, well-kept grounds and an adjacent partially wooded center made this area an attractive setting for the residences of Hammond's successful industrialists and businessmen.

(6) Forest Avenue District
This district is bounded by Hohman Avenue, the Little Calumet River, the Indiana state line and 165th Street. In this well-preserved area of narrow avenues, large homes, well-kept grounds, and ornamental street lights stand a number of homes built by industrialists after World War I. The Forest Avenue district remains a fashionable residential area of the city.

(7) "Little Red School House"
169th Street and Kennedy Avenue
Built of local limestone and brick in 1869, the schoolhouse is the oldest restored building in Hammond. Built largely through the efforts of Joseph Hess, founder of the small German community of Hessville, the structure has served as a schoolhouse, the presidential campaign headquarters for William Jennings Bryan, a polling place, a community hall, a house of worship, a funeral parlor, and currently as a meeting place for public groups. Now owned by the Hessville Historical Society, the structure has its original bell and row of double desks. Open by special arrangement for tour groups. Call (219) 844-7627.

(8) Calumet Room, Hammond Public Library
564 State Street

After a number of attempts and failures to establish a Hammond Historical Society, in 1960 residents of Hammond succeeded. One of the major activities of the society is centered in the Calumet Room of the new Hammond Public Library. Here the curator supervises a growing collection of pictures, manuscripts, old publications, newspapers, and reference works that relate to Hammond's past. People interested in Hammond's history will find this an excellent resource.

The library of the Calumet campus of Purdue University is developing archives and special collections with strong emphasis on the history of the Hammond-Calumet region.

179. East Chicago

Hy US-12

East Chicago originated from the plans of a group of wealthy financial promoters and businessmen, who organized the Standard Steel and Iron Company, primarily as a real estate venture, in 1887. Aware of the growing crunch in industrial sites in South Chicago, some of the organizers may have had a steel plant in mind. They understood the broad appeal that industrial sites would have to a wide variety of industries that wanted to locate close to Chicago's great distribution network, near cheap lake transportation, and in the midst of a growing mid-continental market.

To develop their South Chicago site, the entrepreneurs proposed to build a ship canal from Lake Michigan south to the Grand Calumet River, a pier into the lake, and a beltline railway to connect their projected industrial city with other railroads in the Chicago area. Work on the railway and the canal began optimistically in 1888. In 1889 the town of East Chicago was incorporated. In 1893 it became a city. Industries found the new location congenial. A railroad car wheel plant, a farm machinery company, a horseshoe factory, and a chemical company had been established here before the panic of 1893 threw the country into economic chaos.

The busy Indiana Harbor Ship Canal where ore carriers dock for unloading very close to the blast furnaces. Courtesy the East Chicago, Indiana, Chamber of Commerce.

The town's real growth began with the establishment of the Inland Steel corporation at East Chicago in 1901. From the beginning it was East Chicago's largest employer, and it grew rapidly. The corporation purchased ore holdings near Hibbing, Minnesota. From open hearth furnaces Inland Steel progressed to a blast furnace operation in 1907. In 1911 it purchased its own ore carriers and operated them between Duluth and the Indiana Harbor Ship Canal. Employment at the plant grew from 1,200 in 1904 to 7,000 in 1924. Inland Steel rapidly ran out of land sites for plant expansion and resorted to building out into Lake Michigan. Construction stopped where the water was 22 feet deep, the point where state jurisdiction ended and a federal navigable waterway began.

The development of Indiana Harbor, the eastern section of East Chicago, paralleled the building and expansion of Inland Steel. In the early years of the century it was a good deal like a western mining town, filled with cheap restaurants, boardinghouses, saloons, and gambling establishments, according to Powell A. Moore. Inland Steel constructed some housing for its managerial staff, but unskilled workers found their own accommodations. Slum areas developed around the mills, where the immigrants of the pre–World War I years—Poles, Hungarians, Austrians, Czechs, Rumanians, Yugoslavs, and Greeks—lived in overcrowded, substandard homes. East Chicago's population in 1910 was 53 percent foreign-born. Unskilled immigrant labor made the factories and mills of East Chicago hum. After the outbreak of World War I, and especially after immigration restriction in the 1920s, Mexicans and unskilled Black workers from the South filled many of the lowest paying jobs.

With the completion of the projected beltline railroad in 1906 and progress on the Indiana Harbor Ship Canal, more industries located in East Chicago. While never a one-industry city, East Chicago from early in its history produced primarily steel and metal products, with petroleum products and chemicals in a position of secondary importance. In time Standard Oil's refineries spread from Whiting into East Chicago, and other oil companies located their refineries there as well. In 1929, 45 major industries employed 25,000 workers. The year before, Indiana Harbor became a world port.

The steel industry at East Chicago grew in importance during and after World War II. In 1979 Inland Steel employed 22,000 workers and was by all odds the largest manufacturer. Jones and Laughlin Steel Corporation, with 9,000 workers, was the second-largest employer.

Marktown Residences. Photo by Margaret Bogue.

East Chicago has lost population as industrial plants have expanded. In 1930 it had grown steadily for 30 years to a population of 54,700. The 1980 census showed 39,800 residents. Blacks comprise 29 percent of the population and persons of Spanish origins 42 percent.

East Chicago Sites of Interest

It is easy to drive right into the steelmaking and refinery areas by following Hy IN-912 off Hy US-12. This route goes through the Inland Steel mill area and across the Ship Canal and runs adjacent to the Standard Oil Refinery.

(1) Marktown Historic District*
This area is bounded by Pine, Riley, Dickey, and 129th streets and is accessible from Hy IN-912.
In 1914, when Clayton Mark established the Mark Manufacturing Company, a steel plant, he had the Marktown site built for supervisory employees. The village included 103 white stucco structures, stores, dormitories, and residences as well as recreational facilites for children and adults. An elementary school was located nearby. Marktown, as it came to be called, is still used for residential purposes by steel workers, and visitors may walk through its narrow streets to get an idea of what was considered a socially advanced housing development for steel plant supervisors in 1914. The open playground area remains. Marktown stands in stark con-

trast to the surrounding steel mills and oil refineries.

(2) Serbian Catholic Church
4,000 block of Elm Street, just off Columbus Drive (Hy US-12)
This Serbian Catholic church, dating from 1912, and its adjacent community center are interesting reminders of the thousands of immigrants from eastern Europe who moved into East Chicago to work in the steel mills in the early twentieth century. The attractive, neatly kept houses and yards of the surrounding neighborhood are in sharp contrast with the slum conditions of early immigrant neighborhoods. Old World language and Old World ways are still evident.

The refineries at Whiting, as they appear today from IN–912. Photo by Margaret Bogue.

180. Whiting
Hy US-12

Whiting originated as a home village for railroad workers in the 1850s. Until 1889 its economic life was confined to the sale of ice and sand and the entertainment of hunting parties. In the spring of that year Standard Oil began buying the sandy, swampy lands around Whiting as a refinery site for oil pumped from the Lima, Ohio field in which Standard had large investments.

Standard Oil planned originally to refine the Ohio oil at its 100th Street facilities in south Chicago. The sulfur content of the oil, popularly known as "skunk oil," created such a stench that local residents strenuously objected. The company selected Whiting in its search for a less densely populated area where taxes and land values were low and where it would have access to Lake Michigan and to railroad connections.

In May of 1889 Standard Oil construction crews began rearranging the landscape, leveling dunes and ridges and filling in wetlands. The army of construction workers lived in a frontier town atmosphere of boarding houses, saloons, dance halls, mosquitoes, and sand fleas. By Thanksgiving of 1890 the refinery had produced its first shipments of kerosene, the major product until 1910, when demand for gasoline for automobiles caused a shift in all of Standard Oil's production output. It was here at the Whiting refinery that William M. Burton in 1913 developed the Burton cracking process for making gasoline from heavier oils, a major technological development in the oil industry.

The oil refinery became Whiting's major employer, utilizing from 2,500 to 3,000 employees in 1896 and over 4,000 in 1920. Many were American-born, but Whiting in its early years attracted many immigrant workers, principally Slovaks, Poles, and Hungarians. In 1910, 43 percent of the town's population of 6,500 was foreign-born.

Standard Oil of Indiana displayed an interest in the town and its politics. It provided a cemetery and school sites and made major contributions to a community house. It was definitely interested in blocking the attempt of Hammond to annex Whiting. Standard Oil promoted the organization of Whiting as a separate town in 1893. Whiting became a city in 1903 with a population of a little over 4,000.

The Whiting Refinery has grown over the years. Once the Lima, Ohio, oil fields declined in production, the refinery received oil from elsewhere, in 1906 from the Kansas field, and after 1921 from the Kansas, Oklahoma, and Wyoming fields by pipeline.

Over the years refining facilities at Whiting have expanded into areas formerly occupied by residences. As a result the town's population has declined. In 1930 it stood at 10,900, and in 1980 at 5,600.

Whiting Sites of Interest

(1) Memorial Community House
corner of Clark Avenue and Community Court
Community House dates from 1923, when the Standard Oil Company gave the site and $300,000 toward the building. The citizens of Whiting assumed the responsibility for planning, building, furnishing, and management. The two-story red brick building, southern Italian in architectual style, was dedicated as a memorial to Standard Oil workers who served in World War I. It originally contained an auditorium, gymnasium, swimming pool, billiard room, kitchen, banquet facilities, and rooms for social gatherings and reading.

(2) St. John's Roman Catholic Church
Lincoln Avenue and Benedict Street
St. John's is a monument to the importance of the church in the lives of Whiting's immigrants. Responding to the requests of the Slovaks, the largest of the foreign-born groups in Whiting at the turn of the century, a Slovakian priest came to serve their needs early in 1897. Later in that year the newly arrived priest and his parishioners dedicated the first church to St. John the Baptist. The church grew rapidly, from 1,500 members in 1910 to over 3,200 in 1924. The present structure, built in 1930, housed the largest Slovak parish in the Calumet region.

Side Trip to Lockport and Channahon Parkway State Park

Here a side trip away from the lakeshore is suggested for those interested in the Illinois and Michigan Canal, an important linkage between Lake Michigan and the Mississsippi River during the nineteenth century.

181. Lockport

Hy I-80 (Lockport exit)

When the federal government donated almost 300,000 acres of land to the state of Illinois in 1827 to finance the construction of a canal linking Lake Michigan and the Mississippi River, the waterway envisioned by Louis Jolliet in 1673 came closer to reality. The plan was for Illinois to sell the land and use the money for construction. U.S. Secretary of the Treasury Albert Gallatin recommended building such a link as early as 1808, but construction costs presented a formidable problem then and continued to hamper progress after construction began in 1836. Money was not the only obstacle. Compact clay and rock made the going hard for the workers digging the 96-mile canal, primarily with hand tools. Construction crews completed their work in 1848, and the canal opened to traffic in that year.

During its years of heaviest use, the Illinois and Michigan Canal carried over 10 million tons of cargo, mostly on barges, although steamboats occasionally plied its waters. Northern Illinois settlers built their homes with lumber, stone, and nails carried on the canal. Dining tables in Chicago held molasses, sugar, and coffee shipped from New Orleans via the canal, as well as grain and other farm products from western Illinois.

In an effort to solve its sewage disposal problems, Chicago in the late 1860s secured state permission to lower the canal's summit level. Completed in 1871, the deepening sent Lake Michigan water through the canal to carry sewage into the Des Plaines. The scheme worked poorly. In the two decades following, sewage-laden putrid canal water threatened the health of Chicagoans and all who lived along the canal and the Des Plaines and upper Illinois rivers. The Sanitary District of Chicago, created by the Illinois legislature in 1889, opted to construct a new 28-mile drainage channel

The Illinois-Michigan Canal at Chicago. Courtesy Illinois State Historical Library, Old State Capitol, Springfield, Illinois.

from the Chicago River to the Des Plaines at Lockport. Begun in 1892, the wider, deeper channel first carried Lake Michigan's waters to Lockport in January 1900. Because larger barges could use the new Sanitary and Ship Canal, traffic gradually shifted to the new waterway from the old Illinois and Michigan Canal.

Lockport was platted in 1837 after construction began on the Illinois and Michigan Canal. Here stood the administrative headquarters for the canal during construction and throughout its operational history. Here, at the divide between the Mississippi River and Lake Michigan watersheds, workmen constructed the northernmost lock of the canal system in 1845. Canal boats last used the old channel in 1909, but many reminders of the canal era have survived to the present, making the community an excellent example of a nineteenth-century American canal town. Its current population is about 9,000. The main industry is a Texaco oil refinery.

Lockport Sites of Interest

(1) Lockport Historic District*
This historic district, bounded by 7th and 11th Streets and Canal and Washington Streets, includes the Illinois and Michigan Canal Headquarters Building (1837), G. B. Martin Elevator and Store (1850s), Norton's Mill and Warehouse (1848 and 1850), a row of commercial buildings constructed in the 1890s, Norton's Store (1880), Greek Revival buildings on State and Hamilton Streets (around 1850), and Old Central Grade School (1890). Begin your visit to the district at the Canal Headquarters Building.

(2) Illinois and Michigan Canal Headquarters Building*
803 North State Street
The one-story section of this building, the original canal office, was built about 1837 as canal headquarters. It served as the center for engineering and construction, as the canal land office, and, briefly, as a branch of the State Bank of Illinois while the canal was under construction. Completed after the Civil War, the two-story section at the south end of the building served mainly as living quarters for canal and visiting state officials. The Lockport office was operations headquarters throughout the canal's history. The office and living quarters have been restored. The museum housed in the headquarters building, is open all year, daily from 1:00–4:30 P.M. Free.

The Will County Historical Society, located in the Headquarters Building, has a map and sites list identifying 37 points of historical significance in Lockport. Visitors will find this material an excellent guide to the town's historic district, its churches, canal sites, and business and residential structures, and an area of Illinois prairie with many unusual native plants.

Every June, Old Canal Days are celebrated in Lockport with tours of the canal and the historic district and special displays in the Illinois and Michigan Canal Museum.

(3) Public Landings and Will County Historical Society's Historical Complex
8th Street and the canal
At the north landing, where farmers loaded their produce onto canal boats, the Will County Historical Society has located a group of pioneer buildings, including the oldest remaining log cabin in the county.

(4) Lock No. 1 and Lockkeeper's House
1513 South State Street
In 1845 lock no. 1 was constructed of stone quarried in the vicinity. It had a 10-foot lift. The home for the keeper was built three years later.

(5) Former Canal Hydraulic Basin
12th Street at the canal
At this location stood a flour mill and a sawmill owned by Hiram Norton and operated by water power from the canal.

182. Channahon Parkway State Park

access from Hy I-80, I-55, and US-6 (BCFHP)

At this 18-acre park visitors can see the towpath, two locks of the Illinois and Michigan Canal, and the lockkeeper's house at lock no. 6. Canoeists may use the 16-mile water-filled stretch of the canal extending west to Morris, Illinois. The canal towpath serves as a trail for hiking, bicycling, snowmobiling, and cross-country skiing. The locks and towpath have been designated a National Historic Landmark because of the importance of the canal in the development of Chicago and northern Illinois. See site 181.

This print from an 1873 atlas of Will County, Illinois, shows boats on the Illinois and Michigan canal in Channahon Township, a portion of the Canal where the old towpath has been developed for recreational use. From Combination Atlas Map of Will County, Ill. *(Elgin, Ill., Thompson Bros. and Burr, 1873). Courtesy Illinois State Historical Library, Old State Capitol, Springfield, Illinois.*

Selected Bibliography

The Great Lakes and Lake Michigan

Hatcher, Harlan H., and Erich Walter. *A Pictorial History of the Great Lakes*. New York: Crown Publishers, 1963.

Havighurst, Walter. *The Long Ships Passing: The Story of the Great Lakes*. Rev. ed. New York: Macmillan, 1975.

Havighurst, Walter, ed. *The Great Lakes Reader*. New York: Macmillan, 1966.

Quaife, Milo. *Lake Michigan*. Indianapolis: Bobbs-Merrill, 1944.

Regions, States, and Cities

Bald, F. Clever. *Michigan in Four Centuries*. New York: Harper and Brothers, 1961.

Buley, R. Carlyle. *The Old Northwest Pioneer Period, 1815–1840*. 2 vols. Indianapolis: Indiana Historical Society, 1950.

Current, Richard N. *The Civil War Era, 1848–1873* (*The History of Wisconsin,* vol. 2). Madison: State Historical Society of Wisconsin, 1976.

Cutler, Irving. *Chicago, Metropolis of the Mid-Continent*. 2d ed. Dubuque: Kendall/Hunt, 1976.

Dunbar, Willis F. *Michigan: A History of the Wolverine State*. Grand Rapids; Eerdmans, 1965. Revised 1970, 1980.

Howard, Robert P. *Illinois: A History of the Prairie State*. Grand Rapids; Eerdmans, 1972.

Mayer, Harold M., and Richard C. Wade. *Chicago: Growth of a Metropolis*. Chicago: University of Chicago Press, 1969.

Moore, Powell A. *The Calumet Region: Indiana's Last Frontier*. Indianapolis: Indiana Historical Bureau, 1959.

Nesbit, Robert C. *Wisconsin: A History*. Madison: University of Wisconsin Press, 1973.

Pierce, Bessie Louise. *A History of Chicago*. Vol. 1, *The Beginning of a City, 1673–1848*. New York: Knopf, 1937. Vol.2, *From Town to City, 1848–1871*. New York: Knopf, 1940. Vol.3, *The Rise of a Modern City, 1871–1893*. New York: Knopf, 1957.

Smith, Alice E. *From Exploration to Statehood* (*The History of Wisconsin*, vol. 1). Madison: State Historical Society of Wisconsin, 1973.

Still, Bayrd. *Milwaukee: The History of a City*. Madison: State Historical Society of Wisconsin, 1948.

Wilson, William E. *Indiana: A History*. Bloomington: Indiana University Press, 1966.

Geology

Black, Robert F. *Geology of the Ice Age National Scientific Reserve of Wisconsin*. Washington, D.C.. U.S. Government Printing Office, 1974.

Hough, Jack L. *Geology of the Great Lakes*. Urbana: University of Illinois Press, 1958.

Mapping

Karpinski, Louis C. *Historical Atlas of the Great Lakes and Michigan*. Lansing: Michigan Historical Commission, 1931.

Indians

Blair, Emma Helen. *The Indian Tribes of the Upper Mississippi Valley and Region of the Great Lakes*. 2 vols. Cleveland: Arthur H. Clark, 1911, 1912.

Fitting, James E. *The Archaeology of Michigan: A Guide to the Prehistory of the Great Lakes Region*. Garden City, N.Y.: Natural History Press, 1970.

Flanders, Richard E., and James B. Griffin. *The Norton Mound Group, Kent County, Michigan*. Ann Arbor: University of Michigan, 1970.

Hunt, George T. *The Wars of the Iroquois: A Study in Intertribal Trade Relations*. Madison: University of Wisconsin Press, 1940.

Kinietz, W. Vernon. *The Indians of the Western Great Lakes, 1615–1760*. Ann Arbor; University of Michigan Press, 1940.

Mason, Ronald J. *Great Lakes Archaeology*. New York: Academic Press, 1981.

Morgan, Lewis Henry. *League of the Iroquois*. New York: Corinth Books, 1962.

Peckham, Howard H. *Pontiac and the Indian Uprising*. Princeton: Princeton University Press, 1947

Prucha, Francis Paul. *American Indian Policy in the Formative Years: The Indian Trade and Intercourse Acts, 1790–1834*. Cambridge: Harvard University Press, 1962.

Quimby, George I. *Indian Culture and European Trade Goods*. Madison: University of Wisconsin Press, 1966.

Quimby, George I. *Indian Life in the Upper Great Lakes, 11,000 B.C. to A.D 1800*. Chicago: University of Chicago Press, 1960.

Ritzenthaler, Robert E. *The Oneida Indians of Wisconsin*. Milwaukee: Milwaukee Public Museum, 1950.

Ritzenthaler, Robert E. *The Potawatomi Indians of Wisconsin*. Milwaukee: Milwaukee Public Museum, 1953.

Ritzenthaler, Robert E., and Pat Ritzenthaler. *The Woodland Indians of the Western Great Lakes*. Garden City, N.Y.: Natural History Press, 1970.

Trigger, Bruce G. *The Children of the Aataentsic: A History of the Huron People to 1660*. 2 vols. Montreal: McGill-Queens University Press, 1976.

Colonial Period: French and British

Brebner, John Bartlet. *The Explorers of North America, 1492–1806*. New York: Macmillan, 1933.

Kellogg, Louise P. *The British Régime in Wisconsin and the Northwest*. Madison: State Historical Society of Wisconsin, 1935.

Kellogg, Louise P. *Early Narratives of the Northwest, 1634–1699*. New York: Charles Scribner Sons, 1917.

Kellogg, Louise P. *The French Régime in Wisconsin and the Northwest*. Madison: State Historical Society of Wisconsin, 1925.

Kennedy, John H. *Jesuit and Savage in New France*. New Haven: Yale University Press, 1950.

Kenton, Edna, ed. *Black Gown and Redskins:*

Adventures and Travels of the Early Jesuit Missionaries in North America. New York: Longmans, 1956.

Thwaites, Reuben G., ed. *The Jesuit Relations and Allied Documents: Travels and Explorations of the Jesuit Missionaries in New France, 1610–1791*. 73 vols. Cleveland; Burrows Borthers, 1896–1901.

Wrong, George M. *The Rise and Fall of New France*. New York: Macmillan, 1928.

Fur Trade

Campbell, Marjorie Wilkins. *The North West Company*. New York: St. Martin's Press, 1957.

Gilman, Carolyn. *Where Two Worlds Meet*. St. Paul: Minnesota Historical Society, 1982.

Innis, Harold A. *The Fur Trade in Canada*. Rev. ed. New Haven: Yale University Press, 1962.

Johnson, Ida A. *The Michigan Fur Trade*. Lansing: Michigan Historical Commission, 1919.

Lavender, David S. *The Fist in the Wilderness*. Garden City, N.Y.: Doubleday, 1964.

Morse, Eric W. *Fur Trade Canoe Routes of Canada/Then and Now*. 2d ed. Toronto: University of Toronto Press, 1979.

Nute, Grace Lee. *The Voyageur*. New York: D. Appleton, 1931.

Porter, Kenneth Wiggins. *John Jacob Astor, Business Man*. 2 vols. Cambridge: Harvard University Press, 1931.

Rich, E. E. *The History of the Hudson's Bay Company, 1670–1870*. 2 vols. London: Hudson's Bay Record Society, 1958.

Sosin, Jack M. *Whitehall and the Wilderness: The Middle West in British Colonial Policy, 1760–1775*. Lincoln: University of Nebraska Press, 1961.

Stevens, Wayne E. *The Northwest Fur Trade, 1763–1800*. Urbana: University of Illinois Press, 1926.

Lumbering

Alilunas, Leo. "Michigan's Cut-Over 'Canaan,'" *Michigan History Magazine* 26 (Spring 1942): 188–201.

Carstensen, Vernon. *Farms or Forests: Evolution of a State Land Policy for Northern Wisconsin, 1850–1932*. Madison: University of Wisconsin College of Agriculture, 1958.

Current, Richard Nelson. *Pine Logs and Politics: A Life of Philetus Sawyer 1816–1900*. Madison: State Historical Society of Wisconsin, 1950.

Falder, Susan, ed. *The Great Lakes Forest; An Environmental and Social History*. Minneapolis: University of Minnesota Press, 1983.

Fries, Robert F. *Empire in Pine: The Story of Lumbering in Wisconsin, 1830–1900*. Madison: State Historical Society of Wisconsin, 1951.

Holbrook, Stewart H. *Burning an Empire: The Story of American Forest Fires*. New York: Macmillan, 1943.

Hotchkiss, George W. *History of the Lumber and Forest Industry of the Northwest*. Chicago: George W. Hotchkiss and Co., 1898.

Maybee, Rolland H. *Michigan's White Pine Era, 1840–1900*. Lansing: Michigan Historical Commission, 1960.

Tilton, Frank. *Sketch of the Great Fires in Wisconsin at Peshtigo* . . . Green Bay: Robinson and Kustermann, 1871.

Wyman, Walker. *Mythical Creatures of the North Country*. River Falls, Wis.: River Falls State University Press, 1969.

Transportation

Beasley, Norman. *Freighters of Fortune: The Story of the Great Lakes*. New York: Harper and Brothers, 1930.

Bowen, Dana Thomas. *Shipwrecks of the Lakes, Told in Story and Picture*. Daytona Beach, Fla.: Private printing, 1952.

Boyer, Dwight. *Ships and Men of the Great Lakes*. New York: Dodd, Mead, 1977.

Curwood, James Oliver. *The Great Lakes, the Vessels That Plough Them: Their Owners, Their Sailors, and Their Cargoes*. New York: G. P. Putnam's Sons, 1909.

Cutler, Elizabeth F. and Walter M. Hirthe. *Six Fitzgerald Brothers, Lake Captains All*. Milwaukee: Wisconsin Marine Historical Society, 1983.

Elliott, James L. *Red Stacks over the Horizon: The Story of the Goodrich Steamboat Line*. Grand Rapids, Mich.: Eerdmans, 1967.

Hilton, George W. *The Great Lakes Car Ferries*. Berkeley, Calif.: Howell-North, 1962.

Kuttruff, Karl and David B. Glick. *Ships of the Great Lakes: A Pictorial History*. Detroit: Wayne State University Press,1976.

Mermin, Samuel. *The Fox-Wisconsin Rivers Improvement: An Historical Study in Legal Institutions and Political Economy*. Madison: University of Wisconsin Board of Regents, 1968.

Mills, James Cooke. *Our Inland Seas: Their Shipping and Commerce for Three Centuries*. Chicago: A. C. McClurg, 1910.

O'Brien, T. Michael. *Guardians of the Eighth Sea: A History of the U.S. Coast Guard on the Great Lakes*. Washington, D.C.: U.S. Government Printing Office, 1976.

Putnam, James William. *The Illinois and Michigan Canal: A Study in Economic History*. Chicago: University of Chicago Press, 1918.

Ratigan, William. *Great Lakes Shipwrecks and Survivals*. Grand Rapids, Mich.: Eerdmans, 1977.

Schenker, Eric, Harold M. Mayer, and Harry C. Brockel. *The Great Lakes Transportation System*. Madison: University of Wisconsin Sea Grant College Program, 1976.

Shaw, Ronald E. *Erie Water West: A History of the Erie Canal 1792–1854*. Lexington: University of Kentucky Press, 1966.

Wright, Richard J. *Freshwater Whales: A History of the American Ship Building Company*. Kent, Ohio: Kent State University Press, 1969.

Fish and the Lake Habitat

Downs, Warren. *The Sea Lamprey: Invader of the Great Lakes*. The Great Lakes Alien Series, no. 1. Madison: University of Wisconsin Sea Grant Institute, 1982.

Legault, Jim, and Tom Kuchenberg. *Reflections in a Tarnished Mirror: The Use and Abuse of the Great Lakes*. Sturgeon Bay, Wis.: Golden Glow Publishing, 1978.

Van Oosten, John. "Michigan's Commercial Fisheries of the Great Lakes." *Michigan History Magazine* 22 (Winter 1938): 107–145.

Iron

Boyum, Burton H. *The Saga of Iron Mining in Michigan's Upper Peninsula*. Marquette: John M. Longyear Research Library, 1977.

Dunathan, Clint. "Fayette." *Michigan History* 41 (June 1957); 204–208.

Hatcher, Harlan H. *A Century of Iron and Men*. Indianapolis: Bobbs-Merrill, 1950.

La Fayette, Kenneth D. *Flaming Brands: Fifty Years of Iron Making in the Upper Peninsula of Michigan, 1848–1898*. Marquette: Northern Michigan University Press, 1977.

Walker, David A. *Iron Frontier: The Discovery and Early Development of Minnesota's Three Ranges*. St. Paul: Minnesota Historical Society Press, 1979.

Conservation

Engel, J. Ronald. *Sacred Sands: The Struggle for Community in the Indiana Dunes*. Middletown, Conn.: Wesleyan University Press, 1983.

Young, Gordon. "Superior-Michigan-Huron-Erie-Ontario: Is It Too Late?" *National Geographic* 144 (August 1973): 147–185.

A Heterogeneous People

General

Archdeacon, Thomas. *Becoming American: An Ethnic History*. New York: Free Press, 1983.

Dinnerstein, Leonard, and David M. Reimers. *Ethnic Americans: A History of Immigration and Assimilation*. New York: Dodd, Mead, 1975.

Hansen, Marcus Lee. *The Atlantic Migration, 1607–1860: A History of the Continuing Settlement of the United States*. New York: Harper and Row, 1961.

Jones, Maldwyn Allen. *American Immigration*. Chicago: University of Chicago Press, 1960.

Taylor, Philip. *The Distant Magnet: European Immigration to the U.S.A.* New York: Harper and Row, 1971.

Ward, David. *Cities and Immigrants: A Geography of Change in Nineteenth-Century America*. New York: Oxford University Press, 1971.

For essays on specific ethnic groups and bibliographical references, see Stephan Thernstrom, Ann Orlov, and Oscar Handlin, *Harvard Encyclopedia of American Ethnic Groups* (Cambridge: Harvard University Press, 1980).

Chicago

Addams, Jane. *Twenty Years at Hull-House*. New York: New American Library, 1960.

Allswang, John M. *A House for All Peoples: Ethnic Politics in Chicago, 1890–1936*. Lexington: University of Kentucky Press, 1971.

Nelli, Humbert. *The Italians of Chicago, 1880–1920*. New York: Oxford University Press, 1970.

Spear, Allan H. *Black Chicago: The Making of a Negro Ghetto, 1890–1920*. Chicago: University of Chicago Press, 1967.

Townsend, Andrew J. *The Germans of Chicago*. Vol. 32 of *Deutsch-amerikanische geschichtsblätter*. Chicago: Deutsch-amerikanischen gesellschaft von Illinois, 1932.

Milwaukee

Aukofer, Frank A. *City with a Chance*. Milwaukee: Bruce Publishing, 1968.

Conzen, Kathleen Neils. *Immigrant Milwaukee, 1836–1860: Accommodation and Community in a Frontier City*. Cambridge: Harvard University Press, 1976.

Korman, Gerd. *Industrialization, Immigrants and Americanizers: The View from Milwaukee, 1866–1921*. Madison: State Historical Society of Wisconsin, 1967.

Still, Bayrd. *Milwaukee: The History of a City* (cited under Regions, States, Cites).

Swichkow, Louis J., and Lloyd P. Gartner. *A History of the Jews of Milwaukee*. Philadephia: Jewish Publication Society of America, 1963.

Index

Designed by Richard Hendel

Composed by Modern Typographers, Dunedin, Florida

Manufactured by Kingsport Press, Kingsport, Tennessee

Library of Congress Cataloging in Publication Data

Bogue, Margaret Beattie, 1924–
Around the shores of Lake Michigan.

Bibliography: pp. 365–367.
Includes index.
1. Michigan, Lake, Region—Description and travel—Guide-books. 2. Historic sites—Michigan, Lake, Region—Guide-books. 3. Michigan, Lake, Region—History, Local.
I. Title.
F553.B63 1985 917.74'0433 84-40490
ISBN 0-299-10000-6
ISBN 0-299-10004-9 (pbk.)